Facing Globalization
in the Himalayas

Series Note

This volume has been produced with the financial assistance of the European Union (EU). The contents of the book are the sole responsibility of the respective authors and can under no circumstances be regarded as reflecting the position of the European Union.

The Asia-Link Programme was launched at the beginning of 2002 as an initiative by the EU to foster regional and multilateral networking among higher education institutions in EU Member States and South Asia, South-East Asia, and China. This five-year programme, which had a total budget of 42.8 million Euro, aimed to provide support to European and Asian higher education institutions in the areas of human resource development, curriculum development, and institutional and systems development.

Facing Globalization in the Himalayas: Belonging and the Politics of the Self

GOVERNANCE, CONFLICT, AND CIVIC ACTION: VOLUME 5

Edited by

**Gérard Toffin
Joanna Pfaff-Czarnecka**

www.sagepublications.com
Los Angeles • London • New Delhi • Singapore • Washington DC

First published in 2014 by

 SAGE Publications India Pvt Ltd
B1/I-1 Mohan Cooperative Industrial Area
Mathura Road, New Delhi 110 044, India
www.sagepub.in

SAGE Publications Inc
2455 Teller Road
Thousand Oaks, California 91320, USA

SAGE Publications Ltd
1 Oliver's Yard, 55 City Road
London EC1Y 1SP, United Kingdom

SAGE Publications Asia-Pacific Pte Ltd
3 Church Street
#10-04 Samsung Hub
Singapore 049483

Published by Vivek Mehra for SAGE Publications India Pvt Ltd, Phototypeset in 10/12pt Sabon by RECTO Graphics, Delhi and printed at Saurabh Printers Pvt Ltd, New Delhi.

Library of Congress Cataloging-in-Publication Data

Facing globalization in the Himalayas : belonging and the politics of the self / edited by Gérard Toffin, Joanna Pfaff-Czarnecka.
    pages cm. — (Governance, conflict, and civic action ; volume 5)
    Includes bibliographical references and index.
    1. Ethnic groups—Himalaya Mountains Region. 2. Group identity—Himalaya Mountains Region. 3. Nationalism—Himalaya Mountains Region. 4. National characteristics. 5. Globalization—Himalaya Mountains Region. 6. Himalaya Mountains Region—Ethnic relations. I. Toffin, Gérard. II. Pfaff-Czarnecka, Joanna.
    DS485.H6F33   305.80095496—dc23   2014   2013050062

ISBN: 978-81-321-1162-7 (HB)

The SAGE Team: Supriya Das, Archa Bhatnagar, Rajib Chatterjee, and Dally Verghese
Cover photograph: Computer class in Kabhre, Nepal (front), Kathmandu (back)
Photo courtesy: Prasant Shrestha

Contents

Preface

Seven years ago, a team of anthropologists, historians, linguists, sociologists, and geographers was invited to participate in a collaborative project geared at grasping the present-day dynamics of belonging in the Himalayan region. While launching this project, we anticipated the need to understand the notion of belonging and to inquire into its dynamic nature under present-day globalized conditions of mobility and rapid social change. In the meantime, 'belonging' has emerged as a key concept in academic research and in public debates.

Our team met for a first round of discussions in March 2007 in New Delhi at the India International Centre (IIC). Out of this meeting resulted our well-received book, *The Politics of Belonging in the Himalayas: Local Attachments and Boundary Dynamics* (2011), published in this series. The present volume is the result of a second round of deliberations that took place in August 2008 at the Centre National de la Recherche Scientifique (CNRS) conference centre in Fréjus, France. The organizers of this second round, including the editors of this volume together with David Gellner from the University of Oxford, ensured continuity within the team, while inviting some new colleagues to cover a broad range of Himalayan subregions. We also brought in additional expertise to help us grasp the current globalization processes that thoroughly affect the constellations of belonging. Most chapters constituting this volume are based on the papers given in Fréjus. Two of the authors, Blandine Ripert and Mitra Pariyar, did not attend the conference, but were subsequently invited to submit a paper.

We are very grateful to our contributors for taking part in the in-depth Fréjus discussions and for expanding on their contributions based on their initial presentations. A number of colleagues played an important role in shaping our project by chairing sessions, in their capacity of discussants, as well as by joining in the discussions. They were Véronique Bouillier (CNRS), Martin Gaenszle (University of Vienna), Gisèle Krauskopff (CNRS), Keshav Maharjan (University of Hiroshima), Charles Ramble (École Pratique des Hautes Études), Phillippe Ramirez (CNRS), Anne de Sales (CNRS), Joëlle Smadja (CNRS), Deepak Thapa (Social Science Baha, Kathmandu), and Nirmal Tuladhar (Centre for Asian and Nepalese Studies at Tribhuvan University, Kathmandu).

Our undertaking would not have been possible without the support of the CNRS (Centre d'études himalayennes, UPR 299) in Paris and in Fréjus, the French Foundation Maison des Sciences de l'Homme (MSH), Paris, the British Academy, the German Research Foundation (DFG) through its Collaborative Research Programme (SFB 584), which was run by Bielefeld University, Germany, and last but not the least, the European EU-Asia-Link programme of the European Commission (Brussels) that contributed important impulses to this endavour. Hinnerk Bruhns (MSH), in particular, warmly encouraged the project from the very beginning and has given us useful advice and suggestions regarding its organization. We are grateful to David Gellner, University of Oxford, who invited us to include this book in MIDEA series, published by SAGE Publications. Finally, we would like to thank Bernadette Sellers (CNRS, Centre d'études himalayennes) and Michael Patterson for improving the style of some chapters.

Gérard Toffin and Joanna Pfaff-Czarnecka
CNRS, UPR 299/Bielefeld University

Chapter 1

Introduction

Globalization and Belonging in the Himalayas and in Trans-Himalayan Social Spaces

GÉRARD TOFFIN AND JOANNA PFAFF-CZARNECKA

INTRODUCTION

This book explores the new horizons produced by ongoing global-ization around the world and the impact of these processes on the repertoires and practices of belonging in the Himalayan region as well as in trans-Himalayan social spaces in Asia and in the West. It is widely accepted today that forces of globalization significantly affect Himalayan peoples' lives. We know little, however, about the present-day reconfigurations in human sociability resulting from its impact on this region and its inhabitants. Similarly, little is known about collective dynamics in translocal and transnational social spaces and we are, to a large extent, ignorant of the resulting tensions involved in personal choices, longings, and aspirations in individual confrontations within collective constellations of belonging. Scholarly preoccupations with globalization usually privilege top-down macro perspectives. If interpersonal relations, local solidarities, and attach-ments are perceived at all, they are seen as mostly helplessly adjusting to the powerful wind of change brought about by international and national politics, by neo-liberal forces as well as by development and humanitarian interventions. Individual and collective rationalities and strategies as well as politics that are geared towards expanding the individual and collective room for manoeuvre have so far received insufficient attention in Himalayan research.[1]

This volume, building on our previous edited collection, *The Politics of Belonging in the Himalayas: Local Attachments and Boundary Dynamics*,[2] published in this same series in 2011, reflects the recent dynamics of globalization and transnationalization in Himalayan societies by observing and analyzing how Himalayan people make sense of the changes that are radically transforming their lives. We are mainly interested in social practices, including the ways in which changing values, norms, and ideas are at work, and how social practice shapes an implicit or explicit change of ideas. We pay particular attention to the personal life chances and to the intimate and emotionally charged forms of socializing in collective constellations. These are of interest in localized Himalayan contexts, but we also observe their expansion into transnational social fields.

This volume's inquiry focuses on the notion of belonging. We propose this concept as an analytical tool for reflecting upon the modalities and the interplay of commonality, mutuality as well as the diverse emotional and material attachments under conditions of rapid social change (for a thorough outline of these concepts, see Pfaff-Czarnecka, 2011; Pfaff-Czarnecka and Toffin, 2011; and Croucher, 2004). By analyzing both individual and collective trajectories, the chapters collected here seek to uncover the implicit and explicit politics of the individual and collective self in processes of (trans)migration, in activism responding to global challenges, and within the particularly dynamic religious sphere where different belief systems and modalities of *Vergemeinschaftung*, that is, different ways of incorporating people into social constellations, come to compete with each other in the quest to win over followers.

Through the prism of belonging, we are able to uncover crucial shifts in the meaningful collective constellations reproduced and evolving in the global era. The individual chapters delve into the realm of local Himalayan life-worlds and show how their horizons have stretched far beyond the confines of particular villages and regions. Numerous chapters document the tremendous scope of the Himalayan mobilities produced through travel, work, trade, the use of new communications media, and by new forms of knowledge, possibilities, and aspirations.

The volume's emphasis on mobility, change, flux, and social reconfigurations does not ignore the durable nature of social ties, their strength, and their persistence (see Lien and Melhuus, 2007).

Indeed, it conceptualizes belonging, that is, the emotionally charged social location, as perennially in tension between stability and change. The value of belonging lies in the continuity of cultural models, with people sharing norms, networks, and practices, and relying on routines. Such groupings as a 'family', 'village', 'neighbourhood', 'religious community', and 'ethnic group' build on long-lasting solidarities, histories, as well as aspirations pointing towards the future. The factual force of belonging stems from the well-established modalities of interaction—that goes without saying—and from shared values that are considered perennial. But they are challenged by globalizing forces, rendering them weaker and more fragile, while simultaneously also buttressing their resilience. In any case, under the current conditions of rapid social change, belonging has come under siege: it is challenged; it loses its self-evident property; it appears to be invaluable and therefore instigates protective measures.

The authors of this volume bring to light the fact that the Himalayas are still regarded as very remote, if not peripheral, regions of today's world society. The following chapters reveal how confrontations with the 'external world' occur under conditions characterized by significant impediments and restrictions. Yet, this region is rapidly changing and increasingly connected to the rest of the world through a series of links investigated in the following chapters. The states and societies located in this mountain range in particular have undergone major changes in terms of openness, interconnectedness, and transnationalization (see our 2011 Introduction). The authors report pronounced power differentials, social (including ethnic) boundary-marking, and societal hierarchies that shape individual and collective choices and practices. Several contributions describe how marginality and exclusion impinge upon collective processes and how they shape the overt and covert politics of social positioning.

This opening chapter introduces the main notions and concepts at work in analyzing these processes and gives an account of the chapters collected in this volume—written by eminent scholars who have been carrying out research in this region for many years. It also presents an overall synthesis of the phenomena of globalization in the Himalayan range in connection with various forms of belonging, both old and new. As a first step and before focusing on these remote regions, we turn to the concept of globalization.

REPERTOIRES AND MODES OF GLOBALIZATION

Globalization (in French, the term 'mondialisation' is often substituted) describes processes through which closer contact is established between human societies and which generate a *wider circulation of goods, money, people, ideas, and cultures across national borders*. The concept may be defined in several ways, but the most accepted designation emphasizes the *integration of economic, political, and cultural systems across the globe*. The links between local or national social relations as well as global ones, in other words local/global relationships and entanglements, have intensified. According to Steger (2009: 15),[3] globalization can be defined as "the expansion and intensification of social relations and consciousness across time and space, while time and space themselves are dramatically compressed". Or, more succinctly, it may be thought of as a long-term but accelerating historical process of growing worldwide interconnectedness (Pieterse, 2009).

Globalizing forces are sometimes considered to be an all-powerful process, totally undermining the importance of local and even national boundaries. Some analysts foresee a world where a growing variety of social activities will take place irrespective of the geographical location of participants. Everything will have to be thought of as global. Such a view, of course, is inadequate. We are far from the idyllic vision of a global village in which everyone is connected to everyone else. Globalization does not mean that the world economy is now integrated into a single space. Homogenization is at best superficial. Macro-studies which tend to formulate such types of generalization pay insufficient attention to ethnographic particularities or to changes and continuities that exist below the global level on a local, regional, or national scale. A world without boundaries is a naïve concept. Even in the West, the European Union, one of the most advanced examples of regional integration, has not established long-lasting, salient forms of solidarity and a sense of collective belonging among Europeans.

The globalizing process also covers reactions against the ongoing homogenization buttressed by globalizing forces, resulting in a persistence of old-established forms of attachment, to an ethnic group, a region, and a country. *Globalization is therefore a multifaceted process*, encompassing a large range of fields, geographical, demographic, political, technological, linguistic, religious, and cultural.

The definition of such a broad term, with multiple and fluid meanings, is obviously problematic. Globalization covers such a wide range of phenomena that it has rapidly become a blanket notion easily cited for all sorts of things that are indeed sometimes quite different. Some even speak of a cliché, "an all-purpose catchword in public and scholarly debate" with multiple connotations (Lechner and Boli, 2000: 1).

However, when broadly understood, globalization does apply to a distinctive transformative process which can be ascertained in the field whether by an economist, a geographer, a sociologist, or an anthropologist. Connectivity and interdependence between human societies across national borders are among the key notions conveyed by the term. Improved transportation as well as the rapid surge in the use of new communication media, in particular the Internet, now widely used in South Asia and almost all over the Himalayas, even in remote rural zones, is one of the most striking examples of how space is being compressed. Among the urban middle classes, whether Indian or Nepalese, mobiles and the Internet-based social networking site Facebook, with its hybrid English–Nepali or English–Hindi fluid language employed by its users, are much sought-after and much-used modalities of situating oneself and of communicating with others. These phenomena have transcended old boundaries and imposed new types of links. The new circulatory dynamics of the contemporary world have also produced new patterns of migration, a globalizing labour market, and a number of ideological shifts. The influence of external cultural models is multifarious: the Bollywood cinema industry coexists with Westernized forms of cultural consumption as well as with an increasing influence of South-East Asian or Hong Kong products. In the same way, western and far-eastern TV channels are a powerful means of spreading foreign cultural models and expenditure. All these vehicles for globalization compete with each other and also interpenetrate each other. They are part of a wider *cultural politics of globalization*.

Manifold 'local responses' to globalization have been recorded in social science research. A great deal of attention was geared towards grasping cultural forms of incorporation that impinge upon individual and collective positioning. After lengthy debates over the question of whether globalization instigates cultural homogenization or rather heterogenization, academic writing has devoted a lot of space to the notions of 'hybridization' (Bhabha, 1994) and 'vernacularization' (Merry, 2006), that is, the process of translating external notions into a local cultural canon (e.g. explaining human rights norms through local values), and in particular, its modalities. The analyses collected in this volume allow us to conceptualize these processes more accurately. We suggest four repertoires or options of cultural translation or *vernacularization* and argue that the main interconnected repertoires of cultural globalization oscillate between the following:

- *Universalization*: Defining particular cultural elements as 'fitting' into global repertoires or as expressing universal values. Peter Brook's mise en scène of the Mahabharata can be interpreted as such a claim. Universalization also takes place when local grievances turn into claims drawing upon global legal repertoires. With the expansion of human rights, particularist claims—for example, claims to ethnic monopolies over specific territories or resources—can be expressed in a universal language highlighting democratic values.
- *Particularism*: Stressing the uniqueness of one's culture. Examples of particularism are claims of the uniqueness of traditional value systems such as the 'Asian Values'—as embraced by the Malaysian government at the end of the last millennium and thought incompatible with universal human rights. This claim accorded well with the American Anthropological Association's critique of the Universal Declaration of Human Rights (starting in 1947 in reaction to a draft document) that resulted in the debate over universalism versus relativism.
- *Cultural reform*: For instance, abandoning rituals involving blood sacrifices in order to appear 'more civilized'. Cases are reported in many regions of the Himalayas, especially in Nepal, where new concerns about animal welfare and the pointless suffering of animals have emerged, for instance, under the influence of various strands of both Buddhism and neo-Hinduism. Other examples can be mentioned, such as movements for the replacement of expensive 'superstitious' rituals making way for new forms or types of practices or beliefs, and today's trend among many Himalayan people (as elsewhere in the world) towards new types of therapists, undermining traditional priesthoods. UNESCO's concern for 'heritage' protection, whether

material or immaterial, has also had a tremendous impact on all these regions.

- *Revivalism*: Highlighting cultural elements considered essential for the continuity of a collective group and of its cultural and religious forms while incorporating new elements vital for their survival under changed circumstances. The revival of Theravada Buddhism, the invented traditions by ethnic groups in relation to their history, and discourses on ethnicity can be mentioned as examples.

We make this set of distinctions for its heuristic value. In fact, these phenomena and forces are, for the most part, interconnected. Take, for instance, the Hindutva movement in India that stresses pride in Hinduism and claims a dominant position for this religion in Indian and Nepalese cultural, religious, and political affairs. In many ways, it embodies a plainly chauvinistic anti-globalist trend, rejecting Western influences and values, attacking Christianity and its converts, and acquiring particularistic overtones. Yet, historically, the rise of this Hindu nationalist current and of its political party, the Bharatiya Janata Party, is concomitant with economic liberalization in India, the gradual breakdown of state control, and the increasing integration of the country into the global economy. Some analysts associate Hindutva's success directly with the cultural and political assertion of the growing urban middle class, favoured by the expanding market economy. This parochial manifestation of culture can be seen as a reaction against globalizing forces in India. Moreover, its leaders do not hesitate to use modern media and electronic equipment to communicate and spread their message throughout the Indian diaspora, considered here in the sense of spreading of people originally belonging to one nation or having a common culture over the world. What we have here is therefore a combination, full of contradictions, comprising universalization, Hindu revivalism, and religious reform. Interestingly enough, the Hindutva movement is very strong in the western Himalayas, particularly in Uttarakhand, and it has played an important, more or less hidden, role in the monarchical Shah rule in modern Nepal.

This example also indicates that globalization is closely intertwined with modernization (see Choedon, 1995), both processes being two sides of the same coin. Globality is often seen as time-space-compression (Harvey, 1989; Giddens, 1990) made possible by the availability of modern infrastructures. The spread of values of modernization has been greatly buttressed by modern means of transmission and by the power of the Western centres to utilize them. Recent debates on 'multiple modernities' (Eisenstadt, 2002) and 'entangled modernities' (Therborn, 2003) take up the complex interrelation between globality, modernity, and Westernization. As the example of Hindutva reveals, its success came about partly through opposition to Westernization while simultaneously taking advantage of modernization: in particular new communication channels improving the expansion of ideas and contacts, but also the openness of the public sphere.

GLOBALIZATION IN THE HIMALAYAS: THE ARCHITECTURE OF THE BOOK

The 16 chapters of this volume are organized in five thematic sections, following our inquiry into the widening scope of globality and its increasing bearing upon local contexts. It starts off from the local social spaces in the Himalayan region towards their widening aperture on to the global level. The first section, "Shifting Horizons of Belonging", probes the opening up of Himalayan societies to the world, concentrating here upon local contexts from where supra-local interconnections (see Chapters 2 and 4 by Ripert and by Dollfus) as well as the interdependencies with other local social spaces in the Himalayan region are forged (see Chapter 3 by Shneiderman).

The second section, "Migrant Experiences in South Asia and Beyond", points out translocal processes developing well beyond the scope of the Himalayan region. The chapters analyze relations of belonging that are re-shifted but also reinforced through economic interdependencies. Chapters 5 and 7 by Sharma and Bruslé show that migrant social formations are not confined to the economic sphere. Through interrelating with foreign employers and through connecting with other workers, new perceptions and positionings come into being. For many migrants from the Himalayas, their sense of belonging is challenged and comes to light during encounters with fellow-workers while abroad. It is furthermore reinforced by jointly engaging in ritual practice, as Pariyar, Shrestha, and Gellner demonstrate (Chapter 6).

The chapters by Bruslé and Pariyar et al. are also important bridges for capturing Himalayan transnationality going well beyond the South Asian region. The section "Creating Transnational Belonging" takes this reflection further. The chapters inquire into the global scope of workers' (Hausner's Chapter 8) and students' (Sijapati's Chapter 10) migrations from the Himalayas; the localization of migrant practices at the places of arrival as, for instance, in the form of communal politics (see Campbell's Chapter 9) and the enfolding of transnational social spaces forged by migrant organizations (see Hangen's Chapter 11).

While some of the previous chapters draw our attention to the influence of transnational processes on Himalayan localities, the chapters comprising the fourth section, "Globality and Activist Experience", definitely reverse the direction from 'local-outward' to 'local-inward' and address the local effects of globalization forces. Chapters 13 and 14 by Subba and by Arora, respectively, discuss the impact of external interventions bearing upon local societies when infrastructural projects result in dispossession and displacement of local populations. The local contestations are to be seen, here, as engagements in global dynamics through local interactions and negotiations, instigating internal conflicts and drawing upon transnational activists' networks. Letizia's Chapter 12 also progresses from the global to local, showing how indigenous activists work towards religious change within their constituencies while simultaneously connecting to global religious movements and operating their organizations transnationally.

The final section, "National Reconfigurations", focuses upon the state as mediating between the global and the local and as decisively shaping globalization processes. Chapters 16 and 17 (by Mills and Hutt, respectively) demonstrate the persisting power of states, either guarding their borders and controlling territorial allegiances, or organizing their populations in 'joint' national projects of collective becoming. In Turin's Chapter 15 in this book, the state is the addressee of ethnic politics that—among other things—critically addresses doctrines of common belonging through linguistic homogenization.

Throughout the book, three mechanisms—*connectivity*, *interdependence*, and *openness*—are important features of globalization impinging upon the relations of belonging. *Connectivity* is an omnipresent feature of contemporary Himalayan societies. The collected contributions discuss the main domains where connectivity increasingly shapes social practices. Connectivity evolves within transnational social spaces of ethnic communities that increasingly stretch across continents (see Hangen, Pariyar, Shrestha, and Gellner, Sijapati). Another dimension of connectivity has emerged in transnational activist networks in the field of critical social movements opposing large infrastructural projects (Arora, Subba). Also, Campbell's discussion of the cultural politics of representation (Chapter 9) indicates how Nepalese activists forge ties with local municipalities in order to accentuate their presence in the United Kingdom. Chiara Letizia's chapter demonstrates the substantial intensification of connectedness of believers in the religious realm. At the same time, she shows how religious belonging instigates connectivity far beyond national borders, that is, between people from different ethnic backgrounds and from different regions of the world.

Interdependence is apparent especially in the economic realm. Labour migration thrives and reinforces economic relations. Bruslé (Chapter 7), Sharma (Chapter 5), Shneiderman (Chapter 3), and Hausner (Chapter 8) provide accounts of economic entanglements coming about as Himalayan people join companies abroad as a labour force. Transnational work relations are accompanied by the forging of new social ties. These ties bridge national boundaries, as workers from different regional and national backgrounds are thrown together, and find themselves dependent on each other. Critical protest movements, relying upon the division of labour, also create interdependencies.

Both connectivity and interdependence enhance the *openness* of Himalayan societies. Blandine Ripert's account of Christianization among the Tamangs of central Nepal in Chapter 2 reveals the scope of openness to external influences in this very remote social world. Her study brings to light the fact that external influences have already been a characterizing feature of this society for centuries. According to her, new communicative channels are not a precondition for external influences to 'enter' a remote Himalayan world; they just intensify the process of cultural interpenetration. Ripert also clearly shows the importance of local reflection as well as local practices for mediating social and cultural change. Therefore, our notion of 'openness' of local Himalayan societies does not mean a total exposure to supralocal impacts and inspirations—as also other chapters reveal (Dollfus, Pariyar, Shrestha, and Gellner).

EARLY FORMS OF GLOBALIZATION
IN THE HIMALAYAS

The novelty and the uniqueness of the present globalized trend is a subject of debate. Historians insist on the continuity between the contemporary configuration and the premodern period. Others (mainly geographers and economists) stress the novelty of the present-day situation: for them, contemporary globalization is an entirely new epoch mainly defined by market capitalism and the consequent weakening of the nation state. Whatever the case may be, early forms of globalization cannot be denied. One can argue, for instance, that *ancient forms of cosmopolitanism* (i.e. inclination to accept the other and endorse diversity within traditional social spaces)[4] *and hybridization* have only been exacerbated and generalized by the new transnational forces, especially with the new forms of communication and high-speed transportation from one place to another. Still, the contemporary magnitude in the flow of goods, information, and capital across huge areas of the earth's surface has no parallel in previous eras.

In order to understand the current global reconfigurations it is important to historicize the present realities and to acknowledge the existence of early forms of globalization. In the 1960s–70s, Fernand Braudel already stressed the emergence of an 'économie-monde', or a 'modern global system', connecting all regions of the world from the 16th century onwards. Mobility and circulation are nothing new in the Himalayan region. Trade has always linked different regions, sometimes situated very far from each other. Since ancient times, exchanges between the arid north Tibetan plateau and the luxuriant southern plains of the Indo-Gangetic valley over the passes crossing the Himalayan range have been a conspicuous feature. Over the centuries, they have induced considerable interconnectivity and acculturation processes between different Himalayan communities. Ideas, people, and goods were exchanged on these routes, crossing more or less fixed political boundaries, and corresponding to various historical periods.

Naturally, these initial links were framed by the mountainous topography. It must be recalled within this context that the Himalayas are characterized by a series of steep north–south valleys separated by mountain ranges, all of which have allowed little contact between adjacent population settlements, especially in high-altitude regions. Over the centuries, these physical aspects have tended to favour vertical communication, from north to south or south to north, to the detriment of horizontal exchanges, from east to west, and vice versa. The Himalayas are thus connected to the Indo-Gangetic plains and to the Tibetan plateau by old trading routes, along which important market and political centres flourished long before the unification of Nepal in the 18th–19th centuries or long before the expansion of the British Raj into South Asia. Three of these routes may be mentioned: the one passing through Ladakh in the west, the Kathmandu Valley in the centre, and Sikkim in the east. They have all played a primary role in various fields, economically, politically, and culturally.

One could also and perhaps more topically stress the transnational links in premodern Nepal, especially in the case of the Kathmandu Valley, on the lines of what has been written by Serge Gruzinski (2004), the French historian of Latin America, about the globalization of the world in the 16th–17th centuries. Obviously, during the Malla period the Kathmandu Valley formed a plural world in terms of language, society, and culture. Maithili, a language from the low plains, distant from the Malla kingdoms, was chosen by the kings as one of the literary languages, even if it was not understood by local people. Even today, some local theatrical plays dating from this period use dialogues in this language, interspersed with Hindi. The Malla civilization of the 16th–17th centuries was based on a wide circulation of ideas, people, and texts, differing greatly from a totally enclosed and insular territory. Catholic missionaries, Tibetan monks and scholars, and people from the hills (farmers, mercenaries, etc.) were present and intermingled with Brahmanical gurus and *shastris* from the Indian border districts. Kings frequently called upon these different priests and intellectuals. They themselves took their wives mainly from small neighbouring kingdoms to the south, in particular from Kooch Bihar, in today's Indian State of West Bengal and some districts of present-day Assam. Here we witness, as in many parts of India, the meeting of a cosmopolitan Sanskrit culture (spreading over many parts of the Indian subcontinent and beyond in the East) and an original local, indigenous tradition (see Pollock, 2006). It is noticeable that the creation of such interconnected and intermixed social and cultural spaces owes little or nothing to the expansion of Western civilization throughout the world. It has evolved according to its own logic, unaffected by European forces. When speaking of globalization, we are thus addressing a phenomenon that has spread dramatically over the last two decades and can be better viewed as an acceleration of former processes. We need to recognize and compare these ancient traditions of cosmopolitanism (Nandy, 2002) with present-day changes, in particular in matters of attachment to collective forms of belonging.

During the end of the 19th century and the beginning of the 20th century, places such as Varanasi, Calcutta, Kalimpong, Darjeeling, and Dehradun evolved as significant centres distinguished by a heterogeneous range of cultures. Structurally, these areas were characterized by pronounced ethnic and cultural boundary lines. These inter-mixed urban spaces have been crucial in the course of the overall modernization of the Himalayan economy, the process of democratization, and the diffusion of new ideas. They have transmitted modern notions of social justice and equality, and have been important sites for creating national and regional identity. In addition, such early external centres of migration have introduced complex forms of banking procedures, the raising of funds, marketing, and trade structures, all of great import to the economy. By and large, they have played a decisive role in the political history and in the socio-economic changes taking place in the remote kingdoms of the Himalayas.

Such geographical and historical traits have to be taken into account when considering today's Himalayan countries. They have engendered early forms of globalization with regard to ideas, trade and goods, religion, and civilization. Two chapters of this book address some of these issues directly or indirectly: Mark Turin, in his chapter on linguistics (Chapter 15), and Martin Mills (Chapter 16), on previous forms of globalization in 17th- and 18th-century Tibet.

THE GEOGRAPHY OF GLOBALIZATION IN THE HIMALAYAS

Globalization does not apply everywhere in the same way and with the same strength. There are major differences in this respect between, say, rural areas and cities, Bhutan and Nepal, remote areas and Tarai or the Kathmandu Valley. Consequently, the impact of globalization has to be studied in historical as well as spatial terms.

Each Himalayan country has had its own past and configuration in these matters. The studied region must be considered in plural terms. The Tamangs studied by Blandine Ripert (Chapter 2) and the Thangmi analyzed by Sara Shneiderman (Chapter 3) are not exposed in the same way to globalization as the Gurungs living in the United States discussed by Susan Hangen (Chapter 11) or Nepali nurses in the United Kingdom (Hausner, Chapter 8).

India has opened her borders to overseas markets and Western influences for a long time, and more decisively since the colonial period. Yet, as an independent country, she liberalized her economy only from the 1990s onwards. Its impact on the world is now as important as the impact of the world on her.[5] After being secluded for more than one century, Nepal opened most of its territory to the world in the 1950s. Its exposure to foreign aid and tourism[6] since that period has accelerated the process of globalization considerably. Bhutan still lags behind in terms of connectivity with the outside world, since this small country lays emphasis on its own cultural values (e.g. the 'Gross Happiness Index') with a peculiar strength and restricts access to only a small number of outsiders (Hutt, 2003). Yet it has adopted a more democratic political system recently (2008), a process sponsored by the palace. As far as Tibet, annexed by China in 1959, is concerned, globalization in many ways still equates with a progression of Sinization, that is, supra-local influences. However, the Tibetan diaspora in the Himalayas, India, and all over the world results from transnationalization.

In each of these countries, the flow of capital and goods is extremely uneven according to the areas, mountainous or plains, rural or urban, etc. People living in urban areas of Kathmandu and the Pokhara valleys of Nepal, Darjeeling, Kalimpong, and Gangtok of north-eastern India, to limit the scope to some areas, are much more enmeshed in the processes of global modernity than other regions, even if they receive remittances from migrant workers abroad. Many other groups or communities remain isolated and marginalized, in the rural and mountainous regions of Far Western Nepal, for instance. Global interconnectedness is thus not experienced by all people to the same extent or in the same way. What strikes one, on the contrary, is a *fragmented and partial globalization*, where urban settlements are more affected by the new forms of interconnectivity, while rural areas are far behind. This applies to the Himalayas as to other regions of the world.

To take just one example of the unequal pace of globalization, Pyangaon—an archaic village in the Kathmandu valley—regularly visited by G. Toffin from the 1970s, could be mentioned. This locality is an example of a *lasting traditional community and territory* within a region undergoing tremendous change. Though social rules have become more fragile, social boundaries as well as familial ties are still preserved. To supplement their income, Jyapuni peasant women now weave sweaters with wool imported from New Zealand, while still observing basic social rules, such as territorial endogamy. The dialect spoken exclusively within the boundaries of the village is still in use by local children, despite schooling links with neighbourhood Newar and high Parbatiya Nepali-speaking castes living in the locality. In this village, as in many others of the Himalayan range, more localist forms of belonging are still extremely active and determine social and cultural life. Globalization is present in Pyangaon, through television, mobile phones, schooling, Westernized clothing, etc. But it affectsthe younger generation more than the older members of the community and it remains limited to some sectorsof social life. Remarkably enough, this village is located only 16 km from the large city of Patan.

Globalization tends to marginalize former ways of life and old techniques. In the village of Pyangaon, the male population formerly specialized in making bamboo containers used to measure mainly cereals. This activity was closely linked to the identity of the village (the Nepali name of the locality itself was derived from it), and was associated with an old economy of bartering handicraft bamboo products against grain. This speciality has nearly collapsed, as have many other aspects of their material life and of the traditional dress, which is worn at present only during festivals and ceremonies, as a testimony to the old times and tradition. However, the forces of globalization transform also these old lifestyle elements in their own way. Pyangaon is at present quoted by the Nepali newspapers as an exemplary model tourist 'heritage' village (*paryatakiya kshetra*) (*Kantipur*, 10 June 2010). Its inhabitants are invited to maintain their own craft tradition in order to attract foreigners and be included in tours. Very recently, a local Development and Conservation Committee (*Pyangaon Bikas tatha Sanrakshan Samiti*) has been created. It aims to train young local people in the making of bamboo measuring boxes in order to revive this ancient technique and old-fashioned artefact.

BELONGING AND GLOBALIZATION: RECONFIGURATIONS AT WORK

Our central purpose in this book is a better understanding of the new forms of attachments at work. We are also concerned by the nature of the social links in the modern changing societies characterized by a persistence of 'traditional' social forms—that most Himalayan dwellers seek to maintain.

The main objective is therefore to study the *reconfigurations of local Himalayan societies* that have been instigated by the recent years of general globalization, as well as the new patterns of exchange and movements of population. Translocal and transnational trends have progressively opened up the local and more or less enclosed societies situated more often than not in remote regions, which are difficult to access owing to their mountain environment. These dynamics have changed local perceptions and generated shifting horizons of attention and attachment, with their own specificities. Interestingly enough, the external, mostly Western, elements have been reinterpreted, translated, and reincorporated in the traditional social world. There is a continuous conversion of global cultural forms into vernacular ones, and vice versa. Hybridization and intermingling are ubiquitous in these translocal contexts.

Some chapters document new types of choices, resulting, for instance, in embracing a new religion (Ripert, Chapter 2). Through the lens of belonging, this author is able to demonstrate how individual conversions coalesce into a collective pattern. When increasing numbers of individuals embrace a new religion, established patterns of communal authority are called into question—as her example from the Tamang community indicates. Individual decisions to migrate have also created collective patterns of change as Bruslé's (Chapter 7) and Sharma's chapters (Chapter 5) reveal. Bruslé's data show that, quite unexpectedly, the Nepali migrants in the Gulf come to reflect upon their belonging to their ethnic and caste groups, to their regions and to Nepal. Sharma (Chapter 5) reveals how the strategic responses of Nepali migrants to Mumbai to livelihood insecurities in the hills are shaped by local perceptions of belonging on the one hand and a quest to experience life outside their village on the other. The individual explorations of modernity (in the young men's understanding) become intertwined with their attachments to their natal villages, families, and friends. Individual room for manoeuvre is explored against the backdrop of filial loyalties and obligations. Hausner (Chapter 8) describes individual migrations of Nepali nurses to the United Kingdom, and highlights the numerous restrictions imposed on Nepali workers by legislation imposed on particular national categories of migrants depending on their national 'regimes of membership'. While concentrating on comparatively privileged migrants going from Nepal to the US for study, Sijapati (Chapter 10) explores the individual options of students coping with financial restrictions, social boundaries, traditional codes of conduct, and longing for home in Nepal, while seeking incorporation as newcomers into the American society.

The studies by Hangen (Chapter 11) and Pariyar, Shrestha, and Gellner (Chapter 6) endorse the collective trends narrated in the literature on transnational social spaces. Migration tends to alter, but often also to enhance collective ethnic, religious, or national constellations. Away from home in the Himalayas and in new homes in the Himalayan diaspora all over the world, collective belonging is, for instance, reinforced by religious practice and simultaneously shaped by ritual requirements, bringing members together through ritual performance. Religious transnationality appears as a highly dynamic, instigating ritual invention. Religious belonging has become a vehicle for reinforcing social ties and for coping with the difficult question of not being socially displaced while abroad. As Pariyar et al. argue, religion intersects with other dimensions of individual and collective socialization such as citizenship and organization along caste or ethnic lines.

Reconfiguration can also be studied more specifically from the viewpoint of spaces and territories, which is a major source of belonging. For instance, political conflicts and diverse governmental decisions have displaced over recent years a number of individuals dwelling in the Himalayas. New spaces, especially configured for them, have been allocated to these migrants. Such territories are characterized by dramatic changes from the traditional type of settlements from where the persons in exile were coming from. Among these refugees, one can mention the Tibetan people who fled Tibet after annexation of their country by the Chinese (1959), the Nepali Bhutanese (Lhotshampas) who were expelled or fled from Bhutan after new policies on national culture and citizenship were implemented by the authorities in the 1990s,[7] and the Nepali nationals displaced during the Maoist armed conflict in Nepal (1996–2006). In the last case, the displaced people (called *bisthapit* in Nepali) settled in cities and district headquarters where security was supposed to be well managed. The refugee camps which have been established here and there[8] have caused considerable alterations in the experience of life and give rise to fundamental changes in the spatial contours of social existence of these people in exile. One intriguing example is provided by exiled Tibetans in western India through the interconnections with transnational Buddhist activism (Peot, 2005: 21).

In her chapter on Tibetan nomads, Pascale Dollfus (Chapter 4) highlights the importance of territory for the sense of belonging among Changpas of Ladakh who pursue a mixed agricultural and pastoral livelihood. As non-nomadic agriculturists, they fall within a territory and occupy a *yul* (territory) protected by its own territorial gods. She describes their dramatic shift over the last decades from a mobile existence to a settled and urban lifestyle. She focuses mainly on a village 10 km from Leh, the capital of Ladakh, named Kharnaling, where they have established a permanent urban settlement. In this new space, which is not described as a 'village' but as a 'colony', the former nomads try to invent a new lifestyle, and to free themselves from the stereotypes of ruthlessness and filthiness associated with them in common Ladakhi discourse. Some of them, however, have to earn their money playing the role of true Changpas nomads disguised in folk attire and performing on stage for cultural exhibits.

Labour migration towards the urban centres as well as various conflict-induced waves of migration have also created new settlements located mostly in marginal places and border zones. These peripheral spaces introduce new forms of spatialization. For the sake of analysis, these peripheral spaces can be called *outplaces* (Toffin, 2010). Among such sites are slums, squatter settlements, resettled enclaves, and so forth. Labour camps in Gulf countries where migrants live in buildings or camps provided by their employers also belong to this category (Bruslé, 2010). The key features of most of these spaces are their non-permanent and transitory nature, the vulnerability and poverty of the populations as well as the new forms of belonging characterized by the wider inter-ethnic and inter-caste connectivity that they generate, and often by a high degree of politicization. Their uncertainty has a serious impact on education, economic conditions, and the exercise of citizenship rights. More often than not, the people settled there are urban or national pariahs.

They are prone to conflictive situations and are easily manipulated by political leaders and organizations.

Shneiderman's chapter provides deep insights into economically marginal and socially fragile circular existences. Spatial marginalization is reinforced by the precariousness of material endowment of those dwelling away from their original home. Her chapter is particularly valuable in showing individual families' ways out from the state of manifold exclusion. Transnational activism along with politics of 'social inclusion' embraced by development agencies have buttressed the collective sense of the self (also translating into 'identity politics' in the Indian framework of affirmative action), while labour migration increasingly contributes towards ending economic exploitation and social exclusion.

PATTERNS OF MIGRATION: PAST AND PRESENT

Today, migration is part and parcel of the Himalayan social landscape—as the Nepalese example reveals. It is estimated that between 4 and 6.5 million Nepalese people nowadays work permanently or temporarily outside the country (Bruslé, 2010: 16). In the Nepalese hills, every family has a relative who has migrated, either temporarily or permanently, either abroad, to Kathmandu, or to the Tarai. Mountain and hill villages are incapable of feeding their growing number of inhabitants. Simultaneously, consumerist expectations, often relating to modernization and Westernization, increase the importance of remittances all the more. Today, migration is an even more important component of the livelihood strategies in most Himalayan villages than it was it the past centuries. The subject is so extensive and significant that an outstanding special issue of the *European Bulletin of Himalayan Research* was recently devoted to probing these questions (2010: 35–36). The present volume is devoted in large part to this multifarious phenomenon.

Again, these transregional and international migrations are nothing new. Mobility has pervaded the life of almost all Himalayan people for years (see Messerschmidt, 1976; Sagant, 1978; Lewis, 1993; Riaboff, 2002; and Strawn, 1994).[9] An itinerant form of living—travelling from one place to another—is reported from various regions in ancient periods. For a long time now, the Himalayan mountains and hills have been a region of intense migration from north to south (and sometimes the reverse), as well as from west to east (see Rizvi, 1999). There has been substantial seasonal migration to the plains in order to make up for the low income of mountainous areas and to cover the needs of local rural societies throughout the year. Such a quest for food and additional sources of income has created durable exchanges across the Himalayan region.[10] In addition, rulers in Nepal have repeatedly provided inducements to encourage people to migrate to under-populated areas and to transform forests into arable land, especially throughout the 19th century (Regmi, 1976)—which resulted in the high degree of ethnic intermixing in the north-eastern parts of India. These old forms of relationship have linked the mountains and hills to the plains in many economic, political, and cultural fields. Old and more recent migrations have connected Himalayan areas across national borders. The chapters written by Shneiderman (Chapter 3) and Pariyar, Shrestha, and Gellner (Chapter 6) in the present volume document this phenomenon. Yet, the migrations from the hills to southern districts have increased dramatically over recent years (Shrestha, 1990). In Nepal, permanent migrations to the Tarai and to urban areas have been constantly on the rise since the 1970s so that the once mountainous Nepalese population is today mostly made up of plain-dwellers.

Among the destinations of Nepalese migrants abroad, India has been the foremost and remains a major one, while Nepal, at the same time, was receiving a number of Indian migrants and workers. Historically, the British colonial authorities have recruited 'Gurkha' soldiers in Nepal from the early 19th century onwards (Caplan, 1995). These recruitments, which reached a peak during the two World Wars, have been a first step towards a globalization of manpower. Later on, from the second part of the 19th century, if not earlier, a number of Nepalese have established themselves in Darjeeling, Sikkim, southern Bhutan, and in other regions of northeast India, for economic (but also sometimes political) reasons, for instance, to work in tea estate companies. Others were recruited (and are still employed) as cooks or guards (*chaukidar*), in the fast-growing urban areas of the plains (Pfaff-Czarnecka, 1993; Thieme, 2007; Sharma, this volume [Chapter 5]). Over the last two decades (1990s and 2000s), new destinations have opened up: the Gulf region and Malaysia, but also South Korea, Japan, the US (between 80,000 and 150,000 Nepalese individuals and increasingly also Lhotsampas in the US alone) as well as a number of Western countries. The United

Kingdom continues to be a very popular destination for Nepalese nurses, despite its increasingly restrictive policies and regulations (see Hausner, Chapter 8). A growing number of Nepalese are now migrating abroad. The number of Nepalese seeking work abroad had considerably increased during the Maoist conflict (1996–2006), which caused the local people to flee and owing to the declining carpet industry, which employed a great number of persons until the early 1990s.

THE 'HIMALAYANS' IN THE WEST

With the Himalayan people travelling farther and farther, migrations to the West present some specific characteristics which need to be investigated in present and future research (cf. Hangen [Chapter 11] and Sijapati in this volume [Chapter 10; Gellner, 2013]). The effects of remittances in the economies of the various countries concerned are considerable. The Nepalese working abroad sent 4,500 millions of US dollars to Nepal through various channels in 2011–12 alone. This figure represents, according to the Nepal Rashtra Bank, more than 25 per cent of the gross domestic produce. This figure represents, according to the *Nepal Rashtra Bank*, more than half of the national income. It would go up significantly if legal and banking provisions were made to facilitate foreign remittances for deposits and investments in the country, as asked by for by non-resident Nepali associations.

Though the life of the migrants residing in Europe and North America seems to be easier than those in the Gulf or in some parts of India, because of the economic development of these countries, the level of employment is restricted mainly to low-qualified economic sectors, restaurant, hotels, domestic service, and so forth. It is noticeable that migrants in these countries find it necessary to organize themselves in groups. The network of Nepalese associations overseas plays a vital role in maintaining a sense of dignity and a deeper sense of connectedness among the migrant community. Its members periodically organize social and cultural events such as picnics, conferences, Dasain parties, Losar, that is, New Year celebrations, etc., which bring the Nepalese immigrant diaspora together. In this manner, migrants preserve their culture or even work towards its revitalization and new inventions of tradition, and their children rediscover their 'roots' and rearticulate their identities as members of diasporic communities. Also, Nepalihood or Nepaliness (*nepalipan*) is often recreated through these links in such a way that original *places* and *cultures* are totally dissociated, though frequently reinforced in the diasporic imagination (sometimes translating into indigenous activism) or forging new spaces of belonging (see Campbell, Chapter 9). "These networks serve as a form of social capital that recent arrivals draw upon to receive assistance, including in finding housing, gaining access to employment, and understanding the ins and outs of life in America" (Sijapati, 2010: 144). Moreover, all over the world the migrant minorities have created de-territorialized 'homelands' abroad, sometime on ethnic lines, such as the Gurung Association described by Susan Hangen in her chapter on the US (Chapter 11). In this case, ethnic identification and the sense of belonging are strengthened through migrant practices.

One of this volume's chapters narrates migrant practices in less collectivist terms though. Hausner's (Chapter 8) inquiry into a number of Nepalese nurses (all female) repeatedly uses the term 'solitude'. Unlike the overwhelming body of migrant literature, Hausner highlights the female migrants' sense of alienation. These women not only find it difficult to socialize in the places of 'arrival', but also suffer under pressures from home where they cannot engage in care activities they offer strangers in the United Kingdom. The analysis points to difficulties in entering or establishing networks and in finding access to communities where they can engage in religious practice and festive activities. At the same time, Hausner suggests that an important dimension of identity and belonging comes to life through professional standing and commitment. Thus-achieved commonalities and attachments—that are likely to create a strong sense of belonging—have not yet been discussed in detail in the literature.

The advancement of communication technologies and electronic mass media plays a crucial role within these migrant communities. Skype, low-cost overseas phone lines, email, capital transfer and flows, instantly linking different places in different countries or continents, are widely used to maintain a link with the native country. They create a new space—a cyberspace—where borders and boundaries are overcome, producing a virtual de-territorialized space. For its users, the Web is a source of new expectations, new interests, and new prospects. The annihilation of distance goes together in this case with a contraction of time (see also Inda and Rosaldo, 2002).

Such combined compression implying simultaneity and instantaneousness contain far-reaching implications for human experience of life. For instance, the Internet allows migrants settled in the Western countries to sustain and nurture ties with their families dwelling in Nepal or in India. Both sides regularly send each other photos or video clips of ceremonies and other familial meetings (Sijapati, 2010: 139). Relatives thus participate vicariously in familial events. In addition, the Internet has become a site of political engagement among Nepalis living abroad. It has been used in the past and is still used today to create awareness among both Nepalis and non-Nepalis about political causes, such as pro-democracy movements, protest against the 2005 King Gyanendra's takeover, families affected by the Maoist conflict, and so on. While geographically distant, the Nepali diaspora is thus able to play a role in the current political affairs and changes in Nepal.

These population movements, therefore, create new regional and transnational links, connecting distant countries. They impinge considerably upon the parameters of belonging and their changing nature, in terms of religious and political allegiances. We can contrast these more fragmented and fluid experiences with the traditional bounded sense of attachment to a locality felt in most rural societies of the Himalayas. Diasporic contexts alter traditional forms of belonging. Migrations abroad tend to change the patterns of mutuality and interaction between kin, friends, and neighbours. The new networks, the channels and the routes of migrations, the ways people speak of their migrations, and how they feel about it are particularly interesting to study in this context. The collected chapters answer a number of questions: What are their impressions of the old and new places where they stay abroad? How do migrants get together abroad? How do they choose their companions? What happens if they lack contact with their countrymen? What difference does it currently make that kinship and communal ties stretch over very long distances? How are new loyalties forged and old ones maintained? How do migrants cope with regard to political and civic involvement at home as well as at their place of residence? The experience of new territories and social spaces felt and faced by migrants abroad has been particularly important to document in the following chapters. In other words, the changing Himalayas opened up social and cultural possibilities, as well as a reconceptualization of the very notions of spatiality and territory.

STATE BOUNDARIES

Under the conditions of globalization, the persistence of national boundaries is a remarkable phenomenon. In the Himalayas as everywhere, the process of globalization still largely takes place within the framework created over the centuries by the historical emergence of the nation state. The tenacity of national boundaries is sometimes fortified by the forces of globalization. It can be seen as a sort of counterpoint to the global, but is in fact one of its consequences. Four chapters in this volume illustrate this tendency.

One important instance where state boundaries continue to reinforce collectivizing effects is in the field of *linguistic nationalism*. Mark Turin's chapter in this book (Chapter 15) concurs with Paul Brass who sees language movements as "inherently and necessarily associated with the modern state and modern politics" (2004: 353), but brings to light yet other types of effects—that equally take place within national confines. In his view, Brass's statement holds both at the level of national state-building around a language (sometimes even more than one), as well as the counter-assertion by language activists that citizenship and nationhood need not be predicated on a sole speech form. In fact, he argues, if the process of nation formation were not so linguistically homogenizing, local language movements would probably not have emerged with such force and vigour. His chapter is a fascinating account of recent linguistic dynamics in everyday practices as well as in ethnic activists' conscious attempts to revive their native languages. As he contends, the resultant amalgam is a heterogeneous blend of linguistic forms and elements, and a performative strategy that is rapidly gaining ground in Sikkim as well as in Nepal's urban centres. Such linguistic fusions have a bearing upon peoples' (multiple) belonging, allowing for reflecting upon one's own 'origins' through a preoccupation with one's mother tongue, while shaping one's own minority position within a national space.

Hutt's contribution (Chapter 17) focuses upon belonging in relation to an institution (monarchy) and the individual (the monarch) who embodies that institution. This reflection takes national boundedness as a point of departure, simultaneously admitting that fewer and fewer states in the world derive their unity and common belonging from the power of the monarch and the relationship to the monarch. From among the last Himalayan monarchies the kings of Ladakh, Sikkim, and several other once-autonomous Himalayan realms are now mere figures of history. Until 2008 the Shahs of Nepal and the Wangchucks of Bhutan were the sole survivors; now only the Wangchucks remain. His discussion seeks to demonstrate that concepts of belonging can help us understand why the monarch of one Himalayan nation state (Nepal) has been dethroned and socially displaced, while another (that of Bhutan) appears to have secured the future of his line for at least another generation.

Tibet's case, discussed by Martin Mills (Chapter 16), also closely relates to the question of national boundaries, their location and their enclosing and encompassing nature. Within the confines of China's boundaries, the status and the scope of the Tibetan Autonomous Region continues to be a highly conflictive and polarizing topic—as the scholarly debates also reveal. Mills presents the Tibetan question as a puzzle and addresses two concerns. First, he examines the relationship between the idea of the Greater Tibet, the spread of its borders, and the understating of the constructions of its commonalities and the broader distribution of Tibetan solidarities. Second, he embarks upon the question of how such ideas of belonging—through commonality and solidarity—relate to actual events in Tibet's past. He is interested in the genesis and meaning of historical claims and processes of thought and practice impinging upon the sense of territorial belonging. He suggests that *belonging* is a mode of performance that acts as the necessary precondition for identity claims. The identity claims act, in turn, to obscure the conditions of their own genesis, by legitimizing them on the grounds that particular people, practices, and places intrinsically and always (or at least for a very long time) have 'had' a certain quality. These claims can be understood as acts of distancing vis-à-vis the overpowering collectivization enforced by the Chinese state.

Nepalese nationalism, sustained formerly by royalty, would be another instance of persistence of national boundaries in this time of globalization. The belongingness of Nepali citizens to their country is a quite strong and widely shared feeling among the population, especially in the hills, even if the issue of federalism is presently on the forefront of the political scene and a crucial demand for a number of ethnic minorities as well for the Tarai's inhabitants (cf. *infra*). This feeling is sustained by communist political parties, such as the Maoists (UCPN (M.)) and CPN (UML), and often used as a political means for gaining electorates. Nationalism in Nepal is mostly associated with the notion of 'Nepaliness', *nepalipan*, in opposition mainly to Indian and Madhesi people from the Tarai plains belt. It is reminiscent of the 19th-century period of Nepalese history and its prevailing xenophobic way of thinking against everything coming from abroad. The suspicion towards 'non-Nepali' is still at work in discussion within the Constituent Assembly, especially in relation to rules of citizenship, in case of one of the parents being a non-Nepali citizen. It is also at stake for issues related to double citizenship, a core demand of Non-Resident Nepalis (NRNs) living abroad. These Nepalese were until very recently nearly ignored. The 'Non-resident Nepalese Association' has been officially recognized only in 2011 and it is only after years of consisting lobbying that the government finally promulgated the Non-Resident Act in August 2007 (Sijapati, 2010). Yet this Act remains silent on the question of dual citizenship. Nepalese authorities hesitate mainly because they fear giving Nepalese citizenship to Indians through distorted and illegal means.

As far as transnational migrations are concerned, they seldom encourage a sense of world citizenship, but rather reinforce local nationalist feeling. This applies also to religious feelings: despite the rise of new Hindu sects displaying more general and syncretistic forms of beliefs and practices, Hinduism has been increasingly manipulated during recent decades by national political parties, in the Gangetic plains as well as in the Himalayas, under the Hindutva movement. In other words, the erosion of national boundaries within SAARC countries is extremely limited.

Sondra Hausner's analysis reveals yet another important aspect of state boundaries reinforced by national immigration policies and legal regulations. The Nepali nurses—unlike professionals from India or from the Philippines—do not fit into national contingents allowed to enter the United Kingdom and join its labour force. Under these legal constraints, highly qualified Nepali nurses can only enter the United Kingdom under the pretence of being students and find employment far beneath their expertise. This results in lower pay and, equally importantly, in a reduced chance of forging meaningful social bonds while abroad.

THE DISCOURSE OF ETHNICITY

Another aspect of 'deglobalization', characterized by collective closure, is the widespread wave of entrenched communalism and ethnicity discourses all over the globe. Ethnic revivalism has become a successful mobilization formula and a permanent element of political communication, discouraging other unitary or more citizen-oriented initiatives. In India and Nepal, ethno-separatist movements have been increasingly vocal. As in other parts of our globe, the rise of ethnic voices and autochthonous movements in the Himalayas is one of the major phenomena in the last decades and an important aspect of changes in local contemporary societies (see Geschiere, 2009; Li, 2000, spoke of a "global conjuncture of indigeneity"). Since the early 1990s, ethnic groups, labelled locally *Adivasis/Janajatis*, have been at the forefront of the political scene. In Nepal, ethnic groups represent a large part of the population (about 37 per cent). In India, the number of ethnic minorities is significantly smaller, but ethnic activism is still on the rise, especially targeting the affirmative action and quota system. In the former kingdom of Nepal, the shift from the former Shah/Rana assimilationist policy to a democratic regime more receptive to cultural diversity has opened a space for ethnic groups to put forward their claims for better self-representation and 'state restructuring' (see Gellner et al., 2008). The ethnic *Adivasi/Janajati* organizations demand separate autonomous units, based on ethnicity, even if the population realities of the concerned territories—with their much more intermixed and heterogeneous populations—are different from those asserted by ethno-activists. Such demands have been increasingly acknowledged in the new nation-building process ('New Nepal') and have become an intrinsic element of the political debate. These topics invite us to reconsider the relationships between ethnicity and the nation state that involve embattled spatial dynamics. These dynamics are crucial for understanding the present-day reconfigurations in new constellations of belonging. Ethnic activists' claims to localized territories are buttressed by depictions of strong communal solidarities and a persistence of traditional values, norms, and practices. These depictions stand in a very interesting relationship to the ethnic horizons stretching globally. In this vein, ethnic self-representations and solidarities work as global infrastructures for maintaining social ties while drawing upon new ideas and networks for maintaining the traditional forms of life (Rycroft and Dasgupta, 2011).

The *ethnic idiom*, based on old-fashioned ethnographic concepts and ideologies born in the 19th century, tends to portray each ethnic group as a *collective self*, with its own territory, its own language, its own culture, and so on. These ethnic communities highlight mutuality, relations of reciprocity within the group, common history, a sense of equality (as opposed to the caste system), autochthony, as well as indigeneity. The last aspects suggest special rights of ethnic groups towards certain territories, despite early migration movements from elsewhere and the diversity of the populations living in nearly every geographical zone. Ethnic activists celebrate difference and the strength of the self-organization of their 'communities'. Their leaders are aspiring to reshape the state after centuries of what they call the 'internal colonialism' or the 'imperialism' of the high Hindu castes. Numerous attempts at rewriting history have occurred, sometimes inventing new *vamshavali* chronicles or searching for indigenous scripts. By and large, such revisionist narratives have resulted in downplaying the role of other groups as far as the rights to the land are concerned, in particular. Some such cases have been documented in the previous volumes of this Governance, Conflict, and Civil Action series, in particular in Volume 2. In northeast India and in Nepal, these indigenous claims are or were more or less explicitly associated with various insurgency movements, in conflict with the central state.

This *return of the local* in the Himalayas—a process echoing Geschiere's and Li's observations in other parts of the world (2009)—is a fascinating phenomenon for understanding present-day preoccupations with the ways that feelings of belonging are created (Robertson, 1995). Seen in a wider context, there is an interesting contrast among the apparent compression of space at the international level, the assertion of ethnic territories (through the federal system in the political agenda), and the reinforcement of ethnic boundaries. Local histories and world histories are becoming increasingly intertwined (Trouillot, 2001). The dream of a global world is accompanied by praise in favour of bounded homogenous territories. These forms of communalism and violent discourses of ethnicity obviously represent a new quest for belonging, in reaction to current streams of globalization and the wide encompassing changes affecting most of areas in Asia.

Ethnicity, which is vocal all over the world, increasingly thrives upon *transnational connections*. The upsurge over the last three decades of the notion of *autochthonous* ('born from the earth') and of *indigeneity* in global political arenas is a remarkable phenomenon. These two notions have become a globally dominant discourse.

Ethnicity and minority rights are on the agenda of the United Nations and a part of their policy in favour of endangered local cultures. This international organization apparently may not have realized that in supporting such causes, they are in fact backing basic distinctions between autochthons and others, that is, perpetuating a form of exclusion. Indigenous tribal identity and world recognition are closely interconnected.

CHANGING RELIGIONS, NEW TRENDS, AND TRANSNATIONAL ASPECTS

All over the Himalayas, *religion anchors identity*. It shapes personal and group forms of belonging more than any other traditional bonds crossing national and political boundaries. Religion is therefore an important field of inquiry to ponder when addressing contemporary sociopolitical transformations that affect shifts of identities and belonging. Changes in this domain have been considerable over the last decades: they operated simultaneously in many spatial and temporal registers. New religious movements or trends were established in the Himalayas, sometimes with great success. Although conversion to other religions is not yet recognized and legalized in Nepal, freedom of beliefs and practices is at present much better protected and enshrined than ever before in this country. Since the fall of the absolute monarchy in 1990, Christianization—proseltiyzation was traditionally banned—is on the rise in Nepal. The return of the democratic political model and the new freedom of conscience and self-organization have given Christianity new opportunities in the districts and among diverse ethnic groups and castes. As in India, Christianity's egalitarianism is particularly attractive to people belonging to lower castes or to marginalized ethnic groups. Christianity is the fastest growing faith community in Nepal (though its followers still represent less then 1 per cent of the population according to the much-challenged 2001 census). In this book, Blandine Ripert (Chapter 2) gives the example of the Tamangs of Nuwakot and Dhading, where a significant number of conversions have taken place in recent years.

The spread of the Theravada form of Buddhism is another significant example of religious change over recent decades. Theravada expanded in Nepal first among the Newars of the Kathmandu valley (in the 1930s), benefiting from multiple strands of communication between Nepal and Thailand (and sometimes Burma). For decades, there was a constant movement of leaders, money, and literature, particularly between the two countries. Buddhist high-caste Newars thought by this means to 'purify' their own Mayahanist and Vajrayanist traditions and priestly practice, which after centuries of existence had been moulded in Newar culture and adopted to local exigencies (LeVine and Gellner, 2005). In this book, Chiara Letizia (Chapter 12) documents the spread of this religious movement among Tharus and Magars, two ethnic groups mobilized in *Janajati* politics. Such a conversion represents an important shift as these two ethnic groups do not have any traditional link with Buddhism themselves, at least in recent histories, but rather with Hinduism. The promoters of Buddhism in the Tharu and Magar districts of Nepal insist on the need to stop calling on Brahman priests for rituals. As a matter of fact, for many *Janajati* intellectuals, Buddhist modernism offers a strong and positive response in a pan-Indian and modernizing form to the domination of the high cases, particularly the Brahmans, in all spheres of Nepalese society (Krauskopff, 2009: 251).

It is worth mentioning another religious trend linked to trans-national movements: the growing importance of some Hindu sects (Sai Baba, Iskcon, Pranami) to the detriment of more traditional and ritualistic forms of popular Hinduism in Nepal. These sects, whose adherents put more emphasis on a universalistic religious discourse (uniting, for instance, Christian, Muslims, and Hindus), prosper in the contemporary Himalayas, particularly in its central and eastern reaches. Some of them highlight a reformist aspect of Hinduism, more respectful of women's roles and much opposed to the caste system, for instance, fitting the democratic atmosphere and present preoccupations of society. Here, as in other domains, links between India and Nepal still prevail. Indian religious leaders affiliated to a specific sect, or famous yoga teachers tour Nepal to instruct and encourage followers. Large sums of money are transmitted across the border to support religious activities in India or Nepal, especially the building of schools, medical clinics, and other social welfare projects (Toffin, 2012).

Finally, our volume also highlights the *development of new forms or religiosity* and religious practices, less focused on temples, statues, and rituals. Some are linked to a guru, such as Ram Dev, Vikasananda, and Ravi Shankar, to mention but a few. But others, especially the Japanese sects of Reiki and Jorei, which are very influential in Nepal urban areas, do not place the founder of their organization at the centre of their community. Most of these groups are open to all religions and castes. They insist on meditation, yogic exercises, what they called the 'art of living', naturotherapy, spiritual powers, and sometimes massage. They are also linked with healing practices that challenge traditional Himalayan therapists and old categories of priesthood. These examples indicate that select supralocal influences such as religious innovation are welcomed by larger sections of local populations. They are often in contradiction with the political defiance between Nepal and India and the resilience of political borders between the two countries. In some cases, these external influences are appropriated and reformulated in more local or national terms.

Globalization is involved in these religious changes in at least two aspects. First, such transformations highlight a wide circulation of ideas beyond state boundaries that are facilitated by modern forms of communication, TV with its specialized religious channels in particular. Second, people's new aspirations in these matters reveal a shift in the politics of the self. They are less encapsulated within traditional bonds of caste, ethnicity, and family. They are more exposed to external trends from abroad and more open to syncretic ideas, which have often been identified by specialists of religious issues as New Age worldwide Hinduism. Urbanization, for instance, detaches young people, men and women, from their families, and gives rise to both opportunities and challenges with respect to the direction of livelihoods independent from one's relations. At the same time, these new influences tend to reinforce communal ties.

RESISTANCE TO GLOBALIZATION

Other globalizing forces have raised numerous forms of protest throughout the Himalayan range. Many movements have positioned themselves as explicitly 'anti-globalization' (Baviskar, 2008). Well-known protests include those against dam-construction and other hydropower projects, as well as fighting efforts by international companies to impose patent rights over Himalayan plants. These Himalayan contestations and the individual as well as collective bearers of such protest movements have become famous (and even notorious) throughout the world. Himalayan protest movements are of particular interest because locally instigated actions in small mountain villages have become known throughout the South Asian subcontinent and well beyond this region. The Chipko protests (India, western Himalayas), providing the most famous example, have served as a role model for protest movements in other parts of the world. This example reveals that globalization cannot be perceived as a one-way process, initiated in some remote locale and simply pressing upon local life-worlds. Local microcosms can be a source of dynamics that eventually acquire a transnational or global dimension.

Another important field of inquiry lies in people's perceptions of how global forces impinge upon their circumstances and how local life-worlds are to be protected against external intrusion. The chapters written by Arora and by Subba (Chapters 13 and 14, respectively) indicate which rationales and what political language are in the forefront when villagers and their leaders express and attempt to justify their dissent and their demands. In the Himalayan contexts they discuss, embattled perceptions of the 'local' come to light. How is local belonging related to commitment, and how do the exponents of the movements assess what is 'good' and what is 'bad' for the well-being of their communities? The chapters show that we cannot expect one answer, but many.

Local social spaces are significantly altered by development interventions, in particular, by large-scale projects. The Himalayas, lacking many types of natural resources found in other regions of the world, are rich in water. Governments in all the adjacent Himalayan states have partnered either with international funding bodies (such as the Asian Development Bank) or with transnational corporations and national business entrepreneurs in transforming water into power. These efforts resulted in numerous infrastructural projects of so far unknown magnitude. In order to make such projects possible, plans were developed to build huge water dams, roads, and channels. This altered the availability of water—an already scare resource. Populations were asked to move elsewhere, providing financial compensation in exchange for lands and homesteads, and above all, for the loss of local belonging. The chapters by Subba and Arora document these changes, causing internal conflicts, loss of properties, displacement, loss in command over the collective homelands, and instigating critical movements challenging these overwhelming measures (see also Pfaff-Czarnecka, 2007). Both contributions examine these measures and struggles, and analyze them from the perspective of belonging. They indicate how in times of stress, local attachments become all the more meaningful, and how struggles against gigantic projects encourage local societies to grow together. These Himalayan *anti-globalization protest movements* also shed light upon the channels, networks, and interrelationship with external allies. Who plays an intermediary role in coining ideas and in designing modes of action? Do villagers and city-dwellers throughout the Himalayan region partner with each other and do they exchange information on the possible impact of projects, on demands to be made as well as on the most effective forms of protest action?

Subba and Arora's contributions reflect upon how seemingly local projects that overtly resist globalization in fact derive their resources externally. In particular, movements geared at protecting minority cultures, local languages, and religions often thrive on transnational networks, engage in international human rights forums, and derive funding from international institutions such as development agencies. After all, resistance to globalization may also be found in covert forms. The chapters reveal how villagers, eager to maintain their established relationships to external actors such as international donor agencies, feign consent to their action plans, while pursuing their hidden agendas that may aim at impeding projects from successful implementation. Subba's chapter (Chapter 13) gives a startling account to what extent such external interventions undermine local consensus. Whatever internal conflicts and rivalries existed before infrastructural interventions were planned, these have been significantly aggravated recently.

More generally, anti-globalization and pro-globalization lobbies have emerged in South Asia, as in other parts of the world. For the former, globalization is taken as being synonymous with economic liberalization, of Westernization and Americanization. It includes environmental group struggles for nature preservation. Pro-globalization lobbies argue, on the contrary, that such a process brings far more opportunities for practically everyone. Some people hold that the interconnected and globalized world facilitates their fight against social inequalities and discrimination. For instance, the Vice-Chancellor of Pune University (Narendra Jadhav), a Dalit himself, frequently claims in a most convincing manner how helpful the liberalization of his country was in dealing with caste discriminations and its fight for better social integration (Paris, 2007).

THE POLITICS OF THE SELF AND MULTIPLE VOICES

In studying the various processes of globalization, it is worth considering the psychological aspect of individuals and their personal trajectories. Based on ethnographic data, this method introduces a more personal and inner approach of the experiences of globalization/ belonging than the more abstract concepts of society and culture. Without documenting what can be called 'persons-in history' and the subjectivity of action's repertoire, important aspects of the all-pervading social transformations, their significance for people, would be beyond the scope of this volume. The aim is to give more comprehensibility to the social *through the* individual—its positionality and situatedness as well as the social horizons as unfolding from an individual standpoint.

To defend this viewpoint, it is important to remember that, in traditional contexts, the self is more or less encapsulated within cultural particular patterns. It is formed by practices and discourses within a larger sociocultural ensemble created by the end of childhood through rituals and other socializing practices that distilled cultural principles for the neophyte. That is not to say that in such so-called traditional societies persons do not exist from the sociological point of view: they do resist, suffer, oppose each other, but even then, the stress is on the group, on relatedness, on norms and stereotypes to be respected, on rules established by ancestors to reproduce, etc. In a premodern Newar town of the Kathmandu Valley or in a Magar village of the Nepalese hills, daily living time is, for instance, greatly predetermined by religious and social notions.

On the contrary, in diasporic, modern urban settings and other globalized social contexts, selves are less fixed and more exposed to change (Liechty, 2010). The networks of former students, of neighbours, sport, human rights and cultural groups, political parties, and professional associations are generally more informal and fluid than the former corporate groups based on primal forms of belonging. They disseminate more individual-centred values. One can thus observe a sharp proliferation of identity discourse and claims in post-1990 Nepal in light of broader structural transformations. To take an example, Nepalese urban modernist middle class, especially Newars, are much more exposed than before to new forms of Buddhist meditation (*vipassana*) that invest ethical agency in the individual conceived as a bounded and autonomous whole. These new religious trends tend to transform subjectivities and selves. They illustrate in a powerful manner a shift from personhood defined collectively or by ritual in the Newar Vajrayana Buddhist life-world to the individual sphere (Leve, 2011: 852).

By and large, when societies are in transition, when conditions of flux dominate, individuals are more open to conflicting values and more reflexive regarding the force of collective boundaries. Less subjugated to collective and communal rules, they are constantly negotiating their places in new cultural economies and normative systems. Nepalese migrants in Qatar recreate a network of relations with their other national companions in a way not so dissimilar from former village bonds, but at the same time different. They invent solidarities matching new necessities and responding to new forms of interest. As stressed here by Tristan Bruslé (Chapter 7), they experience new types of interdependence. These migrants are *in between*: between several positions and humanity, between citizenship and its denial. Working abroad is in many ways a process of disidentification or declassification. Migrants experience a feeling of dishonour (*beijat* in Nepali), they endure painful experiences abroad, disillusion, and a sense of loneliness (see also Hausner's chapter). People are thus in the process of reworking objectification and a sense of themselves vis-à-vis others, forging identities from available resources. "Individuals are engaged in creating, maintaining, switching, or changing their personal and cultural identities to meet various needs and life strategies" (Ghimire, 1998: 195).

Reconstructions of personal identities in response to globalization make up a wide and appealing field of research (Skinner et al., 1998). Current changes have introduced greater opportunities for realizing individual goals free from old forms of belonging. In addition, people increasingly formulate notions of themselves—they appropriate, contest, or resist certain identities. They potentially have more freedom to choose as individual actors in relation to new circumstances. This is what we call here *the politics of the self* and this implies that more attention is to be paid to *agency* in relation to culture and society. The basic fact of individuals being socially constructed in all types of situations has to be recognized. Though a person is always shaped by others and the encompassing world, self has not to be seen as only an embodiment of cultural forms. This may sound like a truism, but too many publications continue to engage in methodological collectivism. A range of various contentious situations sometimes engender behavioural disorders, unpredictable conduct, narratives of suffering, as well as protests against cultural and political systems. This has happened in the past, in premodern time, but it is far more frequent in the present day. In other words, it is crucial to link the debate about globalization to the politics of the self and to place these interrelations at the centre of the inquiry. The interplay between individuals and others, self and culture, between the subjective and the social, in the process of forming solidarities, obviously opens fresh windows of inquiry and understanding. Discourses continually shape and reshape human subjectivities. Volumes 2 and 3 of the present MIDEA series dealing with the personal trajectories of activists, politicians, and rebel leaders are particularly remarkable in this respect (Gellner, 2009; 2010).

Yet, in most cases, there is no clear divide between culturally expected rules and the new experiences of life among individuals living in globalized situations. Most Himalayan people living in a Nepalese urban or a diasporic context feel attached to a family, a caste, a neighbourhood, with expected rights and duties, even if they live temporarily far from these collective units. They are in permanent contact through modern means of communication with friends and relatives remaining at home. At the same time, they adopt a more wandering type of life, working in an unusual climate belonging to a different culture. Such bonds, celebrated at every familial event and in daily life, and experienced during every social occasion with people from outside, have powerful emotional appeal. However, the same persons see themselves as being alienated individuals whose identities are not essentially tied to groups and communities, floating in an anonymous whole constituted by other persons. In other words, the selves are more often than not the source of multiple voices, a source of multiplicity. This confrontation between a communal world view, linked with traditional values, and a more individualistic world view, is not new. Yet it is strengthened by modern conditions of life and ongoing globalization.

BELONGING TO THE HIMALAYAS

A final question remains to be addressed: the attachment of local people to the Himalayas as a regional entity. Do persons living within the Indian, Nepalese, or Bhutanese borders have the feeling, beyond their national sensitivity, to be attached to the 3,000-km-long Himalayan range? The question is difficult to answer. As with most mountainous regions of the world, the Himalayas, first of all, are constituted of fragmented, compartmentalized geographical zones, with little communication between the various adjacent valleys. The account of national sentiment in Nepal has a long history of enduring divisions, separateness, and military conquest. It can be designated as a quest towards unity since only the end of the 18th century, namely, over the past 200 years. This quest is far from being achieved. It can even be claimed that the unitary forces towards national integration are undergoing, in the present situation, a crisis of decomposition of what has been unified over the last decades.

Second, this question highlights the opposition between upland and lowland regions. Studies of specific mountain areas have almost invariably been contextualized within an integrated picture of highlands in contrast to an 'other', the lowlands. Himalayan societies are markedly different from the adjacent lowlands of South Asia, in the same way as the people of highlands Southeast Asian differ from those of the plains. This plains–mountains dichotomy persists despite globalization and the manifold translocal dynamics resulting in a significant influx of mountain populations to the adjacent plains. It is still deeply rooted in everyday life, in discourses and in widespread stereotypes. In the plains, the Himalayas are often synonymous with backwardness, political underdevelopment, anachronism, and marginality on the world stage. A form of distinctiveness is attached to the two geographical milieux, with identificatory referents from both sides. However, each Himalayan country has a lowland area, characterized by a higher potential of resources and the existence of different populations than those inhabiting the mountains or the hills. In India, the regional capital of the Uttarakhand state is, for instance, Dehradun, located in the valley and not in the hills. In the same way, in the eastern part of the range, Darjeeling district includes one tarai subdivision, and Kalimpong's main administrative centre, Siliguri, is located in the plains. Such inclusion within regional or national borders raises a number of conflicts where the notion of belonging to the mountains, to *himal* or *lek* as it is called in regional languages, plays an important role.

Third, the question of belonging to the Himalayas, as a source of identity and assertiveness, raises the issue of the attachment of these populations to wider political or regional zones, such as to South Asia or to the Asian world, for instance, as opposed to Western countries. This sense of awareness is obviously more developed in urban areas, among the middle class, than among peasants living in the hills. It plays a role in the process of globalization, even if it cannot be opposed, as some authors claim, radically to a an alternative process of what can be called 'asiatization'. In other words, in the urban areas (and sometimes also in rural zones), globalization comes as much from the East as from the West.

From a geographical and ethnographic viewpoint, there is no doubt that the Himalayas can be defined as a periphery, a marginal space between China and India, or Central Asia and South Asia. Though it has been for long a zone of passage through several passes between these wider geographical and cultural ensembles, its mountainous structure has maintained this region at most as a 'global periphery'. Yet, as will be shown in the following pages, this periphery is now quickly being transformed by the intensified contacts and globalized interconnection with the rest of the word. The shifting relations of belonging within trans-Himalayan social spaces make this possible.

NOTES

1. We would like to thank David Gellner, Michael Hutt, Tanka Subba, and Mark Turin for helpful comments on a draft of this introduction.
2. The title of the book can be translated into Nepali as: *Himalaya Bhekma Sampradayik Rajniti.*
3. Cf. also Fisher (2011: 4).
4. See Nandy (2002: 160–61); for a wider contemporary reflection on cosmopolitanism, see Vertovec and Cohen (2002).
5. On globalization in India, see Assayag and Fuller (2006). On collective identities, see Jodhka (2001).
6. "Tourism seemed to have encouraged conservation of the physical environment by introducing ecological awareness to the permanent residents and by promoting cleanliness" Ives (2004: 166).
7. On Bhutan, see Rinzin (2006: 22):

> Bhutan is in a critical phase of transition. As a formerly closed society it is opening up to the global world. Internally a process of decentralisation and political democratisation has been set in motion. A draft constitution is currently discussed all over the country. As a consequence the hierarchical structure of power will change into a more egalitarian one.

8. The Maoist armed conflict in Nepal has displaced an estimate of 600,000 people, of which 250,000 still live in the country (Ghimire, 2010: 91). *Bisthapits* displaced persons live mostly in Dang, Banke, Kathmandu, Lalitpur, and Bhaktapur, sometimes in riverside settlements.
9. On the Tibetan migration in Kashmir, see Riaboff (2002).
10. Cf. Strawn (1994: 25–36) and Hutt (2003).

REFERENCES

Assayag, Jackie and Chris Fuller (eds). 2006. *Globalizing India. Perspectives from Below*. London: Anthem Press.

Baviskar, Amita (ed.). 2008. *Contested Grounds. Essays on Nature, Culture, and Power*. New Delhi: Oxford University Press.

Bhabha, Homi. 1994. *The Location of Culture*. London: Routledge.

Bruslé, T. 2010. 'Nepalese Migrations: Introduction', *European Bulletin of Himalayan Research*, 35–36: 16–23.

Caplan, Lionel. 1995. *Warrior Gentlemen: Gurkhas in the Western Imagination*. New York, Oxford: Berghahn Books.

Choedon, Yeshi. 1995. 'Impact of Modernization on Society and Culture of Sikkim', in K. Warikoo (ed.), *Society and Culture in the Himalayas*. New Delhi: Har Anand Publications.

Croucher, Sheila L. 2004. *Globalization and Belonging. The Politics of Identity in a Changing World*. Lanhman: Rowman & Littlefield Publishers, Inc.

Eisenstadt, Shmuel Noah. 2002. *Multiple Modernities*. New Brunswick: Transaction Publishers.

Fisher, James F. 2011. *Globalization in Nepal. Theory and Practice*. The Mahesh Chandra Regmi Lecture (2011). Kathmandu: Social Science Baha.

Gellner, David N. (ed.). 2009. *Ethnic Activism and Civil Society in South Asia* (Governance, Conflict, and Civic Action 2). New Delhi: SAGE Publications.

———. 2010. *Varieties of Activist Experience: Civil Society in South Asia*. (Governance, Conflict, and Civic Action 3). New Delhi: SAGE Publications.

Gellner, David N. 2013. 'Warriors, Workers, Traders and Peasants: The Nepali/ Gorkhali Diaspora since the Nineteenth Century', in D. Washbrook and J. Chatterjee (eds), *Routledge Handbook of South Asian Diaspora*, pp. 136–50. London: Routledge.

Gellner, David, Joanna Pfaff-Czarnecka, and John Whelpton. 2008. *Nationalism and Ethnicity in a Hindu Kingdom*. Kathmandu: Vajra Books.

Geschiere, Peter. 2009. 'Introduction. Autochthony. the Flip Side of Globalization', in Peter Geschiere (ed.), *The Perils of Belonging. Autochthony, Citizenship and Exclusion in Africa and Europe*. Chicago: University of Chicago Press.

Ghimire, Anita. 2010. 'Caught between two Worlds: Internal Displacement Induced Dilemma in Nepal', *European Bulletin of Himalayan Research*, 35–36: 91–106.

Ghimire, Premalata. 1998. 'Crossing Boundaries: Ethnicity and Marriage in a Hod Village', in D. Skinner (ed.), *Selves in Time and Space: Identities, Experience and History in Nepal*. Lanham: Rowman & Littlefield Publishers.

Giddens, Anthony. 1990. *The Consequences of Modernity*. London: Polity Press.

Gruzinski, Serge. 2004. *Les Quatre parties du monde. Histoire d'une mondialisation.* Paris: Editions de la Martinière.

Harvey, David. 1989. *The Condition of Postmodernity.* Oxford: Basil Blackwell.

Hutt, Michael. 2003. *Unbecoming Citizens—Culture, Nationhood, and the Flight of Refugees from Bhutan.* New Delhi: Oxford University Press.

Inda, Jonathan and Renato Rosaldo. 2002. 'Introduction: A World in Motion', in Jonathan Inda and Renato Rosaldo (eds), *Anthropology of Globalization*, pp. 1–34. Oxford: Blackwell.

Ives, Jack. 2004. *Himalayan Perceptions—Environmental Change and the Well-Being of Mountain Peoples.* New York: Routledge.

Jodkha, Surinder S. 2001. *Community and Identities. Contemporary Discourses and Politics in India.* New Delhi: SAGE Publications.

Krauskopff, Gisèle. 2009. 'Intellectuals and Ethnic Activism: Writings on the Tharu Past', in David N. Gellner (ed.), *Ethnic Activism and Civil Society in South Asia*, pp. 241–68. New Delhi: SAGE Publications.

Lechner, Frank J. and John Boli (eds). 2000. *The Globalization Reader.* Oxford: Blackwell.

Leve, Lauren. 2011. 'Identity', *Current Anthropology*, 52(4): 513–35.

LeVine, Sarah and David N. Gellner. 2005. *Rebuilding Buddhism. The Theravada Movement in Twentieth-Century Nepal.* Cambridge: Harvard University Press.

Lewis, Todd T. 1993. 'Himalayan Frontier Trade: Newar Diaspora Merchants and Buddhism', in Charles Ramble, Martin Brauen, Beatrice Miller, and Gérard Toffin (eds), *Anthropology of Tibet and the Himalaya*, pp. 165–78.

Li, T. 2000. 'Articulating Indigenous Identity in Indonesia: Resource Politics and the Tribal Slot', *Comparative Studies in Society and History*, 42(1): 149–79.

Liechty, Mark. 2010. *Out Here in Kathmandu. Modernity on the Global Periphery.* Kathmandu: Martin Chautari Press.

Lien, Marianne Elisabeth and Marit Melhuus. 2007. *Holding Worlds Together: Ethnographies of Knowing and Belonging.* New York, Oxford: Berghahn Books.

Merry, Sally Engle. 2006. *Human Rights and Gender Violence. Translating International Law into Local Justice.* Chicago and London: Chicago University Press.

Messerschmidt, Don A. 1976. *The Gurungs of Nepal: Conflict and Change in a Village Society.* Warminster: Aris and Phillips Ltd.

Nandy. 2002. *Time Warps, Silent and Evasive Pasts in Ancient Indian Politics and Religion.* London: Hurst and Company.

Peot, Adam. 2005. *Waking up in Dharamsala: An Inquiry into the Stories of Young Westerners Who Have Sought Buddhist Wisdom in Northern India.* Lund University: Center for East and South-East Asian Studies.

Pfaff-Czarnecka, Joanna. 1993. 'Migration under Marginality Conditions: The Case of Bajhang', in O. Schwank et al. (eds), *Rural-Urban Interlinkages: A Challenge for Swiss Development Cooperation*, pp. 97–109. Zürich: INFRAS/IDA.

———. 2007. 'Challenging Goliath: People, Dams, and the Paradoxes of Transnational Critical Movements', in H. Ishii, D.N. Gellner, and K. Nawa (eds), *Political and Social Transformations in North India and Nepal (Social Dynamics in Northern South Asia)*, vol. 2, pp. 421–526; Japanese Studies on South Asia 6. New Delhi: Manohar.

———. 2011. *From 'Identity' to 'Belonging' in Social Research: Plurality, Social Boundaries and the Politics of the Self.* Frankfurt: Vervuert.

Pfaff-Czarnecka, Joanna and Gérard Toffin. 2011. 'Introduction: Belonging and Multiple Attachments in Contemporary Himalayan Societies', in J. Pfaff-Czarnecka and G. Toffin (eds), *The Politics of Belonging in the Himalayas. Local Attachments and Boundary Dynamics*, pp. xi–xxxviii. New Delhi: SAGE Publications.

Pieterse, Jan Nederveen. 2009. *Globalization and Culture*. Lanham, MD: Rowman and Littlefield.

Pollock, Sheldon. 2006. *The Language of the Gods in the World of Men: Sanskrit, Culture, and Power in Premodern India*. Berkeley: University of California Press.

Regmi, Mahesh Chandra. 1976. *Landownership in Nepal*. Berkeley: University of California Press.

Riaboff, Isabelle. 2002. 'The Bod of Kabön (Jammu and Kashmir, India)—How to be a Buddhist in a Hindu Land?', in Katia Buffetrille and Hildegard Diemberger (eds), *Proceedings of the Ninth Seminar of the Iats, 2000, Volume 9: Territory and Identity in Tibet and the Himalayas: Tibetan Studies in Honour of Anne-Marie Blondeau*, pp. 325–40. Leiden, Boston, Köln: Brill.

Rinzin, C. 2006. *On the Middle Path: The Social Basis for Sustainable Development in Bhutan*. Utrecht 2006 (Nederlandse Geografische Studies 352).

Rizvi, Janet. 1999. *Trans-Himalayan Caravans—Merchant Princes and Peasant Traders in Ladakh*. New Delhi: Oxford University Press.

Robertson, Robert. 1995. 'Glocalization: Time-space and Homogeneity and Heterogeneity', in Featherstone et al. (eds), *Global Modernities*, pp. 23–44. London: SAGE Publications.

Rycroft, Daniel J. and Sangeeta Dasgupta (eds). 2011. *The Politics of Belonging in India. Becoming Adivasi*. London: Routledge.

Sagant, Philippe. 1978. 'Ampleur et profondeur historique des migrations Népalaises', *L'Ethnographie* II, CXX: 93–119.

Shrestha, Nanda. 1990. *Landlessness and Migration in Nepal*. Boulder: Westview Press.

Sijapati, Bandita. 2010. 'Nepali Transmigrants; an Examination of Transnational Ties among Nepalese Immigrants in the United States', *European Bulletin of Himalayan Research*, 35–36: 139–53.

Skinner, D., A. Pach III, and D. Holland (eds). 1998. *Selves in Time and Place. Identities, Experience, and History in Nepal*. Lanham: Rowman & Littlefield Publishers, Inc.

Steger, Manfred B. 2009. *Globalization, a Very Short Introduction*. Oxford: Oxford University Press.

Strawn, Christopher. 1994. 'Nepali Migration to Bhutan', *European Bulletin of Himalayan Research*, 7: 25–36.

Therborn, Göran. 2003. 'Entangled Modernities', *European Journal of Social Theory*, 6(3): 293–305.

Thieme, Susan. 2007. *Social Networks and Migration: Far West Nepalese Labour Migrants in Delhi*. Berlin, Münster, Wien: Lit-Verlag.

Toffin, Gérard. 2010. 'Urban Fringes: Squatter and Slum Settlements in the Kathmandu Valley (Nepal)', *Contributions to Nepalese Studies*, 37(2): 151–68.

———. 2011. 'The Propagation of a Hindu Sect in India and Nepal. The Krishna Pranami Sampraday', *South Asia: Journal of South Asian Studies*, 34(1): 1–30.

Toffin, Gérard. 2012. 'The Power of Boundaries. National and Transnational Horizons among Krishna Pranamis of India and Nepal', in John Zavos, Deepa Reddy, Pralay Kanungo et al. (eds), *Public Hinduisms*. New Delhi: SAGE Publications.

Trouillot, Michel-Rolph. 2001. 'The Anthropology of the State in the Age of Globalization. Close Encounters of the Deceptive Kind', *Current Anthropology*, 42(1): 125–38.

Vertovec, Steven and Robin Cohen. 2002. *Conceiving Cosmopolitanism. Theory, Context, and Practice*. Oxford: Oxford University Press.

PART I
SHIFTING HORIZONS OF BELONGING

Chapter 2

Improbable Globalization

Individualization and Christianization among the Tamangs

BLANDINE RIPERT

We could try to understand the vast processes of globalization by approaching them through a particular place. The idea would be, then, to show how such processes leave their mark on local realities, how it is *internalized*—in the words of Olivier Dollfus (1997)—within a particular location and finally how it functions through a cluster of mediations and influences on a specific population, on localized individuals, within a relatively limited—and in this case rather bounded—social space among the Tamangs of two districts of Central Nepal. This case represents only one of the innumerable faces of globalization, but it is improbable in that it is so far removed from the globalized images that are so routinely mediatized throughout the world. It is also geographically remote, a location that could almost seem to belong to another world at one of the ends-of-the-earth. Globalization processes have made their mark on these Tamangs, not via media that are sometimes likened to super-highways, but via a particular network of steep mountain paths in the Himalayas. Which is precisely the interest of this case: Seeking to understand what is happening in this remote region, accessible only after several days' walk—as is often the case in the Himalayas—and which seems to be completely outside the great contemporary circuits of exchange. It is a region with no access to electricity, roads, or telephones, and where there is no expectation of witnessing the more pronounced effects of the processes of globalization. It is not a region whose inhabitants live in total autarky, however, nor are they deprived of exchange with other populations or exposure to the changes that affect the rest of the world. This has never been the case, nor can it be said that this population has never experienced transformations in the past. In fact, within the space of two or three centuries, they have changed from a nomadic lifestyle tied to animal husbandry, to a culture based on slash-and-burn agriculture and, finally, to a sedentarized existence on the mountain slopes.

In this chapter, I will attempt to summarize the transformations that I have observed among the Tamangs in Dhading and Nuwakot districts in recent decades by describing how they can be understood as participating in globalization. In this vein, my analysis will also raise questions about the Christianization of a large number of them, a concomitant process related to globalization. Based on the spoken accounts of Christian converts, I will then turn to some of the consequences of these changes for collective belonging and the ways in which changes in belonging stemming from processes of globalization have played—or not played—a role in religious conversions.[1] The approach through the belonging concept, as defined by Pfaff-Czarnecka and Toffin (2011), helps to go beyond the idea of identity constructions: we shall see for example that belonging allows fast movements, depending on context and changes.

The Tamangs, coming from the North, apparently migrated across the flanks of the Himalayan mountains several centuries ago. Their language is of Tibeto-Burman origin, and they are divided into two different groups—the Western Tamangs (studied by Toffin, 1976a, 1976b, 1986b; Höfer, 1981; Holmberg, 1989; Fricke, 1994; Campbell, 1997) and the Eastern Tamangs (Steinman, 1987, Tamang, 1995). My field observations focused on two valleys settled by the Western Tamangs, the Ankhu Khola and the Salankhu Khola, which are situated at the foot of the Ganesh Himal range in the districts of Nuwakot and Dhading northwest of Kathmandu. The villages in this area are effectively mono-ethnic (with only a few families of blacksmiths from an Indo-Nepalese Parbatiya sub-caste also present, and Ghales, who are there assimilated to the Tamangs). This contrasts with the lower valley, where a variety of groups and castes coexist. The Tamangs' traditional social organization centres on the differentiation of exogamous clans. The collective interest of the group, in this case of the local sub-clan, overrides that of the individual. In this region, the Tamangs collectively employ an agro-sylvo-pastoral system of subsistence farming on the slopes surrounding their villages, which are between 500 and 3,000 metres in altitude, with a population of 1,500–4,000 inhabitants. Although their fields are worked on by nuclear families, they were traditionally farmed according to a community-based system in which the individual does not choose either the crop or the agricultural calendar, owing primarily to the practice of range pasturing that follows the harvests. Until the 1990s, the region's Tamang inhabitants typically produced adequate crops to sustain their needs for 6–8 months of the year. Some members typically left for seasonal or temporary migrations in the north of the Indian subcontinent, bringing back enough grain to nourish their families for the remainder of the year. The occasional rare monetary surpluses were spent on collective religious rituals such as funerals and weddings and in this way were redistributed. There was also little accumulation of either individual or familial wealth, and little investment in agricultural operations (Dobremez, 1986).

Although Nepal's 'entrance into the world' began in 1950, when its borders were opened after having been closed to foreigners since 1769, it was in 1991, after the collapse of Nepal's partyless Panchayat regime and the writing of a new democratic constitution, that a second round of political and economic openness became possible. As a result, in the 1990s there followed a long series of concurrent transformations that, while not necessarily inter-connected, each had repercussions for the other in an uncoordinated way that differed depending on the specific locality. These changes included the democratization of Nepal, mass politicization, the growth of the *Janajati* movement, the expansion of the market economy, the introduction of foreign (mostly Chinese)-manufactured goods into local markets, substantial influx of foreign aid, the proliferation of NGOs in economic and political competition with the government, the rise of mass tourism, and the delayed and somewhat limited arrival of the Asian agricultural 'Green Revolution'.

In the Tamang villages that I describe here, this 'opening to the World', in the sense of Jacques Lévy et al. (2008), manifested itself through the introduction of new ideas, new techniques, and manufactured products that were disseminated by the villagers themselves, who have increasingly travelled in the rest of the world, in search of answers to the problems that they were experiencing at home, among which were the consequences of high population growth.

A variety of agricultural innovations inspired by the Asian Green Revolution enabled a series of technical and financial improvements, the most notable of which was a substantial rise in crop yields, which doubled on average within 10 years (from 1984 to 1994) in Salankhu Khola, as well as an increase in the practice of crop rotation. The consequences of these innovations were numerous, rapid, and consequential, and they culminated in the replacement of community-based practices by individual innovations.[2] From a spatial perspective, these transformations triggered increasing subdivision of land and the dispersal of living areas that had previously been clustered together, and ultimately the fragmentation of farmland that had always been farmed by the entire community. The management of space became increasingly privatized on several levels, from cultivated parcels of land to inhabited areas (Smadja, 1995; Ripert, 2009). The organization of labour was in turn altered in response to these changes, and community-based practices that were widespread among the Tamangs, particularly in terms of agricultural labour (Toffin, 1986a), disappeared as they too became individualized. To take one example: traditional mutual-aid groups have often been replaced by remunerated piece-work, which has subsequently come to be considered more efficient. The traditional practice of range pasturing of the fields after harvest that involved the entire community has also been abandoned and even forbidden in some villages.

The village economies of Salankhu Khola and the lower part of Ankhu Khola have been profoundly transformed, and most families have become self-sufficient for food, as confirmed by follow-up observations of farms between the 1980s and the 1990s, and by interviews conducted in the 1990s. The ability to accumulate even a modest monetary surplus now brings choices about how the money is spent. Because it is no longer solely devoted to buying food, both the function and status of money have significantly changed. By tradition, savings from labour migrations were primarily applied to grain purchases to cover for the several-month shortfall in the families' agricultural production. In earlier times, in the exceptional event of a monetary surplus, the handful of comparatively wealthy individuals were expected to spend their modest savings on religious ceremonies. Social recognition was thus achieved through a profusion of offerings while also ensuring that wealth was redistributed to an extent within the community.

The sudden arrival of low-cost manufactured goods at local markets connected by road to Kathmandu, such as Trisuli Bazar and Dhading Besi (located from two to five days' walk from the region mentioned), confronted villagers with unfamiliar choices. Because money was no longer restricted to sustenance, it became available for purchases of goods such as plastic and aluminium utensils, flash-lights, plastic tarpaulins, rope, corrugated tin, paint, nails, radios, cameras, clothing of a wider variety, shoes, and sunglasses. Villagers carry these new goods home on their back.

The new status of money is readily apparent during interviews, but it is above all observable in villagers' practices. Newly acquired products within nuclear families have come to be more highly valued than collective expenditures at the level of the clan or village. In just a few years, a large number of new objects have appeared in the vil-lages; such acquisitions are often exhibited with great pride by their owners. Analysis of their discourses indicates that these expenditures are now thought of as more useful and more durable than collective expenditures, which have abruptly become the focus of criticism, in particular the food purchases that were shared during collective religious rituals. It is now preferable in the eyes of villagers to possess a fine urban-style house, topped with corrugated, tin roofing and brightly painted, and to wear jeans and shoes, than to spend money on religious ceremonies.

However, recent access to consumer goods made possible by improved means of transportation and market expansion and by the new functions of money are not the only explanations for changed views of collective expenditures. Other factors have provided even greater exposure to the processes of globalization.

Since the 1990s, Tamangs' seasonal and temporary migrations to foreign countries have substantially increased, thus alleviating severe demographic pressures. Although migrations are not a recent phenomenon among Nepalese from the hills (for example, see Toffin, 1976a; Sagant, 1978; Acharya, 2000), destinations are increasingly distant, extending beyond the Indian subcontinent as far as Southeast Asia in the 1990s and, since the early 2000s, the Gulf nations. Not only are there more migrants than before among the Tamangs, but they now tend to migrate for longer periods, even causing occasional conflicts with the agricultural calendar and at times emptying the villages of men. It is possible today to refer to the fragmentation of Tamangs' living space, as they range across Southeast Asia to the Persian Gulf in search of temporary labour under often gruelling conditions.

Economic migrations are a powerful vector of social change[3] that exposes these Tamangs to economies, cultures, and ideas that are extremely remote from their own and integrate them into the global economy as some of the world's cheapest day-labourers. As they discover developed countries about which they had no previous idea, villagers also become sensitized to their own extreme poverty. New ideas about waste, profitability, loss of time, and profit emerge in the discourses of these migrants when they return to their villages. While they travel, the Tamangs seem to compare their social organization and their religious system to practices that they observe elsewhere in the world. This exposure to other realities modifies their sense of belonging as Tamang, as Nepalese, and as global citizens. As I showed in another chapter (Ripert, 2013), migration can have a strong impact on links between belonging and territory. The emergence of new types of mobility seems to have altered their perception of group belonging and of village territoriality, thereby leading, in some cases, to renewed assertions of identity.[4]

During the same decade as this series of significant agricultural and economic transformations, Nepal became democratized in the wake of a popular insurrection in 1990. On the local level, this has led to remarkable political changes, and notions such as freedom and individual political choice—as opposed to community or clan-level choices—have radiated outward from the capital to the villages, as was evident from numerous interviews conducted during local elections (cf. Ripert, 2000). The elections in the 1990s brought a new generation to power that has contributed to the blurring of traditional social boundaries and rules. It was during the 1990s that the first batch of children to attend school in the Tamang villages of the region came to adulthood, and, unlike other villagers, these 'educated youth'[5] knew how to read and write and were imbued with references and values that were radically different from those of their elders. Their schooling has to a certain extent secularized how they represent the world and modified their interactions with the natural environment. Scientific school subjects, which have become increasingly prominent in the new school textbooks since the 1990s, have also rationalized their ways of knowing (Ripert, 2009). Learning Nepali, the national language, and the markers of a shared culture and history that suffuse textbooks has *Nepalized* these young Tamangs, leading them to perceive Tamang culture from an increasing distance, and even to degrade it openly in dialogues with their elders. In the 1990s, the sense of belonging to a wider society took precedence over belonging to the Tamang group among youth who were, at the same time, denigrating Tamang skills and way of life (that will change in the 2000s). This was in contrast to what was happening in Kathmandu Valley, where Tamangs and other groups were very much involved in *Janajati* recognition and indigenous activism (Gellner, 2007, 2009; Gellner et al., 1997; Tamang, 2009). During many occasions in the 1990s, I tried to discuss with villagers about these ethnic claims, but the youth as well as the elders answered that they were not concerned or not aware of what was going on. None of them spoke of Tamsaling, the autonomous territory claimed by the ethnic group, for example.[6]

Being educated has given young people new authority owing to their literacy and their Nepali language skills. Surrounded by illiterates, they are able to some extent to dominate the rest of the population. Traditional forms of authority were until recently based on clans and communal chiefs recruited from among the descendants of the founding ancestor of a given locality. Despite administrative reforms, the former chiefs of local sub-clans had retained power over the community by being elected by the village committees, but the political rise of educated youth has caused this traditional power structure to dissolve and diminish the familial authority of elders. Educated youth have also become important agents in the Christianization process, filling the role of 'local pastors' owing to their ability to read the Bible to older villagers.

These transformations have unfolded in the span of only a few years, and they were made possible only by exposure to the processes of globalization, even if it was discontinuous and indirect and sometimes arrived at a walking pace up steep mountain paths. The changes have also profoundly altered the Tamangs' understanding both of their immediate environment and of their role in the wider world. The fact that their religious understanding of the world has also changed is illustrated by their discourse concerning 'traditional' religious practices and their desire for change following exposure to other practices. Officially Buddhists, but following traditions founded on three non-competing religious traditions, they have recourse to three types of specialists. The Buddhist lamas are masters of the house and officiate mainly over life-cycle rituals or specific situations, for example against natural disasters. *Bompo* shamans are responsible for curing the ill, and *lambu* priests, whose tradition is said to be tribal, intervene with earth deities but also during ordinary rituals. There is no Hindu figure who formally officiates, but elements of the Hindu gods are integrated into the pantheon and religious festivals. Educated youth, teachers, doctors, and foresters are now in competition with traditional religious specialists, creating a new division between the domain of religion and domains of knowledge comprising now education, politics, health, and the management of natural spaces, domains over which religious specialists, particularly the lamas and shamans, formerly held authority.

Traditional religious specialists are challenged on a number of points, albeit not for their religion. Shamans, or traditional healers, are particularly criticized for being less medically effective than Western medicine (of which the villagers have a very high opinion, even if they ultimately have little access to it) and above all for demanding too many blood sacrifices. Lamas' legitimacy is grounded upon magical powers—making it rain, or stopping sleet, for example—and contradicts the rational approach of the educated youth, who would prefer scientific evidence of their power over nature. The secularization of knowledge among the youth causes them to see the world around them differently, and a number of young people have denounced the cult of earth deities and other natural divinities and evil spirits, which they consider to constitute 'blind faith' and 'superstition' (*andha-bishvas* in Nepali).

The knowledge of traditional religious specialists has become less powerful because young people can now read and write, depriving lamas of a monopoly on literacy. The young suspect them of having only phonetic knowledge of the ancient texts they recite, pretending to read them during ceremonies without actually understanding them. The closing of Tibet and the Tibetan diaspora have weakened the knowledge networks between lamas and the great Tibetan masters, with whom communication has broken down, even if the masters have found shelter not so far away in the monasteries of Kathmandu.

The relationship between knowledge and transmission is even more profoundly unsettled, radically opposing the lamas and the educated youth. One major difference is that the lamas do not divulge their knowledge freely to the uninitiated, whereas the teaching received by educated youth is completely open. In addition, the lamas' sacred texts are inaccessible to the population because they are written in classical Tibetan. It is interesting in terms of belonging that the Tibetan language, and particularly classical Tibetan, has lost much of its status among villagers, especially the youth and is considered to be untranslatable, unlike Nepalese or English. In the context of their strong desire to belong to the broader world, this representation of Tibetan as untranslatable and even useless pointedly illustrates how distant villagers feel from their Tibetan origins and echoes the young people's demands to abandon localisms, to which they feel they no longer belong. It is interesting to compare this to the fact that Tamang pastors use the Nepali translation of the Bible instead of the readily available Tamang version, which is admittedly difficult to read owing to the complicated transliteration of Tamang—which has no written form—into the Devanagari alphabet. Pastors also position themselves at a distance from their mother tongue, which they contend is poorly adapted to the new sacred texts. In Ankhu Khola, some pastors were resuming their preaching in Tamang, but most of their speeches in church and prayers were only in Nepali.[7]

The increased political and economic exposure to the outside has exacerbated criticism of the lamas for maintaining practices tainted by local singularities and a blend of different traditions without wanting to—or being able to—explain their meaning. For example, the dance figures included in certain rituals are particularly denigrated because they are viewed as non-Buddhist. At the end of the 1990s, many villages of Salankhu Khola stopped celebrating the *Tsechu* festival, for example, because it was considered too expensive and villagers said nobody cared any more.[8]

Villagers consequently no longer show respect for the lamas and can occasionally even be heard to mock them and denounce their supposed incompetence. They are often accused of only thinking of drinking and demanding animal sacrifices that are officially condemned by Buddhism. The lamas have internalized this critical discourse and, at times, even denigrate themselves and question the efficacy of their own rituals. Ultimately, traditional specialists' competence, knowledge, legitimacy, and effectiveness are questioned, particularly in terms of their rituals' costs but also compared to new experts, whether religious or non-religious.

Arguably, this context provided fertile ground for a new religious system. Local Buddhism could have evolved towards a more ortho-dox form that was cleansed of Tamang peculiarities and syncretism,[9] which could probably have averted a massive conversion of the population. But in the 1990s, there was no such spread of Theravada Buddhism in this region and instead Tamangs encountered Protestant missionaries during this critical period, producing a far more radical transfer of religions. After an absence of two centuries,[10] missionaries had returned to Nepal explicitly in order to convert groups that were marginalized by central power and by the dominant Hindu populations, specifically targeting Tibeto-Burman language groups, among them the Tamangs.

The Tamangs in this area have converted in great numbers to Christianity since the 1990s.[11] Although several missionaries moved into the country after its opening in the 1950s and the 1990s, to this day they have little presence in this Tamang region. According to my observations and interviews with both converts and non-converts, it is primarily economic and political transformations that have enabled these Tamangs from Ankhu Khola to embrace a new religious belonging. All the conversion narratives I heard among Tamangs of this region were based on a story of somebody who was sick, who went to the lama and to the shaman who asked for several animal sacrifices. Impoverishment and disease then led the family of the sick person to look for another way to get cured—a way that was less expensive and more efficient. A neighbour heard of a Christian not far away who led them to a local pastor who cured the patient with free prayers and sometimes by placing his hands on the head of the sick person.[12]

Gradually blood sacrifices, offerings, and rituals perceived as expensive have become widely condemned, while increasing value has been attributed to individual expenditures. The cost of traditional rituals is tabulated and criticized and judged to be too expensive, particularly when compared to the new uses for money. The villagers assert that they are no longer prepared to spend such large sums for rituals, and they simultaneously question their effectiveness. In such a context, the proposals of a few missionaries, offering what was perceived as a less expensive means of protection from evil and bad spirits (which cause illness for a Tamang), were enough to be welcomed by the villagers.

Although the Tamangs warmly welcomed the advances of missionaries, their success is arguably due to the fact that their belief system seemed to complement ongoing transformations. Tamang converts report considering Christianity better adapted to the newer economic, political, and social forms that they value, especially among the young and migrants. They claim that Christianity is more 'effective', a belief stemming from their perception of the West's success and Christianity's more 'rational' practices and conception of the world, and ultimately what is viewed as its more 'modern' and universal outlook. The Tamangs thus employ a homogeneous discourse to justify their conversion that involves rational calculation of the costs of rituals relative to their perceived effectiveness. The personal nature of Christian prayers is appreciated, and the Tamangs also enjoy not having to pass through the mediation of an expert, which is consistent with the general individualization of other practices referred to earlier. Indeed, although individualization preceded Christianization—a subject that deserves more careful investigation in terms of the social and political structures in place in each village—Christianization has in turn further reinforced the individualization of practices through baptism and prayer for example. But as Nima Ghising (cf. note 6) also underlines (personal conversation), the Tamang traditional belief system, such as the idea of *mang* (evil spirits), of life after death, and biblical accounts of these themes, could also be one of the factors for their opting for Christianity. As Westerners, we often see conversion as a rupture with previous beliefs, as depicted in St Paul's conversion on the road to Damascus. Viroulaud (2004) tried to show that among Magars, exorcism practices in the Pentecostal Church could take the same forms of ancient possession cults, as a way to make local their new Christian belonging.

Mapping the spatial distribution of these diverse transformations and comparing it to the geographical location of Christian conversions shows that the least transformed villages were also the last to convert, that is, the villages of the upper valley of the Ankhu Khola, suggesting that economic, political, and social changes were conditions that made conversion possible. Conversions in the upper valley were also more often collective—where the power structure has remained more traditional, decision-making has remained collective, as opposed to villages lower in the valleys, where the notion of individual choice, especially concerning politics or religion, is more widespread.

The collective character of conversion is especially striking in the upper valley and is reminiscent of other transformations, including changes in agriculture experienced by villagers. The most common pattern involves the introduction of an innovation by a single actor in such a way that it seems accessible to everyone, eventually leading to adoption by the entire village. For instance, a villager coming back home from migration brings a new seed in his bag. It might change the timing of his agricultural practices, so he will spend most of his harvest in giving seeds to others until they adopt the seed. In villages in which the community remains the point of reference, a change only has meaning if it involves the collective. This particular trait of the upper valley can be visualized by examining the geographical spread of Christianity. In the communities of Tipling and Laba, for example, the spatial pattern of recent conversions shows that a centralized political will is at work, with conversion rapidly radiating outward in a star-shaped pattern from the main village to the territory's hamlets. A financial penalty might even be imposed on those who continue to consult shamans for example, as happened in Tipling. Alternatively, in villages that have chosen not to convert, becoming Christian is violently condemned, as in Burang. This pattern contrasts with the lower-altitude villages surrounding Rigaon, where Christianity spread in waves over a period of 30 years from the hamlet where the first conversions occurred, without relying on collective decisions among resident families.

Other factors have contributed to the Christianization of the Tamangs of this region. During the same decade in which Christianity was spreading, the government and NGOs, and occasionally missionaries, financed the construction of free health-care clinics. As a result, when a person fell ill, they consulted a doctor and occasionally addressed a prayer to the Christian God. This solved the problem of the fear of evil spirits and evil-doing deities tempted to avenge themselves for being neglected by the population.[13] The spread of Christianity also follows the pattern of construction of new hospitals and schools, a process further accelerated by certain missionaries who made schooling outside the valley available to children.

Having become Christian, these Tamangs have a sense of belonging to a larger and more universal society than to the Tibetan culture that they have come to denigrate.[14] They are reminded of their remote Tibetan origins when they are referred to by Indo-Nepalese populations as *Bhote*, which they experience as a pejorative term, and Tamang converts see Christianization as a means of avoiding this association (even if they are perceived as belonging to a cow-consuming religion, like also the Bhote). Anyway Christianity is thus perceived by Tamangs as a means of escaping their social circumstances while remaining part of a relatively egalitarian social structure, which would not be the case if they converted to Hinduism, from which they feel 'naturally' excluded.

But the fact of having become Christian can later cause problems of belonging for the Tamangs when they are faced with non-Christianized Tibeto-Burmese populations, especially other Tamangs. These confrontations occur during stays in the lower Nepalese valleys or during more distant migrations. For example, none of the Christian Tamangs belong to the *Tamang Ghedung Shang*, an association in which to be Tamang also means to be Buddhist.[15] In the villages where only part became Christian, as Nima Ghising has observed in Kanchanpur, one of the obvious consequences of conversion on collective community life can be observed at the death of a family or clan member. Every relative has a role to play in the death rites but converts are not permitted to play their role and vice versa.

Irrespective of conversion being collective or individual, however, the new religious landscape appears to be highly fragmented. Various Christian religious denominations have proliferated within each village, which takes on traits that mirror a clan-based, segmented society. If a clan converts and adopts a denomination, another clan will adopt a different denomination[16] from among the array of alternatives, which include Baptists, Presbyterians, Evangelicals, Pentecostalists, and Methodists, among others. This has led to the proliferation of places of worship in the villages—21 in Rigaon, 12 in Jarlang, and 10 in Laba, for example. This societal fragmentation and the redundancy of parishes mirror the subdivision of physical space referred to earlier. These phenomena can be tied to the individualization of practices, but they are also related to the absence of ordained clergy and the relatively high degree of autonomy of each local congregation. Local 'pastors' sometimes even shift from one spiritual affiliation to another or draw their inspiration from several different denominations.

Individualization can be observed at the familial and individual levels, and in agricultural practices, in new economic, political, and religious forms that are given importance at the expense of a community that is losing its solidity and taken-for-grantedness. The 'other' is increasingly defined by the size of one's house and its architectural style, whether modern or not, as well as by one's clothing—Tamang or market-bought—and by the consumer objects that one possesses or does not possess, the trips taken, the schooling received, rather than because of the clan, the lineage, or alliances by marriage.

Ultimately, what can be observed among the Tamangs of this region is a community transformed into a society, a change that occurred in Europe only after a long process that was intricately connected to increasing control exercised over the physical environment and the differentiation of social functions, processes that took place in Central Nepal over a span of roughly 15 years. There has also been a breakdown in the social separation between outlying localities (e.g. remote mountain villages) and cities, not owing to the construction of infrastructure, but through the emergence of new behaviours and influences brought back from the city. In tandem with the individualization process, new forms of social differentiation have appeared as new social divisions have formed—between men and women, and between the schooled and the uneducated, for example—in a community previously considered, at least by some anthropologists, as rather homogeneous and egalitarian compared to neighbouring Hindu societies (Toffin, 1986b: 42; Holmberg, 1989, 2007). Furthermore, we observe a spatial differentiation, making spaces increasingly specialized. It is also possible to observe the rejection of local peculiarities associated with efforts to become integrated into Nepalese civil society, amid a process of linguistic, cultural, and social Nepalization during the 1990s. It should be added that the process of Christianization has provided a means of jumping from the local directly to the global. This leap has the advantage of allowing the Tamangs to avoid a full sense of belonging tied to the national level, which, because it is Hindu-dominated, would marginalize the Tamangs, who are held to be impure by the dominant Hindu castes. Finally, there is an observable coalescence between differentiation within the Tamang community and the simultaneous process of homogenization towards a national or even broader model thought to be more universal, a dual process of both homogenization and differentiation, and of integration and resistance. But at the same time, my most recent observations suggest that these shifts in belonging could be unstable and rapidly reversed, becoming not far from identity revivalism under particular circumstances, after a long and distant migration, for example, that enables individuals to reconsider their own cultural and identitary belongings when they feel far from their home villages. In the mid-2000s, indeed, young migrants were much more interested in their Tamang background and in the village narratives they shunned only 10 years back. Furthermore, Tamang who were no more living in their village and had not converted to Christianity were considering reviving the *Tsechu* festival next to their new house.[17]

NOTES

1. Data for this chapter are drawn from fieldwork conducted during several periods totaling 20 months between 1993 and 2006. I also used data from a 1980s research project called "Programme Versant", in a comparative perspective. The methodology used includes anthropological and geographical research techniques.
2. For detail on these innovations and their agricultural, economic, and spatial consequences, see Ripert (2009).
3. The diasporic context is especially propitious to religious transformations, leading to reflexive processes: to be Hindu in Great Britain, Sikh in Canada, but also Nepalese in India or Santal in Assam is no longer as obvious as several studies of diasporic communities in the Indian subcontinent have shown. On other consequences of migration, see for example, Thapa (1990), Seddon et al. (2001), and Krengel (1997).
4. I showed in that chapter that during the first period of distanciation, Tamang identity was often denigrated by young migrants, fascinated by the lights of the city. It's only after having been away for few years, often after having experienced loneliness and disappointment, that could be observed a revival of interest in their collective identity and ties to their 'reenchanted' village. In the mid-2000s, they were for the first time returning to the village with the will to record the songs, the stories of the elders, etc. Some were even trying to publish small books on local narratives, which was totally absent in the 1990s. It would be interesting to pursue this research and try to understand why there was this 'delay' of 10–15 years compared with other groups of Tamangs in Kathmandu Valley or also Eastern Tamangs, who got involved much earlier in ethnic recognition and the *Janajati* movement.
5. I use the term 'educated youth' to refer to villagers between 15 and 30 years of age who distinguish themselves from others by having attended school in the village and later in the city. They can read and write and have been marked by the national culture acquired during their schooling.
6. I quote Mukta Tamang: "The territory of Tamsaling is employed by the Tamang movement not only to articulate political demand for relative autonomy and compensation for historical injustices within Nepal, but also to build a global network of people forming a virtual Tamsaling" (2009: 283).
7. Nima Ghising, who conducts PhD research among Christian Tamangs in Kanchanpur, told me Nepali has become there a 'religious' language (something like Latin formerly within Roman Catholicism) for villagers who never talk Nepali among themselves. Every single activity that has to do with church or Christianity, whether it be personal prayer or corporate worship, is carried out in Nepali. None of the Tamang Christians pray in Tamang.
8. *Tsechu* (tg.) is a four- to five-day festival, relating the war between Gorkha and Tibetan Kings. Part of this festival is danced by the villagers, with horse disguises.

9. According to Bechert (1992), this evolution of Buddhism has taken place elsewhere in Nepal with the spread of Theravada Buddhism, especially among the Newars in the Kathmandu Valley. This spread reached Ankhu Khola, but only since the 2000s, as a reaction to Christian conversion (for details, see Ripert, 2004).

10. See Vannini (1977) and Shah (1993) for more details on the history of Christian conversion in Nepal.

11. Although a massive conversion movement in this area took place in the 1990s, when religious conversion became tolerated in the country, the first conversion I recorded in this region occured in 1967, a Tamang from Kutal (a hamlet of Rigaon on the west bank of Ankhu Khola) coming back home from work as a porter in a trekking agency of Pokhara. During his migration he met a Protestant priest and came back home with a few Christian leaflets. In the late1990s, I evaluated the number of Christians in Dhading district at 20,000, two-thirds of whom were Tamangs from Ankhu Khola (Ripert, 1997).

12. This basic frame, not detailed here, is very similar to the story of Dorje Ghale, from Tipling in the Upper Ankho Khola, related by Fricke (2008: 41–46).

13. Lucile Viroulaud (2004) among Magars and Nima Ghising (personal conversation) among Tamangs, who worked on Pentecostalism in Nepal, report that most of the people converted because of the fear of bad spirits, with an emphasis on healing and exorcism.

14. In a wider perspective, it is interesting to note that Tibetan origins of Tamangs seem totally absent from the national history reconstruction the Tamang activists promote (cf., for example, the synthesis Mukta Tamang describes, 2009).

15. This association has been strongly suported by a Tamang originating from Ankhu Khola, who than became involved in various government positions in the Panchayat system and after 1990. Males of his family were traditionaly lamas in his village and he was fiercely opposed to the conversion of Tamangs to Christianity.

16. On this question of belonging to different Christian demominations depending on clan membership, see Ripert (1997).

17. I heard about such initiatives in 2006 in Trisuli bazar and in the Tamang suburb of Kathmandu.

REFERENCES

Acharya, M. 2000. *Labour Market Development and Poverty (with Focus on Opportunities for Women) in Nepal*. Kathmandu: Thanka Prasad Acharya Foundation in Co-operation with Friedrich-Ebert *Stiftung*.

Bechert, H. 1992. 'Report on a Study of Buddhist Revival in Nepal', in B. Kolver (ed.), *Aspects of Nepalese Traditions*, pp. 181–92. Stuttgart: Franz Steiner.

Campbell, B. 1997. 'The Heavy Loads of Tamang Identity', in D.N. Gellner, J. Pfaff-Czarnecka, and J. Whelpton (eds), *Nationalism and Ethnicity in a Hindu Kingdom: The Politics of Culture in Contemporary Nepal*, pp. 205–35. Amsterdam: Harwood Academic Publishers.

Dobremez, J-F. (ed.). 1986, *Les collines du Népal Central, écosystème, structures sociales et systèmes agraires*, 2 volumes. Paris: INRA.

Dollfus, O. 1997. *La Mondialisation*, p. 167. Paris: Presses de Sciences Po.

———. 1990. 'Le système monde', in R. Brunet (ed.), *Géographie universelle*. Paris: Hachette/Reclus, Tome I *Mondes nouveaux*.

Fricke, T. 1994. *Himalayan Households: Tamang Demography and Domestic Processes* (2nd, expanded edition). New York: Columbia University Press.

———. 2008. 'Tamang Conversions: Culture, Politics, and the Christian Conversion Narrative in Nepal', *Contribution to Nepalese Studies*, 35(1): 35–62.

Gellner, D.N. 2007. 'Caste, Ethnicity and Inequality in Nepal', *Economic and Political Weekly*, 42(20): 1823–28.

———. (ed.). 2009. *Ethnic Activism and Civil Society in South Asia*. New Delhi: SAGE Publications.

Gellner, D.N., J. Pfaff-Czarnecka, and J. Whelpton (eds). 1997. *Nationalism and Ethnicity in a Hindu Kingdom: The Politics of Culture in Contemporary Nepal*. Amsterdam: Harwood.

Höfer, A. 1981. *Tamang Ritual Texts I: Preliminary Studies in the Folk-Religion of an Ethnic Minority in Nepal*. Wiesbaden: Steiner.

Holmberg, D.H. 1989. *Order in Paradox: Myth, Ritual and Exchange among Nepal's Tamang*, p. 265. Ithaca: Cornell University Press

———. 2007. 'Outcastes in an "Egalitarian" Society: Tamang/Blacksmith Relations from Tamang Perspective', in R.B. Chhetri and L.P. Uprety (eds), *Observations on the Changing Societal Mosaic of Nepal. Occasional Papers in Sociology and Anthropology*, vol. 10, pp. 124–40. Kirtipur: Tribhuvan University.

Kollmair, M., S. Manandhar, B. Subedi, and S. Thieme. 2006. 'New Figures for Old Stories: Migration and Remittances in Nepal', *Migration Letters*, 3(2): 151–60.

Krengel, M. 1997. 'Migration and the Danger of Loss: Some Aspects of Cultural Identity in Kumaon/Indian Himalaya', in I.M. Winiger Stellrecht (ed.), *Perspectives on History and Change in the Karakorum, Hindukush and Himalaya*, pp. 171–88. Cologne: Rüdiger Köppe Verlag.

Lévy, J., P. Poncet, B. Beaude, R.E. Dagorn, M. Dumont, B. Ripert, M. Stock, O. Vilaça, D. Andrieu, and K. Hurel. 2008. *L'Invention du monde, Une géographie de la mondialisation*. Paris: Presses de Sciences Po.

Pfaff-Czarnecka, J. and G. Toffin (eds). 2011. *The Politics of Belonging in the Himalayas. Local Attachments and Boundary Dynamics*. New Delhi: SAGE Publications.

Ripert, B. 1997. 'Christianisme et pouvoirs locaux dans une vallée tamang du Népal Central'. *Archives de Sciences Sociales des Religions*, EHESS-CNRS, 99: 69–86.

———. 2000. '*Dynamiques spatiales et transformations de la société, L'exemple des Tamang du Népal central*', Thèse de géographie, Université Denis Diderot - Paris 7.

———. 2004. 'Le "lama pasteurisé", Vers de nouvelles figures d'autorité religieuse chez les Tamang de l'Ouest', in V. Bouillier and C. ServanSchreiber (eds), *De l'Arabie à l'Himalaya, Chemins croisés en hommages à Marc Gaborieau*. Paris: Maisonneuve & Larose.

———. 2009. 'Parcelling of Land, Privatisation along with Collective Management of Space and Resources on the Salme Mountainside', in J. Smadja (ed.), *Reading Himalayan Landscapes over Time. Environmental Perception, Knowledge and Practice in Nepal and Ladakh*, pp. 467–92. Institut Français de Pondichéry: Collection Sciences Sociales 14.

Ripert, B. 2013. 'Redefining Belonging and Bonds to Territory: Multiple Forms of Mobility and Itineraries among the Tamangs of Central Nepal', in J. Smadja (ed.), *Territorial Changes, Territorial Restructurings in the Himalayas*. New Delhi: Adroit Publishers.

Sagant, P. 1978. 'Ampleur et profondeur historique des migrations saisonnières népalaises', *L'Ethnographie*, pp. 93–119. Paris: CNRS, Gabalda.

Seddon D., G. Gurung, and J. Adhikari. 2001. *The New Lahures: Foreign Employment and Remittance Economy of Nepal*. Kathmandu, Nepal: Nepal Institute of Development Studies.

Shah, S. 1993. 'The Gospel Comes to the Hindu Kingdom', *Himal*, September–October: 35–40.

Smadja, J. 1995. 'Sur une dégradation annoncée des milieux népalais: initiatives villageoises pour remplacer les ressources forestière', *Nature, Sciences et Sociétés*. Paris: n 3, 3:190–204.

Steinmann, B. 1987. *Les Tamang du Népal, usages et religion, religion d'usage*. Paris: Recherche sur les civilisations, ADF, p. 310.

Tamang, M. 2009. 'Tamang Activism, History, and Territorial Consciousness', in D.N. Gellner (ed.), *Ethnic Activism and Civil Society in South Asia*, pp. 269–90. New Delhi: SAGE Publications.

Thapa, P. 1990. *Nepal: Socio-Economic Change and Rural Migration*. Delhi: Vikas Publishing House Pvt. Ltd.

Toffin, G. 1976a. 'The People of the Upper Ankhu Khola Valley', *Contributions to Nepalese Studies*, II, 3: 34–46.

———. 1976b. 'The Phenomenon of Migration in a Himalayan Valley in Central Nepal', in *Mountain Environment and Development*, pp. 31–44. Kathmandu: University Press.

———. 1986a. 'Mutual Assistance in Agricultural Work among the Western Tamang of Nepal: Traditional and New Patterns', in K. Seeland (ed.), *Recent Research on Nepal*, pp. 83–96. Schriftenreihe, 'Internationales Asien Forum', Band 3, Weltforum Verlag, München-Köln-London.

———. 1986b. 'Unité de parenté, système d'alliance et de prestation chez les Tamang de l'Ouest (Népal)', *Anthropos*, 81: 21–45.

Vannini, Fulgentius. 1977. *Christian Settlements in Nepal during the Eighteenth Century*. New Delhi: Stylish Printing Press.

Viroulaud, Lucile. 2004. *Une minorité chrétienne en pays magar (Népal)*. Doctorat in Anthropology from Paris X Nanterre University. Unpublished work.

Chapter 3

Circular Lives

Histories and Economies of Belonging in the Transnational Thangmi Village*

SARA SHNEIDERMAN

Kumaiko ghumai, Chhetriko jal, Newarko lekhai, Thangmiko kal.
"The Kumai's treachery, the Chhetri's trap, the Newar's forgery, the Thangmi's scalp".
—Proverb heard in Thangmi areas of Nepal[1]

Chiyako botma sun phulchha.
"Gold blooms on the tea bush".
—Popular Nepali saying about Darjeeling

THE MISSING *BAMPA*

"I think you are ready to visit Khaldo Hotel", Rana Bahadur said to me conspiratorially one day in 2004 at the very end of my first extended stay in Darjeeling, in the Indian state of West Bengal. Over the past several months, my eyes had often rested on the endless

* This chapter draws upon research funded by Fulbright, the National Science Foundation, the Social Science Research Council, American Council of Learned Societies, St Catharine's College (Cambridge) and Yale University. Earlier versions were presented in Fréjus; at the Centre of South Asian Studies Seminar, University of Cambridge; and at the Anthropology Research Seminar Series, Goldsmiths, University of London. I thank participants at those events along with Bir Bahadur Thami, Suren Thami, Mark Turin, and the Thangmi communities of Nepal and India for all of their contributions to this work over time.

hotel signboards that dotted the bazaar's steep lanes. There were the colonial curlicues of the Windamere at the top of Observatory Hill, the fruity-coloured hues of the Amba Palace down in the centre of town, and the Lunar Hotel's long, narrow sign atop a high Clubside building, pointing skyward towards its namesake. But, Khaldo Hotel did not sound familiar. "Where's that?" I asked. "You know, you keep asking where the Thangmi labourers who come every year from Nepal stay. I'm trying to tell you that they stay at Khaldo Hotel". This revelation provoked both curiosity and frustration in me. In spite of the congenial roadside friendships I had struck up with many of the migrant Thangmi porters from Nepal who spent their days outside looking for work, I had not yet been invited to their homes. This experience diverged sharply from what I had come to expect from my work with other groups of Thangmi in both Nepal and India, and I had been unable to solve the mystery of where they all went at night. So I swallowed my irritation and followed Rana Bahadur down the hill.

As we came to a busy intersection that I had walked through many times before, he crossed the road and ducked under a low metal archway that appeared to lead into a standard concrete building. But, instead of heading up the stairs, he ducked again into an opening so low that I had trouble getting through the entryway with my large backpack. We entered a tunnel-like passageway of the same height. As my eyes adjusted to the darkness, I shivered—it was several degrees colder in here, and very moist—and focused on the point of light coming from Rana Bahadur's cigarette lighter. After turning a few corners, I started to hear voices, and soon we came upon a family of four sitting in front of a wood-burning fireplace etched into the concrete floor. The woman was making tea and nursing a baby, while the man arranged some bags stuffed into a corner. An older child darted back and forth between his two parents. I was relieved when Rana Bahadur sat down by the fire and indicated to me to do the same, since the ceiling was not more than 4 feet above the floor and I was uncomfortably hunched over. "Welcome to Khaldo Hotel", Rana Bahadur said with a smile, and introduced me to the couple. "They are the proprietors here, you see. They rent this whole place every year"—he gestured further into the darkness—"and rent out rooms to the rest of them for fifty rupees a month". With the smile fading into a wry grin, he continued, "It's a 'full-service hotel', you see, with meals, laundry, and any other facilities you need included".

I quickly realized that *khaldo* (N) meant "hole in the ground", and that the appropriately named "hotel" was in fact a subterranean warren of rooms in a defunct portion of Darjeeling's colonial sewer system.[2] A corrupt government official managed to collect rent on the whole place from the Thangmi couple with whom we now sat. They were, in turn, somewhere in the middle of the pyramid scheme, collecting rent from approximately 150 Thangmi of all ages who spent the cold winter months living underground in a windowless cave where there was no room to even stand up. Nonetheless, upon their return to Nepal, these tenants talked about the joys of Khaldo Hotel to would-be migrants back home. This year's residents were promised a free meal next year for every new renter they brought in.

Khaldo Hotel's dingy concrete walls could not be more different from the Thangmi houses of stone, mud, wood, thatch, and the occasional corrugated aluminium dotted across the rugged green hills of Nepal's Dolakha and Sindhupalchok districts. As one of the country's poorest and most socially excluded groups by any standard,[3] most Thangmi survive on small plots of property that yield barely enough grain to feed families for half the year. Despite their limited resources, Thangmi villagers tend to take pride in their houses, seeing them as the embodiment of their attachment to the territory on which they live. Houses are the physical manifestation of their inhabitants' clan lineages; clan identification is often defined in terms of household, rather than individual, membership. In this sense, houses are an essential anchor of identity, demarcating the exclusively Thangmi domestic space of human action that determines both the quality of everyday life and the tenor of Thangmi relationships with the divine world of clan and territorial deities.

In Nepal's oldest Thangmi houses, some of whose residents can trace their family lineages back over a century—to the era when regular migrations to Darjeeling began—the hearth is marked by the *bampa* (T), a large piece of flat rock rammed vertically into the floor. The *bampa*'s primary present-day function seems to be as a windbreak to protect against the drafts that blow through rough-hewn doors left open in even the most inclement weather; however, conjecturing about the *bampa*'s erstwhile ritual purpose is a favourite pastime while seated around the fire. Many Thangmi are eager to recover (or re-imagine) the long-forgotten significance of this single distinctive feature of Thangmi domestic design, from which one of the female clan names also derives. One popular explanation in contemporary Thangmi activist circles is that the solid, heavy stone is a symbol of both Thangmi resilience in the face of oppression and their attachment to the land on which their houses stand. As we sat on the cold floor around the Khaldo Hotel fire, Rana Bahadur invoked these multiple meanings with a terse but revealing statement, "It's just like a Thangmi house, isn't it? Only the *bampa* is missing".

His words helped me understand the complex mixture of social, economic, and personal motivations that compel so many Thangmi to leave their homes in Nepal every year, where "the air and water are clean"—a stock phrase offered immediately by many Thangmi migrants when asked what they like most about their home village—to travel for days, cross the border into India, live for several months in the underground urban squalor of a place like Khaldo Hotel, and carry back-breaking loads up and down the bazaar's sloping roads. At the end of the season, these migrants return to Nepal for several months (which are often punctuated with short trips across Nepal's northern border to China's Tibetan Autonomous Region [TAR]) before starting the whole process all over again. As a symbol of the twin experiences of oppression and attachment to territory that characterize Thangmi identities in Nepal, the *bampa*'s absence in migrant abodes such as Khaldo Hotel highlights the "push" and "pull" factors that contribute to Thangmi desires both to travel away from and then return to their home villages. In Darjeeling, there has historically been a lower incidence of land-based economic exploitation, and social oppression is comparatively minimal, thereby creating stronger prospects for a positive sense of belonging in one regard. Yet owning property, however small, and the economic and spiritual attachment to territory that such ownership generates—underpinning another important aspect of Thangmi belonging in Nepal—remain nearly impossible for Thangmi in India.

THE PRAGMATICS OF CROSS-BORDER MIGRATION

This chapter explores the pragmatics of Thangmi cross-border circular migration, locating its historical roots in the twin experiences of economic exploitation and social exclusion.[4] Following the trajectories of these phenomena into the present, I adapt the notion of 'belonging' from the European sociological contexts in which it has been most robustly deployed (Christiansen and Hedetoft, 2004;

Yuval-Davis et al., 2006) to the Himalayan and South Asian ethnographic contexts in a discussion of the practical aspects of Thangmi migration and its affective results. In the European context, "the politics of belonging" has largely been used to describe the forms of exclusion and inclusion that permanent immigrants who have left their home countries experience in the multi-cultural states which are their adopted homes. Applied to the Himalayan and South Asian contexts in which Thangmi migration takes place, the concept can usefully encapsulate the forms of inclusion and exclusion that people experience in their home countries, and the migrations that such experiences may compel them to undertake. At the same time, the Thangmi case contributes to on-going attempts to balance, on the one hand, the importance of single nation-states as frameworks within which belonging is defined and, on the other hand, the forceful ways in which such frameworks are unsettled for those who move across national borders on a regular basis (Basch et al., 1994; Guarnizo and Smith, 1998; Levitt, 2001).

With their homeland in Nepal's Dolakha and Sindhupalchok districts, a large settled migrant population in Darjeeling district of India's state of West Bengal, and a temporary migrant population in the southern reaches of China's Tibetan Autonomous Region, the Thangmi are a Himalayan ethnic group of approximately 30,000, for whom circular migration itself has become a feature of belonging.[5] Census data from 1872 provides the earliest evidence of a Thangmi population in India, suggesting that the Thangmi have been crossing the Himalayan borders for at least 125 years. The history and on-going circumstances of Thangmi circular migration provide a window into the transnational aspects of belonging in the Himalayas over time. Current migrations from Nepal to Indian city centres, the Middle East, the United States, and beyond are now receiving substantial academic attention (Seddon et al., 2001; Seddon, 2002; Graner and Gurung, 2003; Thieme, 2006; Bruslé, 2010, this volume); however, the causes and effects of these more recent routes of migration can be better understood when contextualized within the long history of trans-Himalayan migration between Nepal and the adjoining border regions of India and China that Thangmi experiences exemplify. The history and literature of the Nepali "diasporic" experience in northeast India is also well-documented (Onta 1996, 1999; Hutt, 1997, 1998; Chalmers, 2003; Sinha and Subba, 2003; Subba et al., 2009); yet, the same cannot be said of the contemporary cross-border connections between people of Nepali heritage in India and Nepal.

Here I take an initial step towards filling these gaps by tracing the history of what we might call the "translocal" (Guarnizo and Smith, 1998; Anthias, 2006), "periphery-to-periphery" migration that results in Thangmi "transnational social formations" (Guarnizo and Smith, 1998: 27) built in corners of Nepal, India, and China, far from any of those countries' political or economic centres. At the same time, I hope to broaden the parameters of the discussion of "transnationalism", which has largely focused on migrations from the so-called "peripheral" locations to cosmopolitan centres. Towards this end I suggest that scholarship seeking to understand the full complexity of contemporary "transnational social spaces" (Pries, 2001) must look beyond the global cities that comprise the focal point for this literature, exploring the complete range of geographical and social scales on which such spaces may be embedded in villages, towns, and regional centres. Moreover, rather than focusing on the "newness" (Pries, 2001) of such transnational social spaces, I seek to historicize contemporary formations in relation to long-term patterns of mobility, both geographical and social.

Building upon the notion of recognition that I have developed elsewhere (Shneiderman, 2010, 2011), here I conceptualize belonging as the perceived affirmation of the social self, in terms of both its existential presence (Graham, 2005) and its potential for transformative action, which derives from a subjective experience of recognition from a range of agents. These might include the divine world, the state, members of one's own diverse collectivity, or broader constellations of collectivities functioning on local, national, regional, and transnational scales. Rather than conceptualizing belonging as a singular relationship between an individual and a bounded nation-state, ethnicity, or community, I define belonging as a multiple category that is cobbled together from the affective experiences of recognition in diverse locales, vis-à-vis a range of actors.

Conceptualizing belonging in this manner expands analytical frameworks that have emerged from the anthropology of migration, such as Michael Kearney's notion of the "articulatory migrant network" (1986: 353). Focusing primarily on the economic implications of migration, Kearney builds upon Meillasoux (1981) to suggest that "households may reproduce themselves by participating in two spheres of production" (1986: 342), with the result that "two generically distinct economies become articulated in large part by circular migrant labor" (1986: 344). Kearney highlights the need for studies "of such complex articulation for an entire community ... that deals with the corresponding articulation—in the second sense—of these variable socioeconomic activities and the corresponding changes in culture and consciousness" (1986: 355). In the 25 years since Kearney wrote, the literature in this field has of course burgeoned, but the turn towards diaspora, transnationalism, and deterritorialization as framing concepts for such analyses has moved away from the careful consideration of how multiple modes of reproduction—both economic and social—come to articulate with each other through the experiences of circular migrants. Here I suggest that we might productively return to Kearney's framework to consider more closely the articulatory nature not only of the economic dimensions of circular migration but also of the social and cultural transformations that such circular movements, particularly those across national borders, effect. From this perspective, we can understand belonging as a process of articulation, which unfolds in the "spaces of cultural assertion" (Gidwani and Sivaramakrishnan, 2003) that, for people like the Thangmi with whom I work, emerge through the experience of circular migration.

To emphasize the intertwined political economies and kinship networks that characterize Thangmi experiences of cross-border circular migration, I borrow the term 'transnational village' from Peggy Levitt (2001). The Thangmi situation is not an exclusively 'diasporic' one, in which migrants leave home to permanently settle elsewhere, but rather one in which the social and economic parameters of home villages are simultaneously augmented and maintained by the experience of migration. I suggest that although Thangmi migration initially began in response to economic and social pressures, in the present circular migration is often a lifestyle choice.[6] Such choices suggest that 'Thangminess' has become grounded in a transnational economy of belonging in which experiences of, or at the very least, knowledge of, the particularities of multiple locations makes one's identity complete.

Put simply (and of course there is a great diversity of individual experiences), Thangmi are 'richer' in Nepal than in India in terms of property ownership and cultural resources, but 'poorer' in terms of social inclusion and political resources, to which Thangmi in India have far greater access. Time spent in the TAR adds another dimension, which although typically short (for most not more than one month at a time due to Chinese regulations), provides a reflective vantage point from which many Thangmi consider their long-term options in the other two countries. Acknowledging the contingent national histories that have led to different experiences in each location illuminates how both social and economic imperatives influence the pragmatics of cross-border migration, pushing and pulling in different directions to create the circular lives that many Thangmi choose. By continuing to move between Nepal, India, and the TAR, circular migrants make the best of three different, but equally challenging, worlds.

The experiences of moving between multiple nation-states, as well as the interaction with multiple socio-political frameworks that such movement entails, become in themselves paradigmatic features of Thangmi identity in action, both for those who move and for those who stay put in one country or another.[7] Migration strategies are often determined at the household level, with some members migrating regularly, while others stay in one place. Kinship and community networks bring settled and migrant Thangmi into regular contact, and in the bazaars of Darjeeling and Dram (the TAR border town adjoining Nepal, also known as Khasa), 'Thangmi' is often used as a generic term to refer to migrant porters, just as the term 'Sherpa' has come to mean 'mountaineer'. To their distress, relatively well-educated Thangmi born in Darjeeling who have never carried a heavy load find they are often assumed to be circular migrants from Nepal simply because of their name. In this way, the fact of circular wage migration impinges on the self-identities of all Thangmi, regardless of their individual economic or social positions.

In the transnational Thangmi village, notions of belonging as a whole are premised upon the simultaneously occurring experiences of property ownership within a caste-based agrarian system in Nepal, and the social mobility made possible by the comparative impossibility of private property and the concomitant absence of rigid land-based social hierarchies in Darjeeling. In other words, important aspects of Thangmi belonging are produced on both sides of the border, but neither set of experiences is complete without the other. I am not suggesting that all Thangmi experience both worlds equally, but rather that 'Thangminess' is produced in a synthetic process through which diverse individuals, with as many life experiences in as many places, enact different pieces of the transnational puzzle to create an overarching framework of belonging, which allows each individual to make sense of their particular piece.

BELONGING IN A TRANSLOCATIONAL WORLD

Using the rubric of 'belonging', with its focus on the 'intersectionality' of different interests in a 'translocational' world (Anthias, 2006; Yuval-Davis et al., 2006), helps to clarify the interplay of forces at work in the Thangmi context. Moving beyond what they see as the fundamentally static nature of concepts such as 'diasporic identity' and 'hybridity'—which, despite recognizing multiple identities, still compartmentalize those identities into separate, block-like components—theorists have used the notion of 'belonging' to emphasize instead the processual intersectionality of people's experiences in different locations at different times. Belonging adds an emotive and experiential component to the rights-based notion of citizenship and an individual aspect to the group-based notion of ethnicity.

Furthermore, "Belonging and social inclusion ... are closely connected ... It is through practices and experiences of social inclusion that a sense of a stake and acceptance in a society is created and maintained" (Anthias, 2006: 21). 'Social inclusion' (or *samabesikaran* in Nepali) has recently become a buzzword within development discourses in South Asia, which tend to conflate the noble goal of such inclusion with the process of realizing it. As Hilary Silver explains (2010), the concept of social inclusion originated in a European policy context, and its applications elsewhere do not always take full account of the local histories and dynamics of inequality. Furthermore, "with all the attention to the participation of the excluded", Silver writes, "it is easy to elide these processes of policy-making with the policies themselves" (2010: 200). In the development-driven 'social inclusion' discourse in South Asia, the importance of measurable indicators at the national level are frequently over-emphasized, while the continued prevalence of deeply ingrained, localized practices of exclusion are glossed over. By adding an experiential, emotive aspect to the indicator-driven discussion of inclusion, adapting the concept of 'belonging' to the South Asian setting encourages a necessary critical engagement with such discourses.

Thangmi live along a continuum of mobility—ranging from those who have never left Nepal or India to those who are constantly on the move, and everything in between. These experiences are shaped by specific histories of exploitation and exclusion, territorial attachment and movement, at the individual, familial, and communal levels. Each Thangmi life is framed both by nation-state boundaries and by the ever-available prospect of moving across them. Discussions of belonging must therefore be carefully calibrated to the wide range of not only geographical but also social locations that frame Thangmi experiences at different moments: the nation-state, the village, the hamlet, the city, the bazaar, the tea plantation, the ethnic organization office, the district magistrate's office, and so on. If belonging is understood to be only the practice and experience of social inclusion at the political level of the nation-state, then many Thangmi have historically felt that they do not 'belong' in Nepal. Despite the fact that most own property and hold the paper trappings of Nepali citizenship, until very recently, few Thangmi believed that they had the capacity to transform the political landscape of Nepal in ways that might grant them a greater sense of belonging. It was this sense of rigidity, the lack of potential for change at the national level—no prospect of belonging—which compelled many older Thangmi to first undertake the journey to India. Yet recalling the figure of the *bampa* as a symbol of both resilience and rootedness, these same people felt very strongly that they belonged in their territory, in their villages, in localized places where they had long defined their own terms of belonging in relationship and resistance to local interethnic status hierarchies.

Upon arrival in India, Thangmi have not immediately experienced a greater sense of inclusion at the national level. In fact, their identification as 'foreigners'—Nepalis—and their typically low economic status have marked them as outsiders. Nonetheless, the lack of rigid status hierarchies in Darjeeling has long afforded them an opportunity to craft their own sense of belonging through community organizations and political action, creating the potential to secure recognition at the national level. For instance, the first Thangmi ethnic association in Darjeeling was registered in 1943, whereas the first such organization in Nepal was founded only 45 years later. As Rhoderick Chalmers has noted, in comparison to Nepal, "within India ... there was more potential for the founding of associations with implicit or explicit political aims, or at least social/religious reformist intentions" (2003: 207). It was in large part this potential for future belonging, the hope that their children would not have to fight so hard for social inclusion, that kept and continues to keep Thangmi coming back to India. This sense of potential political belonging at the national level in India (which until very recently was lacking in Nepal) paired with the strong sense of security in local, territorially based belonging in Nepal (which continues to be weak in India) creates a powerful recipe for a "transnational social formation" of belonging. The reproduction of this formation, this transnational village, with all of its social, economic, and cultural prerogatives, depends on the continuation of circular migration. As Creighton Peet noted in his 1978 study of migration, culture, and community in the Thangmi homeland area of Dolakha district, Nepal, "... migration has in part served as a mechanism for culture maintenance for the Thamis" (1978: 461).[8]

SITUATED HISTORIES OF EXPLOITATION AND EXCLUSION IN NEPAL

The epigraph with which this chapter began is a well-known Thangmi saying which paints a stark picture of the exploitation that many Thangmi feel characterizes their historical position within Nepal's interethnic socioeconomic order.

Kumaiko ghumai, Chhetriko jal ... The term *Kumai* designates the Western branch of the Upadhaya Brahmin caste. Members of this group were some of the earliest high-caste settlers in histori-cally Thangmi-populated areas of what are now Nepal's Dolakha and Sindhupalchok districts. Along with several Chhetri families, the Kumai began to arrive in the 19th century as the Shah dynasty expanded its eminent domain over previously quasi-independent parts of Nepal.[9] In the proverb, Kumai and Chhetri are both cari-catured as slippery characters who exploit their Thangmi tenant farmers by giving them the run-around (*ghumai*) or entrapping them in a net (*jal*).

... *Newarko lekhai* ... The Newar community of Dolakha bazaar has historically occupied a position of economic and social domi-nance in the area. As an important entrepôt on the Kathmandu to Lhasa trade route, Slusser suggests that the town of Dolakha was most likely first developed as a Licchavi settlement (1982: 85), and then became an independent principality ruled by the ancestors of today's Dolakha Newar population.[10] An inscription located inside the Bhimeshwor temple complex in Dolakha dated 688 in the Newar calendar of Nepal Sambat (AD 1568) includes a list of three social groups within the community at the time: *praja, saja,* and *thami.* Vajracharya and Shrestha (2013 VS: 98) suggest that *praja* refers to the Newar population, *saja* describes the ethnically Tibetan inhabitants of the higher villages of Dolakha, such as the Sherpa and Tamang, and *thami* refers to the Thangmi. This inscription singles out the Thangmi as the only group who must pay taxes to the Newar rulers on demand, suggesting that a Thangmi community has resided in the villages surrounding the market town of Dolakha since at least the 16th century. This potentially exploitative relationship was codified in writing (*lekhai*).

... *Thangmiko kal* ... Thangmi narratives suggest that before they became subject to Bahun, Chhetri, and Newar domination, they held large swathes of *kipat* (N), ancestral property recognized by the Nepali state as the exclusive domain of individual ethnic communities (Regmi, 1976). By the middle of the 18th century, although Dolakha remained nominally independent, the area's villagers came under the jurisdiction of King Jagajjaya Malla's tax collectors. Documents show that several villagers registered complaints of harassment against his tax-collecting officials (Regmi, 1981: 12–13). During the same time period, the tradition of awarding military officials and civil servants land tracts as *jagir* (N) in lieu of cash payment began. After Prithvi Narayan Shah annexed Dolakha, this practice became commonplace, with army officials receiving payments in land that had previously been farmed by Thangmi inhabitants of the area. The redistribution of land accelerated under the rule of Prime Minister Bhimsen Thapa, when in 1862 VS (1805–06 AD) he confiscated 82 *khet* (N), or 8,200 *muri* (N), of rice land in Dolakha as *jagir* for the army (Regmi, 1981: 15).[11]

By the mid-1800s, high-caste families originating from regions further west began migrating to Dolakha. After first settling in the area on such *jagir* tracts, many of the less-scrupulous new migrants began appropriating further lands by acting as moneylenders to their Thangmi neighbours. Charging high interest rates of up to 60 per cent per annum, such moneylenders made it difficult for Thangmi farmers to pay back their loans, and when a borrower defaulted, the lender would foreclose on his land. Furthermore, in a trend prevalent throughout eastern Nepal during that period, the newcomers enclosed *kipat* land by taking advantage of the Nepali state's emerging regulation of landholding through the *raikar* (N) system of tenure, which recognized the transferable and taxable nature of private property for the first time in such areas (Regmi, 1976: Chapter 10).[12]

In this way, many Thangmi either went deeply into debt and/or became tenant sharecroppers on portions of the land that they had previously controlled. However, most families were able to hold on to enough arable land to feed themselves for several months of the year. With insufficient land to survive, but too much to abandon, the economic scenario in Nepal's Thangmi villages at the end of the 19th century encouraged circular migration as a means of maintaining traditional lands, while augmenting their agrarian yield with cash income.

THE BEGINNINGS OF MIGRATION TO DARJEELING AND BEYOND

... *Chiyako botma sun phulcha* ... At roughly the same historical moment that the appropriation of Thangmi land accelerated in the mid-19th century, new income-generating opportunities began to emerge in Darjeeling. In 1835, the British took control of this virtually uninhabited tract of forested land, which had earlier changed hands several times between the ruling powers of Nepal, Bhutan, and Sikkim. Darjeeling's strategically situated ridgeline, which overlooked the plains of Bengal to the south and the mountains of Sikkim to the north, was to become a bustling hill station for holidaying colonial administrators—known as the "Queen of the Hills"—and the centre of colonial tea production (Kennedy, 1996; Q. Pradhan, 2007). When the British first surveyed the area in 1835, they recorded a total population of only 100 (Samanta, 2000: 21), and these were largely indigenous semi-nomadic members of the Lepcha ethnic group. Building infrastructure required workers, and the tea industry founded in the mid-1850s called for especially vast human resources. This is where the Thangmi and other Nepalis came in.[13]

Many of the earliest Thangmi migrants came to work on tea estates. First one or two men from a single village would establish themselves as trusted workers, and might eventually be promoted to the role of overseer and recruiter. Travelling back to Nepal every few years, they would return to the plantations with fresh new labour procured through their kinship networks. The tea plantation of Tumsong (often pronounced Tamsang) is a case in point, where the first Thangmi overseer arrived from Dolakha's Lapilang village in the late 1800s. Many Darjeeling Thangmi can trace their ancestry back to this individual. Tumsong tea plantation maintains a majority Thangmi labour force to this day, due to the rules of tenure and inheritance that have governed tea plantation jobs and accommodation since the colonial era.

Another important feature of Darjeeling's colonial tea economy was that almost all large tracts of land were owned either by government or by private tea companies, with small allotments granted to plantation workers on which they had temporary rights, but could not own.[14] This meant that there was no prospect of property ownership for Thangmi migrants, who encountered for the first time a mode of economic production different from the agrarian, subsistence farming economy they had known in Nepal. As the protagonist in Lainsing Bangdel's Nepali-language novel *Muluk Bahira* ('Outside the Country') describes the situation he encountered in India upon emigrating from Nepal, "Although there was no land or kipat [ancestral land exempt from taxes] in Mugalan [India], one could earn enough to feed one's stomach" (as cited in Hutt, 1998: 203).[15]

Besides tea, Darjeeling's other major attraction was the British army recruitment centre, which opened in Darjeeling in 1857. Enlistment in the Gurkhas became a prize objective for many young men from Nepal's so-called 'martial races', a group from which the Thangmi were excluded. The recruitment officers Northey and Morris dismissed them as "coarse in appearance, and the inferior of the other races in social and religious matters, they do not merit further description" (1928: 260). But this did not stop some Thangmi from joining up under assumed names and living a double life as Rai, Gurung, or Magar.

The British preference for certain 'races' did not seem to apply to non-enlisted men responsible for road building and other support services, and many Thangmi were contracted by the army and paid a daily wage for their work. Substantial numbers of Thangmi worked in Darjeeling, Sikkim, Assam, and as far as Bhutan and Arunachal Pradesh in road-building groups, which for many defined their migrant experience. When asked where they worked, many older Thangmi said simply, "*Hami* road *ma gayo* [We went to the road]".

Often, they did not know the names of the specific places in which they worked, and the English term 'road' was used to denote transient road-building sites, which were a focal point of their experience. The rapid development of Darjeeling and its environs, through the powerful combination of tea, resorts, roads, and a strategic border to defend, led to astronomical population growth in the area. According to Kennedy, Darjeeling "experienced the most rapid rate of growth on record for nineteenth-century Bengal" (1996: 184). By 1881, 88,000 residents of Darjeeling had been born in the district, comprising more than 60 per cent of the total district population (Samanta, 2000: 22).

It is difficult to determine how many of these were Thangmi. The 1872 Census of India lists 13 Thangmi language speakers in Darjeeling, a number which had risen to 319 by 1901 (Grierson, 1909: 280). However, these numbers are just the beginning of the contentious politics of the census for Thangmi in both India and Nepal, and must be taken with a grain of salt. Due to self-misrepresentation as members of other groups (largely for army recruitment purposes) and the preference for the Nepali language as a *lingua franca* in Darjeeling's multi-ethnic context, it is likely that these census figures, which are based on language rather than on ethnicity, under-represent the real numbers of Thangmi. Thangmi were as eager as the rest to be included in the pan-Nepali political identity that was emerging in Darjeeling at the time, with the Nepali language as its cornerstone; hence, speaking Thangmi in public was not a popular practice.

PRE-1950 NARRATIVES OF MIGRATION: SEEKING EMPLOYMENT AND INCLUSION

Each of the narratives presented in this section emphasizes different particular life experiences that led to migration, but all have in common a desire to leave the challenging economic situation of land pressure and debt in Nepal, and the social exclusion and oppression that accompanied it. They highlight the relatively unstructured, unhierarchical nature of Darjeeling society at the time, at least when compared to Nepal. In addition, since everyone in Darjeeling was a migrant—the area was virtually unpopulated until 1835, and private property ownership was highly restricted due to the dominance of the tea estates—the opportunities for land appropriation, a dynamic endemic to Nepal's agrarian setting, were reduced in Darjeeling's emerging cash economy.

Bir Bahadur, who was born in Dolakha's Lapilang village and engaged in circular migration for many years before finally settling in Darjeeling, explained:

> My father had a loan. I came back here [to Darjeeling] after paying it off. In one month, it accrued Rs. 10 interest on Rs. 100. It was a loan from Lapilang's *maila* [N: middle-brother] headman. In those days, they really oppressed us. Because they were rich and we were poor, they had us harnessed to the plow like oxen. It's not like that here [in Darjeeling].

Bir Bahadur's pride at being able to pay back his father's loan after a few seasons of work in Darjeeling was evident, and it demonstrates one of the economic imperatives which initially made circular migration an attractive strategy for many Thangmi from Nepal. By earning cash in Darjeeling, where migrants could keep costs low by staying in cheap accommodation like Khaldo Hotel and then using it to pay off debts back in Nepal, Thangmi could ensure that their ancestral property was not appropriated by creditors. As another migrant who paid off debts with Darjeeling-earned cash put it, "we were able keep our *bampa*"—that hearth-side stony icon of resilience and territorial attachment. However, most earned just enough to pay off their debts and maintain the status quo, but not to actually transform the socioeconomic order. As Creighton Peet observed:

> For the majority of Thamis ... circular migration has brought just enough income to pay off debts and regain some economic independence from the moneylenders and large landowners. Much of their earnings go, in fact, into the hands of their wealthy Bahun-Chhetri patrons and thus help to support this latter group's dominant position in the community. (1978: 461)

This assessment matches Kearney's more general observation that rather than leading to improvement as one might expect, "remittances perpetuate status quo underdevelopment" (1986: 47). To understand why circular migration continues, then, we need to look more closely at the impact of what Peggy Levitt calls 'social remittances' (2001), and the transformative potential for the new forms of 'body politics' that Gidwani and Sivaramakrishnan (2003) identify as emergent in the process of circular migration itself.

Harka Bahadur, an elderly stalwart of the Thangmi community in Darjeeling, who became known as '*Amrikan*' because he had worked with American soldiers in the Burma theatre of World War II in an army support role, described a different scenario. His parents' relatively substantial property holding in Nepal became inadequate due to a surfeit of sons, leading him to test the greener pastures of Darjeeling's cash economy. As the youngest of six brothers, Amrikan knew that he would have little chance of inheriting an adequate piece of ancestral property. Based on his research in Nepal, Peet concluded that birth order and family size were not in themselves predictive of who might migrate (1978: 386). However, my data from Darjeeling shows that men like Amrikan were very conscious of their particular constellation of family size, sibling order, and land inheritance as they made choices for on-going circular migration or permanent settlement in Darjeeling. It was not that Amrikan's position at the bottom of a big family's age-status order led him inevitably to migrate to Darjeeling and ultimately settle there; for many other migrants, superficially similar backgrounds led to different choices, like those of the man who decided to settle in Darjeeling because "my youngest brother 'ate' all of our land". Rather, each individual's family situation strongly conditioned the range of options that they might choose.

Amrikan described his first impressions of Darjeeling as follows:

> When I first came here, while I was looking for work, I could tell Thangmi from their faces, and I would ask, "Are you Thangmi?" and when they said, "We are Thangmi" I would ask, "Where are you from?" and when they said "We are from Dolakha Dui Number", then we knew each other.[16] That was a good time. Ethnicity was not that important, it was only much later that there was any competition. At that time, you could earn one or two *anna* [N: coin = 1/16 of a rupee] a day, putting it all together in a week you'd have 10 or 15 *anna*. In this place full of money, we were all equal.

Amrikan's description, although perhaps unrealistically utopian, suggests that in Darjeeling, social exclusion was not the insurmountable problem for Thangmi that it had been in Nepal. The fixed agrarian hierarchies that Thangmi migrants had known in their village homes came unmoored in this 'place of money', where everyone had an 'equal' chance.

Silipitik, a senior figure in Dolakha's Pashelung village, who engaged in circular migration for most of his life, but eventually settled in Nepal, described his contrasting experiences in the two countries as follows:

> Over there, no one talked about caste or ethnicity unless you were in the army. Here, everyone is always harping on about it, who is high and who is low, who is big and who is small. There everyone just worked hard. I remember a speech I heard once in Judge Bazaar [one of Darjeeling's central public squares], where a man said, "Here, there is no caste and no ethnicity, no high and no low. Here, there are only two categories we need to know about, male and female. There are no other divisions in our society."[17] I liked what he said so much, I never forgot it. There, it really was that way, here it never will be. I only came back because I had no brothers and had to care for my mother and our land when she got old, otherwise I would have stayed in that place where people could make speeches like that.

Silipitik's nostalgic reminiscences of this speech, which he repeated to me on several occasions, seemed to encapsulate a powerful moment in the development of his own awareness of the different frames that Nepal and India respectively offered for the articulation of belonging. Both in listening to the speech and in reflecting on it years later, he became aware of the ways in which his own life was marked by the hierarchies and structures of each location and nation-state he had experienced in his life of circular migration, and the choices he had ultimately made between them.[18]

Silipitik, like most other Thangmi migrants, had been to Tibet several times before ever going to Darjeeling. Although they would travel north from their Himalayan border homes to the towns of Dram/Khasa and Nyalam/Kuti (as the towns were called in Tibetan and Nepali, respectively) to trade their grain for salt several times a year, the Thangmi never developed trading conglomerates like those well-documented among the Sherpa, Newar, Thakali, and Manangi communities. Instead, they would travel alone or in small groups on the rough mountain trail that, in just a few long days of walking, brought them directly over the mountains to Khasa and Kuti.

Dhanbir, a Thangmi man from Dolakha who had been to Tibet 17 times before the border closed, described his most enduring memories of the place as follows:

The Tibetans called us Rongsha or Rongba [Tibetan: lowlander]. They didn't think we Thangmi were different from other Nepalis. Everyone from this area traveled up there: Thangmi, Newar, Tamang, even Bahun and Chhetri. The Tibetans were friendly and didn't seem to differentiate between ethnic groups, either within their own community or among Nepalis.

From an outsider's perspective at least, in Tibet, as in Darjeeling, the particulars of ethnicity did not seem to matter in the same way as they did back in Nepal.[19] Certainly, Thangmi were different from Tibetans, but they were not immediately placed in a low-status category, nor were they taken advantage of. Thangmi joked about how Tibetans could not differentiate between Newar and Thangmi, who often travelled up from Dolakha at the same time. Some Thangmi had Tibetan *mit* (N)—a fictive kin relation created between trading partners from different ethnic groups. This fact was often recounted to me to emphasize the relatively non-hierarchical nature of Thangmi relationships with Tibetans. In these ways, the local status hierarchies which structured Thangmi lives in Nepal were unsettled by their contrasting experiences in Tibet as well as in India.

The proximity of many Thangmi villages to Khasa and Kuti meant that until the Sino-Nepali border was closed in the 1950s, most immediate trading needs were taken care of in these Tibetan towns (Shneiderman, 2013). Between these trading trips to the north and wage labour carried out in Darjeeling, there was little need for Thangmi to go to Nepal's capital city of Kathmandu. Few Thangmi visited the city until much later. An urban census that I conducted with research collaborator Bir Bahadur Thami (no relation to the Bir Bahadur quoted earlier) in 2006 identified just under 400 Thangmi who defined themselves as permanent residents of the city. These facts suggest that the Nepali nation-state, with Kathmandu at its political centre, was not the most prominent frame of reference in which Thangmi defined their sense of belonging. Rather, they had a trans-Himalayan sense of belonging, grounded in particular localities of Dolakha, Sindhupalchok, Darjeeling, Sikkim, Khasa, Kuti, and beyond. As argued above, maintaining this transnational formation of belonging—and the economic strategies that supported it—depended upon regular movement across borders, rather than upon strong legal or emotional ties to any single nation-state.

Why did so many Thangmi continue to practice circular migration instead of severing ties with Nepal and settling permanently in India, as significantly higher numbers of other ethnic groups of Nepali heritage did?[20] With apparently so much in common with other migrants from Nepal to Darjeeling—many of whom also experienced economic exploitation and social exclusion—one wonders why the Thangmi relationship to the place followed a somewhat different trajectory. Several factors seem to have been at play. First of all, the Thangmi population numbers in Darjeeling were tiny compared to those of other groups. For example, the 1872 Census, which enumerated 13 Thangmi speakers, also listed 6,754 Rai, 6,567 Tamang, and 1,120 Newar. With so many more members, the other ethnic groups were better situated to recreate their communities in full in a new location. Many Thangmi, by contrast, may have felt uncomfortable settling permanently in a place where they were so few in number, and it was difficult to create social networks and maintain cultural practices. Second, although one tea estate did have a majority Thangmi workforce, as described above, this was an exception rather than the norm. In general, most Thangmi survived on short-term wage labour and did not receive the right to settle on tea estate property. Combined with the lack of easy access to lucrative army jobs, these factors meant that compared to the other groups, Thangmi existence in Darjeeling was relatively insecure from a long-term perspective, although the short-term earnings could be substantial.

Ultimately, although the structures of social exclusion so prevalent in Nepal were substantially softened in Darjeeling, the reality was far from Amrikan or Silipitik's nostalgic descriptions of an egalitarian utopia. While "those entering Darjeeling ... were free from the Muluki Ain promulgated in Nepal" (Pradhan, 2004: 11)—free from the *structures* of oppression as legislated by the Nepali state—they were not necessarily free from the *practices* of oppression that travelled with migrant Nepalis to Darjeeling. Such hierarchies did not disappear overnight, and despite the potential for economic mobility, the Thangmi continued to be treated as low men on the social totem pole by other Nepali migrants. As the Nepali community in Darjeeling began to fashion a self-consciously modern ethnic identity within India in the early 20th century, its scions sought to excise evidence of 'backwardness', of which poor migrant labourers from Nepal, like most Thangmi, were constant reminders. Rhoderick

Chalmers suggests that, "An inevitable concomitant of the emergence of a more concrete and precisely defined conception of Nepaliness was the parallel development of new paradigms of exclusion" (2003: 172). In this kind of environment—where Thangmi were not so badly exploited and excluded as they were in Nepal, but were not exactly included either—perhaps it made good sense to hedge their bets by maintaining their claims to the small pieces of property in Nepal on which their sense of territorial identity was premised.

NATION-STATES ON THE RISE AND THE MAKING OF MULTIPLE CITIZENS

Three historical events around 1950 radically altered the political contexts that framed Thangmi transnational social formations: Indian independence in 1947, and the ensuing Indo-Nepal Friendship Treaty of 1950; Nepal's first period of democracy in 1950–51; and China's occupation of Tibet from 1950 onwards, which led to the closure of Nepal's northern border for the better part of a decade. Each of these events marked for its respective country the transition to a modern nation-state. Both ideas of citizenship and of national boundaries were redefined, affecting the ways in which Thangmi circular lives were structured.

The 1950 Indo-Nepali Friendship Treaty for the first time defined the notion of citizenship in a way that mattered for Thangmi circular migrants. Article 7 of the treaty created trouble for all Indian citizens of Nepali heritage, since "According to the treaty every Nepali-speaking person in India is a temporary citizen of the country" (Timsina, 1992: 51) and "those who are Indian nationals cannot easily prove their citizenship when the Treaty makes no distinction between them and Nepalese nationals" (Hutt, 1997: 124). For Thangmi moving back and forth between Nepal and India, the concept of a singular citizenship in one nation-state was new, as was the very idea of a clearly bounded nation-state which accorded citizens 'rights' in exchange for exclusive allegiance. As Yuval-Davis et al. put it, "citizenship has not always been related to a nation-state" (2006: 2).[21]

The late Latte Apa, Darjeeling's senior Thangmi shaman during my fieldwork, who was originally from the village of Alampu in Dolakha, explained:

When we first came, we did not say 'this is Nepal' and 'this is India'. We had to walk for 10 or 12 days through the hills, and one day was no different from the next. It was only when we saw the train that we said, 'This must be India'. We knew that there was no train in Nepal. And then there were the *saheb* [the British]. They did not come to Nepal. Only after they left was there trouble. Then people said "Are you Indian?" and we had to think about it.

Many Thangmi described the early 1950s as a challenging time to be in India. Questions of national allegiance were on the table, and given the fact that many Thangmi were indeed only 'temporary citizens' of India, those who wanted to stay felt particularly hard-pressed to demonstrate their Indianness. It was at this historical juncture that some Darjeeling Thangmi, such as the family of the Tumsong tea plantation overseer, intentionally attempted to sever their ties with their brethren in Nepal in order to assimilate their linguistic and cultural practices to the Indian mainstream. As Tumsong's current patriarch explained to me, "My father said, 'Our family has been here for generations. You are not to talk with those from Nepal. We do not need the Thangmi language or shamans, those are for the *pahar* ['hills', a derogatory term for Nepal], not for India'". Other Thangmi took the opposite approach, deciding that this was the moment to return permanently to Nepal, with the promise of democracy and land reform there offering the tempting prospect that the social order might become more flexible. Such returnees took with them all that they had learned from their experiences in India, and in many cases remained both socially and economically linked to Darjeeling, sending their children to work there later while slowly expanding their property base in Nepal with the money they had earned.

For the vast majority, however, these changes were only a temporary disturbance until they came to understand the new system(s) and realized that they could procure at least some of the documents of citizenship in both locations. Such documents did not change others' attitudes towards them—in India they would always be stereotyped as Nepali, and in Nepal those born in India would be stereotyped as outsiders—but these papers did provide legal instruments with which to maintain property ownership in Nepal while simultaneously working in India.

Neither Nepal nor India grants citizenship automatically at birth. Citizenship does not just happen to you. Rather, in Nepal it must be 'made' (N: *nagarikta banaunu*), while in India, people speak of 'registering' themselves as citizens. These processes can make it difficult to obtain papers, but they also accord agency to prospective citizens to choose which combination of documents they want to possess. Many Thangmi originally from Nepal alluded to the fact that obtaining some Indian documents—particularly voter registration cards—was not difficult, since from the first post-Independence elections onwards, local politicians in Darjeeling had viewed circular migrants as a secret weapon with which to boost their voter base, and were therefore eager to register them as voters. Although the ration card was supposed to precede the voter card, with the latter issued on the basis of the former, many Thangmi apparently went the other way around, obtaining a ration card by showing their voter card and complaining that they had not received or had lost the former.

In Nepal, the *nagarikta* citizenship document must be applied for after the age of 16 years on the basis of one's father's citizenship document in the locality in which he is, or was, registered. As long as the father holds citizenship, the son is entitled to it in that locality regardless of whether he was born there or has ever lived there.[22] For Darjeeling Thangmi families, keeping the inheritance of *nagarikta* alive became an important strategy to maintain landholdings in Nepal, since non-Nepali citizens may not own land. Many young Thangmi men born in Darjeeling described their first trip to Nepal as a rite of passage at the age of 16 years or soon thereafter to 'make' their citizenship and visit their family's ancestral land holdings. This practice has clearly been going on for generations, because several of the men who told me such stories had fathers, grandfathers, and great grandfathers born in Darjeeling—but all still held Nepali *nagarikta*. Most recently, Nepali citizenship has become a much sought-after commodity for Thangmi from India who wish to work abroad in the Middle East or beyond, since popular wisdom holds that it is much easier to obtain a visa as a Nepali than as an Indian. In all of these ways, holding at least partial papers from more than one country has become the norm, rather than the exception, for many Thangmi. Few people I interviewed seemed to feel conflicted over their obligations to more than one nation-state. Rather, they felt that given their level of social exclusion at the national level in Nepal, and their lack of property ownership in India, both states in a way owed them the opportunity to also belong to the other.

While notions of citizenship and national borders were being defined between India and Nepal, the Chinese occupation of Tibet led to the closure of the northern border across which Thangmi had long travelled. The opening of a newly redefined border in 1960 radically altered Thangmi sensibilities of their national positionality, as this quotation from Dhanbir illustrates:

> In those days, Kuti [Nyalam] was closer and easier to reach than Kathmandu. We did most of our business in Kuti. We did not think of Kuti as a very different country, although it was high up in the mountains and people spoke a different language, like they did in Dolakha and Sailung [where Newar and Tamang were respectively spoken]. There was no 'border' or 'checking'. You had to store your *khukuri* [N: large curved knife] with local headmen when you arrived and pay tax to them when you left. But suddenly the border closed and everything changed. We heard that the Chinese had come and now Kuti was theirs. We could not go. From then on we had to go to Kathmandu, before that there was no reason to go there.

Political changes in a neighbouring nation-state contributed towards reorienting Thangmi relationships with their own; with Kuti inaccessible, Thangmi began travelling to Kathmandu more regularly to procure basic goods, and concomitantly began to conceptualize themselves as citizens within Nepal's national framework. However, there were no roads from the Thangmi region to Kathmandu until the mid-1960s,[23] and even then, walking to Kathmandu from Thangmi villages still required up to a week—not much less than going all the way to Darjeeling. Moreover, there were few immediate opportunities for work in Kathmandu, since the labour jobs that Thangmi would have been qualified for were already filled by others (largely by low-caste Jyapu Newar and Tamang from villages closer to the city). This meant that although Kathmandu became the desired destination for short-term trading, the closure of the Tibetan border did not have much effect on established patterns of circular migration to Darjeeling.

The changes in Tibet, however, did present one other option to a very small sub-group of Thangmi who lived at the northernmost fringe of the region, right up against what was to become the Sino-Nepali border in the Lapchi area. In 1960, China and Nepal entered into a series of boundary agreements and treaties, which included a strategic trade of two villages previously in Nepal for two villages previously in Tibet.[24] Although they were a minority in these predominantly Sherpa villages, a small number of Thangmi families were affected by these events. Along with the rest of the villagers, they were provided the option of staying in their homes and becoming Chinese citizens (with no easy option for dual citizenship, since China enforced borders and paperwork rigorously) or moving away to remain Nepali citizens. A small number of Thangmi chose to become Chinese, but in doing so they essentially gave up their ethnic identity and assimilated to the dominant Sherpa group in the area, who were listed as ethnic 'people' by the national classification projects of Chinese ethnology in the 1950s.[25] Many other Thangmi derided the choices of these individuals at the time, but they were forced to reconsider later when China leapt ahead of Nepal economically. During my fieldwork in the TAR in 2005, I documented a small number of Thangmi from Nepal who were attempting to claim Chinese citizenship in Nyalam and Dram through certification as Chinese Sherpa, usually by way of marriage to bona fide Chinese citizens, but occasionally through protracted residence on temporary labour permits. Those trying to claim Chinese citizenship were only a very small percentage of the much larger numbers of Thangmi who spent one month at a time in this Sino-Tibetan-Nepali border zone, taking advantage of China's economic strength to boost their earnings from Darjeeling and other emerging locations closer to home.

THE FUTURE OF CIRCULAR MIGRATION AND THANGMI BELONGING

Since the 1950s, ideals of national identity have become ever clearer in all three countries in question. Constitutions have been promulgated, national languages promoted, and the symbolic repertoire of national hegemony solidified. Although in some circumstances, Thangmi have sought to evade, or even subvert, such state-promoted paradigms for belonging, the more enduring image that emerges from the narratives here is one of what we might call circular citizens (Shneiderman, 2010). Over time, Thangmi have cobbled together a complex sense of belonging that relies upon a balance of rights and obligations lived out in the diverse localities of their transnational village. That village is embedded simultaneously in multiple nation-states, upon all of which Thangmi individuals feel they have the ability to make different, but complementary, claims. Neither complete citizenship nor total belonging is ever attained within the borders of a single state; rather, circular citizenship entails regular movement across nation-state borders in order to piece together the differentiated prospects for belonging that each national framework offers. At the time that I conducted fieldwork in Darjeeling in 2004–05, circular migration was alive and well. In fact, both the numbers of Thangmi migrants in India and China and the duration of their stays had increased due to the Maoist-state conflict in Nepal. Yet Nepal's civil conflict, along with other local, national, and international dynamics of development and migration, has also brought about a new set of opportunities for Thangmi in Nepal. These dynamics have combined to create a substantial out-migration of high-caste individuals and families from Dolakha and Sindhupalchok. Some have gone to Kathmandu, while others have moved to Charikot (Dolakha's district headquarters) or Bahrabise, both emergent regional centres, to start businesses or work in government or development jobs. Still others have joined the growing number of international Nepali migrants going to study or work in urban India, the Middle East, Southeast Asia, the US, and Europe. All of these lifestyle transformations require capital—to buy land in Kathmandu, invest in a business in a regional town, or finance a ticket abroad—so over the last decade, many of the high-caste landowners of the region have divested themselves of substantial portions of their property. In response, in an example of what Tania Li has called indigenous 'microcapitalism' (2010), Thangmi have begun buying pieces of land vacated by those who once used it as a tool of exploitation against them.

Where has the money for such purchases come from? In part from newly emerging sites of wage labour closer to home—a Thangmi-owned slate mine in Alampu,[26] chicken farms and furniture factories in Charikot, hydroelectric plants in Sindhupalchok, and local road construction projects, to name a few—which allow workers to keep more of their hard-earned wages by living and eating at home. Some individuals have also availed themselves of low-interest loans from micro-credit institutions such as the Agricultural Development Bank in order to finance such purchases, which they are then able to pay back over time with money saved from being able to live off their own land.

As Bir Bahadur, one of the early migrants, said about the changed situation in Nepal from his vantage point in Darjeeling, "Now they can't oppress us, the Thangmi have won and the Chhetri have all gone to Kathmandu". He had heard about these shifts from his nephews, who continued to travel back and forth between Nepal and India. Why were they still doing so if the environment was indeed now more favourable in Nepal? "It's fun to travel with my friends and see how things are done in other places. Also I don't have to eat off of my parents' land", said one young migrant. Another older man added, "It's how we Thangmi enjoy ourselves".

Recalling that choices for circular migration were historically diversified across families throughout the entire transnational social formation, a range of options continues to be available and desirable in specific circumstances. Even for families who have recently expanded their land-holdings in Nepal, an actual increase in grain yield may take several years to realize, and in the meantime, it is helpful if young, able-bodied members live away from home and feed themselves for several months of the year.[27] Moreover, the trends of 'micro-capitalism' and economic development closer to home are new enough that they have yet to benefit substantial numbers of Thangmi. Finally, although Nepal's civil conflict created opportunities for some, the uncertainties and pressures that came along with it made others want, or need, to leave. For all of these reasons, circular migration has continued to be practiced by many Thangmi, as a way to 'enjoy' (N: *ramaunu*) an otherwise difficult life by seeing other parts of the world, and perhaps most importantly, other parts of one's own community. As the choice of such expressions indicates, some component of belonging may be found in the camaraderie of migration itself.

Turning from the economic to the social, prospects for national belonging in Nepal—'social inclusion'—have improved substantially with the political transformations of the last several years, and many Thangmi have sought to capitalize on these opportunities by engaging in political activism within the frameworks of both ethnic and party politics, as I have discussed elsewhere (Shneiderman and Turin, 2004; Shneiderman, 2009). But again, such activities are part of a larger transnational social formation, and many of those Thangmi individuals most involved in politics in Nepal trace their activist interests to the initial experiences of social inclusion and political activism in India, where the potential for such practices of belonging were visible far earlier. As a former general secretary of the Nepal Thami Samaj explained:

It was only when I went to visit my relatives in Darjeeling and Sikkim in the late 1990s that I understood that we had rights which we could demand from the state. At first I wanted to stay there, it was so exciting. But then I thought, "We can do this in Nepal too, slowly such things will become possible".

He, like an increasing number of travellers in both directions, did not go to India for wage labour, but for what we might call 'belonging tourism' in which they went to see how the other half lived. In the other direction, Thangmi born and bred in India also began visiting Nepal regularly in the late 1990s as transportation improved and they became interested in cultural heritage for the purposes of their Scheduled Tribe application to the Indian state (see Shneiderman and Turin, 2006b; Shneiderman, 2009).

One of the things that Thangmi from India are usually most eager to see on visits to Nepal is old Thangmi houses with the *bampa* intact. Recently, a group of politically active Thangmi in Dolakha, many of whom are also part of the buy-back-the-land trend, has developed a proposal to make one of the oldest houses in Dolakha with its prominent *bampa* a museum and 'cultural heritage site' (as the proposal calls it in English) for Thangmi everywhere. Funding has been sought from local, national, and international organizations in both Nepal and India. For Thangmi from India, this idea would fulfil their desires for a link to ethnic territory and ancestral property, as well as being a recognizable cultural heritage site. For Thangmi in Nepal, it would signify resilience, and their slow but sure progress towards ending land-based exploitation and achieving social inclusion. For those who continue to move back and forth, this particular house and *bampa* would mark just one point of belonging among many.

NOTES

1. I am grateful to Tanka Subba for suggesting this translation.
2. Nepali words are designated with (N); Thangmi words with (T). Turner defines *khaldo* as 'hollow, hole, pit, depression; ravine' (1997 [1931]: 121).
3. The Nepal Inclusion Index (Bennett and Parajuli, 2008) locates the Thangmi close to the bottom of every indicator out of 78 caste/ethnic groupings analyzed.
4. For a useful explication of the origins and applications of the term 'social exclusion', see Daly and Silver (2008).
5. See Shneiderman and Turin (2006a) and Shneiderman (2009, 2010, 2011) for more information about the Thangmi.

6. Alpa Shah (2006) makes a related argument about the social and cultural aspects of internal labour migration from Jharkhand to the brick kilns of other states in India.

7. The 2001 Nepal census enumerated just less than 22,000 Thangmi in Nepal, whereas a census conducted by the Bharatiya Thami Welfare Association counted approximately 8,000 Thangmi in India, primarily in the states of West Bengal and Sikkim. It is hard to know what proportion of either those counted in Nepal or India in fact moves between the two countries.

8. 'Thangmi' are often referred to as 'Thami', especially by the Nepali and Indian states and members of other ethnic communities in both countries. Their preferred ethnonym in their own language is Thangmi, which I use except when citing other works using 'Thami'.

9. In nationalist histories, Prithvi Narayan Shah's 1769 "unification" of Nepal is cited as the moment of the modern nation's birth. However, in ethnic and regional activist tellings of Nepali history, "domination" often replaces "unification", and the latter is debunked as a "myth".

10. The earliest written record from the area dates to 1324 AD, in which the town is mentioned as the refuge destination for a deposed Mithila prince who died en route (Slusser, 1982: 259). By 1453 AD, Dolakha was under the control of King Kirti Simha (Regmi, 1980: 136).

11. *Khet* means simply "wet cultivated field", while *muri* is a specific measurement of a field's yield, equalling approximately 160 pounds of harvested grain.

12. See also Caplan (2004 [1970]) and K. Pradhan (1991) for broader discussions of these dynamics in eastern Nepal.

13. Migration from the hills of Nepal to Darjeeling was by no means an exclusively Thangmi phenomenon. Members of virtually every one of Nepal's caste and ethnic groups made their way to Darjeeling and other parts of India during the same historical period (see Hutt, 1997, 1998). What remains unique about the Thangmi situation, however, is the ongoing prevalence of cross-border migration, a practice engaged in only minimally by other groups.

14. See Chatterjee (2001) for details of this system.

15. Tanka Subba (1989) provides an overview of economic relations in Darjeeling.

16. *Dui Number* "Number Two" was the Nepali administrative zone within which Dolakha district fell before the country's reorganization into 75 districts in the early 1960s.

17. Silipitik could not identify the speaker or political context of this event.

18. I am aware that this representation of Darjeeling's tea economy as relatively egalitarian stands in contrast to much of the sociological literature on the production of tea in India, which represents the tea industry as a highly classed domain rife with exploitation (Bhowmik, 1981; Chatterjee, 2001). Recall that here the contrast is between Darjeeling and Nepal, and my point is that although class-based exploitation may indeed have been, and continue to be, a feature of tea production in India, such dynamics were not tied to group identity and territory in the same way that they were in Nepal. Therefore, I suggest that tea plantation workers in India possessed a modicum of social mobility that far exceeded that available in Nepal, where people felt fixed in both geographical and social place.

19. Tibetan societies have their own social hierarchies, which may not have been evident to Thangmi within the relatively short and superficial context of trading relationships.
20. Hutt cites a 1974 survey, in which out of 411 ethnically Nepali residents of Darjeeling tea estates, 48 per cent had never travelled outside the district and only 13 per cent had ever visited Nepal (1997: 123).
21. Hutt's summary of the Nepali language literature of migration confirms this point: "There are very few references in these texts to the political entities of Nepal and India: the émigrés move between Pahar and Mugalan" (1998: 202).
22. In 2006, Nepal's citizenship laws were revised to allow women to pass on citizenship to their children as well. The fieldwork cited here was conducted before the new legislation was implemented.
23. The Arniko Highway from Kathmandu to Lhasa, which runs through Sindhupalchok, was completed in 1966, and the linked Jiri road from Khadichaur to Dolakha was completed only in 1985.
24. For details see Shneiderman (2013).
25. See Mullaney (2010) for a detailed description of these projects. The Sherpa are not one of China's 56 *minzu*, or "nationalities", but are listed as "Xiaerba" in the separate category of *dzu*, or "people" of the Tibetan Autonomous Region.
26. See Dipesh Kharel's award-winning film *A Life with Slate* and his accompanying MA thesis (2006).
27. The Nepal Inclusion Index shows that Thangmi indicators for nutrition and education have indeed recently improved (Bennett and Parajuli, 2008).

REFERENCES

Anthias, F. 2006. 'Belongings in a Globalising and Unequal World: Rethinking Translocations', in N. Yuval-Davis, K. Kannabiran and U.M. Vieten (eds), *The Situated Politics of Belonging*, pp. 17–31. London: SAGE Publications.

Basch, L.N., G. Schiller, C. Szanton Blanc (eds). 1994. *Nations Unbound: Transnational Projects, Postcolonial Predicaments, and Deterritorialized Nation-States*. New York: Gordon and Breach.

Bennett, L. and D. Parajuli. 2008. *Nepal Inclusion Index: Methodology, First Round Findings and Implications for Action*. Unpublished manuscript.

Bhowmik, S. 1981. *Class Formation in the Plantation System*. Delhi: People's Publishing.

Bruslé, T. 2010. 'Introduction' (Special issue: Nepalese migrations), *European Bulletin of Himalayan Research*, 35–36: 16–23.

Caplan, L. 2004 (1970). *Land and Social Change in East Nepal: A Study of Hindu-Tribal Relations*. London: Routledge.

Chalmers, R. 2003. '*We Nepalis': Language, Literature and the Formation of a Nepali Public Sphere in India, 1914–1940*. Unpublished PhD Thesis, School of Oriental and African Studies. University of London, London.

Chatterjee, P. 2001. *A Time for Tea: Women, Labor and Post/Colonial Politics on an Indian Plantation*. Durham: Duke University Press.

Christiansen, F. and U. Hedetoft (eds). 2004. *The Politics of Multiple Belonging: Ethnicity and Nationalism in Europe and East Asia.* Hants, England: Ashgate.

Daly, M. and H. Silver. 2008. 'Social Exclusion and Social Capital: A Comparison and Critique', *Theory and Society*, 37: 537–66.

Gidwani, V. and K. Sivaramakrishnan. 2003. 'Circular Migration and the Spaces of Cultural Assertion', *Annals of the Association of American Geographers*, 93(1): 186–213.

Graham, L. 2005. 'Image and Instrumentality in a Xavante Politics of Existential Recognition: The Public Outreach Work of Etenhiritipa Pimentel Barbosa,' *American Ethnologist*, 32(4): 622–41.

Graner, E. and G. Gurung. 2003. 'Arabko Lahures: Nepalese Labour Migration to Arabian Countries', *Contributions to Nepalese Studies*, 30(2): 295–325.

Grierson, G. 1909. *Linguistic Survey of India.* Delhi: Motilal Banarsidass.

Guarnizo, L.E. and M.P. Smith. 1998. 'The Locations of Transnationalism', in Michael Peter Smith and Luis Eduardo Guarnizo (eds), *Transnationalism from Below.* New Brunswick, NJ: Transaction Publishers.

Hutt, M. 1997. 'Being Nepali without Nepal: Reflections on a South Asian Diaspora', in David N. Gellner, Joanna Pfaff-Czarnecka, and John Whelpton (eds), *Nationalism and Ethnicity in a Hindu Kingdom: The Politics of Culture in Contemporary Nepal*, pp. 101–44. Amsterdam: Harwood Academic Publishers.

————. 1998. 'Going to Mugalan: Nepali Literary Representations of Migration to India and Bhutan', *South Asia Research*, 18(2): 195–214.

Kearney, M. 1986. 'From the Invisible Hand to Visible Feet: Anthropological Studies of Migration and Development', *Annual Review of Anthropology*, 15: 331–61.

Kennedy, D. 1996. *The Magic Mountains: Hill Stations and the British Raj.* Berkeley: University of California.

Kharel, Dipesh. 2006. 'Heavy Loads Toward a Better Life: Thami Slate Miners in Alampu, Northeast Nepal'. Master's Thesis, University of Tromso, Norway.

Levitt, P. 2001. *The Transnational Villagers.* Berkeley: University of California Press.

Li, T. 2010. 'Indigeneity, Capitalism, and the Management of Dispossession', *Current Anthropology*, 51(3): 385–414.

Meillasoux, C. 1981. *Maidens, Meal and Money.* London: Cambridge University Press.

Mullaney, T. 2010. *Coming to Terms with the Nation: Ethnic Classification in Modern China.* Berkeley: University of California Press.

Northey, W.B. and C.J. Morris. 1928. *The Gurkhas, Their Manners, Customs and Country.* London: J. Lane.

Onta, P. 1996. 'Creating a Brave Nation in British India: The Rhetoric of Jati Improvement, Rediscovery of Bhanubhakta and the Writing of Bir History', *Studies in Nepali History and Society*, 1(1): 37–76.

————. 1999. 'The Career of Bhanubhakta as a History of Nepali National Culture, 1940–1999', *Studies in Nepali History and Society*, 4(1): 65–136.

Peet, R.C. 1978. 'Migration, Culture and Community: A Case Study from Rural Nepal'. PhD Thesis, Columbia University, New York.

Pradhan, K. 1991. *The Gorkha Conquests.* Oxford: Oxford University Press.

————. 2004. New Standpoints of Indigenous People's Identity and Nepali Community in Darjeeling (The Mahesh Chandra Regmi Lecture). Kathmandu: Social Science Baha.

Pradhan, Q. 2007. 'Empire in the Hills: The Making of Hill Stations in Colonial India', *Studies in History*, 23(1): 33–91.

Pries, L. 2001. 'The Approach of Transnational Social Spaces: Responding to New Configurations of the Social and the Spatial', in Ludger Pries (ed.), *New Transnational Social Spaces*, pp. 3–36. London: Routledge.

Regmi, M.C. 1976. *Landownership in Nepal*. Berkeley: University of California Press.

———. 1980. *Regmi Research Series Cumulative Index for 1980*. Kathmandu: Regmi Research Series.

———. 1981. *Regmi Research Series Cumulative Index for 1981*. Kathmandu: Regmi Research Series.

Samanta, A.K. 2000. *Gorkhaland Movement: A Study in Ethnic Separatism*. Delhi: A.P.H. Publishing Corporation.

Seddon, J.D. 2002. 'Foreign Labour Migration and the Remittance Economy of Nepal', *Critical Asian Studies*, 34(1): 19–40.

Seddon, J.D., J. Adhikari and G. Gurung. 2001. *The New Lahures: Foreign Employment and Remittance Economy of Nepal*. Kathmandu: Nepal Institute of Development Studies.

Shah, A. 2006. 'The Labour of Love: Seasonal Migration from Jharkhand to the Brick Kilns of Other States in India', *Contributions to Indian Sociology*, 40(1): 91–118.

Shneiderman, S. 2009. 'Ethnic (P)reservations: Comparing Thangmi Ethnic Activism in Nepal and India', in D.N. Gellner (ed.), *Ethnic Activism and Civil Society in South Asia*, pp.115–41. London: SAGE Publications.

———. 2010. 'Are the Central Himalayas in *Zomia*? Some Scholarly and Political Considerations across Time and Space', *Journal of Global History*, 5(2): 289–312.

———. 2011. 'Synthesizing Practice and Performance, Securing Recognition: Thangmi Cultural Heritage in Nepal and India', in C. Brosius and K. Polit (eds), *Ritual, Heritage and Identity: The Politics of Culture and Performance in a Globalised World*, pp. 202–45. London: Routledge.

———. 2013. 'Himalayan Border Citizens: Sovereignty and Mobility in the Nepal-Tibetan Autonomous Region (TAR) of China Border Zone', *Political Geography*, 35: 25–36.

Shneiderman, S. and M. Turin. 2004. 'The Path to Janasarkar in Dolakha District: Towards an Ethnography of the Maoist Movement', in Michael Hutt (ed.), *Himalayan People's War: Nepal's Maoist Rebellion*, pp. 77–109. London: Hurst & Co.

Shneiderman, S. and M. Turin, 2006a. 'Revisiting Ethnography, Recognizing a Forgotten People: The Thangmi of Nepal and India', *Studies in Nepali History and Society*, 11(1): 97–181.

———. 2006b. 'Seeking the Tribe: Ethno-Politics in Darjeeling and Sikkim', *Himal Southasian*, March–April, 19(2): 54–58.

Silver, H. 2010 'Social Inclusion Policies: Lessons for Australia', *Australian Journal of Social Issues*, 45(2): 183–211.

Sinha A.C. and T.B. Subba (eds). 2003. *The Nepalis in Northeast India: A Community in Search of Indian Identity*. New Delhi: Indus Publishing Company.

Slusser, M.S. 1982. *Nepal Mandala: A Cultural History of the Kathmandu Valley*. Princeton: Princeton University Press.

Subba, T.B. 1989. *Dynamics of a Hill Society: The Nepalis in Darjeeling and Sikkim Himalayas*. Delhi: Mittal Publications.

Subba, T.B., A.C. Sinha, G.S. Nepal, and D.R. Nepal (eds). 2009. *Indian Nepalis: Issues and Perspectives*. New Delhi : Concept Publishing Company.

Thieme, S. 2006. *Social Networks and Migration: Far West Nepalese Labour Migrants in Delhi*. Münster: Lit Verlag.

Timsina, S.R. 1992. *Nepali Community in India*. Delhi: Manak Publications.

Turner, R.L. 1997 (1931). *A Comparative and Etymological Dictionary of the Nepali Language*. New Delhi: Allied Publishers Limited.

Vajracharya, D. and T.B. Shrestha. 2013 VS (1974–1975 AD). *Dolakha-ko Aitihasik Ruprekha*. Kathmandu: Institute of Nepal and Asian Studies.

Yuval-Davis, N., K. Kannabiran, and U.M. Vieten. 2006. 'Introduction: Situating Contemporary Politics of Belonging', in N. Yuval-Davis, K. Kannabiran, and U.M. Vieten (eds), *The Situated Politics of Belonging*, pp. 1–14. London: SAGE Publications.

Chapter 4

Being a Ladakhi, Playing the Nomad

PASCALE DOLLFUS

SEDENTARY FARMERS AND NOMADIC PASTORALISTS

Bordering Tibet on the north and on the east and Pakistan-occupied Kashmir on the west, Ladakh is India's northernmost area. The region covers nearly 58,000 square kilometres, Aksai Chin excluded.[1] The population speaks Tibetan dialects and numbered 232,864, divided almost equally between Buddhists and Muslims, according to the 2004 Census.

In this arid, cold area with land elevations ranging from about 2,600 to 6,000 metres, a complex system of irrigation channels bringing water from the glaciers to feed oases allows the cultivation of barley, together with some wheat and peas, and animal husbandry. Indeed, nomadic pastoralists constitute a very small minority numbering about 1,200 persons. They are located on the southeastern edge of Changthang at an average altitude of 4,500 metres above sea level. Generally speaking, the so-called 'Northern Plain' refers to the dry, high-altitude plateau, which covers about 1,600 kilometres starting from the Chinese province of Qinghai in the east, through central and northern Tibet, to Ladakh in the west (Goldstein and Beall, 1990: 4). Within Ladakh however, it denotes the region which extends along the Indo-Tibetan border from Lake Pangong in the north to the Spiti confines in the south.

Altitude rather than aridity is the determining environmental factor and the basis of a unique system of pastoralism.[2] Sedentary farmers and nomadic pastoralists do not compete directly or indirectly for land resources and water, unlike in the arid-zone belt, which extends from the west coast of Africa, through the Middle East and Central Asia, to very near the east coast of Asia, and where the dividing line between fields and pasturages, between the 'sown' and the 'unsown', is a shifting one. They control distinct territories separated by several days' walk over high passes and deserts, and have very little contact. Farmers living in the surrounding villages only come very exceptionally to the camps to fetch unused fertilizer, which abounds in the empty pens. Besides, the nomads do not bring their herds to the villages in autumn to graze on stubble in the harvested fields, thereby fertilizing the soil with the dung left by the animals.[3] They do not, however, live in autarchy. In days past and present, they have depended on sedentary folk both for bartering or selling their pastoral products and for building their supplies of food grains and other essential commodities (tea, sugar, spices, steel cooking utensils, and so forth). Men were traditionally carriers and traders. They brought salt and borax previously collected from the salt lakes in western Tibet, as well as wool to Zanskar, where they exchanged them for barley and wooden wares. These long-distance caravans made up of hundreds of goats and sheep as described by observers at the turning between the 19th and 20th centuries are now a thing of the past.[4] The trans-Himalayan trade, which had in any case been operating at no more than half-throttle since the mid-20th century with the Chinese occupation of Tibet in 1949 and the closure of frontiers for political reasons following the Sino-Indian war of 1962, was given a coup de grâce with the development of modern means of transport and communication, and the introduction of the Public Distribution System in 1983.[5] With the availability of basic goods brought by trucks to the depots there was no longer any need to travel vast distances to get them.

"WE ARE SHEPHERDS"

Contrary to Yorüks from Turkey, for instance, whose self-ethnonym means 'those who walk', nomads from Ladakh do not define themselves by their mobility or the absence of a fixed dwelling. They describe themselves as *lug rdzi*, a word meaning 'shepherd'—literally 'keeper' (*rdzi*) of 'sheep' (*lug*), but which is commonly used in a wider sense and refers to any herdsman. According to the etymological meaning of the word nomad, which is derived from the Greek verb *nemein* (to put out to graze), herding is paramount in their identity. When accompanied by a qualifier, the root-word *rdzi* declines as *g.yag rdzi* 'yak herder', *ra rdzi* 'goatherd', *rta rdzi* 'horse herdsman' but also *thags rdzi* 'weaver', with *thags* referring to a loom and *rdzi* in this compound-word replacing the nominalizer *mkhan*, which is used among sedentary populations. Among highland pastoralists, weaving is the second economic activity after cattle breeding. In contrast to central and western Ladakh, it is practised by both sexes but on different looms.

Identity has an inherent separative and classifying logic. By describing themselves as shepherds, Changthang nomads focus on what they hold to be of central importance and which constitutes all their wealth: their herds. Pastoral knowledge and the possession of livestock are identificatory referents. Among farmers, mastering the handling of a swing plough wins everyone's admiration, whereas here the size of the herd and the ability to raise it are valued. Looking after herds is not merely an economic activity, it defines a way of life discernible in daily gestures and words: in the vocabulary used to describe precisely and name livestock which is much richer than the one used by sedentary farmers in the valley, expressions are used by shepherds to address each animal in the herd individually in order to encourage it or give it an order.

As the main, if not unique, wealth for the herdsman, livestock is omnipresent in the prayers offered to the gods by the nomads. Thus, lineage deities are asked to "put an end to the plague and stop the recurrence of illness among people and cattle", "cut the losses and increase the number of yaks, sheep and goats", and make "the summer drum—that is the thunder—of excellent virtue and auspiciousness vibrate" and "the rain fall on time to water high meadows and favour livestock growth". Furthermore, the primacy of livestock farming is also visible on votive stones laid on prayer walls, which are erected alongside footpaths and near encampments. These record the exact number of prayers recited by such and such a member of the community in the hope of being purified of their sins and the pollution caused by activities specific to herdsmen: milking, shearing, marking, castrating, slaughtering, and tanning.

To discriminate and recognize are inseparable abilities. Nomadic pastoralists focus on this rejection of agriculture in order to stand out from the Others, those they call *rmo pa*, 'ploughmen' or *zhing bat mkhan*, 'the ones who till fields', and whose life is ruled by farming, since cattle breeding comes way behind as merely supplementary to farming activities.[6] They denigrate the 'work of earth and stone' (*sa las rdo las*) as 'difficult' (*dkags po*) and 'laborious' (*lcin te*, lit. 'heavy'). They perceive it as a series of unpleasant and repetitive tasks: so many hours spent ploughing, sowing, irrigating, weeding, harvesting, threshing, winnowing, then roasting and grinding grain to get just a few kilos of barley flour. They put to the fore their freedom—freedom to come and go, to have time to laze in the sun, to chat, to play dice and card games, in contrast to how peasants are subjugated, rooted in the land, and not even masters of their movements or time. Along with the Pala nomads of western Tibet quoted by Goldstein and Beall (1990: 48), they might say,

> The grass grows by itself, the animals reproduce by themselves, they give milk and meat without our doing anything, so how can you say our way of life is hard? We don't have to dig up the earth to sow seeds nor do any of the other difficult and unpleasant tasks that the farmers do. And we have much leisure time.[...] As I have told you several times, the farmers' lifestyle is difficult, not ours.

BELONGINGNESS AND TERRITORY

In Ladakh, the territory occupies a central place in building the identity of both individuals and collectives. Ethnonyms, for instance, are not based on the names of clans or ancestors, as is often the case elsewhere in the Himalayas; they are built on place names to which one adds the nominal particle—*pa*, which means belonging to and is used to express membership of a country, religion, or profession.

To define oneself when referring to the Other, one's geographical location comes first with reference to one's native land, *pha yul* (fatherland) or *skyes yul* (birthplace) taking precedent over one's place of residence whenever these two differ. Interestingly enough, this is even the case for peripatetic communities such as itinerant musicians or religious mendicants. Similar to the French word '*pays*', *yul* can mean a village, a country, or a province; a land, a region, or realm. It denotes any territory constituting a defined geographic reality and inhabited by a community. When there is no inhabitant, this has to be specified through the addition of *stong pa*, an adjective meaning 'empty'. According to the context, the place where one is speaking and the knowledge available to the interlocutor, the place referred to as *yul* may indicate a more or less vast entity. Thus, a person will introduce themselves as being from quarter A, from hamlet B, from village C, from valley D, from region E, and even from nation F—in this case India, known in Ladakhi as *rgya dkar*—especially if he is abroad.

For sedentary farmers, *yul* in its primary sense means village. It is an uninterrupted territory (often the watershed of a body of water which keeps it alive), further defined by its permanence through generations. Conceived of as a concentric and centred world, it is clearly demarcated by religious buildings constructed through the inhabitants' piety: chortens (reliquaries), cairns, or low stone prayer walls. These sacred landmarks show the way and draw borders between an inside, which is organized and controllable, and an outside, which is largely untamed and potentially hostile. Within its limits, only its members, 'those belonging to', have the right to use both rare resources such as water and the vegetation, and supposedly endless resources such as sand and stones. Land is continually being used over time and in the space marked out within a property.

Nomads are not, as has too often been said, 'men from nowhere' who walk wherever their fancy takes them. They also fall within a territory. Though they break camp and move with their herds about 6–10 times a year to gain access to grass and water, each community has a well-established pattern of grazing migrations and claims exclusive access to grassland at a specific time of the year. In the same way, nomadic pastoralists belong to a *yul*, which occupies a physical space protected by its own territorial gods, and with its own customs by which they expressly distinguish themselves from others. However, contrary to sedentary folk, they visualize the world in which they live as an open space, built around several locations along with the resources the latter have to offer. Furthermore, they do not conceive of it as a static and permanent entity set within frozen boundaries, but as a living body. At any time, the territory can be displaced, reconstructed, enlarged, or reduced owing to variations in water and grass resources; to an increase or decrease in the number of men or animals; to economic or political events such as war or government policy; but also in response to divine summons.[7]

THE CHANGPAS OR 'THOSE FROM THE NORTH'

In Tibetan nomenclature, sedentary people are *rong pa*, 'those of the valleys', or *zhing pa* 'those of the fields'; nomads are *brog pa*, 'those of the high pastures'. In Ladakh, both appellations are built on place names, whose primary meaning has been changed. By a synecdochical process, the Changpas (*byang pa*) 'those from the North'—are generally understood to be nomadic people, even if they account for less than 20 per cent of the population of the Changthang region, which consists mainly of folk pursuing a mixed agricultural and pastoral livelihood. It contrasts with the Ladakhpas (*la dwags pa*), 'those from Ladakh'[8], referring in this context to central Ladakh—as the term Nepal may refer to the Kathmandu Valley—and synonymous with sedentary folk. A similar opposition had already been made in the early 16th century by Mirza Haidar. This military general, whose forces occupied Ladakh, thus wrote in his historical narrative, *Tarikh-i-rashidi*, that the inhabitants were divided into two sections: the *Yulpa* that resided in villages and the *Champa*, meaning 'dwellers in the desert', who were nomads.[9]

Despite its name, Changthang, commonly understood as 'Northern Plain', is less of a vast level plain and more of an endless stretch where rugged ranges and ragged bluffs alternate with deep valleys and plains of varying sizes. In addition, it is not located to the north of Ladakh, but to the east. Taking this fact into account, linguist S. Koshal (2001: 15 and 169) puts forward another etymology. The name would have its origin in the archaic form of the classical Tibetan word *che ma* meaning sand, and *thang*, which means plain; thus, the name *Che-thang* means sandy plains, which through the passage of time has given it its current name Changthang.

Although this may be so, the sedentary people's choice of the term 'Changpas', 'Northerners', to refer to nomadic pastoralists is not devoid of meaning. As Retaillé remarks (1997: 39), "Le nom de lieu assurant la vigueur du stéréotype en donne la position et cela suffit à une géographie largement imaginaire qui se développe en marge du monde réellement parcouru et vécu, et qui lui sert de rebord, d'horizon de référence. C'est la fonction du nom de lieu d'afficher le contenu qu'il recèle."[10] The Tibetan government-in-exile thus promoted the name Dharamasala and not MacLeod Gunj, which was redolent with British imperialism. As Anand (2002) points out, Dharamsala, also spelt Dharmashala based on the Sanskrit word dharma ('religion') and *shala* ('house'), resonates well given the fact that the Dalai Lama resides there and that it is home to several religious institutions. Its association with spiritualism and faith makes it more appealing to the Western tourists too. Furthermore, the word in popular Hindi refers to 'a temporary home' and this temporariness has been a central motif in the Tibetan diaspora's discourse on identity. A name is indeed a weapon and its choice is not neutral. For that reason, one way to try to counter a certain stereotyped image is to change the name. Thus in France, the Côtes-du-Nord became the Côtes d'Armor and the Basses-Alpes, the Alpes de Haute-Provence.

Today, nomadic pastoralists contest the label Changpa(s) perceived as derogatory and rude. (In fact, it is commonly used to imply that a person is backward and dirty.) They judge this denomination *btsog po,* an adjective meaning bad in every respect: dirty, untidy, useless, spoiled, naughty, troublesome, perilous, or injurious. They repeat over and over again that they do not inhabit the northern part of Ladakh, but its southeastern borders in southern Changthang. Hence, they ask to be called, if not southerners, at least Changthangpas, 'those of Changthang', which suits them better, or by their specific places of origin (for instance, a person from Kharnak would be known as a Kharnakpa, one from Rupshu as a Rupshupa, and so on). Alas, despite its negative use, the public services still chose the term Changpa (or Champa) to designate them when they were classed as *Scheduled Tribes* in 1989 along with seven other groups together constituting 88.7 per cent of Ladakh's population.[11]

FROM 'THE NOBLE SAVAGE' TO THE BARBARIAN

It is preferable to think of settled or nomadic lifestyles as opposite ends of a continuum with many gradations of stability and mobility, rather than being of two different types. There are various agro-pastoral populations who are semi-nomads or transhumants. Living in high-altitude valleys where only barley can grow, they move with their herds to high pastures, carrying tents with them as soon as the snow melts. Furthermore, people may shift between a nomadic and sedentary lifestyle and back again depending on circumstances. Nevertheless, a remarkably deep-rooted discourse intrinsically sets nomadic and settled populations apart. Man's coming and going do not pose a threat to the perception of how solid the line between the two actually is.

In Ladakh, as elsewhere in the world, the image of the nomad projected by sedentary people is associated with radical otherness, which stirs up both desire and fear. Depicted as different from the rest of the inhabitants, both in their alleged essence and in their means of livelihood, nomads are portrayed as attractive, thanks to their lifestyle, which is seemingly devoid of constraints and perceived as a symbol of freedom; thanks also to their proximity to the mountains—the herdsmen' territory *par excellence*. Indeed, this high-altitude area enjoys a positive charge in the collective imagination. In everyone's eyes and particularly those of city-dwellers, the mountain symbolises a refuge protected from the evils that plague modern society. It is regarded as the archetype of a nature considered good in itself. Folk songs praise the purity of the air in Changthang, the cleanliness of its earth, and the lightness of its water, which, contrary to the heavy water of the river, does not weigh on the stomach. They boast about the quality of the grass covering the pastures, which when very short is even better since the sap diluted in the lush grasslands of the rainiest regions is concentrated there; tasty and nutritious, it does not make animals' stomachs bloated. They praise its multi-coloured flowers adorning meadows like turquoises and corals set in silver reliquaries. They compare its snow-capped mountains to crystal stupas, its lakes twinkling in the sun to silver mirrors, and its countless herds to the stars in the sky, as seen in this excerpt from Thupstan Palden's short novel, *After Thirty Years*, duly subtitled *The flight of values*, and calling upon the youth of Ladakh to preserve and promote its rich cultural heritage.

> O Beautiful Chang Tang Valley
> Surrounded by mountains and lakes
> Vast meadows with flowers and grass
> Yak, sheep, goats and horses all herd together
> Meat, butter, and cheese are our food
> Clean earth, with fresh water and air
> Soft wool and *khulu* (yak hair) clothe us
> Beautiful colors of the flowers surround us
> Sweet smells of the mountain herbs *palu* and *sulu*
> Melodious echoes of the shepherd's song
> Compact and comfortable Nomad tent
> Strong and fast horses for riding

Delicious and healthy milk of the yak
[...]
Vast, beautiful valley
All people and animals are happy there.

In this idealized scene, as though popping up from a repertory of standard images, common to the whole of Tibetan literature, men are described as 'free, healthy, good and happy' like the man in the state of nature depicted by Jean-Jacques Rousseau. In fact, even when sedentary people consider nomads with keen interest, they describe them as 'what we were before'. Nomads are generally believed to be among the earliest inhabitants, and regarded as the archetypical Ladakhis.[12] There is no historical evidence whatsoever for this, but the hypothesis agreed well with the now-superseded three-stage theory associated with 19th-century social evolutionist writings that considered nomadic pastoralism to be an evolutionary stage in human history, following on from hunting-gathering and leading to sedentarization and agriculture.

This portrayal as a Noble Savage, naturally good, protected from corruption from civilization by his isolation, has been taken up by Westerners and raised to the level of a mythical imagery. A surprisingly immutable model, presenting nomads from Ladakh as cheerful men, satisfied with little, having but few wants, whose 'joie de vivre' contrasts with the hostile environment in which they were born thus emerges from the reports of missionaries and British administrators from the 17th century onwards and the accounts by today's travellers posted on the Internet. In this respect, this excerpt from the diary of an army officer, who came to hunt big game in the late 19th century, is exemplary:

> How infinitely superior to them, morally and physically are these wild children of nature, who are, fortunately for them, not yet as corrupted by the vices and evils consequent on a state of semi-civilisation. Strange it is that in a land whose bleak sterile appearance is calculated, one would suppose to depress spirits, such a cheery race of people if found. It seems as though their light hearts were given them by a kind of providence as some compensation for the dreariness of their country.[13]

However, this figure of the Noble Savage, innocent, living happily and in harmony with nature, is coupled with another image, so negative that the first one comes over as positive.[14] This mountain man, undoubtedly solid, is presented as a rough human being, insensitive to the rigours of the climate as well as to vermin. His impetuousness places him on the side of an untamed nature. Shaped in the image of a harsh and impoverished nature, he frightens by his brutality and his strange habits confine him to a marginal and despised position.

In the Tibetan world, the archetypical figure of the idiot is not the peasant, as is the case in the West, but the shepherd, also referred to as 'the northern wild man' (*byang mi rgod*). In Ladakh, he is featured on stage, his face smeared with flour, dressed in a long goatskin or sheepskin robe with the hair or wool turned to the outside, and topped with a ridiculous hat. He cracks his slingshot on the ground and speaks an unintelligible patois (according to its etymology, the barbarian mumbles, producing an incomprehensible spoken language, which sounds like blah, blah). His unfitting gestures and saucy jokes are there to make others laugh. Derived from the same root, the verb 'to laugh' (*rgod byes*) and the adjective 'wild; untamed' (*rgod*) are interlinked.

'US' AND 'THEM': DISCRIMINATION VIA DISCOURSE

By defining nomads through their alleged otherness, eventually through romantically transfigured images, cultural differences have been deemed insurmountable. Prompt to assert their superiority over their neighbours, the inhabitants of central Ladakh, especially those from Leh, the ancient capital where kings used to live in the past and which is today at the core of modern bustling life, look down on those they call Changpas, 'the Northerners'. The former hold many prejudices against these people, though they know them only from afar, having met them just the once at the bazaar. The Changpas—they say—are brusque and speak a different and unintelligible language. Both their way of speaking and their manners are *g.yong po*, an adjective meaning 'hard as wood, iron, or a stubborn person's mouth; rough, rude, impolite'.[15] They eat on the ground, so settlers say of them, stigmatizing with these few words the absence in nomads' homes of low tables and cushions: items of furniture which, in Ladakhi society, testify ostensibly to the position occupied by each and every person. To sit on several cushions in front of two low tables laid one over the other symbolizes a high social rank, whereas to be seated on the floor without even a mat, with a board acting as a table, conversely shows that one belongs to the low-caste artisans: the blacksmiths and the musicians.[16]

Any amusement sparked off by these people described as 'so different' quickly turns into marked contempt, a denigration evident by descriptions made of them in disparaging terms. One can hear the same weary old song, the same old story, the Changpas are dirty; they are covered in lice and fleas; their skin is black, burnt by the sun. They are wanderers: one day here, the next there. They are not used to working continuously for a set number of hours every day or, in short, "They do not know how to work". (Due to this reputation as poor labourers, during harvest time, villagers are very reluctant to employ newly settled nomads seeking jobs.) The Changpas, it is also said, are hot-headed and ruthless people because they eat meat, since men who feed on meat show no compassion. As in our Western civilizations, meat carries the smell of sin. Although this kind of food is popular—a meal without meat is not a proper one—it generates a confused feeling of guilt. In fact, this strong cliché, whereby the Changpas are barbarians and raw meat eaters, appeared along with the first mention of these people in the literature found in Mirza Haidar's personal memoirs:

> The Champas have certain strange practices, which are to be met with among no other people. Firstly, they eat their meat and all other foods in an absolutely raw state, having no knowledge of cooking. Again, they feed their horses on flesh instead of grain.[17]

Through these widespread stereotypes, sometimes fuelled by the nomads themselves, is drawn the recurrent image, already found among urban people in Mesopotamia in the second millennium B.C., and which depicts nomads as being impossible to educate and govern, subsisting entirely on meat, milk, or blood, and ignoring grain, any house structure, or cities.

FACING A CHANGING WORLD

Changthang, like the rest of Ladakh in general, has undergone rapid social and economic transformations over recent decades. In the space of one generation, new networks have supplanted old established trade routes and the nomads' trading partners have dramatically changed. In 1980, motor traffic finally reached Padum, the Zanskar headquarters. Nomadic pastoralists no longer trade with the Himalayan neighbouring populations of Zanskar, Spiti, and Lahoul. Since the opening of the Leh–Manali highway to civilian traffic in 1991,[18] merchants from Leh, mostly Muslims, come in summer by truck or jeep to the camps to buy a supply of butchered animals and the soft undercoat of goats used in the weaving of the famous pashmina shawls. To meet the demand, pastoral production consequently underwent some modifications: over the last 10 years the number of pashmina goats compared to sheep has increased dramatically as a result of this lucrative international market for cashmere. This road, crossing the Rupshu–Kharnak area, which is used from July to October by a large number of vehicles (military convoys, trucks, private and public buses, and jeeps), has enabled this out-of-the-way population to integrate into the urban sphere, has changed its vision of the world, its ambitions and its dreams. Before, any journey to Leh was a real undertaking. It lasted several days whether on foot or on horseback. Now, when the road is open, it takes only a few hours by bus or truck to reach the district headquarters. Therefore, people frequently come and go between the town and the encampments.

In addition, the region which had been closed to foreigners since the 1950s has been re-opened—under certain conditions—to tourism in 1994 (only designated areas are open and entry is controlled via a permit system). In the short summer season, trekkers, mainly from the West, travelling mainly in groups with horses and horsemen, regularly visit the nomads' camps. The Kharnak–Rupshu trek, 'a journey in the highlands of Changthang with nomads and lakes', which is described by guidebooks and travel agencies as one of the most exciting high-altitude treks, is very popular. Though isolated during the long, harsh winter when the passes are closed due to heavy snow, nomadic pastoralists are not cut off from the changing world.

For the last two decades, Leh has experienced the highest urban growth rate in India. Between 1981 and 2001, its population more than tripled in size. Throughout Ladakh, migrants are being drawn towards the district capital where the benefits of 'development', including the building of transport, healthcare, and educational facilities have been focused. Indeed the growth of waged-labour, associated with this development process, is at the root of the increased level of out-migration (Goodall, 2004a, 2007). Nomadic pastoralists have not been immune to this trend. Though the movement of families and individuals from the nomadic communities towards the urban centre is, on one level, another example of the general rural to urban migration affecting the whole region, in this case however, it involves a shift from a mobile existence to a sedentary lifestyle.

Unlike other similar situations that have been witnessed in the Middle East, Mongolia, or Tibet, this sedentarization or rather urbanization has not been forced upon nomads or strongly encouraged by the local administration. It is a voluntary process. Young people disillusioned by their parents' way of life, perceived as 'backward' and 'primitive', take the decision to live outside Changthang. Chaudhuri (2000) once listed the reasons for leaving the highlands—starting with children's schooling, followed by access to health facilities, a shortage of manpower, excess snow, and an easier life for the elderly. Others also mention better opportunities—especially for those who own small herds—wild predators, and the availability of goods and food products—"you have to go to Leh to get it". Indeed, non-economic factors can constrain or stimulate migration.[19]

An increasing number of families lured away by the prospects of city life and a better standard of living have moved down and made their way to the Indus Valley, even though they may be well aware that it is not the promised land and that occupational opportunities have been greatly reduced with the massive arrival of skilled and unskilled itinerant workers from Bihar, Orissa, and Nepal. Ten kilometres from Leh, in Choglamsar, which has sheltered Tibetan refugee camps since the 1970s, they have established a permanent urban settlement, named Kharnakling, 'The Island of Kharnak', because most of its inhabitants originated from this place. Its population shows a relatively balanced age–sex profile, which reflects the fact that this out-migration commonly involves a relocation of the household as a unit. As Goodall (2004b: 195) stresses,

[Kharnakling] is the source of much information flowing back to the mobile community about the opportunities available in Leh. It also acts to facilitate the movement of new cases of migration through providing social support and access to information about available work, thereby easing the transition to sedentary life. This process of chain migration has had serious sequences for the mobile community, as more and more households decide to settle.

Kharnakling is not described as a 'village' (*yul*) by its inhabitants, but as a 'colony', that is a settlement abroad established where a group of people from the same place or with the same occupation live together forming a distinct community within a larger city.[20] Nobody says that they are Kharnaklingpas, that is, 'from Kharnakling', 'belonging to Kharnakling' Interesting enough, no prayer wall, chorten, heap of stones, or other votive edifice marks its gates as is traditionally the case in villages and even in campsites. Indeed, the settlement is not fixed either in its spatial dimensions or in its number; its layout changes as newcomers settle and the population expands. Furthermore, no local territorial god *yul lha* is worshipped in order to protect the place and its inhabitants. With regard to this issue, the birth pollution attitude is a tell-tale sign. Although Ladakhis have fewer qualms about offering a pregnant couple a room in the squatter settlements known as 'housing colonies', which are built in the area surrounding Leh, there are clear and consistent reservations about offering pregnant women rooms in more traditional houses and neighbourhoods. It emerges that people are anxious about the birth pollution they might be exposed to if their tenants go into precipitous labour and deliver at home or the pollution she would bring back upon her return from the hospital. Indeed, they are less concerned about the local deities they might offend in these new settlements.

IDENTITY, BELONGING, AND MIGRATION

In 1931, the Census surveyor wrote in his report, "The Ladakhi are not accustomed to migration to any appreciable extent. In summer a number of European visitors and the Punjab and Yarkand traders go to Ladakh and provide the locals with enough labour which renders emigration unnecessary."[21] Indeed in the past, save for a few merchants settled for business in Tibet and for the children of the royal and noble families, very few Ladakhis emigrated for education or work.[22] Even now, migration to other parts of India and all the more to a foreign country is not common practice among Buddhists or Muslims, irrespective of their economic and social backgrounds. In this respect, nomads are by no means more inclined to move than sedentary farmers described as rooted on their land. Banal ideas associate nomadism with mobility. However, nomadic pastoral mobility, that is mobility as a livelihood tradition involving cyclical movements between encampments within a prescribed area, occurs in a context that separates it radically from migratory movement. It constitutes a strategy that stabilizes resources and populations and whose basic foundation is the appropriation of a territorial base that is established as durably as possible. As Legrand (2007) rightly points out, just as sedentary settlement and following it, nomadic pastoralism puts an end to migratory mobility.

Contrary to other populations on the Indian sub-continent, a large number of whom leave their country to work abroad, especially in the Persian Gulf countries, Ladakhis do not emigrate and rare are those who have left India. The 'culture of migration'[23] is not embedded in societal structures and in no way have migrants come to be seen as some sort of hero. Being a migrant in itself is not a status marker as is the case, for example, among Muslims in Hyderabad (Ali, 2007). Identities ascribed at birth are still more important than achievement, that is, money, education, and occupation. As for marriage opportunities, it is not the status of 'migrant' in itself which widens one's scope of partners, but the fact that the bridegroom (or the bride) lives on the urban fringes, not as a shepherd lost somewhere in the wild highlands.

The shift from a nomadic existence to a settled one is not easy, and life in town is hard. Most migrants sell their livestock beforehand either to butchers or to other herdsmen. Then, they buy land on the outskirts of Leh and build a two- or three-room house for themselves. The land is dry and rocky. Water is scarce; farming or growing vegetables is impossible. Deprived of any animals, except for a few horses kept for tourists, 'those who have come down' (*bab mkhan*) try to earn a living. However, they have limited job options, especially women. In fact, most of them work as labourers—coolies—on construction and road-building sites, or in military camps nearby. When there are no employment opportunities, they make nomadic textiles—saddle-bags, bags, rugs—and sell them in summer to antique dealers with some broken objects and jewellery, dirty enough to look 'authentic'. Some young men work as horsemen during the summer for travel agents and do business as middlemen. They aspire to be drivers and hope that they will be able to earn enough to buy their own truck or taxi. Other men set up a small business.

Belonging connotes being at home. With particular reference to migration, various patterns of belonging are constructed dynamically according to gender, age, economic and social status, or lived experiences. An individual positions him/herself in relation to collectives of both her original community and the place in which they have migrated. Elderly parents whose children have all moved away to Leh and have no choice, but to join them, reminisce about the open spaces of the Changthang, its green meadows, and its clear water. They cannot stand the heat in summer and complain of the number of mosquitoes and flies in dusty and dirty Kharnakling. They have not made this place their own and live there as though on a station platform. They stay at home all day long to prevent any thieves from robbing them when most people are away for the day working or at school. In the settlement abroad established in a larger city, there is no place to meet outside and chat.

Those who have taken the decision to drift away from their native places towards the urban centre try to find their way in Leh society. In order to do this, they play on two registers. On the one hand, they try to rid themselves of any trait that would make them stand out from common Leh people in terms of dress, food, habits, lodging, language, and so forth. In their two- to three-room house, the spatial organization and furniture are very similar to that of sedentary people: low tables, cupboards and shelves with cookware, sofas and armchairs, and TVs and VCRs. Posters of Bollywood movie celebrities (such as Shahrukh Khan), Swiss-like landscapes, and white blonde-haired babies at play adorn the walls. Only the woven rugs thrown over mattresses used as seats recall their previous means of livelihood and nomadic women's excellent traditional skills as weavers. Neither in summer nor winter do men and women dress in their traditional clothes. The former wear Western dress consisting of jeans, t-shirts, and sweaters, while the latter wear *shalwar kameez* (Hindi), a Punjabi-style outfit comprising a knee-length blouse, the *kameez*, worn over loose trousers, the *shalwar*. Both don quilted jackets if needed, even for special occasions such as weddings, receptions, religious festivals, or public gatherings, where it is compulsory to wear traditional clothes in Changthang to avoid the local gods' wrath and punishment. They thus dress like people from central Ladakh. (Indeed, as people emphasize, no local territorial gods rule over Kharnakling and protect its inhabitants.) For instance, women wear blue and red brocade capes and brocade hats rather than a rectangular cape made of red and green felt, lined with white-coloured fleece from kids, or a cape made of red woollen cloth; the youngest dress in Tibetan sleeveless robes over a long-sleeved blouse, available on markets in Leh. In addition, though migrants no longer celebrate any festivals, which in Changthang used to mark the seasonal migration cycle along with the New Year, they have adopted Leh urban practices when celebrating lifecycle rituals. In Kharnak when a child is born, no special celebration is held or grand meal is organized. But when he or she grows older, at 6–7 years of age for a boy and 12–13 years for a girl, a one-day ceremony is performed. The boy gets his first haircut, the girl has her hair plaited and the *perak*, the woman's turquoise headdress, is laid on her head for the first time. In Kharnakling, all these traditions have been left by the wayside. People there, like their urban neighbours, celebrate the 'full month (ceremony)', when a newborn baby reaches the age of 1 month, sending invitation cards to their relatives and neighbours, and throwing a party. They also celebrate birthdays with creamy birthday cakes bought from Leh, candles, confetti, streamers, and paper hats. The same is true for weddings and funerals, which are no longer performed as in the past in housing colonies. On the other hand, they earn money playing the role of the 'true nomad' disguised in curious attire and performing on stage for cultural exhibits.

'TRADITION' AS PREREQUISITES FOR AN INTEGRATED GLOBALIZED MARKET

At the Ladakh Festival celebrated annually to promote "the richness and pageantry of centuries-old customs of the people of Ladakh, their traditions and folk heritage", they are dressed in Tibetan-style costumes. Men wear the common *chuba* overcoat lined with fake tiger or leopard fur and leather boots with the upper part made of felted wool, while women put on a sleeveless gown over a long-sleeved blouse and the rectangular apron, which has never been worn, not even in the past by Ladakhis, whether nomadic pastoralists or sedentary farmers. One or two yak hair tents, all neat and well furnished, are pitched on the exhibition ground for visits. While outside, women seated on wooden stools milk female yaks using a wooden pail, inside the tent; others in their best clothes grind barley using a stone hand-mill. Neither of these utensils is used these days on the high plateaus. Customs performed for tourists' sake, now far removed from their primary function, become marketing commodities. The same is true when new settlers play the wild herdsmen for

advertising campaigns, Bollywood movies, and even documenta-
ries. Thus they recently worked as extras in *The Valley of Flowers*,
a saga about passion, death, and reincarnation directed by Pan
Nalin, and partly shot in Ladakh with "30,000 goats and sheep,
5,000 yaks, 350 horses and 50 Bactrian camels". "I took authentic
nomads to play the bandits" said the Indian film-maker in an interview promoting this Himalayan epic of love and longing. Mounted
on horses, with a fur cap on their tousled hair, men gallop at top
speed, shouting wildly and brandishing rifles. The women look after
the flocks, dressed in long, heavy sheepskin coats, with sheepskin
boots. They are adorned with heavy jewellery, their hair plaited into
numerous braids according to eastern Tibetan customs. Ironically,
yet again, the 'typical' nomad garments they wear are not the ones
they are used to wearing at home, but they pander to the exoticised
representation of the nomad. In doing so, these new settlers are not
reinventing or re-interpreting local traditions in a new setting as can
be observed in diasporic communities for example. They meet the
Other's expectations, firstly, to achieve recognition as artists and,
second, to earn money.

The situation is slightly different for the youngest who have grown
up there and know about life in the highlands mainly through the
tales recounted to them. Kharnakling is more a reference framework
and they have woven a particular, intimate relationship with it. Like
the great majority of Ladakhi children, they attend one of the very
many public schools, which have sprung up over the last decade in
Leh and its outskirts. They live there in hostels, mixing with kids from
all over Ladakh and sponsored by various local or non-local NGOs.
Like their classmates, they hope to be able to do a degree course in
English or Hindi outside Ladakh, in Delhi, Chandigarh, or Jammu
and aspire to get a government job. They eat rice and *chapati*, play
cricket, dance to disco music, and dream of places perceived only
through the distorted image of TV, but they are not sentimental
about the old lifestyle that Changthang symbolizes. Contrary to
their parents, they are reluctant to define themselves as Rupshupas,
Korzokpas, Kharnakpas, or more largely Changthangpas. They
identify themselves as belonging to Leh or to Ladakh.

Indeed changes have always occurred, but over the last two
decades they have been particularly radical and fast moving. In
Changthang, the end of nomadic life, if not pastoralism, seems
inevitable. To take the case of the Kharnak community over the last

15 years, dozens of households have been leaving the high plateaus, thereby reducing the mobile population by 80 per cent. Policies recently designed to reverse the population flow have so far proven unsuccessful. In July 2008, every family, whether settled or still nomadic, owned a plot of building land there if not a house in town: in Kharnakling for the large majority of them. It is too early to say if, among this new generation that has grown up in town, there will be a revival movement. As Pouillon remarks, "la tradition dont on a conscience, c'est celle qu'on ne respecte plus, ou du moins dont on est près de se détacher."[24]

NOTES

1. Claimed by India, Aksai Chin is entirely administered by China since the Sino-Indian War of 1962. Despite this region being nearly uninhabitable and having no resources, it remains strategically important for China as it connects Tibet and Xinjiang.
2. In his typology of nomadic pastoralism, Ekvall (1974: 519) distinguishes the *altitude-zone nomadic pastoralists* found for instance in Tibet from the more widely distributed *arid-zone nomadic pastoralists* who occupy the arid and semi-arid arc of the Saharan area and of the Arabian peninsula.
3. Such practice is widespread throughout the Anatolian and Iranian Plateaus and in Central Asia and India, Digard (1990: 100).
4. For descriptions, see Rizvi (1999).
5. The PDS refers to a network of retail outlets through which the government sells subsidized rice, wheat, and kerosene at fixed prices lower than market prices. The sale of goods is liable to certain conditions: firstly, the buyer must possess a ration card; secondly, purchases are subject to a quota.
6. According to Norman (Unpublished), *brog bat ces* is sometimes used in reference to families that depend on raising livestock as opposed to *zhing bat ces*, "farming".
7. See Dollfus (Forthcoming).
8. Though Ladakhpa(s) is the way the inhabitants refer to themselves, Ladakhi(s)—the Hindi name—is more commonly used.
9. In the same way, in Tibetan Chronicles and census reports, one discriminates *bod pa*, "those from Tibet", and *brog pa*, "those from the pastures", as though the latter were not Tibetan.
10. "The place name that ensures that the stereotype sticks situates it within a largely imaginary geography that develops on the margins of the actual travelled and lived world and is used by it as a reference horizon. The place name's role is to conjure up well-known stereotyped images of the place" (my translation).
11. The Constitution of India grants special status to people who are recognized as "tribes". Such status provides preferential treatment in the attribution of jobs and access to higher education, a compensatory discrimination popularly referred to as Reservation.

12. As Kapstein remarks (2006: 11), the same is true in Tibet. However, both Neolithic sites and the legendary and historical traditions, which locate the birth of Tibetan society in the fertile valleys of southern Tibet, suggest the primacy of agriculture in the development of Tibetan civilization.

13. Anon. *Wanderings and Wild Sport beyond the Himalayas*, May 1888, *India Office Library* IOL. E 39817.

14. Actually, this ambiguity characterizes Ladakh as a whole, where nomads are generally regarded as the archetypical Ladakhis. The region, says Aggarwal (2004: 9), is similarly "described in binary terms, either as a self-sustaining and unique paradise open for adventure, sport and tranquil spiritual self-discovery, a surviving remnant of the glory and mysticism of an unsalvageable Tibet, or else as a backward border on the fringes of India, a stark, hazard-filled wilderness where men of courage battle nature and enemies".

15. Norman's personal communication.

16. This system of hierarchical ranking also exists among pastoralists, but it is expressed in a less-rigid manner and mainly on a horizontal plane: the position occupied at the back of the tent near the altar is the most highly valued.

17. Mirza (1973: 407).

18. The opening to civilians of this road built by the Indian Army during the first Indo-Pakistani war was used by the Indian government to "double" the Srinagar-Leh highway; indeed this road, which is like an umbilical cord linking Ladakh to the rest of India, has become a victim of the Kashmir conflict and of Pakistani threats.

19. See Dollfus (2004).

20. In fact, it does not shelter only people originally from Kharnak, but also from other nomadic places, as well as from remote villages.

21. 1931 Census Series, *Jammu and Kashmir. Village and Townwise Primary Census Abstract. Ladakh District.*

22. In his *Reports on an Exploration on the North-East Frontier 1913* (India Office Library, Mss Eur F157/304 e), Captain Bailey thus notes, "at Tsetang we found a colony of Ladaki Mohamadan traders. There were 20 men, who with their families, totalled about 50 individuals. In Lhasa there are about 800 of their community who suffered considerable financial loss in the fighting between the Tibetans and Chinese."

23. According to Ali (2007), "the culture of migration is those ideas, practices and cultural artefacts that reinforce the celebration of migration and migrants. This includes beliefs, desire, symbols, myths, education, celebrations of migration in various media, and material goods".

24. Pouillon (1991: 712). "The tradition of which we are aware is the one no longer respected or at least from which we are ready to distance ourselves."

REFERENCES

Ali, Syed. 2007. '"Go West Young Man": The Culture of Migration among Muslims in Hyderabad, India', *Journal of Ethnic and Migration Studies*, 33(1): 37–58.

Aggarwal, Ravina. 2004. *Beyond Lines of Control. Performance and Politics on the Disputed Borders of Ladakh, India*. Durham and London: Duke University Press.

Anand, Dibyesh. 2002. 'A Guide to Little Lhasa: The Role of Symbolic Geography of Dharamsala in Constituting Tibetan Diasporic Identity', in P.C. Klieger (ed.), *Tibet, Self, and the Tibetan Diaspora*, pp. 11–36. Leiden: Brill.

Chaudhuri, Ajit. 2000. 'Change in Changthang: To Stay or to Leave?' *Economic and Political Weekly*, 35(1/2): 52–58.

Digard, Jean-Pierre. 1990. 'Les relations nomades-sédentaires au Moyen-Orient. Eléments d'une polémique', in H.P. Francfort (ed.), *Nomades et sédentaires en Asie central*, pp. 97–111. Paris: Editions du CNRS.

Dollfus, Pascale. 2004. 'Vers une sédentarisation univoque? Le cas des éleveurs nomades de Kharnak, Ladakh, Himalaya occidental indien', *Nomadic peoples*, 8(2): 200–13.

———. 2013. 'From a Green Happy Homeland to a Crammed "island": Discussing the Territories of a Nomadic Group Inhabiting the South-Eastern Edge of Ladakh', in J. Smadja (ed.), *Territorial Changes and Territorial Restructurings in the Himalayas*, pp. 317–33. Delhi: Adroit.

Ekvall, Robert B. 1974. 'Tibetan Nomadic Pastoralists: Environments, Personality, and Ethos', *Proceedings of the American Philosophical Society*, 118(6): 519–37.

Goldstein, Melvyn C. and Cynthia M. Beall. 1990. *The Nomads of Western Tibet: The Survival of a Way of Life*. London: Serindia.

Goodall, Sarah K. 2004a. 'Rural-To-Urban Migration and Urbanization in Leh, Ladakh. A Case Study of Three Nomadic Pastoral Communities', *Mountain Research and Development*, 24(3): 220–27.

———. 2004b. 'Changpa Nomadic Pastoralists: Differing Responses to Change in Ladakh, North-West India', *Nomadic Peoples*, 8(2): 191–99.

———. 2007. *From Plateau Pastures to Urban Fringe: Sedentarisation of Nomadic Pastoralists in Ladakh North-West India*. PhD Thesis, University of Adelaide.

Kapstein, Matthew T. 2006. *The Tibetans*. Oxford: Blackwell Publishing

Koshal, Sanyukta. 2001. *Ploughshares of Gods. Ladakh: Land, Agriculture and Folk Traditions*, Vol. 1. New Delhi: Om Publications.

Legrand, Jacques. 2007. 'Migrations ou nomadisme. La glaciation comme révélateur des modèles historiques de mobilité', *Diogènes*, 218: 116–23.

Mirza, Haidar. 1973. *The Târikh-i-Rashîdî of Mirza Muhammad Haidar, Dughlat. A History of the Moghuls of Central Asia*. Patna: Academica Asiatica.

Norman, Rebecca. Unpublished. *Dictionary of the Language Spoken by Ladakhis*.

Pouillon, Jean. 1991. 'Tradition', in Bonte and Izard (eds), *Dictionnaire de l'ethnologie et de l'anthropologie*, pp. 710–12. Paris: PUF.

Retaillé, Denis. 1997. *Le monde du géographe*. Paris: Presses de Sciences Po.

Rizvi, Janet. 1999. *Trans-himalayan Caravans*. New Delhi: Oxford University Press.

Thupstan Palden. 1998. *After Thirty Years*, International Society for Ecology and Culture. Delhi: Jayyed Press.

PART II
MIGRANT EXPERIENCES IN SOUTH ASIA
AND BEYOND

Chapter 5

Migration, Marginality, and Modernity

Hill Men's Journey to Mumbai

JEEVAN R. SHARMA

INTRODUCTION

Migration across the border to India has historically been a significant feature of livelihoods among the poorer households in the middle hills of Nepal. The practice of young men's outflow to India and increasingly to various global destinations is a pervasive phenomenon among the hill households amid a fragile socioeconomic and environmental context (Hitchcock, 1961; Pfaff-Czarnecka, 1993; Macfarlane, 2001; Seddon et al., 2002). Starting with recruitment to the army of the Sikh ruler Ranjit Singh and then into the British army in India, men from the middle hills continue to migrate to major Indian cities in order to make up for low incomes throughout the year. Except for some adult men who work in government agencies or the Indian army, these men mostly work in menial and low-paid jobs in the service and manufacturing sectors mainly as *chaukidars* (security guards), domestic workers, and workers in hotels and restaurants. Adolescent boys start to migrate, often accompanied by others on their first visit or as runaways, as young as 10–12 years old, and continue to travel back and forth until they are old. After the 'departure ritual' in their village (Sharma, 2008), men walk for hours or days before catching a passenger bus often with loud popular Bollywood (Hindi movie) music, which takes them to the bus station close to the border. After crossing the border, men take either bus or train for about 40 hours to their final destination in Mumbai. Over the years, social networks and inheritance have played a crucial role in sustaining the migration cycle between the origin villages in western hills and specific destinations in India (Thieme, 2006; Brusle, 2008). Such a quest for multi-locale livelihoods has created and sustained durable transnational links, connecting very distinct regions, economies, and cultures.

This chapter focuses on the case of male migrants from poorer households who spend a significant part of their life travelling between a rural hill village in western Nepal and the cosmopolitan Indian city of Mumbai. It is an attempt to understand how their migration decisions are shaped by local perceptions of belonging and attachment associated with family loyalties and obligations on one hand, and a quest for adventure and experience life outside their village, on the other. Given that a social requirement for achieving a desired form of manhood among the marginal households in the western hills of Nepal—for being a man—is migrating to India and supporting households by sending remittances, what are the implications of this form of multi-locale livelihoods to migrants' attachment and belonging to their home village in the middle hills? How do migrants balance loyalties and obligation to support their family on the one hand and their involvement in adventure and consumption activities amid very difficult living and working conditions in Mumbai?

The concept of belonging offers a useful lens to address these questions, particularly in relation to transience and fluidity of identity construction of male migrants who travel to the Indian city of Mumbai. It is possible to explore how hill migrants see their migration experience as a way to transcend their status from a young man from a rural area into not just an adult man but also as an adventurer and a cosmopolitan traveller with a wider experience beyond the village life with a strong drive to earn money and support their household back in Nepal. Hill migrants' life is strongly characterized by the 'uncertainty' stemming from the fact that most of them find it difficult to achieve their desired aspiration to turn their expectation into reality owing to difficult working and living conditions in Mumbai.

This chapter is based on an ethnographic fieldwork in a village in Palpa district that I conducted in 2004–05 as a part of my doctoral research (Sharma, 2007), including tracing the experience of young men who take on adult responsibility to travel to find work opportunities in the Indian city of Mumbai.

Following this introduction, the next section argues that the decision-making reveals that migration to India is far more complex than an economic venture and highlights the socio-cultural dimension, particularly the prevailing normative practices, expectations and standards, social roles, and obligations. The chapter then looks at life in Mumbai focusing on my ethnographic fieldwork with a group of Nepali men. This reveals that within the constrained working and living conditions, Nepali men working in Mumbai were seen as trying their luck, exploring possibilities for realizing their dreams, and cultivating new dreams and possibilities of attaining manhood. In many ways, the living and working conditions in Mumbai appear to both empower and constrain men's identities. I conclude this chapter with a few remarks on how hill migrants manage tension between what hill men desired and hoped in terms of their familial obligations to contribute to household subsistence and adventure involved in migration, and the way they encountered the difficult living and working conditions in Mumbai.

Understanding Migration Decisions

The first thing to be said about this movement to India, from the perspective of households in the middle hills, is that there is nothing exceptional about this practice (Sharma, 2008); rather it is simply considered a thing to do as a part of managing their livelihoods. The concept of 'culture of migration' (Cohen, 2004) adequately captures the pervasive nature of migration in the middle hills, which has remained a historical practice among the hill households and that migration decision is a part of everyday experience, and households consider migration as one of the key strategies of managing their livelihoods amid fragile socioeconomic, environmental, and political contexts. A useful question is how do young men and the households make decisions on whether to migrate or not?

Men spoke of migration to India as an escape from the 'difficult situation' (*garo awastha*) and 'hardship' (*dukha*) back home, which at the same time provided them with an opportunity to improve their socioeconomic situations and fulfil their obligation as responsible family men. Irrespective of their ethnic or caste background, it was a common livelihood strategy for men from poor labouring households in the village. The situation of young men in the middle hills is very much similar to that described by Osella and Osella in the context of South India:

> For boys in the poorest labouring families, adolescence hardly exists: they move from an impoverished and deprived childhood in which their parents are unable to protect them from the knowledge of adult realities into a young manhood, which immediately demands that they share their share of responsibility by dealing with those realities. (Osella and Osella, 2006: 40)

Krishna, a young unmarried Bahun of 19 years from the western hill in Nepal was working as a helper in a restaurant in Mumbai, leaving behind his parents and two young sisters back home. When I reached Krishna's house in the village, his father was lying on a mat made of straw (*gundri*) on the *pirhi* (veranda) outside the house. Suffering from diabetes and tuberculosis, he could barely work. Krishna's mother was busy working in the *bari* (non-irrigated field) beside their small hut, while two of his sisters (aged six and seven years) were playing in the courtyard with other children from the neighbourhood. They represented a relatively poor household. Like most Nepali farmers in the middle hills, they owned insufficient land to provide them with sufficient grain for the entire year. Depending on the situation, they had to buy grain for 4–6 months (*besaha*). Krishna's father had been working as a watchman (*chaukidar*) in Delhi for 17 years, which was an important source of income for the household, until he fell ill two years previously and could no longer go back to work. This meant that the responsibility to earn money had come to Krishna and the only option available was to follow the footsteps of his father and other relatives who had been going to India for work. Eventually, Krishna was to go to Mumbai, supported by his uncle who lived next door. He was excited when his mother told him about the possibility of going to Mumbai with his uncle and he immediately accepted it. Though he had heard a lot about life in Mumbai and many of his friends had been to India, he had never had a chance to go there. His uncle took complete responsibility for paying for the travel expenses, accompanying him, and finding work. When I met Krishna in a tea stall next to his workplace in Mumbai, he had been able to send money home on a regular basis for the last couple of years. He was planning to go home in the next three months but expected to come back to work after a month. When asked why he had decided to come to Mumbai, using the phrase *gharko awastha* he said, "The situation of my home was not good, so I came with my uncle to find work". As the only able-bodied man in the family, he felt that he was responsible (*jimmawar*) for earning money and regularly sending it back home to ensure the economic security of his household (*ghar chalaune, ghar herne*). Though he did not feel that it was possible for him to earn a lot of money, he nonetheless felt that it was possible to earn reasonable money and improve the situation of his family back home (*kehi awasta sudharne, kehi ramro hola bhanera*). To him, earning money to support his family was vital to ascertain his identity as a *jimmawar* son (Osella and Osella, 2000). He was particularly concerned about the health of his father and the education and marriage of his two little sisters. While Krishna's situation seemed to have been triggered by his father's illness, the practice of going to India was not uncommon in his family history and immediate social network.

One of the common themes that ran across most of the stories of young men's lives was *bhagne* or running away across the border to India. This practice was gendered, that is, it was always performed by young men and associated with fun, wandering (*ghumne*), and the excitement of seeing a distant place. Boys left home as young as 10–12 years old, without consulting their parents but often with the support of friends or other relatives, to wander around in different places in India. They left in small groups of 2–4 from the village, usually motivated and/or accompanied by another experienced migrant from the village. Those who were unaccompanied by an experienced migrant usually took the address of some of their relatives or neighbours in the destination and lived with their support once they reached there. After spending a few weeks in one or two cities, some of them returned home, whereas others continued to work and came home only after earning money. The clothes, hairstyle, opportunities for rail and bus travel, cash, radio, mobile phone, use of language, movie talk, and the stories of glamour brought back by the migrants who returned to the village during holidays and the ideas of life outside the village which they heard through radio and school textbooks exposed young men to life outside of their village.

While some adolescents continue to leave home without informing their parents, the frequency of *bhagne* had reduced drastically in the last two decades. Children and adolescents were encouraged to go to school, as it was widely believed that schooling opened up new prospects for social and economic mobility. Interaction with the parents and others in the village showed that, increasingly, it was not considered right for the adolescents to run away, which signified deviant behaviour (*bigranu*). In particular, high-caste parents considered that it was a matter of shame (*lajmardo kura*) for the family and they believed that their child must have run away under the influence of others (*aruko laha-lahai ma lagera gayeko*). While schooling was more common and this led to a reduction in *bhagne* from the village, there was evidence that the pressure of schooling itself led to *bhagne* among several young men. From the perspective of those involved, strict discipline, poor performance, and corporal punishment in the school were the major reasons behind their decision to run away.

Although *bhagne* did not always lead to employment, it nonetheless provided a wider experience of travel and offered a wider exposure to young men. They enjoyed the freedom and learned about the wider world away from their home village and away from the strict control of their parents. Young boys spent a few months wandering as runaways and without necessarily being economically productive, and this was socially accepted.

Any fruitful analysis of the social meaning of labour migration to India requires a discussion of how this form of migration is spoken about, discussed, and imagined in the home village. While *India tira jane* was the generic term people used to refer to those who went to work in India, it is useful to discuss different terms—*lahure, jagire, phaltu,* and *chaure*—that are used in the local context to talk about specific meanings associated with men's position vis-à-vis migration status. Discussion of these categories helps us understand the ideas associated with belonging to different forms of masculinities in the local context.

Although the term *lahure* was mainly used for those who went to work in a foreign army and also of the men who went to work as labourers in the Gulf and South East Asian countries in recent years, the term was often used as a generic term to talk about men who went to work outside of Nepal and contributed to the households left behind. It was common to find that the term *lahure* was used to talk about men who went to work in India. In terms of gender, *lahure* exclusively referred to men and not to women.

People used the term *jagire*[1] or *nokari* to talk about the migration of men and women who went to work in professional of semiprofessional jobs, within or outside of Nepal. The terms *jagir* and *nokari* covered the jobs that were considered more or less permanent, or in some cases temporary but ensured a degree of job security and ensured regular payment. Some *lahures* were also known as *jagires*. In certain situations, the term *chaure* was used in the opposite sense as *lahure* or *jagire*, which meant useless or worthless. The term *chaure* in these contexts was used in comparison with *lahure* or *jagire*. In this context *chaure* meant those who worked in a relatively undesired and useless setting in India and were looked upon as 'old', 'weak', and 'wrinkled', whereas *lahure* (mostly among Magars) and *jagire* (mostly among Bahuns) meant those who were in a desired setting, earned respect, and ensured regular salary. *Lahures* were spoken about as men who displayed lots of cash, bravery, and experience of a foreign place and *jagire* were men who were educated and had salaried employment, whereas *chaures* were men who could not display money, and were weak and incompetent.

Importantly, the term *phaltu* was a very common word used to categorize people who were unemployed or worked in relatively undesired manual work with low wages and no job security, which was contrasted to a few commonly known as *jagire* or *lahure* who got more pay, were more intelligent, and had a white collar job with some level of job security. The term *phaltu* meant useless (or those who lacked worth) and was used to talk about unproductive men who could not earn and demonstrate their obligations as men of worth. It was also used to talk about the men who did not do any work but rather wandered around in the village or about the unemployed men in the cities.

All this showed that the experience of moving to India for work had complex meanings in the local conception. The different meanings showed that people used a variety of terms to categorize men who went to India for work depending on the nature of work and the experience they underwent. Although going to India to work as manual workers was more common but comparatively less desired and people often called it *phaltu kam*[2] or *sano tino kam*,[3] it was more desirable for men to go to India in search of work than stay in the village often managing their farm and/or working on others' land, which was commonly referred to as *halo jotne* (literally meaning ploughing in the field) or *bhari bhokne* (literally meaning carrying weight) or sometimes simply *phaltu*. In this sense, going to work in India provided an escape from being referred to under the traditional category of *halo jotne* or *bhari bhokne* and look for opportunities to be referred to as *jagire* or *lahure*.

For many young men, living in the hills of Nepal puts severe constraint on their ability to achieve the ideal model of masculinity. Neither do they wish to work in agriculture and be seen as *halo jotne* or *bhari bokne* nor could they easily find *jagir or* afford attractive migration to the Gulf States or Malaysia. Many are left as *phaltu*. Despite the difficulties, compared to staying back in the village, going to work in India opened up possibilities of being modern and developed, exploring a distant place, and demonstrating the concept of manhood. For those who are unable to prove their worth, they risk being labelled *phaltu*, a category that young men are desperate to avoid.

As in other parts of the world, the context in which young men in the middle hills struggle to achieve their personal goals is not of their own making, and it has changed over the past decades. Over the years, the incorporation of the middle hills into the market economy, as indicated by the commodification of land, labour, and money (Sharma and Donini, 2012; Polanyi, 2001) and the associated ideas of *bikas* (development) and modernity (Ahearn, 2004; Pigg, 1992) have impacted men's lives in important ways.

Subsistence mountain agriculture combined with male labour migration has remained the key feature of livelihoods in the middle hills. "An important aspect of the relationship between India and Central Nepal is the close connection arising from the stringencies of hill agriculture on the one hand and the cash value of Indian employment on the other" (Hitchcock, 1961: 15). Migration and associated remittances have sustained the hill agriculture for decades. However, although subsistence farming remains the most important source of livelihood, at least from the perspective of households who identify themselves as farmers and engage in farming that is aided by income from migrants sending remittances, it is no longer an aspiration among young men in rural Nepal not only because it is not profitable but more importantly because farming signifies a traditional occupation. As a consequence, unlike their previous generation young migrants no longer see the value of migration and associated remittances in supporting subsistence hill agriculture but rather choose to move away from it, although it is possible to spot a few young men attempting cash crops or small-scale livestock enterprises. This can be explained by looking at the effect of development discourses on men growing up in the middle hills. Development discourse that has a particular effect in viewing the rural villages as a traditional place to be left in the past and urban areas as modern places to be desired (Pigg, 1992) has impacted the meanings of agrarian livelihoods and out-migration to cities and towns. Thus, apart from viewing it as physical movement, movement of people out of agriculture signifies a movement in the ideological space of development and modernity. The significance of migration lies in the possibility of what it offers to the individual men who migrate and their households and how it relates to the experience of other men in the community, in the context of discourses of development that has an effect in creating rural and urban areas as social categories of differentiation (Pigg, 1992). A similar observation has been made by Mary Beth Mills in her study on young rural women involved in the migration process in Thailand. She argues that economic compulsion was often not the major driving force behind women's decision to migrate to Bangkok, but rather it was the desire to participate in a 'modern' (*thansamay*) way of life (Mills, 1999).

Although labour out-migration is not a new phenomenon in the middle hills, its nature and socio-cultural meanings have certainly changed over the years in the context of discourses of development and modernity. The shift from the role of labour migration to support subsistence hill agriculture to its role in offering possibilities to escape from it has emerged as a new phenomenon.

LIFE IN MUMBAI

This section examines the life of Nepali men working in Mumbai who faced a complex tension between fulfilling their familial loyalties and obligations as men and consumption in Mumbai, in the face of difficult and exploitative circumstances that often put their identity as men into crisis.

Only a few of them were aware of the difficult working and living conditions before they arrived, when they would find that they would be living in a small room shared with 4–6 others in the middle of a slum community in suburban Mumbai, and work for long hours often in difficult and exploitative conditions. Although the working space of Nepali migrants was in a prominent economic space in Mumbai, often working as watchmen in important banks, companies, hotels, or houses of economically and/or politically influential people, they lived in the invisible peripheries.

In Mumbai, commonly known as *chaukidar* or *gorkha* or *bahadur* most adult men worked as watchmen who were employed in private bungalows, housing colonies, government offices, factories, hospitals, or businesses. Commercialization of the security business under the multinational companies, such as Group Four, meant that the social networks that long formed the basis of a continuous supply of Nepali men to work as watchmen was slowly getting replaced by formal procedures of recruitment.

The working hours of watchmen were not fixed and it was common to see these men working overtime, often up to 15–17 hours a day, to earn more money to enable them to save and send money back to their family in Nepal. The monthly salary of watchmen ranged anywhere between Rs. 2500 and Rs. 5000, but they were able to earn more money by working overtime and doing other work (e.g. taking children to school, cleaning the car, shopping, etc.) for the residents as well as getting occasional tips from the residents. Though most of the watchmen worked long hours, it was not always possible for them dramatically to change their living conditions. Despite this, men I spoke to seemed happy with their jobs though they hoped to find better jobs later. Although a few of them initially felt that the job was difficult and boring, they found it easier as they got used to it. Despite the long working hours, their job as watchmen was particularly important for the flexibility it provided to work overtime and earn more money.

Watchmen were usually given a uniform, a long stick, and a whistle, but this was not always the case. Dressed in a uniform, holding long sticks, and often with a moustache, the watchmen moved around their building, checked cars and people entering the building, and demonstrated their employer's confidence in them. As the owner of the building passed through the gate, they often displayed their obedience and discipline with a salute. The job was considered easier—they frequently called it "stick holding job" (*danda samatne kam*)—when compared to work in restaurants and domestic help that required long hours of work often in difficult conditions. In the words of one Bahun watchman of 48 years, the job was very easy as he did not have to do anything other than be there. But the job also involved loneliness as they spent most of their time standing at the gate and often there was hardly anyone with whom they could talk to, except the domestic workers staying in or visiting the building or watchmen from the neighbouring building. It was almost impossible for them to get to know others intimately. The difficulty of working as watchmen was when they would be attacked by thieves or they were unable to catch the thieves, which resulted in the immediate loss of job or deductions from their salary for a few months. However, it did provide an opportunity to obtain good security and thus recognition as a more capable person, which sometimes led to an increase in their salary.

A growing but invisible workplace for the increasing number of Nepali boys (aged between 14 and 20 years) was to work as domestic workers in middle-class houses in suburban Mumbai[4] or to work as helpers in hotels and restaurants. They often worked long hours although their monthly income ranged from anywhere between Rs. 1,200 and Rs. 2,500, which was significantly lower than the income of older Nepali men who worked either as security guard or as helpers in shops. Often invisible, except when they left the home for 2–3 hours day, young men who worked as domestic workers spent most of their time inside the apartment of their middle-class employers. The job involved loneliness as they spent most of their time working on their own except when they would get instruction from the employer. The owners did not like their workers spending much time outside their apartment block. When instructed by the owner to buy vegetables, a Magar boy of 14 years who worked as a domestic worker always took time out to come to the tea-stand to speak to other Nepalis working in the same locality. Domestic workers spent most of their time preparing and cooking food, cleaning dishes, cleaning the house, and washing clothes. Young men I spoke to did not complain about their work although they did not see domestic help or working as helper in hotels or restaurant as a long-term job and they hoped to find 'better' work (*ramro kam*) in 'office' later.

Within the constrained life of Mumbai, from the perspective of these men, Mumbai was associated with the excitement it offered. For instance, Mumbai was a city of big buildings, public transport, brothels, 'beer bars', freedom, and the film industry. Working in cities like Mumbai offered these men an opportunity to become involved in consumption of what was considered as modern goods and experiences. Thus, one way to characterize life in Mumbai was the transformation that these men went through in their consumption both in Mumbai and back home. Let us look at a couple of examples of consumption practices in Mumbai.

A particular aspect of life in Mumbai was to go sight-seeing to different parts of the city where there were high-rise buildings, places of tourist attractions like the Gateway of India, the sea beach, and occasionally to see the shooting of films or television serials in studios or outside. Commonly known as *ghumna jane*, this involved exploring new places for entertainment. Among the people who stayed in suburban Mumbai, men often went on weekends to watch shooting in film studios with the help of their friends working there. A few men worked in the film industry or at least came with the hope that they would find some work there. A few young men spoke of the desire to work in 'shooting' and watched shooting closely.

One of the things that struck me about Nepali men working in Mumbai was their use of mobile phones. Almost all the Nepali men I met had a mobile phone, except for those who worked as a domestic helper who had no access to phones. Whenever I began to talk to them, a mobile phone would ring with the ring tone of the latest Bollywood song. Although having a mobile phone enabled them to be in touch with each other, it was also very easy for their family members back in Nepal to make phone calls to them. Whenever I sought a favour from my informants to speak to other Nepalis, my informants always took out a mobile phone and made the phone call. The difference in the use was visible when we consider how easy it was for these men to talk to their family; however, it was a long walk for the people in the village to reach the nearest telephone service. The widespread use of mobile phones shows the desire of these men to consume modern goods.

Although not all of them had access, television and movies were popular forms of entertainment among the young men. Whenever there were opportunities (*mauka parda*), young men often watched movies, entertainment serials, news, or cricket. Except for those who worked as domestic workers, other young migrants went to see a movie whenever they were free. A couple of young men told me that they never missed newly released movies, and spent much of their earnings on movies them. They had up-to-date knowledge about movies, movie stars, television serials, and gossip.

CONCLUSION

In this chapter I have discussed the meanings and experiences of migration to India having social and cultural dimensions, particularly within the framework of masculinity (Osella and Osella, 2000). The idea of masculinity appropriately articulates the decision-making, work experience, and how men's identities are reconstituted through the process of their movement. It is possible that the men who do not move may be under pressure to perform other ways of asserting their masculine identity (e.g. joining the Maoist rebels). One important implication of migration for masculinity was that there was a contradiction between the men's desire and obligation to move and the actual experience of movement, under the difficult and exploitative working and living conditions in Mumbai, and the journey that placed strain on their manhood.

There was a tension between what Nepali men desire and hope for in terms of their obligations of becoming a complete man, who could earn money to contribute to the household subsistence, and the way in which they encounter the other side of life in Mumbai. In particular, the constraints due to poor working and living conditions in Mumbai and the exploitation during travel came as a surprise to these men. Low wages, poor living conditions, difficulties involved in travel, and separation from the family meant that most of them found it difficult to realize their dreams.

Furthermore, masculinity in the patriarchal family and community context that rewarded the authority and respect of men was often questioned under the difficult conditions of the journey, destination, and their separation from family (wife, children, and parents). This was an assault on their identity as a man. Therefore, I argue that under the difficult and exploitative conditions of work in India, men's identity was both reconstituted and compromised by their movement to India. Thus, for these men, there was often a tension between the material and symbolic pressure to go to work in India in order to earn money and run the household and the emotional pressure of being away from their families and therefore being unable to look after their parents, wife, or children. In the hill village, men were expected to move as a way to escape from the exploitative social structure that constrained their identity as men. Paradoxically, men might have their masculinity stripped from them once they began to work in India under the prevailing difficult and exploitative conditions.

Despite all these constraints, it was possible to see these men exercising their agency and reconstructing their identity through their experience of adventure and consumption of goods and images that were found in Mumbai. These men were exposed to new forms of consumerism, which was visible in their use of mobile phones, clothing, entertainment, friendship, and the way they manage their money and free time. These consumption practices had an impact on how these men were spoken about, imagined, and categorized in the local context in the hills of Nepal.

From the standpoint of men, this form of migration challenged the marginality of village and life in the village or contributed to the reconstruction of men's identities. At the same time, their experience in the city of Mumbai often reaffirmed their distance from a modern way of life. It is possible that the experience of mobility and its role in reconstructing gender identities help sustain conditions that encouraged a regular flow of hill men to work in Indian cities.

Notes

1. The term *jagir* was a form of land allocation in return for state service, which was a common means of payment to soldiers in the Nepali army in the 19th century. Though these days those who were employed by the state or private agencies did not get paid in the form of land, most of them used the salary to purchase land, which signified their particular relation to the state as servants.
2. It means useless work; work that has does not earn much respect and money.
3. It means small work or work that has low status or value.
4. Known as maids or *bai*s, the wives of some of the Nepali men worked as domestic workers on a part-time basis for 2–3 hours a day in each house, often cooking food, cleaning clothes, and washing dishes. The practice of keeping maids on a part-time basis is a very popular phenomenon in middle-class households in Mumbai.

REFERENCES

Ahearn, L.M. 2004. *Invitations to Love: Literacy, Love Letters and Social Change in Nepal*. New Delhi: Adarsh Books.
Brusle, T. 2008. 'Choosing a Destination and Work Migration: Strategies of Nepalese Workers in Uttarakhand, Northern India', *Mountain Research and Development*, 28(3–4): 240–47.
Cohen, J. 2004. *The Culture of Migration in Southern Mexico*. Austin: University of Texas Press.

Hitchcock, J.T. 1961. 'A Nepalese Hill Village and Indian Employment', *Asian Survey*, 1(9): 15–20.

Macfarlane, A. 2001. 'Sliding Downhill: Some Reflections on Thirty Years of Change in a Himalayan Village', *European Bulletin for Himalayan Research*, 20(1): 105–10.

Mills, M.B. 1999. *Thai Women in the Global Labour Force: Consuming Desires, Contested Selves*. London and New Jersey: Rutgers University Press.

Osella, F. and C. Osella. 2000. 'Migration, Money and Masculinity in Kerala', *Journal of Royal Anthropological Institute (N.S.)*, 6: 117–33.

———. 2006. *Men and Masculinities in South India*. London: Anthem Press.

Pfaff-Czarnecka, J. 1993. 'Migration under Marginality Conditions: The Case of Bajhang', in Dipak Gyawali, Othmar Schwank, Indra Thapa, and Dieter Zürcher (eds), *Rural–Urban Interlinkages: A Challenge for Swiss Development Cooperation*, pp. 97–109. Zürich: INFRAS/ IDA.

Pigg, S.L. 1992. 'Inventing Social Categories Through Place: Social Representations and Development in Nepal', *Comparative Studies in Society and History*, 34(3): 491–513.

Polanyi, K. 2001. *The Great Transformation. The Political and Economic Origins of Our Time*. Boston: Beacon Press.

Seddon, D., J. Adhikari, and G. Gurung. 2002. 'Foreign Labour Migration and the Remittance Economy of Nepal', *Critical Asian Studies*, 34(1): 19–40.

Sharma, J.R. 2007. Mobility, Pathology and Livelihoods: An Ethnography of Forms of Mobility in/from Nepal. *Graduate School of Social and Political Studies*. Edinburgh: University of Edinburgh.

———. 2008. 'Practices of Male Labor Migration from the Hills of Nepal to India in Development Discourses: Which Pathology?' *Gender, Technology and Development*, 12(3): 303–23.

Sharma, J.R. and A. Donini. 2012. *From Subjects to Citizens? Labor, Mobility and Social Transformation in Rural Nepal*. Medford: Feinstein International Center, Tufts University.

Thieme, S. 2006. *Social Networks and Migration: Far West Nepalese Labour Migrants in Delhi*. Münster: LIT publishing house.

Chapter 6

Rights and a Sense of Belonging

Two Contrasting Nepali Diaspora Communities

MITRA PARIYAR, BAL GOPAL SHRESTHA, AND DAVID N. GELLNER

INTRODUCTION

Whether or not a particular group of people feel that they belong in a given place depends, it need hardly be stressed, on a number of factors.[1] Age, generation, and the simple passage of time all play important roles. A group that has barely arrived, however favourable the circumstances, is unlikely to feel fully integrated and is bound to feel the pressures of an unfamiliar cultural and legal environment, as the Oxford UK case discussed here will illustrate. On its own, the simple passage of time is not enough to engender a sense of belonging. Groups that experience systematic and ongoing exclusion from the host society may feel like the paradigmatic stranger in a strange land even if they have been settled for many generations (e.g. South Asians who have been working in the Gulf states for several generations—though one should be careful not to take it for granted that such populations must necessarily be wholly alienated from the place where they live, just because they lack full citizenship rights). The role of succeeding generations, as is well known, is crucial: by the third generation they may even feel so at home in the new environment as to take up cultural and linguistic revival as a conscious choice.

The notion of belonging has recently begun to receive considerable attention as a sociological concept.[2] The concept of belonging manages to combine within it both ideas about ownership, rights (legal and moral), relationships to particular places and people, and subjective senses of well-being. These manifold links to diverse social fields and the very fluidity and processual nature of the concept perhaps explain why it appears preferable (or at least more promising) to some than the overused philosophical notion of identity, with its (on the face of it) de-socializing, homogenizing, and mathematical overtones. One factor that seems to play a key role both in symbolizing people's sense of belonging and in creating it in the first place is ritual. One of us has explored this in relation to Newar people in Nepal (Gellner, 2011): how rites make rights, so to say. It is interesting to see that in diaspora too, ritual (whether one can freely perform it or not; how one performs it) becomes a crucial part of generating belonging (or failing to do so).

The second case to be considered in this chapter, that of Sikkim, illustrates a complex situation where all are citizens, but some have greater rights than others, which gives rise, unsurprisingly, to complex and graded senses of belonging. The South Asian context is one in which different and graded senses of belonging have always existed. These subtle, complex, and overlapping forms of belonging are now, in the modern world, confronted with the pervasive assumption that everyone should have the same rights and that these should be articulated in clear, articulable, and legally enforceable ways. There are therefore sometimes uncomfortable clashes between older ways of articulating identity and the newer ones; and, however these are resolved or held in tension, the stage is set for multiple belongings: as a member of various nested 'ethnic' or otherwise defined groups; as a citizen of one or more nation states; as members of professional groupings (e.g. ex-British soldier), and so on.

THE EX-GURKHAS OF OXFORD

On 29 April 2009 UK Prime Minister Gordon Brown suffered a famous defeat, when an opposition motion was passed allowing all ex-Gurkha soldiers with more than 4 years' service in the British Army to settle in the United Kingdom.[3] Until that time, Gurkhas retiring after 1997 (when Hong Kong was handed back to China) had the right to settle; however, pre-1997 retirees, who, the Ministry of Defence argued, had not formed any lasting attachment to the United Kingdom, did not. A high-profile campaign, with actress Joanna Lumley, the daughter of a Gurkha officer, as its very vocal and effective figurehead, had successfully enlisted the backing of the Liberal Democratic Party, some Conservatives, and much of the conservative British press and general public not normally known for supporting anything that would encourage greater immigration. The argument that soldiers willing to die for the United Kingdom should at the very least have the right to live there had become, in a world more closely globalized than ever before, politically unanswerable.

The post-1997 retirees, by definition a younger group, had already started arriving in the United Kingdom in large numbers following the 2004 decision to allow them to settle in the United Kingdom. The biggest years for arrivals were 2005–07. Today, the largest Nepali communities are to be found in the Farnborough-Aldershot area (Greater Rushmoor Borough Council), in Ashford, Kent, and in Plumstead (east London). The total number of Nepalis in the United Kingdom may be between 100,000 and 150,000. About two-thirds are either ex-Gurkhas or their dependants; the remainder are mainly divided between highly skilled migrants, students, nurses, restaurant workers, and asylum seekers. A few Nepalis (particularly doctors) had already arrived in the 1980s or the 1990s, but the number of people born in Nepal and recorded in the 2001 census was a mere 5,938. By 2008 a survey by the Centre for Nepal Studies UK estimated that there were 72,173 Nepalis in Britain.

According to the Nepalese Community in Oxford (NCO, founded 2006), approximately 100 Nepali families live in Oxfordshire. Some Nepali students had been in Oxford beforehand, but ex-Gurkhas started arriving in Oxford in 2004. Pariyar's survey of 20 families revealed that the largest number of arrivals—45 per cent—occurred in 2006, 25 per cent came in 2007, and only 15 per cent came in 2008. The declining figures for new arrivals over the recent years are in line with falling UK arrivals from Nepal generally (CNSUK, 2011: 7–8).

Ninety per cent of Pariyar's sample consists of permanent residents (holding ILR or 'indefinite leave to remain') and the other 10 per cent have already become British citizens. Of those who had not yet become British, 33 per cent said that they wanted to become British citizens but 39 per cent did not wish to do so. The remaining 28 per cent were undecided. Many of them found themselves in a real dilemma. On the one hand, they did not wish to deprive themselves of facilities such as free healthcare, free education for children, and help with care for the elderly, which were not available back home. More importantly, they saw no prospects for their children in Nepal. But they were not sure whether they would always be welcome in

Britain. They were very nostalgic about their much easier and happier life in Nepal: the savings from Gurkha service and from second jobs overseas, coupled with a regular Gurkha pension, meant that in Nepal they did not need to work hard for subsistence, unlike in the United Kingdom. Many of them also did not like the idea of sundering their official link with their homeland. As one of them remarked, "How could we visit our own country on a tourist visa?" Many would be very willing to become British citizens if the Nepal government assured them that they could keep both passports. (Despite a strong campaign by non-resident Nepalis, the government of Nepal does not yet recognize dual citizenship.)

Many Oxford-based ex-Gurkhas intended to return to Nepal after seeing their children settled in Britain. Chandra Limbu's wife, for example, looked forward to going back because she had grown tired of working as a hotel cleaner.[4] Similarly, Shakti Limbu wanted to return once his only son, currently at school, went to university. However, everyone reckoned that their return would ultimately depend not only on their personal circumstances at the time but also on the situations in Nepal and in the United Kingdom. They would be more inclined to return, for instance, if Nepal acquired a degree of political stability, effectively tackled the problem of insecurity, developed its infrastructure, improved the delivery of public services, and so on. There were a few who explicitly stated that they had made up their minds to stay permanently in the United Kingdom, and again the reasons for this were a mix of personal interests and the situation in both nations. Part of the reason why Kus Bishwakarma was not looking forward to going back to his hometown in Lamjung (in the central hills) was that, as a member of a low caste, he felt that he would still be socially ostracized in Nepal, despite being wealthier than many others in the town.[5] Some thought they would probably have to remain in the United Kingdom because by the time they were ready to return to Nepal their parents there would have died and most, if not all, of their children would be in the United Kingdom.

It was interesting to tease out, beneath the slogans of Gurkha politics, what actually inspired them to emigrate in the first place. Most answers contained a mixture of personal and national issues. As indicated above, the most popular reason for moving to the United Kingdom was the pursuit of better prospects for their children. One ex-Gurkha remarked: "It would be foolish if a Lahure [soldier in a foreign army] did not have any children and yet came here to toil for survival. " Many of them had significant savings from Gurkha service and other jobs overseas; some of them were actually working in Hong Kong, Taiwan, and other places before moving to the United Kingdom. Some blamed Nepal's political problems as well. Shakti Limbu used to run two small factories in the town of Bhaktapur. However, he had to suffer regular extortion by the Maoists and other groups. On a number of occasions, although his life was in danger, he could never rely on the Nepal police. Moreover, the problem of frequent strikes organized by political parties and other groups meant that his factories suffered disruption and profits were inevitably low. Unfortunately, he ran into trouble with his job in the United Kingdom as well. As the financial crisis deepened, a few Gurkhas working as private security officers locally, including him, were made redundant. He struggled to find a new job for several months. This shocked him and his friends in Oxford, who had now learnt the hard way that it was never safe to assume all would go well in the United Kingdom.

Most ex-servicemen in Oxford work as private security officers and a few are bus drivers. About 5 per cent were unemployed at the time of the interviews. The average annual income of those working was £25,000, which is roughly the same as the UK national average. Bus drivers are the highest earners; they could make more than £30,000. Most Gurkha spouses work, most of them as cleaners in hotels or colleges, for a minimum wage.

Migration has brought a profound change in the lives of Gurkha wives. As Subba shows, describing Gurkha families in the town of Dharan, the children are habituated to an easy life; as long as they get support from parents working abroad, they prefer not to work (Subba, 2007: 299). Money earned overseas is rarely invested in income-generating activities. Although she does not refer to Gurkha spouses directly, the same observation is true for them as well. A Gurkha wife in Nepal epitomises the life of luxury, of extravagance, and of prosperity without hard work—a lifestyle impossible for them to achieve once they are in the United Kingdom. The husband's income is generally not sufficient to meet the costs of the household, which means wives were forced to start working outside the home for the first time. Although a few wives managed to evade work on different pretexts, the majority of them were working.

The lack of work experience coupled with the problem of English language skills means that most of the wives end up working as cleaners—the work that their maids used to do at home. There was a well-known case of a group of about eight women who worked for a hotel in north Oxford. The payment of about £6.50 per hour was made not on the basis of the actual number of hours worked but according to the number of rooms cleaned. The expectation was that they should complete 18 rooms in six hours, but most women could not finish this within the stipulated time. Therefore, they worked an average of two hours extra per day to finish the rooms allocated to them, which was not paid. The women and their husbands were fully aware that the system was exploitative, but they dared not complain for fear of losing the job and not finding another one.

Gurkha spouses' attitudes to work differed quite significantly from person to person. Some of them hated having to work so hard to make a living and therefore lamented their migration. But others quite enjoyed the experience of working, despite the physical hardship, because they found it empowering in the sense that they no longer needed to depend fully on their husbands for money. Furthermore, work also gave them an opportunity to come out of the house, explore the world, meet new people, and learn the local language. When asked if they would contemplate working as cleaners in hotels in Nepal, none said they would do it. The reason was that in Nepal such work is categorized as polluting and is therefore bad for their family honour. The same work in Britain was apparently not seen as deleterious to family prestige.

As with many other migrants, remittances are an important link between ex-Gurkhas and relatives back home. Sixty per cent of the population sample regularly sent money to Nepal; the average among those who sent was £1500 p.a. They reckoned it had to be much higher than this for those whose families had not joined them in the United Kingdom. Part of the reason why some of them had stopped sending money to Nepal was that all of their dependants had shifted to Britain. Many respondents eagerly supported small development schemes such as drinking water taps for schools, building or repairing temples for local deities, and so forth, usually in their villages of origin. They also gave small sums of cash to their relatives every time they visited Nepal. Dev Limbu visited his home for 2 weeks in January 2009 and distributed a total of £2,000 to his numerous affinal and consanguineal kin.

Forty per cent of respondents were homeowners, and the figure was likely to rise as many others were in the process of selling a part of their property in Nepal and investing the proceeds in UK houses. A few older Gurkhas, like Subash Rai, struggled to purchase houses as they were denied mortgages because of their age. For economic reasons, they tended to share a house or flat between two families (often not relatives).

The Limbus, from the eastern hills of Nepal, are the predominant ethnic group in Oxford, and most of them live in Rose Hill; the Rais, also from east Nepal, live in this area in significant numbers. A few Magars, Gurungs, and low-caste ex-Gurkhas are settled in different parts of Oxford. There are also Nepalis from other backgrounds not normally recruited to the Gurkhas (Newars, Bahuns).

DASAIN AND THE CONSTRUCTION OF COMMUNITY IN OXFORD

The Dasain festival is the biggest single celebration of the Nepalese religious calendar (corresponding to Durga Puja/Dassera in India). Government offices close for days (as at Christmas/New Year in the West) and everyone who can do so returns home to celebrate the festival with their kin. In recent years (particularly since 1990) it has come to be contested by many from a *Janajati* ('tribal') background because it is strongly associated with Hinduism (and the now defunct monarchy). However, it remains the premier festival and is accepted by almost all Nepalis, even Buddhists, Christians, and Muslims, as a cultural and national holiday.[6]

The former soldiers in Oxford were indeed influenced, to a certain degree, by ethnic politics in general and by the movement for boycotting Dasain in particular. Although most of them had not stopped celebrating the festival altogether, they had nonetheless given up using the traditional red *tika* (vermilion spot on the forehead) and replaced it with a white one. They did this because they trusted their ethnic activists' claims that not wearing *tika* at all or at least not using the traditional red colour was a powerful way of symbolizing their rejection of the hegemonic Hindu order that placed them in a debased position. A counter-myth created by ethnic activists says that the demons slain by Hindu gods and goddesses in the mythical stories were the ancestors of ethnic and indigenous people. For them, therefore, wearing red *tika* would be celebrating the blood of their own forefathers. Not everybody in Oxford took the story to be true, but they were, nevertheless, keen to maintain the distinction between the colours of *tika*, and through this, to fight their subordination to Hindu high castes, although this does not mean much in British society. Moreover, some Gurkhas told me that their families and kin back home had stopped celebrating Dasain altogether. Upon further examination, it became clear that what they actually meant was that their families had stopped observing the festival as a religious affair but had continued with the usual feasting and socializing.

Interestingly, Oxford Gurkhas do not seem to hold a similarly negative attitude to blood sacrifice, although it is the very re-enactment of the slaying of the demons. In fact many of them had a strong propensity for performing sacrifice not just at Dasain but also in their tribe-specific rituals. There were in fact some who did not like the sacrifice as an offering to deities and spirits, but even they missed slaughtering goats, pigs, and chickens at home, particularly on special occasions like Dasain. On the basis of his fieldwork in a Limbu village in east Nepal in the 1970s, Philippe Sagant observed: "One morning the festival opens to the sound of Damai horns. From then on it is one endless round of slaughtering goats and chickens, buffalo and pigs, and going from house to house drinking" (1996: 265).

Every year the executive committee of the Nepalese Community in Oxford (NCO) takes a decision on which festivals of the Nepali calendar to celebrate, when and how. Normally it organizes at least three events annually, including the Nepali New Year and Dasain party (sometimes a combined Dasain–Tihar party), the latter being the most popular. In 2009 there was extended discussion about who should be included as official guests that year and finally it was agreed that the Labour MP for east Oxford, Andrew Smith, should be the chief guest. Other guests included officials from Oxford County Council and representatives of a few private organizations that had contributed small sums of money to run this or other events.

Interestingly all non-Nepali guests were members of the native British population; there was nobody from other communities, such as the British Pakistanis who have a large presence in east Oxford. Much of the 'social field' of the Gurkhas was exclusively within the Nepalis, and often indeed with members of the same tribe or caste. All of them had been commanded by British officers while in military service and most of them still worked with White British people. Though they admitted there had been generally no problem working with them, there was hardly any evidence of them socializing with anybody from a non-Nepali group. A change of attitude could be observed, however, among a few Gurkha children. For instance, Chandra Limbu's younger daughter lived with her Irish boyfriend in her parents' house in Rose Hill. Despite the overt unhappiness of some other Limbus, he and his wife apparently had no problem with the situation. They considered him to be their daughter's de facto husband. They happily included him in Nepali functions such as the Dasain festival and introduced him to other Nepalis as their *juwai* (son-in-law).

The NCO committee set certain rules about the conduct of the Dasain festival, which everyone was expected to follow. Food had to be explicitly Nepali. An ex-Gurkha was ridiculed at one meeting when he suggested including pasta in the menu. Perhaps it might have been acceptable for some other occasion such as the summer barbecue, but it was almost a sin to think about having Western food as part of a Dasain feast. Despite their prolonged work overseas, most Gurkhas remained strictly Nepali in terms of what they ate. Pariyar met not a single Gurkha household that had attempted to prepare English or any other Western dish for dinner; they always took Nepali food with beer at home. The second important rule for the Dasain party was about the genre of music: non-Nepali music and dance music were strictly banned, to the utter dismay of the younger boys and girls who prefer Hindi and English music. Nepali folk or country music was particularly emphasized. This tended to be the inclination of the organizers even in other events. For instance, there was an open dispute between the NCO leader and some young Gurkha boys at the Nepal New Year programme in 2010 because the former did not permit the latter to dance to Hindi and English tunes in the communal dance. Another important rule for Dasain was that people should wear, as far as possible, Nepali national dress—*daura* and *suruwal*[7] for men, and saree for women. Although almost every caste or tribal group has its own distinctive ethnic dress, this was not encouraged for the Dasain party. The overall aim was to maintain a distinctive Nepali flavour to the cultural programme, people's dress, and the cuisine. To a considerable degree participants complied with the wishes of the organizers, though at least two young Gurkha daughters incurred their displeasure by appearing in miniskirts.

The event started in the BMW workers' club in the late after-noon. Light snacks were served with fried goat meat and beaten rice at the beginning; drinks were to be bought from the counter.

This continued for a few hours with people drinking and socializing with each other while enjoying quite loud Nepali folk music. It was indeed an opportunity for many Nepalis to meet up. There was a cultural performance by some Gurkha children involving Nepali songs and dances on the stage. This was followed by a raffle draw. An announcer conducted the whole programme from the stage. Then people queued up for dinner at around 8 p.m. A Nepali catering company based in another town—Farnborough—was given the business of supplying and serving food as specified by the NCO. After this the official guest was asked to address the gathering; this followed the NCO leader's speech in Nepali and English. The programme ended around 11 p.m. following communal dancing.

The greatest irony was that the event, organized for the celebration of a key religious festival of Nepal, did not include any associated ritual or religious observance. There were no Dasain rituals performed, no space or object consecrated, no worship of goddess Durga, no red or white *tika* used. A small lamp was lit on the stage but it was not sacralized, nor was it declared as an offering to the goddess. In fact this could also be interpreted as purely secular, as ceremonial lamps are normally used as a way of opening any Nepali meeting. Most importantly, there was not even the mention of blood sacrifice. Of course, UK law does not permit the public slaughter of animals or birds, so blood sacrifice would not have been possible in any case. But fruits or vegetables can be used as surrogate victims when blood sacrifice is not possible. At the very least they could have put up posters or figurines of goddess Durga and carried out worship with flowers, vermilion, and rice. There was in fact a total absence of discussion of the religious aspects of the event in the NCO meetings preceding the event. It was not just the activists who were not bothered with religious aspects of the function, there was no question raised by any of the over 300 participants. This could also be seen perhaps as a way of avoiding the problem of agreeing on what the appropriate practice would be. Given the widespread diversity of personal preferences and caste/ethnic traditions, it was better to conduct the event in terms of the most neutral and banal symbolism that could offend no one.

The communal, and even political, significance of the festival as celebrated, and the absence of direct religious importance, was evident also from the content of the formal proceedings. The official guests were seated on an allocated table close to the stage; there were formal speeches by the chief guest and officials of the NCO. The NCO leader spoke at length about Nepali culture and tradition, attempting to present the Nepalis in Oxford—Gurkhas and non-Gurkhas—as one community with a common culture, language, religion, and so forth. He did his level best to portray all Nepalis in Oxfordshire as one, united community. He refrained from mentioning internal divisions in terms of caste, tribe, class, education, language, religion, and so on. As a Magar he has his own ethnic language and speaks it well, but he did not utter a word of it. He deliberately attempted to hide the fact that Gurkhas and non-Gurkhas rarely met, that people socialized mostly with other Nepalis from their own caste or ethnic background. He made no reference to the many difficulties Gurkha families face in conducting their religious rituals in Oxford and in the United Kingdom generally.[8]

One example of such difficulties occurred during the second most important Nepali festival, Tihar, which follows Dasain a month later (it corresponds to the Indian Diwali). One of the popular ways of celebrating Tihar festival is through the public performance of Deusi and Bhailo—a special genre of music and dance—where groups of people go house to house chanting ritual songs and prayers. It is customary for host families to offer the performers cash, food, drinks, and so on. This is a popular practice in Nepal; several groups may visit and perform over several days. Some enthusiastic young people wanted to start the tradition and began visiting Nepali houses in Rose Hill. The normal way is to perform in front of the house in as loud a way as possible. They did not dare to do this, for fear that people nearby might complain and call the police. They felt constrained to come into the narrow hallway of the house itself and to sing just a few of the ritual songs in hushed tones. Everyone present knew that it was nothing like Deusi Bhailo in Nepal.

BELONGING, THE HOUSE, AND ANIMAL SACRIFICE

A key site for the generation of one's sense of belonging is the home. One Oxford ex-Gurkha shared his personal experiences as follows:

> I have to not only keep visiting my place in Nepal but also do all I could to support it and my people. Even if I became very rich here and never went back to my society, my *atman* or spirit will go back

where it came from when I die. It could not possibly hang around here because it will not get due respect and space in this country.

Chandra Limbu owned a house in Rose Hill that he had bought the previous year. When asked whether he liked it, his answer was—yes and no. He knew that it was a worthwhile investment. It was not small for his family of four; and he was quite happy with its physical outlook, shape, colour, size of the garden, and other facilities. The house was also close to other Nepali/Limbu houses. In fact he had selected it after being shown many others in the area. Despite all this, he still did not feel that he truly owned this house or that he fully belonged to his house. He explained:

> I know the two could never be compared in terms of property values, but I always get the sense that my house in Rose Hill is never the same as my father's house in our ancestral village in Nepal. To my mind this house is not even equivalent to my father's buffalo shed. This is an important property in local terms and more so in Nepali terms, and yet I do not feel I fully belong here. I tend to think that my true home is in Nepal, and not this one; that it is nothing more than a temporary shelter.

One of the reasons for not feeling at home at his own house was that he believed only his family lived there but his deities and ancestor spirits did not. He felt they did not have a space in his house because it had not been consecrated through 'house warming' rituals according to the Limbu tradition. As Hubert and Mauss (1964) famously claimed, at least occasional human intervention is essential for the very existence of the gods; there is a contractual and mutually beneficial relationship between the two worlds. The edited volume *Man and His House in the Himalayas* (Toffin, 1991), based on an ethnographic study in a variety of locations in Nepal, amply demonstrates that for Nepalis the house is more than a mere physical space for dwelling: it is also the residence of ancestor spirits and deities. Generally the family starts living in a new house only after completing the ritual of installing their ancestor spirits and deities. These gods and deities protect the family, and in return the family has to regularly worship them—often involving blood sacrifice. For instance, Jest (1991: 158) shows, using the ethnography of a *Majhi* or fisherman house in eastern Nepal, that these deities cohabiting with the family can be malicious and can cause misfortunes, death, and destruction in the family if they are not treated well through mandatory rituals. In some cases, the house itself is believed to be a form of deity, which should be appeased. Levy (1990: 331) describes how the Newars of Bhaktapur believe that people should not start living in a new house until blood sacrifice is performed (and the same is true much more widely within Nepal); people fear it could otherwise seek to draw human blood instead through fatal incidents like fire, earthquake, or similar disasters. The same rule applies to new vehicles: blood sacrifice is required before using them so that they may not cause accidents and the resultant flow of human blood. Levy continues: "The close relation of animal sacrifice and threats to humans is experienced by some ... individuals in their late childhood in a deeply felt way" (ibid.: 331–32).

As noted above, the biggest group within Oxford Nepalis is made up of Limbus, a group based in the far east of Nepal, with a largely shamanic religious tradition. According to Sagant (1976: 162–63), Limbu houses are no exception to the rules outlined above. Once a new house is built, or bought, a Limbu spiritual expert called *Phedangma* is summoned to perform the necessary rituals before the house is inhabited. He first ceremonially enters the house and performs elaborate rituals, including the sacrifice of a pig to the main pillar. Blood sacrifice and other domestic rituals are meant to make the key protector deity of the Limbus—Yuma—come and reside in the house; she is believed to live by the main pillar of the house and bear the burden of the house and the whole world. She is responsible for the overall welfare of the family in the house. "The Limbu calendar requires that every household make annual sacrifices, one in November and one in April, to the goddess Yuma; twice a year to Manguenna, to deceased ancestors, and to Nahangma" (Sagant, 1996: 379).

Many Oxford Limbus used to perform some of these key rituals in their houses in Nepal towns, although the calendar would be followed more strictly in villages than in towns. They acknowledge the fact that the performance of these rituals, though mandatory according to their custom, is not possible in the United Kingdom. Firstly, there were no trained *Phedangmas* available in Oxford, or indeed in Britain. Even if they were available, UK laws forbid the slaughter of animals in domestic spaces or anywhere outside licensed venues run by professional butchers. The ban on animal slaughter makes many Limbu rituals—among those who wish to follow the tradition—incomplete. Unlike the Hindu sacrifice for goddess Durga in Dasain, apparently fruits or vegetables cannot be used as surrogate victims in Limbu rituals. Even the simple act of burning a bundle of incense sticks could make the fire alarm go off, which inhibited many informants from performing this simple home ritual.

There was yet another aspect of their living arrangements that many Gurkhas found undermined their sense of belonging in Oxford and the United Kingdom. Many of their affinal and consanguineal relatives were in Nepal, and they were highly unlikely to visit their houses mainly because they would not normally be given visas to attend family rituals and functions in the United Kingdom. Of course, some of them did have a few close relatives living in the United Kingdom, but they did not always live close by. Many practical considerations prevented them from visiting friends and relatives even within the United Kingdom. Furthermore, the size of UK houses that they could afford is too small for family gatherings. The design of UK houses is, in most cases, orientated towards accommodating a nuclear family and is not favourable for hosting an extended one. Most Gurkha houses in Nepal tend to be quite spacious. Besides, they can find places in neighbours' houses, or erect tents in the field in order to host a large gathering. As the ex-soldiers recognized, such arrangements are normally not easy in the United Kingdom; one can certainly not keep guests in a tent in a nearby field.

It should be made explicit that the Limbu house is the epicentre of their rituals and other public functions. "The house is the sanctuary, almost the definition, of the cultural order. Beyond it there is almost nothing" (Sagant, 1996: 9). In Nepal, when special guests arrive, the host family should ceremonially slaughter a pig or similar animal and offer the entire frontal half of the body to the guests to take home. The other half is cooked and eaten in an elaborate feast. This tradition, called *phudong*, is still popular among the Limbus in Nepal; there is an onus on families to observe it for important functions such as weddings and funerals. This cannot be practised in the United Kingdom, for the obvious reason that the killing of animals or birds in the house (or outside) is not permitted.

Oxford Gurkhas miss slaughtering animals so much that they have invented an interesting way of doing it whilst following the health and safety regulations. They have a special arrangement with pig farms in Didcot and Salisbury where they are offered a whole pig as soon as it has been slaughtered. Small groups of ex-Gurkhas took turns to drive to these places, cut and clean the pork themselves, and distribute the meat equally among the members of the pork-buying group. There were quite a few such groups of men in Oxford (women did not participate). It was certainly more than the mere provisioning of pork; everyone looked forward to it when he was on leave. They were prepared to travel long distances to chop a whole pig to pieces; this pork, they claimed, was much tastier than what they could buy in the local supermarkets.

BELONGING AND DEATH RITES IN THE UNITED KINGDOM

It is customary for the death of a Limbu due to unnatural causes like accidents and natural calamities to be treated by a ritual expert, specially trained for dealing with bad events, called *Bijuwa*; there is no elaborate funeral involved in such cases. Natural deaths are dealt with by *Phedangma*s who perform lengthy rituals.[9] According to Oxford Limbus, the very first thing he does is to go into a trance state in order to carry out direct verbal communication with the deceased. In an emotional invocation the spirit of the dead embodied in the *Phedangma* not only spells out the cause of his death but also speaks about his personal experiences, interests, unfulfilled desires, and so forth. His family and friends, who find the words of the spirit medium entirely convincing, sometimes become hysterical. They ask the spirit about whether the deceased had any last wishes and also sometimes about how they should perform the last rites.

Close members of the deceased's patriline act as chief mourners. As instructed by the *Phedangma*, the dead body is prepared in a special way and placed in the house with its head facing a certain direction. Then it is taken to the burial ground in a procession involving exclusively Limbus; people from other castes or tribes are not allowed to touch the body. After the burial, chief mourners ceremonially shave their head, face, and body by the side of a river or stream. They then return and sit in a corner of the house on hay for 3–4 days, observing semi-seclusion and food taboos, again under the supervision of the *Phedangma*.

Within a year of death the family should hold an elaborate final ritual called *khauma* that will help the spirit reach its final destination. All related households—consanguineal and affinal—support the family with free supply of money, food, liquor, buffalo, pigs, chicken, or meat. A pig or male buffalo is sacrificed and its raw head, together with liquor and other food items, is offered to the spirit. Whilst *Phedangma*s spend the nights chanting ritual texts, guests engage in merry-making, drinking, romantic love, and so on. Previously it was held over three nights but now it has been reduced to 1 for reasons of economy. This is a key ritual for any Limbu household. Although such elaborate rituals are not required in the case of unnatural deaths, the funeral involves the sacrifice of a piglet, which is often killed in a cruel manner.

Several Oxford Limbus told Pariyar: "It is easier in life but harder after death in the UK."[10] There was a sense among many Gurkhas and their spouses that they may live richer in the United Kingdom, compared to Nepal, but they would die poorer. It was not difficult to see that elaborate funerals following traditional custom were not going to be possible in the United Kingdom. It is not easy for people from countries like Nepal to fly to the United Kingdom for family visits; even when visa difficulties are overcome, many relatives simply cannot afford the cost of travel. The lack of space in the house for visitors and guests and the unavailability of ritual experts are other key problems. It is not Limbu custom to burn dead bodies, but not all can afford the traditional burial as it is comparatively more expensive in the United Kingdom. It is impossible to keep to the rule of not allowing a dead body to be touched by a non-Limbu, because the UK mortuary law requires that funeral officers do much of the work on the body, including its cleaning, before cremation.

THE NEPALIS OF SIKKIM

We turn now to a very different diaspora population, equally originating from Nepal. This particular group also finds itself outside its homeland—indeed as the original inhabitants of the Kathmandu Valley they find themselves some hundreds of miles and at least a full day's journey away from their place of origin (in the 19th century it would have been two weeks' walk away). On the other hand, Sikkim shares a border with east Nepal. Sikkim had been a semi-independent kingdom, but was incorporated into the Indian Union, as its 22nd state, in 1975.

The people of Sikkim have mixed feelings about being part of the Indian Union: on 16 May 1995, 20 years after the merger of Sikkim into India, Kaji Lhendup Dorji, who played a major role in engineering the merger of Sikkim into India and whose name has become a byword among Nepali speakers for betrayal of one's nation, published a fierce statement urging the Indian Government to return Sikkim to its previous status. Yet on the whole most Sikkimese are reconciled to being part of India, if only because India has poured enormous resources into the fledgling state. There are roads to even the most remote hamlets and the poor receive subsidized rice and cooking gas. Some claim that this high level of government support has made the Sikkimese lazy and dependent.

Nepalis started migrating to Sikkim in the middle of the 19th century. A Newar from Bhaktapur, named Lakshmi Das, was able to lease land from the Chogyal, or King, of Sikkim in 1867. He was entrusted with mining copper in the 1870s and from 1882 with minting coins for the government. He encouraged many Nepalis to come to Sikkim to work in his enterprises. The Nepalis who settled in Sikkim faced no barriers to reconstructing their way of life and were able to carry on rituals as in Nepal. Despite it being a Buddhist country, they continued their own traditions, for example, of sacrificing animals for Dasain, and it would appear that this practice died out around the end of the 1980s. (Most temples in India forbid animal sacrifice.) Today some perform a sacrifice with a vegetable substitute. Locals in Sikkim ascribe the campaign against animal sacrifice to Sai Baba, who is very popular there. In general, Nepalis in Sikkim have assimilated to a larger Hindu-Nepali identity and have adopted the Nepali language as their mother tongue. There is a high degree of intermarriage between different caste and ethnic groups, as in nearby Darjeeling.

Today the population of Sikkim is over half a million, of whom nearly three quarters are of Nepali origin. The Lepchas and Bhutias, treated both in colonial times and after as indigenous to Sikkim with various attempts to prevent their land from being alienated to in-migrating Nepalis, form just one-fifth of the total population.[11] In 1978 only the Lepchas and Bhutias were granted the status of Scheduled Tribes (ST), but Tamangs and Limbus were added to the list in 2002. Around 33 per cent of the post-matriculation educational places in the state are reserved for them. A further 5 per cent of the population are listed as Scheduled Castes (all members of the

Nepali-speaking service castes) and 6 per cent of the educational seats are reserved for them. As the ST status is being diluted by additions to the category, the State Council of Sikkim gave Lepchas the status of 'Most Primitive Tribe' in January 2005. Shneiderman and Turin comment:

> [E]ven the most disadvantaged Lepcha settlements in Sikkim maintain a relatively high standard of living. Dzongu, an officially demarcated Lepcha reservation in north Sikkim, is remote by Indian standards, but still boasts electrified villages, well-run schools, and Community Information Centres with battery-powered computers and broadband satellite connections. Rather fittingly, the Indian reservation system has indeed created a 'reservation'—a discrete homeland territory where only members of Sikkim's Most Primitive Tribe may settle and own land. (Shneiderman and Turin, 2006: 58)

The OBC category was also diluted by adding Bahun, Chhetri, Newar, and Sanyasi in 2001, so the Sikkimese government simultaneously recognized a subcategory of Most Backward Classes (MBC). This included Bhugel, Gurung, Mangar (Magar), Kirat Rai, Sunuwar, Thamil, Jogi, and Dewan (Vandenhelsken, 2011: 95–96).

Under the rule of Chief Minister Nar Bahadur Bhandari (1979–94), differences within the Nepali-speaking population had not been encouraged, and civil servants who supported ethnic groups were discriminated against for promotion. However, when Pavan Chamling came in as Chief Minister in 1994 there was a change of policy in favour of multiculturalism. The various Nepali subgroups were encouraged to relearn their 'original' languages and for a year or so the Government of Sikkim published its proceedings in Newari, Tamang, etc.—which of course the vast majority of Sikkimese Newars, Tamangs, etc., were incapable of reading. Every group sought to have its own language and its own script in a process Arora (2007) dubs 'retribalization'. The obsession, strong in Nepal and even more so in Sikkim, with having one's owns script is labelled 'scriptophilia' by Shneiderman and Turin. The *Sikkim Herald* weekly is still published in thirteen different languages; however, as Arora notes (2007: 206), all this is a question of "linguistic symbolism rather than linguistic proficiency". Some suspect that the encouragement of such retribalization is an elite Indian plot to divide the Nepalis of Sikkim and Darjeeling among themselves (Pradhan, 2005: 22–24).

Very similar processes were occurring at the same time just over the border in Darjeeling district, as has been described by Shneiderman and Turin (2006) and Shneiderman (2009) for the case of the Thangmis. The aim is to achieve the coveted protected status of Scheduled Tribe, though so far most Nepali groups have only the lesser (but still desirable) status of OBC (Other Backward Class).

The Nepalis in Sikkim have been living there for well over a century now, and in some cases for over 150 years. Therefore they believe that they are no less indigenous people of Sikkim than the Bhutia and the Lepcha populations who have the coveted ST status. In so far as most of the Nepali communities, including the Bahuns, the Chhetris, the Rais, the Gurungs, the Magars and the Newars have not received ST status, they feel like outsiders. There is an unspecified line between Nepalese communities, on the one side, versus the Bhutias and the Lepchas on the other. All the Nepalese communities feel themselves somehow closer to each other than to the Bhutias and the Lepchas.

Nepalis in Sikkim show considerable respect and affection towards Nepal and visitors from Nepal. In the words of Suryabir Tuladhar, the priest of the Svayambhu Bhimakali temple in Gangtok, Nepalis in diaspora are fragments of Nepal, but abandoned and forgotten in foreign lands. Whether or not the mainland recognizes them, they believe that they are Nepali in their own right. One finds statues of the famous Nepali poet Bhanubhakta everywhere in Sikkim. Even more surprising, there seems to be a family portrait of the late King Birendra and his family in virtually every Nepali home in Sikkim. One informant said that during Dasain there was a tradition of offering a barley sprout (*jamarā*) in the name of the King of Nepal before distributing them amongst themselves. The respect shown to the King of Nepal was surprising, because the people in Sikkim are physically and politically not bound to Nepal and their ancestors sought in India economic and educational opportunities and political and social freedoms not available in Nepal. It shows how, nevertheless, they are still attached culturally to Nepal.[12]

Despite their love for Nepal and the Nepali people, Sikkimese Nepalis display not the slightest interest in returning to Nepal permanently. Among many reasons, their present prosperous economic and stable political position has given them confidence. For that matter, they are not attracted to other Indian states either. They are not very positive towards others migrating into Sikkim. People of Nepali origin who have migrated to Sikkim from other Indian states in recent times do not feel that the locals treat them well. For instance, Nepalis from West Bengal (Darjeeling, Kalimpong) and from across the border in Nepal come for work, but are not made welcome. Many people in Sikkim consider that people from other parts of India are attracted to Sikkim simply in order to get economic benefits from the state government.

SIKKIMESE NEWARS

Because there are some prominent Newars in Sikkim and there was a history of Newars working for the Chogyal as tax-collectors and contractors, it is believed that all Newars in Sikkim are well off; but in fact there are many who are poor and backward. A survey in 1989 showed a third of Sikkimese Newars to be illiterate. Even the numbers of those with prominent government jobs seem to be in decline as the reservations policy for STs begins to take effect. The Newars therefore are no less inclined to pursue ST status for themselves than anyone else, despite the fact that the Kathmandu Valley's sophisticated urban culture, from which they derive their traditions, could be taken to be the very antithesis of tribal.[13]

Although individuals had been interested in the 1970s and the 1980s, the Newars of Sikkim did not become organized until 1993 when they established the Sikkim Newa Guthi, which was registered with the government the following year. By 1997 it had established branches in various places within Sikkim and had started to invite Newar activists from Kathmandu to help revive long-abandoned or never-practised Newar customs. Of first importance was the observance of Mha Puja, which is the occasion for a motorcycle rally and political speeches in Kathmandu. The Sikkim Newa Guthi also campaigned for OBC status for Newars. In 2003 the Guthi was renamed as the All-India Newar Organisation, Sikkim, in order to emphasize links with Darjeeling and elsewhere. In line with Chamling's language policy, there were attempts to teach Nepal Bhasa (Newari) to Newar children (whose parents spoke to them in Nepali or English); some young Sikkimese Newars were sent to Kathmandu to learn Newari as well.

Along with Bahuns, Chetris, Jogis, and Sanyasis, the Newars achieved OBC status in 2003. Khagendra Pradhan, Chair of the All-India Newar Organisation, Sikkim, wanted to go further. Generally, those seeking to achieve ST status need to demonstrate, in lines with the definitions of the 1965 Lokur Committee, "primitive traits, distinctive culture, geographical isolation, shyness of contact with the community at large, and economic backwardness" (Arora, 2007: 209).[14] With this in mind, Khagendra Pradhan wrote a paper in 2003 entitled 'Inclusion of Newars within the Provision of the Indian Constitution, Scheduled Tribes Status: provision Article 332 & 342'. He put forward the following eleven cultural arguments to demonstrate that the Newars should be considered a tribe:

a) The great veneration shown by the Newars for serpent and the cult of Naga is similar to the tribes of South West India. b) Wa-vel-va and Sumaka sentences are perfectly the same in form and meaning in Newar and the dialect of the tribes of Nilgiri. c) It is to point out here that wooden pulveriser used as agricultural implement by the Newars is similar to that now being used in Malabar. In Newari it is called *Khatti Muga* and is called *Katta Kol* in Malayalam. d) Mulmi section among the Newars are drawn from the Murmi tribes. e) Newars are the descendants of the ancient Kiratas. f) Attention may be invited to the fact that Bhimsen, the epic hero, is regarded as an important deity both by the Newars and the Tamangs. g) Another cultural similarity with the Khasi is the settlement of dispute by water ordeal. h) The Newars' sub-clan Hayu or Vayu originally came from Lanka having left the country after the defeat of King Ravana. The sentimental attachment of the Newars' is found to this mythological King. i) The exchange of betel-nuts in the marriage celebration is similar to the Khasi tribes. j) The ritual of disposing of the dead body of the Newar girl who dies during her first mensuration or Barha similar to the dead body of Palaung woman of Shan States. k) Non-piercing of the nose and non-wearing of nose ornaments are similar to Lepcha, Bhutia and Tibet women.[15]

Like the mouse-eating that the Thangmi of Darjeeling argued to be an original cultural trait of Thangmis in Nepal (Shneiderman, 2009), many of these arguments might be looked at askance by Newars in Nepal. The point is that they are discursive arguments, aimed at achieving a particular bureaucratic classification within the Indian state's regime of preferential entitlements.

CONCLUSION

The two contrasting cases show particular diasporic populations adopting rather different strategies. In the Oxford case, cultural difference is ignored and played down in public forums in order to build a sense of identity that is useful in gaining resources from the local government. Culture is objectified in public staging—sometimes to the annoyance of the young people who do not want to be constrained by nationalist considerations. In more private spheres, however, members of the older generation have a clear sense that they do not belong, because they cannot carry out the rituals that they would at home—either at all (because animal sacrifice is not allowed) or properly (because they fear what the neighbours might say or do).

In the Sikkimese case, settlement dates back much longer. There has been a similar merging of different cultural identities to produce a pan-Nepali one, a process that has gone much further—but not so far as to obliterate internal cultural differences altogether. And that cultural difference is now at a premium, given the differential reservation policies that depend on being able to demonstrate a distinctive cultural identity combined with a history of exclusion. This means that though in fact Sikkimese Newars (like other Nepalis in Sikkim) actually feel strongly that they do belong in Sikkim (to the extent that they do not welcome more recent Nepali arrivals), they are constrained (paradoxically) to try and demonstrate publicly that they do not fully belong and that the state should respond to their demand to allow them the most privileged category of citizenship (namely, that of ST) which they currently lack.

One context—the United Kingdom—may be characterized as weakly multicultural: there is a discourse that values cultural difference but there are no preferential rights. In the other strongly multicultural context—Sikkim—the state accords preferential treatment in matters of considerable import to anyone who values education or state employment. As a consequence, questions of group belonging and cultural classification are potentially crucial for almost every member of society.

NOTES

1. This chapter is based on the MPhil dissertation research of Mitra Pariyar carried out in Oxford in 2009–10 and the postdoctoral research of Bal Gopal Shrestha in Sikkim carried out mainly in 2004. It is also informed by the Vernacular Religion project on which Gellner, Shrestha, and S. Hausner have been working since 2009 (see www.isca.ox.ac.uk/research/social-anthropological-research/ vernacularreligion/). Thanks are due to Joanna Pfaff-Czarnecka for constructive feedback on earlier drafts.

2. See the Introduction of this volume and Pfaff-Czarnecka and Toffin (2011) for overviews. For an introduction to the Nepali diaspora in general, see Gellner (2013).

3. The term 'Gurkha' derives from the hill town of Gorkha, the origin of the Shah dynasty that ruled Nepal until the declaration of a republic in May 2008. It is used to refer to soldiers from Nepal serving in the British and Indian armies, in the Sultanate of Brunei, and in the Singapore police. This chapter concerns only British ex-Gurkhas.

4. All names are pseudonyms.

5. However, it would be wrong to assume that caste discrimination is entirely absent within the Nepalese diaspora in the United Kingdom: see Pariyar (2011).

6. There is by now a considerable literature on the Dasain festival, including on activists' recent attempts to persuade people to boycott it. See Ramirez (1993), Campbell (1995), Krauskopff and Lecomte-Tilouine (1996), Pfaff-Czarnecka (1996), Gellner (1999), Hangen (2005, 2009).

7. A long-sleeved shirt, folded over and tied at the front, with trousers baggy at the top, and tight around the calves.

8. One should also mention that there is a minority of Nepali migrants to the United Kingdom who choose not to participate in such communal events. A survey of 300 households for the Vernacular Religion project suggested that 12 per cent had not attended any religious event (festival) in the last two years and 9 per cent had not attended any non-religious event (e.g. barbecue, football tournament); only 4.3 per cent had attended no such event of either kind.

9. The way in which death rituals are performed, and also the nomenclature used for the ritual specialist, varies from place to place within the Limbu region.

10. In August 2011 (issue 268), *Yuropko Nepalipatra*, a Nepali diaspora weekly, ran a front-page article about the difficulties Nepalis face in dealing with death in the United Kingdom, entitled 'It's not even easy to die'.

11. For earlier studies of Sikkim and Darjeeling, particularly from the Nepali point of view, see Nakane (1966), Pradhan (1982, 2005), Chalmers (2003), Subba (1992), Hutt (1997), Steinmann (2003/04), Arora (2005, 2007), Shneiderman (2009), Vandenhelsken (2011).

12. Such respect was not extended to Gyanendra, who succeeded the throne after the palace massacre of 2001.

13. As argued, for instance, by Gellner (1986, 1991, 1997: 30–34).

14. See also Middleton and Shneiderman (2008) on the ways in which these criteria of backwardness have affected Sikkim and Darjeeling, and are likely to affect Nepal.

15. Thanks to the author for providing Shrestha with the unpublished typed manuscript.

REFERENCES

Arora, V. 2005. 'Being Nepali in Sikkim', *Contemporary India*, 24(1): 54–64.

——. 2007. 'Assertive Identities, Indigeneity, and the Politics of Recognition as a Tribe: The Bhutias, the Lepchas and the Limbus of Sikkim', *Sociological Bulletin*, 56(2): 195–220.

Campbell, B. 1995. 'Dismembering the Body Politic: Contestations of Legitimacy in Tamang Celebrations of *Dasain*', *Kailash*, 17(3–4): 133–46.

Chalmers, R. 2003. '"We Nepalis": Language, Literature and the Formation of a Nepali Public Sphere in India, 1914–1940'. PhD, SOAS, University of London.

CNSUK. 2011. *Directory 2011 of Nepali (Individuals, Businesses and Organisations) in the UK*. Reading: Centre for Nepal Studies UK.

Gellner, D.N. 1986. 'Language, Caste, Religion and Territory: Newar Identity Ancient and Modern', *European Journal of Sociology*, 27(1): 102–48.

——. 1991 'Hinduism, Tribalism, and the Position of Women: The Problem of Newar Identity', *Man* (N.S.), 26(1): 105–25. Republished as Ch. 13 in D.N. Gellner, 2001. *The Anthropology of Buddhism and Hinduism: Weberian Themes*. New Delhi: Oxford University Press.

——. 1997. 'Introduction', in D.N. Gellner and D. Quigley (eds), *Contested Hierarchies: A Collaborative Ethnography of Caste among the Newars of the Kathmandu Valley, Nepal*, pp. 1–37. Oxford: Clarendon.

——. 1999. 'Religion, Politics, and Ritual: Remarks on Geertz and Bloch', *Social Anthropology*, 7(2): 135–53. Republished as Ch. 4 in D.N. Gellner, 2001. *The Anthropology of Buddhism and Hinduism: Weberian Themes*. New Delhi: Oxford University Press.

——. 2011. 'Belonging, Indigeneity, Rites, and Rights: The Newar Case', in J. Pfaff-Czarnecka and G. Toffin (eds), *The Politics of Belonging in the Himalayas: Local Attachments and Boundary Dynamics*, pp. 45–76. New Delhi: SAGE Publications.

——. 2013. 'Warriors, Workers, Traders, and Peasants: The Nepali/Gorkhali Diaspora since the Nineteenth Century', in D. Washbrook and J. Chatterjee (eds), *Routledge Handbook of the South Asian Diaspora*, pp. 136–50. London: Routledge.

Hangen, S.I. 2005. 'Boycotting Dasain: History, Memory, and Ethnic Politics in Nepal', *Studies in Nepali History and Society*, 10(1): 105–33.

——. 2009. *The Rise of Ethnic Politics in Nepal: Democracy in the Margins*. London: Routledge.

Hubert, H. and M. Mauss. 1964 (1898). *Sacrifice: Its Nature and Function*, tr. W.D. Halls. Chicago: University of Chicago Press.

Hutt, M. 1997. 'Being Nepali without Nepal: Reflections on a South Asian Diaspora', in D.N. Gellner, J. Pfaff-Czarnecka, and J. Whelpton (eds), *Nationalism and Ethnicity in a Hindu Kingdom*, pp. 101–44. Amsterdam: Harwood.

Jest, C. 1991. 'How I Built My House', in Toffin, G. (ed.), *Man and His House in the Himalayas: Ecology of Nepal*, pp. 155–60. New Delhi and Bangalore: Sterling Publishers.

Krauskopff, G. and M. Lecomte-Tilouine (eds). 1996. *Célébrer le pouvoir: Dasain, une fête royale au Népal*. Paris: CNRS/Maison des Sciences de l'Homme.

Levy, R. (with K. Rajopadhyaya). 1990. *Mesocosm: Hinduism and the Organization of a Traditional Newar City in Nepal*. Berkeley: University of California Press.

Middleton, T. and S. Shneiderman. 2008. 'Reservations, Federalism and the Politics of Recognition in Nepal', *Economic and Political Weekly*, 43(19): 39–45.

Nakane, C. 1966. 'A Plural Society in Sikkim: A Study of the Interrelations of Lepchas, Bhotias and Nepalis', in C. von Fürer-Haimendorf (ed.), *Caste and Kin in Nepal, India and Ceylon: Anthropological Studies in Hindu-Buddhist Contact Zones*, pp. 213–63. New Delhi: Sterling.

Pariyar, M. 2011. 'Cast(e) in Bone: The Perpetuation of Social Hierarchy among Nepalis in Britain' (COMPAS Working Paper WP-11-85). Available online at www.compas.ox.ac.uk/publications/working-papers/wp-11-85/

Pfaff-Czarnecka, J. 1996. 'A Battle of Meanings: Commemorating the Goddess Durga's Victory over the Demon Mahisha as a Political Act', *Kailash*, 18(3–4): 57–92.

Pfaff-Czarnecka, J. and G. Toffin. 2011. 'Introduction: Belonging and Multiple Attachments in Multiple Himalayan Societies', in J. Pfaff-Czarnecka and G. Toffin (eds), *The Politics of Belonging in the Himalayas: Local Attachments and Boundary Dynamics*, pp. xi–xxxviii. New Delhi: SAGE Publications.

Pradhan, K. 1982. *Pahilo Pahar* (First Watch). Darjeeling: Shyam Prakashan.

———. 2005. *Darjeelingmā Nepālijāti ra Janajātiya Cinārikā Nayā Adānharu* (M.C. Regmi Lecture 2004). Lalitpur: Social Science Baha.

Ramirez, P. 1993. 'Drama, Devotion and Politics: The Dasain Festival in Argha Kingdom', in G. Toffin (ed.), *Nepal, Past and Present*, pp. 47–59. Paris: Editions du CNRS.

Sagant, P. 1976. *Le Paysan Limbu: Sa Maison et ses Champs*. Paris: Mouton.

———. 1996. *The Dozing Shaman: The Limbus of Eastern Nepal*. New Delhi: Oxford University Press.

Shneiderman, S. 2009. 'Ethnic (P)reservations: Comparing Thangmi Ethnic Activism in Nepal and India', in D.N. Gellner (ed.), *Ethnic Activism and Civil Society in South Asia*, pp. 115–41. New Delhi: SAGE Publications.

Shneiderman, S. and M. Turin. 2006. 'Seeking the Tribe: Ethno-Politics in Sikkim and Darjeeling', *Himal Southasian*, 19(2, March–April): 54–58. Available online at www.himalmag.com/2006 (accessed: 16 October 2013).

Steinmann, B. 2003/04. 'National Hegemonies, Local Allegiances: Historiography and Ethnography of a Buddhist Kingdom', *European Bulletin of Himalayan Research*, 25/26: 145–67.

Subba, K. 2007. 'Drug Users of Dharan: Aspects of Marginalization', in H. Ishii, D.N. Gellner, and K. Nawa (eds), *Nepalis Inside and Outside Nepal*, pp. 283–306. New Delhi: Manohar.

Subba, T.B. 1992. *Caste, Ethnicity, State and Development: A Case Study of Gorkhaland Movement*. Delhi: Har-Anand and Vikas.

Toffin, G. (ed.). 1991. *Man and His House in the Himalayas: Ecology of Nepal*. New Delhi and Bangalore: Sterling Publishers.

Vandenhelsken, M. 2011. 'The Enactment of Tribal Unity at the Periphery of India: The Political Role of a New Form of the Panglhabsol Buddhist Ritual in Sikkim', *European Bulletin of Himalayan Research*, 38: 81–118.

Chapter 7

Geographical, Cultural, and Professional Belonging of Nepalese Migrants in India and Qatar

TRISTAN BRUSLÉ

Over the last 10 years, international labour migration from Nepal has become a major social phenomenon. The crave to leave for *bidesh* affects almost all classes of people, both educated and uneducated, rich and poor, city dwellers and peasants. Although temporary migration to India is nothing new, the integration of Nepal in the global labour market leads workers to be confronted with whole new worlds.[1] India still remains the major destination, welcoming a total of between 1.3 and 3 million Nepalese (Kollmair et al., 2006; Thieme, 2006).[2] Ten to 24 per cent of the population over 15 years old live outside the country (ibid.) and, according to the Department of Foreign Employment, about 1.3 million Nepalese work abroad, without counting India (*The Rising Nepal*, 29 June 2009). The latest figures from the Department of Foreign Employment show that since 2006–07, the number of annual departures to foreign destinations has remained above 200,000. Even if there was a slight decline in the offer of work to Nepalese workers during the 2008–09 crisis, the expatriation of workers is again under way, so that in July 2010 the number of Nepalese working in a foreign land, India included, stands at 3 million (Nepalnews.com, 15 July 2010).

Since the beginning of this century, following the trend to emigrate from Nepal, research on Nepalese international labour migration has developed and taken various directions. Migrants' networks, the ways of integrating migrants in host countries, and the economic considerations regarding their work and livelihood abroad have been at the forefront of much research (Adhikari, 2010; Bruslé, 2007, 2008, 2010; Thieme, 2006; Yamanaka, 2007 among others), whereas other research has focused on transnational links (O'Neill, 2007; Sijapati, 2010; Uesugi, 2007) and transnational ethnic movements (Minami, 2007). The study of Nepal's migration policy and the organization and meaning of labour migration (Sharma, 2008; Wyss, 2004) show that migration has long been considered a 'pathology' (Sharma, 2008), with the long-term aim of eradicating it as a social evil. The meaning of migration for rural communities has not yet been explored since its role in changing societies has not been emphasized. The Nepalese State and development agencies are eager to study the economic impact of the remittances migrants send home (see NIDS, 2008, 2010), or migration as a reproduction strategy (see Hollema et al., 2008). Although the effects of migration have been studied regarding gender dimensions (Kaspar, 2005) or on agriculture (Aubriot, 2010; Khanal and Watanabe, 2006), no in-depth village studies have been undertaken about the economic, social, and political changes migration might bring about. Studying Nepalese migrants' ways of belonging helps understand a few facts. First, while in migration, we see that because migrants belong to groups, their own practices in India or in Qatar are influenced by their sense of belonging. According to contexts, belonging is a resource used by migrants in the fulfilment of their migration strategies and aims. Second, understanding migrant's forms of belonging can help the researcher place migrants on the changing map of Nepal, as a rural and agrarian country, and also explain how workers, due to their encounter with people from different districts, view their own country. And finally, given the growing proportion of young men and women whose only expectations are to become migrants and the growing place of the Nepalese Diaspora on the political scene, understanding how migrants feel about belonging to a collective unit that shares mutual values and practices is useful today in understanding Nepalese politics.

I would like to put forward the hypothesis that spending time in India or in a *khadi* country (Gulf) is not a neutral experience, that is, a migrant's character and world views can change due to new experiences abroad. As Kibria (2008: 518) points out, "international migration is widely understood to be a transformative experience, marked by varied and complex shifts of identity". This is confirmed by a migrant: "when they [the Nepalese] come back from a foreign land, their behaviour (*byabahar*) becomes very different". The 'migratory world', a world in itself with its norms, codes, and representations, differs from the world left by the migrants and from the world that surrounds them. Even though men know they will encounter *the Other*, thanks to a culture of migration[3] (Massey et al., 1993; Kandel and Massey, 2002), which is strong among the Nepalese, being a foreigner, living with other people, and having a job that gives them worker status lead them to re-evaluate themselves. Thanks to the confrontation with different places and people, men also realize the particularities of their own identity. This can lead some of them to assert new forms of belonging. What is at stake here is the progressive transformation of Nepalese society through migration processes due to the changing forms of belonging migrants may acquire during their stay abroad. New practices and new expectations enter the life of migrants when they are abroad. Even though economic remittances and their potential effects on the Nepalese economy are mostly what researchers focus on, the 'social remittances'[4] (Levitt, 1998) migrants bring back home may lead to major changes in the society. Among the things learnt abroad are new layers of belonging. They appear to be symptomatic of similar class and professional changes that occur abroad. I will try to explain how 'being in migration' induces a new discourse about 'us' and 'them', them being either other Nepalese from different regions or other nationalities. I will try to assess what in actual daily life reflects the migrants' belonging: how does belonging determine social and spatial practices? It is worthwhile studying this particular aspect on account of two points. First, one should understand how migrants live their lives abroad and how belonging influences their daily practices. The second point, which will not be discussed here and must be regarded as a possible future line of research, is that the practices and ideas learnt abroad definitely have some influence at home. The essential point here is that belonging to a new world, different from that of their parents, leads to visible changes in Nepal, which have an impact on the socio-spatial and economic order of the country.

By belonging, I mean a sense of being part of a shared community, be it the nation, the region, the caste, or the profession.[5] These layers of belonging differ according to the situation in which the migrant finds himself. Belonging, as a form of identity, is difficult to grasp and its different forms or manifestations occur in different contexts.

This contribution is based on fieldwork carried out in Nepal and in India[6] (2001–03) and in Qatar[7] (2006 and 2008). Interviews in Delhi and in Uttarakhand were held among Nepalese migrants from the Far Western Region (mainly Bajura, Bajhang, Baitadi, Darchula, and Kalikot), most of whom work as coolies and watchmen. In Qatar, migrants—interviewed in their dwelling place—locally called the *labour camp*, come from all over Nepal, except for mid- and far-western Nepal. Half of them work in offices (as tea boys, mail boys, photocopy boys, etc.) and the other half are gardeners and are in charge of maintaining public spaces in executive gated communities. All the migrants studied in India and in Qatar are men who come and go between their place of origin and their place of migration.[8] Those interviewed mostly belong to higher castes. About 60 interviews in Nepali, half open interviews, half based on questionnaires, were held face to face with migrants in the rooms where they live. They were recorded and later translated. In India and Qatar, the sample of migrants is not meant to be representative.

I will study different forms of belonging one after the other. For each aspect of belonging, I will try and compare Nepalese people's experiences in India and in Qatar.

SENSE OF BELONGING TO PLACES

Belonging to Nepal

"You can take a Nepali out of Nepal but you cannot take Nepal out of a Nepali"

—*Nepalis in Oregon* website, 2005

In both countries, the Nepalese occupy particular labour niches, which, in the view of the host society, make them a homogenous labour class. In Qatar, the Nepalese now form one of the largest foreign communities. They numbered 266,000 in February 2008 and this number will no doubt reach 500,000 at the end of 2009 according to the Nepalese ambassador in Doha.[9] The context here is one of a country where at least 80 per cent of the 1.5 million inhabitants are not actual citizens. Encountering non-Qataris is therefore very common. After a few months in Qatar, migrants form stereotypes about each foreign community, as they point out their differences. It thus strengthens the feeling of *us* as being different from the rest of one's fellow migrants. Contrary to India, migrants have no possibility at all of becoming Qatari citizens in the long term. On the whole, a worker's *nepaliness* is imposed by government institutions that decide nationality quotas, and by the existence of a *labour camp* accommodation system whereby labourers are segregated into rooms, buildings, and dining halls according to their nationalities. Spatial segregation is based on nationality and social class (Nagy, 2006). Although there is not such strong segregation in India, the Nepalese also occupy particular niches at the bottom of the hierarchy, as watchmen in towns and coolies in Uttarakhand. Their *nepaliness* is useful when looking for a job: it is instrumental for them to show that they belong to Nepal. As such, Indians are keen to enhance the foreignness of the *Bahadur* while the latter differentiate themselves from the *dhotiwala*.[10]

Being Nepalese is not discussed as such by migrants. Belonging to Nepal is implicit, inherent to one's identity when one is abroad. It is the first layer of belonging, the broader one which enables migrants to feel familiar with other fellow countrymen. The *bideshi* status binds all men because one of the reasons for their being in India or Qatar is that these types of economy particularly need the Nepalese workforce. It is thanks to their nationality that they are made welcome and that they can work. In both countries, they can count on their very positive image, inspired by the famous Gurkhas, to carve themselves a labour niche.[11] Having gone from being a peasant to a poorly qualified worker creates a sense of common fate abroad, reinforced by the fact that they tend to work and live together. According to them, Nepal cannot provide them with an adequate means of earning money. "What's in Nepal? Nothing except water", is what is usually heard to explain why migration is a constraint (*badhyata*) one can seldom avoid. This is why ambivalent feelings do exist with regard to their native country, towards which loyalty cannot be discussed but at the same time, grievances are formulated as Nepal cannot provide them with the basic needs and does not help them lead a decent life at home. It also helps migrants identify with each other as Nepalese. A sense of shared belonging is felt when, for example, two men meet by chance and discuss their situation. The question 'what are the reasons for your going abroad' is not raised in a straightforward manner; instead a common history, made up of small plots of land, unemployment, and the lack of a brighter future in Nepal, unites migrants. Belonging to Nepal, speaking Nepalese, and being out of their country make migrants feel that their personal story is a story shared by all of them. Migrants use the expression *Hami Nepali* (we, the Nepalese) to speak about themselves and to differentiate from the local population and from other foreigners. Their daily practices show that their *nepaliness* is something they can count on abroad. It is a mark that is needed and a way of not feeling too lonely amidst others.

Asserting one's belonging to Nepal takes different forms in India and in Qatar. In Uttarakhand, wearing *kurta suruwal* and the Nepalese hat (*topi*) is a strategy for standing out from the local population. It is instrumental in finding work as a coolie, so it must be visible and identified as such by would-be employers. On the contrary, in Delhi, there is no need to wear such an attire, although some men do as they would in Nepal. In Qatar, there is a general tendency not to wear traditional dress, except on special meetings or occasions. In fact, young migrants readily admit that these signs of *nepaliness* are for the older generation, not for them who are keen to adopt a more Western—read modern (*adhunik*)—and standard style of dress. The majority of Nepalese migrants in Doha do not differentiate themselves from the rest of South Asians, who wear a shirt and trousers.

Both in India and in Qatar, belonging to Nepal also means re-creating a Nepalese atmosphere and eating Nepalese food. For these purposes, Nepalese restaurants are places where migrants can get back in touch with their inner citizenship. Such *hotels* number about ten in Qatar. Their names (*Nepali Bhansa Ghar, Sagarmatha, Himalayan Restaurant, Samsara, Nepali chowk*) are immediately identifiable and their food (*dal bhat, momo, sukuti, Newar* dishes) is definitely Nepalese. Situated in the heart of old Doha, they are particularly frequented on Fridays (the only day off in the week) when thousands of migrants meet in a square known amongst them as the *Nepali chowk*.[12] Here, workers turn into salesmen and sell items directly imported from Nepal ('*Top of the world*' T-shirts, *pan masala, surti*, etc.) and pirated Nepalese CDs and DVDs. On another register, private businessmen or associations occasionally organize artistic events (*nepali karyakram*) aimed at the Nepalese community. Nepalese artists come from Nepal and the community's VIPs appear on stage to inaugurate the events in huge theatres. On such occasions, thousands of young Nepalese men, and some women, gather to hear Nepalese folksongs and pop music. Taking part in such programmes is a way of escaping the daily grind, of asserting one's sense of belonging to Nepal, and of taking part in a somewhat modern and new way of entertainment.

In small Uttarakhand towns (Pithoragarh, Almora, Pauri Garhwal, Mussoorie), the Nepalese also have their own restaurants, though on a more modest scale. These are also meeting places where migrants can find 'identity food' but they attract customers according to their regional sense of belonging rather than according to their national sense of belonging, given the fact that only the Dotiyali dialect is spoken.[13]

Lastly, another means of valorizing Nepal as the primary layer of identity is via associations. The Non-Resident Nepalis Association, Qatar branch, is said to represent all Nepalese people in this Gulf country. Its main objective is to become the meeting point for the fifty or so Nepalese associations in Doha and to influence the diaspora-orientated policies discussed in Kathmandu. Nevertheless, it encounters great difficulties in actually speaking on behalf of the people and tends to be viewed as an upper-class association disconnected from the grassroots level.[14] In Delhi, although many associations, linked to Nepalese political parties, claim that they address migrants' needs, temporary migrants from the Far Western Region of Nepal do not take part in their activities: migrants do not understand the benefits of belonging to such associations and find it difficult to identify with the labour class.[15]

Regional Belonging

More than in Nepalese towns where migrants mainly come from neighbouring districts, migrants abroad get to meet fellow compatriots who hail from many different parts of Nepal. This can thus enhance or weaken their regional and district sense of belonging. Do regional stereotypes persist when one has migrated abroad? Is belonging to a particular district or region visible in daily practices?

Regional Belonging and Practices in Qatar and in India: When Region Matters

One of the first pieces of information migrants give about themselves, when they first meet fellow countrymen, is their name (i.e. the name of their caste clan) and that of their district of origin. As ancient royal entities melted into the new Nepalese State at the beginning of the 19th century, districts in Nepal are a major layer of identity for the local population (Ramirez, 2000). They are the second layer of spatial belonging.

In India, village social networks (as sets of interpersonal links) are the basis of belonging and shape temporary migration features such as the choice of destination, the type of job, and the dwelling place. In Kumaon, among Nepalese migrants from the Far Western Region, the use of the Dotiyali dialect in their daily interactions creates a sense of common belonging, and of separateness from other Nepali speakers. Meeting other Nepalese people is not sought after and would also be difficult. Small food outlets in Pithoragarh (Uttarakhand) are named after Baitadi or Darchula districts and almost only welcome people from these districts. As their daily practices lead them to keep to themselves, migrants tend to have very limited notions of the geography of the rest of Nepal.

The Qatar experience is the opposite in that labour camp rooms are full of men from a wide range of districts, spanning east to west, from *pahad* to the Tarai.[16] For almost all migrants, living with other Nepalese people is a first-time experience, which helps them discover their differences and mutual features. The first way of introducing oneself is to say one's name and district of origin: the district is a primary layer of geographical belonging in a situation where one meets a fellow compatriot. Finding out one's interlocutor's district of origin enables a person to categorize him, of course, in terms of his region of origin, but also in terms of his development and modernity (See next paragraph).

The strong vernacular and geographical division between *Madhesh* and *Pahad* can also have spatial consequences in migration. It is especially the case for some *Pahadi*s who find it easier to head for the mountains of Uttarakhand where the environment and people are the same as the ones they left behind (Bruslé, 2008). In one Qatari *labour camp* where many Nepalese lived, rooms are divided between *Madheshi*s (from Janakpur region) and *Pahadi*s. There is very little communication between them, especially since, so they say, their language and food are different.[17] Regional belonging is also conveyed by the use of particular meeting places. As a *Nepali chowk* exists in the centre of Doha, people from Rupandehi and Kapilbastu districts, situated in the Terai, meet at the *Akai roundabout* in the centre of Doha. This spatial division of meeting places recalls the spatial division of working places in Mussoorie, Uttarakhand. In this Himalayan town, migrants from Bajhang and Kalikot have separate areas where they carry loads as coolies. Belonging to a district induces belonging to networks[18] and thus determines the geographical space a migrant lives in.[19]

In both countries, belonging to a district, and using this sense of belonging, through associations or friendships, is a way of finding common traits shared by a great number of people: it can be considered as a resource.[20] In extreme cases for instance, district associations in Qatar collect money for their fellow district members who are in dire need; the latter require money for medical fees or to return home. Beyond any nationality-based solidarity, the district-based one is particularly strong when migrants die and the body has to be repatriated, that is at least the claim made by district associations.

Perceptions of Nepal's Geographical Divisions Coincide in India and Qatar

In Qatar, contrary to what happens in India, migrants are often reluctant to point out differences between districts, as if they were afraid of saying things that might harm Nepalese nationalism: "We are all Nepalese brothers (*bhai*). One must not say 'he is a *madheshi*, he is a *pahadi*'. The most important thing is Nepal". The feeling of *nepaliness* is strong and at a time when clear divisions based on ethnicity are emerging in Nepal, migrants prefer to focus their discourse on what binds them rather than on what divides them.[21] In India, no such precautions are taken when talking about the differences between them and the others: people dare to make distinctions which would not be considered politically correct. Surprisingly, perceptions of these geographical divisions of Nepal and of its people by Nepalese people in both India and Qatar tend to converge. Migrants put forward several characteristics to create a kind of geography of regional representation. Yet the overall and more common characteristics of the mental perception of Nepal shared by all Nepalese people, whatever their region of birth, is a declining gradient of modernity running from eastern to far western Nepal. Even though the word modernity is not actually used, people talk about development (*bikas*), in terms of education, roads, towns, and dress to emphasize the differential receptiveness of the different regions of Nepal to the outside world. These ideas, which are based on genuine marked differences in socio-economic development, also abound in official, political, and media discourses.[22]

First of all, language is a common means of differentiation. Migrants from both the central and eastern part of Nepal acknowledge that their way of speaking (*bolne tarika*) the national language is different from that of the western Nepalese, whereas the latter consider that 'pure Nepali' (*suddha nepali*) is spoken in Jumla. The Far Western Nepalese tend to think that beyond some mid-western districts, Nepali is less spoken to the benefit of tribal languages, such as Tamang or Gurung.

In terms of development, people from the mid-western region, who are seen as western Nepalese (*paschimi*) by people from Jhapa or Morang, are considered to be less modern: they listen to folksongs (*dohori lokgit*), whereas those from the east prefer modern (pop) songs (*adhunik gana*).[23] From the point of view of those from the Far Western Region, Easterners are considered to be more concerned with fashion: they are said to like movies and to dress like *heroes*;[24] that is, they have a trendier lifestyle. As Jeevan B., from Argha Khanci now in Doha, puts it:

> [P]eople from eastern Nepal are smart (*canakh*), they are more advanced than us, people from the west. We have been left behind (*pichadi*). I learnt all of this here. People from the west are straight-forward (*sojho*) and people from the east are advanced (*agadi*). There are many places in difficult (*vikat*) circumstances in the west, places with no facilities (*asubidha*), where people have never seen a car.

However, he states that these differences acknowledged in Qatar and India do not take the form of open conflict between people. Mahendra P., from Jhapa, confirms this vision: "in the mountains of western and far western Nepal, they are all uneducated. Here in Qatar, people from western Nepal do not understand, they say 'what's that for? What should I do (*ke garne ho*)?'"

It must be said that the Far Western Region's perception of Nepal is governed by a limited spatial imagination of their country, as illustrated by these two drawings done by two youngsters in India (see Figure 7.1). They show a hypertrophy of their region of origin compared to the rest of Nepal, which can be considered as *terra incognita*, except for the national capital.[25] For migrants who have never been to Kathmandu, it is common to say that "they would like to go to Nepal". So, the 'east' (*purba nepal*) starts as far west as Dang district. Another country starts beyond that point, a country made up of tribes and dialects opposed to their region, which is viewed as homogenous in terms of castes and languages. The east is a land of development, of wealth, of people who are in the British army, and who readily travel worldwide.

Figure 7.1
**Maps of Nepal Drawn by 15-Year-Old Boys from Bajhang
and Bajura, Now Living in India. New Delhi, 2003**

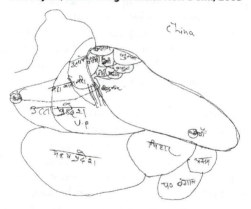

Source: Author.

In such circumstances, belonging to a district and asserting it is a way of categorizing one's group and of entering a hierarchy.[26] In India, people from Baitadi often explain that their district is the most advanced in the region, that the standard of education is higher than that in Bajura, Bajhang, or Kalikot. Yet at the national level, there is a common feeling of inferiority that binds men from the Far Western Region together. A lack of education and a lack of modern facilities do nothing to boost their confidence, as Sher Bahadur R., from Bajhang, expresses it: "even illiterate Nepalese from the east can speak (*bolna saknu*) with literate people from Bajura".

For all migrants, the western region of Nepal is less civilized and less developed, whereas the east is open to international influence and is a modern place. There is a correlation between the perceived level of development of any region and its people. The less developed a region, the more conservative (*rudabadi*) and superstitious (*andha-bishvas*) its inhabitants. The Nepalese from the Far Western Region are conscious of belonging to a lesser developed region and thus of being less educated and less integrated in the outside world. Lastly, the feeling of being despised by Easterners is summed up by this statement: "we (people from the west) call Easterners *dhede*[27] and they call us *pakhe*."[28] Antagonism here is about food and not eating the valuable rice, and about the degree of civilization and of development.

In India, regional stereotypes and district belonging persist because Far Western migrants live and work within their own rather closed society. In Qatar, the vast melting pot helps migrants find more things in common than things that are likely to divide them. Familiarity with one's own world (i.e. people from the same district with whom shared feelings are supposed to exist) can be sought from time to time, by heading to particular places; however, this does not condition daily behaviour as strongly as it does in India.

Home Abroad?

Belonging to Nepal and being a Nepalese represents a protection, a certainty in a world dominated, especially in India, by uncertainty. The ethnic label 'Nepalese' provides them with work but at the same time confines them to the labour class. Even though some migrants in Qatar have the impression of being at home even abroad if their brothers (*daju-bhai*) from Nepal are around them in the same camp or room, after years of migration this feeling is not expressed as often in India. It is particularly reflected in the non-use of the term *ghar* (house) to refer to the dwelling place, which is called *dera* (temporary, rented place). For a foreign place to become home, it requires some spatial appropriation, but also some form of identifying the cultural and professional realm, which is the migrant's lot.

CULTURAL AND PROFESSIONAL BELONGING

Among the things that struck me in Qatar is the fact that names of the dwellers are written on the doors of many rooms in the labour camps. This not only tells us who lives in the rooms but also clearly advertises the harmony of multi-ethnicity and multi-caste life. As migration leads to brand new daily lives for the Nepalese, the question of caste and professional belonging has to be addressed.

Caste Affiliation[29]

Major differences exist between migrants in India and in Qatar with regard to this layer of belonging. In India, both in Uttarakhand and in New Delhi, where migrants from the Far Western Region (mainly Bahun, Chetri, Thakuri, and Dalit) were interviewed, caste relations are of great importance in daily life.[30] Whether men live in close proximity with each other depends on their caste, the dividing line being between higher and lower castes. Most higher-caste men follow strict caste rules in private spaces. In small rooms, water tanks are tucked away in a corner, so that other men do not bump into them. Some high-caste workers, who want to stay away from the pollution and promiscuity of life in town, even choose a job that enables them to live on their own. Thus, the Thakuris from Bajhang whom I met near Pithoragarh explained that they prefer to work in a small quarry and live with fellow Thakuris. They can wear their sacred thread and cook in *dhoti* according to their religious practices. Otherwise, higher-caste migrants rely on restaurants run by a fellow caste member, where they are sure to find pure food. At the opposite end of the spectrum, low-caste Sarkis always live grouped together in small huts in Uttarakhand or in slums in Delhi. It is as if the spatial segregation they experience in Nepal also applies in India. Here, the sense of belonging to a caste does not seem to fade over time. These migrants appear to have no qualms about a stranger witnessing the ongoing consequences of discrimination policies and caste segregation. Although, some literate high-caste men would say that they do not believe in the caste system, they abide by it even while abroad.

In Qatar, contrary to India, migrants interviewed speak reluctantly about discrimination and issues relating to the caste system, except to say that they feel unconcerned by it and that the same blood runs in everyone's veins.[31] The consensus is less about differentiation, as noted in India, than about sameness. Even though talk about the irrelevance of caste distinction is commonplace and reflects a certain change in ideology, a check should be made on whether this translates into less-discriminatory behaviour back home.[32] Living with low-caste people can be disturbing for some, even though this feeling is not expressed directly. For example, Rajesh K. (*Chetri*), 44-years-old in 2008, when explaining who lived in his room, pointed to a bed and whispered to me in a conspiratorial way that it belonged to a Dalit whose family is 'very rich'. He seemed uneasy about sharing his room with someone of lower caste from his own village. Yet he does share food with him, as all workers do over supper in their room. Unlike in Kathmandu (Sharma, 2007: 165), Brahmins in Qatar do not wear their sacred thread. They say that the significance of caste is left behind once they leave the country:

> When we leave home, caste no longer has any meaning, we do not think about it. Thinking about it will give us no advantage. We eat with everyone, we are all friends, there is no benefit (*phaida*) in knowing a person's caste (*jat*). We cannot say "I do not eat impure food (*chokho*)" as happens at home. Here, nobody discriminates (*chuvachut garnu*).

Living together, often without having chosen one's room-mates, implies that in the daily routine caste rules are no longer applicable. However, even though youngsters claim to dislike the system of discrimination, many admit that back home they have to adhere to their parents' rules, seen as more conservative: "My mother suspects that I eat with Kamis. She says that things abroad are different from (*beglai*) what they are in Nepal. In our own courtyard (*agan*) [i.e. house], one must respect the tradition (*parampara*)."

In each migration place, the Nepalese adopt the majority's rule in force and abide by this. It is as though any conflict based on ethnicity or caste is laid aside in migration where resistance to this implicit behaviour may exist but is carefully hidden.

Professional Belonging

In India and Qatar, Nepalese migrants belong to the working class.[33] Abroad, they face their first encounter with the realities of working life governed by strict hierarchical rules and dictated by office hours. The host society considers them as workers who are willing to toil under the sun for hours, for low wages, with no objection. Therefore, their social position is greatly determined by economics rather than by caste or prestige. Yet the gap that exists between the identity attributed by the society in which one lives and the sense of belonging to the working class is not always bridged. Generally speaking, it can be said that nearly all migrants interviewed in India and Qatar come from rural areas and that they and their fathers are peasants.[34] Though the occupation of 'cultivator' is passed from one generation to the next, when abroad the vital link to the village soil is broken. Questions then arise: does being a worker abroad lead an individual to identify with the working class? Is this belonging to the farming world challenged? The question of 'professional belonging' also pertains to the relationship to their village soil and this leads to the question: what kind of space does one belong to? There is no straightforward answer to this question and it differs from Qatar to India.

Work is held in greater contempt in India than in Qatar for various reasons. If we follow Bista (1991), due to the Bahun ideology, manual work in Nepal is regarded with disdain. This is particularly true for higher-caste people in India where all work-related values are highly negative and where compulsion (*badhyata*) explains why men seek work in India for a few months a year. Since India's cultural environment is similar to Nepal's, migrants feel that being a coolie, a watchman, or a road worker is degrading. These jobs are difficult, dangerous, and badly paid. There is little dignity (*ijjat*) in carrying loads in *bajar*s and in living in squalid rooms. Cultural stigmas attached to porterage are expressed by the words *sarma* and *laj* (shame) and may be directly linked to the tradition of low-caste people carrying the wedding palanquin in the Far Western Region (Winkler, 1979). In Delhi, night watchmen complain about being compared to an owl (*ullu*) and of having to beg (*magnu*) for money every month to get their salaries, especially since begging has a low-caste connotation. Finally, it is more difficult and painful to hold down a low-class job in India, whose culture is similar to Nepal's. As working in India is also tantamount to slavery (*gulam*), as mentioned by a few migrants, identifying oneself with the working class is an embarrassment. Being a worker in India means remaining at the bottom of the economic hierarchy, with no social recognition that caste might provide in the village. Compared to the idealistic, cherished vision of a farmer who feeds his family, thanks to his own hard work on his own land, being a worker represents the opposite. One solution adopted by migrants to place some distance between themselves and their occupation in India lies in the vocabulary they use. Migrants will say 'to do the worker' (*laburi garnu*) rather than 'to be a worker' (*laburi hunu*). Another way of rejecting the hated self as a worker is to adopt a new name in India. This is especially the case among lower-caste people who prefer to go by the name of Singh or Thakur to pass unnoticed.[35] Migrants may be considered as having two distinctive professional identities: one inherited and relating to farming, whereas the other is linked to necessity and to low-value work and is rejected. Although migrants come and go[36] throughout their life, they always consider their stay abroad, and thus themselves as workers, as something temporary. They do not join trade unions, even in Delhi where many exist, but which are more geared to permanent Nepalese migrants.

In Qatar, the great distance separating the worker from his hometown is also put forward to explain why migrants do things (such as cleaning toilets) they would not do back home. Working in the Gulf is also described by migrants as a necessity, though many of them also admit that a personal desire to travel, the wish to lead a different life than their parents' drove them abroad. The desire to build a different future for their children is also strong, as Cinta B. explains: "I do not want my son to be a peasant. I want him to study. If my son comes to Qatar, I want him to come as an engineer". Even though many do not have enough food to sustain their own family, there seems to be a lesser proportion of them than among the migrants I met in India. Nevertheless, one thing is clear for all migrants: 'we come to Qatar as workers' (*hami laborma aeko*). What is written on their contract (*labour*) determines the way they think of themselves once they arrive in Qatar, even if they do not know, at least the first time, what it is like to be a worker. Nepalese migrants identify with this collective 'us' because they quickly end up realizing that their individuality as a worker barely exists. As in India, their condition of *majdur* (worker) is seen as similar to that of a slave. 'Who likes to stay in another country as someone else's servant (*nokar*)?' said a young newcomer to Doha. Older migrants also complain about the lack of any possible social upgrading, as if Nepalese migrants were stuck in the labour niche, with no opportunity of ever leaving it. However, the value of work is higher than in India because of what it ultimately enables and because it symbolizes great hope. Men narrate the difficulties of being a cleaner (*cleaning garnu*), yet they overcome their initial reluctance and commit themselves to making a good job of it. Workers from the labour camp I visited have the possibility of taking on a second job, which they call *part-time* and which involves cleaning private houses. They feel that the job is not too undignified, especially in *bideshi* households (i.e. non-Indian) where they are respected (*ijjat*) and earn a good salary. Claiming 'I am a labourer' does not appear to be an embarrassment, even if identification with the working class does not take on a political character in Qatar. Belonging to a union is reserved for Qataris, who make up only 10 per cent of the active population.

Discourses rarely oppose manual labour to agriculture, as was often the case in an oversimplified way in India. Nevertheless, one of the first discussions I had in a labour camp with some young Nepalese was about the sense of shame (*sarma*) associated with cultivating. This surprised me at first and then I came to understand that for many of these migrants, farming can be qualified as 'unmodern'. In Qatar, compared to India, migrants seldom focus on the dignity of agricultural work and rarely emphasize the link between owning fields and producing one's own food. Many of them have a different vision of the future than the migrants I met in India. While they nurture a long-term project in Nepal (buying a house in a town, running a business, or opening a factory), agriculture is no longer appealing. Tensions rise among families when, for example, money sent by a son to buy a plot of land in Kathmandu is used by his father to buy paddy fields in the Terai. The aspirations of different generations change. Such behaviour is also described by Daryn (2003):

Brahmins from the central part of Nepal reject their village identity and contemplate urban life, which is characterized by modernity and equality. Ram B., who arrived in Qatar from Morang district in 2002, puts it this way:

> [D]uring our stay in Qatar, we change mentally. We do not want to plough any more. We can't in any case because we are no longer used to working in the fields. Usually the Nepalese who have worked in Qatar buy land in town. In the village, one has to plough, dig the earth, bring water...we do not have any modern means (*adhunik tarika*) of cultivating, there is no profit (*phaida*) in buying agricultural land.

Whereas, the Nepalese from the Far Western Region dream of staying in their native village to cultivate their own fields or of buying land in the Terai, the migrants I met in Qatar cherish more modern ambitions, given that farming represents old values. This shift from rural inhabitant to city dweller disconnected from agriculture represents a shift in professional belonging and epitomizes the global trend towards towns, which, in the case of the Nepalese, is perhaps accelerated by labour migration to faraway places. Yet one must remember that their aim on returning to Nepal is not to find another job as a worker in a factory, but a job where they are their own boss. The idea of independence in the profession is still strong but is now linked to more 'modern' ways of handling life.

And finally, a word must be said about new ways of consuming that migrants discover in Qatar, and that contribute to making a new sense of belonging, belonging to a youth culture.[37] Spare time in labour camps is used to play carrom, a classic board game shared by South Asians, but also to play with computers, to use mobile phones, CD players, digital cameras, and television. Younger Nepalese migrants spend hours comparing their digital devices, choosing ringing tones for their phone, or sending 'missed calls' to their beloved in Nepal.[38] Among the items brought back to Nepal, digital cameras and mobile phones top the list. Apart from these new consumer products, which are very revealing of the difference between new- and old-comers, men also take an interest in clothing. Such new interests are not likely to reach Far Western migrants in Uttarakhand and in Delhi, unlike what Sharma (2007) says about Palpa migrants in Mumbai. However, these consumer products show that a transition is bound to occur from their parents' low level of consumption to their entry into the consumer society. Experiences abroad[39] play a major part in this transformation, especially for migrants from remote areas.

CONCLUSION: MIGRANTS' MULTIPLE BELONGINGS

When away from Nepal, the Nepalese rub shoulders with people from different geographical backgrounds. They get to know their respective particularities and are aware of the common features they share. In this respect, it can be said that the geographical position of being outside Nepal helps migrants become aware of feelings of belonging they would not express at home. The district as a layer of identification, for example, expands while they are abroad as it constitutes a resource, a means of making friends and of establishing a mutual understanding and familiarity. Whether in India or in Qatar, the daily routine is shaped by migrants' sense of belonging. The Indian experience tends to enhance their identity as a farmer, a member of a special caste, whereas the Qatar experience tends to blur these belongings.

Migrants lead a double life, sometimes antagonistic, in a dual living space. Living abroad may be a reason for leading a life of fewer social constraints as regards social rules, whereas returning to the village means a return to the ideal world as defined by social norms. Working abroad, even though migrants do it for most of their active life, is always thought of as being temporary (*asthayi*) and that is why there is almost no sense of belonging to the host country and little identification with the labour class.

My study also highlights the differences in stereotypes between the regions. If, as appears to be the case, the east (i.e. the would-be 'modern' part of Nepal) is a model and has become a reference of modern life for all other Nepalese people, then a trend seems to have emerged that leads men to identify less with their inherited identity and more with what they personally shape through their *bidesh* experience.[40] Nevertheless, this may not take any collective form. When one studies changes in belonging, from the individual's point of view, the question of the interaction with material ways of dealing with life (one's dwelling place, the kind of house, the kind of job and aspirations) still comes under scrutiny and should be assessed by fieldwork in Nepal.

A question has emerged regarding the creation of a consciousness of world-citizenship. Migrants in India are a long way from achieving this awareness, but in Qatar migrants experience the feeling of being part of the new world of modernism and materialism. Items such as mobile phones or computers (thanks to which migrants assert themselves as *adhunik*) are highly coveted and are a way for those living in rural areas to assert themselves as belonging to a world which is different from their parents'.

NOTES

1. For studies about Nepalese migration in India, see Sharma (2007) and Thieme (2006) among others.
2. It is impossible to obtain accurate figures for Nepalese migrants in India due to the open border and to the absence of any control and of official statistics.
3. The culture of migration can be defined as "the cultural atmosphere that leads many to decide to migrate" (Ali, 2007: 38). It is "those ideas, practices and cultural artefacts that reinforce the celebration of migration and migrants (ibid.: 39).
4. "Social remittances are the ideas, behaviors, identities, and social capital that flow from receiving- to sending-country communities" (Levitt, 1998: 927).
5. I will not study the dimensions of masculinity as have Osella and Osella (2000) regarding Keralite migrants and Sharma (2007) regarding Nepalese migrants in Mumbai.
6. Thirteen months in total: five in Nepal, eight in India.
7. Two weeks in October 2006, three weeks in February 2008.
8. It is worth noting that the same expression 'coming and going" (*aune-jane*) is used in both countries.
9. http://www.kantipuronline.com/kolnews.php?&nid=180417; http://www.myrepublica.com/portal/index.php?action=news_details&news_id=1621
10. Both terms are derogative. Bahadur, as used by Indian employers, is synonymous with coolie and is used to greet any Nepalese person, as if all migrants could be called by a single name. In such a context, the bravery or fierceness of Bahadur, its real meaning, is not referred to and therefore this aspect is not enhanced.
11. It is likely that the inclusion of Nepalese migrants on the Qatari labour market has been favoured by the strong presence of Indian nationals. The relationship between Indians, especially those working in middle and top management, and the Nepalese embodies a historical heritage, given the traditional pattern of seasonal migration from Nepal to India.
12. One migrant even told me that in every corner (*kuna*) of Nepal, everybody knows about Doha's *Nepali chowk*.
13. As most migrants in Kumaon are from far western Nepal, Dotiyali is the lingua franca among the Nepalese. Nepali is used in case they meet Nepalese people from other regions.

14. For example, the NRN (Non-Resident Nepali) day organized on 13 October 2006 at the Nepalese Embassy was only attended by 50 people, mainly chairpersons of associations.
15. See below for a discussion about professional belonging.
16. It must, however, be noted that the number of people from each district differs greatly. Roughly speaking, far western, mid-western, and central regions send far fewer migrants than the western and eastern development regions.
17. This observation is not necessarily applicable to every labour camp in Qatar.
18. It can be noted that district-based associations (often aimed at helping their home region or workers in dire conditions) are commonplace in Qatar, whereas they are non-existent in India. It is as if, in this melting pot where migrants from the same region are scattered throughout labour camps, their sense of belonging to a district is such that it creates a form of guilt towards their home country. This is a common feeling among migrants and prompts them to offer each other mutual help.
19. This statement is confirmed by the fact that in 2001, according to the Nepal census, all migrants from far western districts headed to India.
20. I noticed the same thing in Paris among illegal Nepalese migrants. In a town that is unfamiliar and hard to decipher, finding someone from one's own district is reassuring for new migrants. They have high hopes that meeting people of the same kind will help them solve their lodging and job problems.
21. There are, however, some Qatar-based *janjati* associations.
22. For example, a 'Wild West Triangle' (Rara, Bardiya, Suklaphanta, and Kaptad) programme was launched in 2005 by the Nepal Tourism Board to develop tourism in these remote areas, often considered uncivilized by people from the centre of the country.
23. This was particularly mentioned by a seller of pirated music CDs who goes from one labour camp to another to do business.
24. A *hero* is a male leading actor in a Bollywood movie.
25. One also notes the importance of the district as the base of Nepal's geographical divisions. Such drawings show how the district is a meaningful level of identification for places in Nepal.
26. One's own district or region is often talked about by comparing it with other regions and establishing a hierarchy.
27. Corn eater, a derogatory term (Turner, 1965).
28. Unrefined, rude, villager (ibid.).
29. The features of ethnic belonging have not been studied, although there are at least four *janjati* (Magar, Kirat Yakthung, Tamang, and Tamu) associations in Doha. The fifth one is the Adivasi Janjati Mahasang, which is a grouping of the latter.
30. I have not studied Nepalese *Janjati* associations in India.
31. This kind of normative discourse can be heard very often when talking about caste discrimination. It seems that the theory of no genetic difference between men incites people to spread the idea.
32. It is particularly true for higher-caste Hindus, who constitute 60 per cent of the migrants I interviewed in the Qatari labour camp.
33. There are of course a marginal number of Nepalese migrants who are qualified and have qualified jobs.

34. Cultivation may be a second activity, particularly in the case of low-caste people.
35. This practice is widespread for those wanting to work as cooks and thus pretend to be from a higher-caste background.
36. *Aune-jane* is the expression used to describe temporary migration.
37. See Gardner and Osella (2003); Sharma (2007).
38. A 'missed call' is a way of telling someone 'I'm thinking about you' at no charge: it consists in letting the phone ring once, then hanging up before the other person picks up the phone.
39. In this case, India cannot be considered as much abroad as Qatar.
40. The question is thus raised about the modernization or the Far Western Region through migration.

REFERENCES

Adhikari, R. 2010. 'The "Dream-Trap": Brokering, "Study Abroad" and Nurse Migration from Nepal to the UK', *European Bulletin of Himalayan Research*, 35–36: 122–38.

Ali, S. 2007. '"Go West Young Man": The Culture of Migration among Muslims in Hyderabad, India', *Journal of Ethnic and Migration Studies*, 33(1): 37–58.

Aubriot, O. 2010. 'International and National Migrations from a Village in Western Nepal: Changes and Impact on Local Life', *European Bulletin of Himalayan Research*, 35–36: 43–61.

Bista, D.B. 1991. *Fatalism and Development. Nepal's Struggle for Modernization*, p. 187. Calcutta: Orient Longman.

Bruslé, T. 2007. 'The World Upside-Down: Nepalese Migrants in Northern India', *European Bulletin of Himalayan Research*, 31: 172–83.

———. 2008. 'Choosing a Destination and Work. Migration Strategies of Nepalese Workers in Uttarakhand, Northern India', *Mountain Research and Development*, 28(3/4): 240–47.

———. 2010. 'Who's in a *labour camp*? A Socio-Economic Analysis of Nepalese Migrants in Qatar', *European Bulletin of Himalayan Research*, 35–36: 154–70.

Daryn, G. 2003. 'Bahuns: Ethnicity without an "Ethnic Group"', in M. Lecomte-Tilouine and P. Dollfus (eds), *Ethnic Revival and Religious Turmoil. Identities and Representations in the Himalayas*, pp. 162–73. New Delhi: Oxford University Press.

Gardner, K. and F. Osella. 2003. 'Migration, Modernity and Social Transformation in South Asia: An Overview', *Contributions to Indian Sociology*, 37(1–2): v–xxviii.

Hollema, S., K. Pahari, P. Regmi, and J. Adhikari. 2008. *Passage to India: Migration as a Coping Strategy in Times of Crisis in Nepal*, p. 112. Kathmandu: World Food Programme, Nepal Development Research Institute.

Kandel, W. and D.S. Massey. 2002. 'The Culture of Mexican Migration: A Theoretical and Empirical Analysis', *Social Forces*, 80(3): 981–1004.

Kaspar, H. 2005. '*I Am the Household Head Now*'. *Gender Aspects of Out-Migration for Labour in Nepal*, p. 149. Kathmandu: Nepal Institute of Development Studies.

Khanal, N.R. and T. Watanabe. 2006. 'Abandonment of Agricultural Land and Its Consequences. A Case Study in the Sikles Area, Gandaki Basin, Nepal Himalaya', *Mountain Research and Development*, 26(1): 32–40.

Kibria, N. 2008. 'Muslim Encounters in the Global Economy. Identity Developments of Labor Migrants from Bangladesh to the Middle East', *Ethnicities*, 8(4): 518–35.

Kollmair, M., S. Manandhar, B. Subedi, and S. Thieme. 2006. 'New Figures for Old Stories: Migration and Remittances in Nepal', *Migration Letters*, 3(2): 151–60.

Levitt, P. 1998. 'Social Remittances: Migration Driven Local-Level Forms of Cultural Diffusion', *International Migration Review*, 32(4): 926–48.

Massey, D.S., J. Arango, G. Hugo, A. Kouachi, A. Pellegrino, and J.E. Taylor. 1993. 'Theories of International Migration: A Review and Appraisal', *Population and Development Review*, 19(3): 431–66.

Minami, M. 2007. 'From *Tika* to *Kata*? Ethnic Movements among Magars in an Age of Globalization', in H. Ishii, D.N. Gellner, and K. Nawa (eds), *Nepalis Inside and Outside Nepal. Social Dynamics in Northern South Asia*, pp. 443–66. Delhi: Manohar.

Nagy, S. 2006. 'Making Room for Migrants, Making Sense of Difference: Spatial and Ideological Expressions of Social Diversity in Urban Qatar', *Urban Studies*, 43(1): 119–37.

NIDS (Nepal Institute of Development Studies). 2008. *Nepal Migration Year Book 2008*, p. 90, Kathmandu: NIDS.

———. 2010. *A Final-Report on the Study of 'Remittance Flow and Its Impact on the Economy of Nepal'*, p. 39. Kathmandu: NIDS.

O'Neill, T. 2007. '"Our Nepali Work Is Very Good": Nepali Domestic Workers as Transnational Subjects', *Asian and Pacific Migration Journal*, 16(3): 301–22.

Osella, F. and C. Osella 2000. 'Migration, Money and Masculinity in Kerala', *The Journal of the Royal Anthropological Institute*, 6(1): 117–33.

Ramirez, P. *De la disparition des chefs. Une anthropologie politique népalaise. Collection Monde Indien Sciences Sociales 15–20e siècle*, p. 370. Paris: CNRS.

Sharma, J.R. 2007. *Mobility, Pathology and Livelihoods: An Ethnography of Forms of Human Mobility in/from Nepal*, p. 327. The University of Edinburgh, Anthropology Thesis.

———. 2008. 'Practices of Male Labor Migration from the Hills of Nepal to India in Development Discourses: Which Pathology?', *Gender Technology and Development*, 12(3): 303–23.

Sijapati, B. 2010. 'Nepali Transmigrants: An Examination of Transnational Ties among Nepali Immigrants in the United States', *European Bulletin of Himalayan Research*, 35–36: 138–53.

Thieme, S. 2006. *Social Networks and Migration. Far West Nepalese Labour Migrants in Delhi*, p. 272. Muenster: LIT Verlag.

Turner, A.L. 1965 (1st ed. 1931). *A Comparative and Etymological Dictionary of the Nepali Language*, p. 932. London: Routledge & Kegan Paul Limited.

Uesugi, T. 2007. 'Re-examining Transnationalism from Below and Transnationalism from Above: British Gurkhas' Life Stategies and the Brigade of Gurkhas' Employment Policies', in H. Ishii, D.N. Gellner, and K. Nawa (eds), *Nepalis Inside and Outside Nepal. Social Dynamics in Northern South Asia*, pp. 383–410. Delhi: Manohar.

Winkler, W.F. 1979. *The Evolution of Caste Organization in a Subregion of Far Western Nepal*, p. 380. Madison: University of Wisconsin-Madison.

Wyss, S. 2004. *Organisation and Finance of International Labour Migration in Nepal*, p. 196. Kathmandu: Nepal Institute of Development Studies.

Yamanaka, K. 2007. '"Bowling Together": Social Networks and Social Capital of a Nepali Migrant Community in Japan', in H. Ishii, D.N. Gellner, and K. Nawa (eds), *Nepalis Inside and Outside Nepal. Social Dynamics in Northern South Asia*, pp. 411–42. Delhi: Manohar.

PART III
CREATING TRANSNATIONAL BELONGING

Chapter 8

Belonging and Solitude among Nepali Nurses in Great Britain

The indicators of belonging are not solidly prescribed in any social science discourse, and perhaps they should not be. Belonging is a fluid and palpable experience that will, by definition, vary by subject and over time. With caveats about the dangers of rigid taxonomies in place, however, attempts to establish broad parameters of the experience of belonging—whether in the specific cases we describe here or scaled up to be considered possibly true of the human condition more generally—might be useful.

When they take on the formidable task of defining belonging, Pfaff-Czarnecka and Toffin argue that the experience encompasses (1) "performances of *commonality* ... (2) a sense of *mutuality* ... and (3) material and immaterial *attachments*" (2011: 2). This chapter builds on their project by suggesting that recognizing the exigencies of *location*—or locations—for these parameters grounds us not only in place but also points us towards what is invariably a transitive process between places. Seeing the global as rooted in the local—and then refracting outwards again—is a method recommended by Tsing (2000),

* My thanks to Joanna Pfaff-Czarnecka and Gérard Toffin for patiently encouraging the development of this piece, as did colleagues at COMPAS and the anthropology group at the University of Oxford. Radha Adhikari graciously explained the finer points of the subject to me; I also benefited from comments on earlier versions of the essay when presented first in St. Raphael, and then in Providence, Rhode Island, at Brown University's Population Studies Training Center. David Gellner provided contacts and Bhim Laxmi Sakya offered first-hand knowledge. Martin Kaminer reminded me that professionals outside the academy might be interested, and Ben Eaton offered much care. All errors are mine alone.

who recognizes that our studies necessarily 'take place', be they singly or multiply located.

The case described below charts local networks (or the relative absence thereof) in the global marketplace of health-care providers, specifically nurses. Based on fieldwork with Nepali nurses in Britain and their families in Nepal, it regards how the fields of identity and belonging, singularly and collectively, are experienced and expressed in at least two sets of nation state places. Each may be assessed as a distinct domain in a particular site, but there is also a fluid exchange and interplay between these categories across hemispheres.

Just as two locations of belonging are considered in this essay (Britain and Nepal), two methodologies are invoked: first, ethnographic observation offered material on the conditions of migration and work for Nepali nurses in the United Kingdom, and the kinds of challenges they faced as they tried to settle in—*belong to*—a country that might *become* home (if they were lucky enough to jump over the administrative, financial, and personal hurdles they were to face), but that was not initially their own. Second, the piece contains a policy critique, in that an account of actual people's lives is shown to be at odds with government policies in both Nepal and the United Kingdom.[1] Policy landscapes genuinely aim to find the best solution to social concerns, but in this case, they do not tally with the real-life situation, and in some senses have made people's efforts towards 'commonality … mutuality … and attachment' all the more intractable.

In demographic terms, Britain has an ageing population pyramid, whereby a growing elderly population is projected to need increased geriatric care. But since the 1970s, fewer 'native' women have trained as nurses and health-care providers the elderly need. Nepali women are among the top five nationalities who have migrated to Britain to provide this care. The point of the essay then, is to interrogate the experiences of belonging among Nepali professional women (and suggest that professional belonging should be included among relevant scholarly categories of identity, which in turn need to be multiplied by place), but also to demonstrate a sometimes damaging disconnect between well-intentioned efforts by the British government to enable a multicultural or pluralist society whereby we all belong, on the one hand, and national health-care personnel recruitment policies that precisely prohibit belonging, on the other. Nurses' accounts and experiences cannot easily be reconciled with the well-meaning goals of the UK public health services, however: ostensibly under the protection of nation states on both sides of the globe, it is Nepali professional women who appear to bear the greatest burden of all.

NEPALI MIGRATION TO THE UNITED KINGDOM

In August 2008, the Runnymede Trust reported that the 2001 UK census data counted almost 6,000 Nepalis in Britain (Sims, 2008). At the time, community organizations estimated the number as close to eight times the census data, to number around 50,000. In July 2010, the Centre for Nepal Studies (United Kingdom) estimated over 80,000 Nepalis in the United Kingdom. Undocumented migrants from Nepal or anywhere will likely avoid those asking questions, but these figures may still give us a ballpark number of Nepalis in Britain; although the earlier figure clearly was under-reported, we may also have some indication of the rate at which this figure has grown over the past eight years.

UK Nepali communities differ from Nepali diasporas in other locations, as well as from other diaspora communities in Great Britain, in that UK citizenship was offered to retired Nepali Gurkha soldiers and their families in 2004. Many thousands of Nepali families have migrated legally to England, Scotland, and Wales. Some have been able to buy housing, one significant marker of belonging in any location. Gurkha communities continue actively to discuss fair and equal access to British government benefits, which are sometimes but not always forthcoming; one successful lobbying campaign saw two new Buddhist lamas arriving to serve as chaplains alongside Hindu pandits. Battles continue in the British media about Gurkha pensions and retirement benefits and in the Nepali media (especially among expatriates living in the United Kingdom) about the possibility of dual citizenship—a campaign that should be understood as an insistence that some Nepalis belong in more than one place.

Nepali nurses—all women—migrate to the United Kingdom under different circumstances than do Gurkha family members or university students: they are professional women seeking higher remuneration than they would receive in Nepal or India, and additional training and experience in a career about which they are passionate (*Global Nepali*, 2008). Close to 500 nurses from Nepal have joined the UK nursing register in the past 5 years (Nursing and Midwifery Council, 2006, 2007, 2008); Adhikari estimates that a total of between 700 and 1000 Nepali national nurses are registered and working in the United Kingdom (2008b); many hundreds more have migrated to Britain and await full accreditation. All the nurses referred to in this chapter were trained and qualified in Nepal.

In 2007–08, nurses from Nepal made up the fifth largest number of foreign registrants with the Nursing and Midwifery Council (2008). Despite restrictions in foreign nurse recruitment, the number of Nepali nurses joining the Nursing and Midwifery Council's register annually has remained steady or even continued to grow.[2] When, in 2008, the total number of foreign nurses registering in Britain plummeted to half[3] the previous year's total for political reasons described below—and the number of registrants from other top-ten countries decreased by up to two-thirds—the number of Nepali registrants remained nearly steady (Nursing and Midwifery Council, 2008). Given the dearth of professional nursing opportunities—and the salary levels for health-care providers—in Nepal, there is no doubt that migration is the most appealing option for a Nepali nurse. In an interview in 2008 with two nurses in west London, I was told that more than half—26 out of 45—of their graduating class from one of Kathmandu's most respected nursing schools (attached to Tribhuvan University's Teaching Hospital) had made their way to Britain.[4]

Although absolute numbers are small, the proportional representation of Nepali nurses in the UK Nursing and Midwifery Council register has dramatically increased in the past five years. Less than 10 years ago, in 2003, Nepal did not figure in the top 20 countries of foreign registration until 2003; was listed at number 15 in 2005–06; jumped up to number six in 2006–07; and was ranked number five in 2008 (Nursing and Midwifery Council, 2006, 2007, 2008). Apart from Australia, from where nurse migration is fully legal, and India and the Philippines, which have 'government-to-government' agreements with the United Kingdom, Nepalis are second only to Nigerians as foreign nurse registrants in the most recent register (Nursing and Midwifery Council, 2008). The number of new registrants from almost every other country decreased during this same period. The cachet of migration in Nepal—along with the push factors of almost no work opportunities and extremely badly remunerated jobs—was such that Nepali nurses continued to come in higher numbers even though opportunities for foreign nurses to practice in Britain at the level of their skills and training were decreasing.

PROFESSIONAL BELONGING ON A GLOBAL SCALE: IF YOU CAN'T EXPORT YOUR AGE PYRAMID, IMPORT GLOBAL LABOUR[5]

In Britain, as in most of the world, nursing is an overwhelmingly female profession; in Nepal, it is exclusively so. Since the United States and Europe's women's movement in the 1970s, other professional options have become available to working women in the West,[6] and the so-called 'native' British nursing corps has diminished significantly. In addition, the United Kingdom, like every other state in Euro-America and Japan, has, for the past 20 years, projected a population that would age at a faster rate than it could likely support with its then-current number of elderly carers—especially since the same women who used to care for elderly parents at home were now usually working full time, and not as nurses.

Looking at this wide demographic gap in the projected number of needed nurses, in 2000, Britain's National Health Service announced a recruiting drive for 20,000 foreign nurses, to be hired by 2004, which it subsequently met (Buchan, 2003; 2007). The recruitment policy was astoundingly successful: within 1 year, more than 50 per cent of new nursing registrants in the United Kingdom were foreign. Foreign nurses were the perfect answer to a demographic problem of fewer carers and a proportionately larger (and older longer) elderly population: migrant nurses appeared to be an unlimited labour force of already trained, often hardworking, professional women who would care for an ageing British population; sometimes they were attractive and gentle to boot.

However, policies like those explicit in the Philippines—where the most talented nurses aimed not to work at home but abroad and were supported by their government to do so, in light of the remittances they would send back—gave way to public debates that exporting health-care providers as global labour might jeopardize the provision of health care in home countries. The argument was, and rightly, that economic remittances in the south could not be considered sufficient compensation for the provision of health care in the north if it meant worse health care in the south. In those cases where a sizeable fraction of health-care provider remittances was spent on family members' medical expenses in the home country,[7] the whole system would be shown up as for the exclusive benefit of the north.[8]

Concerns about ethical recruitment were such that the British government did not want to be seen as poaching global health-care labour at any cost.[9] In 2004 (once its recruiting drive had been completed), the Department of Health laid out clear 'benchmarks for international recruiting' unequivocally stating that '[d]eveloping countries will not be targeted for recruitment' (2004: 7).[10] The government also restricted the ability of employers to pay the travel or visa costs of health-care professionals:

> No active recruitment will be undertaken in developing countries by UK commercial agencies ... or by any overseas agency sub-contracted to that agency, or any healthcare organization unless there exists a government-to-government agreement that healthcare professionals from that country may be targeted for employment. (Department of Health, 2004: 10)

The list of developing countries from which nurses were ineligible for recruitment was first published in 2001 and revised in 2004, after which the estimated number of nurses needed in the national health-care system was significantly downsized (Buchan, 2009). In 2006, nurses "were removed from the Home Office shortage occupation list" (Bach, 2010: 99). As of early 2009, every 'developing' nation in the world was on the list, which included 151 foreign countries and exactly mirrored the member roster of the United Nations' list of developing countries. Exceptions—where bilateral Memoranda of Understanding between governments were in place—allowed for recruitment in China, India, and the Philippines (except in certain areas and special cases).

Perhaps unsurprisingly, however, foreign nurse immigration to and registration in the United Kingdom have continued apace since 2004: quite apart from Nepali nurses, approximately 1,000 new African nurses have registered in the United Kingdom every year since 2005.[11] In a span of three years (2005–08), Britain registered more than 30,000 foreign nurses from all over the world. Once a call for labour migration is in place, a network of migrants routed on particular pathways (such as from Kathmandu to London) may be more difficult to stop than policymakers may realize.[12] Seven of the top ten countries from which newly registered nurses came in 2006–07 were on the list of banned states (Nursing and Midwifery Council, 2007). The only way a nurse could now come to Britain was 'of [her] own volition'—meaning, in other words, if she paid for it. In most cases the costs would have to include the help of a private migration agent. In one swift move, the National Health Service downsized, privatized, and outsourced the costs of elderly care onto health-care providers themselves.

So it is not exactly illegal to come as a nurse from a less-developed country; you just cannot be recruited by or work for the UK government or the British NHS. You are on your own. Or rather, you have to come on your own dime, pay your own way, remunerate the agent that places you, work in a private nursing home (or in palliative care rather than in a hospital at skill levels much beneath your experience), and be paid lower wages than your skills would merit. As citizens of states whose currencies are much weaker than the pound you will likely be willing to work for very little—especially as there may be almost no job prospects in your home country. You have to go through the market rather than the government, even though health care is nationalized. You want to work in a hospital, but you are limited to employment in a private nursing home because the hospitals cannot hire you—and there is actually more need for palliative care for an elderly population, which, being brown and female, you are considered well suited to, although you may be a trained nurse with decades of experience.

The great irony of nursing migration is that professional women pose as students, and pay agents to facilitate their move, even though their skills are needed—solicited—by the British government. This construction, surely, constrains a foreign nurse's hopes of belonging. Indeed, according to the British government, she does not belong, either to the country in which she now lives or to the national health-care system in which she now works. All in her own best interest.

Departure and Arrival: Permission, Agents, and Visas

Unlike in the Philippines, where the government has intentionally trained and exported nursing labour, the government of Nepal has worried that sending women overseas might compromise their purity or endanger them. Nepali women could not travel abroad for work until 2001; the ban on travel to the Gulf was not lifted until 2006. Nepali nurses must seek permission from the Nepali Nursing Council to emigrate. In some sense, Nepali nurses have been stymied by both their sending and receiving governments, who appear to want neither to send nor to receive them in the name of their own protection.

Nepali nurses come to the United Kingdom as professional women, but they come on student visas, already a patronizing gesture. Nurses cannot come on labour visas: as we have seen, the UK government cannot formally or informally hire a cadre of Nepali health-care professionals, and labour visas to the United Kingdom are thus unavailable to them. Skilled labour visas (Tier 1 or Tier 2 visas in the United Kingdom; H1 visas in the United States), administered through the central government, do not include nurses from 'third world' countries.[13] Other kinds of labour visas (such as for unskilled labour, including domestic workers) are tied to individual employers, who cannot directly recruit foreign nurses if they wish to be seen as complying with government regulations, and who in turn use not always responsible migration agents to find and place their staff. Agents provide a service to institutions who wish to appear compliant, and they cost their clients—the nurses, not the bureaucracy—a lot of money.[14]

Because only "professionals … who volunteer themselves by individual, personal application, may be considered for employment" (Department of Health, 2004: 7), most nurses who have migrated to the United Kingdom for work since these guidelines were put into place have paid private agents to enable their migration. But these facilitators are not always ethical: the formal ban on recruitment has left the field open for agents whose practices are not properly monitored and who often charge people exorbitant rates to migrate. Networks of private agents, adaptation colleges, and nursing homes have cropped up to fill the gap that government recruitment used to fill: agents now manage the migration, placement, and employment processes of a necessarily isolated individual nurse, who will pay high fees in order to be able to render services that are actually needed of her. Here, as in other cases, legislation designed to protect those seen as less fortunate does not remove barriers but in reality supplements hardship.

Nepali private agents who arrange nurse migration can remain the link to British government structures too intricate for the average layperson to negotiate even years into living in Britain: for example, the gradual progression from student visa to work permit requires guidance and facilitation. It might seem odd that we are mired in a discussion of visa categories and migration management as they refract against belonging—visas seem so administrative, not related to questions of experience at all. And yet this is what my conversations with Nepali nurses focused on: where they had arrived into their professional worlds, as well as local hierarchies, and what obstacles remained to be overcome before they truly fit into—belonged in—the British health-care system.

BELONGING AMONG NEPALI NURSES IN GREAT BRITAIN

Let us create a matrix of belonging through three categories of experience: identity, network, and professional standing. We may consider these elements to indicate one's perception of self, one's links to others, and one's aspirations; they broadly represent what we know of social life and migration processes but they are heuristic variables or categories that are not intended to be exhaustive or fixed.[15] When broken down in this fashion, we see that belonging—or the attempt to belong—does not take place in a singular location but in multiple ones. That is, all three factors in Britain still operate in Nepal, and sometimes affect or are affected by people farther afield too.[16] Belonging in each place has an impact on belonging in the other. A belonging matrix for UK-based Nepali nurses thus poses three categories of experience—identity, network, and professional standing—in each of at least two places.

Identity/Britain

To start with, identity, that most elusive of categories, and in Britain: Nepali nurse identity in the United Kingdom seems first and foremost about being a ... nurse. That my informants were Nepali, and in particular, Newar, was never in question, but the reason for and the focus of their migration to the United Kingdom was to practise nursing, their chosen profession. All were trained at well-regarded Nepali nursing colleges in the 1990s or earlier, and had worked in South Asian hospitals for extended periods of time, a decade or more.

They travelled not to train nor to find work in the first instance, but to advance their professional experience and earn wages in hard currency doing so.

To say that their profession was uppermost in their minds does not denigrate other values or attachments. Being Nepali almost always meant attending Nepali diaspora communal events (such as Nepali New Year or Dasain celebrations), usually religious in nature; being Newar meant collectively celebrating *Mha Puja*, if at all possible. This pattern reflects our traditional understanding of belonging: a person's participation at such events can reify and reinforce a Newar communal identity, or a Gurung or a Buddhist or a Hindu one, even in a diaspora context. Participation, however, was dependent upon professional commitments: nurses often had to forego the social and culinary pleasures of collective *bhoj* or *bhway* because they were on 'duty'. Events were attended when a nurse could plan her work schedule accordingly, by negotiating leave on a particular day (or longer, for a 10-day festival like Dasain).

Natal families of unmarried nurses were sometimes viewed as support, but sometimes as the source of unwelcome pressure to return to Nepal and be closer to home. Marital families also were a core part of women's identities: for UK-based nurses with husbands and adolescent children in Nepal, part of the point of migration was precisely to give their children an opportunity to grow up in the West.[17] Sometimes a nurse might succeed in obtaining visas for her husband and children and the nuclear family might be reunited, even though the assimilation process would have to begin all over again for her dependants. To unmarried informants, the prospects of meeting an eligible Nepali man abroad appeared slim (we offered the idea of *shahdi.com* as one possibility but online dating did not appeal). One nurse did by chance meet and subsequently marry a Nepali man in greater London.

If belonging depends on integral identity, one's category of citizenship or legal status (residence or permission to work) may also be important, as a way to ensure livelihood if nothing else. For all these professional women, identity ultimately appeared linked to structure: the National Health Service and the Home Office in Britain remained the obstacles to belonging in the United Kingdom. Between one and three years into a nurse's stay in Britain, she may graduate from a student visa (when she is permitted to work half-time) and qualify for a work permit whereupon she is legally allowed to work a full week.[18] This transition—from student status to formal work permit—was described as an enormous relief—a significant lifting of 'tension'—when a burden comes off the shoulders. Not only can she earn full-time wages but she can legitimately claim her status as a professional nurse in Britain, by registering with the British Nursing and Midwifery Council. Once a nurse is registered, she properly belongs.

Identity/Nepal

Nursing is a fairly recent professional vocation for women in Nepal; in the 1950s and the 1960s a nurse's white uniform might have been considered foreboding and the profession impure for Hindu women (and being a professional woman was probably neither valued nor seen as entirely appropriate in the first place). Nepali nurses were recruited from the Darjeeling diaspora during that period (Adhikari, 2008a). After *Jan Andolan I*, an increase in private institutions in Nepal's newly liberalized economy meant that training nurses, formerly a state-only regimen, could be privatized in the 1990s. Since 2000, there has been an unregulated mushrooming of private nurse training colleges.[19] Creating new training institutions even when there are not enough jobs is a standard capitalist pursuit, but in this context, nurse training campuses arose at least partly in response to global demand, and with a growing awareness of the potential of economic remittances. The lure of migrating to Great Britain specifically (second only to the United States in the global hierarchy, and with a large Nepali population in place) is such that other forms of identity and belonging—to both people and place—might be voluntarily withheld or suspended among women aspiring to nurse migration.

If, in Britain, primary identity is as a nurse, in Nepal, one primary identity of emigrant nurses is as an Overseas Nurse. A great deal of honour and pride rests on being able to succeed overseas professionally: despite the undeniable hardship of *not* belonging, no nurse I have met returns before she makes it. If a married nurse temporarily puts her professional identity over and above her identity as wife and mother (and invests all available time, money, and energy to facilitate the subsequent migration of her family), an unmarried nurse was concerned not to give in to parental pleas for her return, even in the face of heavy financial burdens, limited work opportunities, and uncertain prospects for the future. Professional identity becomes the way a woman claims herself overseas, far from family.

Once a nurse is professionally established, however—able to afford a plane ticket, and holding a visa status that will not be jeopardized by leaving the United Kingdom—she may visit Nepal. Being able to return to the place where she *really* belongs is a source of enormous relief and delight.[20] (Sometimes parents eventually visit Britain, too; being visited by family in a new location may also enable a greater sense of belonging.) The need to demonstrate having made good, though, can be experienced as pressure: the material objects a woman will bring back to Nepal with her as gifts or as show can cost a good portion of her wages. I have travelled with migrant men and women carrying televisions, phones, cameras, handbags, lipsticks, and coats, in enormous suitcases or in tightly wrapped boxes, intended as gifts for close or extended family members, or for whole households or villages. Commodity capitalism, too, has become a kind of remittance in Nepal.

Networks/Britain

Networks pose a theoretical problem in a matrix demarcated by location because they do not occur in one specific place but by definition are active in multiple sites at the same time: networks transcend and are not confined by space. We can, however, scale them up or down, or move them laterally, to consider Nepali networks in Britain, for example, or to think about how an individual nurse's personal network incorporates both family members in Nepal and group gatherings in Europe. Networks reverberate outward to form overlapping sets of kin, ethnic, and professional circles in Kathmandu, London, Nepal, and the United Kingdom, to name a few locations. And networks change depending on a person's circumstances: a nurse who comes to the United Kingdom on her own, leaving family behind, will forge closer links with other single or solo women like her than she would if she comes with her husband and children to begin with, or successfully negotiates their migration at a later date.

Whether a nurse is alone or with her family, she will likely belong to or participate in religious or ethnic group organizations that reflect her identity. But Nepali nurse networks appear small in Britain because the population is relatively widely dispersed—nursing homes for the elderly are all over the country. The attempt to accrue a steady income (and achieve a degree of belonging) requires women to spend more time in the small towns where they work than in central or urban locations where the Nepali community and festival gatherings are likely to occur.[21]

British Nepali nurse associations do exist, but it can be difficult to attend collective events: a nurse might be on duty, or work a night shift and need to sleep during the day. Online network possibilities for migrant Nepali nurses are not particularly well used, either (*pace* Castells, 1996): zero posts were listed for most of the possible discussion groups on www.nepalinurses.com in August 2008 (one event of note was a Teej festival celebration to be held that month); the website has since expired. The Runnymede Trust also reported that the Siddhartha Nepali Samaj, an organization established for overseas trained nurses, had not had too much success with social events (Sims, 2008): work schedules are heavy and elderly health care is a profession that requires the dispersion of a workforce. Nepali nurses do sometimes attend London celebrations of *Mha Puja* and *Buddha Jayanti* even if they are located some distance from the capital, but especially in the early stages of settling, work comes before anything else and transport is expensive—elaborate attempts to gather can sometimes fail. There is not much time in hand to build or reap the benefits of networks.

Still, anyone who knows about Nepali social connections will not be surprised to know that they are tight in Britain (and that they are active in and connected to family and neighbourhood networks in Nepal, which is really in our second tier of indicators—those experiences of belonging that 'happen' in Nepal, but again, networks are difficult to pin down in any one place). Even if registered professional organizations are not the dominant mode or location of interaction, nurse networks in the United Kingdom do exist among nursing college alumnae, and between friends of connected or neighbourhood families back in Nepal. Professional colleagues in elderly care homes also comprise a network, especially as some institutions are dominated by Nepali staff (in a classic example of 'snowball hiring', possibly combined with employer assumptions that certain nationalities are better suited to specific kinds of work).

Nursing college alumnae networks provide camaraderie and support in the United Kingdom: two young nurses who lived together in a small flat in west London knew each other from their Teaching

College nursing training days in Kathmandu (they also grew up in the same neighbourhood as little girls, they noted, and used to see each other, although they did not personally know each other). Their families were acquainted although they were not from the same *guthi* (one of their families did not belong to any *guthi*, in an unusual case). The two lived together in a family house in London before they moved to a small two-room Hounslow flat, which they kept immaculate, the fridge stocked, at a rent of 500 pounds a month. They much preferred the 'freedom' (and presumably the independence) of their own place, and took a great deal of solace from each other, although one had graduated to a work permit and the other remained at the frustrated status of student, her hours of work limited, and her prospects, for the moment, bleak.[22]

As in any social setting, unanticipated—and transnational—networks may develop. For one informant, sharing accommodation with non-Nepali co-workers (first in London and then in a small English seaside town) meant the novelty of living with nurses (sometimes female and male) of other nationalities, such as Filipinas, Nigerians, or Bulgarians, each with her own culinary tastes and personal style, and the fun of a night out together in a setting new to all of them. Finally, as the carers of elderly people who may not have other social connections, some nurses may find themselves in complex personal or emotional encounters with patients. These circumstances can lead to more intimate social bonds with implications for the inheritance of objects or property. Whether they facilitate or bring about a sense of belonging or attachment will depend on the nurse, the patient, and the specific case under consideration.

Networks/Nepal

Nursing school friendships form one basis of professional and social links for nurses working in Britain; however, diaspora sociality remains very closely linked to family and kin in Nepal. Family networks in Nepal—parents, uncles, husbands, children, and fictive kin—remain the closest ties, even for a woman in Britain. Families likely financed the ventures of migration to begin with and agreed to the child care that would allow the long-term absence of a nurse mother of young or teenage children. If a nurse's family has contacts in Britain, she may not have to rely on an agent for early-stage migration processes, such as being met at the airport or finding a place to stay, and this hospitality can make a big difference in foreign terrain. Networks in this instance are not so much a motivator for migration (Massey et al., 1998), but simply make transitions easier.

Other kinds of networks also need to be considered in the mechanics of migration and the layers or types of belonging they reveal (or inhibit): agents pose their own network about which we know little. Subsidiary networks of agents are partly responsible for maintaining a high (and increasing) flow of nurse migration in the face of significant policy changes (to which agents must adapt, as they did in 2004 by facilitating professional migration through student visas). Agents' fees, however, might counter what Portes calls the 'diminishing costs of migration' (2008: 13): classical theory argues that social networks mean lower costs for migrants, and thus explains the endurance of migration flows even when policies change. But in this instance agents diminish the costs of migration not for the migrant but for the state. In shifting the burden of health-care migration from the state to the migrant, agents become the mediators of professional status.

Navigating the course of belonging in a 'receiving' or 'host' country means that ties to a private agent may remain active even when a nurse is most eager to sever them. The Nepali community in Britain is not large: on one occasion, a gathering of Newars in England included both a nurse who had paid an agent to enable her migration, and the agent she had paid (and for whom, years later, she did not have the warmest of feelings). Belonging, then, may be inhibited in British professionals' settings, and also within Nepali diaspora networks. As isolated women, far from natal or marital families, in awkward social circumstances during ethnic or community religious events, a nurse may at times feel that she does not belong at all.

Professional Standing/Britain

As 'student' nurses, a new arrival must take English language classes and cultural 'adaptation' courses in which all migrant nurses are required to enrol during the early stages of their tenure in Britain. They are also (re-)trained in basic nursing skills. Some sessions appeared to assume no nursing experience whatsoever, as when nurses were trained to draw blood. Informants were generally remarkably good-natured about the number of hours they had to spend in training sessions, except in the domain of nursing. Given the depth of their training and experience in Nepal (and sometimes India), they took offence at the level of skill they were presumed not to have: one nurse exclaimed: "I used to take blood every minute!" Living in England is a desirable goal for many Nepalis, so experienced nurses will migrate there (thus the moral concern on the part of the UK government). But lower levels of skill are required for the work they will likely do.[23]

The two young London-based nurses were not satisfied with their work in a nursing home, and this is a frequent refrain among Nepali nurses working in the United Kingdom; Adhikari calls it a 'dream trap' (2009). They are too well-trained. Of the two, one had worked as a nurse in a major Kathmandu Valley hospital for seven years, and the other had worked in a number of large hospitals in South India. They were frankly bored in a place where their work lives centred on administering pills and monitoring patients. Palliative care did not inspire their passion for work: they would rather be in action. One said her favourite place of work in Patan Hospital was the Intensive Care Unit (although she had also worked in gynaecology and maternity); the other had speciality training in a dialysis and kidney transplant unit. Medical treatment in elderly care homes is very limited: there are no IV lines, for example, and doctors—with whom nurses gain additional technical knowledge—visit only once a week. If migration to Britain is partly about advancing knowledge and skills, nursing home work stymies this objective.

The work arrangement itself for the two women was not bad: they worked in a nursing home nearby (only about 5 minutes away by bus), but it was neither satisfying nor properly remunerated work. The nurse who remained on a student visa after years of experience in both Nepal and India had no clear idea on when her work permit might come through, or why it was taking so long. Her parents sometimes encouraged her to come home: they would implore her to forego the endless administrative trials she faced and return to Kathmandu to marry. But she was determined to stick it out—so much effort, so much money expended so far—in order that she might have something to show. She wanted to succeed as a professional, and obtain higher levels of training or experience, or at least enough money so that it was worth the loneliness and also the enormous sunk cost of visas, migration, and language and adaptation courses. And there was the question of honour: she could not go back before she could prove herself or before she could take enough away to compensate for the sacrifice she felt she had made.

As for any profession, a bureaucratic hierarchy exists regarding which place of employment or institution one finds work with, and at which level. In the United Kingdom, working at an NHS hospital is the Holy Grail, the reason for migration to the United Kingdom, but now entirely unattainable. Over a meal with the two West London nurses, a third, veteran NHS nurse from Nepal recounted the difference in application statistics from the time she applied, in 2000—she was the only applicant when NHS was hiring five nurses—and a recent hire, in 2008, when 45 people applied for a single position; the news was bad enough to curb the appetite of our two young friends, who appeared crestfallen.

A nurse at an elderly care facility in Norfolk took some pride that her title was a nurse, not a carer. She was the lone Nepali staff member in a remote elderly care home in a tiny town far from London and quite isolated. When I went to visit, we met some of her co-workers from Eastern Europe; later she explained that she was 'Nurse-in-Charge' (unlike the two other categories, Carer and Senior Carer). Her rank as a nurse meant that she belonged professionally and she could demonstrate her seniority in new terrain.

Professional Standing/Nepal

In Britain, being a nurse from Nepal usually implies financial and personal hardship, the near impossibility of finding a job with the National Health Service, and the indignities of working on a student visa and being retrained in basic nursing procedures. In Nepal, there is at least a status associated with being an overseas professional. Interestingly and inversely, a degree of national pride about Nepali hospitals remained palpable among overseas nurses in Britain, who claimed, for example, that Nepali public hospitals were much better than those in India and who marvelled at the amount of bureaucracy involved in a profession that they saw as being hands-on. They could not fathom how in Britain there was an elaborate 4-step bureaucratic procedure to summon an ambulance, whereas "in Nepal we called ambulances all the time".

Still, nursing is not seen as a particularly worthy profession in Nepal: new jobs have not been created and government support is limited. Nepali nurses also must obtain formal permission to go abroad (from the Nepali Nursing Council). Of course, they also must seek implicit permission from or an agreement with husbands and family members. But it is the state, not a husband or father, that plays the patriarchal role in this instance; support (or resistance) from families has already been solidly established by the time a nurse begins nursing school and a professional career. What the evidence suggests is that being a transnational migrant means that a professional nurse will be patronized by two governments (Britain's and Nepal's), instead of one.

It is difficult—perhaps something akin to shame—to return to Nepal short of one's goal, no matter how much parents or children may miss a daughter or mother. Personal and family sacrifices in Nepal were made in order to facilitate a nurse's migration abroad: being able to make good on those hopes and dreams is a matter of individual if not family or even national pride. Marriage—the presumed life trajectory for both working and non-working women in Nepal—is either deferred or suspended in order to be an overseas nurse. A married nurse who initially migrated without her husband and children told me that her friends teased her: why had not she come home to Nepal? Did she now have a boyfriend? (Her family eventually obtained visas to join her in the United Kingdom.) Did single nurses plan to marry, eventually? Yes, of course, they told us. But not right now. Right now we are working.

THE FRACTURE THEREIN: THE POSSIBILITY OF NON-BELONGING, OR SOLITUDE

But what of the possibility of not belonging? Those arenas of life we most easily associate with the collective—religious events, for example, or *pujas*—seemed for some nurses to be a private matter, tucked in around the edges of professional aspiration. When I asked a nurse which temple she went to, her response was "Whichever", and when I asked who else attended rituals at the temples in the neighbourhood, she said, "Indians". Religion has not exactly been demoted in this new, migrant context, but its practice has become an individual or solitary pursuit.[24]

Can someone worship alone and still belong? Most certainly; most people do. Does belonging only take place in collectivity? Solitary practice might be considered the inverse of belonging, but there is something to be made of the idea of belonging in oneself, or being comfortable in one's own skin, such that you belong anywhere. This too may be belonging, even if it is solitude.

Solitude may not preclude belonging; nor may belonging be a singular experience. People have a way of finding social connections wherever they might be, and creating bonds for themselves to survive. Belonging to Britain—or being part of Nepali circles in the United Kingdom—can happen in a number of ways. Nepali religious events among immigrants may serve a Durkheimian purpose, for example, by bringing together diverse strands of a single national migrant population (and arguably fostering a common Nepali identity) for Dasain and Nepali New Year. Families may visit from Nepal, or migrate in due course; new generations of Nepalis are born in the United Kingdom, and feel connected to more than one place. Identity and networks determine and are determined by those with whom we connect: mutuality, commonality, and attachment arise in recognition of where and with whom we belong, and these spheres may be multiple.

Policies of Non-Belonging

Nepali nurses voiced their yearnings to belong not in terms of people or places (although distances could contribute to sometimes lonely migration experiences) but through professional aspirations. In their narratives, we see that the concept of belonging must accommodate not only ethnic, kin, and religious identities and the networks that enable and ascribe those identities, but also professional status and a woman's capacity to generate livelihood for her family. Assimilation, to use the sociological policy language that has accompanied studies of migration in the United States (e.g. Guarnizo et al., 2003), would then depend on religious, kin, and cultural identity networks, and also on bureaucratic institutions within which professional women aspire to work. As Bach writes, "nation states continue to exert a powerful influence over the mobility of health professionals" (2010: 95). But British law shifts the burden of recruiting international labour for health-care provision onto the immigrants themselves: the state absolves itself of the obligation to finance the cost of importing a labour force to care for its elderly.

Does migration fracture social networks? No. Personal experience? Not necessarily. Financing health care is perhaps one of the more critical issues of our time; let us ensure that already marginalized migrant women of colour not bear the overhead costs of professional migration to provide global elderly health-care provision. In the interest of fair and equitable working conditions—and the goal of enabling the feeling that they *do* belong—perhaps we can adjust the system slightly, such that women who provide care are themselves benefited rather than burdened. Just because they are arguably the most vulnerable population in the system (migrant women) does not mean they should bear the financial and administrative costs of providing Britain's elderly care.

A system that inhibits belonging does not arise out of malice but out of ignorance. The current or default global market for health-care provision is poised to reproduce the same inequalities all over again, whereby poor women from the south do the least valued work, receive the lowest wages, and are the least supported. The final policy recommendation of a recent report on migrant health-care states we need to "[f]oster public recognition of the ... contribution of care workers" (Cangiano et al., 2009: 208). After all, they are doing our collective work. We would do well to shift our focus and monitor a little more carefully visa, accreditation, and migrant management agents, rather than migrant women themselves.

The question has become not only where is belonging found—in what alternative modes or locations, through which social or electronic organizations and networks—but also how can it be facilitated. If Nepali nurses continue to provide nursing care in the face of increasing needs but fewer nurses trained in Britain—as trained nurses willing to work beneath their skill levels—can we not ensure that travelling as a migrant nurse be a global honour, not an instance of poorly paid and poorly treated women immigrants who must struggle to make ends meet and justify their presence in foreign terrain?[25] This is where the question of belonging belongs.

NOTES

1. Both methods of research for the paper were limited: the ethnographic fieldwork for the paper is in some sense still preliminary, in that it consists of two years of occasional participation in Nepali community events in London and Oxford, a weekend in Norfolk, two visits to Kathmandu, and numerous visits to hospitals.

And the policy landscape (for both migration and health care) is extremely fast-changing; the research for the article was done in 2008–09, and the information was current in October 2009.

2. Seventy-three nurses from Nepal joined in 2004–05, 75 in 2005–06; the number doubles in 2006–07, when 148 joined (Nursing and Midwifery Council, 2006, 2007).

3. This figure is still more significant when one bears in mind that the total work-force of qualified nurses, midwifery, and visiting health staff had increased by 25 per cent between 1997 and 2007 (Bach, 2010: 93).

4. Such a trend has justified the mushrooming of private nursing colleges in Nepal, who have an eye to training nurses for a global market (Adhikari, 2008b), despite the legal and administrative obstacles detailed here.

5. See Kingma (2006) on nurses in the global health-care economy and Bach (2010) on migrant health-care workers in the United Kingdom.

6. Whether we refer to Europe and the United States as the West or the North is a matter of convention.

7. We know this to be the case for 80 per cent of remittance recipients in Mexico, for example (Ray et al., 2005).

8. See Portes (1976) for early work on brain drain.

9. The *Journal of the American Medical Association* reports that a similar policy was under consideration by the American government recently (Gostin, 2008); anecdotal reports suggest that it has already been largely implemented (personal communication with Nepali technician, NYU Medical Centre, New York August 2009). The US Department of Health and Human Services projected in 2002 that the government would need to recruit 800,000 additional nurses by 2020 for elderly care in hospitals and in nursing homes (Gostin, 2008: 1827, based on HHS projections).

10. Once again, Britain was the first country to lay out these guidelines, but the United States may soon follow. Articles expressing such worries in the *New England Journal of Medicine* (Chaguturu and Vallabhaneni, 2005) and the *Journal of the American Medical Association* (Gostin, 2008: 1829) call for 'surveillance' of migrant health-care workers, in the name of 'human rights and global justice'.

11. The *New England Journal of Medicine* reported that 7,000 nurses from Africa registered in the United Kingdom between 2001, when the list was first published, and 2005 (Chaguturu and Vallabhaneni, 2005: 1762).

12. See Tilly (1990) and Massey et al. (1998) for clear expositions of the network theory in migration.

13. See Sassen (1988) and, later, Vertovec (2002) on transnational skilled labour migration.

14. See Anderson and Ruhs (2009) on the notion of semi-compliance to immigration regulations.

15. The list is endlessly malleable: financial status, for example, could be an addi-tional marker of belonging in a given location, or it could be folded into one of the three categories here. Mutuality, attachment, and commonality would at first glance fall within the collective or network category, but of course one's view of oneself (identity) or where one wants to be (aspirations, or, in this case, professional standing) will have an impact on which networks (family, religious, professional, regional) one cultivates or belongs to.

16. One nurse's brother's migration to a European country other than Britain enabled her travel to Scandinavia.

17. Partly for the sake of their children, women with jobs and well established in Nepal move away from their own natal families at a time when elderly parents might need care but for demographic reasons that are the opposite of why developed countries have projected ageing populations—high fertility rates—women from Nepal and other LDCs are usually able to leave elderly parents in the care of siblings. One woman's migration does not usually jeopardize the home care of one's parents.

18. Migration scholars' interest in networks (see below) has of late focused on remittances, in order to track where and how foreign-earned capital is sent 'home' to sending states. But for Nepali nurses in the United Kingdom, years pass before a woman is in a position to earn full-time wages. In the early stage of nurse migration, it is possible that financial returns actually flow the other way in the sending–receiving network (the receiving state receives not only the migrant but also the financial inflow), to help establish a beloved daughter in a new and expensive country. Out-of-pocket expenses to hire agents, buy visas and plane tickets, and pay for the courses that are required prior to UK nurse registration can nowhere near be paid by the half-time work that is permitted on a student visa.

19. Complaints have started in Kathmandu hospitals that wards "were becoming seriously overcrowded with trainees," Adhikari writes. "Professionals started commenting that training standards were compromised, and some hospitals in the Kathmandu valley had more students than the number of hospital beds and patients occupying them" (2009: 22). Given the desirability of an overseas nursing career, however, rates of admission to contemporary Kathmandu nursing colleges are very low. We can gather that talented women are being trained, even in private colleges, such that they could be well qualified for elderly care.

20. One nurse I spoke said she could not return to Nepal until she obtained her work permit: the money required for the plane ticket did not seem worth it. (Also, I suspect, she felt she could not go until a certain hurdle had been jumped and a certain measure of success achieved.) Another nurse, who had already obtained her work permit, opted not to return because the cost of the ticket would cut so far into the savings for which she had come to Britain in the first place.

21. Nepali Nursing Association UK.

22. She did, in due course, obtain a work permit and relocate to an elderly care home in Essex.

23. A long-term labour migration policy oriented towards elderly care might consider the recruitment of more recently trained nurses or nurses with less training given that (1) lower skill levels may be required for palliative care than for tertiary care and (2) new health-care professionals in the United Kingdom are required to undertake basic levels of training in any event.

24. Whether this shift resembles the work ladder she and her fellow nurses have started to climb *a là* Weber's rationalization thesis is something we may wish to pursue.

25. Before we end, let us note that by 'migrants' both scholars and policymakers are referring to labourers who have moved from non-OECD states (Organisation for Economic Cooperation and Development) to OECD ones. Put simply, this construction means people who travel from poor countries—those places that

used to be known as Less Developed economies and are now collectively known as the South, although in some cases they are further north than the North—to rich ones, not the other way around, whose structurally analogous migrants are called 'expats', 'development workers', or 'volunteers'. Migrant is not a value-neutral or a geography-neutral term: no Peace Corps doctor would ever be referred to as a 'migrant health care worker'. Indeed, we might consider using the Peace Corps as a model to facilitate an expatriate Nepali Nursing Corps that could provide elderly care needs all over the world.

REFERENCES

Adhikari, Radha. 2008a. '"If You Have to Clean up Shit, Then It's Best to Do It for Greater Personal Profit!"': The Expansion of the Nursing Education Industry in Nepal and International Migration'. Paper presented at Scottish Centre for Himalayan Research, 1 March, Edinburgh.

———. 2008b. '"The Business Nursing Complex": Understanding Nursing Training in Nepal', *Studies in Nepali History and Society*, 13(2): 297–324.

———. 2009. 'The Dream Trap: Nepali Nurses in the British Health Care System'. Paper presented at School of Oriental and African Studies, Centre for Diaspora and Migration Studies Seminar Series, 18 February, London.

Anderson, B. and M. Ruhs. 2009. 'Semi-Compliance and Illegality in Migrant Labour Markets and Analysis of Migrants, Employers and the State in the UK', *Population, Space and Place*, 16(3): 195–211.

Bach, Stephen. 2010. 'Achieving a Self-Sufficient Workforce? The Utilization of Migrant Labour in Healthcare', in Martin Ruhs and Bridget Anderson (eds), *Who Needs Migrant Workers: Labour Shortages, Immigration and Public Policy*, pp. 87–118. Oxford: Oxford University Press.

Buchan, James. 2003. *Here to Stay? International Nurses in the UK*. London: Royal College of Nursing.

———. 2007. 'International Recruitment of Nurses: Policy and Practice in the United Kingdom', *Health Services Research*, 42(3): 1321–35.

———. 2009. 'Achieving Workforce Growth in UK Nursing: Policy Implications and Options', *Collegian: Journal of the Royal College of Nursing Australia*, 16(1): 3–9.

Cangiano, Alessio, Isabel Shutes, Sarah Spencer, and George Leeson. 2009. *Migrant Care Workers in Ageing Societies: Research Findings in the United Kingdom*. Oxford: ESRC Centre on Migration, Policy, and Society (COMPAS).

Castells, Manuel. 1996. *The Rise of the Network Society: The Information Age Economy, Society, and Culture*, vol. 1. Oxford: Blackwell.

Chaguturu, Sreekanth and Snigdha Vallabhaneni. 2005. 'Aiding and Abetting: Nursing Crises at Home and Abroad', *New England Journal of Medicine*, 353(17): 1761–63.

Department of Health, 2004. *Code of Practice for the International Recruitment of Healthcare Professionals*. Available online at www.dh.gov.uk/publications

Global Nepali. 2008. Care and Share. October/November: 56.

Gostin, Lawrence O. 2008. 'The International Migration and Recruitment of Nurses: Human Rights and Global Justice', *Journal of the American Medical Association*, 299(15): 1827–29.

Guarnizo, Luis Eduardo, Alejandro Portes, and William Haller. 2003. 'Assimilation and Transnationalism: Determinants of Transnational Political Action among Contemporary Migrants', *American Journal of Sociology*, 108(6): 1211–48.

Kingma, Mireille. 2006. *Nurses on the Move: Migration and the Global Health Care Economy*. Ithaca: Cornell University Press.

Massey, Douglas S., Joaquin Arango, Graeme Hugo, Ali Kouaouci, Adela Pellegrino, and J. Edward Taylor. 1998. *Worlds in Motion: Understanding International Migration at the End of the Millennium*. Oxford: Clarendon Press.

Nursing and Midwifery Council. 2006. *Statistical Analysis of the Register*. Available online at www.nmc-uk.org/aDisplayDocument.aspx?documentID=3593 (last date of access: 1 April 2005–31 March 2006).

———. 2007. *Statistical Analysis of the Register*. Available online at www.nmc-uk. org/aDisplayDocument.aspx?documentid=3600 (last date of access: 1 April 2006–31 March 2007).

———. 2008. *Statistical Analysis of the Register*. Available online at www.nmc-uk. org/aDisplayDocument.aspx?DocumentID=5730 (last date of access: 1 April 2007–31 March 2008).

Pfaff-Czarnecka, Joanna and Gérard Toffin. 2011. 'Introduction: Belonging and Multiple Attachments in Contemporary Himalayan Societies', in Pfaff-Czarnecka, Joanna and Gérard Toffin (eds), *The Politics of Belonging in the Himalayas: Local Attachments and Boundary Dynamics*, vol. 4, pp. xi–xxxviii. New Delhi: SAGE Publications.

Portes, Alejandro, 1976. 'Determinants of the Brain Drain', *International Migration Review*, 10: 489–508.

———. 2008. 'Migration and Social Change: Some Conceptual Reflections'. Keynote address presented to COMPAS Annual Conference, 1 July, Oxford.

Ray, Kristin Michelle, B. Lindsay Lowell, and Sarah Spencer. 2005. *International Health Worker Mobility: Causes, Consequences, and Best Practices*. Roundtable paper from working discussion at Institute for the Study of International Migration. Washington DC.

Ruhs, Martin and Bridget Anderson. 2009. 'Semi-Compliance and Illegality in Migrant Labour Markets: An Analysis of Migrants, Employers and the State in the UK', *Population, Space, and Place*. Earlier version available online at www. compas.ox.ac.uk/fileadmin/files/pdfs/WP0630_Ruhs_Anderson_a.pdf (last date of access: 8 October 2011).

Sassen, Saskia. 1988. *The Mobility of Labor and Capital: A Study in International Investment and Labor Flow*. Cambridge: Cambridge University Press.

Sims, Jessica Mai. 2008. *Soldiers, Migrants and Citizens: The Nepalese in Britain*. London: The Runnymeade Trust.

Tilly, Charles. 1990. 'Transplanted Networks', in Virginia Yans-McLauglin (ed.), *Immigration Reconsidered: History, Sociology, and Politics*, pp. 79–95. New York: Oxford University.

Tsing, Anna. 2000. 'The Global Situation', *Cultural Anthropology*, 15(3): 327–60.

Vertovec, Steven. 2002. *Transnational Networks and Skilled Labour Migration*. Transcomm Working Paper Series. Available online at www.transcomm.ox.ac. uk/working%20papers/WPTC-02-02%20Vertovec.pdf

Chapter 9

Culture on Display

Metropolitan Multiculturalism and the Manchester Nepal Festival

BEN CAMPBELL

In 1998 I saw an article in the *Kathmandu Post* reporting a visit to Nepal by the Lord Mayor of Manchester. It was part of the build-up to a festival to be held in Manchester that would celebrate Nepali culture and promote understanding and trade. This took me by surprise as I had been living in the Manchester area for several years but had not heard about this planned event. The first of these festivals had taken place in 1996. By the time the next one was organized, in 2004, I had been given a seat on the festival's organizing committee.

This chapter discusses two of these festivals, and raises issues of belonging to think about processes that can be seen at work in the presentation of Nepali culture both for the diaspora community and for others to enjoy in celebratory mode. There is a kind of festive belonging involved in the way such an iconic place as Manchester's neo-gothic Town Hall is transformed into a partial simulacrum of Kathmandu's tourist bazaar area Thamel. The colours and energy of the stalls, the photographs of the classic landmarks, and the performances of song and dance announce an unmistakable presence of Nepalis, charmingly packaged up for consumers of cultural diversity. The visually impressive combination of retail items, trays of *dal bhat*, and themed programme of events demonstrates how Nepalis can recreate a version of 'belonging' while abroad. This makes an impact both on the participants who reconfirm a belonging in one way or another to Nepal, and on the curious members of the society in which

Nepalis have settled, who witness the shop-window assemblage of a culture on display—in a post-industrial city in northern England.

Is this, though, a culture from 'afar', or something that is partially formed by realities of belonging nearer at hand? Where is the civic centre of gravity in the affective networks of intentional recognition among the participants? The Mancunian Nepali families have children who all speak with the fast, friendly wit-tinged dialect of the locals. They perform national distinctiveness at the festival, within a series of similar events, when the Irish celebration of St Patrick's day, Chinese New Year, and the 'Asian' mela take their turn to hold the attention of the city. The Nepali festival, in other words, belongs comfortably within the mainstream self-image and performance of a multicultural metropolis. However, there are 'backstage' incidents discussed in this chapter, which demonstrate how the 'front stage' performances are controlled and contested in terms of what is deemed permissible for public airing and what possibilities for viewing Nepal are foreclosed. Being Nepalis in the United Kingdom, and marking out performative public space to put across the attractiveness, tenacity, and liveliness of Nepali culture for the new environment of belonging, requires putting together a staged version of what can be considered typical and appropriate elements of life in Nepal. Of necessity, this is made up from a combination of materials and skills available already among the UK and Manchester diaspora, with some special display items, racks of eye-catching and relatively cheap imports of Thamel bazaar clothing and other produce, and select persons brought in from Kathmandu to boost the authenticity of connectedness to the national home. The whole cultural package is given a seal of approval with an ambassadorial visit, to encourage tourism and investment.

The professionalization required for staging multicultural events calls on organizational values that run counter to the energetic goodwill of the mass of voluntary contributors. Although Nepali culture indeed has to be packaged up and commodified in the process of making a festival and providing the public with an experience of varied kinds of consumption that is accessible and enjoyable, the commodity logic has disturbing effects. Professional etiquette, standards, and forms of organization are aspired to for an event of this type, but there are problems where claims to professional levels of remuneration are refused, and voluntary giving 'for the good of Nepal' becomes a rhetoric heard in inverse proportion to the budget for the whole enterprise. The less money available, the more pressure to work for the flag.

Gilroy's (2004) discussion of multicultural capitalist society provides some inspiration for understanding the context of Nepali culture on display in Manchester. He reflects on the role that consuming difference has in late modernity, as compared to old ideas of race. Cultural diversity has become a positive value in UK national and metropolitan public policy since the adoption of integrationist models for immigrant minority groups, giving a new arena for state legitimacy (Favell, 2003); however, Gilroy is concerned with changes in how capitalism reshapes the ideas of embodied difference by which people now fashion their bodies, their selves, and their stylistic allegiances to communities of belonging. Cultural diversity is prominently displayed on supermarket shelves and offers attractive variety for consumption. Gilroy explains how systems of raciological discourse have shifted from colonial economies of racial divisions of labour, (recall how Gurkhas were recruited from 'martial tribes and races'), to difference being expressed by reference to optional consumption styles, which can offer purchasable parts of otherness, in kinds of dietary taste, and musical and hairstyle choices among other potential choices. The case of the engagement with cultural difference enabled by the Nepal festival makes use of 'dominant' municipal registers of cultural affiliation and belonging, with some 'demotic' retail pleasure too (Baumann, 1997).

A tailored package of multicultural consumption was fashioned for the citizens of Manchester to come and appreciate a flavour of Nepali food, song, dance, handicraft, and history. This calls on an understanding of belonging that operationalizes aspired links of mutuality, and attachment in a kind of *jatra* congregation, of formal and informal civic commitment shown by the public that includes British people who have links to Nepal, as ex-Gurkhas, volunteers, mountaineers, and spiritual seekers. The hats, jackets, or clothing made in Nepal stand out from the local shopping centre's offerings, and wearing them can be seen as a badge of boutique niche market access to cultural diversity. The Nepal-branded produce evokes an invitation to the British public as Gilroy argues for black cultural affiliation being indexed by David Beckham's choices of jeans and dark glasses. Being Nepali abroad finds corresponding movements from the host community of recognizing aspired-to relationships of conviviality and mutual participation in a performance of culture.

The mutualisms at work in the relations between diaspora organizations and the local government for enhanced legitimacy (as actors for multicultural citizenship) are clearly of a different kind from those between the festival stallholders and the curious viewing publics. Participation in the acts of performative cultural distinctiveness rubs off on the sense of belonging as a guest in a staged arena of shared community space. This invites formal politeness and corresponding diplomatic gestures of greeting, gift giving, as well as more cash-based exchanges that contribute to the facilitating cosmopolitan ethos that celebrates diversity of this kind. The festival gives an occasion for self-identifying multicultural citizens to present themselves. In important ways, this builds on networks of jobs and entitlement in a 'multicultural sector' of public life, so that people working with immigrant groups, refugees, and asylum-seekers would be attracted to this kind of event. Events such as the Notting Hill carnival have popularized festivals as a vehicle for celebrating contemporary diversity that also evoke historical continuities of festive traditions in the United Kingdom (Olwig, 1993).

There are a number of rhetorical tropes whereby the Nepalis in the United Kingdom can exercise claims of relationship to the British public. Foremost among these is the Gurkha connection, which can inspire cross-generational sentiments of solidarity, especially among older people who have served in the armed forces or whose parents would have told them about Gurkha bravery in the war zones of Burma and Malaysia. This is a historical relationship that can trigger emotive bonds of association that evoke mutuality through episodes of shared historical interdependence, even if a British person has never been to Nepal. Other pathways of mutuality can be built up between Nepalis and the British locals that work through more personalized recognition, for example, individuals who have been transformed by mountaineering or trekking holidays in Nepal. Shangri-la imagery of wondrous experiences and landscapes typically feature in the British visitor's account. People who have been to Nepal as volunteers or workers in the health and development, conservation, and education departments give other reasons for their affection or empathy with Nepalis who have come to the United Kingdom. Nepali interpersonal etiquette is both ritualized and relaxed with regard to strangers, and shows a genius for making foreigners feel welcome in Nepal (by personal warmness and attention, bestowal of kin terms for inclusion in domestic circles, and intimacy with a unique place). The festival in Manchester works to trigger again such sentiments and to deploy orientalizing far-away, magical land imagery to play into the register of integrationist multicultural policy that pretends to facilitate an encompassing logic of civic diversity inclusion (Baumann, 2005).

A further sense in which the Manchester event is a phenomenon that is to do with the near, rather than coming from afar, is that the Nepalis who do attend the festivals (and the other more regular gatherings of the Himalayan Yeti Association in the United Kingdom) are the Nepalis who have 'arrived' and are happy to be seen, as opposed to those who do not want to be conspicuous, or to have their rights for being in the United Kingdom possibly brought into question. In this sense the festival marks the belonging in Manchester (or the United Kingdom more generally) of those who want to distinguish themselves from Nepalis who are present, but without permanent rights or legitimate paperwork. This is important in relation to the question put by the editors of this volume "When do we belong?", and in staging an event of belonging, it is worth noting that internally differentiated markings of presence and absence are produced by the public display of belonging.

Nepalese migration to the United Kingdom has consisted, in the main, of doctors and nurses, restaurant owners and workers, students, and spouses of British men and women who met in Nepal. Since 2009 there has been an increased right for ex-Gurkha soldiers to live in Britain.[1] The 2001 census of 30,000 people of Nepali origin is considered an underestimate, and the likely figure is more probably around 100,000 (Adhikari, 2012). Core concentrations are in Reading and outer London; I have even attended Dasain gatherings in rural Lincolnshire. One estimate is there are roughly 100 organizations formed by Nepalis in the United Kingdom. In Manchester the restaurants are the most visible community, and actively enhance the diversity of South Asian cuisines available in the city. There are half a dozen very fine such restaurants (Rajdoot, Great Kathmandu, Jai Kathmandu, Gurkha Grill, Nepalese Village, Nepalese Kitchen) with others rapidly building reputations. Speaking with some former students at Manchester University, they told me there was an insider–outsider barrier depending on visa status that they had encountered when they had attempted to make contact with the resident Nepali community. As I make plain in later sections, there is a Bahun–Chhetri–Newar predominance both in the organizational life of the Nepali Associations in the United Kingdom and in the cultural forms with which they seek to represent Nepal.

METHODOLOGY AND ETHICS

I am writing as a participant in the social interactions and cultural production that this chapter is concerned with. This does not mean I believe I have done 'proper' fieldwork with the Nepali community in Manchester. Rather than announcing myself as an anthropologist at work, I have been an anthropologist who happens to be a member of the festival organizing committee. Now, there is a twist to this position of distance. For several years I have held a certain theory about the British middle classes. To understand who they are, anthropologically, 'in the round', as social actors expressing their selective individualism, it is not enough to see them at home or at work, but also *in committee*: in evenings spent with cups of tea and biscuits, agendas, apologies, and AOBs. With the ordered environment of a chairperson, a treasurer, a membership list, a newsletter, and a cause, the British middle class person emerges as a social phenomenon, voluntaristically embracing civic responsibilities. This is a function that the habitus of the Manchester-resident Newar community seems to be 'at home' with too.

I have witnessed the inside of committees from village planning response groups, to organic gardeners, cooperative housing projects, anti-racism organizations, and residential groups for maintenance of unadopted roads. Although the context of a committee form enables a certain kind of person-in-public to come through and affords a stage on which matters of importance play around in the personal chemistry of the committee members, there are notably British rules of etiquette and procedure. One of these is not to get too personal and overstep that sensitive frontier marked as encroaching into another's privacy beyond the context of relevance for the given committee's assembling. As a committee member for the festival, I have observed the meetings, attended related 'social functions', but have remained within that persona. So I have not done fieldwork in the way I would expect to if I were to be on a funded project to research the Nepali diaspora, checking facts from different angles, running in-depth interviews, taking up other kinds of roles than committee member, and inserting myself in the flow of events and relationships necessary for a 'holistic' fieldwork experience.

THE MANCHESTER NETWORK

I had come to know some of the Nepali restaurant owners, workers, and their families, in part due to the proximity of the Great Kathmandu restaurant to the former home of Tim Ingold, where anthropology department seminar speakers were often entertained in the mid 1990s. I attended the occasional New Year and Dasain-Tihar social events organized by the Himalayan Yeti Association held at the Manchester Police sports centre.[2] The Himalayan Yeti Association is organizationally based in Manchester where Dasain-Tihar (as one event) and Nepali New Year are celebrated, but it holds further meetings at different locations around the country where groups of Nepalis have settled. I heard of the Nepali language lessons run at a library on Saturday mornings. Then a student at Manchester began working on an MA thesis about the royal family massacre, and she drew me into an evening at one of the restaurants in south Manchester to help launch fund-raising for the forthcoming festival. Here I met the dynamic impresario of the Manchester festival, Puspa Shrestha. Originally from Pokhara, he has lived in Manchester for 30 years. He has an Irish wife, and a daughter. It was his realization that many of the children born to Nepali parents were likely to lose touch with Nepali language competence, that had motivated him to start the language classes. The evening I met him, Puspa told me I should 'give something back to Nepal', and hoped I would join the committee. An evening of entertainment was provided to the invited clientele, including dances by Charan Pradhan[3] who had studied performing arts at a college in Oldham, Greater Manchester, and to add a multi-cultural flavour, there was a belly-dance show by a local woman.

When the 2004 Nepal Himalayan Festival organizing committee met for the first time on a Saturday afternoon in a room at Withington library, a mixed gathering of members of the Nepali community and other invited volunteers was present. The story of the previous festivals was told, and roles within the committee were discussed. The organizational core for the Manchester festivals grew out of the language classes and the group of families that sent children to them. Puspa Shrestha already had some contacts within Manchester City Council in the field of education, and his welcome multicultural face within the predominantly white municipal establishment had prompted encouragement to put on a festival. The first festival had required a strong coalition of Nepalis and non-Nepalis to help put all the necessary elements together organizationally (with advertising and marketing to potential audiences), and in such a way that the programme of events would draw a wider public interest than the appeal of Nepal alone would achieve. Therefore, the *relationship* of British and Nepalis became a common element. The 1996 festival relied heavily on the enthusiasm and public celebrity of Mike Harding to generate interest. Well-known as 'The Rochdale Cowboy',[4] for many years he had a TV show of folk and country music (and is still a DJ on BBC radio 2). He had done a trek in Nepal and spoke of its transformative effect on him. He and Sir Edmund Hillary as the main attractions, with a spectacular formation march of the Gurkha brigade band, provided an attraction for the wider British public to come and make the first festival a success. The main figure to attract the public at the next festival was Doug Scott, the first Britisher to climb Everest, on Chris Bonnington's 1975 expedition.

In the first meeting I attended of the organizing committee, roles were assigned for president, treasurer, secretary, and for the specific task areas of stalls, fashion show, cultural programme, speakers, films, marketing, and publicity. After a good turnout at the first meeting, subsequent committee meetings, held approximately once a month for the year running up to the festival, were less well attended. Attendance rose again closer to the event as stress levels increased. Most of the song and dance programmes consist of performances from Manchester-based families. In 2004 and 2008 the band of the brigade of Gurkhas was not available due to commitments in Iraq and Afghanistan.

Several of the committee's organizational positions were held by 'British' people from the Manchester region, who have developed connections with Nepal and the UK diaspora, and they frequently have other family members who have worked in Nepal. One of these is Dave, who I had supervised for his MA on the Bhutan refugee situation, and who had secured a job with the Oldham town council offering various kinds of provision for people seeking asylum in the United Kingdom. Another 'British' member of the committee is the formidable Linda Sherpa, who spends her time partly in Kathmandu and partly in the high Pennine valley of Rossendale. Her main role is to coordinate the exhibits coming from Kathmandu, including photographs, paintings, and textiles. Others share in the sense of Nepal having affected them powerfully in one way or another, and have ongoing connections with organizations and individuals from Nepal apart from the festival. The very demanding role of festival organizing committee secretary has always been held by an English woman. Both the festivals I participated in struggled to find funding, and the Himalayan-Yeti Association has had to subsidise the event.

On any one occasion, the committee normally consisted of roughly half Nepali and half British people and rarely numbered more than 10. It has run with an ethos of inclusivity and welcome openness to newcomers who have any appropriate idea or skill to offer for the festival. It needs an informality suited to voluntary organizations, with the chairman occasionally having to use firmer nationalist rhetorical methods to improve attendance or require people to perform the tasks they are responsible for. The festival committee is conscious of different communities it needs to mobilize: the Manchester-based Nepalis and UK-wide Nepalis, and the different kinds of interest groups in the Northwest of England who appreciate different elements of the festival programme—mountaineers, back-packer travellers, Buddhists, teachers, and volunteer organizations. In the lead up to the festival, several meetings need to be held in the Town Hall itself to map out activities and coordinate with relevant staff from the city council. In 2008, Nepalis on the committee included the son of the owner of one of the most popular Nepalese restaurants, who took on the role of website manager for the festival, and restored it after a hacker attack. Others are teachers, doctors, nurses, accountants, and travel firm workers. A majority of them are Newar speakers.

CULTURE AND CAPITAL

Funding for the festival is always a difficult issue. A certain amount comes from the city council, which also provides the impressive venue of the Town Hall, but roughly £40,000 is necessary to cover all expenses: paying travel fees and accommodation for speakers and performers, providing audio-visual technical support (all the production and technical costs on the festival site in 2008 came to £13,100), paying for publicity in appropriate media, designing and distributing leaflets and posters, and covering costs of telephone calls, stationary, and postage incurred by committee members. Money comes in from businesses and charity organizations that run stalls, and a charge has been made for tickets to hear the 'big name' speakers.[5] If 'Himalayan' celebrities can be lured to the event, big attendances can be planned for. In 2008 Reinhold Messner, Chris Bonnington, Michael Palin, Roy Lancaster, George Schaller, and the Dalai Lama unfortunately all had schedules over a year in advance, which made them too busy to commit to the festival. A 'public relations' company had joined the committee by the autumn of 2007, and had found a celebrity as the potential main attraction for the Saturday evening: comedian Rowland Rivron who had appeared in a TV show 'Extreme Celebrity Detox' set in a Himalayan location. This had also featured the late Tony Wilson (of Manchester's Hacienda, and Factory Records) and Magenta Divine of the Rough Guide show. The PR company withdrew due to a breakdown in communications with the committee secretary who considered them incompetent. They had booked an interview for the cable TV 'Channel M' on the wrong day prior to the festival, and had failed to place advertisements on time in the regional magazines. (In fact, their main contribution of finding a Saturday main speaker had fallen foul of rights to use footage from the TV programme he had appeared in). Prashanta Tamang, the young policeman from Darjeeling and winner of the Indian Pop Idol competition, was going to be in the United Kingdom at the time of the festival, making three appearances. He would have been a huge draw, but his PR quoted a performance fee of £10,000.

For the 2004 festival, funding bids were put in to arts, and 'community and diversity' organizations, as well as the national lottery. None of these was successful. The evidence for competent account keeping from previous festivals may have been an issue. For the 2008 festival, planning started in early 2007, but even by October 2007, when it is the time for most of the deadlines for many funding bodies, a convincing set of accounts still had not materialized from the previous festival. This was despite talk of 'never again' from non-Nepalis, who held secretarial roles through the previous events, and although there was much exhortation that a more professional stance would be taken for 2008, the principal source of accounting information within the Town Hall network could not be located. He had played a key role in liaising between the festival organization and the city council, and had the most officially prepared set of figures. His previous role within the city council set-up had since been 'outsourced', so he had become freelance and therefore his contact details had altered. Other advice was taken that sponsorship rather than grants should be targeted, but despite applications made to Manchester airport, and companies located in and around the city (Qatar Airlines, Manchester Evening News), Nepali companies (e.g. Khukri Beer), and NGOs such as Water AID, the only bid that had been successful was for a performing arts source to help pay flights for a musical group from Kathmandu.

The festival organization was not completely without support. There was the city council to which a bid for £18,000 was being prepared, and the Himalayan Yeti Association's executive committee had put up £10,000 as a figure to draw on as running costs for getting the event moving. The Asian mela receives £16,000 every year from the city council, and does not even put on the range of programme the Nepali festival offers; hence, some of the Nepalis claim they are due a similar figure. Bargaining is conducted to ensure no disadvantage occurs. In 2004 the European election clashed with the festival dates, and being therefore deprived of use of the Great Hall within the building, where voting papers are counted and kept, the committee made known its sense of grievance, that the festival would be unduly deprived of the key venue as a result. A claim for compensation was even contemplated, until the main debating chamber and other considerations were made available to improve matters.

In March 2008, less than three months from the festival, it still looked like the only funding was £5,000, coming from the city council. At this point corporate contacts within the Nepali community were approached. The Nepal embassy was to be asked for assistance too.

At the April meeting, late in the day, I suggested I could ask Canon (who lent the cameras used in my recent film project) if they would be interested to sponsor the festival. The committee members rapidly set the price at £20,000 for the whole event to be named 'The Canon Nepal-Himalaya Festival', which would go out in all the publicity and be emblazoned on a banner in front of the Town Hall for two weeks. It transpired this was too little time for Canon to respond.

With so little money to play with, up to the last minute bookings at hotels were being cancelled, or relocated to cheaper venues.

THE DIASPORA CONTEXT OF CULTURE ON DISPLAY

The festival's cultural content reflects locally available talents and the cultural preferences of the organizing committee, which tend to serve dominant rather than demotic diaspora demographics and registers of cultural life. Asylum seekers and transient kitchen workers are not greatly in evidence at the events hosted by the Himalayan Yeti Association. None of my Tamang contacts in the United Kingdom have ever felt inclined to come to the events organized in Manchester. One of them, who is working as kitchen staff in an English east coast holiday town, is happy enough to be taken for a Chinese there, and not worry about correcting others' ideas of his national origins. Conditions of work for many Nepalis are extremely demanding. Talking with some of the restaurant workers has impressed on me the long hours of toil involved: "People in Nepal think if you have work in UK you will be happy. They have no idea how much you have to work, only work."

Doctors and teachers are prominent among the professional Nepalis living in the United Kingdom who belong to the association. Others work in IT, and the restaurant business. I have not done research to see if marriages have a greater frequency among UK-resident Nepalis, or whether as Werbner (1999) found for Pakistani families in Manchester, subcontinental marriage partners are preferred.

The Association has evolved an annual calendar for gathering together at different times. Apart from the Nepali New Year and Dasain-Tihar celebrations, there is a growing taste for British-styled activities such as the summer picnics held at Tatton Country Park in Cheshire, when family outdoor entertainments include egg-and-spoon races, and weekend walking holidays in the Lake District, or Wales. Visits to the hills and mountains are written up as 'making a successful attempt' on mount Snowdon. Reading the report of these trekking expeditions in the newsletter *Namaste* is like a playful transposition of tropic roles in the Himalayan trekking literature (and given Ortner's (1999) historical analysis of Nepalis challenging the expeditionary hierarchies, this makes logical sense)—with committee member Mark as the trusty local 'guide'. In the Peak District, they even find a hill village to visit named Ilam.

The children of Nepalis who migrated in the 1970s and the 1980s have been thoroughly socialized into the ways of the ritual cycle of putting culture on display:

"we have all performed our national service" (dancing on stage over the years).

There is an almost *swadeshi* pride in the ability of the UK-based Nepalis to put on a convincing show of national culture without needing to fly plane-loads of performers from Kathmandu, which is anyway an unreliable method for presenting Nepali culture abroad. As the committee president put it in relation to the festival:

> you can never rely on Nepal for providing contributors and stalls. You can only rely on what we can provide from this end.

There are difficulties regarding the decision over who can travel and about who can qualify as a transnational cultural actor (Ong, 1999). The 2008 festival secured funds for tickets for the musicians mentioned earlier, but the UK visa-issuing office in New Delhi only agreed to issue visas just to stop our unrelenting committee member's daily telephone calls. The visa office had initially turned down the applications, despite no evidence of previous untoward visa experience from the applicants.

On the other hand, the local density of Nepalis in the catering business close to Manchester presented a dilemma for choosing which business would provide the *dal bhat tarkari* for the festival. Sensitive diplomacy was required in deciding who was to get the contract. This was one of the few roles undertaken by Nepalis, which would have to be professionalized, as it needed an efficient service to take money from the public, rather than be managed through volunteers. At the same time, the Nepali restaurant community who did not get the contract were not to be let off lightly. They were being systematically reminded to be present at the festival when their restaurants were closed, and they were off work. A full turnout was required.

The president took considerable risks in calculating who was valuable to the cultural programme, to such an extent that requests for professional terms of remuneration were refused, but not so as to offend the performer. One person was told he 'should not ask for £800. We can't pay'. At the December meeting the president said this person should not charge for his services and "must make his contribution *as a Nepali*".

In contrast, and perhaps revealing something of the priorities chosen in staging another culture in a foreign land, through ritual management of visible formal roles, a full professional rate was going to be offered to someone from the Manchester BBC studios to play the role of master of ceremonies and introduce each act in the cultural programme (an aspiration for locally dominant prestige validation that could be termed 'Mancritization'). In the end, it was a West Indian woman with a music and stage background, known to a committee member, who did this job instead, as a friendly gesture.

Getting close to the festival date, and with the programme more or less in shape, the festival committee president visited Kathmandu, over the Christmas holiday period, for meetings with the Minister of Culture, and the Tourism Board.

The *Namaste* issue of April 2008 announced the forthcoming festival while marking the death of Sir Edmund Hilary; "the festival continues Sir Hilary's mission, as it seeks to raise awareness of Nepal and its people's need, while celebrating the mystery and rich culture of one of the most captivating places on this planet".

But what are the Nepali people's different needs, of those who are in Britain? One Nepali I have spoken with, who had been a Masters student at Manchester University, did not feel welcomed by those with a more permanent footing in the United Kingdom. He implied there was a barrier facing people who turn up temporarily from Nepal. Furthermore, there is little evident *Janajati* presence at the association's events. Thanks to Yarjung Gurung, who gave a shamanic inauguration for the 2004 festival, he organized for the impressive Tamu Pei Sang group to come for a day to the 2008 festival and take the Town Hall by storm with their dramatic choreography of Gurung dance styles.

It is obvious how the diaspora's hierarchies are performed in the seating arrangements at the meetings in the police sports centre—with suits and ties seated at tables, and leather jackets milling around at the back.

MULTICULTURAL CITIZENS

[I]f mobile subjects plot and manoeuvre in relation to capital flows, governments also articulate with global capital and entities in complex ways. I want to problematize the popular view that globalization has weakened state power. While capital, population, and cultural flows have indeed made inroads into state sovereignty, the art of government has been highly responsive to the challenges of transnationality. (Ong, 1999: 7)

If two Nepalis find each other [in another country], there will be three organisations. (Ambassador to UK Murari Raj Sharma)

There was an important speech given by the newly appointed ambassador to the New Year meeting of the Himalayan Yeti Association in April 2008. Witty and with sharp observations, he was very comfortable with the role of speaking to the congregation at the police sports hall. He made a very positive presentation, in English, about the formation of the provisional government in Kathmandu and the democratic progress this represented for the country. With hardly a pause he pointed out this was now an excellent opportunity to invest in Nepal's future, and in particular highlighted the financial returns being made from investing in small hydroelectric ventures. He strongly encouraged events such as the festival to make the British community aware of the local Nepalis, and spoke of the general benefits of getting involved in school governors boards, and health organizations, so that people in local positions of power would come to know about the Nepalis, and if situations arise that require help or advice from local politicians, there is already some recognition from previous points of contact.

For the new ambassador, and many involved in the festival, there was no issue of being any less Nepali by living abroad. Providing a cultural window onto Nepal was recognized as a strategy for local belonging, but what limits were experienced about acceptable cultural images, or political messages? At one point, a key committee member was arguing for inviting the biggest names possible to speak at the festival. He was not worried about political repercussions if we were to invite the Dalai Lama, "We don't care what the Dalai Lama says, we only want him to sell the festival".

Back in 2004, there had been a concerted attempt to thwart my plan to show 'The Killing Terraces' among other documentary films on the civil war in Nepal, showcased through the biennial 'Film South Asia' festival in Kathmandu. Emails poured in, suggesting this was a partisan, unbalanced view of the Peoples War, and should not therefore be shown. The role of the festival, I was told by one vociferous non-Nepali member, was to promote Nepal, not to detract from its image, and 'keep the political situation out of it'. Others argued that the citizens of Manchester include many who would be curious to know more about the background to the shifting global image of Nepal—from Shangri-la trekking destination to the Maoist battle zone. My argument that an emerging, confident journalistic movement in the country was something to be celebrated was loudly contested in email exchanges. The films were shown, in a side room, keenly watched by many Nepalis for the first time. A vote did not need to be forced, as the debate was mostly conducted among the non-Nepali members, with the president trying 'to keep everyone on the committee happy'. Further interventions to censor the views of Nepal on show came in discussions of appropriate topics for the programme of talks. Admonishments were made by the president to Nepalis, not to think they can 'stand up in front of British audiences' and say what they like.

In the 2008 festival, the funding crisis led to another confrontation. What did and did not appear on the final leaflet, who was acknowledged and thanked, and who was not, needed close reading. Certain energies to promote the inclusion of specific elements in the programme were deemed not to warrant mention, as only contributions to the general festival production, not private passions pursued in apparent favour over other options, deserved recognition. As for an expenses claim submitted by one committee member, there was a special meeting called:

> Nobody disagrees she hasn't worked hard ... [but] it cannot be on a professional basis.... We do appreciate her input. We cannot afford the bill.... The Association has taken years to build up its reserves.

The total expenses incurred by the 2008 festival were £10,500 more than incomings. The attempt to raise funds by the volunteer committee had been severely hampered by the committee's inability to locate credible figures from the previous festival (given the committee's haphazard record keeping—the old figures were found two weeks before the new festival). The reorganized freelance agent job status of the key interfacer with the Town Hall administration meant he submitted his bill and expenses to the committee for a discrete job of work, which had included applying to the council for the funds to cover his administrative role. This professionalized enclaving within the work of the festival organization, and over-reliance on one broker to mediate with the Town Hall, hindered the festival management and left others who had dedicated hundreds of hours of work, feeling unfairly situated on the voluntary/professional axis of multiculturalism.

DISCUSSION

In considering the relations of cultural translocation in this chapter, do the Nepalis present a coherent face to the 'host' society in an exchange of inter-national regard? Alternatively, how does the shifting locatedness of diaspora unpick the contours of culture and redistribute a sense of belonging? My argument is that Nepalis appear to be quite successful players of the multicultural game for belonging in the 'integrationist' political environment of global metropolitan society. By putting an authentic culture on display, they are possibly doing much more: "Cultural continuity appears in and as the mode of cultural change" (Sahlins, 1993: 19). As Baumann (1992) argues for South Asians in London, the use of cultural symbols is as much for others to recognize and respond to, as for 'intra-group' readings.

If the question is asked 'who is the Manchester festival for?', the answer has to be a range of people with both dominant and demotic cultural interests (Baumann, 1997). When I visited the office of the British Council in Lazimpat in 2007, to distribute information leaflets about the festival, the council official I spoke to asked the question 'Why Manchester?', with a mixture of surprise and possibly disdain. Not high in the affections of people wanting to promote respectable images of touristic England, it is mostly in the national profile for reasons of gun crime, football, rock music, and gay lifestyles. Yet it is a highly globalized city within a region that has experienced a post-colonial reinvention, where the old industrial landscape has given way to a consumption service economy, including hiking and mountaineering in the nearby areas of the Peak District and Lake Districts. In the old mill towns outside Manchester there have been episodes of rioting by disaffected Asian youth. As a beacon of enlightened multicultural tolerance and generosity, Manchester's council needs to present an image of inclusivity. Thus, the functional happenstance of a political centre looking for disciplined 'ethnic' communities to interact with, a constituency of professional multiculturalists, a market of leisure-oriented people, many of whom have been on trekking holidays and expeditions to Nepal, all come together in ways that Olds and Thrift (2005: 271) have written about in terms of a functionality of happening, a coming together, rather than cause and effect.

The Nepalis who participate and attend do so on the one hand to enjoy the public occasion of *their* culture taking the stage, providing an occasion for British-resident Nepalis to see themselves as a public 'in the public', occupying the attention of civic dignitaries, given broadcast space on the media, and additionally, doing so in a way that connects with a large number of non-Nepalis. Just looking at the stalls arranged in the elegant rooms of the Town Hall, it is obvious how many professional and self-appointed 'friends of Nepal' there are, doing voluntary work, enabling development projects, promoting spiritual causes, and marketing tourism. The several thousand people who attended enjoy the colours, sights, films, and talks about Nepal, but it is within the embrace of officialdom, surrounded by the solid iconography of old Mancunian burghers and the pictured narratives of great institutional scenes in the history of this global epicentre of industrialism that the self-confident and coincidentally new republican members of the Nepali community celebrate their diasporic capacity to be simultaneously of here, and there.

And yet there is a big mediation provided by and for non-Nepalis for the festival. The festival needs 'crowd-puller' names, and none of those suggested were Nepali (apart from Prashant Tamang, the Darjeeling pop idol). In the absence of providing a big media star, my own role was to provide a set of speakers for the discerning populace (many thanks to Michael Hutt and Charles Ramble), and reveal something of the wealth of knowledge about Nepal among academics to share with the tax-payers who enable this knowledge production. Along with the academics, artists, and NGO actors, the figures of Mike Harding, Edmund Hilary, and Doug Scott (more recently Joanna Lumley) can be seen to epitomize a very particular kind of an experience of personal transformation by contact with Nepal. This emotional, intimate, biographically re-scripting dimension of the image of Nepal in the eyes of the British public could be heard in the conversations of animated festival visitors, sprinkled with some of them wearing visible marks of identification, from the old British Gurkha emblems, to handbags and headgear bought in Thamel or Phewa Tal.

The selling point of Nepal is a distinct kind of exotic symbolic capital (made tangible through cheap retail products and tourism services), which enables numbers of non-Nepalis to find points of solidarity through personal narratives of peak-ascents, of spiritual, military, scientific, and educational journeys, and simply pleasurable association. Photogenic landscapes and celebrity self-publicity against the backdrop of picturesque traditional people sell in popular culture.

The Manchester Nepalis were not worried about this aspect for the sake of promoting a successful event. For the British public of course, there is an added sentimental paternalism derived from the Gurkha relationship (the Liberal Democrat Party leader Nick Clegg asserted if Gurhkas can die for Britain they should be allowed to live in Britain [White, 2009]). The Manchester festival aims to take care of all these sensibilities, and in the process offer the event as an example of the dream of a multicultural public sphere: for generous and responsive local government fortified by well organized and civically disciplined ethnic communities (Baumann, 1995). However, this dream is not so cheap in the end. People who give their energies and time to bring the dream alive for a couple of days are not receiving equal rewards. Some stand to gain prestige, some will receive commercial rates and consultancies, some will gather material for academic papers, some will have received applause, but others worked long hours to pull the strands together, keep the committee up to date, turn promises and offers into real commitments, and manage the difficult interface between regimes of standards acceptable to voluntary organizations, and those expected of professional practice. Each festival has seen an inordinate burden of organizational toil fall on the shoulders of non-Nepali women.

Multiculturalism in the United Kingdom is an industry that offers largesse to those communities that will present themselves as organized, and work to fulfil the picture of inter-ethnic harmony—a picture at variance with undesirable aspects of global society, of violence against asylum seekers, and riots against British fascists or police in towns close to Manchester. The performance of Nepali culture is not then politically innocent. Soysal's (1994) argument from other 'ethnic' organizations in Europe is that these diaspora reflect a strong trace of the host society's framework for managing its relationship to 'immigrant' communities, and especially by resources and policy constructions in which cultural diversity is modelled as a beneficial phenomenon, congruent with general civic values. This does not mean that the principles of multiculturalism need to be strongly articulated beyond vague sentiments of respect for difference within shared civic values. Anderson comments that

> even multiculturalism's defenders often have little clue of what it really is, or does. Multiculturalism is not only a heap of colours, it is a machine with cogs that whirr. It not only fuses, but keeps apart.

It doesn't so much discriminate as direct a choreography of cultures. Much like a latter-day, benign sort of empire, where all races and cultures play a minor part in the symphony of power. (Anderson, 2006)

Whereas some (e.g. Favell, 2003) see multiculturalism as rescuing the nation state, others perceive a different phenomenon: "long-distance nationalism is reconfiguring the way many people understand the relationship between populations and the states that claim to represent them". After the sway held by nationalism in the 20th century, which required two World Wars and the United Nations to become hegemonic "a new form of state has emerged that extends its reach across borders, claiming that its emigrants and their descendants remain an integral and intimate part of their ancestral homeland, even if they are citizens of another state" (Glick-Schiller and Fouron, 2002: 357).

All these possibilities need to be considered in situated, 'everyday' state practices of multiculturalism, and the interrogative concept of belonging can bring focus and nuance to processes of change that are far from adhering to set types. It is not as if the kinds of transnationalism demonstrated by some Nepalis are reflecting a generic type of transnational actor. In the opening-out for others to gaze at the Manchester festival, the symbolic capital and global branding of Nepal and the Himalaya through Gurkhas, Sherpas, and pagodas, but also seeing citizens confronting state power and replacing a monarchy with a republic, contrasts notably with the discussion of transnationalism in Ong's *Flexible Citizenship* talking of "a border-running Chinese executive with no state loyalty"(1999: 135–36), who "readily submit to the governmentality of capital, while plotting all the while to escape state discipline" (1999: 135).

The Nepalis in Manchester, rather, are happy to take on the role of hosting the other dispersed members of their national community abroad, and grounding the event in their newfound spectacular temple of civic belonging. Manchester's resident Nepali community is hardly more than a 150 people, but the political need from the local state, the self-selected community of interest from the region in Nepal, and the good name in which Nepal is held (despite poverty, politics, and paucity of media coverage) have converged to generate an event of very hybrid manufacture desired by locals and neo-locals. Werbner has re-joindered accusations (Barry, 2000) of multiculturalism as a conspiracy of state engineering by arguing:

multiculturalism is a rather messy local political and bureaucratic negotiated order, responsive to ethnic grassroots pressure, budgetary constraints and demands for redistributive justice. It is bottom-up rather than top-down. This also means that there is no single 'just' blueprint for multiculturalism, even in a single country and certainly between countries... In different countries, multiculturalism refers to different struggles, depending on minority demands for recognition and a share of state or local state budgets. Beyond the struggles for local recognition, however, we need to recognise that multiculturalism has also become a global movement.... (Werbner, 2005: 761)

Within the history of Nepalis living in Britain, there is an important interplay of rhetorics about national conviviality, compatibility, and mutual respect, which can be genealogically tracked back to the mid-19th-century relationship to the British state. New terms of recognition and symbolic capital of contemporary value are projected through culture on display. What goes on display can become a matter of anthropological curiosity, even contrivance. However, I could not contrive the presence at the festival of other Nepalis in the United Kingdom, for whom this festive display represents an aspiration for visible citizenship they cannot entertain on account of the scrutinizing of their residence documents this could invite and their marginal ethnicity among Nepalis. For such people who have little affective belonging to the state of Nepal, a visit to the Dalai Lama's public audience in Scotland provided a greater incentive to take a couple of days off work than attend the elite-flavoured event in Manchester.

CONCLUSION

The term 'belonging' appears in Modood's book on multiculturalism (2007) to help navigate the space between formal legalistic notions of citizenship and old ideas of culture that cling to pre-immigration notions of national identity in Europe. It brings an affective dimension to understand how diaspora communities can develop positive relationships to European national cultural life beyond civic rights and economic benefits. As with much multiculturalist literature, Modood's primary concern is with the relationship of Muslim people to European societies, and the normative potential for overcoming stigmatized and conflict-laden perceptions. In contrast, the Nepali diaspora case appears to offer an unthreatening vision of multi-cultural integration with pleasure at the fore. There is more of a two-way traffic between ethnic British and ethnic Nepalis living in Britain. With the entrepreneurial spirit of northern England, and its predilection for public congregation, multiculturalism has provided a platform for an international consumption of difference brought to the doorstep, and a rationale for civic repopulation of urban Europe.

The Nepali festival in Manchester persuaded me of the need to view multiculturalism in the context of the dynamics of particular cities and relationships. 'Why Manchester?' was the bemused question from the British Council official about the location of the festival. It is a very good question, and already begins to explain that a dynamic based on a very different political and social landscape in Northwest England lent an impetus to the city council to demonstrate it would part-fund and encourage the local Nepalis and their friends and associates to make a show of their belonging to Manchester, at the same time as their affective belonging to Nepal. Multiculturalism is not the same thing in London and Manchester due to regional political history, but to dig beneath the encompassing discourse of multiculturalism as policy for managing societies of migration, the questions posed by belonging abroad point to demotic struggles in principles of commercial rationality and cultural commitment that leave little room for *Janajati* migrants who do not find a welcome place in national narratives. Multiculturalism glitters with colourful variety in the supermarkets and local government brochures, as a reinvented form of consumption and of political legitimacy; however, between its happy images of staged conviviality, its aspirations for encompassing diversity are limited by the national brands on offer, its potential for giving recognition by segregating communities, and neglect of demotic opportunities for belonging that are not reliant on donning national dress.

NOTES

1. As a historical footnote, it is interesting to look back on the fact that political coalition organized for the Gurkhas' right to live in the United Kingdom in April 2009 was the first parliamentary vote in the United Kingdom that brought the Conservative and Liberal Democrat leaders David Cameron and Nick Clegg, respectively, together with a successful outcome, after which they went on the next year to displace Gordon Brown's Labour Party from government.

2. These have moved to the local Irish Community Centre after the police introduced a rule that any food served on the premises had to be provided by the police's regular caterers. One event when the meal of rice and curry English style was offered, was enough to cause the relocation to the *dal bhat*–friendly venue of the Irish community.
3. Having heard of me, Charan had searched me out, and found my house in the Pennine hills simply by asking in the local town where 'the man from Nepal' lived.
4. Rochdale is one of the industrial mill-towns set beside the Pennine hills in Greater Manchester.
5. This was dropped at the 2008 event, as tickets cost money to run, and are difficult to control in the busy event.

REFERENCES

Adhikari, K.P. 2012. *Nepalis in the United Kingdom: An Overview*. Reading: CNSUK.
Anderson, R. 2006. 'Multiculturalism at Work'. Available online at www.open-democracy.net/arts-multiculturalism/london_3652.jsp (last date of access: 12 May 2009).
Barry, B. 2000. *Culture and Equality: An Egalitarian Critique of Multiculturalism*. Cambridge: Polity Press.
Baumann, G. 1992. 'Rituals Implicate "Others": Rereading Durkheim in a Plural Society', in D. de Coppert (ed.), *Understanding Rituals*. London: Routledge.
———. 1995. 'Managing a Polyethnic Milieu: Kinship and Interaction in a London Suburb', *Journal of the Royal Anthropological Institute*, 1(4): 725–41.
———. 1997. 'Dominant and Demotic Discourses of Culture: Their Relevance to Multi-Ethnic Alliances', in P. Werbner and T. Modood (eds), *Debating Cultural Hybridity: Multicultural Identities and the Politics of Anti-Racis*, pp. 209–25. London: Zed Books.
———. 2005. 'Grammars of Identity/Alterity: A Structural Approach', in Baumann and A. Gingrich (eds), *Grammars of Alterity/Identity*, pp. 18–51. Oxford: Berghahn.
Favell, A. 2003. 'Integration Nations: The Nation State and Research on Immigrants in Western Europe', in *The Multicultural Challenge*. Comparative Social Research, 22: 13–42.
Gilroy, P. 2004. *Between Camps: Nations, Cultures and the Allure of Race*. London: Routledge.
Glick-Schiller, N. and G. Fouron. 2002. 'Long-distance Nationalism Defined', in J. Vincent (ed.), *The Anthropology of Politics*. Oxford: Blackwell.
Modood, T. 2007. *Multiculturalism: A Civic Idea*. London: Polity Press.
Olds, K. and N. Thrift. 2005. 'Cultures on the Brink: Reengineering the Soul of Capitalism—on a Global Scale', in A. Ong and S. Collier (eds), *Global Assemblages: Technology, Politics and Ethics as Anthropological Problems*, pp. 270–90. Oxford: Blackwell.
Olwig, K.F. 1993. *Global Culture, Island Identity*. Chur, Switzerland: Harwood Academic Publishers.

Ong, Aihwa. 1999. *Flexible Citizenship: The Cultural Logics of Transnationality*. Duke University Press.

Ortner, S. 1999. *Life and Death on Mount Everest*. Princeton: Princeton University Press.

Sahlins, M. 1993. 'Goodbye to Tristes Tropes: Ethnography in the Context of Modern World History', *Journal of Modern History*, 65(1): 1–25.

Soysal, Y. 1994. *The Limits of Citizenship: Migrants and Postnational Membership in Europe*. Chicago: University of Chicago Press.

Werbner, P. 1999. 'Global Pathways. Working Class Cosmopolitans and the Creation of Transnational Ethnic Worlds', *Social Anthropology*, 7(1): 17–35.

———. 2002. 'The Place Which Is Diaspora: Citizenship, Religion and Gender in the Making of Chaordic Transnationalism', *Journal of Ethnic and Migration Studies*, 28(1): 119–33.

———. 2005. 'The Translocation of Culture: "Community Cohesion" and the Force of Multiculturalism in History', *The Sociological Review*, 53(4): 745–68.

White, M. 2009. 'Gurkhas Vote: Gordon Brown Never Stood a Chance against Joanna Lumley'. Available online at www.guardian.aco.uk. (last date of access: 7 May 2009).

Chapter 10

Being and Belonging

Mapping the Experiences of Nepali Immigrants in the United States

BANDITA SIJAPATI

INTRODUCTION

It was a few years ago that a friend became one of the successful recipients of the Diversity Visa (DV)[1] that would allow him and his family to emigrate to the United States. By participating in the DV lottery, he had indicated his preference to live and work in the United States rather than in Nepal. Although his appeared to be a pragmatic choice, his wife could not hide her excitement at the prospect of being able to relocate to her 'dream country'. This Nepali couple is one of the many who continue to enter the United States because of the enduring narrative of an 'Immigrant America'. Although this narrative conjures up an image of a 'welcoming America' and reinforces its appeal as a multicultural society, migration to the United States has also recently become an issue of heated public debate with the rise in hostility, suspicion, and fear targeted against migrants, especially from Asia, Latin America, and Africa.

By looking at the case of Nepali youths who have come to the United States, in this chapter, I seek to delineate the ways in which these recent migrants have been mediating through the 'social fields'[2] of America that is juxtaposed between multiple contradictions—the image of a welcoming country and the realities of increased racism and xenophobia; heightened transnationalism as well as efforts to incorporate and socialize immigrants into American society and its values and traditions. I will argue that the concepts of assimilation and incorporation, which put the onus on the individual or the community, are not well suited to explain the diverse experiences of these youths whose lives in the United States are informed not only by their own sense of wanting (or not wanting) to be incorporated into American society but also by various external forces in Nepal as well as in the United States, which are beyond their individual control.

More specifically, I will first describe the ambiguity that surrounds the lives of Nepali immigrant youths as they negotiate the interface of two societies, Nepal and the United States; the pain they feel in defying some elements of Nepali traditions while seeking to incorporate those considered 'American'; and their struggle to carve out a legitimate space for themselves in American society. Second, I will also show how the foreign status accorded to these youths, despite their efforts to acculturate and assimilate; the experiences of being thrust down to the lowest rungs of the workforce; and a life of exclusion from mainstream America, have led Nepali youths to harbour a growing sense of 'being in America' but not 'belonging to America'.

BEYOND ASSIMILATION AND INCORPORATION: THEORETICAL FRAMEWORK

The United States has often been described as a 'permanently unfinished' society (Portes and Rumbaut, 2006). Every year, thousands of immigrants and refugees, especially from Asia and Latin America, are legally admitted into the country, while an equal number of them either enter the country clandestinely or overstay their visas and become 'illegal aliens'.[3] Along with the large influx of migrants, there has also been increased suspicion, and even fear, among native-born Americans who regard newcomers as a threat to the integrity of American culture and a source of 'decay in their quality of life'. For instance, in his book, *Who Are We? The Challenges to America's National Identity*, Huntington (2004) argues that immigrants, especially Latinos, are posing a major threat to the 'cultural and political integrity of the United States'. Whether one is critical of immigration or in favour of it, the central question that remains revolves around issues of immigrant incorporation and assimilation, that is, how well have the immigrants been able to adapt and assimilate themselves into American culture and society?

An overview of the literature on immigrant incorporation indicates at least three main propositions. First, the straight-line assimilationist theory, also formulated as the 'melting pot theory', maintains that through regular and close social interactions, ethnic groups will be able to 'unlearn' and abandon their cultural practices and rituals, and embrace the core values of mainstream American culture. This, they argue, would mean that assimilation of immigrants into 'mainstream' American life is not only inevitable but also desirable both for the nation and for the immigrants (see also Huntington, 2004; Alba and Nee, 2005).

Recently, however, scholars, especially those who have studied first-generation post-1965 immigrants, suggest that although for some immigrant groups, 'structural' assimilation has been possible, that is, they participate in mainstream economic and educational institutions, 'cultural' assimilation has not been achieved because of the continued ethnic identification maintained by these groups as well as the continued prevalence of racism in the United States (Merenstein, 2008). Accordingly, these theorists have used the concept of 'segmented assimilation' to argue that contrary to the unidirectional proposition made by the 'straight-line' assimilation theorists, different groups of immigrants assimilate into different sectors and subcultures of American society; however, that assimilation, even if second-, third- or fourth-generation, will eventually occur (Gans, 1992; Zhou, 1999).

In contrast to the assimilationist paradigm, pluralist models posit that instead of assimilating into the melting pot, ethnic groups continue to maintain their own identity, leading many to conceptualize American society as a 'salad bowl' while speaking of race and ethnic relations in the United States (Glazer and Moynihan, 1970). Furthermore, pluralists also argue that cultural pluralism is a desirable outcome because it allows immigrants and the America-born to enter American political structures as ethnic groups and accordingly make demands, thus promoting democratic governance (Glazer and Moynihan, 1970). In this regard, the pluralists argue that ethnicity and a different cultural background are assets and not a liability to a group's progress.

Contrary to these assimilationist and cultural pluralist paradigms, recent scholars on immigration have pointed to the dangers of viewing assimilation and pluralism as mutually exclusive processes and instead argued that 'multiple exposures' to different sociocultural contexts will evoke more complex responses in contrast to these dualistic conceptualizations. For instance, Phinney (1990: 509) suggests that "ethnic identity is not a linear construct" but that it is possible for individuals to maintain a strong ethnic identity while also identifying with mainstream American culture.

Accordingly, current perspectives on immigrant assimilation and adaptation have begun to focus on the ways in which immigrant groups maintain identities and allegiances across national boundaries rather than parting with them (Basch et al., 1994; Appadurai, 1996; Levitt, 2001; Rumbaut, 2002; Levitt and Schiller, 2004; Grewal, 2005). Popularized by Basch et al. (1994: 7), the term 'transnationalism' used to describe this phenomenon refers to the processes by which immigrants "forge and sustain multi-stranded social relations that link together their societies of origin and settlement". Based on these dynamics, these scholars argue that the transnational flows of people, goods, and money give rise to what are variously defined as 'transnational communities' (Portes, 1997), 'transnational migration circuits' (Rouse, 1995), 'transnational social fields' (Basch et al., 1994), 'transnational village' (Levitt, 2001), 'transnational attachments' (Rumbaut, 2002) or even 'accommodation without assimilation' (Gibson, 1988). Collectively, all these terms are used to understand how the experiences of immigrants are shaped by the back-and-forth movement and communication between host- and home-societies, multiple cross-border social networks and linkages, immigrant communities' desires to preserve their home culture amidst encounters of racism and discrimination in the host society, cross-border flow of money and goods in the form of commercial linkages, remittances, and so on.

On the issue of transnationalism and identity in particular, drawing from anthropological literature that suggests that cultures are not discrete, bounded entities fixed to bounded spaces or territories, scholars on transnationalism conceive of cultures and identities as being 'deterritorialized' (Basch et al., 1994; Appadurai, 1996; Olwig and Hastrup, 1997). However, these scholars caution that to say that identities are deterritorialized is not to say that national identities have become defunct. Instead, national identities, particularly in the form of 'diasporic nationality', continue to arouse fervent loyalties even within the diaspora (Basch et al., 1994; Appadurai, 1996), and in some instances re-territorialization of identity may even occur, thus leading to a paradoxical situation where strong attachments to home coexist within a global framework of identities and attachments (Basch et al., 1994; Appadurai, 1996; Olwig and Hastrup, 1997). In terms of conceptual framework, I will use the concepts of incorporation/assimilation as well transnationalism to understand Nepali youths' sense of belonging in the United States. Such a synthetic approach is necessary because the former seeks to cultivate a sense of belonging in the host society whereas the latter erodes such conceptions by fostering attachments and commitments to more than one nation at the same time. In keeping with these emphases, I will delineate the dimensions of Nepali transnationalism while mapping the ways in which concepts of assimilation and incorporation are affected by forces of transnationalism, especially when migrants simultaneously inhabit two worlds—the host country and the home country. In doing so, I show that neither the unidimensionality nor simple dichotomy, between the host country and the home society, or between assimilation and transnationalism, is an appropriate frame for analyzing the lives of these immigrant youths. Instead, these youths are operating "more or less simultaneously in a variety of places" (Foner, 2000: 176).

BACKGROUND ON NEPALI STUDENTS

In middle-class Nepali society, especially in the capital, Kathmandu, it is quite common to find children who either have left home to 'study abroad' or are in the process of preparing to leave. Newspapers, magazines, and billboards in Kathmandu are inundated with messages advertising assistance for study abroad programmes and vying with each other to claim the best success rate in preparing and sending students abroad for higher education. Quite clearly, middle-class families in Nepal believe that the 'rite of passage' for the future of their children would be to prepare them to leave Nepal for education in some other country, preferably in the West. This trend of youth going abroad for studies has become so ingrained into people's repertoire of behaviours and values that families believe it to be the best way and perhaps the only way to elevate their children's, and their own, social and economic status. As such, families of youths preparing their children for study abroad are willing, in many instances, to spend all their life investments, sell their assets, and even go into debt, only in the hope that after receiving a foreign degree, their children will be better positioned economically as well as socially. One of the most favoured destinations in this regard is the United States.[4]

Although there is no reliable data on the number of Nepali immigrants living in the United States, especially since many of them enter on a student or tourist visa and overstay their visit, there are figures available for those entering the United States for higher education. Over the past decade, students from Nepal to the United States have increased dramatically (see Figure 10.1). According to the Institute of International Education/Opendoors, in the 2010/11 academic year, 10,301 students from Nepal were studying in the United States. Even though this is an 8 per cent decrease from the previous year, Nepal is the eleventh leading place of origin for students coming to the United States.[5] This figure of 10,301 amounts to slightly more than 28 students per day.

Although it is beyond the scope of my paper to explore the reasons for this trend, there are a few obvious factors which have contributed to this development. These include, among other things, the poor state of national institutions, prestige of a foreign degree, possibilities of long-term migration, political instability in Nepal, etc.,

Figure 10.1
Number of Nepali Students in the United States

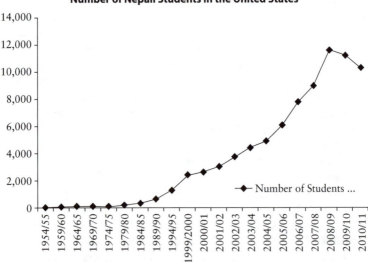

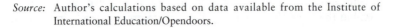

Source: Author's calculations based on data available from the Institute of International Education/Opendoors.

combined with the stated and unstated objectives of the US government and academic institutions to attract foreign students such as getting benefits from diversifying college campuses, soft diplomacy, possible immigration of professionals that would help meet the country's labour needs in certain fields like engineering, computer science, mathematics, etc.

Extrapolating from past trends as well as the reasons for going to the United States for higher education, it will suffice to say here that the number of Nepali youths in the United States can only be expected to grow in the future. However, despite these increasing numbers, a study conducted in 2008 on assimilation in the United States showed that Nepalis are the least-assimilated group. With the composite assimilation index value of 8, Nepalis had the lowest value of all the foreign-born migrants, representing a total of 119 countries.[6] In this chapter, I will seek to explain some of the processes that would account for this apparent discrepancy between increasing number of youths seeking to go to the United States and their low levels of assimilation into American society.

BELONGING IN THE UNITED STATES

Michael Walzer (1992: 17) argued, "This [USA] is not Europe; we are a society of immigrants, and the experience of leaving a home-land and coming to this new place is an almost universal 'American' experience. It should be celebrated". Despite this widely prevalent American narrative of celebrating diversity brought about by the influx of immigrants, the realities and experiences of immigrants with American society as well as the American state do not reflect this image of 'immigrant America' (see also Ngai, 2004; Maira, 2008). In this section of the paper, I will explore some of the ways in which this disjuncture—the simultaneous embracing as well as eschewing of America and American society—manifests itself in the everyday experiences of young Nepalis in the United States.

Shattered Dreams

Nepalis generally enter the United States with the hope of making it big in the 'land of opportunity' and living the American Dream.

Influenced by Hollywood as well as Bollywood[7] renditions of life in America, Nepalis conceive of the United States as a materialistic utopia. This type of fantasy about America is not uncommon or completely unwarranted either because as Prashad (2000: 92–93) argues, the "good graces of [an] expanding 'global' media" is that its "reach is worldwide but ... content is frequently the fantasy of the American Dream" and even though the media does not "manipulate reality; it simply frames U.S. life to show it at its best".

For Nepalis, their first impression of the country upon arrival is invariably spectacular—the complex network of highways, luxury cars, bright lights in the streets, smooth roads, large shopping malls, all things grand and promising when compared to Nepal. However, this honeymoon period oftentimes is soon shattered as they negotiate their way through the challenges of living in America, as can be glimpsed in Kanchan's story below.

> I come from an upper middle-class Bahun family from Kathmandu. I came to America to pursue my undergraduate studies in the metropolitan area of Washington DC. I had received partial scholarship but had to pay half of my tuition fees and living expenses. I wanted to be independent and not a burden on my family, and so the first thing I did the day after I came to the U.S. was to look for a job. I considered myself fortunate enough to find one immediately at a fast-food restaurant.[8] My excitement about starting a job and earning 5 dollars an hour—about 300 [Nepali] rupees an hour at that time—was, however short-lived when my manager at the end of the work day told me to clean the toilet. I felt like telling the manager, "I am a Bahun, I have never cleaned the floor, let alone a toilet," but there was nobody I could say that to. (Personal Communication)

Kanchan is not the only one who had to do something they never even considered doing in Nepal. Because of the kind of living and travel expenses required, the majority of Nepalis entering the United States come from middle- to upper middle-class backgrounds. Most of these individuals would not have even 'lifted a stick' in terms of physical work (*sinka pani uthako chhaina*), as the Nepali saying goes, but in the process of making available to themselves the economic and educational opportunities encoded in the narrative of the 'American dream', they end up working as low-wage workers, mostly in the service sector. In particular, youths like Kanchan, who have to self-finance their education, work in Indian restaurants, fast-food joints, grocery stores, nail parlours, day-care centres, and so on.[9] Some of them rationalize the 'indignity' of taking on such jobs by reassuring themselves that it is only temporary and that 'one day they would be able to make their dreams come true', as one participant mentioned. The ruthlessness of immigration laws, however, is such that it does not allow individuals the luxury of choice in what they can do. Given the necessity of having to work full time to finance their studies, many youths lose their legal status as 'full-time students' when they do not attend college/university full time even for one semester.[10] This immediately relegates them to the status of an 'illegal alien'. This process of becoming an 'illegal alien' is a quite common phenomenon, as seen in Naresh's story.

> I came to America to pursue my undergraduate studies in electrical engineering. I arrived in Nebraska but transferred to [a community college in] New York City after a year, thinking that it would be easier to find a better-paying job in New York. Upon arriving in New York, I worked in several places, from restaurants to grocery stores, before finally settling down as a bus boy in a Korean restaurant...The first semester after moving to New York City, I had managed to enroll as a full-time student at the community college with my savings from the summer. However, in the following semester, I had to drop out since I could not pay the 4,500 dollar tuition fee. I was short of 1,500 dollars and with a snap of the finger, I lost my student status and with it, my dreams of becoming an engineer... As an illegal worker, I now find myself in fear all the time—being caught by immigration officials, being reported by somebody, being deported... I fear everyone. (Personal Communication)

Naresh's story attests to the way in which from being a country of dreams, America becomes a place where the hopes and aspirations of young Nepali immigrants are quickly crushed. From being promising students with passionate dreams and aspirations, the young are quickly relegated to the status of 'illegal aliens'.

As illegal immigrants whose lives are marked by the imminent threat of deportation, these youths not only are thrust on to the lowest rungs of the workforce where they are subject to exploitation and isolation but are also excluded from the polity and hence experience 'multiple marginalizations' (Ngai, 2004; Maira, 2008). For example, like Naresh, many others, including Deepak, said that his illegal status had kept him in 'a state of constant fear—fear that somebody would report him to the INS,[11] fear that he would never be able to go back home to Nepal, fear that he would never be able to see his family, fear that he would always be forced to work in Indian restaurants illegally and under exploitative conditions', and so on. These experiences of exploitation and marginalization as 'illegal aliens', embedded in the narratives of many Nepali youths, are one of the most prevalent ways in which Nepali immigrants realize that they do not belong in the United States and do not have a future here, at least not the one they had envisioned for themselves when they first came to America.

Morality, Hardships, and Struggle

As scholars on transnational migration have argued, in order to understand immigrants' relationships with the host society, it is essential to first understand the norms and rules that govern their own native culture since it is through these that immigrants experience, decipher, and make sense of their experiences in the host nation. For instance, Thapan (2005: 32) argues,

> ... the immigrant's native categories of perception, i.e., the *habitu* ... while being socially produced within a specific context, however, continue to mediate the experience and understanding of changing objective conditions. Thus, even when the individual migrates, a native paradigm predefines, in a sense, one's interpretation of the new situation in the host country, and one tends to use the same tools and resources to think in and perceive a changed world.

As Roma, a junior at a private university in the Washington DC Metropolitan Area, recalled,

> When I was preparing to come to the United States on a full scholarship, my family was very anxious even though they were visibly very proud of me. My mother called up all my relatives to announce my achievement which was kind of embarrassing. But, then, there was a lot of anxiety as well. In particular, I think my father was really worried because I was after all a girl, still unmarried, had just turned nineteen and was about to venture into a faraway place. My father, the night before I was scheduled to leave, came to me and said, "I am really proud of you and I know you will not disappoint your family by forgetting who you are [i.e., a Nepali]." That was all he said and even

though I just nodded my head at that time, I had promised myself then
and there that I will not disappoint him. (Personal Communication)

Roma proudly told me that she has not "forgotten [her] father's
words", and is still a Nepali, which she interpreted as meaning
"working hard, excelling in school, deferring to elders, acceding
to parental wishes, dressing up modestly, and more importantly,
not entering into relationships with Americans (*laughs*)". All in all,
Nepalis consider it desirable to structurally assimilate into American
society through educational and professional success, but nevertheless refrain from cultural assimilation into mainstream American
culture and values that stress individual choice, freedom, independence from family, etc.—values considered as being at odds with the
Nepali ethos.

Having said that, the demanding nature of life in America compels
many Nepalis to engage in activities they consider immoral or wrong.
The following narrative of Simran, a 25-year-old woman originally
from one of the urban centres outside Kathmandu, is emblematic of
the dilemmas Nepali youths face as they seek to negotiate their lives
in the United States while retaining the norms, values, and cultures
of Nepal.

I was unable to keep up with my studies and work at the same time,
so I was forced to drop out of school. Even then it was hard. Being a
female and living in a dangerous city like New York is always risky.
You cannot just work anywhere or work till late at night. Paying
my rent even though I shared accommodation with other Nepali
girls was difficult ... I have now moved in with a Nepali man who is
married, has children[12] and is much older than myself. I know that
there is no question of us getting married at any point but I had no
choice.... By living with him, I at least don't have to worry about my
living expenses.... I feel really ashamed of myself. Whenever I talk
with my parents on the phone and lie to them about how well I am
doing in my job as an assistant manager in a business firm, I feel like
crying.... Not only am I lying to my parents but I am doing something
so disgraceful that I am ashamed to even look at myself in the mirror.
(Personal Communication)

For Simran, being involved in an illicit relationship is something
that she would not have otherwise done had she been anywhere else
but America. Accordingly, for her, "America is a place where I lost
my virtue and the morals that I was brought up with."

In addition to their own sets of values and ideas that individuals are socialized into in Nepal, these values and norms are reinforced by existing Nepali networks in the United States. These networks, comprising families, friends, acquaintances, and so on, as I will explain in the next section, are of significance because they are usually the first points of contact for most of the youths when they land in the United States, and continue to be the most important arena for social engagements in their sojourn abroad. Invariably, the social mores, codes of conduct, values, and norms guiding these networks are those that have been transplanted from Nepal with very little, if any, elements of American values or norms added.[13] Sangeeta, a 25-year-old woman who lives in Queens, New York, is dating a Bangladeshi male. She said,

> My boyfriend and I never meet in Queens even though we both live here. I worry about being seen by other Nepalis. You know Nepalis have not left their gossiping habit back in Nepal ... I cannot afford to be seen with a Muslim man[14] because, after all, I have to live here [among the Nepali community]. (Personal Communication)

As Sangeeta's narrative elucidates, for many Nepalis who live in Nepali ethnic enclaves, the fear of reprisal or ostracism from families back home and/or the Nepali community in the United States is very pervasive, indicating how, despite being away from home, Nepalis constantly find themselves negotiating with what are considered Nepali values and codes of conduct. However, not all the Nepalis I interviewed have undergone the same experiences and treatment. For one, the rules governing these social networks are more exacting and discriminating against women than they are for men, with the former being subjects of continual gossip and speculation, whether real or perceived. However, the cumulative impact of this set of norms of ethnic networks, their conventions, and governing rules is that it affects the immigrants' sense of belonging in the United States, which is nevertheless governed by the culture, norms, and values of Nepal.

"You Do Not Belong Here"

Like other immigrant groups, when Nepalis come to the United States, whatever their ulterior motives might be, they seek the 'American Dream'. An integral part of that dream is the belief in America's meritocratic system coupled with the narrative of an 'Immigrant America', or a 'multicultural America'. This vision leads many to believe that social mobility in America is possible for anyone who is willing to work hard for it and emerges as one of the major rationales for wanting to come to the United States (Merenstein, 2008). However, as scholars on immigration and race relations in the United States have argued, the often unspoken understanding of what it means to be an American in most cases has been implicitly reserved for 'European-American', or simply, 'white American' (Feagin, 2000; Devos and Banaji, 2005; Golash-Boza, 2006). As a result, the opposition or the difference, real or perceived, between citizens and immigrants "feeds and sustains racist expressions of hatred on the basis of nationality" (Bhavnani, 1993: 34–35, quoted in Thapan, 2005: 47).

Considering the case of Nepalis, upon arriving in the United States, they have in them a deep sense of desire to succeed in their educational and professional endeavours, belong to America, and gain acceptance. This desire shapes the experiences of many Nepali youths as they seek to internalize what they view as the social norms, values, and traditions of American society and culture. In general, because of the pervasive nature of American media, this often means emulating American pop culture. Pranab, a 25-year-old male, described his initial efforts at integrating into American society in the following way:

> I wanted to come to America so badly that when I finally made my way to the United States, I told myself that I will leave behind my Nepali way of life and follow the American culture. I started to listen to hip-hop music. I started subscribing to *Sports Illustrated*. I began to play play-stations—that is very American, right? I watched American football. But after a while, I started to yearn for Bachchu Kailash and Narayan Gopal[15]... I quickly came to realize that it is not in me to only listen to hip-hop or watch American football. I mean, I still enjoy them but I am a Nepali, too, and I will never fully be an American no matter how much I try because I simply won't be allowed to, I simply won't be accepted. (Personal Communication)

When I later asked Pranab why he thought that he 'won't be allowed to' be an American, his answer was simple: he had tried very hard but does not have single white American friend he is close to. "If I were accepted, then I would have friends who I hang out with, who are Americans; people who I watch football with, who are Americans ... but that is not the case."

Pranab's anecdote symbolizes the ways in which many Nepali immigrants initially seek to acculturate and even assimilate themselves into what they believe to be the American way of life. Among other things, this initial attempt soon gets thwarted when these individuals start getting differential treatment because of their skin colour, their accent, and their status as 'foreigners', ultimately leading to the realization that "whiteness is a prerequisite for assimilation into [the] dominant culture" (Golash-Boza, 2006: 31; see also Feagin, 2000; Levitt, 2001; Devos and Banaji, 2005). For example, Shekhar, a student at a public university in Washington DC mentioned,

> When I came here, I sought to be as 'American' as possible. I joined a frat group in college and was heavy into drinking, partying, etc. As a result, my grades were affected.... Gradually, I came to realize that I was not being accepted by my circle of friends either. For them, I was just somebody they could ridicule and laugh at for my brown skin, foreign accent, and 'un-American' ways. What could I expect from a group of largely white males from privileged backgrounds, right? (Personal Communication)

In general, youths who are enrolled full time in college, especially those who live in the dorms (as opposed to Nepali enclaves), were the ones who mostly talked about experiences of racism and discrimination on a daily basis. This is not to say that discrimination and racism are more prevalent at these sites, and absent outside the four walls of academic life. On the contrary, these individuals, through their coursework and interactions with faculty members and peers, are more adept at identifying practices of racism and discrimination as opposed to their other Nepali counterparts who are either oblivious to it or even insist on the 'racelessness' of American society.

One of the most prevalent experiences these individuals, primarily youths who were still 'legal', described was of hearing hurtful comments from peers and outsiders, such as 'brownie' and 'over-fried chink'.[16] Other experiences such as being followed around by department store clerks, being questioned by security guards, etc., are much too common to merit recounting. However, when these individuals, unknowingly or on purpose, do something considered as being 'American', such as watching football or talking with an American accent, they are called 'coconut'[17] by their Nepali compatriots.

Thus, it is also important to bear in mind that the discriminatory practices outlined above are not limited to 'white' Americans practicing racism and discrimination against Nepalis or other groups. In fact, so institutionalized is the form of discrimination and racism in the United States that oftentimes it is people from minority groups who perpetuate and exercise these practices against other immigrants. For instance, one of my participants, who is currently working in an Indian restaurant in New York as an 'undocumented' worker, mentioned,

My boss treats me like a slave just because I am from Nepal while he is from India. He makes me work long hours and expects me to always follow his orders.... For him, I am just a *Bahadur*[18] and nothing else. But I have no other option because he is the only hope that I had for starting my green card process. (Personal Communication)

Despite this realization, only a few individuals spoke of resisting racism or discrimination targeted at them. Bikash is a 20-year-old male studying at an elite private institution in DC.

I am tired of people asking me about my plans of returning. I get really riled with the question and on various occasions have even told people, "Why should I go back? This country does not belong to you either—it belongs to the Native Americans." (Personal Communication)

For him and others alike, questions about when they plan to go back are 'their [Americans'] way of telling you that you do not belong here'. In fact, many scholars have also interpreted the question of returning 'home' as being racist (Talpade-Mohanty, 2001: 487). In this regard, as Bikash's rejoinder suggests, and as Bhatia (2007: 9) argues, the 'home' question can 'act as [a] destabilizing force that questions their [immigrants'] sense of home and their belongingness' in the United States.

Increased Racialization of South Asians

As has been documented by many scholars, the process of racialization of brown-skinned individuals heightened in the aftermath of the 11 September 2001 attacks even though exclusion of minorities was pervasive long before (Grewal, 2005). More specifically, as Ewing (2008: 1) points out, in the days following the attacks, some members of the American public, including leaders from the Christian right and radio talk show hosts, were quick to generalize threats from Al-Qaeda to include 'anyone who might look Muslim or Arab'. Because of the increased racialization and racial profiling of brown-skinned individuals, the more educated among the Nepali youths often expressed discontent, as elucidated in the experience of Akash, who works as a part-time salesperson in a department store in the West Coast while also attending an elite private institution.

> Once, a client came to me and started asking me about what I do. When I told him that I am working as well as going to school, the client asked sarcastically if I was attending flying school.[19] Since then, I have been more conscious of the color of my skin and even when I am in public places, I think about what the other person might be thinking of me.... When I am using public transport, I think about whether or not the person sitting next to me is freaking out thinking that the subway or the bus will blow up anytime soon.... (Personal Communication)

During the course of the fieldwork, other Nepalis also maintained that by virtue of the colour of their brown skin, they have been experiencing more racist undertones in their day-to-day living in the United States. The experiences in these narratives, seemingly trivial, mundane, and non-violent, nevertheless provide hints of racism or discrimination, which serve as a significant barrier against the incorporation and assimilation of young Nepalis in America. Not only do they prevent many Nepali immigrants from feeling that they can carve out a space for themselves in America but, as Akash pointed out, also serve as a 'constant reminder that this [America] is not their home'.[20]

Equally disconcerting has been the fact that this form of racism experienced on a daily basis is given public legitimacy by the likes of Pat Buchanan announcing, "Our [White-American] culture is superior to other cultures, superior because our religion is Christianity". The ramification of such nativist xenophobia in the public domain, as pointed out by Ross (1994), is that it gives "permission to [disaffected people to] practice a kinder, gentler white supremacy" (see also Merenstein, 2008). In such an environment where xenophobic sentiments are receiving public validation and racism against brown-skinned individuals is on the rise, most Nepali youths only spoke of anger and frustration yet found themselves unable to respond to, or address and resist such racial or discriminatory treatment. In particular, the 'fear of losing their immigrant status or being deported' has left many Nepalis in a state of despair.

However, in a seeming contradiction, some youths have been seeking to redress the problem of discrimination by practicing what is called 'reverse assimilation', that is, reinforcing ethnic or national identity, especially in benign terms, rather than assimilating into mainstream America. As Gagan, a student in New York, mentioned,

> I cannot pretend to be an American because I would not pass as a white. I am a 'brownie' and have a distinct accent.... But then I don't want to be mistaken for being a Muslim or an Arab either. The 'war against terror' has been waged against Muslims but Nepalis are not Muslims[21] and we need to highlight that.... (Personal Communication)

This need to assert Nepali identity, especially in opposition to Islam, is one of the many ways in which Nepali transnational organizations in the United States have been harbouring conservatism, especially one espousing Hindu orthodoxy (see also, Sijapati, 2010).

BEING WITHOUT BELONGING

As can be surmised from the discussion above, there are notable contradiction in the lives and aspirations of Nepali youths in the United States. On the one hand, the experiences of most immigrant youths are marked by exclusion and marginalization from mainstream America, which cause most of them to consider Nepal, and not the United States, as the place where they ultimately belong. Yet, Nepalis not only seek to enter the United States in increasing numbers but also foresee building a career in the United States and settling there for a 'few years', that is, until they are able to save enough money that would allow them to do something meaningful in Nepal. And, in fact, many of them, whether legal or illegal, are consumed by the idea of adjusting their status and becoming legal immigrants, whether by reinstating their student status, receiving 'green cards', that is, permanent residency, obtaining asylum,[22] or even naturalizing as American citizens.

How can this contradiction be explained? During the course of my fieldwork when I had asked my participants about why they had left Nepal, the reasons, as will be described below, were many, including the prospects for better educational attainment and economic opportunities. However, when I asked them why they have chosen to remain in the United States despite their experiences of hardships, struggle, discrimination, prejudice, etc., the answer often was a shameful smile or an awkward silence, suggesting that they were embarrassed or even apologetic. Evidently, for most of these Nepalis, as suggested by political theorist Honig (2003), the enduring narrative of America as a land of immigrants "[allows] disaffected citizenry to experience its regime as [being nevertheless] choice worthy."

So, what are the different ways in which Nepalis negotiate their being in the United States, particularly by accepting that remaining in the United States is 'choice worthy', despite the adversities they experience in their everyday lives? In the sections that follow, I present the rationales provided by my participants. It is unclear to me whether these responses, to use Bhatia's (2007: 3) terminologies, are forms of 'strategic justifications, denials, deflections, resistance, or acceptance'; but whatever they may be, these are ways in which Nepalis are exercising their agency to provide meaning to the contradictions they experience in their daily lives.

Benefits of American Lifestyle

The appeal of the United States to Nepali youths can be derived almost exclusively from the 'American lifestyle'. As Jyoti, one participant, mentioned and others echoed,

> You can get anything you want ... clothes, variety of food, good education for children, cars, music ... basically everything as long as you pay for it. You don't have that in Nepal, no matter how much I am willing to pay, I simply cannot get electricity in my village until and unless the government builds a grid. Similarly, if I need milk, I can simply go to a grocery store and buy it. I don't have to stand in line to get a bottle of milk like you sometimes have to in Nepal.... The amenities that you receive in America are simply not available in Nepal. (Personal Communication)

The benefits immigrants receive from new kinds of earnings, modern capital, and technology unavoidably attract as well as legitimize their being in the United States. For those who have received training in highly specialized technical fields, the prospect of finding employment commensurate with their educational attainment is simply not available in Nepal. Others, with families, especially children, mentioned their desire to remain in the United States for the future of their children. As one of my participants, an undocumented worker who recently had a child, mentioned, "It is not easy raising a family as an illegal worker. I work seven days a week driving cab for at least 10–14 hours a day. But my son was born here and is a citizen of this country. Hopefully, he will be able to bear the fruits of my labor."

In addition to these reasons for wanting to remain in the United States, which generally hold true across the board among Nepali youths, for women, the reasons run deeper. For many of them, in addition to the fulfilment of material wants and needs, the financial and psychological autonomy they enjoy in the United States is a source of liberation.

In fact, some women in my study even claimed that the sense of autonomy they feel is worth the experiences of distress they undergo from being separated from family and friends or the hardship they have to endure in their everyday dealings. However, given the daily experiences of marginalization, social isolation, and exclusion, in most cases, Nepalis, after a short interval, give up their earlier hopes of fully integrating into American society (even after naturalization) and instead choose to live marginalized lives.

Disenchantment with Nepal and Nepali Politics

A major impetus for young Nepalis leaving for the United States is the political instability in the home country. Because of the recent political turmoil in Nepal caused previously by the Maoist conflict, and now by the uncertainty of the future of the state structure, young Nepalis also claimed that they are doubtful about whether or not they would like to return to Nepal in the immediate future, despite their deep commitment to it. Others were reluctant because of the constant insistence from their parents that returning to Nepal would not be a worthy option because of the political as well as the dismal economic situation in the country. In fact, Suraj even said,

> My parents keep on saying that the best return for the investment they have made on me would be for me to get American citizenship through which I can also bring them over.

Still others cited issues of corruption, nepotism, and discrimination in Nepal, to name a few, that barred them from opting to return to Nepal. In fact, "*Nepal ma gayera pani ke garne?*" [What is there to do in Nepal even if we were to return?] was a response that was repeatedly mentioned by almost all of my participants. The disenchantment with the socio-political realities of Nepal was more pervasive amongst youths from marginalized groups. As Suman, a Dalit youth in DC, mentioned,

> While I was in Nepal and even when I first came to the U.S., I hardly ever used my last name to introduce myself since I did not want to be discriminated against.... People [admittedly, Nepalis who are 'non-Dalits'] are hesitant to share an apartment with me, eat with me, hang out with me or marry me. But who cares? If I do not find Nepalis, I will find Americans. They do not care whether I am a Dalit or not. These things do not matter for Americans, they treat everyone equally. (Personal Communication)

As can be deduced from this anecdote, youths like Suman, who are less aware of the various layers of race relations in the United States, uphold the belief that mainstream America would be more amenable to their lower caste or ethnic status than their counterparts in Nepal or fellow Nepalis in the United States. Evidently, these experiences not only serve as reminders to youths from marginalized groups about the nature of discrimination they had once faced in Nepal and/or likely to face if they were to return, but also instil in them the belief that the discriminatory treatment in Nepal is much worse than what they receive in the United States.

Image of America as a Raceless Society

On the issue of experiences of racism and discrimination in the United States, whereas some Nepalis, as I have highlighted above, claim that their experiences in Nepal were far worse than those in the United States, for many others, racism in America simply 'does not exist'. Evidently, on the one hand, the reluctance to admit that they have been exploited or discriminated against makes it easier for Nepalis to justify their being in the United States. On the other hand, some individuals are simply unaware of one's status in the racial hierarchy in the United States and, hence, on many occasions, fail to recognize subtle forms of prejudice, discrimination, and racism targeted against them, the non-white 'other'.

In general, as was the case in Levitt's study (2001) of Dominicans in Boston, Nepalis, by and large, have different understandings of race and discrimination from the way in which they are constructed and enacted in the United States. For them, 'blacks are poor because they are lazy, do drugs or engage in violence'. Pointing to an African-American man who was panhandling in a New York City subway, Shankar told me,

Look at him, we have to struggle so much to maintain our legal status, to find a job where questions about our legal status are not asked, and this man, even though he is a citizen and has the luxury to work anywhere he chooses to is simply not making use of the opportunity. I do not understand why people say that Americans are racist, these people ['Blacks'] are simply lazy. (Personal Communication)

Evidently, these Nepalis tend to believe that racial differences occur in polarized black-white terms. They claim that they themselves are impervious to discrimination because they are 'not black'. In the absence of deeper understandings of the complexity of race relations in the United States, it is thus not difficult to find Nepalis who proudly introduce themselves as 'Mexicans' and thereby believe that they have effectively surpassed being discriminated against![23]

In the same vein, the less educated among the Nepalis also claim to have successfully overcome exploitation and discrimination in the United States by being able to find a job that is 'more respectable' than what other Nepalis are doing. When Bimala told me that she works six and a half days a week from 8 a.m. to 6 p.m. in a carpet repair shop, and gets a weekly salary of $300, I instinctively asked her how she feels about being exploited like that. She quickly retorted, saying:

I don't think I am being exploited. My managers are nice to me. I am lucky to have found such a respectable job in Manhattan. If I had worked for some Indian in Jackson Heights then the pay would have been much less. And, plus, it is not like I am holding somebody's feet like you have to in a nail parlor or cleaning after somebody else's kid [as a babysitter].... Many [Nepali] women ask me if my manager would hire more people.... And, who is to say what is good or bad? In America, everyone has to do all kinds of work. In fact, no job is more superior than any other.... (Personal Communication)

In addition to youths engaged in menial jobs, the other group that also claims to be living in a 'discrimination-free' and 'meritocratic' society are successful individuals, especially those in the technical and scientific fields of study. When I asked Chandra, a student of electrical engineering, about his experiences with others and how he thought they viewed him, he replied curtly, "No different than anybody else," and further added, "I have been able to do so well in my classes here that all my classmates and professors hold me in high regard and to them it does not matter what I am besides the fact that I am one of the best, if not the best student in the class". Based on his own success, Chandra also believes that America is a 'colour-blind', meritocratic society and 'if you really work hard, then there are no barriers or ceilings that you are likely to face because of your ethnicity, race or nationality' (see Bhatia, 2007 for a similar phenomenon amongst middle-class Indian professionals). These narratives of Chandra and others like him corroborate Fordham's (1991) argument that in an effort to gain acceptance by the dominant group, academically successful students from minority groups often employ the strategy of racelessness wherein they seek to assimilate into the dominant group by emphasizing sameness and de-emphasizing differences (e.g. Chandra's argument about engaging in 'scientific endeavours' where differences based on 'physical traits' become irrelevant).

Still others argued that rather being prejudiced against, Nepalis, many of whom resemble Indians, are often typecast as a 'model minority' and hence in privileged positions instead of in a marginal status. These individuals surmised that by relying on their 'privileged' status as model minorities, they are somehow are able to overcome the discrimination and prejudice targeted against them as 'others'. However, as scholars studying race and Asian immigrants note, these very model minorities are often treated as foreigners who are unable to assimilate and are only seldom able to penetrate the upper-class status of the whites (see Bhatia, 2007 for an elucidative account of the experiences of Indian professionals leading the 'American Dream' in suburban America. See also Ong, 1996; Prashad, 2000; Merenstein, 2008).

The Evolving Multicultural America

Related to the earlier point on the perceived 'racelessness' of American society, some Nepali youths also rationalized their being in the United States by drawing on the demographic reality of multiculturalism in the United States. In fact, cognizant of the rhetoric of diversity and multiculturalism promoted in college campuses and universities throughout the United States as a response to "the 'politics of recognition' of American multiculturalism" (Kurien, 2004), Nepali youths claimed that 'there is space' in the American cultural milieu to assert different kinds of ethnic, regional, or religious identifications. As Aditya, a Limbu who is pursuing his education in computer engineering in New York, mentioned,

> Yes, in the United States, there is an appreciation of diversity. Despite the history of racism, especially against the Blacks, Americans are at least trying to overcome their racist past...there is equal opportunity in this country no matter what your ethnic background is. (Personal Communication)

Evidently, aware of the increasing rhetoric of multiculturalism, these youths based out of areas like New York and Washington DC are at ease in their heterogeneous metropolitan environment. In fact, their perception of an evolving and multicultural America is endorsed by what Sanjek (1992) calls 'ceremonies of incorporation' or 'rituals of inclusion' (Sanjek, 2000), whereby, through events like International Day, Kathmandu nights, South Asian Day, etc., featuring ethnic foods, music, and costumes and languages, young Nepalis believe that they will eventually be able to carve out a space for themselves in America.

Insisting on the evolving nature of the American metropolis and the increasing diversity of New York City's social groups, another participant added, "There was a time when Italians in this city were treated as the 'other' but now they are considered 'white' together with the dominant group. So, things are changing, you know…" In fact, insisting on the extremely diverse social context of New York City and Washington DC, these youths collectively sought to view themselves not as 'outsiders' but rather as part of the ethnic mosaic that has come to define these metropolitan areas.

Nepalis as 'Alien Citizens'

Broadly speaking, as mentioned earlier, there is a strong desire amongst Nepalis to be incorporated into American economic life even amongst those who were becoming increasingly aware that cultural assimilation in the United State is simply not possible for them. In fact, Nepali youths constantly struggle to get better jobs and lead more comfortable lives. Similarly, as I have mentioned earlier, despite the ultimate aim to return to Nepal, some Nepali immigrants even naturalize as American citizens. However, naturalization has not meant that Nepalis who are now bearers of American passports are exercising 'substantial citizenship'. One of the main reasons for this disjuncture is that most of these youths view the acquisition of American citizenship mostly in terms of convenience. For instance, Sheetal said,

> We took American citizenship only because we figured that there were so many benefits that we could get as a citizen, like easier access to loans, easy entry into other countries when we go out for vacation, etc.… I personally do not care about political participation and I have not yet practiced my voting rights. I would rather go and vote in Nepal because I care about political issues in Nepal much more than I do out here. (Personal Communication)

As Sheetal's example indicate, many Nepalis take American citizenship only for reasons of convenience and that acquiring American citizenship has no influence on their perceived identity as Nepalis. Scholars have often described this type of attitude as 'passport identity' (see Magat, 1999) or 'flexible citizenship' (Ong, 1996) where people take the citizenship of another country only because it would allow them to reap benefits bestowed by that state to its citizens.

In all such cases in my study, individuals who had naturalized had, however, not relinquished their Nepali citizenship (i.e. Nepali passport) even though it is illegal by Nepali law to hold dual citizenship.[24]

Amit rationalized retaining his Nepali passport by arguing that he should not be required to get a visa to visit his home [Nepal]. In fact, many Nepali youths who are seeking to acquire American citizenship or permanent residency do not view their desire to acquire American citizenship as conflicting with their sense of identity as a Nepali, their commitment to Nepal, or their plans to return to Nepal. Based on these dynamics, it is clear that Nepali immigrants are joining the ranks of 'alien citizens'—immigrants who have formal American citizenship but who nevertheless 'remain alien in the eyes of the nation' either because they themselves refrain from engaging in the American mainstream or because they are not allowed to because of racism, discrimination, etc. (Ngai, 2004: 8).

'Nourishing Non-Belonging'

Finally, irrespective of their experiences in the United States, their legal status, or their views about the current situation in Nepal, all the participants in my research invariably expressed their desire to eventually return to Nepal where they ultimately belong. With these future visions, it is not surprising then that, as in Magat's (1999) study of Israeli immigrants in Canada, many Nepalis, even those who have lived in the United States for a long time, have started to 'nourish non-belonging' in the United States by instead developing stronger ties with friends and families in Nepal, engaging more with social and political activities in Nepal despite the distance, and deepening Nepali social networks in the United States itself. In my other writings (see Sijapati, 2010), I have turned to this issue at greater length, so it will suffice to say here that these transnational ties give a sense of purpose and self-worth to these immigrants amidst the daily experiences of marginalization, social isolation, and exclusion in the United States.

CONCLUSION

In this chapter, I set out to explore the experiences of Nepalis in the United States by delineating the ways in which they have been negotiating the interface of two societies, Nepal and the United States. In doing so, I have presented the struggles that surround the lives of these youths as they seek to fulfil their educational and economic goals, often leading to the espousal of American culture and lifestyle but rejecting others considered to be 'distinctly American'. In the process of navigating their lives in America, these youths are also engaged in simultaneously rejecting, reconciling as well as adhering to the norms, values, and mores of Nepali culture and society.

In conclusion, I would like to point to a few propositions that can be drawn from this chapter, which has both theoretical and practical implications. First, the synthetic framework of utilizing transnationalism and assimilation/incorporation used in this chapter makes evident that neither of these terms on their own are useful in understanding the experiences of Nepali youths. This is because assimilation assumes that immigrants will abandon their ties with their home country and instead identify with the cultures, traditions, values, and institutions of the host country, which clearly is not the case for Nepali immigrants. On the one hand, while the aspirations of many Nepalis are marked to some degree by the desire to assimilate and be accepted by mainstream America, the experiences of discrimination and 'othering' on a daily basis serve as reminders to them that they are not equals in American society, leading these immigrants to seek ways of developing a stronger sense of belonging with their home country rather than in the United States.

While harbouring transnational ties with family, friends, and communities in Nepal may allow many immigrants to navigate through racial, social, and other sense of exclusion and marginalization from mainstream America, the need to be incorporated and assimilated into American society, even if it means in superficial terms (such as holding an American passport), is, however, quite pressing for the immigrants' everyday survival in the United States. In this regard, whereas home country ties in the transnational might be 'optional' for immigrants, ties with the 'host country' cannot be easily erased, particularly because of the ramifications that it has on one's being able to continue living in the United States.

Second, this analysis shows that in the post-modern era, there is a need to differentiate between 'being' and 'belonging'. Nepalis not only want to enter the United States in increasing numbers but also want to extend their periods of stay. However, this sense of 'being' in the United States and participating in and enjoying the amenities that life in America has to offer does not affect an individual's sense of belonging, which clearly is attached to their home country—Nepal.

Finally, the case of Nepalis shows that there is no 'monolithic minority experience' in the United States and the ways in which Nepali youths seek to navigate through life in America is affected by the socio-economic status of the immigrants themselves. For instance, the way in which a college-educated Nepali reacts to racism in the United States is significantly different from a youth who has dropped out from college and works in an Indian restaurant to survive. Although the latter may not even realize what being 'racialized' means, the former in an academic setting has available to him/her many institutional mechanisms to address it if he/she chooses to. In this regard, while talking about immigrants and belonging in post-modern era, there is perhaps a need to expand the concept of belonging to include 'selective belongings' to mark how the sense of belonging varies across groups within an immigrant community.

NOTES

1. The Diversity Immigrant Visa (DV), also known as the Green Card lottery, is a lottery programme that is administered annually by the Department of State among individuals from countries with low rates of immigration to the United States. The programme makes available 50,000 individuals with a United States Permanent Resident Card every year. Accessed from travel.state.gov/visa/immigrants/types/types_1322.html on 13 April 2009.
2. Levitt and Schiller (2004: 1009) describe transnational social fields as "a set of multiple interlocking networks of social relationships through which ideas, practices, and resources are unequally exchanged, organized and transformed".
3. The term 'illegal alien' is used in policy and legal circles in the United States, to identify a foreign natonal who has entered the United States without legal permission, or who legally entered but is now out of status especially since they have overstayed their terms of the visas.
4. Others include Australia, the United Kingdom, China, India, etc. Alongside the United States, the other most favoured destination is Australia, particularly because of part-time employment opportunities. In 2007, the Australian education services reported a 504 per cent increase from the previous year in the commencement rates of Nepalis.
5. The highest is China with 157,558 in 2010/11 followed by India, South Korea, and Canada. Countries which are either much larger in terms of population size than Nepal and/or economically much better-off such as Germany, the United Kingdom, and Brazil rank lower than Nepal.
6. Since the most common way in which Nepalis enter the United States is through student visas, I am taking the assimilation index for the entire Nepali population in the United States as a proxy to discuss issues of assimilation of my population group. The Composite Assimilation Index for the Nepalis was 8, which was the

lowest value for all the foreign-born immigrants from 119 different countries represented in the study. This relatively low value shows that Nepalis are much less integrated than migrants from other South Asian countries who are also recent migrants to the United States. For instance, the composite Index for Bangladesh, Sri Lanka, Pakistan, and India is 18, 20, 28, and 16, respectively. It is important to note that for the Nepali immigrants, assimilation is high on the economic domain (Economic Index Value=88), followed by Cultural, which equals to 57 and the lowest value is for civic (equal to 14), which means that naturalization rates and enlistment in military service are very low among Nepalis. See Vidgor (2008) for more details.

7. As the Hindi film industry centered around Bombay (Mumbai) is called.

8. Menial labour jobs are not difficult to find, especially in large cities like Washington DC, where employers recruit people without seeking legal papers that would establish their eligibility to work.

9. It is important to note here that while some immigrants who are employed at these jobs are also enroled in full-time study, a majority of them have dropped out of school and are now only working.

10. According to immigration regulations in the United States, to maintain their visa status, a student is required to register full time every quarter or semester of the academic year (excluding the summer) and make sufficient progress towards a degree until the study is completed.

11. What was earlier known as the INS, or the Immigration and Naturalization Services, has now been revamped as the United States Citizenship and Immigration Services (USCIS) under the Department of Homeland Security.

12. The man's wife and children are in Nepal while he too is living in the United States illegally.

13. This is because, on the one hand, Nepali immigrants, like many other immigrants, feel the need to portray their community as homogenous, and as having 'high moral values' and deep cultural roots, which often reflect an 'ahistorical' conception of the home that is untainted by 'western culture', but on the other hand, because most Nepalis have very little contact with the American mainstream, it is not surprising that they are able to incorporate few, if any, elements of American values or norms into their lives.

14. The anti-Muslim sentiment, which is notably shared by most Nepalis, is at one level a reflection of Hindu–Muslim tensions pervasive all across South Asia. However, in the case of Nepal in particular, the irreducible difference between the Hindus and Muslims also needs to be understood in light of the fact that the Nepali nation state until 2007 was defined as a 'Hindu monarchy' and most Nepalis had little contact with Muslims.

15. Famous Nepali singers who gained fame during the 1960s and the 1970s but continue to occupy a key standing in Nepal's musical and cultural scene.

16. 'Over-fried chink' is a derogative term used to signify Nepalis, who in comparison to other South Asians have 'smaller' eyes like East Asians do, yet are equally brown-skinned as other South Asians.

17. 'Coconut' is a racial slur, meaning 'brown from outside and white from inside'.

18. 'Bahadur', a term meaning 'brave' in many South Asian languages, including Nepali and Hindi, is commonly used in northern India to refer to Nepalis working in India, many of them as guards, and is considered a slight by many Nepalis.

19. The connotation here is that if Akash were going to 'flying school' he could possibly be a terrorist since some of the individuals involved in the 11 September terrorist attacks had been students at flying schools in the United States.

20. Drawing from various sources, Maira (2008) identifies that there were 700 reported hate crimes against South Asian Americans, Arab-Americans, and Muslim Americans, including four homicides (of which two involved South Asian American), in the three weeks following 11 September 2001. Similarly, the Council on American–Islamic relations reported that it had documented 960 incidents of racial profiling in the five weeks after 9/11, with hate crimes declining but incidents of airport profiling and workplace discrimination on the rise.

21. The claim that 'Nepalis are not Muslims' is a common attitude even in Nepal despite the fact that almost 5 per cent of Nepalis are Muslims (Census, 2001).

22. In the aftermath of the political conflict in Nepal, many Nepalis who have overstayed their visas have sought asylum on the grounds that they have been victimized by the Maoists or the government. While some of the asylum cases are genuine, others have been patently fabricated, as I myself was able to discover first hand when asked to serve as an 'expert witness' a number of times.

23. I have come across many Nepalis who say that they tell people that they are Mexicans so that they are not treated as 'blacks' or 'Indians'.

24. Although illegal, retaining 'dual' citizenship is a common practice among Nepalis. As of August 2009, only 249 people with foreign citizenships had renounced their Nepali citizenship although there are an estimated 30,000 foreign citizens. See "Govt mulling multiple-entry visa to NRNs," www.nepalnews.com, 6 August 2009, accessed on 7 August 2009.

REFERENCES

Alba, Richard and Victor Nee. 2005. *Remaking the American Mainstream.* Cambridge, MA: Harvard University Press.

Appadurai, Arjun. 1996. *Modernity at Large: Cultural Dimensions of Globalization.* Minneapolis, MN: University of Minnesota Press.

Basch, Linda, Nina Glick-Schiller, and Cristina Szanton-Blanc. 1994. *Nations Unbound: Transnational Projects, Postcolonial Predicaments and Deterritorialized Nation-States.* New York, NY: Routledge.

Bhatia, Sunil. 2007. *American Karma: Race, Culture, and Identity in the Indian Diaspora.* New York, NY: New York University Press.

Bhavnani, Kum-Kum, 1993. 'Towards a Multicultural Europe?: "Race", Nation and Identity in 1992 and Beyond,' *Feminist Review,* 45: 32–42.

Devos, Thierry and Mahzarin R. Banaji. 2005. 'American = White?', *Journal of Personality and Social Psychology,* 88: 447–66.

Ewing, Katherine Pratt. 2008. *Being and Belonging: Muslims in the United States since 9/11.* New York, NY: Russell Sage Foundation.

Feagin, Joe R. 2000. *Racist America: Roots, Current Realities, and Future Reparations.* New York, NY: Routledge.

Foner, Nancy. 2000. *From Ellis Island to JFK: New York's Two Great Waves of Immigration*. New Haven, CT: Yale University Press.

Fordham, Signithia. 1991. 'Racelessness in Private Schools: Should We Deconstruct the Racial and Cultural Identity of African-American Adolescents?', *Teachers College Record*, 92: 470–84.

Gans, Herbert. 1992. 'Second-Generation Decline: Scenarios for the Economic and Ethnic Futures of the post-1965 American Immigrants', *Ethnic and Racial Studies*, 15: 173–93.

Gibson, Margaret A. 1988. *Accommodation without Assimilation: Sikh Immigrants in an American High School*. Ithaca, NY: Cornell University Press.

Glazer, Nathan and Daniel P. Moynihan. 1970. *Beyond the Melting Pot: The Negroes, Puerto Ricans, Jews, Italians, and Irish of New York City*, 2nd ed. Cambridge, MA: MIT Press.

Golash-Boza, Tanya. 2006. 'Dropping the Hyphen? Becoming Latino(a)-American through Racialized Assimilation', *Social Forces*, 85: 27–55.

Grewal, Inderpal. 2005. *Transnational America: Feminisms, Diasporas, Neoliberalisms*. Durham, NC: Duke University Press.

Honig, Bonnie. 2003. *Democracy and the Foreigner*. Princeton, NJ: Princeton University Press.

Huntington, Samuel P. 2004. *Who Are We? The Challenges to America's National Identity*. New York, NY: Simon & Schuster.

Kurien, Prema. 2004. 'Multiculturalism, Immigrant Religion, and Diasporic Nationalism: The Development of an American Hinduism', *Social Problems*, 51: 362–85.

Levitt, Peggy. 2001. *The Transnational Villagers*. Berkeley, CA: University of California Press.

Levitt, Peggy and Nina Glick Schiller. 2004. 'Conceptualizing Simultaneity: A Transnational Social Field Perspective on Society', *International Migration Review*, 38: 1002–39.

Magat, Ilan N. 1999. 'Israeli and Japanese Immigrants to Canada: Home, Belonging, and the Territorialization of Identity', *Ethos*, 27: 119–44.

Maira, Sunaina. 2008. 'Flexible Citizenship/Flexible Empire: South Asian Muslim Youth in Post-9/11 America', *American Quarterly*, 60: 697–720.

Merenstein, Beth Frankel. 2008. *Immigrants and Modern Racism: Reproducing Inequality*. Boulder, CO: Lynne Rienner Publishers.

Ngai, Mae M. 2004. *Impossible Subjects: Illegal Aliens and the Making of Modern America*. Princeton, NJ: Princeton University Press.

Olwig, Karen Fog and Kirsten Hastrup. 1997. *Sitting Culture: The Shifting Anthropological Object*. New York, NY: Routledge.

Ong, Aihwa. 1996. 'Cultural Citizenship as Subject-Making: Immigrants Negotiate Racial and Cultural Boundaries in the United States', *Current Anthropology*, 37: 737–62.

Phinney, Jean S. 1990. 'Ethnic Identity in Adolescents and Adults: A Review of Research', *Psychological Bulletin*, 108: 499–514.

Portes, Alejandro. 1997. 'Immigration Theory for a New Century: Some Problems and Opportunities', *International Migration Review*, 31: 799–825.

Portes, Alejandro and Rubén Rumbaut. 2006. *Immigrant America: A Portrait*, 3rd ed. Berkeley, CA: University of California Press.

Prashad, Vijay. 2000. *The Karma of Brown Folk.* Minneapolis, MN: University of Minnesota Press.

Ross, Loretta. 1994. *White Supremacy in the 1990's.* Atlanta, GA: Center for Democratic Renewal.

Rouse, Roger. 1995. 'Questions of Identity: Personhood and Collectivity in Transnational Migration to the United States', *Critique of Anthropology*, 15: 351–80.

Rumbaut, Rubén. 2002. 'Severed or Sustained Attachments? Language, Identity, and Imagined Communities in the Post-immigrant Generation', in Peggy Levitt and Mary C. Waters (eds), *The Changing Face of Home: The Transnational Lives of the Second Generation*, pp. 43–95. New York, NY: Russell Sage Foundation.

Sanjek, Rocher. 1992. 'The Organization of Festivals and Ceremonies among Americans and Immigrants in Queens, New York', in Åke Duan, Billy Ehn, and Barbro Klein (eds), *To Make the World Safe for Diversity: Toward an Understanding of Multicultural Societies*, pp. 123–94.

Sanjek, Roger. 2000. *The Future of Us All.* Ithaca, NY: Cornell University Press.

Sijapati, Bandita. 2010. 'Nepali Transmigrants: An Examination of Transnational Ties among Nepali Immigrants in the United States', Special double issue: Nepalese migrations. *European Bulletin of Himalayan Research*, 35–36: 139–53.

Talpade-Mohanty, Chandra. 2001. 'Crafting Feminist Genealogies: On the Geography and Politics of Home, Nation, and Community', in Ella Shohat (ed.), *Talking Visions: Multicultural Feminism in a Transnational Age*, pp. 485–500. Cambridge, MA: MIT Press.

Thapan, Meenakshi (ed.). 2005. *Transnational Migration and the Politics of Identity.* New Delhi: SAGE Publications.

Walzer, Michael. 1992. *What It Means to Be an American*, 1st ed. New York, NY: Marsilio.

Zhou, Min. 1999. 'Segmented Assimilation: Issues, Controversies, and Recent Research on the New Second Generation', in Charles Hirschman, Josh Dewind, and Philip Kasinitz (eds), *The Handbook of International Migration: The American Experience*, pp. 825–58. New York, NY: Russell Sage Foundation Publications.

Chapter 11

Global Gurungs

Ethnic Organizing Abroad*

SUSAN HANGEN

At City Hall in New York City, on a sunny Sunday afternoon in September 2002, a group of about 30 people gathered to attend a workshop on accessing health-care services in New York, sponsored by an organization called the Gurung (Tamu) Society, Inc., USA.[1] The group was composed mostly of recent Nepali immigrants. Women were mostly dressed in saris and lungis, though a few sported jeans or skirts. Men wore business casual dress pants and shirts. The president of the organization, a man in his thirties who works in the technology industry, introduced the presenters, including the health director, at the Mayor's office and officials from the city health department and a hospital in Queens, a borough in New York.

One official from the Queens hospital, an African-American man named Mr. Johnson, decided to introduce himself to everyone in the audience. He shook hands with the first person and asked him for his name: "I'm Akash Gurung", replied the man. "Gu-rung", he repeated slowly, "Did I get that right?" "Bala Ram Gurung", answered the next man. "Ah, another Gurung!" he said, surprised. After meeting Gurung after Gurung, he paused and asked the room, "Okay, wait—is *everyone* here a Gurung?" Laughter broke out, and one man explained: "We are all members of the same ethnic group; Gurung is the name of an ethnic group in Nepal and we all have that as our last name. But we aren't all directly related". As he absorbed

* The author thanks all members of the Gurung (Tamu) Society Inc., USA, for assisting her with this project. Tika Gurung, who was in a leadership position in the organization for several years, has been especially helpful.

this information, Mr. Johnson spotted me on the other side of the room and referring to my non-Nepali appearance joked, "Okay, let me guess—you're Gurung too?" "Well actually I'm married to a Gurung, so ..." I began, and everyone laughed.

This incident speaks about the challenges that Gurungs face in seeking recognition from the wider society in the United States, where surprisingly few people are familiar with Nepal, and even fewer have heard of the numerous small ethnic groups there. According to the Gurung Society's unofficial estimates in 2009, there are only about 500 Gurungs, out of about 20,000 Nepalis, in the New York metro area.[2] The Gurung Society was formed in 1999 when the population of Gurungs was even smaller. By examining this organization, I seek to contribute to our understanding of how Nepali migrants to the United States create forms of belonging.

It was not inevitable that Nepalis outside of Nepal would organize along ethnic lines. In fact, the first organizations created by Nepalis in the United States in the early 1980s, such as the Association of Nepalis in America and the America-Nepal Friendship Society, did not refer to these ethnic groups and emphasized belonging to the Nepali nation. In the late 1990s, however, Nepalis abroad began forming associations for particular ethnic groups in addition to those that represent Nepalis as a whole. By 2009, there were 30 organizations of Nepalis in New York city, and half of these were based on a Nepali ethnic, caste, or regional identity rather than representing the Nepali community as a whole. This shift appears to have occurred in most countries where there are large Nepali communities. Gurung organizations now exist in New York and other major metropolitan areas in the United States, the United Kingdom, Australia, Hong Kong, and Japan, and other scholars have discussed organizations representing other Nepali ethnic groups in Japan (Yamanaka, 2007) and Hong Kong (Minami, 2007).

Most of these ethnic organizations were formed after the year 2000, when Nepalis began to arrive in New York in greater numbers. Yet the increasing numbers of Nepali immigrants in New York cannot fully explain why organizations have taken this particular focus and form. The evolving political context in Nepal and the interests of some Nepali migrants in participating in that political arena from a distance are crucial for understanding the changing character of Nepali migrant associations. Thus, we must ask why belonging to particular ethnic groups as they are labelled in Nepal remains salient for Nepali migrants and what the references to these ethnic groups mean in this new context. In this chapter, I aim to answer these questions by examining the activities of the Gurung Society and their social and political effects.

The concept of belonging can illuminate some of the meanings of the Gurung Society for Gurungs in New York. Belonging refers to the various forms of attachment that people create in their relationships and to the sense of mutuality and commonality that emerges from those relationships. The idea of belonging encompasses attachments to various collectivities such as families, ethnic groups, nations, states, or organizations (Pfaff-Czarnecka and Toffin, 2011). The existence of organizations in New York that reference the ethnic groups in Nepal, like the Gurung Society, indicates that ethnicity is a salient marker of belonging in the context of migration. Yet the label Gurung in New York calls forth multiple forms of belonging that are not simply transferred from Nepal. As I explore further below, the idea of belonging to a Gurung community has come to hold meaning both through transnational political activities as well as through activities that take place within the United States.

MIGRANT ASSOCIATIONS AND TRANSNATIONAL POLITICS

Since the 1990s, scholars have focused on understanding the transnational activities of migrants, examining how migrants "… act in a field of social relations that links together their country of origin and their country or countries of settlement" (Glick Schiller et al., 1992). Migrants can engage in many different forms of transnationalism, from sending remittances to consuming media focused on the homeland or campaigning for political candidates from afar. Furthermore, different migrants engage in transnationalism through diverse channels: some migrants may be primarily involved in transnational kinship networks, whereas others are involved in transnationalism through institutions (Levitt et al., 2003). Individual migrants participate in these networks with varying degrees of intensity and formality.

Scholars have identified migrant associations as one of the key sites of institutionalized transnational activities. Many of the activities of migrant associations fall into the broad category of transnational politics, which refers to the various ways that migrants directly participate in the politics of their country of origin from their location across border, including voting, campaigning, or participating in political debates (Ostergaard-Nielsen, 2003). These migrant associations often engage the administration and political parties of the sending state (Itzigsohn, 2000) but may also work with non-state actors, such as social movements organizations, in the sending state. Although transnational activities are now a mainstay of immigrant organizations, these organizations continue to play a role in addressing the needs and interests of migrants in their new countries (Owusu, 2000; Levitt et al., 2003; Ostergaard-Nielsen, 2003; Odmalm, 2004). Migrant organizations thus operate at multiple levels and are oriented towards several social and political contexts.

The Gurung Society exemplifies this pattern as it operates in multiple social and political contexts, and is oriented both towards the political and social spheres of Nepal and the United States. First, I examine the transnational dimensions of the Gurung Society and show how it calls forth a form of belonging to the political sphere of Nepal. It does so by engaging with non-state actors, specifically with organizations that are key players in the indigenous nationalities' (*Adivasi/Janajati*) social movement in Nepal. Some of the Gurung Society's activities, such as the celebration of Lhochhar, illustrate this connection to the indigenous nationalities movement. Gurungs also send DVDs produced by the Gurung Society to Gurungs in Nepal and other places, contributing to the sense of belonging to a Gurung diaspora. Second, I examine how the Gurung Society facilitates other forms of belonging within the United States. The organization seeks to forge connections between Gurungs in New York so that they can provide a support structure for each other, replacing in part the role that kin and other affiliates played for them in Nepal. The Gurung Society also responds to the challenges that Gurungs face in working and surviving in New York, and seeks recognition for Gurungs from the dominant society there.

GURUNGS ABROAD

In Nepal there are about half a million Gurungs, but Gurungs have migrated to other countries in Asia, as well to the Middle East, Australia, America, and Europe. Gurungs, like many other Nepalis, have long sought foreign employment as a means of earning cash to supplement their agricultural livelihoods. For Gurung men in particular, from the 19th century onwards, foreign employment has often meant serving in the Gurkha regiments of the British or Indian armies (Caplan, 1995). Gurungs migrating outside Nepal now include both men and women who work at a wide variety of jobs.

The number of Gurungs and other Nepalis who are living and working in the United States and elsewhere outside of Nepal has increased in the last decade. This trend is related to the heightened political and economic crises there, fuelled by the decade-long Maoist insurgency that displaced hundreds of thousands of people from rural areas and led to 13,000 deaths (Seddon et al., 2001). The New York metropolitan area is one of main regions where Gurungs have settled in the United States, and the Gurung organization asserts that there are at least 200 Gurungs there now. Other places in the United States where Gurungs cluster are Boulder, Colorado, with about 200 Gurungs, and Boston, MA, where there are about 100 Gurungs.

Most Gurungs, like many Nepalis in the New York area, do not arrive with immigrant visas; they enter on student or tourist visas and then overstay these visas. While many of these individuals were professionals in Nepal, they settle for jobs in the low-end of the service sector in New York. Women often find employment in nail salons and babysitting; men work as limousine or taxi drivers, and in restaurant and retail positions. Many seek to legalize their status here and some have successfully done so. A few Gurungs are legal permanent residents of the United States and hold professional positions in the New York area; these individuals typically have undergraduate and/or graduate degrees from the United States.

The purpose of the Gurung Society in New York as stated in the by-laws, is "to preserve, encourage and enhance social, economic and cultural heritage and cooperation among Gurung (Tamu) people living in and outside the United States of America". The organization upholds this mission by carrying out projects that connect Gurungs in New York City, such as the annual summer picnic, and the New Year celebration, Lhochhar, which I discuss below. They also seek to connect Gurungs throughout the world. One example of this effort is the organization's website, www.Gurungs.org,[3] described as "an online village of Gurungs and friends of Gurungs". It presents a list of Gurung organizations and events throughout the world, and photos of New York Gurung events. Finally, the organization sponsors projects that help Gurungs integrate into the United States by helping them deal with the challenges they face there.

People become members of the Gurung organization by contributing $25.00 per family per year, or a one-time fee of $500.00 per family to become life members. As of 2009, there were about 15 life members and more than 100 members. Of the roughly 500 Gurungs in New York, about two dozen people, mostly men, play an active role in steering the organization and can be considered the core members of the organization. These core members include the executive committee of the organization, which consists of the president, vice president, secretary, treasurer, co-treasurer, and 12 other individuals. The executive committee serves for a two-year term and is selected by the previous executive committee.

Most of the executive committee representatives are men and all have legal immigration status in the United States. Of the four men who have been presidents of the organization since it was founded, two were educated in the United States whereas the other two are retired British army soldiers. Many of the core members lack valid immigration documents, and they have refrained from accepting leadership positions because they do not wish to attract the attention of immigration authorities.

The organization's project of preserving Gurung culture and encouraging cooperation among Gurungs is complicated by the fact that this is a heterogeneous community. They are fragmented by differences in religious identity, as many Gurungs follow Hinduism, whereas others assert that Gurungs are really Buddhists or should follow shamans. Clan distinctions also divide Gurungs: some argue that 'real Gurungs' must come from one of four clans, and disregard another set of 16 clans who also claim to be Gurung. People from the Gurung heartland in the western part of Nepal who speak the Gurung language often view those from the east, who only speak the Nepali language, as less authentically Gurung. Gurungs from the northern region of Manang are often regarded as constituting a separate community though they use the last name Gurung. While people refer to these distinctions in New York, the official policy of the Gurung Society is to invite all people who call themselves Gurung to become members and to even allow non-Gurungs to belong to the organization as 'friends of Gurungs'.

Furthermore, not all Gurungs have the same expectations of the Gurung Society. The core members have somewhat different goals for the organization than the other Gurungs in the community. The core members are the most engaged in the transnational political activities of the organization. For many other Gurungs, the Gurung Society exists primarily to connect them to other Gurungs in the United States and to assist them in times of crisis.

TRANSNATIONAL ACTIVITIES

In this section, I explore some of the Gurung Society's transnational activities, particularly those activities through which Gurungs in New York engage with the Nepali political and social spheres. The emergence of the Gurung Society and other ethnic organizations outside Nepal is related to the rise of the indigenous nationalities (*Adivasi/ Janajati*) movement in Nepal since the People's Movement of 1990 established a multi-party democracy. This movement has mobilized marginalized ethnic groups to work to end the dominance of high-caste Hindus in the state, to gain greater political representation, and to revitalize their languages, religions, and other cultural practices, which had withered under the assimilationist strategies of the Hindu state (Pfaff-Czarnecka, 1999; Hangen, 2007).

Organizations of indigenous nationalities have proliferated in Nepal; among the hundreds of such organizations, representing about 60 different groups of indigenous nationalities, there are more than 50 Gurung organizations. These organizations work towards ending ethnic inequality and engage in activities that seek to define and promote a distinct Gurung culture. These organizations have played an increasingly central role in defining what it means to be Gurung in Nepal, and participating in the activities sponsored by these organizations is now an important way of expressing Gurung identity. The growth of the indigenous nationalities movement and the organizational forms it has spawned made the project of expressing Gurung culture and identity abroad compelling. Leaders of the Gurung Society and other ethnic organizations in New York see their organization as part of the Nepali indigenous nationalities movement and assert that Gurungs belong to the wider community of indigenous nationalities.

The formation of organizations based on ethnic identity in the context of migration can be directly linked to debates over the definition of the Nepali nation that have flourished in Nepal since the launch of democracy in 1990 (Sharma, 1997; Whelpton, 1997). The indigenous nationalities movement rejected the old model of a nation based on a Hindu monarchy and the Nepali language with a multicultural secular ideal escalated. Thus for some migrants, organizations that claimed to represent all Nepalis were suspect. One Gurung Society leader explained his perception of the more general Nepali organizations as follows: "They say those organizations are for all Nepalis, but when you look at the board it is not so. They sponsor Hindu religious programs. It is hard for our ethnic groups to get comfortable in that situation". For supporters of the indigenous nationalities movement, the overwhelming presence of high-caste Hindus at the helm of these other organizations suggests that these organizations espouse a definition of the Nepali nation in which high-caste Hindu culture is equated with Nepali culture.

Building on the transnational influence of the Nepali indigenous nationalities movement, many organizations representing indigenous nationalities in New York came together in 2006 to create a coalition, called the Federation of Indigenous People's of Nepal in America (FIPNA). The Gurung organization was not among the founding organizations but later joined FIPNA. FIPNA replicates the organization in Nepal that has been the main engine of this social movement, the Nepal Federation of Indigenous Nationalities (NEFIN), comprising 59 ethnic organizations. FIPNA was founded after a prominent ethnic activist from Nepal, Parsuram Tamang, who was at one time chair of NEFIN, visited New York for the annual meeting of the United Nations Permanent Forum on Indigenous Peoples. Although there is no official link between FIPNA and NEFIN, FIPNA representatives consulted with NEFIN members when creating their by-laws, and FIPNA has hosted talk programmes for members of NEFIN and other indigenous nationalities organizations when they visit New York.

The Gurung Society also engages in other forms of transnational politics. Forming the Gurung organization has enabled Gurungs in New York to be visible as a community to Gurung political representatives who visit from Nepal, and thus to attempt to influence politics in Nepal through them. For example, when two Gurung politicians, Dev Gurung, a minister in the Maoist government and a member of the central committee of the Maoist party, and Sita Gurung, a Constituent Assembly member from the Nepali Congress party, visited New York in April 2008, the Gurung Society sponsored a series of public presentations and small dinner gatherings so that their members could interact with these people. Unlike some other Nepali organizations in New York, the Gurung Society does not promote any single political party. Rather, they view all Gurung politicians as role models for other Gurungs, as there are relatively few Gurung politicians, and as individuals who would support Gurung issues.

Leaders of the Gurung Society explained that these events served as a way of educating Gurungs in New York about current political issues in Nepal, and thus keeping them connected to Nepal. Many of the conversations at these events dwelled on the progress and challenges of the indigenous nationalities movement and considered how to advance Gurungs in Nepali society. The representatives of the Gurung Society would not be able to gain access to these leaders so easily in Nepal, where more people compete for their attention.

Gurung organizations inside and outside of Nepal influence each other. The existence of Gurung organizations outside of Nepal was an important factor in the decision to establish a federation of Gurung organizations in Nepal and beyond in 2000, the Gurung (Tamu) National Coordination Council. When the Council held a conference at which all organizations met in 2003, they asked Gurung organizations in New York, Hong Kong, the United Kingdom, and Japan to contribute funds to cover the expenses of the meeting. The Gurung Society in New York contributed about $1,400 to the event, and asked that their funds assist in enabling women and youths to attend.

The strong connections between the Gurung organizations in Nepal and the one New York are evident in the largest project of the Gurung organization in New York, the celebration of Lhochhar. Lhochhar (meaning the changing of the year, as *Lho* means year and *chhar* means change in the Gurung language) celebrates the Gurung New Year in a 12-year cycle. Lhochhar is an excellent example of an 'invented tradition' (Hobsbawm and Ranger, 1983), a fundamentally new cultural project that suggests continuity with the past. Since the mid-1990s, Gurung organizations in Nepal have transformed what was a minor and varied celebration followed by some Gurungs in western Nepal into a major public celebration shared by all Gurungs. They sponsor huge celebrations in various cities, and in Kathmandu, the festivities are held in the capital's largest convention centre and attended by thousands of Gurungs from all over Nepal. Activities at the four-day-long festival include speech contests, motorcycle rallies, archery contests, Gurung dress contests, *dohori* song fests (competitive singing duets), and a large outdoor feast. Lhochhar is celebrated on the fifteenth day of the Nepali month of Poush, which falls in late December.

Celebrating Lhochhar advances the wider political projects of Gurung organizations in several ways. Gurung activists promoted Lhochhar to replace the major national Hindu holiday, Dasain, with Lhochhar as the central holiday of the year for Gurungs. Celebrations of Lhochhar invoke a calendar system that differs from the state's official 'Hindu' *vikram sambat* calendar, and thus challenged the idea of the Nepali nation as fundamentally Hindu. When many sweeping symbolic changes were implemented after the people's movement of 2006, the government recognized Lhochhar as a public holiday.

The celebration of Lhochhar also provides a potential source of unity for Gurungs, who are fragmented in multiple ways, including religion, language, and regional origin. Lhochhar suggests that they share a unique system of structuring time, and by extension a distinct history. By privileging time as a key component of identity, Gurungs create a sense of unity across space. Lhochhar is a ritual that incorporates Gurungs living abroad into the Gurung community. Gurungs may live in various parts of Nepal and around the world, but they all observe the same beginning of the year.

The Gurung (Tamu) Society, USA, began holding Lhochhar celebrations shortly after it was established in 1999, and it remains the organization's central activity. Lhochhar celebrations outside Nepal are not long-held traditions 'from the homeland'. Many Gurungs celebrated Lhochhar, especially in this major way, for the first time outside of Nepal, following efforts of Gurung organizations in Nepal in the mid-1990s to promote Lhochhar as part of a revitalized and unified form of Gurung culture. The Lhochhar celebrations are evidence of the Gurung Society's participation in a transnational conversation about the meaning of Gurung identity. By celebrating Lhochhar, Gurungs in New York symbolically connect with Gurungs elsewhere in the world. The celebration makes being Gurung salient in New York by providing a space and activity through which Gurung identity is performed and through which Gurungs connect with each other.

The six celebrations of Lhochhar in New York I attended between 2002 and 2010 were similar in spirit and structure. Indeed, the sequence of events at these celebrations is similar to that of most other large, public Nepali gatherings in New York. I briefly describe the event I witnessed in December 2003 to give a sense of these events. The party was held at a glitzy function hall, sparkling with crystal chandeliers and mirrored walls, in the basement of an Indian restaurant in Queens. Over 150 adults purchased tickets at the door and numerous children attended the event as well, for free. People chatted in small groups while eating snacks; many men hovered near the cash bar. The highlight of the evening was the 'cultural programme' of songs and dancing, lasting over two hours. An elaborate Indian buffet feast followed, at about 11 p.m. After dinner, people danced to Nepali and Hindi pop music until 2 a.m.

Despite the Indian venue and cuisine, the celebration was devoted to enabling Gurungs in New York to gain a sense of belonging to a Gurung community. A large replica of the circular 12-year calendar hung on the front wall, reminding those attending that Gurungs have their own calendar. Furthermore, over half of the people at the party were wearing what they referred to as 'Gurung dress', using the English word 'dress'. Gurungs in New York wear this clothing only at Lhochhar, unless they are performing a Gurung dance on a stage at some other Nepali gathering. I first saw these outfits not while living with Gurungs in eastern Nepal in the 1990s, but at the Lhochhar celebration in Queens in December 2002. Around the year 2000, Gurung organizations in Nepal determined which clothing would constitute 'traditional' Gurung dress, loosely based on historical evidence and on the sartorial practices of some Gurungs in mid-Western Nepal. When wearing these outfits, Gurungs invoke the notion of ancestral customs and a unique history, thus underscoring the temporal dimension of identity.

The project of representing Gurung identity is also explicit in the cultural programme (*sanskritik karyakram*), a term that describes an event at which people, ideally, perform 'traditional' dances and/ or songs on a stage. Some performances are designated as 'Gurung dances': these are based on either traditional dances or choreographed to Gurung language songs, and performed in Gurung dress. Gurung dances make up no more than a third of the performances in these cultural programmes. The bulk of the performances make no pretence of presenting a 'traditional' or unique Gurung culture and refer in some way to Nepali culture: performers dance to Nepali folk or film songs, croon Nepali pop songs, and perform skits or comedy routines in Nepali. Performers have also delivered magic shows to

American popular music, and break-danced to hip hop songs in English. Furthermore, while most of the performers are Gurungs at these events, some are other Nepalis.

The variety of performances and performers encompassed in these programmes present an elastic definition of Gurung culture: such hybridity characterizes many diasporic cultural practices and identities (Chaudhry, 1998; Dwyer, 2000; Anthias, 2001). This hybridity was unproblematic for Lhochhar organizers and audience members. When I asked organizers of the New York programme if there have been discussions concerning whether non-Gurungs should perform at Lhochhar, or debates over what forms of culture should be presented at the programme, they responded that these were not crucial issues for them. The audience appeared similarly untroubled by these issues: they responded as enthusiastically to the magic shows and hip hop dances as they did to the Gurung dances. Whatever people do can be considered Gurung culture within the space defined by Lhochhar celebrations. That the category Gurung is reinforced is sufficient.

THE EMERGENCE OF A GURUNG DIASPORA

Recently, Gurungs outside Nepal have begun to view themselves as part of a global Gurung community, or diaspora. The concept of diaspora holds that some contemporary migrants come to see themselves as belonging to a third social space, a diaspora. For the diaspora, as James Clifford (1997: 250) wrote, "decentered lateral connections may be as important as those formed around a teleology of origin/return". Diasporas emerge from efforts to stitch together peoples who are dispersed in more than two places, creating the idea that these people form a community despite their lack of spatial unity.

In some studies of diasporas, the homeland is often taken to automatically generate a diaspora, meaning a group of people who are living away from their common place of origin and yet continue to identify as belonging to that place. For example, scholars often calculate the size of 'a diaspora' by enumerating people with shared ancestry living outside of their country of origin (Brubaker, 2005). As Brian Axel argues, scholars mistakenly consider the homeland to be the primary context of diaspora, and refer to it as an archive of facts to explain the culture of the diaspora (Axel, 2004: 29). In fact, the new countries of residence and the global spaces that emerge when people in different countries communicate with each other are also important contexts in understanding the emergence of a diaspora.

As both Axel and Brubaker argue, diaspora is better understood not as a concrete group of people with shared ties to a distant land but as a form of social practice: "a globally mobile category of identification" (Axel, 2004: 27), or "an idiom, a stance, a claim" (Brubaker, 2005: 12). By viewing diaspora as a social practice, rather than as an already-existing entity, the focus of analysis shifts to explaining how the idea of a diaspora comes into existence. Following this interpretation of the diaspora, I examine some the cultural activities through which Gurungs make claim to this form of belonging. In the vision of the Gurung community as a diaspora, Nepal is a reference point that gives Gurung identity salience rather than the container within which Gurungs exist. A Gurung diaspora is not generated by the mere fact that Gurungs share a homeland in Nepal.

The emerging idea of a Gurung diaspora stems from the politicization of Gurung identity since 1990 and the increasing availability of forms of media that make a Gurung diaspora plausible. Scholars have noted that new media forms, especially digital media and the Internet, are a key element in the production of diasporas (Axel, 2004; Schein, 2004; Ignacio, 2005; Ong, 2008). Dispersed Gurungs are able to connect through various media forms, giving Gurung identity salience even in settings like the United States in which there are relatively few Gurung individuals and in which Gurung is not a recognized category.

The production and circulation of DVDs of Lhochhar is one media-based cultural practice that contributes to the production of the diaspora. Gurung organizations throughout the United States, and in Japan, Hong Kong, and London, create videos or DVDs of Lhochhar celebrations. The Gurung Society in New York hires Nepali videographers and editors for these events. Organizers request that people do not film the event themselves so that there is one collective DVD of the event. These DVDs are official representations of community events, in which individuals are represented as members of a Gurung community.

The content of the dozen DVDs that I have seen is similar in significant ways. Each opens with a title, announcing the Gurung organization, year, and city of the celebration, then proceeds to shots of the city in which the celebration takes place: the New York DVD begins with scenes of taxis rushing down avenues full of bright lights, followed by a sweeping view of The Statue of Liberty and other famous buildings. Scenes of organizers preparing for the big event, and people arriving and buying tickets, followed by scenes of people socializing and eating snacks, are also common. The cultural programmes, presented with only minor edits, take up the bulk of these films. Occasionally, shots of the audience are interspersed with the performances, particularly when an individual is singing. After scenes of people standing in line for the buffet and eating, the films end with the guests dancing under strobe lights to upbeat Nepali pop music. The standard plot of these DVDs creates the idea that wherever Gurungs are in the world, they are engaging in the same activities at the same time.

Some Gurungs compared these DVDs to 'home videos' that they take themselves. This comparison is appropriate because these DVDs contain many close-up shots of people attending the event. These scenes enable these DVDs to serve as a means of connecting with friends and family members in distant places. Most Gurung organizations' websites feature photo albums of Lhochhar and other Gurung events: individuals anywhere can access these pictures and identify and connect with friends and family members they have not recently met.

Members of the Gurung Society in New York order and distribute 300 copies of the DVD. These DVDs are not commercial products; they are sold at cost exclusively by the Gurung Society. People purchase DVDs for themselves and they serve to commemorate their participation in community life. People occasionally view these with their own families and often play them to entertain guests who come to their houses for meals. Often, people purchase multiple copies and then send them to friends and family members in other places. One man, Sitaram Gurung, told me he bought 12 copies, which he sent to family members in Hong Kong, the United Kingdom, and Nepal, and to friends in various cities in the United States. He explained that he sent DVDs to his parents because, "We haven't met our parents in a long time…. My brother and I came here in 1995 so it has been eleven years. This is like sending a home video. It feels closer than just calling on the phone. My son was very young when we came here. Now he is eighteen. They can see him".

Gurungs send these DVDs to each other partly because they serve as a form of communication: they supplement telephone calls, photographs, and email to communicate with friends and family far away. Several Gurungs expressed that sending these DVDs is a way for people to meet with their distant family members. Like Sita Ram, they emphasized the emotionally charged dimensions of this media, stating that it 'feels closer than just calling'.

It is not immediately clear why they perceive these DVDs to be a more intimate way of 'meeting' those who are far away than phone calls. These DVDs lack the immediacy of phone calls. Furthermore, the voices of individuals are muted in these DVDs, with the exception of the people on stage in the cultural programmes. The DVDs rarely feature conversations between those who attend the programme or have individuals address comments to imagined viewers of the video. In these DVDs, the connection between Gurungs throughout the world takes place through visual images. The image allows people to imagine the diaspora, and serves the same role as the voice does in the context of an FM radio programme that connects people in Kathmandu with their friends and relatives abroad through phone calls on the air, described by anthropologist Laura Kunreuther (2004). In this radio programme, the voice underlines the connection between distant people by making them 'present' to one another. At another level, broadcasting the voice in public space of radio airwaves conjures the presence of the diaspora. Similarly, people in the Gurung Lhochhar DVDs become virtually present for the viewer, whereas the circulation of these images allows people to gain a sense of belonging to a global community of Gurungs.

The emotional force of this media derives from the presentation of more life-like appearances of loved ones than in photographs. These DVDs produce a kind of intimacy because they enable people to simulate a shared experience. Viewers may virtually attend the same Lhochhar celebration that their friends or relatives attended by watching it themselves. The DVDs can also introduce Gurungs who have not actually met. One Gurung man who lives in New York reported that when he attended a function in Nepal, several people whom he had not met before approached him and, to his surprise, said they recognized him from the New York Lhochhar videos.

This virtual sharing of experience and the idea that there is a single global community of Gurungs is enhanced through the exchange of DVDs with multiple people. Thus, people end up with collections of DVDs from Lhochhar celebrations in multiple places and can 'attend' and see images of friends and kin at multiple ceremonies. These DVDs symbolically connect individual Gurungs in major cities, and provide a body of evidence that indexes the existence of Gurung diaspora.

The celebration of Lhochhar contributes to a sense of a diasporic Gurung community by suggesting that Gurungs are bound together in a unique system of time even if they are spatially dispersed. Lhochhar DVDs simulate simultaneity, as Gurungs living throughout the world can imagine that they were all celebrating Lhochhar at the same time. Often Lhochhar cannot be celebrated on the exact same day, due to the demands of local schedules. Nonetheless, these DVDs underscore the idea that there is a temporal unity to the Gurung community, and thus contribute to a sense of belonging to a Gurung diaspora.

GURUNG BELONGING IN NEW YORK

In addition to forging links with Gurungs in Nepal, the Gurung Society in New York is concerned with connecting Gurungs in New York, and with integrating Gurungs into the political and social life of the United States. As one of the founders of the organization explained, "People have a very busy life here and they don't have time to meet. The organization creates a way for people to get together. We've all met so many people that we didn't even know were here at these events. Most people from our community who are here don't have legal status and they have to work long hours. The new year celebration and the summer picnic provide a break in the busy lives".

The two major annual events that the Gurung Society sponsors, Lhochhar and the summer picnic, provide settings for Gurungs to meet each other or to renew friendships. Unlike at the Lhochhar celebration, there are no performances at the picnic and no one wears Gurung outfits. However, the summer picnic provides Gurungs with a better opportunity to connect with one another since there is no need to focus on a performance. Also, non-Gurungs may attend or participate in the Lhochhar celebration but only Gurungs join the picnic, with the exception of a few non-Gurung friends or spouses of Gurungs, such as myself. On this occasion in June or July, several hundred Gurungs travel by bus from Queens to a park in a more rural area of the New York metropolitan area and spend the day cooking and eating Nepali food, including the staples of rice and lentils, along with spicy grilled meats. Occasionally the organizers set up activities such as tug of war or volleyball but the focus of the day is chatting with others at the picnic.

While these social occasions may fulfil the Gurung Society's mission of promoting and preserving Gurung identity abroad, they also lay the groundwork for what many Gurungs view as the primary role of the Gurung Society: providing a form of social support to Gurungs in New York. They hope that the Gurung community in New York will replace ties of village and kinship for them in this new context, where their social networks are much thinner than they were in Nepal. Gurungs often request the Gurung Society to assist them in resolving a variety of problems, such as immigration issues or disputes over loans between Gurungs. When an elderly Gurung woman who had recently arrived from Nepal was missing for three days, the Gurung Society mobilized people to search for the woman, who was eventually found.

Most commonly, Gurungs request the Gurung Society to provide funds when illnesses strain their family's financial resources or when Gurungs die and families wish to send the bodies to Nepal. The leadership of the Gurung Society has thus far declined to use Gurung Society funds in these cases. Such demands, they reason, could be limitless and would deplete the organization's funds, preventing it from performing activities that could benefit Gurungs as a community. However, the Gurung Society assists these people by asking other Gurungs to donate money directly to these individuals. For example when a young man with an unemployed wife and two small children became terminally ill, the Gurung Society coordinated fundraising efforts to make up for his lost wages and cover his medical bills. Several hundred people, mostly Gurungs, attended his funeral, and they contributed enough money to cover the funeral expenses and to assist his family.

The leadership views the organization as providing community development through projects that they hope will improve the position of all Gurungs, whether in New York or in Nepal, rather than assistance to individuals. To this end, they have sponsored activities such as the health information workshop described at the beginning of the chapter, classes for Gurung youths in New York to prepare for college entrance exams, and have contributed funds to build schools and provide scholarships in Gurung villages.

The Gurung organization has attempted to use structures and resources available in the United States to assist Gurungs and to achieve recognition for the Gurung community within the dominant society. In July 2001, the Gurung organization in New York officially became a non-profit organization by acquiring 501 3(c) status. One leader in the organization explained that the tax advantages of this status were important, but that the main benefit of this status is that the Gurung organization is "sanctioned by the community and by the new country.... It gives us a certain level of legitimacy in the eyes of our members and in the wider society". In this man's interpretation, the organization's 501 3(c) status confers recognition on the organization and on Gurungs as an ethnic group. It offers them an importance that a small community would not otherwise have. He explained that it had enabled Gurungs to gain access to city officials and the resources they could offer: "No one asks how many people you have. If you have a registered organization, they will come and pay attention to you."

In order to secure this status, the organization had to demonstrate that it was committed to providing public services for Gurungs in New York and in Nepal. Initially, most of the Gurung organization's projects were cultural; after becoming an official non-profit organization, starting in 2002, the Gurung organization began holding workshops focusing on housing, employment, immigration law, and health care, like the event I described in the introduction. These workshops provide recently arrived Gurungs with practical information about how to survive and meet basic needs in the context of the United States. As such, these workshops facilitated the integration of Gurungs into the dominant society.

At another level, Gurungs also sought recognition from the state through these workshops. Gurungs saw it as important to represent themselves as responsible and trustworthy people after the attacks on 11 September 2001, when immigrant groups in the United States came under new waves of discrimination and suspicion. While Nepalis as a group were not targeted, several Nepali immigrants faced severe mistreatment due to the heightened xenophobia in the United States. Perhaps the most well publicized of these cases was that of Purna Raj Bajracharya, who was arrested for videotaping outside an office in Queens in October 2001, and held for three months in solitary confinement on the grounds that he was suspected of being involved in terrorism. Nepalis in New York were discussing the plight of this man long before the story made the cover of the *New York Times* in 30 June 2004 (Bernstein, 2004).

When I asked members of the Gurung Society how they had been affected by the events of 11 September 2001, they remarked that it gave an urgency to long-standing concerns about the precarious status of the numerous Gurungs whose visa status in the United States is 'in question'. As one leader told me, "It put the issue of immigration on the front burner.... There was a sense of helplessness now more than ever. Before, deportation was a far distant fear." These workshops were a way for the Gurung Society to address these fears by representing Gurungs as responsible people who are willing to respect and work with the state.

The Gurung Society has also aimed to establish recognition for Gurungs by the dominant society when they have donated money to the American Red Cross and other charities in the aftermath of the tsunami in Sri Lanka, Hurricane Katrina, and the earthquake in Haiti. Although these causes were not directly related to the mission of the Gurung Society, Gurung Society leaders sought to demonstrate that Gurungs are good citizens and hoped that the representatives of these organizations would be familiar with their ethnic group as a result of these donations.

CONCLUSION

Several social and political contexts shape the diverse activities of the Gurung Society in New York: the indigenous nationalities movement in Nepal, the Gurung diaspora, and the United States. Of greatest relevance for understanding the very form of this organization is the influence of the indigenous nationalities movement in Nepal. Without that movement as a reference point, Gurungs in New York would most likely not have founded an organization that is centred on Gurung identity.

The Gurung Society created one of the many paths for migrants in New York to participate in political forms of transnationalism. Transnationalism instigated by the Gurung Society takes place through the projects of the Gurung Society, such as the Lhochhar celebrations or events with Gurung politicians who visit from Nepal, or informally, as when people send the Lhochhar DVDs to family and friends in distant places. Yet the Gurung Society is also concerned with connecting Gurungs who live in New York and with the problems that Gurungs face as migrants in the United States. By interfacing with the dominant society in the United States, the organization seeks to gain access to public services such as health care for its members and to gain recognition as Gurungs from that society.

The idea of belonging to a Gurung community is multidimensional and is experienced in various ways by different people who call themselves Gurungs in New York. There are several different ways that belonging is created, or at least evoked, through the activities of the Gurung Society. For most people, the idea of belonging to the Gurung community meant access to a kinship-like network that people could rely upon in times of trouble. For the core members and leaders of the Gurung Society, the assertion of belonging to a Gurung community is also a commitment to political projects to end ethnic inequality and increase the visibility and political power of indigenous nationalities in Nepal. Some Gurungs who do not support the indigenous nationalities movement dislike this aspect of the Gurung Society and stated that they would prefer that it not be involved in these 'divisive' activities. Finally, there is an emerging idea of Gurungs as a Nepali ethnic group that belongs to the constellation of ethnic minority groups in the United States, and that should be recognized by the dominant society.

These multiple ideas of belonging are further complicated by the fact that Gurung individuals who take part in the activities of the Gurung Society do not only think of themselves as Gurung. Some are also involved in FIPNA, the federation of indigenous nationalities organizations in New York described above. Some Gurungs also take part in pan-Nepali organizations, such as Adhikaar, which advocates for the rights of Nepali migrants as workers and as residents of the United States, and the Alliance for Human Rights and Democracy in Nepal. They participate in fundraising for political parties in Nepal. Others are involved in civil society and political activities, which do not prioritize their identity as Gurungs or as Nepalis at all; for example, they take part in a restaurant worker union in New York, and work for campaigns for US presidential candidates. Gurungs abroad thus have multiple forms of belonging that have salience in different contexts, and these other identities may become more important in the future. The Gurung community abroad will persist to the extent that the Gurung Society and other organizations like it continue to make belonging to a Gurung community meaningful in both the transnational context and in the new societies where Gurungs live.

NOTES

1. The ethnonym Tamu is the Gurung word for the Gurung ethnic group. The term Tamu became more popular with efforts to revitalize Gurung identity after 1990. Yet the name Gurung remains more widely used within the community both in New York and in Nepal. Most people call the organization 'The Gurung Society', omitting the term 'Tamu'. In this chapter, I follow this common practice and refer to the organization as the Gurung Society.
2. According to the United States Census of 2000, 11,715 people born in Nepal were residing in the country in the United States in that year. A 2006 report by UNIFEM and NIDS estimated that there were 22,000 Nepalis in the United States (UNIFEM and NIDS, 2006).
3. Last date of access 6 June 2010.

REFERENCES

Anthias, Floya. 2001. 'New Hybridities, Old Concepts: The Limits of Culture', *Ethnic and Racial Studies*, 24(4): 619–41.

Axel, Brian Keith. 2004. 'The Context of Diaspora', *Cultural Anthropology*, 19(1): 26–60.

Bernstein, Nina. 2004. 'In F.B.I., Innocent Detainee Found an Unlikely Ally', *The New York Times*, 30 June, 1: B6.

Brubaker, Rogers. 2005. 'The "Diaspora" Diaspora', *Ethnic and Racial Studies*, 28(1): 1–19.

Caplan, Lionel. 1995. *Warrior Gentlemen: 'Gurkhas' in the Western Imagination*. Providence: Berghahn Books.

Chaudhry, Lubna. 1998. 'We Are Graceful Swans Who Can Also Be Crows': Hybrid Identities of Pakistani Muslim Women', in S.D. Dasgupta (ed.), *A Patchwork Shawl: Chronicles of South Asian Women in America*. New Brunswick, NJ: Rutgers University Press.

Clifford, James. 1997. *Routes: Travel and Translation in the Late Twentieth Century*. Cambridge, MA: Harvard University Press.

Dwyer, Claire. 2000. 'Negotiating Diasporic Identities: Young British South Asian Muslim Women', *Women's Studies International Forum*, 23(4): 475–86.

Glick Schiller, Nina, Linda Basch, and Cristina Blanc-Szanton. 1992. 'Transnationalism: A New Analytic Framework for Understanding Migration', in N.G. Schiller, L. Basch, and C. Blanc-Szanton (eds), *Towards a Transnational Perspective on Migration*. New York: The New York Academy of Sciences.

Hangen, Susan. 2007. *Creating a 'New Nepal': The Ethnic Dimension*. Policy Studies, Vol. 34. Washington, DC: East-West Center Washington.

Hobsbawm, Eric and Terence Ranger (eds). 1983. *The Invention of Tradition*. New York: Cambridge University Press.

Ignacio, Emily. 2005. *Building Diaspora: Filipino Cultural Community Formation on the Internet*. New Brunswick, NJ: Rutgers University Press.

Itzigsohn, Jose. 2000. 'Immigration and the Boundaries of Citizenship: The Institutions of Immigrants' Political Transnationalism', *International Migration Review*, 34(4): 1126–54.

Kunreuther, Laura. 2004. 'Voiced Writing and Public Intimacy on Kathmandu's FM Radio', *Studies in Nepali History and Society*, 9(1): 57–95.

Levitt, Peggy, Josh De Wind, and Steven Vertovec, 2003. 'International Perspectives on Transnational Migration: An Introduction', *International Migration Review*, 37(3): 565–75.

Minami, Makito. 2007. 'From *Tika* to *Kata*? Ethnic Movements among the Magars in an Age of Globalization', in H. Ishii, D.N. Gellner, and K. Nawa (eds), *Nepalis Inside and Outside Nepal*. New Delhi: Manohar.

Odmalm, Pontus. 2004. 'Civil Society, Migrant Organisations and Political Parties: Theoretical Linkages and Applications to the Swedish Context', *Journal of Ethnic and Migration Studies*, 30(3): 471–89.

Ong, Aihwa. 2008. 'Cyberpublics and Diaspora Politics among Transnational Chinese', in J.X. Inda and R. Rosaldo (eds), *The Anthropology of Globalization: A Reader*. Malden, MA: Blackwell Publishing.

Ostergaard-Nielsen, Eva, 2003. 'The Politics of Migrants' Transnational Political Practices', *International Migration Review*, 37(3): 760–86.

Owusu, Thomas. 2000. 'The Role of Ghanaian Immigrant Associations in Toronto, Canada', *International Migration Review*, 34(4): 1155–81.

Pfaff-Czarnecka, Joanna. 1999. 'Debating the State of the Nation: Ethnicization of Politics in Nepal—A Position Paper', in J. Pfaff-Czarnecka, D. Rajasingham-Senanayake, A. Nandy, and E.T. Gomez (eds), *Ethnic Futures: The State and Identity Politics in Asia*. London: SAGE Publications.

Pfaff-Czarnecka and Toffin. 2011. 'Introduction. Belonging and Multiple Attachments in Contemporary Himalayan Societies', in *The Politics of Belonging in the Himalayas: Local Attachments and Boundary Dynamics*, pp. iv–xxxviii. New Delhi: SAGE Publications.

Schein, Louisa. 2004. 'Homeland Beauty: Transnational Longing and Hmong American Video', *Journal of Asian Studies*, 63(2): 433–63.

Seddon, David, Jagannath Adhikari, and Ganesh Gurung. 2001. *The New Lahures: Foreign Employment and Remittance Economy of Nepal*. Kathmandu: Nepal Institute of Development Studies.

Sharma, Prayag Raj. 1997. 'Nation-Building, Multi-Ethnicity, and the Hindu State', in D.N. Gellner, J. Pfaff-Czarnecka, and J. Whelpton (eds), *Nationalism and Ethnicity in a Hindu Kingdom: The Politics of Culture in Contemporary Nepal*. Amsterdam: Harwood Academic Publishers.

UNIFEM and NIDS. 2006. *Nepali Women and Foreign Labour Migration*. Kathmandu: UNIFEM and NIDS.

Whelpton, John. 1997. 'Political Identity in Nepal: State, Nation, and Community', in D.N. Gellner, J. Pfaff-Czarnecka, and J. Whelpton (eds), *Nationalism and Ethnicity in a Hindu Kingdom: The Politics of Culture in Contemporary Nepal*. Amsterdam: Harwood Academic Publishers.

Yamanaka, Keiko. 2007. '"Bowling Together": Social Networks and Social Capital of a Nepali Migrant Community in Japan', in H. Ishii, D.N. Gellner, and K. Nawa (eds), *Nepalis Inside and Outside Nepal*. New Delhi: Manohar.

PART IV
GLOBALITY AND ACTIVIST EXPERIENCE

Chapter 12

Buddhist Activism, New Sanghas, and the Politics of Belonging among Some Tharu and Magar Communities of Southern Nepal*

CHIARA LETIZIA

INTRODUCTION

Globalization, as Sheila Croucher (2004) has shown, affects the condition and contours of belonging, that is, the mechanisms for negotiating belonging and available options for belonging. Globalization affects the reality and the awareness of human interconnectedness across borders, and thus enhances the capacity for individuals to imagine themselves as members of a global world. Just as globalization can enhance the capacity of world citizenship, it can also facilitate the maintenance and flourishing of particular identities and attachments (Croucher, 2004: 190), break old forms of belonging, and provide the conditions for the creations of new forms. The case studied in this chapter shows how a shift to Buddhism among some ethnic groups in a context of ethnicization of Nepalese

* This chapter is based on a four-month fieldwork in Nepal in 2003–04 funded by the Fondation Fyssen and on three subsequent short fieldworks in 2007, 2008 (supported by the University of Milano-Bicocca), and 2009 (financed by the Newton Fellowship of the British Academy). I interviewed Tharu and Magar Buddhist intellectuals based in Kathmandu, Tharu and Magar Buddhist priests based in Udayapur, Saptari, Nawalaprasi, Rupandehi, and Dang districts, and Kathmandu-based Newar activists involved in the spread of Buddhism in those districts. Parts of this data have been already published in Letizia, 2005 and 2007. Much of the material of this chapter was presented originally in 2006 at the research unit 'Milieux, sociétés et cultures en Himalaya' in Villejuif, Paris. I am grateful to David Gellner, Joanna Pfaff-Czarnecka, Gérard Toffin, and Philippe Gagnon for their comments on earlier versions of this text.

politics (a phenomenon closely linked with the global recognition of ethnicity and to the transnational Buddhist networks) has created the space for local activists to encourage new forms of belonging for the members of their groups.

Religions are a major factor of belonging and globalization, crucial for tying people together and shaping a sense of communality among believers, thereby contributing to the emergence of a global imagination[1] (and since its beginnings in the 5th century BCE, Buddhism was premised on the notion of a supraterritorial world community). In some cases, this gives rise to a sort of paradox, in which universalist doctrines can be observed as the tools that define local identities.

In the case presented here religion is viewed as a field of contending politics of belonging, which I define (following Sheila Croucher) as "the processes of individuals, groups, societies and polities, defining, negotiating, promoting, rejecting, violating and transcending the boundaries of identity and belonging" (2004: 41). In Nepal, where Hinduism had been assimilated with national identity for two centuries (until 2006),[2] religion is intrinsically political (Hangen, 2010: 132). A religious transformation is therefore loaded with potential for what I will call 'oppositional' belonging.

This chapter deals with the diffusion of Buddhism among two ethnic groups of Nepal, the Tharus and the Magars, who have been influenced by Hinduism for many centuries and who have been announcing a collective shift to Buddhism since the 1990s.[3]

I will examine how a local shift to Buddhism among these groups in some Tarai districts, encouraged by local activists, was a result of and connected to transnational modernist Buddhism (through a Theravada Buddhist revivalism among Newars of Kathmandu Valley and through manifold connections with global Buddhism). The political context of this religious shift has been the post-1990 rise of ethnic movements against the domination of high-caste Hindu groups in the State. This ethnicization of politics in Nepal is itself a result of the global opportunity structure created by the adoption and implementation of international conventions and declarations (such as the Indigenous and Tribal Peoples Convention, 1989, or the UN Declaration on the Rights of Indigenous Peoples) and by the networks established for the mobilization and development of ethnic groups.

The politics of belonging have been led by Tharu and Magar ritual specialists and Buddhist activists who have played a prominent role in domesticating and transforming Buddhist notions. These 'brokers' have conveyed new messages in apparently old structures, and have shaped new forms of belonging through religious rituals and the affirmation of a Buddhist common past.

OUTLINE OF THE CHAPTER

During fieldwork in 2003 in the eastern Tarai, I noticed the growing presence of an 'alien' Theravada Buddhist activism, ritual performance, and education in Rupandehi, Saptari, and Udayapur districts: this included hearing Tharu villagers chant the formula for 'taking refuge' in Pali[4] or being told by a Tharu Buddhist ritual specialist that the 'stupa-shape' of their earth mound house shrine was clear evidence that they had always been Buddhists without being aware of it;[5] observing the five-coloured international Buddhist flag on the roof of every Magar house between Butwal and Bhairawa;[6] visiting a stupa and a new Buddhist monastery (*vihara*) built with Taiwanese funds, awaiting a statue from Thailand;[7] and attending a camp where young Magar boys and girls were taught how to perform Buddhist rituals and told to give up Brahmin priests and blood sacrifices.[8] Such examples give a sense of the much wider Buddhist network involved.

In the first section of this chapter, I give a brief account of the channels and networks through which Buddhist ideas and practices were conveyed. A key to this process was the prior establishment of Theravada revivalism within the Newar community, and subsequent missionary work of Newar Buddhist monks and lay activists among other Nepalese groups. This first part will provide a simple overview, since many publications already deal with this subject.[9]

Second, I will explain how Buddhist language was combined with ethnic activism: I will identify the political context of ethnic movements that made the missionary activity successful and will describe briefly key elements of the discourses of some intellectuals and ethnic leaders which made Buddhism become a tool to develop manifold forms of belonging.

In the third part, I will describe the role played by the local ritual specialists of some Tharu and Magar communities of eastern Tarai, who work as missionaries in their communities. I will show how these ritual specialists do not merely receive and transmit the values of Buddhism, but also actively process and reshape these external Buddhist influences, adapting them to the local culture.

ORIGIN, GLOBAL NETWORKS, AND CHANNELS OF THE BUDDHIST REVIVAL IN NEPAL

The Newar Reform

Before its recent arrival in Tarai-based Tharu and Magar communities, Theravada Buddhism first travelled through the Newar community, where it was introduced in the 1930s as a reform of traditional Newar Buddhism.[10] This reform intended to purify Newar Buddhism from magical practices, sacrifice, and caste distinctions, to reintroduce monasticism, and to educate the laity in Buddhist doctrine. LeVine and Gellner have shown that the first Nepalese Theravadins engaged in a process of 'religious domestication' (2005: 62–65), selecting certain features of Vajrayana Newar Buddhism in order to make their message locally acceptable: the provision of alternatives to established Hindu and Vajrayana practices helped Theravada broaden its appeal. Two aspects of this process are significant for my purposes here:

(1) The prominent role of the laity in the administration of the Buddhist monasteries (*viharas*), which monks had to allow because Newar Buddhism involved the laity in the running of the traditional monastery (*baha*);

(2) The involvement of Theravadins as ritual specialists: even if they were determined to eliminate the baroque Vajrayana rituals, monks began to assume certain functions of Vajracarya household priests, such as the administration of life-cycle rituals (Kunreuther, 1994; Hartmann, 1996; LeVine and Gellner, 2005: 65; Gellner, 2010).

I will show how these two aspects have become central to the diffusion of Buddhism in Tharu and Magar communities, where lay Buddhist activists play a prominent role and conduct Buddhist life-cycle rituals.

Buddhist Modernism

The Theravada Buddhism that spread among the Newar community has been referred to as 'Buddhist modernism'[11] or 'Protestant

Buddhism'.[12] It took shape in the late 19th and early 20th century in Ceylon, where, under the influence of (and in reaction to) colonialism and Christian missionary activity, and with an active Western influence, Buddhism was rationalized, modernized, and re-formulated as nationalist, missionary, and anti-occidental, by Anagarika Dharmapala and the Maha Bodhi Society he founded in 1891 (Gombrich, 1988; McMahan, 2008).[13]

In Nepal many characteristics of Buddhist modernism as developed by Dharmapala became influential. They include the development of Buddhist missionaries; the central role given to lay people, making social activism and meditation a duty for monks and lay people alike; the importance given to Buddhist education and to publishing; the portrayal of Buddhism as scientific and rational, the condemnation of 'blind faith' (*andha-vishvas*);[14] the importance given to meditation and to the philosophical aspects of teachings, in opposition to ritualistic types of Buddhism; the advocacy of social reform;[15] and the criticism of other religions, in particular Hinduism and Christianity.

The 'anti-Hindu' feature of Buddhist modernism and its promulgation as a means of social liberation was prominent in the discourse of another important protagonist of this movement: Bhimrao Ambedkar, the leader of the Indian Dalits. In 1956, he publicly converted to Buddhism and converted 500,000 of his disciples as well.[16] Ambedkar presented his message of social emancipation under the guise of religion, adopting a ritual of collective conversion, thus making it more accessible to a largely illiterate population. Ambedkar chose Buddhism for various reasons: first, it was an indigenous religion, born on Indian soil. Second, he saw in the Buddha the prototype for the fight against Brahminism.[17]

The conversion of Dalits to Ambedkar Buddhism in Maharashtra and the adoption of Buddhism by Tharus and Magars in Tarai have many points in common. As we will see, the anti-Hindu elements and the idea of conversion as a tool of freedom from a position of inferiority in a religiously defined hierarchy are also found in the discourses of Nepalese Buddhist activists.

The Buddhist Ethnoscape

Theravada Buddhist modernism reached Nepal through what Steven Kemper refers to as the 'Sinhala Buddhist ethnoscape' (Kemper, 2005).[18]

Kemper remarks how Sinhala monks have scattered around the globe, forming a worldwide network, which, among other things, is theravadizing local systems of belief and practice, such as in Malaysia, Singapore, Vietnam, and, as we will see, in Nepal. Extending beyond and sometimes interspersed with the Sinhala Buddhist ethnoscape lies a broader Buddhist ethnoscape (Kemper, 2005: 23).

Both ethnoscapes were fundamental for the early Theravadins in Nepal. Gellner and LeVine have remarked that the effects of Buddhist modernism reached Nepal through the influence of Anagarika Dharmapala and his Maha Bodhi Society: the entire first generation of Nepalese Theravadins received their first ordination from the Maha Bodhi Society monks in India.[19] Likewise, the objectives of the Buddhist Society of Nepal, published in 1951, were for the most part adapted from the Maha Bodhi Society programme (Kloppenberg, 1977: 307). Sources of Buddhist influence in Nepal were not limited to the Maha Bodhi Society: a number of transnational Buddhist organizations followed in its wake, such as the World Fellowship of Buddhists (WFB), founded in Sri Lanka in 1950: Nepal hosted two of the WFB annual conferences. Nepalese monks and nuns travelled worldwide to strengthen ties with Buddhist institutions, to study, and to receive ordination.[20]

The links which Asian Buddhist traditions have increasingly forged among themselves in the 20th century are still contributing to and sustaining Buddhist activism in Nepal: financial support for the development of Buddhism in Nepal is currently offered by Buddhist institutions and devotees from Taiwan, Thailand, Burma, and Sri Lanka, and Nepalese monks and nuns travel regularly to these countries for their education.[21] The manifestations of these East–East connections and of Buddhist global connections are very tangible in Nepal and are coalesced in Lumbini, the birthplace of the Buddha, which shares with Bodh Gaya in India the role of centre of gravity for global Buddhism.

The Broadening of Buddhist Proselytization

The early years of Nepalese Theravadins were marked by internal persecution: under Rana rulers, Nepal was constituted explicitly as a Hindu Kingdom. Ranas assimilated Hinduism to national identity, and aggressively supported traditional Hinduism against modernist reforms, outlawing proselytization and conversion.[22] Though successive constitutions never ceased declaring conversion illegal,[23] as the years passed Buddhism found itself in a privileged position compared to other religions like Christianity and Islam, considered as foreign and dangerous. Buddhism came to be considered as a sub-sect of Hinduism: the Buddha was now venerated as an incarnation of Vishnu. At the end of the Rana regime, in 1951, Theravada monks received permission to practice and to preach freely, and in 1952 the festival of Buddha Jayanti was recognized as a national holiday. In 1985, the government of Nepal formed the Lumbini Development Trust and Lumbini was inscribed as a world heritage site of UNESCO in 1997. These international and national political opportunities made Buddhism a legitimate option for the ethnic activism which started shaping the Nepalese political realm around 1990. In a context of ethnic claims against a State that continued to call itself Hindu, the Buddhists emerged on the national scene as a major force in the big campaign for a secular state led by ethnic activists and religious minorities.[24] Although the 1990 revolution prompted a first constitutional recognition of Nepal's ethnic, linguistic, and cultural diversity, it did not succeed in overturning the official characterization of Nepal as a 'Hindu' State.

Some young Newar Buddhist activists, who felt that their struggle for secularism had failed, then created an association of young Buddhists (*Yuba Bauddha Samuha* in Kathmandu, or YBS).[25] They organized meetings in the Theravada monasteries, where they invited the leaders of the different ethnic groups. The campaign for a secular state thus allowed religious and political activists from all ethnic groups to come into mutual contact, and together they set a goal to increase the number of Buddhists in the National Census. Thanks to Taiwanese funds, these encounters brought about the creation in 1995 of the Himalayan Buddhist Education Foundation (HBEF). The mission of this foundation was to provide Buddhist education and to promote Buddhist morality among the different castes and ethnic groups of Nepal (*Smarika*, 2006).

The 'Buddhist Awareness Camps'

One of the first proposals of YBS was the 'Buddhist Awareness Camp' (Bauddha Jagaran Prashikshan Shivir) project (LeVine and

Gellner, 2005: 234–35). These residential camps, directed at all ethnic groups, constituted the principal channel through which Newar activists helped spread Buddhism among the Tharus and Magars. One of the founders of YBS, Keshab Man Shakya, wrote that the idea of these camps came to him while he was studying in America, when he observed the Wednesday activity and programmes of a local church (Shakya, 2006).

I will consider here only the camps organized especially for Tharus and Magars. Held in villages, these camps were always organized in partnership with ethnic associations. The teachings were given not only by monks but also by lay instructors of the same ethnic group as the participants, in their own language. The instructors did not limit themselves to teaching Buddhist doctrine (the five precepts, the three refuges, the four noble truths, and the life of Buddha), but also gave lectures demonstrating the historical link between Buddhism and Tharu or Magar societies, and presenting Buddhism as an agent of progress for Tharu and Magar communities.

The Buddhist awareness camp of Banepa held in 1995 illustrates well the synergy between different activists: the monk Asvagosha taught the life of the Buddha, whereas the militant intellectual M.S. Thapa Magar, leader of the national association of Magars (Nepal Magar Sangh), gave a speech on Buddhism and Magar community; meanwhile, activist Tharu Syaram Chaudhary spoke on Buddhism and Tharu society, the Newar activist Gehendra Udas spoke on Buddhism in Nepal, and Lok Darshan Bajracharya talked about Buddhist activities in the international context. Thus, starting from the religious Theravada context of the monk's speech, the lessons progressively opened up to Buddhism among ethnic groups in Nepal and finally extended the horizon to the transnational scene (HBEF Newsletter, 1996).

A pamphlet containing an invitation to participate in a camp organized in Kailali district in 1997 underscores the particular link between the Buddha and Nepal, the universality of Buddhist teachings, and the lack of local education:

> Buddha, the son of Nepal, is not only a Nepalese god; he is the light of the Asian continent. Maybe you know that the light given by the Buddha is not only a guide for Asian people: his light of peace has spread to the whole world. In Europe and in America, Buddhist monasteries have been built and people are studying Buddhist teachings

and are leading a happy life following these teachings. However, it is so sad to see that there is darkness under the lamp: we are not progressing, we are caught up in illusion, we are not leading a peaceful life following the teachings of Buddha. Since we have realized this, we invite you to a camp of Buddhist Awareness. (Buddhist Awareness Camp, 1997, my translation)

These camps operated until 2001, when Maoist insurgency caused these activities to stop. They are now slowly restarting. Meanwhile, many local camps were organized by local Tharu and Magar activists, without the supervision of YBS.

THE ADOPTION OF BUDDHISM BY THARU AND MAGAR LEADERS AND INTELLECTUALS

Buddhism and Belonging to One's Group

Following the fall of the Panchayat regime in 1990, Nepal experienced a great flowering of ethnic activism seeking to achieve greater recognition of cultural, religious, and linguistic differences, and denouncing the domination of Brahmins in the political, educational, religious, and economic spheres.[26] The main association established to push these issues was the Nepal Janajati Mahasangh (Nepal Federation of Nationalities, NEFEN).[27] The neologism *Janajati* came to refer to the ethnic minorities oppressed by the Hindu state and was translated into English as 'nationality'.[28]

Some *Janajati* leaders, and among them Tharu and Magars, relied on Buddhism in their movement against a two-century-long process of Hinduization and in their need to answer the basic question which characterized the renaissance of ethnicity: "Who are we?", or, in the language of the preceding Panchayat regime: "What is our religion, our language, our common history?" The growing fame of Buddhism both on the global scene and at the national level made it a worthy choice as a tool of belonging and as an alternative to Hinduism. Being Buddhist was presented as being more authentically Magar or Tharu.[29] Buddhism therefore contributed to the effort of these groups to constitute their identity subjectively as a single ethnic group in a multi-ethnic state, a common identity that the different groups with the same ethnonym scattered in the country had never shared. Kham Magars living in the western part of the country do not share any cultural feature with the Magars of eastern Nepal, and there has always been a wide gap between the common symbols and practices of Tharus of eastern Tarai and Tharus living in the far west.[30] However, the reference to Buddhism and to a common ancestor, the Buddha, as I will show later, enabled activists to actualize a new sense of belonging transcending locality. As Tharu activist Ramanand Prasad Singh recalls: "We used to go from one district to another to inform others about their own common origin" (Guneratne, 1998: 761). The same happened for Magars: Buddhist activists started visiting their far western counterparts, contributing to the creation of this imagined belonging.

Buddhism as Oppositional Belonging

The sense of belonging provided by Buddhism did not stop at the single group level: Buddhism provided a common denominator to the *Janajati* as a whole. *Janajati* were at first united by a negative definition: the fact of not being Hindu, of being (or wanting to be) outside of the social hierarchy based on Brahminical values. The notion of *Janajati* was connected to the notion of the *adivasi*: *Janajati* were there before Aryan intruders came to Nepal bringing Hinduism. Therefore, the *Janajati* were not Aryans, not *varna*, not Hindu. From this, only a small step was required to propose a model of a Mongolian, egalitarian, and Buddhist *Janajatis*.[31] The advantages of choosing Buddhism were multiple: to be recognized as indigenous (using the United Nations terminology and discourse),[32] it was important to have always lived in Nepal, but many *Janajati* groups had myths that traced back their origins to Tibet, or Rajasthan. But proving a group's descent from the Buddha helped prove its autochthony, since the Buddha was born in Nepal.[33] This proof has become central in Tharu and Magar Buddhist activism, since Siddhartha was born in Lumbini, a region currently inhabited by Tharus and Magars as well.

The advantage of being Buddhist was also to be practising an authentic Nepalese religion, different from foreign religions such as Islam and Christianity, and yet adhere to a religion which, historically and doctrinally, was set in opposition to Brahminism and which the activists presented as modern, egalitarian, and humanist against a Hinduism perceived as discriminatory and superstitious. This notion of Buddhism as a modern, rational, and progressive religion fitted well with the emphasis placed by many ethnic associations on modernizing, promoting education, and abandoning 'backwardness' (Krauskopff, 2003).

Activists were therefore putting in operation an 'oppositional' belonging that was simultaneously defining inclusion (we: Buddhist, Mongol, indigenous, oppressed, democratic, egalitarian, rational) and exclusion (them: Hindu, Aryan, invaders, oppressors, reactionary, discriminatory, superstitious).

To sum up, Buddhism united several Nepalese ethnic groups as opposed to the Hindu State, thus expressing an identity by way of negation—the affirmation of being non-Hindu—and including at the same time a dimension of social emancipation: the choice of non-Hinduism was intended to reject a position of inferiority in the religious hierarchy imposed by the State. As a positive choice, Buddhism offered a notion of salvation identical to that found in Ambedkar Buddhism: conceived not as the release of the individual from the world, but in terms of a strong social and political commitment.[34] The modernist ideas connecting the soteriological message of Buddhism with such commitment, combining individual development and social reform, and considering social service as the fruit of meditation and compassion, were the nexus which allowed Buddhism to be included in activists' agendas in their struggle for democracy, social inclusion, and ethnic recognition.

These considerations motivated ethnic leaders to adhere to this propagation of Buddhism, at a time when they wanted to redefine the identity of their own ethnic group and, simultaneously, their belonging to the *Janajati* group. Leaders of Magar and Tharu associations chose to take up and propagate Buddhism. The first international conference of the Magars, held in Jhapa district in 1998, declared Buddhism as their religion: a special branch of the Nepal Magar Sangh (the national association which represented Magars in the NEFIN), named Nepal Magar Sangh Bauddha Seva Samaj ('Buddhist Service Society of Nepal Magar Association'), was formed in order to deal with Buddhist activities, under the guidance of two Magar intellectuals, M.S. Thapa Magar and Dev Bahadur Rana. For its part, the national association of Tharus, Tharu Kalyankarini Sabha (the association that today represents the Tharus in the NEFIN),[35] created a committee of specialists to conduct research on and to spread awareness of Buddhism in the Tharu community; this committee operated under the guidance of the prominent intellectuals Ramanand Prasad Singh and Tej Narayan Panjiyar.[36]

The shift to Buddhism was not as a result of a shift in beliefs; at the beginning, it was a nominal and collective one, made in the context of a campaign for the National Census, and later it became a shift in ritual practices. National censuses show how religion has become one of the most burning issues in Nepal. In the past, Hinduism was the majority religion in almost all districts; however, Theravada activists organized big campaigns in order to convince their groups to change these figures, to which Tharu and Magar national associations adhered.[37] Tharu and Magar activists followed the direction of their respective national organizations to mark their 'religion' as 'Buddhist' in the 2001 national census, despite the total absence of a Buddhist tradition among them.[38]

Many times during fieldwork, I heard the story of people who dated their 'conversion' to Buddhism to the date of the official declaration of their leaders. In Rupandehi and Nawalparasi districts, I visited some Buddhist monasteries that had been constructed with funds collected by the local community but which then remained dormant while the new Buddhists waited for someone to give Buddhist teachings.

Total ignorance of Buddhist doctrine or the absence of a personal conversion was not considered as an important fact when declaring that the collectivity was Buddhist; however, two other aspects were considered fundamental: the question of origins and the transformation of ritual.

Origins: Rewriting History

To justify collective adherence to Buddhism, Tharu and Magar activists felt it was necessary to prove that the Buddha himself belonged to their group respectively and that Buddhism was their ancestral religion before they were 'violently forced' to become Hindu. For both groups, the adoption of Buddhism was presented as a return to origins, a progressive awareness of their Buddhist past (Letizia, 2005).[39]

Magar and Tharu intellectuals thus produced new histories of origin, which run counter to the previous 'sanskritized' histories and where the upper castes were no longer considered as models to emulate. They wanted to prove their Buddhist past with the contribution of scholars and the help of archaeological and historical data. For example, the Tharu intellectual, Ramanand Prasad Singh, refuses to acknowledge the previous myth of the Rajput origin of the Tharus and affirms their Mongolian origin. According to him, the name 'Tharu' would derive from 'Sthavir', the name of the elder disciples of the Buddha, and in which case the Tharus would be the descendants of Buddha's clan, the Shakya. This theory is presented as the 'true story' of the Tharus (Singh, 1988).[40] As Krauskopff (2009b: 260) writes, this new story mirrors the previous myth, following the same need of a prestigious origin, but affirms the autochthony of Tharus, erasing the exteriority suggested by the provenance from Rajasthan.[41]

Another important intellectual Tharu, Tej Narayan Panjiyar, contributed to the rewriting of the history, by underscoring the Buddhist heritage: he affirmed that, in the past, the Tharus found refuge in Kathmandu in order to escape the persecution of Brahmins in the region where the Buddha was born (Krauskopff, 2009b: 262).[42]

Conversely, a Magar intellectual, M.S. Thapa Magar, traced in his book a very complicated history to demonstrate that Buddha, Ashoka, and the Licchavis were Magars and he postulates a Mongolian origin for all of them (Thapa Magar, 2002).

As mentioned earlier, a noticeable characteristic of these stories is that they operate a reification of ethnic categories and consider Magars and Tharus, respectively, as socially uniform groups, eliminating the remarkable and obvious differences (cultural, linguistic, and social) between the different groups which share the same ethnonym.

As Krauskopff notices (2009a, 2009b), these 'stories' use the traditional register to produce a truth and, at the same time, insert themselves in a modern political discourse, adapted to a contemporary and global contexts. The intended recipients of these stories written by urban intellectuals and sometimes published in English are not (or not only, since the message clearly reached them) the villagers of Udayapur or Nawalparasi; these stories aim at a wider audience: members of other ethnic groups, national politicians as well as a global audience of foreign scholars and international ethnic activists. These intellectuals compete with Brahmins on the field of history and erudition, and they look for national and foreign scholars' endorsement of their stories. As one of these historians, Subodh Kumar Singh, told me in 2007, when I asked him why he was writing in English: "Because Brahmins have destroyed Nepal's history and even foreign scholars have been influenced by them and don't know the real past. We Tharus must write our own history; otherwise we will not survive. We cannot let others write our own history."

Changing Rituals

Rituals are the first point of attack of the Buddhist activists working among the Tharus and Magars. They try to convince people not to perform animal sacrifice any more, not to call Brahmin priests to perform rituals,[43] and not to celebrate the main Hindu festival of Nepal, Dasain.[44] Secondly, an attempt is being made to change the life-cycle rituals, by providing a substitute Buddhist version.

How do Magar and Tharu Buddhist intellectuals justify a change of ritual? M.S. Thapa Magar, interviewed in 2004, argued as follows:

> Despite the influence of the Brahmins, the Hindu religion could not establish deep roots, except for the rituals; but rituals are only a tradition. With time, traditions change and adapt to the situation. Even if religious practice can change all the time, the philosophy of the religion does not change. People who follow different traditions can share the same religious philosophy. Buddhists from Japan, China, Korea, Tibet and Nepal share the same religious philosophy, but their cultural tradition and their rituals are different.

M.S. Thapa Magar distinguished the intrinsic and unchangeable Buddhist philosophy of Magars, which they have in common with Buddhists of Asia (now forgotten and to be revived), from the rituals that can be changed because they are just superimposed traditions adapting to the historical moment. Following this logic, since rituals have already changed once, they can very well be changed again.

Here is a more pragmatic perspective, expressed in the words of the politician Gore Bahadur Khapangi, former president of the Nepal Magar Sangh, when he was still a prominent Magar leader:[45]

> The Nepal Magar Sangh declared that the Magars must be converted to Buddhism. At this time, we are working to apply this rule in the field. The most important thing to do is to replace the Brahmin. That is the first duty of the Magars. If we don't change the content of the ritual, that is not so important. What is important is that the officiating

person be changed. Sometimes, when there is no one else, I celebrate myself. We are in the process of changing and making a transition from a Hindu way of celebrating the ritual to a Buddhist procedure, but all this is done very gently; it takes some time.

THE LOCALIZATION OF BUDDHISM AMONG THE THARU AND MAGAR COMMUNITIES OF EASTERN TARAI

The Formation of Local Buddhist Associations

At the end of each Buddhist awareness camp, the participants promised to spread Buddhist awareness in their home districts. After the above-mentioned camp of Banepa in 1995, Tharus and Magars founded branches of the Buddhist association in their respective districts.

The Udaypaur Yuba Bauddha Jagaran Samithi ('Youth Buddhist Awareness Committee of Udayapur') was founded by Tharus in Deuri VDC, in 1996, with the slogan: *Buddha dharmako prachar prasar ra bauddha ka upadesh* ('Publicity for Buddhism and its teachings'). The first president of this association, Vasudev Choudhary, came in contact with Buddhism via the Tharu Kalyankarini Sabha and participated in the first Buddhist camp in Kathmandu where he met Theravada monks and nuns as well as the Newar members of YBS. Inspired by the books by Ramanand Prasad Singh and Tej Narayan Panjiyar, he created in his home in Deuri village a Buddhist library. Bringing Buddhism to the Tharus became the mission of his life.

The local branch of Nepal Magar Sangh Bauddha Seva Samaj in Rupandehi district was formed in 1999. Its president, Tulsi Regmi Magar, did not know the first thing about Buddhism at the moment of his election. He told me how he had to take a temporary initiation in a *vihara* in Butwal, in order to study Buddhism, and recalled how the leaders of Nepal Magar Sangh were pushing the local members to attend Buddhist training camps at the Kirtipur Vihar in Kathmandu (Image 12.1).

These activists started working in their respective districts with a twofold activity: looking for evidence of the Buddhist origin of their group and specializing as Buddhist priests.

Image 12.1
Tulsi Regmi Magar, President of the Nepal Magar Sangh Bauddha Seva Samaj Branch in Rupandehi District Shows to the Students the Schedule of a *Uapa* Training Program Held in Saljandi, Kapilavastu District in 2007

Source: Author.
Note: Tulsi Regmi Magar's lecture will concern the doctrine of dependent origination, represented in the image visible in the background.

The Quest for Evidence of Buddhist Origins

The relentless search by local Buddhist activists for proofs of the new story of their origins, in order to show the evidence to the people of their village, is itself a proof of the priority they gave to the 'truth of the origins'.

The main objectives were:

(1) To prove that Buddha was Magar or Tharu, and to scrutinize his life to find out traces of Tharu or Magar traditions or language.

For example, they postulated that: "When Buddha's mother Mayadevi was pregnant, she gave birth to Buddha in Lumbini on the way to her parents. In Magar tradition, when a woman has a child, she has to go to her parents"; "We know that the Buddha ate pork meat before dying. Pork meat is the most delicious food for Magars". "The jewels of Buddha's mother that you can see on Buddhist statues are identical to the jewels that we Tharu women used to wear".

(2) To prove that Tharus or Magars' customs are related to Buddhism. They analyzed the local traditions and the local territory to show that some practices and sites had traces (or relics) of a Buddhist past and inversely, that there was no trace of Hinduism in them:

"The earth mound at the entrance of the Tharu house has the same shape as a Buddhist shrine"; "In the altars of Tharu houses, one never finds a single Hindu statue";

"Archaeologists found remnants of Buddhist statues in this small Devi temple and discovered that this is a temple dedicated to Buddha's mother. No Hindu sacrifice can be done here anymore."

(3) To prove that the somatic characteristics and moral qualities of Magars/Tharus reveal their natural Buddhism.

"We Tharus are honest and innocent, as we have the nature of the Buddha; we are naturally Buddhist without having the concept of being Buddhist"; "We Magars have the same Mongolian face as the ancient statues in Sarnath."

To be naturally Buddhist means to have the physical traits of the Buddha, to be a descendant of the Buddha, or to have the same moral qualities as the Buddha; it seems that Tharu and Magar activists are making a cultural operation to naturalize themselves as Buddhists.

The discovery of a Buddhist past and the quest for proof of such are presented as scientific endeavours (to the point of quoting the presence of similar DNA between Tharus and Lord Buddha) and as a question of awareness and education necessary to operate a social transformation.[46]

Lumbini provided a strong proof in this quest for evidence: the head of the Tharu village of Gularya considers his trip to Lumbini as the key event that convinced him of the Tharus' Buddhist past: "I was struck by the similarities between the objects in Lumbini museum and our traditional artefacts", he recalls. The trips to Lumbini also led the villagers to align with a religion that appeared fascinatingly international: "We were fascinated by all these pilgrims and temples of all the countries of the world, we were proud to be part of such a great tradition," recall some members of the Tharu women's association of Kathmandu whose visit of Lumbini marked the starting point of their Buddhist activism. Thus, the villagers seemed to be relying on a global Buddhist centre to validate their local Buddhist belonging.

Ritual Specialists: The New Sangha

As requested by their Kathmandu-based leaders, Magar and Tharu local activists organized themselves to change their life-cycle rituals by providing substitute Buddhist versions as follows: while the Hindu structure was retained, the Brahmin was replaced by the Magar or Tharu lay ritual specialist, who celebrated the life-cycle rituals following a Buddhist ritual handbook, and read texts in Pali, the language of the Theravada Buddhist Canon, instead of Sanskrit. The Pali suttas were now chanted and translated into Nepali by the ritual specialist. Among the Magars, these officiants were called *Uapas*,[47] and among the Tharus they were called Tharu pandits.[48] The ritual specialists whom I met were almost all men, schoolteachers among the Tharus, and retired soldiers among the Magars.[49] The handbook requires some proficiency in reading Nepali and Pali, which probably explains why Tharu pandits are all teachers: many of the aspirant Tharu pandits of Udayapur did not speak or read Nepali well enough.[50] These ritual specialists are thus among the most cultivated people in their village, and often maintain the only library of the village, full of free publications from Taiwan, China, and Malaysia, and also magazines published by Nepalese Theravada monks.

These Tharu and Magar ritual specialists have formed a network and they know each other because either they were trained in the same camps of 'Buddhist Awareness' or together they took a temporary ordination in some *vihara*. In turn, they organized other camps in the districts where they each became instructors.

In 2004, they were very few in number: four or five Tharu pandits in all Udayapur and no more than five *Uapas* in all Rupandehi, and they had to travel in order to serve the families. The number of *Uapas* is increasing rapidly, as new *Uapas* are being trained with courses that last from two to five days. In Nawalparasi, Magar *Uapas* numbered more than 150 in 2007 and they offered their services to Tharus as well; I observed that they were becoming less and less linked to their own ethnic group and more united with Tharu pandits in their Buddhist mission. It is for this reason that I suggest that these new ritual specialists are members of a new *sangha*, a group which has the practice of Buddhism in common and which transcends the ethnic group's traditional boundaries.

Magar *Uapas* are supported by the Nepal Magar Baudha Seva Samaj, created especially to attend Buddhist affairs. The *Uapas* have founded local branches of Baudha Seva Samaj and can rely on the efficient network of Nepal Magar Sangh to spread their information and invitations to the camps. The young girls and boys who came to the *Uapa* training camp (*uapa prasiksan kareikram*) in which I participated in 2007 were all children of members of the Nepal Magar Sangh. After the training camp, the Nepal Magar Sangh provided *Uapas* with a certificate of accreditation and a series of forms for the rituals they perform (birth and marriage certificates, etc.). *Uapas* of Rupandehi are more and more independent and organize camps on their own.

As for the Tharus of Deuri in Udayapur, they do not offer any course: participating in a Buddhist camp is sufficient to become a Tharu pandit. They are much more isolated than their Magar counterparts are and have maintained much stronger contacts with the YBS in Kathmandu. They depend on members from YBS to organize a camp and they have suffered from interruptions to these programmes owing to the People's War. They still have a small *sangha* of Tharu pandits, which meets every month to share the problems they might experience in their practice.

Missionary Activity

Uapas and Tharu pandits move from village to village to celebrate rituals and to conduct their missionary activity, which includes:

(1) Criticism of the 'blind faith' of Hindu practices and an invitation to adopt a rational, responsible attitude;
(2) An injunction to stop calling on Brahmins and to save money by using their *own* Buddhist priest instead;
(3) The news that important scholars have discovered the truth about their true religion.

For example, Vasudev Choudhary, the Tharu pandit in Deuri village (Udavapur district), addressed the villagers in the following way:

> Do not call the Brahmin, he cheats you; he tells you that your deceased father will go to heaven only if you offer him money, animals, or land, but that is only superstition: the deceased will go to paradise only if he has performed good deeds during his life! Keep all the offerings for your family and, to celebrate the ritual, call me instead, because I belong to your group, I am your *kutumba*[51] and I will celebrate a simple ritual for you without asking any form of compensation.

Rim Bahadur Srish, *Uapa* in Kirtipur village (and responsible for the *Uapas* in Nawalparasi and Kapilavastu), scolded people for indulging in 'superstitious behaviours':

> Why do you believe that goddess Sarasvati gives us knowledge? If you close all your books, and wait for some knowledge from her, do you expect to get it? If you separate a wife and a husband, and ask God for a baby, do you think he will give it? Nothing is impossible, but we need to work hard to obtain what we want, not relying on blind faith or on gods. In this new Nepal, we should understand that one must work and avoid bad actions in order to be happy and successful; Buddha teaches us that we have to be responsible and not simply believe what we hear, but to experience personally whatever has been taught to us.

Mahesh Choudhary, Tharu pandit in Motigara (Saptari district), told me:

> I visit the villagers and I announce that scholars have discovered the truth that we are Buddhists; I explain to them the connection between us and the Buddha, which was hidden from us and that we have forgotten. I go with them to the village shrine and I show them the Buddhist vestiges; they believe me and they ask me how to perform the rituals and then I give them the Buddhist ritual handbook.

The exhortations and preaching of the *Uapa* and Tharu pandits are usually delivered on the occasion of rituals. Where the community already has built a little Buddhist temple (usually called *gumba*), these Buddhist activists can organize the life of the little Buddhist community around it, and thereby create opportunities for preaching.

For example, they can invite the community to gather and recite the Five Precepts and the Three Refuges at Purnima and Aunsi (the days of the full and new moon, respectively) and at Buddha Jayanti (the festival celebrating the birth, enlightenment, and passing away of Gautama Buddha). In a few places, the community began practising meditation at the temple instead of celebrating the Hindu festival of Dasain.

Except for the aspects more linked to ethnic claims, the Buddhist message sounds awkward to the majority of the villagers. They will listen to it because *Uapas* and Tharu pandits are usually respected members of the community, and their message can be perceived as authoritative. If the person presenting the message to the villagers lacks the necessary authority, he risks being laughed at and marginalized. The news that scholars have discovered that the Tharus and the Magars were Buddhists is a source of authority. My own presence has sometimes been a support for the vacillating authority of some Tharu pandits, who could show the villagers that the Buddhist cause was even attracting foreigner scholars.

While talking of the positive effect of Buddhism in their own lives, and asserting the positive effect Buddhism will have on their societies, many of these ritual specialists mentioned the difficulties they experienced in spreading their message in villages where Hindu traditions were strong. Problems occurred at times of weddings, such as when only one of the families of the bride or groom was already Buddhist and the other family insisted on having the usual Hindu ritual.

The positive response came principally from the young and from women, whereas the elders, especially among the Tharus, reacted quite badly. For example, a Tharu pandit in Udayapur district was told: "You are changing our young ones, please let us die first and then you can do what you want". However, the opportunity to reduce expenses by calling a member of one's own group instead of having to make costly offerings to the Brahmins is well appreciated by the villagers.

The process of Buddhist diffusion can be seen as quite superficial; for instance, it can be seen in the name that some Tharu villagers from Saptari district gave to the new Buddhist officiants: they called them *bahun* ('Brahmin'). Similarly, the Magar villagers from Nawalparasi called them *lama*.

Lal Bahadur Chaudari (Tharu pandit at Mainaha, Saptari) complained:

Here, there is a Maithili Jha Brahman and they call me only when he is not available. They don't see any difference and call me *bahun* too: they know simply that when it's me I recite a Buddhist *sutta* and when it's him, he recites a Hindu *mantra*.

Tharu pandit Vasudev Choudhary told me about the difficulty of celebrating a Buddhist funeral ritual:

> People suffer and they ask me in anguish where are the *pinda*s (small rice balls offered to the dead). I reply that to believe that one can recreate the body of a dead person by offering a *pinda* during ten days, is pure imagination. I tell them to free themselves from these imaginations and that the Buddha has taught us to doubt everything that has not been personally experienced. I tell them that they should concentrate on avoiding doing things that are harmful to others and to themselves, and on doing what is good to themselves and others. There are traditional families that hesitate to change, but when they are told that what they are doing is not really following their ancestors, sometimes they are convinced.

Many Tharus were afraid or felt guilty when they switched to Buddhism, especially if they were the first in their village. A discouraged Tharu pandit summarized his difficulties in this way: "To attempt to teach Buddhism to the Tharus is like being a mouse attempting to put a collar on a cat".

The contrast between the villagers and the pandits or *Uapas* does seem to fit within the two ideal types distinguished by Timothy Fitzgerald in his ethnography of Buddhism in Maharashtra villages, namely what he calls 'village Buddhism' and 'intellectual Buddhism' (1994: 19–23). The former refers to the kind of Buddhism which has not really changed anybody or anything very radically, in which the identity is of a purely communal kind and concerns the identity of a caste group in relation to other castes. Buddhists may have changed some practices, but still they recognize caste hierarchy, practice endogamy, commensality, and even untouchability. Alongside the ostensibly Buddhist practices, such as the chanting of the Three Refuges and the Five Precepts on Purnima and Jayanti days, they may still continue to worship the old Hindu gods. Intellectual Buddhism, on the other hand, is typical of educated Buddhists who tend to emerge as leaders of the village Buddhist community. Some of them have taken a short training at some Buddhist temple in the performance of simple Buddhist ceremonies, enabling them to act as Buddhist *pujari* for the local community. For them, Buddhism means equality, rejection of caste discrimination and of 'blind faith', and acceptance of scientific rationality, modern education, and democracy. Some of them, who are involved in meditation and in the study of Buddhist scriptures and are close to Buddhist monks, focus more on the soteriological message of Buddhism, but still link it with a strong social commitment.

The Ritual Handbook

All Tharu and Magar ritual specialists in eastern Tarai districts own a Buddhist ritual handbook (*samskar paddhati*), which is strictly followed during the rituals and during the training of new officiants. The book was written by Dharma Ratna Shakya, a Newar Buddhist scholar and social activist who played a key role in establishing the first curriculum for teaching Buddhism in Nepal (Pariyatti Siksa) (Shakya, 2003). He wrote this book at the request of *Janajati* leaders who were eager to have a handbook on which to base the change of their rituals.[52]

This handbook is a concrete example of the invention of a Buddhist tradition through the adaptation of values (mediated by Newars) exterior to the local culture.

The original version written by Dharma Ratna Shakya contained only ten basic rituals, which did not take into any account the local rituals of the recipients of the book. In 2003, Magar *Uapas* of Rupandehi formed a committee to decide which of the many missing Magar rituals should be included in the book. The committee had to decide which part of Magar traditions was compliant with a Buddhist taste and thus acceptable, and which part was unacceptable 'blind faith'.

Some rituals like *rudri puja* or *satya narayan puja* were targeted as Hindu and superstitious and then rejected,[53] whereas other rituals like the ritual for ending the period of mourning (*kryapatti chokine*) and the engagement ritual (*teki halne*) were included in the book. The worship of the lineage deity (*kul puja*), which usually implies sacrifice, was included but changed: animal sacrifice was replaced by the recitation of one of the edifying stories on 'Why One Should Avoid Sacrifice'.

Even when a ritual was considered acceptable, there remained the problem of how to perform it in a Buddhist manner. The practical solution adopted was that the setting should be the same for all the rituals: the same ritual space (*mandap*), the same water pots (*kalash*) symbolizing Buddha Dharma and Sangha, the same chanting of the Precepts and the Three Refuges at the beginning of the ritual, and the same recitation of a *sutta* at the end.

Tharu pandits faced similar problems: they did not know many of the rituals in the book, and none of their own rituals appeared in the book either. They studied the rituals proposed and tried to find a correspondence to their own system; for example, the ritual called *vratababandha* (the major initiation ritual for all twice-born Hindus) meant nothing to them, but they realized the corresponding ritual of tonsure was included in their tradition and so agreed that they were already practising a Buddhist tradition without being aware of it.

Tharu pandits of Saptari explained to me that they gave themselves a general rule that all things for which they did not find any precise instruction in the book were to be performed 'as they were', but in all cases fire sacrifice (*hom*) and blood sacrifice were to be removed.

The interpretation and integration of the ritual handbook led to a negotiation of the following: (1) What could be classified as Hindu (and so to be abandoned); (2) What had been considered Hindu until now, but in fact was not and could be easily recognizable as Buddhist (and so to be kept and slightly modified); and (3) What was purely Buddhist and accepted as such. Although the previous categories were subject to considerable vacillations (to the point that the lineage god ritual was accepted), the only fixed point affording no debate was that sacrifice was a Hindu practice to be entirely condemned. This latter point turned some Buddhist activists into rather zealous cultural reformers.

Conveying Teachings within the Hindu Structure of Ritual

The *Uapas* and Tharu pandits themselves said that they were not celebrating pure rituals, whatever this might mean, but that they were performing them 'half-Hindu, half-Buddhist' (*adi hindu adi bauddha*) in order to be more accepted by the community, which at times could still require a fire sacrifice or a *pinda* offering for the *sraddha*.[54]

They all agreed that these rituals had kept a Hindu structure and that sometimes the change consisted simply in replacing the Brahmin priest with a Buddhist priest and replacing the Sanskrit mantra with the Pali *sutta*, and that sometimes the only hint of Buddhism was the presence of an image of the Buddha in the ritual space (Image 12.2).

These substitutions can be interpreted as a part of a process of assimilation, that is an incorporation of new cultural elements without making any fundamental changes in worldview or practice. However, I noticed in a number of instances that the performance of the ritual actions as prescribed in the ritual handbook was accompanied by anecdotes, moral teachings, and elements of doctrine.

Let us take the example of the Buddhist Magar *sraddha* ritual, celebrated in Butwal in 2004 by the *Uapa* Purna Bahadur Thapa, vice president of the Nepal Magar Bauddha Sewa Samaj of Rupandehi. While celebrating this ritual, which had a basically Hindu structure,

Image 12.2
A Buddhist Wedding in the Tharu Village of Jaljale, Udayapur District

Source: Picture taken by author.
Note: The image of Buddha in front of the bride and groom gives a discrete Buddhist flavour to an entirely traditional ceremony. The celebrant is Tharu *Pandit* Ram Lagaan Panjiyar, a nephew of Tej Narayan Panjiyar. Their influential family has facilitated the spread of Buddhism in the local community.

Purna invited people not to cry and to be aware of the Buddhist truth of *anicca*, the impermanent nature of all things. In this case, he told the story of a mother asking the Buddha to save her son from death; the Buddha answers that he will help her only when she will bring him some rice from a house where nobody has ever died.

During a camp of training for new *Uapas*, Purna explained to the participants what makes a good *Uapa*: he/she has to know the Suttas and many Buddhist stories; should be strong during the funeral, even if the family suffers; and should provide Buddhist teachings. During the procession to the *ghat*, the *Uapa* has to remind the bereaved family about the impermanence of all beings, that nothing can come with us at the moment of death, and explain that Buddha teachings are the only support in that moment. Finally, at the cremation *ghat*, the *Uapa* should give a teaching from the meditation on the decomposition of the body.

What I want to underscore here is that although the structures seem to have remained the same, the ritual has increasingly become an occasion for teaching the doctrine, thanks to these oral additions. In my opinion, this transformation of ritual into a form of Buddhist teaching is a very interesting and new phenomenon and may lead to disconnecting ethnic activism from Buddhist practice, so that proselytization of Buddhism will become a goal of its own.

There are hints of this possible transformation: in 2004 the *Uapas'* discourses were focused on a fierce anti-Brahminism and on the need to free the Magars from the domination of Hinduism, whereas in 2008 I noticed a strong emphasis on moral teachings, on the fight against superstitions, and on the notion of personal responsibility. East–East Buddhist connections are also contributing in detaching the local Buddhism of Magars and Tharus from its ethnic preoccupations and in opening it to a wider scene.

The teachings given during the rituals and the camps flow right through the networks of transmission of Buddhism first identified above. They are taken from the Buddhist literature that *Uapas* and Tharu pandits receive from the Theravada monasteries of Kathmandu or from the many free publications coming from Malaysia and Taiwan, in English or Hindi translation. *Uapas* and Tharu pandits make use of these networks for the benefit of their own sons and daughters as it is not unusual for them to send their sons and daughters to the Theravada monasteries for a temporary ordination or as *bhikkhus* and *anagarikas*, hoping to see them leaving to Burma or

Thailand for a Buddhist education (as poor Newar families have done since 1990). Finally, Chinese and Thai statues, ornaments, and incense burners brought by foreign pilgrims have started appearing in small Tharu and Magar Buddhist monasteries—concrete reminders of the wider Buddhist ethnoscape.

CONCLUSIONS

The linking of transnational Buddhist modernism with ethnic activism in the evolving political context of Nepal has created a space for Buddhist activists to build new forms of belonging for the members of Tharu and Magar communities.

Tharu and Magar ritual specialists and Buddhist activists have played a prominent role in the assimilation and domestication of Buddhist notions, making them more acceptable to locals. They have mediated and localized Buddhism through two means, which are deriving principally from the dominant Hindu culture: (1) new Buddhist rituals modelled on Hindu structures, and (2) references to a mythology of an original Buddhism, which as Krauskopff (2009b) argues depends more on a Hindu model of origins, where belonging must be defined in terms of a genealogy and descent.

Both the new rituals and the new mythology of origins provide simultaneously different levels of belonging: to an individual group, to a collection of groups, and to an international community. The affirmation of a Buddhist past provides a fundamental truth about belonging for a single group, underscoring its prestigious ancestry, asserting its uniqueness, authenticity, and its indigenousness, and which offers elements of commonality to otherwise scattered groups having in common no more than an ethnonym. At the same time, this Buddhist common past offers an 'oppositional' bonding to all the groups that share the label of *Janajati*, who define themselves as non-Hindus in a set of opposition to the dominant groups and share the Buddhist modernist commitment for social inclusion and justice. The affirmation of an original Buddhism also shifts the belonging to the global Buddhist world, which can inspire or validate the local adhesion. Although the Buddhist past of Tharus and Magars is invented and constructed, this does not make it less real: quite on the contrary, these histories of origins provide a truth about belonging, which is quintessentially political, a starting point for the politics of belonging.

In the same way, the rituals define the dual criteria of belonging to and exclusion from a single group: on the one hand by including 'our people' ('relatives', *kutumba*s) as ritual specialists and excluding Brahmins as outsiders, and on the other hand by accepting some ritual procedures as Buddhist and excluding some others as Hindu. The ritual activity also creates a new group to belong to, that is, the Buddhist *sangha*, which transcends the ethnic group's traditional boundaries because it is constituted by the ritual specialists of different ethnic groups who have in common the practice of Buddhism. This group, involved in the study of Buddhist ritual and doctrine, easily feels the connection with the transnational world of Buddhist education and knowledge dissemination.

The adoption of both the Hindu structures of ritual and the mythology of origins are indeed forms of domestication. However, in my opinion, these traditional tools, which lie halfway between a Hindu model and a Buddhist innovation, carry the seeds of a transformation and convey new messages in old structures. As we have seen, during the new rituals there is an opportunity to spread the teachings and in the new historiographies there is passage from a discourse on ethnic origin to a discourse on a Buddhist universalism.

It is possible to label as contradictions the obvious differences between the rationalist values taught by Theravada monks and Newar activists during the camps (i.e. religion as the responsible choice of the individual) and the values of ancestry conveyed by the historiographies of Magar and Tharu intellectuals, not to mention the collective conversions decided by the ethnic associations.

I, however, think that these 'contradictions' stem from the fact that Buddhism is working as a bridge between the old and the new, that it refers to a multilayered meaning of 'being Buddhist', and that it becomes an interface through which different horizons or levels of belonging interact:

(1) To be Buddhist is to redefine one's belonging to a group in search of its own identity, and in the process of rewriting its history, creating the truth of a Buddhist past and a common prestigious ancestor (the Buddha), and rooting itself as *adivasi* on the land where he was born. (In addition, this eventually also opens the individual to a connection to the international

indigenous movements.) The reference to the common origin of groups like Magars or Tharus helps solidify the existence of these groups sharing the same ethnonym, whereas they previously never had a common identity, and enables the individual to feel part of a unique group. Being Buddhist enables a collective dimension for these groups in their search for a (new) identity.

(2) To be Buddhist implies belonging to a *Janajati* group opposed to a (formerly) Hindu state still largely controlled by dominant Hindu groups. To be Buddhist is to express a negative identity (the affirmation of non-Hinduism) and implies at the same time a dimension of collective social emancipation.

(3) Thanks to the mediation of the rituals and of the discourse of activists, there is a fostering of a new sense of belonging to a wider community: as a member of a Buddhist *ecumene* in Nepal (creating links to every other Buddhist group, whether Tibetan, Tamang, or Newar) and as a member of an international Buddhist community, sharing the same Dharma (beyond the 'superficial differences of traditions') with people of other nationalities, whether they be Americans or Chinese.

NOTES

1. As Jim Beckford (2001) suggests, it is important to put in perspective the problematic adaptation strategies of religions faced with globalization. Religions have surely been 'structured' by the international context, but they have been also one of its structuring elements, and they have sometimes prepared, contributed, and announced globalization.
2. Nepal was declared a secular state by the restored House of Representatives on 18 May 2006, a few weeks after the successful People's Movement. Nepal's secular state status was reiterated in the Interim Constitution promulgated in January 2007 and finally by the Constituent Assembly on 28 May 2008.
3. On the adoption of Buddhism among Magar and Tharu ethnic groups, see Krauskopff, 2003, 2009a, 2009b; Lecomte-Tilouine, 2002, 2009, 2010; Letizia, 2005, 2007. The shift to Buddhism among Gurungs described by Susan Hangen presents striking similarities with the case studied here (Hangen, 2010: 132–51).
4. Tharu VDC of Jogidaha, Saptari district. *Buddham saranam gacchami dhammam saranam gacchami, sangham saranam gacchami* (I take refuge in the Buddha, in the *dharma* and the *sangha*), the threefold recitation of which is the minimum commitment that makes one a Theravada Buddhist.
5. Village of Deuri, Udayapur district.

6. The flag (popularized by Colonel Olcott as a symbol of international Buddhist unity) was adopted by the World Fellowship of Buddhists in 1950 as the flag of Buddhists throughout the world.
7. In Prasabani, a Tharu village in Saptari district.
8. In Saljhandi, Rupandehi district.
9. See Bechert and Hartmann, 1988; Leve, 2002; Gellner, 2002; LeVine, 2005; LeVine and Gellner, 2005; Gellner and LeVine, 2007.
10. As Gellner remarks, most of the early Theravadins were not modernists: they did not reject Vajrayana's traditions as some do today (2010: 174; see also Leve, 2002); rather, they sought to revive Newar Buddhism.
11. Heinz Bechert established the term 'Buddhist modernism' (Bechert, 1966, 1984, 1990), describing it as a movement that reinterpreted Buddhism as a 'rational way of thought' that stressed reason, and which popularized and democratized meditation and the rediscovery of canonical texts. This movement de-emphasized ritual and folk beliefs and practices, and was linked to social reform and nationalist movements.
12. Richard Gombrich and Gananath Obeyesekere coined the term Protestant Buddhism to suggest that modernizing Buddhism both protested against European colonization and Christian missionization and adopted elements of Protestantism (this-worldly asceticism, a code of ethics for lay people, and an emphasis on doctrine and education with disdain for superstition and intercession of gods and demons) (Obeyesekere, 1970; Gombrich, 1988: 174; Gombrich and Obeyesekere, 1988: 5–6).
13. On Dharmapala, see Sangharakshita, 1980; Gombrich, 1988: 188–91; Kantowsky, 2003.
14. *Andha-vishvas*, a literal translation of 'blind faith' was the neologism introduced by Swami Dayananada Sarasvati, the founder of Arya Samaj, to translate 'superstition' (Bharati, 1970).
15. Dharmapala transposed the Buddha's liberation of ancient Indians from Brahmin priests into the Dhamma's liberation of modern Sinhalese Buddhists from Christian ones. In Nepal, this became the liberation of ethnic minorities, the *Janajati*, from Brahmin domination.
16. See Zelliott, 1992; Jondhale and Beltz, 2004.
17. Ambedkar chose for his conversion the time of Dassehra (leaving Hinduism during the most important Hindu festival) and the year 1956, marking the 2500th anniversary of the *parinirvana* according to the most accepted (though wrong) chronology.
18. Appadurai (1996) uses 'ethnoscape' to refer to people on the move: migrants, tourists, refugees, and students creating a landscape of networks not confined to territorial or national boundaries. Even if Appadurai leaves out missionaries as such, Kemper notes very convincingly that "Buddhist monks constitute a globalizing force as important as any other moving group" (Kemper, 2005: 23). Missionaries are brokers of religio-cultural boundaries of these ethnoscapes, using a wide variety of media to create and broadcast their message.
19. Persecuted by Rana rulers for having caused conversion, early Nepalese Theravadins spent long years in exile and training abroad, and began to develop foreign networks, which were continued later.

20. Bhikkhu Amritananda, one of the first Nepalese *bhikkhu*s, travelled abroad to Theravada countries, and to Mongolia and Vietnam, to strengthen ties with Buddhist institutions that might provide training for Nepalese novices (LeVine and Gellner, 2005: 67). Nepalese novices received invitations and sponsorships from Buddhist institutions in Burma, Sri Lanka, and later in Thailand and Taiwan as well. These links abroad became essential to the growing order of nuns, who could not receive full ordination without their connection with the Foguang Shan (Mahayana) sect of Taiwan (LeVine, 2005: 64–71).

21. Taiwanese funds (from the Foguang Shang Monastery and wealthy individuals) were particularly important for the broadening of Buddhist proselytizing efforts in Nepal, through the Himalayan Buddhist Education Foundation (LeVine and Gellner, 2005: 259–61).

22. Since 1935, proselytizing and conversion have been prohibited under the civil code, which specifically forbade the spread of beliefs that "ruined the religion traditionally practised by the Hindu community" (Gaborieau, 1994: 63).

23. Constitution of the Kingdom of Nepal 2047 (1990): Part 3.19, Right to Religion. The article remained unmodified in the Interim Constitution 2063 (2007); the ban on conversion still appears in current constitutional drafts and the new Criminal Code submitted to the Parliament in January 2011.

24. It may appear surprising that a religious minority would campaign for a secular state, but secularism in Nepal is not so much the separation between the Church and the State as a demand for the equal recognition of all religions practiced in the country and the abolition of the special state-sponsored primacy given to Hinduism (Gellner, 2001: 338). In this campaign, secularism was not a retreat from or rejection of religion: the concept was redefined as "the institutional instantiation of freedom of religion and religious equality" (Leve, 2007: 94). On secularism in Nepal, see also Toffin, 2006 and Letizia, 2011.

25. For the early history of the YBS told by its founders, see *Smarika*, 2006.

26. See Gellner et al., 1997; Lecomte-Tilouine and Dollfus, 2003; Hangen, 2007 and 2010. For a discussion on the rhetoric of the ethnicizing discourse of *Janajati/ Adivasi* organizations, see Toffin, 2009.

27. In 2003 the Nepal Janajati Mahasangh changed its name to Nepal Janajati Adivasi Mahasangh, inserting the term *adivasi*, 'indigenous people'. Its English name was changed to NEFIN (Nepal Federation of Indigenous Nationalities).

28. On the definition of the term *Janajati*, see Gellner and Karki, 2008: 110–14.

29. As Toffin and Pfaff-Czarnecka (this volume) notice, ethnic discourses oscillate between particularism and universalism: members of ethnic groups highlight the uniqueness of their cultures, but to do so, most ethnic activists seem to be using the same cultural repertoires and to be making similar claims. This is particularly true in the shift to Buddhism; for example, Gurungs share the same discourse as the one related here for Tharus and Magars (Hangen, 2010: 132–51): thus, becoming not Hindu (=Buddhist) means simultaneously to be a more authentic Gurung/Magar/Tharu. This uniqueness and authenticity does not seem to be undermined by the fact that many groups with manifestly different traditions refer to the same ancestor and religion.

30. As Guneratne observes, "the Tharus are culturally and linguistically very heterogeneous: they share no common cultural symbol, such as language, or religion,

or even a common myth of origin on which they might anchor their imagining community" (1998: 752).

31. On the effort to represent identity in racial terms (opposing Aryans and Mongols) by the ethnic political party Mongol National Organization, see Hangen, 2005b and 2007.

32. After the UN declared 1993 as the year of the Indigenous Peoples, *Janajati*s started to stress their groups' indigenousness (Gellner and Karki, 2008: 110). In 2007, Nepal ratified the 'Indigeneous and Tribal Peoples Convention, 1989' (C169), which recognizes various important rights to 'indigenous' people.

33. Other Nepalese groups (and among them many Magars and Tharus) reaffirmed other traditional indigenous religions, like Kirant religion, Bon, shamanism, and 'natural religion' (see Schlemmer, 2004; Lecomte, 2010).

34. The idea of 'converting' or 'reclaiming' Dalits for Buddhism, as in India, has not been pushed or adopted as a policy by the Dharmodaya Sabha, the Buddhist Society of Nepal. The Newars, who control how Buddhism is represented in the country, accept *Janajati*s as fellow Buddhists, but seem uncomfortable with the idea of a big influx of Dalit Buddhists. Efforts to create coalitions of Janajati and Dalits may have been impeded by the fact that the category of indigenous peoples excludes Hindu caste groups, which, *Janajati*s argue, are non-natives originating from India (Hangen, 2007: 20, 51).

35. For the Tharu Kalyankarini Sabha (Tharu Welfare Society), see Guneratne, 2003: 139–88.

36. On the role and activity of these two Tharu intellectuals from Saptari district, who engaged in rewriting the history of the Tharu, see Krauskopff, 2009a and 2009b. Both Panjiyar and Singh have passed away, but their family members continued their work: Ramandand Prasad Singh's son, who lives in Kathmandu, continued his father's work, publishing books on Buddhism and Tharu history (Singh, 2006 and 2010), while many members of Panjiyar's family support Buddhist activism in Udayapur district.

37. The same type of activism can be observed today for the 2011 Census and seems to remain captive to the logic of pro-Hindu state activists, who argue that Nepal should be a Hindu state because 80 per cent of Nepalis are Hindus.

38. The campaign was partially successful (with 25 per cent of the Magars declaring Buddhism as their religion) but the adoption of Buddhism was not the only alternative available: many activists were considering Magars as 'nature worshippers', practitioners of the 'Religion of Nature'. For the opposition Naturism/Buddhism, see Lecomte-Tilouine, 2009 and 2010.

39. Ambedkar (1948) recasts untouchables as 'broken men' who converted to Buddhism in 400 AD and were ostracized and tyrannized by Hindus. Their refusal to return to Brahminism was punished by the stigma of untouchability. The present conversion of Tharus and Magars to Buddhism appears similarly presented as a return to a previous (and lost) agency.

40. Ramanand Prasad Singh wrote in English, more for a local educated and foreign audience than for the members of his group; however, later his writings have been translated into Nepali and widely distributed in the Tharu community (Choudhary and Choudhary, 1997) and recently posted to Tharu websites like tharus.org and tharuculture.blogspot.com.

41. Ramanand Prasad Singh's son, Subodh Kumar Singh, wrote a book along the same lines entitled *The Great Sons of the Tharus: Sakyamuni Buddha and Asoka the Great* (Singh, 2006) and more recently wrote "The remnant of the Shakyas and Koliyas is the Tharu community of today, and the culture that was practised during the time of the Buddha is still followed by the Theravadin Tharus. It is the culture that helped to preserve their identity" (2010: 157).

42. Panjiyar translated into Tharu the *Grihi Vinaya*, the moral code for Buddhist lay-people, written by Amritananda, one of the first Nepalese bhikkhus (Krauskopff, 2009b: 263).

43. These exhortations echo some of the 22 vows that Ambedkar added to the five traditional Precepts for the lay Buddhist, which for the most part show a desire to reject Hindu traditions, as for example: "I will never get any samskar (life-cycle ritual) performed by Brahmins" or "I will not regard Brahma, Visnu and Mahesh as Gods nor will I worship them". The 22 vows are listed in Jaffrelot, 2000: 204–05.

44. The boycott of Dasain was a central issue of the entire *Janajati* movement, as has been shown by Susan Hangen (2005a).

45. i.e. before he became a government minister in the period of royal autocracy 2004–06.

46. The search for historical and scientific evidence of this Buddhist past was so intense that my presence was seen as a contribution to their efforts. For example, I was welcomed by a militant at a Tharu Kalyakarini Sabha meeting in 2004 with the explicit request: "With your research will you help us to prove that Tharus are anthropologically and biologically Buddhist?"

47. *Uapa* means in the Magar tongue 'instructor, master', and has come to mean priest.

48. My observations are limited to a few districts and do not account for all Tharus and Magars of Nepal. Nevertheless, in 2009 I noticed that Tharu Buddhist activists had gone as far as Dang Valley, where a Buddhist camp was held in the same year. Many Tharus were 'informed' that 'Tharus are Buddhists', and many were proud to have a statue of the Buddha in the newly constructed Tharu local museum. The head of the village was impressed by the fact that Buddhism was explained as a rational and scientific philosophy, very similar to the Marxist approach. He affirmed: "Our life history and traditions match the life story of the Buddha and we should not change anything of our traditions to become Buddhists". As far as Magars are concerned, the *uapas* of Butwal are organizing Buddhist camps for Magars of Myagdi, Baglung, and Surkhet districts. It is likely that this process will extend to many districts other than the ones I visited.

49. I was told that there are some women working as *Uapas* (called Mapas) and as Tharu pandit, but I have not met any of them yet. However, the number of Mapas may grow: in the formation camp for *Uapas* I observed in 2007, the majority of participants were women.

50. The role of these new Buddhist ritual specialists is strikingly similar to that of the Buddhist *pujari* of Ambedkar Buddhism in Maharashtra, where in many villages a local person such a schoolteacher who may have done a training course performs simple Buddhist *puja* in the *vihara* and teaches Ambedkar Buddhism (Fitzgerald, 1997: 228–29). This being said, I have no data at this time referring to contacts between the Nepalese Buddhist activists and the Ambedkarite ones.

51. Kutumbas are the in-laws. Vasudev here stresses the importance to make the ritual 'totally ours', celebrated by 'one of us' a relative.
52. The book contains Pali *suttas* that are chanted and translated in Nepali (the translation is chanted as well). As mentioned above, the book requires some proficiency in reading Nepali and Pali, which probably explains why Tharu pandits are all teachers.
53. The fact that the committee declared a ritual superstitious and excluded it from the book did not change anything in practice: families still ask for these rituals and many *Uapas* accept to celebrate them 'just to please them since they are ignorant of their true tradition and still are attached to the wrong one' (Interviews with the *Uapa* Purna Bahadur Rana, Butwal, 2004 and 2007).
54. In the ritual setting, the Magar *Uapas* of Rupandehi put five Kalasas (ceremonial vessel) representing, respectively, Buddha, Dharma, Sangha, Pitris (ancestors), and Kuldeuta (lineage deity).

REFERENCES

Ambedkar, Bhimrao Ramji. 1948. *The Untouchables: Who Were They and Why They Became Untouchables*. New Delhi: Amrit book Co.
Appadurai, Arjun. 1996. *Modernity at Large; Cultural Dimensions of Globalization*. Minneapolis: University of Minnesota Press.
Bharati, Agehananda. 1970. 'The Use of "Superstition" as an Anti-Traditional Device in Urban Hinduism', *Contributions to Indian Sociology*, 4: 36–49.
Bechert, Heinz. 1966. *Buddhismus, Staat und Gesellschaft in den Ländern des Theravāda- Buddhismsus*, vol. 1, Berlin: Alfred Metzner (Vol 2: 1967. Wiesbaden: O. Harrassowitz. Vol. 3: 1973, Wiesbaden: O. Harrassowitz).
———. 1984. 'Buddhist Revival in East and West', in H. Bechert and R. Gombrich (eds), *The World of Buddhism*, pp. 273–85. London: Thames and Hudson.
———. 1990. 'Buddhistic Modernism: Its Emergence, Impact and New Trends', *Business & Economic Review*, 14: 93–104.
Bechert, Heinz and Jens-Uwe Hartmann. 1988. 'Observations on the Reform of Buddhism in Nepal', *Journal of the Nepal Research Centre*, 8: 1–30.
Beckford, J. 2001. 'Perspectives sociologiques sur les relations entre modernité et globalisation religieuse', in J-P. Bastian, F. Champion, and K. Rousselet (eds), *La Globalisation du Religieux*, pp. 273–82. Paris: L'Harmattan.
Buddhist Awareness Camp. 1997. *Bauddha Jagaran Prashikshan Shivir* Dhangari, Kailali, 2054 BS Pus 13–15 (tract).
Choudhary, Ram Lagan and Hari Prasad Choudhary. 1997 (2053 BS). *Siddharta Gautam Tharu jatika tye?* (Was Siddharta Gautama a Tharu?). Lalitpur: Pragatishil Tharu Yuba Sangathan.
Constitution of the Kingdom of Nepal. 2047 (1990). (Online: Supreme Court of Nepal). Available online at http://www.supremecourt.gov.np/main.php?d=law material&f=constdef2047 (accessed: 13 February 2012).
Constitution of Nepal, Interim 2063 (2007). (Online: Nepal Law Commission). Available online at: http://www.lawcommission.gov.np/en/prevailing-laws/

constitution/Prevailing-Laws/Constitution/Interim-Constitution-of-Nepal-2063-%282007%29/ (accessed: 13 February 2012).

Croucher, Sheila L. 2004. *Globalization and Belonging: The Politics of Identity in a Changing World*. Oxford: Rowman & Littlefield.

Fitzgerald, Timothy. 1994. 'Buddhism in Maharashtra: A Tri-partite Analysis—A Research Report', in A.K. Narain and D.C. Ahir (eds), *Dr. Ambedkar, Buddhism, and Social Change*, pp. 17–34. Delhi: B.R. Publishing Corporation.

———. 1997. 'Ambedkar Buddhism in Maharashtra', *Contributions to Indian Sociology*, n.s. 31(2): 226–51.

Gaborieau, Marc. 1994. 'Une affaire d'Etat au Népal. Depuis deux siècles le prosélytisme chrétien et musulman', *Archives des sciences sociales des religions*, 87(1): 57–72.

Gellner, David N. 2001. 'Studying Secularism, Practising Secularism. Anthropological Imperatives', *Social Anthropology*, 9: 337–40.

———. 2002. 'Theravāda Revivalism in Nepal: Some Reflections on the Interpretation of the Early Years', *Studies in Nepali History and Society*, 7(2): 215–37.

———. 2010. 'Initiation as a Site of Cultural Conflict among the Newars', in Zotter and C. Zotter (eds), *Hindu and Buddhist Initiations in India and Nepal*, pp. 167–81. Wiesbaden: Harrassowitz Verlag.

Gellner, David N., Joanna Pfaff-Czarnecka, and John Whelpton (eds). 1997. *Nationalism and Ethnicity in a Hindu Kingdom: The Politics of Culture in Contemporary Nepal*. Harwood Academic Publishers: Amsterdam.

Gellner, David N. and Mrigendra B. Karki. 2008. 'Democracy and Ethnic Organizations in Nepal', in D.N. Gellner and K. Hachhethu (eds), *Local Democracy in Nepal and South Asia*, pp. 105–27. New Delhi: SAGE Publications.

Gellner, David N. and Sarah LeVine. 2007. 'All in the Family: Money, Kinship and Theravada Monasticism in Nepal', in R.B. Chhetri and L.P. Uprety (eds), *Observations on the Changing Societal Mosaic of Nepal*, Vol. 10 pp. 141–73. Occasional Papers in Sociology and Anthropology. Kathmandu: Central Department of Sociology and Anthropology, Tribhuvan University.

Gombrich, Richard, 1988. *Theravada Buddhism: A Social History from Ancient Benares to Modern Colombo*. London: Routledge.

Gombrich, Richard and Gananath Obeyesekere. 1988. *Buddhism Transformed: Religious Change in Sri Lanka*. Princeton: Princeton University Press.

Guneratne, Arjun. 1998. 'Modernization, the State, and the Construction of a Tharu Identity in Nepal', *Journal of Asian Studies*, 57(3): 749–73.

———. 2003. *Many Tongues, One People: The Making of Tharu Identity in Nepal*. Ithaca-London: Cornell University Press.

Hangen, Susan I. 2005a. 'Boycotting Dasain: History, Memory and Ethnic Politics in Nepal', *Studies in Nepali History and Society*, 10(1): 105–33.

———. 2005b. 'Race and the Politics of Identity in Nepal', *Ethnology*, 44(1): 49–64.

———. 2007. 'Creating a "New Nepal": The Ethnic Dimension', *Policy Studies*, vol. 34. Washington: East-West Center.

———. 2010. *The Rise of Ethnic Politics in Nepal. Democracy in the Margins*. New York: Routledge.

Hartmann, Jens-Uwe. 1996. 'Cultural Change Through Substitution: Ordination Versus Initiation in Newar Buddhism', in S. Lienhard (ed.), *Change and*

Continuity: Studies in the Nepalese Culture of the Kathmandu Valley, pp. 355–65. Torino: Edizioni Dell'Orso.

HBEF Newsletter. 1996. *The Newsletter of Himalayan Buddhist Education Foundation* 1. Chakupat-Lalitpur-Kathmandu: M.B. Shakya.

Jaffrelot, Christophe. 2000. *Dr. Ambedkar. Leader Intouchable et père de la Constitution Indienne*. Paris: Presses de Sciences Politiques.

Jondhale Surendra and Johannes Beltz (eds). 2004. *Reconstructing the World. B.R. Ambedkar and Buddhism in India*. New Delhi: Oxford University Press.

Kantowsky, Detlef. 2003. *Buddhists in India today: Descriptions, Pictures and Documents*. New Delhi: Manohar.

Kemper, Steven. 2005. 'Dharmapala's *Dharmaduta* and the Buddhist Ethnoscape', in Linda Learman (ed.), *Buddhist Missionaries in the Era of Globalization*, pp. 22–50. Honolulu: University of Hawaii Press.

Kloppenberg, Ria. 1977. 'Theravada Buddhism in Nepal', *Kailash*, 5(4): 301–22.

Krauskopff, Gisèle. 2003. 'An "Indigenous Minority" in a Border Area: Tharu Ethnic Associations, NGOs, and the Nepali State', in D.N. Gellner (ed.), *Resistance and the State: Nepalese Experiences*, pp. 199–243. Delhi: Social Science Press.

———. 2009a. 'Intellectuals and Ethnic Activism: Writings on the Tharu Past', in D.N. Gellner (ed.), *Ethnic Activism and Civil Society in South Asia*, pp. 241–68. New Delhi: SAGE Publications.

———. 2009b. 'Descendants du Bouddha. La construction d'un passé bouddhiste par des intellectuels tharu (Népal)', in G. Krauskopff (ed.), *Les faiseurs d'histoires. Politique de l'origine et écrits sur le passé*, pp. 247–74. Nanterre: Société d'Ethnologie.

Kunreuther, Laura. 1994. 'Newar Traditions in a Changing Culture: an Analysis of Two Pre-pubescent Rituals for Girls', in M. Allen (ed.), *Anthropology of Nepal: Peoples, Problems and Processes*, pp. 339–48. Kathmandu: Mandala Book Point.

Lecomte-Tilouine, Marie. 2002. 'La désanskritisation des Magar; ethno-histoire d'un groupe sans histoire', in M. Carrin and C. Jaffrelot (eds), *Tribus et basses castes. Résistance et autonomie dans la société indienne*, (Purushartha 23), pp. 297–327. Paris: Éditions de l'EHESS.

———. 2009. 'Ruling Social Groups—From Species to Nations: Reflections on Changing Conceptualizations of Caste and Ethnicity in Nepal', in D.N. Gellner (ed.), *Ethnic Activism and Civil Society in South Asia*, pp. 291–336. New Delhi: SAGE Publications.

———. 2010. 'To Be More Natural than Others. Indigenous Self Determination and Hinduism in the Himalayas', in M. Lecomte-Tilouine (ed.), *An Exploration of the Categories of Nature and Culture in Asia and the Himalayas*, pp. 118–55. Delhi: Social Science Press.

Lecomte-Tilouine M. and P. Dollfus (eds). 2003. *Ethnic Revival and Religious Turmoil in the Himalayas*. New Delhi: Oxford University Press.

Letizia, C. 2005. 'Retourner au bouddhisme moderne des origines: remarques sur la diffusion du bouddhisme Theravada chez les Tharu et les Magar du Népal', *Annales de la Fondation Fyssen*, 20: 69–78.

———. 2007. 'Réflexions sur la notion de conversion dans la diffusion du bouddhisme Theravada au Népal', in P. Beaucauge and D. Meintel (eds), *Social and Political Dimensions of Religious Conversion, Anthropologica*, special issue, 49(1): 51–66.

Letizia, C. 2011. 'Shaping Secularism in Nepal', *European Bulletin of Himalayan Research*, 39: 66–104.

Leve, Lauren. 2002. 'Subjects, Selves, and the Politics of Personhood in Theravada Buddhism in Nepal', *Journal of Asian Studies*, 61(3): 833–60.

———. 2007. '"Secularism is a Human Right!" Double-Binds of Buddhism, Democracy, and Identity in Nepal', in M. Goodale and S.E. Merry (eds), *The Practice of Human Rights: Tracking Law between the Global and the Local*, pp. 78–113. Cambridge: University Press.

LeVine, Sarah. 2005. 'The Theravada Domestic Mission in Twentieth-Century Nepal', in Linda Learman (ed.), *Buddhist Missionaries in the Era of Globalization*, pp. 51–76. Honolulu: University of Hawaii Press.

LeVine, Sarah and David N. Gellner. 2005. *Rebuilding Buddhism: The Theravada Movement in Twentieth-Century Nepal*. London: Harvard University Press.

McMahan, David L. 2008. *The Making of Buddhist Modernism*. Oxford: Oxford University Press.

Obeyesekere, Gananath. 1970. 'Religious Syncretism and Political Change in Ceylon', *Modern Ceylon Studies*, 1: 43–63.

Sangharakshita, Bhiksu. 1980. *Flame in Darkness: The Life and Sayings of Anagarika Dharmapala*. Pune: Triratna Grantha Mala.

Schlemmer, Grégoire. 2004. 'New Past for the Sake of a Better Future: Re-Inventing the History of the Kirant in East Nepal', *European Bulletin of Himalayan Research*, 25–26: 119–44.

Shakya, Dharma Ratna 'Trisuli'. 2003 (2060 BS). *Bauddha samskar paddhati* (The handbook of Buddhist rituals). Butwal: Nepal Magar Bauddha Seva Samaj.

Shakya, Keshab Man. 2006 (2063 BS). 'Yuba Bauddha Samuha ra dharma nirapeksako abhyana' (The Youth Buddhist Group and the campaign for secularization), *Smarika*, Kathmandu: Dev Ranjit.

Singh, Ramanand Prasad. 1988. *The Real Story of the Tharus*. Kathmandu-Lalitpur: Tharu Samskriti.

Singh, Subodh Kumar. 2006. *The Great Sons of the Tharus: Sakyamuni Buddha and Asoka the Great*. Kathmandu: Babita Singh.

———. 2010. *Community That Changed Asia*. Lalitpur: Babita Singh.

Smarika (Souvenir). 2006 (2063 BS 1127 N.S.). Special issue published on the 25 years anniversary of Yuba Bauddha Samuha, Kathmandu: Dev Ranjit.

Thapa Magar, M.S. 2002 (2059 BS). *Prachin magar ra akkha lipi* (Ancient Magars and the *akkha* script), 1st ed. 1992 (2049 BS). Lalitpur: Briji Prakasan.

Toffin, Gérard. 2006. 'The Politics of Hinduism and Secularism in Nepal', *Studies in Nepali History and Society*, 11(2): 219–40.

———. 2009. The *Janajati/Adivasi* Movement in Nepal: Myths and Realities of Indigeneity, *Sociological Bulletin*, 58(1): 25–42.

Zelliott, Eleanor. 1992. *From Untouchable to Dalit: Essays on the Ambedkar Movement*. New Delhi: Manohar.

Chapter 13

Power Projects, Protests, and Problematics of Belonging in Dzongu, Sikkim*

INTRODUCTION

This chapter deals with the protests by local tribe against a 280 mega watt (MW) electricity generation project in Talung valley of Dzongu, a Lepcha reserve in North Sikkim and believed to be a sacred landscape for the Buddhists. This chapter is also about the problematics of belonging that emerged and divided the local tribe horizontally following the acquisition of land for the Panang Hydro-Electric Project by the state government on the strength of a colonial Act. In particular, it brings out the clash of the traditional (social and legal) notions of ownership and belonging with the new notions of moral and ideological ownership.

Drawing on materials from Nepal and India, Joanna Pfaff-Czarnecka (2007) questions the prevailing tendency in the existing literature to depict the protests against power projects as well-integrated and smooth. She shows how complex and fragmented the character of these arenas is and how human rights abuses and everyday problems are contested and negotiated. What further draws her study close to this work is her engagement with "diverse logics of

* I am thankful to those Lepchas of Dzongu who came to Shillong for different purposes and shared their concerns and views with me but have wished to remain anonymous. I am particularly thankful to my student Charisma K. Lepcha for helping me with whatever little documentation that has gone into the preparation of this chapter. Finally, I must express my gratitude to Dr Anindita Dasgupta, Associate Professor and Deputy Dean at Taylor's University, Malaysia, and the editors of this volume for their valuable suggestions for revision of this chapter.

action and the internal conflicts within protest movements" (2007: 2). Indeed, in Sikkim too, there was not only an ideological opposition to the big dams *per se*, but several of those who sold the lands and/or belonged to the ruling party supported the project. The unsettled questions of sustainable development like whose development, who pays for whose development, what are the social, environmental, and cultural costs of development, and so on did not seem to bother those who supported the dam or those who remained mute spectators while several young and educated Lepcha youths risked their lives by going on indefinite hunger strike. Also very pertinent in the case of Dzongu is the politics of cultural survival circumscribed around the idioms of a 'vanishing', 'primitive', and 'endangered' tribe.

Jeremy Bird, former senior advisor to the World Commission on Dams (WCD) Secretariat, puts the dam debate in a slightly different perspective: "The intensifying controversy surrounding large dams is not about the technical designs, but their social and environmental consequences and the decision making processes that lead to their construction... At the heart of the dams debate are issues of equity, governance, justice and power" (2001: 2). Indeed the large dams like the Panang Hydro-Electric Project in Dzongu do not take into account issues of equity, participatory development, and access of the Project Affected People (PAP) to decision-making. The World Bank certainly knows the 'social and environmental consequences', but while on the one hand, in developed countries it has stopped funding such mega dams as the Hoover Dam, on the other hand, in developing ones it continues to support large dam projects. It is also argued that the agencies outsourced by the Indian government often manipulate their data to make the proposals acceptable to a funding agency like the World Bank, which would otherwise pull out of such projects, as it indeed did in the case of the Narmada project. Indeed, a country like India is still enamoured by the Nehruvian idea of big dams as 'the temples of modern India'.

Almost all scholars writing on large dams view them as a consequence of globalization (Mittleman, 1998; Osman, 2000; Aravinda, 2000; Bird, 2001; Kala, 2001; Raghunandan, 2003; Sheth, 2004, etc.). While the displaced tribal societies are seen as helpless victims of globalization, some like Aravinda also show how the Indian state and its apparatuses, including its judiciary, are in hands and gloves with the forces of globalization. One important aspect of the residual impact of globalization, which has not received much attention of the above scholars, is the transfer of technology and human resources from the developed to the developing countries because these are thought to be lacking in India. If one looks at the technological aspects (in terms of mechanized inputs) required for building such dams, one realizes that most of the technology incorporated is Western and the project managers are usually Western technocrats. Furthermore, before any big dam is commissioned, the Memorandum of Association requires by law that the construction companies employ the local population, sometimes to the extent of 50 per cent, which is never honoured. The usual argument given by multinational companies is that the local people lack skills and efficiency and hence their participation is limited to them being employed as menial labour, which is often a strategy for keeping the local people off from all such development sites, be it mining, steel factory, or hydel project. A very important dimension of the Memorandum of Association is also regarding the construction company contributing a part of its profits to the development of the local region and its people. The contribution largely differs from state to state, but normatively what has emerged is that the construction companies are able to also subvert this important clause in connivance with the local authorities, political and administrative. Another important dimension thus is dependency creation by the forces of globalization. It also appears from the vast literature on the subject that a lot of protests against the forces of globalization are because the PAP, who are mostly tribals, are given uncultivable lands in lieu of their fertile farmlands or given no lands at all because the government is not obliged to give land-for-land compensation under the National Rehabilitation and Resettlement Policy of 2007. In fact, it is not just about land but cultivable land or such land which forms the basis of their livelihoods, be it the Enclosure movement in 17th-century Britain or the Narmada Bachao Andolan (NBA) in India, and also what values—economic, symbolic, political, or class—communities attach (or do not) to it.

Although the national policy of 2007 has failed the PAP in protecting their basic human rights, the case of Haryana shows that a given provincial state can come up with a policy that is highly favourable to the affected people. For instance, the rehabilitation package for dam-related displaced persons offered by Haryana includes payment of Rs. 15,000 per acre per annum for 33 years with an annual increase of a fixed sum of Rs. 500 (Collins, 2011).

Another crucial aspect pertains to cultural costs. The lives of the people living near rivers or estuarine climate are governed by the river. In India, the river is seen as 'life giving'; it is a source not only of water but also of livelihood. Thus, the rivers govern the lives of those living near it: their material culture, their livelihoods, their cropping patterns, their social life, folk songs, dance forms, etc., all revolve around the river. While local cultures are celebrated in the post-modernist era, they face serious disruptions due to forced globalization. The role of civil societies is also becoming important in such arenas today, at least at some stage where the local resistances are co-opted by civil society activists, in which case often different meanings are attached to such resistances. This perhaps happens because local leaders are often unable to comprehend the ideology of development, issues of sustainable development, and politics of globalization, nor are they always capable of undertaking analysis of the cultural cost and benefit of a project in their midst. Indeed, not much work has been done on why some of these movements are co-opted by civil societies and some others are not, nor does any work seem to exist on the complexities that globalization creates in local notions of belonging.

THE POTHOLES OF THE PANANG HYDRO-ELECTRIC PROJECT

According to the Detailed Project Report (DPR), Volume I, the proposed project "is envisaged to utilize the flow of the Talung Chu,[1] a tributary to the Teesta River for the generation of electrical power in a run-of-river hydropower development" (SMEC, 2006: 1). 'Utilization of the flow of river' perspective actually shows the mindset of policymakers, who see river as a resource to be tapped, which seemingly continues to shape their opinion in contemporary times. This project is part of the 50,000 MW hydroelectric initiatives, which include the much-criticized linking of the rivers project because of its dangerous would-be consequences. The Preliminary Feasibility Report (PFR) for this project in North Sikkim was prepared by the National Hydroelectric Power Corporation Ltd. (NHPC) in 2004, which recommended a 50-m-high concrete gravity dam on Talong Chu, which easily makes it a large dam according to the standards set by the International Commission on Large Dams (ICOLD). The water from the dam would be conveyed to a 200 MW power station located at the confluence of Talung Chu and Rongyong Chu. Talung Chu originates in the Talung glacier of the Kanchenjanga range of the Himalayas. The total length of this river from origin to the proposed dam site is 30 km with a steep gradient. According to different official reports, the total area likely to be affected by the Panang Hydel Project varies from 54 to 63 hectares (hereafter ha).

In the DPR mentioned earlier, Sikkim has been seen as a state endowed with huge hydroelectricity potential. Of the total 2820.7 MW potential, the state has so far harnessed only 95.7 MW and 510 MW is under execution. As many as 10 such schemes with a potential of 1,569 MW are under investigation in the state and an additional list of 13 schemes with a total capacity of 646 MW has been drawn by the Central Electricity Authority for possible execution in future. On why the Panang project was proposed, the DPR states that there is an urgent need for generating hydropower 'to provide additional generation capacity in the eastern region', which includes states like Jharkhand, Bihar, Orissa, and West Bengal. Thus, the electricity to be generated is not for Sikkim but for the regional grid. Hence, questions like whose development and who pays for whose development are relevant in this case. It needs no big imagination to visualize that though development will happen in Sikkim, the benefits will largely flow outside the state, leaving the state and its population to grapple with issues of development and environment. This has been the story elsewhere and this is going to be the story of North Sikkim as well.

It is therefore important that policy initiatives have built-in consensus of the local people and are not imposed; however, as per the National Rehabilitation and Resettlement Policy of 2007 referred to earlier, the affected families do not have the right to say 'no' at the time of determination of the project site and there is no provision for consultation with the affected families during the preparation of the Social Impact Assessment and Environmental Impact Assessment reports.

If the DPR is read alongside the Environment Impact Assessment (EIA) report prepared by the Centre for Inter-Disciplinary Studies of Mountain and Hill Development, Delhi University, one would notice innumerable anomalies, making both reports doubtful (CISMHE, 2006a). Not only are the ethnographic details full of errors, or the names of some places spelt wrongly in the two reports, but even the technical details do not match. For instance, the DPR says that Teesta originates in glaciers at an altitude of 8,500 m whereas the EIA says that it does at an altitude of 5840m, which is about 3000 m less. Similarly, the longitude and latitude figures or the hydrological data on the project site do not match in the two reports. The travesty of the entire process is the total disregard of policymaking bodies for the local people and their concerns.

The EIA report, on page 179, says that the "total affected families due to various activities of the Panang Hydro-Electric project are 80", which is misleading. What the records show is that 80 families have sold varying amounts of land for the project. The impact report does not include those families that are going to lose access to various natural resources due to their immersion. These figures also do not include those who would be affected in terms of culture, religion, language, and leisure when they come in direct contact with large numbers of people from outside with different languages and cultures, who are likely to dominate the local culture or cause tension between the local people and the outsiders because the latter usually have a sense of superiority over the former, and the local society is numerically too small and geographically too dispersed to be able to absorb the outsiders.

Furthermore, this report does not say how frequently and violently might the landslides occur in future due to dam-related activities, such as tunnelling and blasting of rocks. Since Sikkim Himalayas are geologically rather fragile and hence earthquake- and landslide-prone, it is difficult to understand the rationale of building large dams there. The other worry is the carelessness of the implementing agencies and the inability of the regulatory authorities to safeguard the interests of the local people. There are several instances of failed promises, such as the offer to give 80 per cent employment to locals in the Rangit Hydel Project commissioned about 10 years ago. There is also a serious threat to several villages posed by cracks in the reservoir walls of the Teesta Stage V Project commissioned recently.

Finally, according to the EIA report, the lands acquired from the 80 families vary from 0.0020 to 0.7340 ha and the total private land acquired is 26.5620 ha, excluding the school land of 0.046 ha, which also comes under the project. Out of 80 families, 45 belong to Lingthem village, 21 to Lingzya village, and the remaining 14 to Sakyong-Pentong village. 63.06 per cent of the total land required for the project is acquired from Lingthem, 25.92 per cent from the second, and the remaining amount from the third village. All the owners belong to the Lepcha tribe. The total figure for private lands given above does not match with the figures for private land for the project given on the blueprint of the project, which shows the plot numbers and amount to be acquired for the project. According to the blueprint, the figure for private land is 36.2450 ha plus underground private land amounting to 5.6090 ha. The total forest land, which belongs partially to both Kanchenjanga Biosphere Reserve and Kanchenjanga National Park, amounts to 16.3520 ha surface land and 4.3934 ha underground land. The grand total of all the land required for the Panang Hydro Project, according to the blueprint, is 62.5994 ha, which is much more than the amount of land stated in the DPR. The deficit land is most likely to be met in a manner that may lead to further encroachment of private land and protected forest.

This implies that construction will be carried out partially on a demarcated biosphere and national park, which highlights the apathy of governance in India, which seemingly has two sets of rules: one, for pursuing its own development agenda and the other, for the people. This could also be read as disregard of law by the law-implementing agency itself in the name of 'public purpose' or the supposed larger good of the nation.

It may be further noted that the above land has been acquired by invoking a colonial Act called the Land Acquisition Act of 1894. The National Rehabilitation and Resettlement Policy of 2007 clearly upholds the sovereign power of the state under this Act to apply the concept of 'eminent domain' to forcibly acquire any private property in any part of the country in the name of 'public purpose'. However, the following paragraph indicates that Dzongu is not just any other part of the country that could be taken over by the state by evoking the above Act.

On 27 September 1954, Maharaja Tashi Namgyal issued a notification stating "General Public is hereby informed through this notification that His Highness the Maharaja of Sikkim has strictly banned entry of any trader/agent from outside the Dzongu area, into the Dzongu area" (Notification No 665/P.S.). On 30 August 1956, he issued a proclamation not only making the transfer of all lands from the Lepchas and Bhutias to the Nepalis during the past 25 years invalid but also made all such transactions illegal in future (Sikkim Code, Vol. II, Part 1, pp. 91, 92). For protection of the indigenous people of Sikkim, the king issued another notification on 24 March 1958 that says: "...it is hereby ordered that any out-sider, (non-indigenous) settling and/or carrying on any occupation in the prescribed areas without a permit issued by the Sikkim Darbar shall be liable to imprisonment upto six months" (Notification No. 3069/O.S.). Later, in 1965, a general Order was issued concerning the protected areas in Sikkim clarifying that no new people were allowed to reside in these areas and people intending to enter for visit or work needed to obtain a permit (Sikkim Code, Vol. III: 88). The reserved land was protected by the country's laws and no other community could stay in Dzongu permanently. It is said that even the king of Sikkim offered prayers to the Talung monastery from outside the reserved area (Roy, 2007).

The state obviously does not see Dzongu in the same perspective as the people there do or the kings of Sikkim did. However, the only thing the anti-dam activists can perhaps do is to challenge in the court of law the procedures that are laid down for acquisition of private land under the Act, provided that the same is not followed by the state.They can also perhaps serve as watchdogs but they cannot stop it even if it is going to defile their sacred landscape or threaten the very existence of their culture, religion, and language.

THE AFFECTED CITIZENS OF TEESTA[2] (ACT)

The protests against the power projects in Dzongu were spearheaded by an organization called the Affected Citizens of Teesta, which was established on 18 July 2004. According to Pema Wangchuk (2007), the editor of English daily from GangtokNOW, it was "a progression of the Joint Action Committee formed by the same group to protest Teesta Stage V HEP (hydro-electric project) in the year 2002".

The Affected Citizens of Teesta (ACT) was established under the leadership of Athup Lepcha, former minister of environment and forests, government of Sikkim, with the help of Lepcha youths of Dzongu who were studying in Mangan, Gangtok, Kolkata, and other parts of India. Initially ACT held many awareness camps and protest meetings to stop possible damage to the biodiversity, environment, and demography of North Sikkim on account of the hydel projects. Its main objective was to protest against the state government's deci-sion to grant permission to several companies for hydel projects in North Sikkim. At no stage of the protest did ACT raise the issues of resettlement and rehabilitation because, unlike in the case of Narmada projects, the Lepchas of Dzongu did not face any threat of physical displacement, which is used by authorities to legitimize the project and paint the activists as anti-development. The state also created a bubble of hopes and aspirations in the minds of local people regarding prosperity and employment. Indeed, the activists were at pains to explain that they were not against development but only against mega hydel projects because such projects were harmful to them. Without the support of NGOs like the Concerned Lepchas of Sikkim (CLOS), Sangha of Dzongu (SOD), Citizens' Forum of Sikkim (CFS), and the Sikkimese Association for Environment (SAE), the protest would perhaps not have lasted even for a month not just because there was a cleavage within the Lepcha community between those who supported the dam and those who opposed it but also because there was virtually no opposition party member to support the activists in the state assembly of 32 members.

Much water has flown down the Talong Chu in North Sikkim since the protests by some young Lepcha activists under the banner of ACT started in 2007. The attitude of the Chief Minister of Sikkim towards the protesters was initially like that of President George Bush against terrorists (Lepcha, 2008), but he apparently changed later if scrapping of 11 hydroelectric projects from this Himalayan state, including four from Dzongu in North Sikkim, is anything to go by. While the reasons for scrapping so many projects are reportedly the failure of private companies from outside Sikkim to prepare detailed project reports (DPRs), or execute the projects on schedule, or obtain the mandatory clearance from various government departments, the reason for not scrapping the Panang project could be the fact that the state's position was strengthened by a 400-odd-page, pink-covered DPR submitted in April 2006, which was reinforced by a 200-odd-page Environmental Impact Assessment Report (CISMHE, 2006b) and a 100-plus-page Environmental Management Plan Report prepared by CISMHE, Delhi University. He was also under pressure from the central government to get the pending hydel projects of the state started. For instance, according to a letter written to the Chief Minister of Sikkim, dated 5 June 2007 by Montek Singh Ahluwalia, the then Deputy Chairman of Indian Planning Commission, out of the 26 medium/large hydro projects in the state, DPRs had been prepared for 19 only. The Deputy Chairman in the letter urges the Chief Minister of Sikkim to "take quick action for expediting these projects". The letter further urges him to complete by 2009–10 Lachung Phase-II (3 MW), Mangley (2 MW), Relli Khola (12 MW), and Rongli Khola (5 MW) projects initiated during the Tenth Plan. The above letter partly explains the desperation of the Chief Minister of Sikkim to complete the various hydel projects in the state. Otherwise, Pawan Chamling, who was awarded by the Centre for Science and Environment, New Delhi, as the 'greenest chief minister of India' a few years ago and whose green initiatives in Sikkim have received a lot of praise from different quarters, was expected to be a lot more sensitive towards the protection of the environment of Sikkim. Left to himself, he would perhaps have scrapped the Panang project as well. Although he virtually had no opposition in the state assembly, he would perhaps not like to offend, leave alone antago-nize, the Buddhist Lepchas and Bhutias of North Sikkim by pushing a project into their territory much against the wishes of the local people there. There is also an apprehension among the activists that even the Chief Minister may not be able to stop some of the scrapped projects from being restored in the near future either under the pressure of the central government or on the direction of the Sikkim High Court where some private companies have gone challenging the decision of the state government to scrap several hydel projects.

Meanwhile, the Independent Committee on Big Hydro Projects in Sikkim, consisting of members representing various environment-related NGOs from New Delhi, West Bengal, and Assam, also surveyed the projects in Sikkim and suggested, in a letter dated 22 May 2008 and addressed to the Chief Minister of Sikkim, that the government of Sikkim should suspend all such projects at least for five years and instead prepare micro hydel projects, which were welcome by the ACT activists as well. The position of ACT was also endorsed, among others, by Medha Patkar, the legendary leader of the NBA fame, during her visit to Sikkim in April 2008.

THE 'SACRED' TALUNG VALLEY

This valley is located below Mt. Siniolchu (6,888 m) and Mt. Lhamo Anden (5,200 m) and falls under the Lepcha reserve called Dzongu. The importance of the valley lies not only in its sacred landscape, as nicely constructed by Arora (2006) and corroborated by Little (2008), but also in its rich biodiversity, history, and art. The Talung

Monastery located in the valley is not just one of the most sacred institutions for the Buddhists but also a historic institution. As early as in 1909, Claude White, the Political Officer in Gangtok, wrote the following on this monastery:

> Talung Monastery is one of the most sacred monasteries in Sikhim (sic), and is full of very beautiful and interesting objects of veneration, nearly all real works of art. During the Nepalese invasion of 1816, many of these objects were removed from other monasteries and brought here for safety, and have remained here ever since. Unlike most monasteries, an inventory is kept and most carefully scrutinized from time to time by the Maharaja, and owing to these precautions, the collection has remained intact.
>
> Here is preserved the saddle and saddle-cloth of the Joch-chen Lama, the first Lama to enter Sikhim from Tibet, several fine thigh-bone trumpets and some splendid specimens of "Rugen" (apron, breastplate, circlet and armlets), exquisitely carved from human bones, a beautiful set in silver gilt of marvelously fine workmanship of the Tashi Tagye, or eight lucky signs, as well as many other altar vessels and vestments. Here also are all the old dancing dresses and ornaments, beyond comparison finer than any I have ever seen in other monasteries in Sikhim. (1909/2000: 66–67)

Geoffrey Gorer (1938), an anthropologist who lived in Lingthem village located in the Talung valley of Dzongu for three months in 1936, describes not only the valley's virgin forests but also its everlasting myths. John Morris, who lived in the same village at the same time with Gorer, writes that his first view of the Talung valley was in the spring of 1936, on his way to Mt. Everest, and it was "one of the most spectacular sights in the whole Himalaya" (1938: 7). He further writes that "In all other parts of Sikkim the people (Lepchas) had intermarried with Tibetans and Nepalis to such an extent that they had lost all traces of tribal consciousness. Not so, however, in the Talung; for this valley formed part of the Maharaja's personal estate and none but Lepchas were permitted to own land or to settle in it" (ibid.: 8).[3]

The valley still looked very beautiful, especially when a thick fog filled the valley every morning, in 1987 when the present author lived in the same village as Gorer and Morris did in 1936. Although some patches of land near the Talong river were converted into paddy fields, the terraces actually enhanced the beauty of the valley.

Cardamom cultivation, which was indeed extensive in this valley, was practiced in such a manner that the forest cover was not disturbed and was instead used to provide fertility, shade, and humidity, all of which were very important to their cardamom plants.

SACRED LANDSCAPE, PROFANE LAND[4]

VibhaArora, who did her doctoral research in Talung (spelt Tholung by her) valley, writes extensively on the valley's sacred landscape. According to her, "...not a single leaf or a pebble can be taken away from this sacred area. Pilgrims are instructed to even dust their clothes and shoes for any loose leaves and twigs, as otherwise the Tholung spirits would get angry and make them sick...only holy water and offerings returned by the lamas can be taken back as divine blessings" (2006: 65).

In a certain sense, all forests in the eastern Himalayas are sacred landscapes because the people living in and around them—be they Buddhists like Lepchas in Dzongu or Hindus elsewhere—are aware of the deities and spirits living in the forests. This is even true of the Khasi Christians of Meghalaya, Northeast India, although they may not perform any rituals or make offerings to placate those deities and spirits the way Hindus or Buddhists do. The elderly men and women are also aware of the myths and legends associated with the forests. But while forests are sacred landscapes, the sale of lands by 80 Lepcha families in Talong valley indicates that land is apparently not so and therefore can be disposed off. This is perhaps why they had no 'sacred dilemma', so to say, about the sale of their lands. None of those who sold their lands thought that some deity reigning over their lands would be angry and punish them instantly or later, nor any of them ever thought that it was a 'sin' to do so or it would invite the 'curse' of their ancestors. If at all, some of them were worried about the secular consequences of selling their land, such as the influx of people with different cultures and languages into their area and the consequent erosion of their own cultures and languages. Although some Lepchas thought that it would be difficult for them to protect their culture and traditions for long, they were worried that their forests would be plundered, their hills scarred, and their rivers vanished into tunnels due to the hydel projects. Some men also worried about the closure of the prospect of fishing in Talong river, which is a more popular hobby than hunting among the Lepchas of Dzongu.

Regarding land in Dzongu, it may be recalled that up until 1957, there was no cadastral survey and the Lepchas there had no registration certificates to prove which or how much land belonged to them. Everyone in the villages, however, knew which land was whose and who owned how much land in local units, which were based on the amount of seeds or number of days a pair of bullocks was used for ploughing a field. No one ever questioned if a plot of land 'belonged' to someone in the village. Occasional quarrels between brothers or neighbours over alleged encroachment or cattle trespass were known, which showed how carefully their 'invisible' boundaries were actually protected. Thus, ownership of land was more social than legal, but land was never a commodity, not because it was 'sacred' but the very concept of buying and selling land was alien to the Lepchas of Dzongu. Even the Lepchas from outside this area could not buy lands or settle there.

They cultivated the commercially lucrative species of large cardamom called Golsai in the lower altitudes, which fetched very good prices in the market and the less lucrative small cardamom called Ramsai in the altitudes above 1,000 metres approximately. During the last two decades or so, however, there was less enthusiasm among the Lepcha owners about growing cardamom due to the increasing problem of pests, which they found difficult to control, and dependence on the labourers from Nepal for cultivation of their cardamom and paddy fields. Many Lepcha families in Dzongu had no one to work in their fields and they were forced to lease their lands to the Nepalis in rather unfavourable terms for themselves. Even those Lepcha families who cultivated such fields themselves were often compelled to mortgage the same to the Marwari traders living in Mangan town, the headquarters of north district of Sikkim. These traders often gave advance to the cardamom growers in Dzongu at a time the growers needed money the most, which made them vulnerable to exploitation.

This perhaps partly explains why most Lepchas of Dzongu were willing to sell their land for the hydel projects. They were paid @Rs. 16 per sq. foot of dry land and Rs.18 per sq. foot of paddy land (Dutta, 2007; Lepcha, 2008). There was no bargain and the rates were decided by the revenue department of the state government. Price was never an issue because they were getting a lot more than what they expected. But there were two important issues with a bearing on the protest: one, there was a division between those whose lands were bought and those whose lands were not required to be bought, and two, there was a division even among those whose lands were bought, as Kerry Little has shown. According to him, some landowners felt that they were tricked into selling their lands whereas others declared in public that they sold their lands willingly (2008: 241).

They may well have sold their lands willingly, but it appears that they did so without knowing how much land they were actually selling and for what price. This was perhaps quite expected because sale or purchase of land had never taken place before and their unit of measurement was not in terms of hectares. In other words, the decision to sell their lands was not based on informed consent of the owners and, hence, the deal was in a sense not ethical, although it might as well have been legal. Yet, they seem to have considered themselves lucky, for they could sell their lands at a 'fabulous' price. They were least aware of what they had lost and would be losing in the future. It was also learnt how quickly some of those who sold their lands finished the money by repaying debts, drinking factory-made beers, and indulging in gambling, which is quite similar to the findings of Kabita Rai in the Kali-Gandaki "A" Project discussed in detail by Pfaff-Czarnecka (2007: 439) or that of Raghunandan among the displaced tribes of Narmada Valley (2003: 53).

It was legitimate for those who sold their lands in Dzongu to ask why the other Lepchas from Dzongu or outside it were protesting against the sale of lands that did not 'belong' to them, which is fine if belonging is understood in the traditional sense. In their perception, a piece of land belongs to someone because he has inherited it from his father, who in turn had inherited from his father, and so on. If he belongs to a patrilineal clan (*p'tsho*) of Dzongu and is a legitimate heir, he is the owner of a piece of land there. That piece of land simply 'belongs' to him in the sense he can build his house on it, grow any crop on it, keep it barren, or 'defecate on it', as one of the sellers from Dzongu put it. If any cattle strays into his field and destroys his crop, he has the right to compensation and this right is honoured by other villagers including the offender. He may not have a certificate to prove it because the land may still be in his father's or grandfather's name, but everyone in the village knows who owns how much land and where. "Do they (protestors) know where my land is located? Do they know the boundaries of my land? How big is my land? What was my father's name?" The seller from Dzongu whom I interviewed in Shillong replied agitatedly when I was trying to argue on behalf of the ACT activists.

However, it is equally legitimate for others to criticize, on moral and ideological grounds, those who sold their lands or the state government, which acquired the land for the project. They have a moral and ideological right to oppose the sellers and the government because large dams, in their perception, have many hidden environmental and cultural costs, some of which may show up only at a later stage. All those who share this ideology, even if they do not belong to the Lepcha tribe or Buddhist religion or Dzongu area for that matter, have their moral right to protest against the hydro-electric projects in Dzongu, as indeed many people from outside Dzongu and even outside Sikkim did.

CONCLUSION

The coming of power projects to Dzongu, North Sikkim, has given rise to new issues of belonging in the region. The conventional understanding of 'belonging' as a form of social and legal ownership has been challenged by a new form of ownership that I may call 'moral' or 'ideological' ownership. However, since the concept of moral or ideological ownership is rather new among those who opposed the state government's decision or the decision of those Lepchas who sold their lands in Dzongu, the protest was conceptually handicapped from the very beginning. Most anti-dam activists had grown up with the same notions of social and legal ownership and belonging as those who had sold the lands. That made their anti-dam protest conceptually weaker than it would otherwise be because most of them were yet to come to terms with new ways of looking at issues of ownership and belonging. Their protests would perhaps have been stronger if the Lepchas of Dzongu had not agreed to sell their lands at all and the state government was forced to invoke the Land Acquisition Act of 1894. It would then be easier to pitch a 'primitive' (officially declared so by the state government in 2006) tribal community against the state and mobilize not only the members of such a community across the region but also engage all those who sympathized with the Lepchas or Buddhism or were against large dams morally or ideologically. However, when there was a large group of Lepchas who supported the hydro-electric project either because they sold their lands or because they were supporters of the ruling party in the state, the issue of belonging was further entangled.

To give the devil its due, the flip side of globalization seems to be the fact that the very act of opposing the hydel projects in their sacred landscape generated amongst Lepchas of Sikkim and outside, if not among all Buddhist communities there, a sense of belonging to the place and its culture, as it did among the indigenous peoples of Sarawak in Malaysia (Osman, 2000: 987–88). The symbolism of a 'primitive', 'threatened', 'vanishing', or 'endangered' tribe was exploited by the more educated among them to muster the support of their own community members as well as the neighbouring communities. They also constantly reassured their supporters that their movement was not against development, as the state government made it out to be, but against mega development projects that are likely to vandalize the abode of their gods and goddesses to benefit the outside people.

It might also do well to remember what Amita Baviskar writes in her celebrated *In the Belly of the River* (2004) about activism against the construction of big dams. In the postscript to the second edition, she writes that when the dam was eventually built, the main supporters of the anti-dam movement, who were largely middle-caste landowners and educated *adivasis* with resources for their relocation, were cared for while the poor people were ignored. When the fight was lost, nationwide activists just moved on to other issues elsewhere.

NOTES

1. Tolung is also spelt as Talung (Gorer, 1938) and Tholung by others (see Arora, 2006). *Chu* in Bhutia language means water or river, whereas it, spelt as *chyu*, means mountain in Lepcha language.
2. Teesta is the biggest and most important river of Sikkim and Talong Chu is an important tributary to it.
3. Gorer and Morris have produced two very readable monographs on Lepchas based on Lingthem village in Talung valley. The changes in the village since they wrote their monographs have been studied by a Lepcha anthropologist after 50 years or so (see Gowloog, 1995).
4. It appears that lands were communally owned in the past when the Lepcha economy was characterized by hunting, gathering, and shifting cultivation but all lands except the monastery land are individually owned today. However, in the land revenue department's records the names of all individual owners may not

exist. The person whose name is recorded may have long died and no mutation of the plot owned by him may have taken place. Such a land may have been divided among his heirs by him before his death or by the village headman after his death without corresponding changes in the revenue office records. Such social owners are, however, recognized as legal owners even by the revenue officials.

REFERENCES

Affected Citizens of Teesta (ACT). Available online at www.actsikkim.com. Accessed: 24 February 2012.

Aravinda, L.S. 2000. 'Globalisation and Narmada People's Struggle', *Economic and Political Weekly*, 35(46): 4002–05.

Arora, Vibha. 2006. 'The Forest of Symbols Embodied in the Tholung Sacred Landscape of North Sikkim, India', *Conservation and Society*, 4(1): 55–83.

Baviskar, Amita. 2004. *In the Belly of the River: Tribal Conflicts over Development in the Narmada Valley*. New Delhi: Oxford University Press.

Bird, Jeremy. 2001. 'Globalisation and Water Resource Management: The Changing Value of Water'. AWRA/IWLRI-University of Dundee International Speciality Conference, 6–8 August.

Blueprint for 300MW Panang Hydro Electric Project.

CISMHE. 2006a. *Environmental Management Plan of Panan H. E. Project*. Prepared for Himagiri Hydro Energy Pvt. Ltd.

———. 2006b. *Environmental Impact Assessment of Panan H.E. Project*. Prepared for Himagiri Hydro Energy Pvt.Ltd.

Collins, Andrew. 2011. 'Haryana Policy: Rehabilitation and Resettlement of Land-owners'. Available online at www.theteamwork.com/.../2016-49-haryana-policy-rehabilitation (Accessed: 24 February 2012).

Dutta, Soumik. 2007. 'Lepcha v Hydropower', *Himal Southasian*, 20(9): 34–36.

Gorer, Geoffrey. 1938/1984. *The Lepchas of Sikkim*. Delhi: Cultural Publishing House.

Gowloog, R.R. 1995. *Lingthem Revisited: Social Change in a Lepcha Village in North Sikkim*. New Delhi: Har-Anand Publications.

Kala, Pablo. 2001. 'In the Spaces of Erasure: Globalisation, Resistance and Narmada River', *Economic and Political Weekly*, 36(22): 1991–2002.

Lepcha, Charisma K. 2008. 'Dzongu in Dilemma', *The NEHU Journal*, 6(1 and 2): 121–26.

Letter No. DCH/11/07/4506 dated 5 June 2007 written by Montek Singh Ahluwalia to Shri Pawan Chamling.

Little, Kerry. 2008. 'Lepcha Narratives of Their Threatened Sacred Landscapes', *Transforming Cultures eJournal*, 3(1). Available online at http://epress.lib.uts.edu.au/journals/TfC

Mittleman, James H. 1998. 'Globalisation and Environmental Resistance Politics', *Third World Quarterly*, 19(5): 847–72.

Morris, John. 1938. *Living with the Lepchas: A Book about the Sikkim Himalayas*. London: William Heinemann Ltd.

Osman, Sabihah. 2000. 'Globalization and Democratization: The Response of Indigenous People of Sarawak', *Third World Quarterly*, 21(6): 977–88.

Pfaff-Czarnecka, Joanna. 2007. 'Challenging Goliath: People, Dams, and the Paradoxes of Transnational Critical Movements', in H. Ishii, D.N. Gellner, and K. Nawa (eds), *Political and Social Transformations in North India and Nepal*, vol. 2. Delhi: Manohar.

Raghunandan, D. 2003. 'Environment and Development under Capitalist Globalisation', *Social Scientist*, 31(9/10): 36–57.

Roy, D.C. 2007. 'Dzongu: The Present Day Mayel Lyang of the Lepchas', *Aachuley* (A Quarterly Lepcha Bilingual News Magazine published by the Lepcha Literary Organization, Kalimpong).

Sheth, D.L. 2004. 'Globalisation and New Politics of Micro-Movements', *Economic and Political Weekly*, 39(1): 45–58.

SMEC India Pvt. Ltd. 2006. *Detailed Project Report, vol. I: Main Report*. Prepared for Himagiri Hydro Energy Pvt. Ltd.

Wangchuk, Pema. 2007. 'Lepchas and Their Hydel Protest', *Bulletin of Tibetology*, 43(1–2): 33–57.

White, J. Claude. 1909/2000. *Sikkim and Bhutan: Twenty-One Years on the North-East Frontier 1887–1908*. Delhi: Asian Educational Services.

Chapter 14

Weepingsikkim.blogspot.com

Reconfiguring Lepcha Belonging with Cyber-belonging

VIBHA ARORA

This chapter analyzes the discourse of Lepcha socio-political belonging and their perceived cultural marginalization, which has been circulated since June 2007 by select Lepcha activists as part of their multi-sited protest in place and in cyberspace against the hydropower development of River Teesta in Himalayan Sikkim and North Bengal. Lepcha socio-political belonging in Dzongu is not merely asserted in discourse, but enacted and transformed in place and cyberspace. The effective use of emails and blogging has strengthened the political activism of these select Lepchas, permitted greater Internet networking, and simultaneously reconfigured their 'local' belonging as *the Lepchas* by conferring a cyber-belonging on them. Weepingsikkim. blogspot.com has reconfigured them as custodians of the indigenous Sikkimese culture and the environment.

I began this chapter by introducing the ethnographic region and the Lepchas to our readers. Sharing international borders with Nepal in the west, Bhutan in the east, Tibet/China in the north, and the state of West Bengal in the south, the contemporary Himalayan state of Sikkim joined the Indian union in 1975 and the Northeast council in 2002. It is an economically backward region and enjoys the status of being a special category state of India.[1] It is completely dependent on receiving preferential funding from the national government. A democratically elected super-active state government has been entrusted with the responsibility of engineering economic development and modernizing Sikkim's population.

Any development strategy has to take cognizance of Sikkim's ethnic and religious divisions, and the differential sense of belonging and territorial attachment of these diverse groups. Demographically, Sikkim is a multi-ethnic society inhabited by roughly 22 Indo-Tibetan and Indo-Aryan groups. Out of its total population of half a million persons (540,493) in 2001, about 20.6 per cent are enumerated as Scheduled Tribes[2] whereas the Scheduled Castes (exclusively of Nepali origin) comprise about 5 per cent of Sikkim's population. Buddhists comprise a large minority of approximately 27 per cent whereas 68 per cent of the total population are Hindus,[3] 3 per cent are converted Christians, and some Muslims settled there recently (Census, 2001). Political discourse historically and presently define the main ethnic boundary to be between the indigenous groups, namely the Bhutias and Lepchas who enjoy Scheduled Tribe status and the diverse ethnic groups who have varying migration histories from Nepal and all of whom are termed Nepali in an aggregate sense. However, more recently, tribal and ethnic divisions are responding to the official administrative discourse categorizing groups into Scheduled Tribes, Scheduled Castes, and Other Backward Classes (refer to Arora, 2007a for details).

Who are the Lepchas? The Lepchas term themselves *Rong* (a Lepcha word meaning ravine-folk or the dwellers of the valley) and they define themselves by their association with the sacred mountain Kanchenjunga, that is regarded as the source of their knowledge, culture, religion, wealth, and resources, and the place of their origin. Hence, their self-perception contains a strong place-based identity and these cultural roots are periodically affirmed in rituals. Their social networks and sense of socio-cultural belonging are reinforced by preferential land ownership laws and their historic habitation in particular locales, which altogether enable them to demand entitlements as an indigenous group. They are the autochthones in their self-perception (Tamsang, 1983; Foning, 1987; Gowloog, 1995), although anthropological discourse debates this status.[4] The government of Sikkim and India has acknowledged their indigenous status and this recognition determines their relation with other ethnic groups. In 1972 they were accorded Scheduled Tribe status and in 2005 they were recognized as 'Most Primitive Tribe' by the Government of Sikkim.[5] Presently, the Lepchas live in Sikkim, Kalimpong, and the Darjeeling Hills of north Bengal in India. Until 1835, these areas were part of the undivided kingdom of Sikkim

(Arora, 2008c). They also reside in some parts of west Bhutan and in the Illam district of Nepal. Within Sikkim, the Lepcha community is not regionally concentrated but quite scattered in its multi-ethnic villages, excepting Dzongu, which is an exclusive Lepcha reserve and in some parts of North Sikkim.[6] In the contemporary period, they are not a homogenous community, but an internally differentiated group. By religious affiliation, they are subdivided into followers of Buddhism, Shamanism, and Christianity.[7] Linguistically, they belong to the Sino-Tibetan family, the Tibeto-Burman subgroup, and the Kachin family (Thurgood et al., 1985). They are primarily agriculturists and only a minority are engaged in government employment.

In the first section, I discuss the competing discourse of hydropower development in Sikkim in order to outline the fundamental cleavages that have shaped the emergence of opposition to hydropower projects planned on River Teesta and the main turning points. The Affected Citizens of the Teesta (ACT) and other environmentalists are protesting against the undemocratic imposition of these projects. On the one hand, local activism and political networking have been complemented by the sending of periodic delegations to represent their concerns to ministers and politicians in Calcutta and Delhi, and on the other hand, ICT has been used to propagate their dissent at a global level. In the second section, I explain the significance of Dzongu for Lepcha culture and the need to preserve it. It spatially expresses and is the locus of their socio-cultural belonging. Here, I reveal the critical reasons and the explicit events whereby a historic tribal reservation has been transformed into a 'holy land', such that for protecting its sanctity Lepcha leaders are even prepared to sacrifice their lives.

Not all Sikkimese citizens and not all Lepchas are protesting as claimed on the blog and in popular discourse; hence, it is a social movement of an ecologically conscious minority. So we must distinguish between the voice(s) of a locality for the outside world (a simplified message) from the complicated message circulating in private conversations among its members (Cohen, 1982: 8). This injunction is especially useful in understanding the message weepingsikkim.blogspot is disseminating to the wider world. The final section accentuates the positive role of Internet activism (blogging) for disseminating the activist perspective globally. The blog chronicles their public campaign and struggles against the state government of Sikkim; it is an expression of their technopolitics.[8]

I argue that the idea of territoriality and cultural belonging is much enriched by the inclusion of an idea of cyber-belonging, which enables these protesting Lepchas to participate in wider debates, draw political strength from other ongoing social movements against hydropower development of rivers in South Asia, and effectively use new ICT technologies to give a global frame to their human rights as an indigenous group.

DEVELOPMENT VISION AND EMERGENT VOICES OF PROTEST FROM HIMALAYAN SIKKIM

The *Human Development Report* that was published in 2001 highlighted the achievements of democratic Sikkim and stressed the untapped revenue potential of hydropower (Lama, 2001), along with the lack of employment and business generation in Sikkim. In the recently released *Sikkim Development Report*, the state government, in collaboration with experts, has identified hydropower, tourism, and international trade through the Nathu-La, as the panacea for Sikkim's human and economic development (Planning Commission, 2008). The state government repeatedly asserts that power generation is critical for rural electrification, meeting the growing urban domestic consumption, generate industrial employment, and to promote tourism. Although micro-hydropower projects can meet domestic demands, they certainly cannot become big revenue generators. This explains the government's favourable slant towards hydraulic gigantism and cascade development of River Teesta.

The decision to construct multi-purpose mega projects on River Teesta is guided by the perceived necessity to achieve economic growth through the sale of power (Lama, 2001). Unlike Bhutan, Sikkim has not been able to sell any power but on the contrary needs to buy power for its domestic consumption (Planning Commission, 2008: 27). The Teesta River, originating in the Himalayan glaciers in the Himalayan heights of 8,598 m, rapidly flows downstream, cutting deep gorges to drop 213 m in Melli within an aerial distance of 100 km (Pandit, 2007: 4–8). Its perennial waters and cascade present a rich opportunity for power generation. There is tremendous scope to export and sell power generated through hydropower projects over River Teesta and other tributaries and streams (Planning Commission, 2008: 117).

Documents outlining development vision and periodic human development reports indeed play a vital role in persuading that human and economic development is happening at the ground while legitimizing (un)popular development policies to the national government and the wider world (on Sikkim refer to Lahiri et al., 2001; Lama, 2001; Planning Commission, 2008). Such reports may often not capture the mood and sentiments of what kind of development is needed and what is acceptable to the people in whose name they are being framed and disseminated. The state government reiterates the employment-generating, huge revenue-earning potential of these multi-purpose hydro projects, but it has neither the necessary skilled personnel to design and manage nor the resources to finance them. This explains the soliciting and approval of private investment in these hydropower projects.

Most of the hydropower projects in Sikkim are indeed located in ecologically sensitive regions that are rich in biodiversity. The state government and the project developers have argued that they have secured the necessary clearances from the Ministry of Environment and Forests (although the carrying capacity studies of the Teesta basin were completed and submitted in December 2007).[9] In his speech on 15 August 2007 celebrating India's 60th Independence Day while addressing a public gathering, Sh Pawan Chamling said,

> Lots of water flowed down the river Teesta and Rungit, but we never understood its importance, now we will generate huge revenue through this flowing water.

The Chief Minister has repeatedly stated that neither the sanctity of Dzongu would be undermined nor will migrants be allowed to settle there. The Sikkim government is committed to protecting the rights of the indigenous Lepchas who were formally recognized as the Most Primitive Tribe in 2005. To counteract activism and delegitimize it, the state government has repeatedly declared that although guided by the majority interest, it is quite concerned about the Lepcha minority and is committed to protecting the integrity of Dzongu despite implementing hydropower projects therein.[10] The government has asserted that the number of families who would be displaced by these hydropower projects was not large either. The government regards the hydropower protests to be disruptive, ethnically divisive, anti-development, and anti-Sikkimese.[11]

At this point, we must remember that the agitating activists have been voicing their concerns not recently, but ever since 2001. Admittedly, opposition was neither as vocal nor as strong as in recent times. In 2006, some of the activists were persuaded to call off a massive rally they had planned for on 12 December after the Chief Minister assured them that he would review the projects located in Dzongu.[12] The leaders decided to launch formal protests after the government started land-acquisition activities in Dzongu in 2007. If the interests of the Lepchas are safeguarded, then why are they opposing the Teesta projects? What are the central arguments of current struggles against state-approved hydroelectric projects on River Teesta? Are these protests merely a resource-struggle for the Lepcha minority having vested interests? How are they opposing state-directed hydraulic development of the Teesta river? The activists' banner proclaiming, "In the name of development, do not make us refugees in our own homeland [Sikkim]" and another asserting, "Dzongu is the holy land of the Lepchas. Lepchas have the responsibility to protect it," challenge definitions of what constitutes public interest in Sikkim and exemplifies cultural politics over natural resources (Arora, 2007b, 2009).

The diverse groups living in the project area are internally divided into pro- and anti-dam supporters and this issue has split the Lepchas. What began as concerns of a few culturally committed educated and ecologically conscious Lepcha youth have snowballed into pertinent debates on belonging and indigeneity in Sikkim's landscape,[13] complemented by a renewed demand for preserving its cultural heritage and designing sustainable development projects that are implemented in a participatory manner. It is the perceived threat to their cultural roots and the possibility of Dzongu being irrevocably transformed that have united large number of scattered Lepchas residing in Sikkim and Darjeeling into a community. Some of the Lepcha political representatives are supporting the government due to vested interests and have been motivated by greed. Roughly one-third of the Lepcha community within Dzongu has vocally opposed these projects, whereas another one-third of the community has been wavering or unconcerned, and roughly one-third has been seduced by the government assurances. This explains why, despite reservations and heavy campaigning by activists, the ruling government's candidates did not lose the 2009 elections in Dzongu. The lack of vocal expression of dissent is not due to consent but due to fear of government repression. There have been ups and downs within this movement and public support has been variable over the past few years.

It is impossible for me to detail all the events and sites of struggle here in the limited space of this chapter. Hence, I restrict myself to mentioning turning points and focusing on historical moments. Formal protests against hydropower projects proposed and under construction on River Teesta[14] commenced on 20 June 2007 at Bhutia-Lepcha House at Gangtok with an indefinite *satyagraha*[15] by three Lepcha youth[16] affiliated with the Affected Citizens of the Teesta (ACT)[17] and the Concerned Lepchas of Sikkim (CLOS) with the support of the Sangha of Dzongu. Among those three youth, Dawa Lepcha and Tenzing Lepcha's *satyagraha* began on 20 June 2007 and lasted for 63 days.[18] I was in Sikkim conducting fieldwork at that time and have subsequently followed their multi-sited struggle in space and cyberspace, as many of the leaders are long-standing collaborators.

The leadership and membership core is drawn from the Lepcha group, but not completely since some other environmentally conscious Sikkimese youth and their organizations (such as Sikkim Association for Safe Environment–SAFE) have supported these agitations. The Bhutia leaders of the earlier hydropower agitations against the Rathongchu project namely Chokie Topden[19] and Sonam Paljor have motivated, supported them with material and human resources, and helped them strategize.[20] However, the protests have inordinately focused on Dzongu and not as much on other stages of the Teesta cascade.[21] The activists predominantly are young Lepcha men and women along with Buddhist lamas. Many of these youth have participated in the historic relay hunger strike. The activists have creatively combined Gandhian methods of non-violence and resistance (Arora, 2008b) and creatively used Shamanic and Buddhist rituals to give religious sanction to their protest activities. They have been uncompromising, "we will accept nothing less than a complete scrapping of hydropower projects in Dzongu". They have repeatedly demanded that the government should commission an interdisciplinary comprehensive review[22] of the entire Teesta project plan before commencing construction. Over time they have withdrawn their opposition to micro hydropower projects that are environmentally benign and located outside Dzongu.

The protests have been largely peaceful and non-violent unlike the Gorkhaland movement in the neighbouring Darjeeling Hills, which has thrown the entire region into turmoil repeatedly. However, about 38 activists, including 11 monk activists, were arrested when they participated in a peaceful rally on 2 October 2007 and attempted to offer silk-scarves and garland the Gandhi statue on M.G. Marg in Gangtok.[23] The government and the activists have tried to negotiate but not very successfully.

After their demands were repeatedly rejected, the heroic duo of Dawa and Tenzing began the second round of their indefinite *satyagraha* in March 2008 along with Ongchuk Lepcha who fasted for 86 days with them.[24] On 13 June 2008 just a few days prior to the first anniversary of their first *satyagraha*, Dawa and Tenzing broke this second *satyagraha* that lasted for 96 days. They were given a government notification announcing the withdrawal of letter of intent given to four hydropower projects located in Dzongu[25] and an invitation to negotiate. However, the relay *satyagraha* was not stopped since the controversial 280 MW Panang project was not cancelled. In fact, the Chief Minister laid the foundation stone of the 1,200 MW Teesta III project at Chungthang (North Sikkim) in June 2008 amidst protests. Teesta III is considered the largest of the mega projects planned on River Teesta and this project had not yet secured clearance from the Central Electricity Authority. Hence, all construction activities of this project explicitly violate existing and acceptable norms.[26] The blasting activities carried out in sensitive geological areas of North Sikkim have led to loss of human lives, endangered animal lives, caused considerable distress to people and loss of livelihood, and damaged property in the area.[27]

The struggle of these brave activists has been protracted. Their relay hunger strike was formally withdrawn on 27 September 2009 after a historic period of 915 days upon receiving an official letter from the Chief Secretary inviting them for peaceful talks and meaningful negotiations. The activists firmly declared at this juncture of their struggle that their agenda was non-negotiable and they want the government to abandon the Panang and Teesta Stage IV in Dzongu, since both are located in the heart of Dzongu and encroach into the Kanchenjunga biosphere reserve.[28]

What have been the modes and instruments of organizing dissent and galvanizing public support for their cause? Localized struggles and rallies within Sikkim have been reinforced by oppositional movements and rallies organized by the Lepcha Associations of Kalimpong and Darjeeling Hills of North Bengal,[29] and the staging of demonstrations in collaboration with other civil society organizations not merely in Sikkim and north Bengal but also in Delhi.[30] The leadership has tried a range of methods and at various levels to persuade and pressurize the state and central governments into reconsidering its position. They have filed legal petitions in the National Appellate Authority at Delhi to question the grant of necessary environmental clearances,[31] repeatedly sent delegations to convince the state government into commissioning a review of the environmental impact of these projects, attempted to generate public debate, and argue for a better relief and compensation package for the affected and displaced families. Through multi-sited struggles in space and cyberspace, these activists have laudably galvanized public sympathy for their ongoing struggles at the regional, national, and international levels. A pivotal role has been played by weepingsikkim.blogspot, which is the virtual chronicle of their movement. I discuss this in the final section of this chapter.

The petitions submitted by the activists time and again have stressed loss of biodiversity, threat to their cultural roots, damage to sacred places, loss of livelihood, and violation of indigenous rights. The leaders point at rampant corruption, misuse of government funds to guarantee and underwrite loans taken by dubious private companies that have absconded with money, and the widespread violation of environmental regulations in the name of national development.[32]

Environmental concerns dominate the objections raised by the agitating Lepchas with the government, but cultural survival is the paramount concern framed by their oppositional discourse. They contend, "mega projects in Dzongu are not sustainable development, but the sustainable destruction of Dzongu."[33] Leaders spearheading opposition contend that they already are a vanishing tribe and likely to be vanquished with the implementation of Teesta projects in Dzongu (Arora, 2008a, 2008b). Time and again, they emphasize how these hydropower projects contravene the constitutional safeguards enshrined in Article 371F.[34] They highlight that special provisions were inserted into the Indian Constitution in 1975 to safeguard the unique cultural and religious heritage of the indigenous people of Sikkim.[35] The activists accentuate the disruptive impact of the projects on the social and cultural heritage of the indigenous people of Sikkim, especially the Lepchas, after the settlement of migrant labour from other parts of India. They stress that projects implemented in Dzongu would result in the disappearance of their endangered cultural and religious traditions and desacralize their sacred landscape.

The blog entry of 28 November 2007 interconnects the activists' demand to save Dzongu with the UN resolution of 13 September 2007 to protect the rights of indigenous people and India's declared commitment to protect and safeguard the indigenous, which also includes the Lepchas. The leaders have cleverly used these international conventions to elicit sympathy and argue that their indigenous rights are being undermined within Sikkim. They have been successful in garnering support from the Sikkim Bhutia Lepcha Apex committee and the Akhil Bharatiya Adivasi Vikas Parishad, which is the national body for tribals.[36] Civil Society organizations supporting environmental movements and resource-related struggles for justice such as Kalpavriksh, South Asian Network for Dams, Rivers and People (SANDRP), Delhi Forum, Intercultural Resources, River Basin Friends, Legal Initiative for Forests and Environment (LIFE), and Centre for Organisation, Research and Education (CORE) Manipur are providing strategic support and helping the activists overcome any feelings of powerlessness (Arora, 2009: 107). Political parties such as members of Congress I in Sikkim burnt an effigy of the Sikkim Governor V. Rama Rao protesting at the government apathy towards the peaceful environmental movement,[37] while several members of the Communist Party of India (M) have visited Gangtok to extend moral and political support to them.

An independent six-member expert committee of civil society activists and environmentalists spent a few days in Sikkim in May 2008. The group lauded the government's decision to shelve four projects located in Dzongu while recommending the freezing of a decision on Panang and an evaluation of sustainability of commissioned projects prior to undertaking the construction of new projects. Their rationale is clear—if the project's life is not even going to be 30 years due to heavy siltation in tunnels and dams, then there is no point in commissioning them, and degrading the environment and dislocating people are avoidable. In April 2008, none other than the renowned environmentalist Medha Patkar visited Gangtok to extend moral support to these *satyagrahi*. She acknowledged the critical need of safeguarding the environmental and cultural heritage of the Lepchas. In November 2009, noted environmentalist and leader of the Tehri-dam protests, Sunderlal Bahaguna, commended the Teesta activists and criticized the Sikkim government for destroying forests and disturbing the fragile ecology of Sikkim.[38]At the international level, the activists have elicited admiration from members affiliated to the International Rivers Network, World Mountain People's Association, Ecotibet,[39] and the Sikkimese Diaspora settled as far as in Canada and Australia, as is evident in their postings on the blog.

DZONGU AND (RE)CONFIGURING LEPCHA BELONGING

During my short-term fieldwork visits to Sikkim between 2006 and 2008, many Lepchas were vocal that these hydropower projects would de-root and decentre them from their heartland, Dzongu, and cause the disappearance of their sacred river, the Teesta. Is Dzongu just a piece of real estate available for commercial exploitation?[40] As the Coordinator of Affected Citizens of Teesta (ACT), Tseten Lepcha commented, "these hydro projects are being touted as harbinger of immense money and prosperity but they will make us a minority in our own homeland". Generally, the activists argue that state development policies in the shape of mega hydropower projects impinge on their territorial and emotional belonging.

The root metaphor galvanizing opposition is that 'the Lepchas belong to the land and the land belongs to them'. The activists' banner repeats their appeal not to reduce them into becoming displaced refugees in their homeland.

> Real Estate Classified: Wanted Arable/agricultural land that can nurture and sustain approximately 40,568 people of a vanishing tribe that are on the verge of displacement and extinction due to the construction of a hydroelectricity project in their backyard.

Indigeneity is defined by territorial claims and ancestral roots and practice of a particular cultural politics located in claims over the landscape. Inhabited by around 7,000 Lepchas, Dzongu is located at the margins of the state. Thinly populated, Dzongu is regarded as one of the most backward underdeveloped areas of Sikkim, which is governed by some restrictive laws. Formulated during the colonial period, these protective laws confer exclusive rights of habitation and land-ownership on Lepchas who have historically resided here. Dzongu-land enjoys the status of being an exclusive Lepcha reserve.[41] All land transactions in Dzongu are restrictively permitted between residents of Dzongu. Even Lepcha residents of Sikkim and North Sikkim are not allowed to buy land here. Descent and genealogy define Lepcha belonging in Dzongu. Even intermarriage with non-Dzongu Lepchas and other residents of Sikkim or other Indians leads to loss of residency-membership and all rights to land ownership. "All of this is a question of a particular kind of identity, an identity of rootedness, of genealogy as it relates to territory" (Friedman, 2004: 69).

Why would the Lepchas want to remain here far removed from modern civilization with its seductive amenities? In *Belonging*, Anthony Cohen explained, "to remain in these communities is itself an expression of commitment, and commitment is sustained by the continuous elaboration of culture" (1982: 6). Ethnicity and locality are both expressions of culture (Cohen, 1982: 3). To be a Dzongu Lepcha is to be a *real* Lepcha and I was constantly advised during even my first visit to Sikkim in 2001 to talk to Lepchas who have continued to live there by choice in order to really know what it means to be a Lepcha. The sense of belonging, "of what it means to belong, is constantly evoked by whatever means comes to hand, the persistent production of culture and attribution of value becomes an essential bulwark against cultural imperialism of the political and economic centres" (Cohen, 1982: 6). Dzongu is located at the periphery. The inhabitants of Dzongu[42] are politically, demographically, socio-economically marginalized, and culturally dehumanized as forest-dwelling backward nature-worshippers.[43]

Belonging to a locality far from being a parochial triviality is very much a cultural reality than is the wider association with a region or nation (Cohen, 1982: 10), whereas belonging implies much more than merely having been born in a place (Cohen, 1982: 21). "We may die in our efforts but we will not see our land being plundered by capitalists," declared *satyagrahi* Dawa Lepcha from his hospital bed at Gangtok in August 2007. "Dams over Dzongu will be built over our dead bodies", proclaimed the banner on 6 January 2008 that marked the 200th day of their relay hunger strike and public opposition. The Lepchas of Sikkim are spatially scattered and with intermarriage with Bhutias and Limbus, conversion to Buddhism, and modern education, they have lost their cultural moorings to a large extent everywhere, except in Dzongu.[44] The Lepchas of Kalimpong are more politically conscious, linguistically and culturally aware of being a Lepcha, but never represented as the *real* Lepcha to me. They do not have a locality of belonging and cannot press for indigenous homelands unlike the populous migrant Nepalis who are violently agitating for a Gorkhaland state and the partition of West Bengal. Dzongu is a historic reserve located in the restricted access area of North Sikkim that the Lepchas consider the cradle of their culture. Unlike the Rathongchu activists (Arora, 2006b), the activists opposing the Teesta projects lack religious writings supporting their claim of Dzongu being a *holy land*. Anthropological literature acknowledges Dzongu to be a Lepcha reserve with sacred sites but it has never been regarded a religious landscape and centre of pilgrimage until now. Its cultural importance is adequately documented in myths and anthropological literature (Gorer, 1938; Siiger, 1967; Siiger and Rischel, 1967; Kotturan, 1976, 1983; Arora 2006a, 2007b, 2008a). As a locality it constitutes the locus of their cultural roots, materially signifies their indigeneity, and expresses their belonging in the landscape. It is sacred and holy in this wider sense. Located on the path leading to their *mayel-lyang* (paradise), Dzongu contains many sacred sites used to worship protective place-deities and 12 Buddhist monasteries, including the Tholung temple preserving the famed three-centuries-old sacred relics and religious treasures of Lhatsun Chenpo (see Arora, 2006a, 2010).[45]

All places have the potential to become sacred centres and beliefs and practices ebb and flow transforming and creating new sacred centres while the value of other centres may diminish—even Shangri-La's are always in the making (Arora, 2010). Recently in April 2008, Dzongu was transformed into a pilgrimage centre after 500 Lepchas[46] living in neighbouring Darjeeling and Kalimpong dressed in their traditional attire under the leadership of their tribal associations attempted a three-day 'long march' to their holy land on 14 April 2008. This pilgrimage-march started after the offering of prayers at Tribeni shore in Kalimpong, which is the confluence of the Teesta and Rangit rivers.

"We are basically going to a pilgrimage to our holy land and this march will create an awareness of the significance of this place to everyone", explained Azuk Tamsangmoo.[47] At Rangpo on the Sikkim border, after walking in pouring rain for nearly 8 hours, they were welcomed by a Lepcha lama, who incidentally is *satyagrahi* Dawa Lepcha's father. The procession-march was bolstered with another 300 Sikkimese Lepchas[48] joining their ranks. About 200 policemen deployed to maintain law and order at Rangpo greeted the youthful fraternity's peaceful entourage that merrily sang Lepcha songs and danced. The pilgrims proceeded towards a prearranged public rest-house at Singtam for a night's rest. There they discovered that they had been viciously locked out. The next two days were confusing and shattering for these pilgrims comprising youth who had peacefully walked from Kalimpong to reaffirm their ancestral roots in Dzongu. The leader of the People's Movement and noted environmentalist Medha Patkar had intended to join these rallyists and walk in unity with them to Dzongu. However, the government of Sikkim imposed Section 144 in the interest of maintaining law and order at Gangtok and diverted this rally towards Dikchu. At Dikchu there were some verbal and physical clashes between the anti-project and pro-project groups supported by the ruling SDF party. These clashes were immediately controlled by the police. The Lepcha leaders decided to abandon their original plan to enter Dzongu, since they did not want to encourage internal dissension within the Lepcha community.[49] Therefore, Medha Patkar met the marchers at Rangpo and travelled to Gangtok to extend her support to the *satyagrahi*s and address a press conference there. She declared, "every community must have a right to concede or not to concede to any project and this is what the Indian constitution has granted".[50]

Belonging is related to parameters of inclusion and exclusion, sentiments, and affirmation of connections (Pfaff-Czarnecka and Toffin, 2011). The participation of Lepchas of Kalimpong and Darjeeling in these protests begets further questions on locality and belonging. They are concerned about the future of their community and the loss of heritage. Some of them are even Christians, yet displaying solidarity with the protesting Lepchas of Sikkim. Who belongs to Sikkim and who is weeping for Sikkim? These questions require us to differentiate between 'ethnic' belonging and 'political' belonging or civic membership that is defined by contractual membership and citizenship (see Thomas, 2002; Brettell, 2006). Citizenship and nationality are distinct conceptions and cannot be conflated. Historically, Darjeeling was part of undivided Sikkim whereas Kalimpong had been part of the Bhutanese kingdom. Today, the Lepchas of Kalimpong and Darjeeling are not Sikkimese as they do not have Sikkim citizenship certificates. Yet they have an ethnic belonging in Sikkim and affective connection with Dzongu, which continues to be the focus and locus of their ancestor worship rituals. Politically all Lepchas belong to India and have Indian citizenship, but cultural belonging is not the same as their local-political belonging. The rise and violent expression of the Gorkhaland movement in May 2008 in the neighbouring Darjeeling Hills have raised further questions in the realm of belonging. In contrast to the indigenous Lepchas and Bhutias of this region, some Nepalis only have contractual civic membership at a minimum, and affective belonging with Sikkim and India may or may not even be manifest. The emergent demand for a separate Gorkhaland does indicate that Nepalis of India now have a political belonging, which needs a place-expression.

The emergence of protests in North Bengal, and in Lachen and Lachung in North Sikkim inhabited largely by Sikkimese Bhutias, does substantiate the claims of these activists that they are fighting for others and not merely for the rights of the Lepcha community. The title-graphic of weepingsikkim.blogspot blog depicts a man dressed in Tibetan clothes paying homage to a couple dressed in traditional Lepcha attire with a snowy mountain in its backdrop. An adjacent caption identifies this image as a depiction of the iconic statue of unity, which symbolizes the ethnic unity of the Lepchas, Bhutias, and the Nepali with the sacred mountain Kanchenjunga acting as the witness of this pact. Interestingly this historical depiction materially represents the ethnic unity of the Lepchas and Bhutias, while occasionally in the past it has included the Limbus, but nowhere does any oral or written discourse acknowledge the Nepali to be part of this ethnic-pact.

Are these activists intending to mislead or reconfigure the discourse of cultural belonging in Sikkim? As one admirer stated, "the people who are doing the hunger strike, theirs is the voice of Sikkim. Let us help this voice reach its goal. If you consider it carefully, they are representing each one of us because the consequences that nature unleashes in its fury will have to be borne by all irrespective of any strata of society. That is the law of nature".[51] In my opinion, the virtual contextual narrative projects a more inclusive definition of belonging, by naturalizing and affirming the formal Sikkimese citizenship of the Nepali, and in encouraging them to demonstrate it expressively by protecting it—as an expression of cultural belonging in Sikkim.[52]

Belonging here is redefined by a role-acceptance to protect Sikkim from others/Indian migrants who will marginalize and uproot the people to whom Sikkim rightfully belongs. In this narrative stance, those who are not anguished by the deleterious and environmentally destructive impact of these hydropower projects do *not* belong to Sikkim. The Nepalis may not be considered indigenous to Sikkim; nevertheless, these activists are beckoning them to rise up and protect Sikkim as an expression of belonging to Sikkim. Some Web-postings do confirm that the activists enjoy support from some Nepali individuals and leaders such as Biraj Adhikari, J.B. Poudyal, Bhim Prasad Nepali, and Dilip Kumar Pradhan.[53] The ethnic associations of the diverse groups included in the Nepali category are maintaining a distance from these agitations.

It will be erroneous to assume that all Lepchas are aware or wanting to express their cultural belonging in terms of protest against the hydropower protests. There persist competing discourses within Dzongu and in Sikkim. The local government elections in Sikkim in October 2007 did not indicate that the ruling party forming the state government of Sikkim had become so unpopular in Dzongu despite activists campaigning against them. Other scholars who visited Dzongu in April 2008 mention the divisions and polarizations within Dzongu.[54] The residents of Lachen already have accepted the money given out as compensation for land, and voices of protest have died out there by now. Nor can I ignore the fact that the Lepchas long-march in April 2008 was confronted by some other Lepchas and people of Sikkim demanding the implementation of hydropower projects to promote Sikkim's development. Land compensation has been released to those whose land was acquired for Panang in April 2008. According to the agitating activists, this has caused social tensions within Sikkim. Compensation has divided families, with many people within a family not getting a share since their name is not on the title deed, although they are dependent on it for their livelihood.[55]

> There are signs of social tension and problems for future in the quite peaceful land due to no land no money situation topping with no education and qualifications and no job.[56]

An emotionally saddened Tseten Lepcha coordinating these agitations had confessed to me as far back as in December 2007 while sitting on a *dharna* in Delhi:

> [V]illages are divided, clans are divided, friends and well-wishers are divided and worst of all families are divided. Dzongu has become like

the India before the East India Company came to India. We are divided for the interest for outsiders who promise prosperity while taking away our land, our culture, the environment, and our very identity.

WEEPINGSIKKIM.BLOGSPOT.COM: CHRONICLE AND EXPRESSION OF CYBER BELONGING

I have never found these resource-poor, numerically weak, politically inexperienced Lepcha youth activists to be dispirited in their fight against the powerful Sikkim government and its associate power project companies such as the National Hydroelectric Power Corporation.[57] In early December 2007 during a *dharna* staged at Delhi,[58] the leaders admitted that they had never expected their relay hunger strike to be protracted nor had they collected necessary funds to sustain it. While admitting that a dearth of resources constrained their capacity to organize a large-scale campaign and strengthen their oppositional politics, they acknowledged the positive role of the Internet in propagating their dissent. Localized struggles can engage with national and international agencies through Internet activism. ICTs are recognized to be a powerful tool for non-elites, marginalized, resource-poor groups that enables them to communicate, influence public opinion, network, and garner support for their cause. Technopolitics can create and strengthen insider communities when these are not only locally connected but also spatially dispersed globally (Kahn and Kellner, 2005). Here I will explicitly acknowledge that in a scenario where the majority of people in Sikkim neither use nor have access to the Internet, cyber-activism can merely provide an alternative space to voice protest. It cannot supplant place-based activism and force the government into accepting their demands.

Unlike other blogs, weepingsikkim is not an individual's chronicle. The blog is an interactive portal and several youth have taken turns to become its webmasters and upload reports, news coverage, and report various activities and document narratives. It emerges as an interactive virtual space in which some concerned 'Sikkimese' are documenting the ongoing protests and chronicling their actions, their struggle, and dilemmas. It functions as a virtual diary chronicling oppositional arguments and protest events staged in multi-sited space (Gangtok, Dzongu, Delhi, Kalimpong, etc.) while simultaneously enabling the activists to Internet work with other social movements and instantaneously. However, the blog's right column contains an important disclaimer declaring, "We would also like to clarify that http://weepingsikkim.blogspot.com/ is not the official website of ACT (Affected Citizens of Teesta) and we do not have any political affiliations or belong to any political party or any other group as such." The blogger/webmaster(s) of weepingsikkim declares that they seek to educate the public about Sikkim's fragile environment and create awareness about the adverse impact of hydropower projects. The contextual justification for the blog is given thereon in terms of the following:

> It began the day our friends Dawa, Tenzing and others decided to go on an indefinite strike last June [2007] and appeal to the Government of Sikkim on the dangers of mega Hydropower dams and the ecological degradation and social impact that it would bring to Sikkim and Dzongu in particular. It is dedicated to them and the courage and conviction they have had in standing up for a noble cause and going hungry all these days. Dawa and Tenzing went hungry for 63 days earlier and now are on a second indefinite hunger strike....

Place-based politicking and territorial belonging will continue to be critical for successful activism on these local issues. However, the Internet provides these Lepcha activists with an alternate instrument of political struggle and a tool of democratic opposition and information-dissemination. The right column of the blog indicates the number of days this blog has clocked, its political stance with its affiliations with the Affected Citizens of Teesta (www.actsikkim.com) website and another website savetheteesta.com, details about the list of hydropower projects planned on the Teesta river and public and private investors in these projects, and like-minded networks such as International Rivers Network (www.irn.org), Kalpavriksh, Narmada Bachao Andolan (www.narmada.org), South Asian Dams Rivers and People (http://www.sandrp.in/), Nespon (www.nespon.org), and so on. The blog connects to the Sikkim government official website containing the soft copy of the Carrying Capacity Study of Teesta River Basin (www.sikenvis.nic.in/ccstb.html) and the ongoing media coverage in various news channels. Video and films are uploaded in the left column, allowing readers to see and judge for themselves about what is happening in remote Sikkim without the need to travel to it.

Emails on activist networks and blogging circumvent the official government perspectives and mass media that censor reports and protest activities or give them marginal column space and coverage.[59] The scalar of their struggle is a locality involving local actors; nonetheless, the invocation of multiple localities engaged in similar struggles around the world transforms them into global actors (Sassen, 2004: 883). Blogging has enabled local politics to network and situate themselves in global politics, overcome their peripheral geographical position, and counteract government apathy by actively carving an alternative public sphere.[60] Any feelings of isolation and alienation among these activists are effectively counteracted by their interlinking with other activist websites, which confirm the global dimension of their local struggle and provide them a cyber belonging. Global digital linkages enable "place-specific politics with a global span" (Sassen, 2004: 654).

The internal tensions within the Lepcha community are elided in this space. The Lepchas become eponymous with the Sikkimese in this cyberspace as they narrate the story of their struggle and enact their role as true custodians of the earth; their local belonging is reconfigured and recast with their cyber-activism; they present themselves as protectors of the fragile Himalayan environment and as a vanishing indigenous group. The blog rouses all those living in Sikkim to awaken and join the movement against the Teesta projects. It seeks to encompass all those who are inherently Sikkimese and remind them of their duty towards protecting its landscape. Cyberspace becomes a stage for these Lepcha activists to express and an instrument to claim a global belonging as vanguards of a fragile environment. The other Lepchas who are not aligned with these protesting activists are not perceived as *being* Lepcha in this narrative. The other citizens who are not fighting for protecting Sikkim's environment and for the integrity of Dzongu are not *the* Sikkimese. The profound impact of the blog can be assessed in the fact that on 15 August during his public speech, the Chief Minister of Sikkim explicitly decried the activists' engagement in 'cyber-war' while labelling the leaders of these protests as being anti-national and anti-Sikkimese.

CONCLUSION

My discussion has highlighted the relatedness of groups with locality and belonging, differentiated between socio-cultural belonging and nationality, then explained the intimate relation between the expression of political and cultural belonging by analyzing Lepcha activism, and indicated the transformation of place-based identity and belonging with cyber-activism. Blogging has enabled the Lepchas living on the peripheries of the Indian state to situate themselves in global networks of oppositional politics. I have demonstrated how political activism to protect cultural roots in specific localities has circumscribed Lepcha identity and discourse, yet cyber-activism has enabled them to transcend locality and transform themselves into vanguards of Sikkim and garner national and international support for preserving their cultural heritage.

Scholars asked me during the 2008 conference held at Fréjus whether I had anything new to offer to the debate. There are other environmental movements, such as Narmada Bachao Andolan and the Tehri dam protests (and Rathongchu hydel protests in Sikkim), that have effectively used Gandhian methods and relay hunger strikes to oppose the government along with legal action to pressurize the government. The numerical minority status of the indigenous Lepchas, the lack of their resource base for funding and organizing protests against a resource state government and private developers, their creative use of ICTs to obtain wider support and network with other environmental movements, and the indigenous people all these factors do make their case quite poignant and interesting. Very few environmental movements have been successful in countering government development plans in India, and the possibility of an insignificant Himalayan tribal minority forcing an all-powerful resourceful government to shelve planned projects is very bleak. Yet, the Rathongchu and the Teesta hydropower protests organized by the indigenous Lepchas (and Bhutias) are classified as those exceptions where the ambitious hydropower development plans of the government were countered and some, if not all, the hydropower power projects were shelved. Environmental movements and activists in South Asia have acknowledged this to be an achievement. The partial success of the activists in stopping Dzongu from being blasted and dammed definitely makes the story of their struggle fascinating; nonetheless, it is their effectiveness in accruing a cyber-belonging and demonstrating the connection between local and global belonging that marks them as exemplars. My discussion on Weepingsikkim. blogspot.com has attempted to broaden the conceptual horizons of belonging by integrating cyber-belonging into it.

NOTES

1. SCS receive substantial financial support from the central government in the form of 90 per cent as grants and 10 per cent as loans. This ratio is 30 per cent grants and 70 per cent loans for non-special category states (Lahiri et al., 2001: 44–45).
2. This does not include the Limbus and Tamangs, who were given Scheduled Tribe status in 2002.
3. The majority of the Hindus of Sikkim have ethnic-national origins in neighbouring Nepal. However, post 1975, many Indians settled in Sikkim are included in this category.
4. Gorer (1938: 35) follows Lepcha self-definition but H. Siiger and J. Rischel (1967) agree with L.A. Waddell, who has argued that the Lepchas have Indo-Chinese origin and they migrated to Sikkim by way of the Assam Valley.
5. During the early 1990s, politically conscious Lepchas revived several rituals to affirm their symbolic connections with Sikkim's landscape, and politically stake a claim over its resources as the 'sons of the soil' and oppose the political economic control of the Nepali majority (Arora, 2007a: 214).
6. Both Land Revenue Order No. 1 (issued by Charles Bell in May 1917) and Tashi Namgyal's proclamation on North Sikkim (30 August, 1937) safeguard Lepcha interests by placing restrictions on settlement of other ethnic communities (excepting Bhutias) in North Sikkim and the sale and purchase of land there (refer to Arora, 2007a).
7. Shamanism or *mun* (in Lepcha) is considered their original religion. In the 14th century, after the migration of the Bhutias to Sikkim, the majority were converted to Buddhism. With the arrival of the Christian missionaries in the 19th century, they converted in large numbers in Darjeeling but only in small numbers in Sikkim (see Arora, 2007a: 198).
8. Technopolitics refers to politics that is mediated by technologies such as broadcasting media or the Internet (Kahn and Kellner, 2005: 95).
9. The recommendations of the Carrying Capacity Report have been discussed in other articles (see Arora, 2008a, 2009).
10. For further details, refer to Arora (2008a).
11. Speech of Chief Minister Pawan Chamling given on 15 August 2007.
12. Personally communicated by Tseten Lepcha, the Working President of ACT.
13. Being indigenous has a corollary duty of protecting and safeguarding the landscape from other exploiting outsiders.
14. Initially, 26 projects are listed on the ACT website, with some of them listed as under construction while for others letters of intent were issued. These projects were expected to generate an estimated 3635 MW. The Carrying Capacity Report mentions 30 projects. At the time of writing this chapter this number had dwindled to about 18 projects.

15. A Hindi word broadly translated as a hunger strike. Gandhi transformed this mode of protest during India's independence struggle. Since then this method has been widely deployed in Asia as a protest weapon of the weak against government repression.

16. Tsering Ongchuk, who also inaugurated the *satyagraha*, withdrew after about five days and was replaced by others participating in a relay hunger strike.

17. Their website defines them to be "an organization of the indigenous Sikkimese citizens to protect the land and the people against the threat of devastation of the biodiversity hotspot (Khangchendzonga biosphere reserve), endangering the demographic profile of the indigenous primitive Lepcha tribes and the right to live in one's own homeland in dignity and security in the name of development harbingered by numerous mega hydropower projects at one go" (refer to http:// www.actsikkim.com/).

18. It was hailed to be exemplary by the Gandhian social activist Medha Patkar of the Save the Narmada Movement (*Narmada Bachao Andolan*). She applauded their efforts in an email she wrote to the political advisors of these activists.

19. She tragically died in a car accident on 6 April 2009 in South Sikkim. Her death has been publicly mourned by the activists in local media and on this blog.

20. Refer to Arora (2006b) for details on the Rathongchu movement and details about these leaders.

21. Contrary to all public perception, this movement has drawn limited support from the Sikkimese Bhutias and even Nepalis affected by these Hydropower projects.

22. The review committee for the 280 MW Panang Project comprising nearly only government officials submitted a report in May 2008 stating that the project was sustainable. This was confirmed by government officials and blog entry dated 9 May 2008.

23. See blog entry of 4 October 2007.

24. He had to withdraw due to medical reasons.

25. The 90 MW Ringpi, 33 MW Rukel, 120 MW Lingza, and 141 MW Rangyong projects were shelved.

26. Personal communication of activists and government officials of the Power department. Blog entry for 20 May 2008.

27. Refer to ACT's petitions submitted to Mr Jairam Ramesh, the Union Minister for Environment, 18 January 2010.

28. Refer to blog entry of 1 October 2009.

29. Public rallies have been organized in Kalimpong and Darjeeling in support. For instance, refer to blog entry for 31 July 2007 and 9 October 2007.

30. Refer to blog entry for 11 December 2007.

31. Personal communication from Dawa Lepcha, General Secretary ACT, who also has filed petitions in the National Appellate Authority challenging these projects.

32. Refer to Sikkim express article and blog entry dated 26 December 2009.

33. Blog entry dated 9 May 2008.

34. The continued implementation of these laws was acknowledged to be critical by the Indian government in 1975 when Sikkim was incorporated into the Indian Union (refer to Arora, 2006c, for details).

35. The blog entry dated 19 October 2007 highlights these. Refer to Arora (2006c) for discussion on Article 371F.

36. Lyangsong Tamsang, the President of the Indigenous Lepcha Tribal Association, has been successful in mobilizing their support after making a strong presentation on Dzongu at their 14th National Conference at Jaipur in October 2007. The President of Akhil Bharatiya Adivasi Vikas Parishad, Mr Somjibhai Damor, later visited Sikkim and publicly extended organizational support to these activists. This meeting was reported in the newspapers. Refer to blog entry of 11 October 2007 for details and pictures of this public meeting.

37. Tseten Lepcha, who was earlier the Coordinator of ACT and currently is the Working President, was formerly the General Secretary of the Congress I branch in Sikkim. To establish the apolitical stance of the agitations, Tseten resigned from his post in July 2007. The Lepchas have met Congress I representatives such as Rahul Gandhi and Mani Shankar Aiyer to convey their concerns to the ruling coalition at the national level.

38. See blog entry for 13 November 2009.

39. An environmental NGO of Tibetans—see ecotibet.org for further details.

40. "Can Dzongu (a pilgrimage place for Lepchas), be bidded to private businessmen for hydropower?" encapsulates this sentiment lucidly. Cited in the weepingsikkim blog entry for 22 December 2007.

41. With the exception of one Tibetan clan—the Nangpa—Dzongu has been entirely inhabited by Lepchas for over a century (see Arora, 2006a).

42. Figures communicated by government and cited by blog entries (for instance see 23 March 2008). Many of the youth are studying in schools at Mangan and Gangtok and some youth are working in other parts of Sikkim. With cardamom plantations in a state of crises and no longer profitable, many youth are being forced to migrate in search of employment to other parts of Sikkim.

43. Many of its residents are the first generation of Lepchas who have gone to school and benefited from modern hospitals, telecommunication, and transportation facilities introduced in Dzongu in the last decade.

44. I have discussed the Bhutianization of Lepchas and the recent trends of retribalization.

45. Lhatsun Chenpo was an eminent Dzogchen master of the 17th century and regarded the chief propagator of Nyingmapa Buddhism in Sikkim.

46. Blog entry cites the number to be 650 Lepchas, 16 April 2008.

47. He is an influential member of Rong Ong Prongzom, which is the Lepcha Youth Association. I have met him in the course of his several visits to Delhi when delegations have come to submit memorandums of requests to ministers at Delhi. He also participated during the *dharna*s at Jantar Mantar in Delhi in December 2007 and is one of the key players in spearheading the movement in Kalimpong.

48. Blog entry cites this number to be 350 Lepchas, 16 April 2008.

49. Refer to Blog entry for 16 April 2008 and news reports.

50. Medha Patkar, cf. blog entry 17 April 2008.

51. Chewangmit from Melbourne. See blog entry for 2 August 2007 on weepingsikkim. blogspot.com

52. In an earlier chapter, I have highlighted how the indigenous Lepchas-Bhutias have denied the Nepali a belonging in Sikkim by continually underplaying their politico-economic contribution and emphasizing their lack of affective-symbolic identification with its 'sacred' landscape (Arora, 2007a).

53. Refer to blog entry of 15 October and Biraj Adhikari's posting on 19 October 2007.
54. Personal communications of some scholars who wish to remain anonymous.
55. Blog entry dated 25 April 2008.
56. Dawa Lepcha cf. blog entry dated 25 April 2008.
57. The expenses of organizing the social movement are being met by a few Lepchas from their personal resources, with majority being unemployed youth; therefore, sustaining the campaign or organizing big rallies and events have been difficult.
58. On 5–6 December 2007 a 30-member delegation of Lepchas (including lamas) from Sikkim, Kalimpong, and Darjeeling with support of the Delhi Lepcha Association and other civil society organizations staged a sit-in at Jantar Mantar to bring national attention to their protests.
59. Much of my recent interaction and information elicitation was enabled by extended chatting.
60. They have become an integral part of the global indigenous people's movement.

REFERENCES

Arora, V. 2006a. 'The Forest of Symbols Embodied in the Tholung Sacred Landscape of North Sikkim, India', *Conservation and Society*, 4(1): 55–83.

———. 2006b. 'Texts and Contexts in Sikkim, India', in E. Arweck and P. Collins (eds), *Reading Religion in Texts and Context: Reflections of Faith and Practice in Religious Materials*. Aldershot: Ashgate.

———. 2006c. 'The Roots and the Route of Secularism in Sikkim', *Economic and Political Weekly*, 23 September, 41(38): 4063–71.

———. 2007a. 'Assertive Identities, Indigeneity and the Politics of Recognition as a Tribe: The Bhutias, the Lepchas and the Limbus of Sikkim', *Sociological Bulletin*, 56(2): 195–220.

———. 2007b. 'Unheard Voices of Protest in Sikkim', *Economic and Political Weekly*, 42: 3451–454.

———. 2008a. '"In the Name of Development, Do Not Make Us Refugees in Our Own Homeland"': Contestations around Public Interest and Development Planning in Northeast India'. *Proceedings of the International Conference of Planning History, University of Chicago, 2008*.

———. 2008b. 'Gandhigiri in Democratic Sikkim', *Economic and Political Weekly Economic and Political Weekly*, 20 September, 43(38): 27–28.

———. 2008c. *Routing the Commodities of the Empire through Sikkim (1817–1906)*, Commodities of the Empire Working Paper No.9, Open University and London Metropolitan University, United Kingdom, ISSN: 1756-0098.

———. 2009. '"They Are All Set to Dam(n) our Future": Contested Development through Hydel Power in Democratic Sikkim', *Sociological Bulletin*, January–April, 58(1): 94–114.

———. 2010. 'Walking the Shangri-La Sikkim Trail', in Debal K. Singha Roy (ed.), *Surviving Against Odds: The Marginalized in a Globalizing World*. Delhi: Manohar.

Brettell, C.B. 2006. 'Political Belonging and Cultural Belonging: Immigrant Status, Citizenship, and Identity among Four Immigrant Populations in a Southwestern City', *American Behavioural Scientist*, 50: 70–99.

Cohen, A. 1982. *Belonging: Identity and Social Organization in British Rural Cultures*. Manchester: Manchester University Press.

Foning, A.R. 1987. *Lepcha: My Vanishing Tribe*. Delhi: Sterling Publishers Ltd.

Friedman, J. 2004. 'Globalization, Transnationalization, and Migration: Ideologies and Realities of Global Transformation', in J. Friedman and S. Randeria (eds), *Worlds on the Move: Globalization, Migration, and Cultural Security*. London: I.B. Taurius.

Gorer, G. 1938. *Himalayan Village: An Account of the Lepchas of Sikkim*. London: Michael Joseph.

Gowloog, R.R. 1995. *Lingthem Revisited: Social Changes in a Lepcha Village of North Sikkim*. New Delhi: Har-Anand Publications.

Hooker, J. 1891. *Himalayan Journals or Notes of a Naturalist*. London, New York and Melbourne: Ward, Lock, Bowden and Co.

Kahn, R. and D. Kellner. 2005. 'Oppositional Politics and the Internet: A Critical/ Reconstructive Approach', *Cultural Politics*, 1: 75–100.

Kotturan, G. 1976. *Folk Tales of Sikkim*, 1st edition. New Delhi: Sterling Publishers.

———. 1983. *The Himalayan Gateway: History and Culture of Sikkim*. New Delhi: Sterling Publishers.

Lahiri, A., S. Chattopadhyay, and A. Bhasin. 2001. *Sikkim: The People's Vision*. Gangtok and Delhi: Government of Sikkim and Indus Publishing Company.

Lama, M.P. 2001. *Sikkim: Human Development Report 2001*. Delhi: Government of Sikkim, Social Science Press.

Pandit, M.K. 2007. *Carrying Capacity Study of Teesta Basin in Sikkim: Executive Summary and Recommendations*. Centre for Interdisciplinary Studies of Mountain and Hill Environment, University of Delhi.

Pfaff-Czarnecka, Joanna and Gérard Toffin. 2011. 'Introduction: Belonging and Multiple Attachments in Contemporary Himalayan Societies', in Joanna Pfaff-Czarnecka and Gérard Toffin (eds), *The Politics of Belonging in the Himalayas: Local Attachments and Boundary Dynamics*, Vol. 4, pp. xi–xxxviii. New Delhi: SAGE Publications.

Planning Commission. 2008. *Sikkim Development Report*. New Delhi: Planning Commission, Government of India and Academic Foundation.

Sassen, S. 2004. 'Local Actors in Global Politics', *Current Sociology*, 52(4): 649–70.

Siiger, H. 1967. *The Lepchas: Culture and Religion of a Himalayan People. Part I*. Copenhagen: National Museum of Denmark.

Siiger, H. and J. Rischel. 1967. *The Lepchas: Culture and Religion of a Himalayan People. Part II*. Copenhagen: National Museum of Denmark.

Tamsang, K.P. 1983. *The Unknown and Untold Reality about the Lepchas*. Kalimpong: Lyangsong Tamsang and Mani Printing Press.

Thomas, E.R. 2002. 'Who Belongs? Competing Ideas of Political Membership', *European Journal of Social Theory*, 5: 323–49.

Thurgood, G., J.A. Matistoff, and David Bradley (eds). 1985. *Linguistics of the Sino-Tibetan Area: The State of the Art*. Canberra: Department of Linguistics, the Australian National University.

PART V
NATIONAL RECONFIGURATIONS

Chapter 15

Mother Tongues and Language Competence

The Shifting Politics of Linguistic Belonging in the Himalayas

MARK TURIN

INTRODUCTION

'Hypocrisy is the essence of snobbery', says the protagonist and narrator of Alexander Theroux's *An Adultery*, 'but all snobbery is about the problem of belonging' (1987: 212). Although literary rather than sociological in genre, Theroux has identified the same process that Nira Yuval-Davis, following John Crowley, describes when she defines the politics of belonging as the 'dirty business of boundary maintenance' (2006: 203). Identities and statements of belonging are often formed, revised, and challenged at boundaries and borders (whether spatial, geographical, political, or—as I will suggest—linguistic), in large part because these are sites of accentuated political valence and heightened emotional attachment.

The now considerable corpus of literature on belonging has addressed the formation of ethnic categories, the rootedness of identities, and the interface of politics, power, and passion in the construction of a sense of self and the imagining of a nation. However, these studies are still predominantly European in focus and remain strangely quiet on issues of language identity and linguistic belonging. In *Globalization and Belonging*, Sheila Croucher is critical of the fact that:

identity is invoked as an explanation, but little effort is made to explain or understand identity itself ... the origins or essence of identity is taken for granted or rendered irrelevant. (2004: 36–37)

A similar critique may also be made for language: it is often cited as an integral component in personal identity formation and portrayed as central to concepts of belonging, but routinely under-analyzed. Drawing upon linguistic examples from across the Himalayan region, including Bhutan, Nepal, and the Indian state of Sikkim, I aim to situate language competence as important determinants and constituents of belonging. To do so, I first bring the literature of linguistic anthropology and identity to bear on the writings on belonging; I then turn to recent events in Nepal (and briefly in the United States) as examples of the emotive power of linguistic attachment; and finally, I discuss census-taking and surveys as classifying and classificatory tools that record, and even help to create, a sense of belonging.

I should end this introduction with a note to the effect that both the form and the substance of this chapter have changed from a presentation of field data on Sikkim (as envisaged) to a position on ways of thinking about belonging that explicitly incorporate language.[1] In part, this shift is an explicit attempt to avoid rehearsing the tired territory of identity politics, but it also stems from my reading of the literature on belonging and out of an increasing conviction in the utility of the concepts of linguistic competence and language heritage in making sense of belonging.

SITUATING LANGUAGE IN BELONGING

Linguistic anthropologists are acutely aware of the importance of language in the construction of personal and private identities, and the different modalities that shape such formations, but have said little about belonging. As we know, languages have been heavily implicated in the formation and formalization of nation states, with nation-building exercises across Europe and Asia predicated on unifying and binding people together using a single language, with a belief that national identity and a sense of belonging would naturally ensue. As de Varennes (1996) has shown, the process by which emergent European nation states imposed a single national language on linguistically diverse populations in the interest of fostering national unity has strong parallels in post-colonial Asia, where similar approaches, in the name of 'language planning' and unity, have foisted monolingual policy on multilingual communities. In many European nations, the 'naturalization' test for aspiring citizens requires that candidates demonstrate a communicative competence in the national language. In such cases, the ability to speak a language can act as a gatekeeping device to determine membership of a nation.

Reflecting on linguistic belonging, Bonnie Urciuoli summarizes one position as suggesting that "people act in ways that are taken as 'having' a language, which is equated to 'belonging' to an origin group" (1995: 525). This statement would resonate strongly with many ethnolinguistic activists and *Janajati* (indigenous nationality) organizations in Nepal, who believe that a one-to-one correlation between language and ethnicity (and the inalienability of both) exists, essential for the promotion of a distinct group identity within a nation state. As Urciuoli goes on to point out, however, language and group identity should not, by definition, be considered as isomorphic, and 'people do not always see language shift vitiating their cultural identity' (1995: 533). As I illustrate in this chapter, language shift is a dominant feature in the identity landscape of Sikkim, where language heritage, acting as shorthand for ethnicity, can trump linguistic competence in instilling and maintaining a sense of belonging.

Although Nepal (a diverse nation state home to many ethnolinguistic communities) and Sikkim (India's least populous and second smallest state) differ massively in scale and their historical trajectories, the utility of comparison between the two endures because their populations continue to draw on similar sets of ideas and narratives of belonging, in large part because they believe that they share elements of a common past. Furthermore, if we prioritize borders as highly articulated sites for creating ideologies of belonging, the Nepal–Sikkim border can serve as a useful case in point. As Urciuoli continues:

> Border-marking language elements are locational markers: They assign people a place, often opposing places between those who 'have' the language and those who do not. Borders are places where commonality ends abruptly; border-making language elements stand for and performatively bring into being such places. (1995: 539)

Even though state borders can become sites of highly articulated and performative displays of belonging, Andreas Wimmer (2008) reminds us that national boundaries are neither ahistorical nor uncontested. Working through his taxonomy of how actors are able to change ethnic boundaries and even redraw social borders, we can begin to conceive of national borders as 'notional borders', seeing them as important objects of inquiry in their own right rather than as rigid territorial units. Presenting a range of strategies that have been used for 'making and unmaking ethnic boundaries' (2008: 1043), Wimmer looks beyond typology and taxonomy to imagine an 'agency-based model of ethnic boundary making' (2008: 1046), one that could well be developed for application to linguistic boundaries and language borders.

In a volume on language and national identity in Asia, Andrew Simpson explores how language 'is and has been relevant for the cultivation of nationalistic feelings of belonging' (2007: 3). He makes the point that language differences are not only more accentuated at national borders but that language itself is often invoked in boundary keeping and maintenance:

> As a symbolic marker and index of individual and group identity, language has the potential to function as an important boundary device. (2007: 1)

One notable difference between Nepal and Sikkim is in their experience of migration: Nepal has a tradition of 'sending' migrants, whereas Sikkim is a state that has accepted and 'received' them, even building itself on their labour. Peter Sutton observes that:

> As migration increases and monocultural nation-states become obsolete, cultural identity becomes more complex, less tied to a geographical location, more individualized, and less static. (1991: 136)

The different historical experiences of migration may, in part, account for the different expressions of linguistic belonging as they are articulated in Sikkim and Nepal. Yet Nepal to Sikkim migratory movements are in themselves unusual: in his influential 2006 book *A Nation by Design*, Aristide Zolberg illustrates how most labour migration brings in people who differ culturally, linguistically, ethnically, and religiously from the bulk of the established population already settled in the host country. The story of the Nepali migration to the eastern hills of India, however, is more one of ethnolinguistic continuity than rupture, unlike most other modern migratory narratives.

In Sikkim, the loss of speech forms and the process of language shift are popularly presented as unavoidable by-products of the juggernaut of global progress and development, whereas in Nepal, the continued vibrancy of minority mother tongues has been associated with their remote and sequestered status. This opposition, at least in the popular imagination, is fleshed out to the extent that Sikkim is often portrayed in the press as modern, literate, educated, and connected, whereas the ethnolinguistic homeland areas in Nepal are widely described as remote, backward, and traditional. My point here is not to endorse such descriptions, but to reflect on them for what they tell us about the forms of belonging that individuals and communities may invoke or be subjected to, and what these ideological formulations tell us about the different nation-building exercise in Nepal and India.

Patterns of language shift as well as transformations in linguistic identities are familiar territory for linguists. The late Michael Noonan, writing about Chantyal-speaking villages in western Nepal, suggested that their 'relative isolation and poverty' might contribute to 'the retention of the language' (1996: 130). Although out-migration may even prolong isolation for those left behind, in-migration brings individuals together in unexpected ways, sometimes creating new speech forms and often elevating regional tongues to the status of *lingua franca* or *Verkehrsprache*.

Over the last two decades, some linguistic anthropologists have turned their investigations away from semiotics and 'ethnographies of speaking' to refocus on the ways that speech communities maintain and manage their borders to create a sense of cohesion or group belonging. Michael Silverstein has referred to this repositioning as "the dynamic linguistic anthropology of what we might term 'local language communities' investigated as dialectically constituted cultural forms" (1998: 401). This approach takes literally the proposition that, through group action,

> people participate in semiotic processes that produce their identities, beliefs, and their particular senses of agentive subjectivity. It considers culture to be a virtual—and always emergent—site in socio-historical spacetime with respect to the essentialisms of which such agents experience their groupness. (Silverstein, 1998: 402)

Although phrased somewhat differently, these concerns effectively dovetail with the emerging field of research on belonging. When Nira Yuval-Davis describes belonging as a 'thicker' concept than that of citizenship, suggesting that 'it is not just about membership, rights and duties, but also about the emotions that such memberships evoke' (2004: 215), it reminds us of Silverstein's words. In short, we must position language practice and linguistic identification within discussions of belonging, and connect with linguists and anthropologists for whom speech forms and the emotions that they elicit have long been explicit objects of study.

HINDI VERSUS NEPALI, OR ENGLISH AND DZONGKHA AS 'GLUE'

Paul Brass writes of language movements as 'inherently and necessarily associated with the modern state and modern politics' (2004: 353). This statement holds both at the level of national state-building around a language (sometimes even more than one) and at level of the counter-assertion by language activists that citizenship and nationhood need not be predicated on a sole speech form. In fact, if the process of nation formation were not so linguistically homogenizing, local language movements would likely not have emerged with such force and vigour.

When effective politicians invoke the emotive, political, and boundary-maintaining power of language in the rhetoric of their speeches, they also use specific languages to lay claim to domains of belonging. Just as minority language identities are often forged because of struggle and protest in opposition to dominant linguistic ideologies mandated by the nation state and underwritten by its legislation, the speakers of hegemonic languages may assert themselves when they feel insecure or under threat. A timely illustration of such a tension was Nepal's first Vice President Parmananda Jha's oath taking in Hindi in 2008, which unleashed five days of angry demonstrations in Kathmandu and a lawsuit against him in the country's Supreme Court.

Vice President Jha asserted that Hindi was widely used in Nepal and should be classed as an official language. 'I translated the oath into Hindi so as to convenience the people of southern Nepal, who speak such languages as Maithili, Bhojpuri, and Awadhi. And Hindi is considered as our medium language', he told the BBC.[2] However, most analysts agree that Jha's primary motive for speaking in Hindi was political (perhaps even at the request of the Madhesi Janadhikar Forum, whose leaders have a policy of debating in Hindi at public events), and that he was only secondarily invoking a linguistic right to speak in a language easy for Tarai-dwellers to understand. If his objective had been to generate a sense of belonging and inclusion, as he was asked by the newspaper *Naya Patrika*, why did he not take the oath in his native Maithili, in the manner that Matrika Yadav had done, and avoid the political fallout? Jha's answer was that he even uses Hindi to converse with his wife, a Bhojpuri speaker, which would make Hindi their family *lingua franca* and therefore a language inextricably bound up with his personal sense of self and emotional and familial belonging.

To situate this debate in its proper context, we should recall that Maithili has come to be regarded as one of Nepal's minority languages, whereas Hindi is still perceived by many Nepalis to be a dominant and domineering language primarily associated with India, even if it is spoken by over 105,000 Nepali citizens as a mother tongue (as reported in the 2001 Census of Nepal). Such associations make Jha's decision to speak Hindi provocative, earning him a reputation in some circles as politically expedient. In the heightened political context of Parmananda Jha's oath taking, columnist Prashant Jha's riposte in the *Nepali Times* focused on the Vice President's linguistic choice rather than the symbolic associations that he was invoking:

> How is Hindi a Nepali language when Pahadis use it to communicate in the Tarai, but is an Indian language when Madhesis use it to speak to each other or in public? (2008: 10)

To clarify: at issue with Parmananda Jha's choice of language was not that it was linguistically incorrect (from a dispassionate perspective, his choice might even be commended), but that it was widely perceived to be politically inappropriate and even inflammatory, evinced by the fact that 'once all sides met their political objectives, the confrontation fizzled out' (Jha, 2008: 10).

The caustic backlash by some commentators to the Vice President's choice of language (in both *langue* and *parole* in this case) illustrates the force unleashed when politics intersects with language. It also reminds us of the ever-emotive power of linguistic attachment and confirms the special place that some accord the Nepali language in the collective imagining of what it means to be Nepali, and thus belong to Nepal (see Chalmers, 2007). Writing in *Kantipur*, journalist Dhirendra Premarshi was shocked by 'Madhesi leaders who start blabbering in Hindi' and proposed that Jha's effort to 'sideline Nepali is being seen by many as a matricidal act' (translated and reported in the *Nepali Times*, #411, page 6). Premarshi's polemical point was that within the borders of Nepal, Nepali is 'spoken' but Hindi can only be 'babbled', and then only as an alien and degraded speech form. Far worse, in fact, Hindi speaking is a desecration of the motherland and therefore anti-national (leaving aside any allusions to the matricide of the Palace Massacre of 2001).

In his detailed coverage of the events that followed, writing for *Kantipur.com*, commentator Puran P. Bista remained perplexed by Jha's inexcusable mistake:

> Obviously, the vice-president who speaks perfect Nepali deliberately uttered Hindi instead of reading the text in Nepali. (4 August 2008)

Bista's position echoes sentiments heard across the political spectrum in Nepal: although speaking Hindi spontaneously and without mal-intent may be pardoned, why would someone who is able to speak Nepali choose not to do so? How should such flagrant disregard for national sentiment be understood and forgiven? The answer is that to some it was unforgivable, with Nepal's Supreme Court deciding a year after the event that Jha must retake the oath in Nepali for it to have legal and constitutional weight.

These strong reactions are reminiscent of another ongoing and heated debate played out in a distant country whose principal language is as unthreatened and secure as Nepali, but is nevertheless perceived by an increasingly vocal minority to be under attack: English in the United States. In the United States, and to a lesser extent in Nepal, the self-consciousness of the nation is flagged by the use of a common language as an indelible part of its heritage, and, as Pier Guiseppe Monateri has written, 'as a constituent of its cultural peculiarity' (1999: 124).

While in its 200-year history, the United States has never yet seen fit to adopt an official language, a campaign to 'officialize' English has gathered momentum in recent years, 'resting on the claim that the most successful and dominant world language is threatened in its bastion: the USA' (Monateri, 1999: 124). However, as Zolberg has shown, a sense of North American linguistic fragility is far from new, with many US leaders (including Benjamin Franklin and Thomas Jefferson) expressing deep concerns about growing immigration from the German empire, as the German language that the migrants carried with them was considered to reflect a culture incompatible with republican democracy.

In June 1995, Newt Gingrich informed a group of Iowa business leaders that: 'English has to be our common language, otherwise we're not going to have a civilization' (Thursday, 8 June 1995, in section A, page 22 of the *New York Times*). Only a few months later, Robert 'Bob' Dole, gearing up to be the Republic presidential candidate, announced to the 77th national convention of the American Legion in Indiana:

> Insisting that all our citizens are fluent in English is a welcoming act of inclusion. We need the glue of language to help hold us together. We must stop the practice of multilingual education as a means of instilling ethnic pride or as a therapy for low self-esteem or out of elitist guilt over a culture built on the traditions of the West. (Dole, 1995)

There are many rhetorical flourishes worth analyzing in Gingrich and Dole's proclamations, in particular the promise of a Babel-like end of society if the shared tongue is lost, the apparent oxymoron that 'inclusion' can somehow be 'insisted' upon, and Dole's choice of the term 'glue' for the collective sense of belonging that language instils. Besides the ideological posturing, though, these strident statements echo a common concern that plurilingualism and particularly bilingual education programmes are a force of social decomposition and national disunification, fuelling a change 'from a nation of individuals to a loose conglomeration of groups' (Croucher, 2004: 192). The sum of these atomized and individualized identities, the argument supposes, will no longer cohere into a sense of belonging and would also effectively exclude Spanish-speaking citizens in the United States.

The underlying positions in this debate are elegantly analyzed in an article by Aristide Zolberg and Long Litt Woon, entitled 'Why Islam is like Spanish'. Arguing that both Islam and Spanish have become metonyms for the perceived dangers of immigration—namely, a loss of cultural identity, disintegration, separatism, and communal conflict—the authors show how Islam in Europe can be understood as structurally similar to Spanish in the United States. In the United States, 'the English language emerged very early on as a crucial unifying element, entrusted with the mission of balancing ... diversity' (1999: 7). Seen from this perspective, then, the expanding reach of Spanish, the 'common speech of an expanding population', feeds 'fantasies of a malignant growth that threatens national unity' (ibid.).

Although geographically removed from our present focus on the Himalayas, the apparent incongruity between a language's unmistakable strength and its assumed vulnerability in North America is worth a moment's reflection, as it resonates with sentiments expressed across the Himalayas, but played out differently in each nation. Alessandro Simoni suggests that the Bhutanese state has endorsed a 'division of labour' between English and Dzongkha, in which English is a 'code of rules' (2003: 52) and the 'tool required for operating the legal machinery borrowed from the West' (2003: 51), whereas Dzongkha maintains the position of "social glue", of defense against cultural alienation, of brick stone of national identity [sic]" (2003: 52). Although such clear domains of use may be what the Bhutanese authorities desire, can such divisions ever be so clear-cut? Moreover, where does this leave Nepali, a language spoken as a *lingua franca* by so many Bhutanese of all ethnic backgrounds and a speech form about which Simoni and the national powers of Bhutan are regrettably silent? It appears that the Bhutanese authorities have resorted to patrolling their socio-linguistic borders by invoking purism and tradition, demarcating their boundaries with legal mechanisms such as the 2005 constitution, which positions Dzongkha as the only national language.

We should recall that all projects involving ethnic categorization and linguistic classification are fraught with taxonomic, political, and ideological problems, often compressing complex and highly local ethnolinguistic identities into standardized checkboxes. There is a sizeable literature on 'colonial linguistics', which lays bare the power relations involved in mapping 'monolithic languages onto demarcated boundaries' (Errington, 2001: 24). Nation-building projects not only objectify languages through documentation but also inhibit the spread of some speech forms in the name of elevating a favoured vernacular to the status of national or official language. For the moment, we may focus on the emotive rather than on the hegemonic side of classification through surveying and census-taking, described so elegantly by N. Gerald Barrier in his writing on Imperial India:

> Thus from its beginning a census acts to reshape the world it will examine and in this way is not simply a passive instrument ... individuals find themselves firmly fixed as members in various groups of a particular dimensions and substance. Thus the census imposes order, and order of a statistical nature. In time the creation of a new ordering of society by the census will act to reshape that which the census sought merely to describe. (1981: 74–75)

CENSUS AS CLASSIFICATION, SURVEYS TO CREATE BELONGING

A census is the single most important statistical operation for most national populations. Although the methodology and motivations for the decadal census in Nepal and India are similar, the questions that are posed are not equivalent. The Indian census enumerates for mother tongue but not for ethnicity, whereas the Nepali census seeks responses in both categories, and has recently included an additional question on bilingualism. For those who work in cultural Tibet, it may be relevant to note that the 1990 census of China collected 15 categories of information for each individual, one of which was 'nationality', but that there was no question on language (Jianfa Shen et al., 1999: 176).

According to census enumerators and statisticians, only a census can provide 'uniform information both about the country as a whole and about individual areas' as the continuity of statistics from census to census 'shows how conditions are changing over time' (Sillitoe and White, 1992: 142). A baseline linguistic survey can be a helpful, and usually additional, tool for effective policy planning in education, media, and the public sphere. The decadal Indian census returns very little data on monolingualism, bilingualism, and multilingualism, and does not investigate the levels of retention of officially recognized minority languages.

The Linguistic Survey of Sikkim (LSS), administered through the Namgyal Institute of Tibetology in Gangtok with the support of the Department of Human Resource Development (formerly Education) of the State Government of Sikkim, was designed to generate a better understanding of the complex reality of language use and to evaluate language teaching in government and private schools across the state. When I initiated the survey in 2004, there was still no official confirmation that the Central Institute of Indian Languages (CIIL) in Mysore would undertake a new national linguistic survey. The go-ahead for the 'New Linguistic Survey of India' came only in late 2006, and more recent reports indicate that the implementation has been held back because of funding troubles.[3]

According to an early report in *The Hindu*, the New Linguistic Survey of India would involve at least 10,000 linguists and language experts, nearly 100 universities, and would be conducted over a period of 10 years at a cost of ₹280 crore, with the aim of describing and documenting each speech variety in the nation. The announcement of this massively ambitious project was good fortune for those involved in the LSS, because it permitted a refocusing on the issues that most interested us: mother tongue instruction, language competence, heritage identity, and belonging.

Over a period of a little over a year, the linguistic survey field team travelled to Sikkim's four districts visiting more than 120 of the state's 157 secondary schools and administering a 29-question survey on language use to over 17,000 students and teachers. Included in the survey were questions on which language(s) the respondent speaks with his or her parents, grandparents, and siblings; which languages a respondent's kin speak with one another; how many languages the respondent could speak and write, and which ones; questions on the different domains and registers of language use (songs, lists, numbers, TV); and which language the respondent identifies as his or her mother tongue. A survey form is enclosed as an appendix to this chapter for readers interested in the questions. Some of the findings and their implications for discussions of belonging follow below, but I would first like to focus on the issue of self-classification.

The contrast between etic statements about belonging and emic experiences of belonging is not new: 'interviews fail to get at the difference between peoples' professed and actual behavior' (Collins, 1988: 304). Most censuses and surveys rely exclusively on respondent statements and are almost by definition non-ethnographic. The literature on the formulation of census questions indicates a movement towards recognizing the virtues of respondent-led classification rather than concealing it as a methodological flaw. Although not referring explicitly to census-taking, Joane Nagel's point that 'the extent to which ethnicity can be freely constructed by individuals or groups is quite narrow when compulsory ethnic categories are imposed by others' (1994: 156) is well taken. Although identities and belonging may be assigned by organizations, states, census bureaus, politicians, and dominant social groups, individuals and groups are 'not merely passive recipients in the process' (Croucher, 2004: 40), and some consciously choose to subvert classificatory systems that are imposed on them. Permitting, or even encouraging, respondents to classify themselves works to equalize relationships of power and, as the discussion below illustrates, may even generate a more interesting dataset.

In Mauritius, for example, the 'onus of ethnic classification was thus shifted from the enumerator to the individual' making the census far more effective (Christopher, 1992: 59), whereas a report on the configuration of the 1991 census of Great Britain recommended that the form of a question 'should enable people to identify themselves in a way acceptable to them' (Sillitoe and White, 1992: 148). Returning to linguistic surveys, Paul Brass endorses such realignment:

> I believe that the only fair and honest census of languages is one that accepts what the respondent says and notes it down. My point is simply this: the decisions concerning grouping, classification, recognition, are ultimately political decisions, not scientific linguistic ones. (2004: 367)

As the data below illustrate, the results of the Linguistic Survey of Sikkim are not scientific evaluations of competence in a language, but rather statements of linguistic belonging.

PRELIMINARY FINDINGS FROM THE LINGUISTIC SURVEY OF SIKKIM

There are three main findings of the survey to be discussed here. First, the identification of a mother tongue; second, the process of language shift; and third, the issue of multilingualism and education.

Question 7 of the survey asks respondents 'Which languages can you speak?' whereas question 22 asks 'Which language is your mother tongue?' The results of these two questions are shown in the following table:

	Can speak the language (%)	Mother tongue (%)
Nepali	94	67
English	74	1
Hindi	67	7
Bhutia	7	10
Lepcha	5	6
Limbu	3	4

A few points are worth drawing attention to. First, the table can be divided into two categories: languages with more speakers than mother tongue claimants, versus languages with more mother tongue claimants than speakers. The first cluster includes Nepali, spoken (to some level) by nearly all surveyed school-going students in Sikkim, but claimed by only two-thirds as a mother tongue; English, claimed as a mother tongue by only 1 per cent of the school-going population, but spoken by three-quarters (to some degree of proficiency); and Hindi, which follows a similar pattern to English, albeit less extreme.

The most interesting results are to be found in the second half of the table in the responses for Bhutia (also known as Denzongke, Löke, and Sikkimese), Lepcha (also enumerated as Rongaring), and Limbu (variously spelled as Limboo, but also returned as Subba): all three are claimed by more young people as a mother tongue than can speak them. At first glance, this claim appears to be contradictory, at least from the perspective of linguistic competence: How can an individual profess to have as a mother tongue a language in which he or she has no declared proficiency? Are these respondents, particularly the Bhutia students for whom the differential is the greatest (3 per cent), not subverting the survey to bolster their numbers for political gain? Unpacking this apparent inconsistency lies at the heart of understanding linguistic belonging in Sikkim.

The autochthonous languages of modern Sikkim—Bhutia, Lepcha, and Limbu—are at present severely endangered. Besides a few notable areas (parts of North Sikkim for Bhutia, the Dzongu reservation for Lepcha, and West Sikkim for Limbu), these three languages are spoken by an ever-dwindling number of people, and the majority of children from these communities have only basic proficiency at best. The first census of Sikkim dates back to 1891 when Sikkim was under British colonial rule. The total population of Sikkim was then recorded as 30,458, of which a little over one-third constituted the indigenous Lepcha and Bhutia populations. This early census and some later surveys recorded ethnic affiliation only, and contained no explicit data on which languages were spoken or by how many people. According to the 1931 Census, out of a total population of 109,808, 12 per cent were Lepcha and 11 per cent were Bhutia, the rest mainly Nepalese. The 1961 Census reported that 43 mother tongues were spoken in Sikkim, whereas the 1971 Census Report gave the percentage of population by language, according to which speakers of the Nepali language constituted about 64 per cent, whereas the Lepcha and Bhutia languages were each spoken by about 11 per cent of the total population. On 17 October 1977, the Sikkim Official Language Act was passed by the Governor of the State, adopting Nepali, Bhutia, and Lepcha as 'the languages to be used for the official purposes of the State of Sikkim'.

There are a few general points worth making about the census statistics for language and ethnicity collected from Sikkim at decadal intervals over the course of a century. First, there is no doubt that many Lepchas and Bhutias, two of Sikkim's Scheduled Tribes, are now speaking ever more Nepali and Hindi. Second, many of those individuals more recently recorded as speaking Nepali as their mother tongue are members of non-caste and non-Hindu ethnic groups of Nepalese origin, that is Tamang, Gurung, Rai, and others. Third, disaggregated language data from 2001 are expected to confirm the trend towards Nepali, a linguistic shift occurring across other parts of the Indian northeast as well as within Nepal itself. Finally, we may wonder why the Bhutia speech community decreased since the 1960s whereas the Lepcha speech community remained relatively stable, according to government figures, at least. A working hypothesis is that the difference between the speech patterns and language retention of these communities can be attributed to their different economic statuses and locations. Many Bhutias have had better access to education over the last 40 years, and some of their larger population concentrations are increasingly urban (correlated with a decreased use of their ethnic mother tongue). In contrast, the Lepcha community is still largely rural, providing an ongoing context for the mother tongue to be spoken, particularly in protected or remoter areas such as Dzongu.

As competence in Sikkim's traditional mother tongues has declined, however, their status has begun to shift from spoken vernaculars forming a part of a lived ethnic identity, to symbolic markers of an ancestral heritage, and elements of emotional belonging. Yuval-Davis' observation that belonging 'becomes articulated and politicized only when it is threatened in some way' (2006: 196) is very pertinent to the language shift observed in Sikkim, in which a growing attachment to the 'idea' of a mother tongue is directly related to its decline in use as a speech form.

Alongside these emotional attachments are important political motivations that underlie claims of linguistic belonging. Even though the Lepcha, Limbu, and Bhutia languages are on the wane as spoken vernaculars, these speech communities have waged successful campaigns to be accorded 'Scheduled Tribe' status, and an application is presently under review for Lepchas to be classified as a 'Primitive Tribe'. An integral component of such applications is the existence, both real and abstract, of a mother tongue. Declining utility and diminishing speaker numbers, then, do not necessarily threaten the inalienable connection between a tribe and their traditional language and their 'right' to have a mother tongue.

Fernand de Varennes is a respected authority on such 'rights' of linguistic minorities, whose comprehensive 1996 work aimed to establish language rights as fundamental human rights, once and for all. Using case studies of international human rights law to illustrate how minority languages and their speakers can be protected, he makes a compelling case for three areas of human rights legislation being pertinent and appropriate to linguistic claims: the right to freedom of expression, the right to non-discrimination and the right of individuals to use their minority language with other members of their community. Although his fighting prose is certainly a boon to language activists around the world seeking to preserve, promote, and revitalize endangered speech forms that have been marginalized in the name of nation building, the field data from Sikkim open up a new avenue of inquiry: the 'right', perhaps even the need, to have, own, and deploy a language, specifically as a mother tongue, without using it.

From observations during the survey process and analysis of the returns, students answered the question on their mother tongue in a number of different ways. Some wrote down what language they spoke at home, others wrote down the name of the language that they thought they should speak at home, some read the question as another way of asking for their ethnicity (mother tongue in lieu of caste or tribe), and some understood it to be a question on heritage and origin. Others simply asked their teacher what to put down. In other words, respondents answered this open-ended question by filling it with whatever meaning they found most appropriate.

The issue of language shift has been variously understood, explained, and defined by different writers, but is traditionally characterized as a process in which both *langue* and *parole* are systematically simplified. Individuals move from functioning as full speakers with complete grammatical and pragmatic command to being 'semi-speakers' with reduced verbal dexterity. Eventually, all competence drains away, leaving only a residual smattering of specialized vocabulary (food words, kinship terminology, or elements of ritual vocabulary), and often a strong sense of attachment to a heritage identity as a former speaker.

Language activists such as Philippe van Parijs accentuate the hegemonic aspects of this process, talking of the 'displacement of local by national languages' and underscoring the assertion of state power (2000: 218). In this argument, language shift or replacement is seen as a product of projects of modernity: languages can coexist for centuries when there is little or no contact between groups, but the 'nicer people are with one another, the nastier languages are with one another' (van Parijs 2000: 218). Once a particular language has taken the lead, more and more people will converge towards the same vernacular, quickly promoting it to the level of a *lingua franca*.

The processes of linguistic convergence and language shift are in fact not as straightforward as van Parijs would have us believe. 'Language shifts are inextricably tied to shifts in the political economy in which speech situations are located' writes Urciuoli (1995: 530), and Sikkim is undergoing a period of profound social, economic, and political upheaval.

There are effectively three *linguas franca* or *linguae francae* in Sikkim—Nepali, English, and Hindi—all of which operate in different functional domains of use yet constantly intersect with one another. The pragmatic utility of all three languages in Sikkim—Nepali in the bazaar, English in school, and Hindi on television and in Central government offices—prevents any one of them from becoming overly dominant. In the process of language shift, then, which Sikkim is undergoing, a region can experience an explosion of plurilingualism.[4] In anything other than abstract models, one language does not give way to another overnight, and a number of speech forms remain in use for long periods of time until the linguistic residue settles. Data from the linguistic survey of Sikkim would support this analysis: while only 2 per cent of the respondents reported as speaking five or more languages, 20 per cent claimed to speak four languages, 63 per cent three languages, 11 per cent two languages, and under 4 per cent only one language.

The speech of some Sikkimese students would offend the ear of a language purist: young men and women pepper their Lepcha or Bhutia with Nepali verbs, English sentiments, and Hindi conjunctions, in much the same way that urban, educated elites in Nepal can be heard to do. The resultant amalgam is a heterogeneous blend of linguistic forms and elements, and a performative strategy that is rapidly gaining ground in Sikkim as well as in Nepal's urban centres. Is this but another indication of language shift or a sign of the emergence of a hyphenated linguistic identity? And what do such linguistic fusions mean for belonging?

In Sikkim, language competence and purity do not have primary roles in the maintenance of individual identities and in the construction of a sense of group belonging. But then Sikkim is not one of India's 'linguistic states' in the model of Gujarat, Tamil Nadu, or West Bengal, where the 'internal reorganization of much of its territory … has been a deliberate attempt to consolidate populations of speakers of regional languages and concentrate these in administrative units, helping promote the strength of [these] languages' (Simpson, 2007: 25). In Sikkim, ethnic and linguistic identities are not oppositional (i.e. 'he is Tamang, but he doesn't speak it'), rather they are more incorporative (i.e. 'although she's Lepcha, she speaks Nepali pretty well'). Additionally, linguistic identities are increasingly understood and expected to be complex.

Perhaps as a consequence of massive in-migration, considerable intermarriage between groups, an administration that recognizes and rewards diversity, the presence of sufficient resources to avoid intense ethnic competition, or a combination of all of these conditions, there is an almost post-modernist rejection of 'totalizing meta-narratives', and in their stead an acknowledgement of the 'multiple, shifting and, at times, nonsynchronous identities' that are the norm for individuals (May et al., 2004: 10). In Sikkim, then, speaking a language—or perhaps more saliently, 'not' speaking a language—is not a diagnostic marker of ethnic identity or belonging. Linguistic belonging increasingly lies not in performance, but in history. From a legal perspective, one may speak of the 'right' to not use and not speak a language, but invoke it nevertheless as a primary form of symbolic attachment. As one student answered my clearly naive query on the apparent disconnect between his avowed lack of proficiency in a language and his answer to question 22 of the survey: 'Of course we have a mother tongue, I just don't speak it'.

However, if spoken or written competence is not so highly prized, why are so many students learning their ancestral language in schools across Sikkim? Along with other commentators, I have congratulated the Sikkimese government for offering minority languages as subjects in the school curriculum. To be clear, the medium of instruction across Sikkim is English, but Lepcha, Limbu, Newar, or Rai (and many other languages) may be taken as additional subjects by students who hail from these communities. Yet we should not assume that the students who opt for these classes are actually being taught the language in order to use it, or that they are being steeped in the performative skill that true competence entails. Rather, through the prism of language, they are learning mostly heritage, culture, history, and ancestry. In fact, these students are 'learning belonging', because the utility of such languages to young Sikkimese is now as markers of belonging rather than as vernaculars for daily use. Moreover, it is precisely because these languages now have emotional, symbolic, and political importance, rather than practical utility, that the Government of Sikkim can afford to teach them. Once again, we hear an echo of Zolberg's writing on the history of migration to the United States, where he demonstrates how the development of cheap printing technology (in Sikkim we may think of school books as well) led to a proliferation of newspapers in the immigrants' mother tongues, contributing to the formation of hyphenated identities.

We should therefore not be surprised when initiatives to bring Newar teachers from Kathmandu (cf. Pariyar, Shrestha, and Gellner's chapter, this volume) to teach Nepal Bhasa in Sikkim fail, as the aims of the instructors and the students are most likely quite different: Newar teachers come to these classes to revive their language among migrant Newars in Sikkim, whereas the latter attend the classes to learn the symbols and metaphors of ancestry. In Nepal, by way of comparison, where minority languages are still spoken, language competence continues to be a core marker of ethnic and individual identity for most speakers.

ELITES, CLASS, AND BELONGING: FURTHER AVENUES FOR INQUIRY

The results of the Sikkim language survey offer interesting insights into a number of issues, including correlations with gender, region, age, and kind of school (government or private), but there is no space to address these here. The full results will be provided to the Sikkimese government in the future. For now, I would like to conclude with a few thoughts on elites and their relationship to language.

David Gellner (1997) has noted the incongruity in the positions taken by language and culture activists in Nepal who promote the use of indigenous languages but pay for their own children's education in Nepali or even English medium schools. Are such activists claiming the right to a language at the same time as asserting the right not to speak and propagate it? As Simpson has noted, this reflects a wider trope across South Asia, and may even hold true for national languages, where one finds 'elite groups in many countries who may function almost fully in English and are perceived as being considerably detached from other members of their ethnic groups and may not be not proficient in the national language of their country' (2007: 16). This inconsistency has not escaped the attention of more grassroots language campaigners, who perceive ethnic elites to be jealously guarding their proficiency in the very languages that have helped further their own advancement while at the same time wanting, or even needing, the homeland language to be maintained by their rural cousins. Such advocacy positions can become conflicted and contested, as Yuval-Davis notes for what she calls 'political agents', who:

> struggle both for the promotion of their specific position in the construction of their collectivity and its boundaries and, at the same time, use these ideologies and positions in order to promote their own power positions within and outside the collectivity. (2006: 204)

In the case of Nepal, it is almost a truism to suggest that articulations of language identity grow and change as competence in the speech form declines. As Sheila Croucher reminds us, 'inherent in the concept and practice of belonging is the related reality of fear of not belonging' (2004: 40), and for many non-speakers of a language, a sense of emotional belonging is all that can be rescued from the ashes of dwindling linguistic proficiency.

For Tamangs who speak Tamang, or among Newars for whom Nepal *Bhasa* is still the reality of daily familial interaction, language remains embedded in practice, and the belonging that it indexes continues to be implicit. However, for members of such communities who have little or no competence in their traditional or heritage mother tongue, what matters is the existence, ongoing vitality of, and even belief in the language rather than their ability to speak it. Language has become heritage and an inalienable right, and belonging can become invoked in more explicit ways as a consequence.

Related to the issue of competence is that of purity, which once again appears to matter more to non-speakers than it does to speakers. How often does one hear a fluent speaker of Thangmi complaining about the pervasiveness of Nepali loan words in his language? Not very often, because the incorporation of loan words from Nepali or Newar may not even be noticed, or if it is, then promoted as a practical strategy for linguistic survival. In fact, as some have argued, the incorporation of loan words is a key strategy for ensuring the continued vibrancy, relevance, and longevity of smaller languages whose lexical inventories were historically modest.

Where does this leave English as it is spoken in Nepal and Sikkim? The short answer is that English continues to be a language of class and education, its role in education being fired by 'pragmatically driven public demand' (Simpson, 2007: 15). English is not a language of territorial identity in traditional terms, but is very much a language of globalized access, which makes English almost anti-territorial. English is also a language of belonging and group attachment, but belonging to a class rather than an ethnicity. In Sikkim, English is additionally the medium of instruction in all schools, breaking down elite associations somewhat, although not entirely. At face value, at least according to the national Indian narrative underscoring the equality of access, the prevalence of English as a medium of instruction benefits all communities. In reality, as de Varennes has shown, it is a false argument to suggest that by imposing a single language upon all individuals, the state is in effect treating everyone equally. The range of aptitude in English is enormous across Sikkim, illustrated by the fact that only 74 per cent of all students surveyed claim to speak English whereas 88 per cent write it. Which language the remaining 12 per cent write in when their teachers are instructing them in English is up for debate.

Schools themselves are important sites and sources of belonging, creating associations of community through instruction and curricular content. In Sikkim's government schools, when students learn Lepcha or Bhutia, local cultural content is only one component of what is taught. As they progress through school, books on Lepcha culture gradually give way to narratives of national history written in Lepcha.

Belonging, then, 'necessitates and implies boundaries' (Croucher, 2004: 40), and schools are just one location where these boundaries can be instilled and reproduced. Belonging does not just happen, but requires action and agency, and is achieved through boundary maintenance. 'Social actors bring into being a sense of boundedness, which may also map onto a border', writes Urciuoli (1995: 531), but some communities transcend borders and many boundaries exist only in the mind. The Lepchas of Sikkim, for example, patrol multiple boundaries comprising the various aspects of their identity against encroachment from outsiders: their exclusive status as a primitive tribe, their homeland reservation of Dzongu against hydropower interests, and their political and cultural rights in Sikkim—a state that many Lepchas believe originally 'belonged' to them. At the same time that this Lepcha sense of belonging is being maintained, even supported by the state, a sense of Indian belonging is being produced, and the two processes are not mutually exclusive. Local languages such as Bhutia and Lepcha, then, are co-opted into the larger regional and national project of creating a sense of Indian belonging: becoming Indian through being Sikkimese, becoming Sikkimese by being Lepcha. Andrew Simpson makes a related point when he argues that:

> A strengthening of national identities in Asia based on local language and culture might therefore also not be an unlikely by-product of increased globalization in certain instances. (2007: 27)

Although the borders between Nepal and India are very real, they are also very thin, and in some ways the countries may be seen to be converging in how they approach attachment and belonging. In Nepal in particular, the identity landscape is fast changing. In his study of

Chantyal over a decade ago, Noonan observed that 'knowledge of the language is no longer at the core of ethnic identity, as it once must have been' (1996: 135) and that "'Chantyalness', therefore, does not include the ability to speak Chantyal among its characterizing features" (1996: 133). It is only a small step from this to having a mother tongue in which one has no mastery.

Paul Brass's statement that 'it is probably more often the case that one defends one's mother tongue when one cannot speak at all or well a language of wider communication' (2004: 365–66) is not borne out or supported by the examples that I have provided in this chapter. On the contrary, I would suggest that it is usually the elites who defend languages—sometimes even languages that need no defence such as English and Nepali—while marginalized monolinguals aspire to bilingualism. No surprise then, that battles for linguistic representation are not usually fought by the politically marginalized if linguistically competent, but waged rather by the politically strong (if linguistically incompetent) who invoke the rights of the disenfranchised in order to construct their own sense of belonging to a community of speakers whose language they may not speak.

APPENDIX

Namgyal Institute of Tibetology   Gangtok, Sikkim

Linguistic Survey of Sikkim:
Part I - Language in Education and Schools

Date:

1. What is your full name ? _____ Male / Female

2. What is the name of your school ? _____

3. In what class do you study ? _____ 4. How old are you ? _____

5. How many languages can you speak ? _____ 6. How many languages can you write ? _____

7. Which languages can you speak ? _____

8. Which languages can you write ? _____

9. Which language(s) do you speak with your mother ? _____

10. Which language(s) do you speak with your father ? _____

11. Which language(s) do your parents speak together ? _____

12. Which language(s) do you speak with your grandparents ? _____

13. Which language(s) do your grandparents speak together ? _____

14. Which language(s) do your parents speak with your grandparents ? _____

15. Which language(s) do you speak with your brothers and sisters ? _____

16. Which language(s) do you speak with your school friends in break ? _____

17. If you have to write a letter, which language do you write it in ? _____

18. If you have to write a shopping list, which language do you write it in ? _____

19. If you know any songs, in which language(s) are they ? _____

20. If you know any poems, in which language(s) are they ? _____

21. If you watch TV, in which language(s) are the programmes that you watch ? _____

22. Which language is your mother tongue ? _____

23. Which languages are you now learning in school ? _____

24. Which of these languages is most important to you, and why ? _____

_____

25. If you could study only one language, which one would you choose ? _____

26. What do you want to do when you graduate from school ? _____

_____

27. Where are you from ? _____

28. How many brothers and sisters do you have ? _____

29. What is your religion ? _____

NOTES

1. My thanks to Eve Danziger, Joanna Pfaff-Czarnecka, Charles Ramble, Sara Shneiderman, Tanka Subba and Gérard Toffin for helpful comments and constructive feedback on earlier iterations of this chapter.
2. http://news.bbc.co.uk/2/hi/south_asia/7528454.stm
3. I am grateful to Tanka Subba for bringing this delay to my attention.
4. I am grateful to Charles Ramble for reminding me that such evocations of multilingualism with different speech forms accorded different domains of use is not new. Charles V, the King of Spain and Holy Roman Emperor (1500–58), is alleged to have remarked 'I speak Spanish to God, Italian to Women, French to Men, and German to my horse.'

REFERENCES

Barrier, Norman Gerald. 1981. *The Census in British India: New Perspectives*. New Delhi: Manohar.

Bista, Puran. 2008. 'Vice-president Who Misread the Nepali Text', *Kantipuronline*, 4 August 2008. Available online at http://www.kantipuronline.com/kolnews.php?&nid=155865

Brass, Paul R. 2004. 'Elite Interests, Popular Passions, and Social Power in the Language Politics of India', *Ethnic and Racial Studies*, 27(3): 353–75.

Chalmers, Rhoderick. 2007. 'Nepal and the Eastern Himalayas', in Andrew Simpson (ed.), *Language and National Identity in Asia*, pp. 84–99. Oxford: Oxford University Press.

Christopher, A.J. 1992. 'Ethnicity, Community and the Census in Mauritius, 1830–1990', *The Geographical Journal*, 158(1): 57–64.

Collins, James. 1988. 'Language and Class in Minority Education', *Anthropology & Education Quarterly*, 19(4): 299–326.

Croucher, Sheila L. 2004. *Globalization and Belonging: The Politics of Identity in a Changing World*. Oxford: Rowman & Littlefield.

Dole, Bob. 1995. Remarks prepared for delivery, American Legion Convention, Indianapolis.

Errington, Joseph. 2001. 'Colonial linguistics', *Annual Review of Anthropology*, 30: 19–39.

Gellner, David N. 1997. 'Introduction: Ethnicity and Nationalism in the World's only Hindu State', in David N. Gellner, Joanna Pfaff-Czarnecka, and John Whelpton (eds), *Nationalism and Ethnicity in a Hindu Kingdom: The Politics of Culture in Contemporary Nepal*, pp. 3–31. Amsterdam: Harwood.

Jha, Prashant. 2008. 'Manufacturing mistrust', *Nepali Times*, 411: 10.

Jianfa Shen, David Chu, Qingpu Zhang, and Weimin Zhang. 1999. 'Developing a Census Data System in China', *International Statistical Review*, 67(2): 173–86.

May, Stephen, Tariq Modood, and Judith Squires. 2004. 'Ethnicity, Nationalism and Minority Rights: Charting the Disciplinary Debates', in Stephen May, Tariq

Modood, and Judith Squires (eds), *Ethnicity, Nationalism and Minority Rights*, pp. 1–23. Cambridge: Cambridge University Press.

Monateri, Pier Guiseppe. 1999. '"Cunning Passages". Comparison and Ideology in the Law and Language Story', in Rodolfo Sacco and Luca Castellani (eds), *Les Multiples Langues du Droi Européen Uniforme*, pp. 123–41. Torino, Italy: Editrice L'Harmattan Italia.

Nagel, Joane. 1994. 'Constructing Ethnicity: Creating and Recreating Ethnic Identity and Culture', *Social Problems*, 41: 152–76.

Noonan, Michael. 1996. 'The Fall and Rise and Fall of the Chantyal Language', *Southwest Journal of Linguistics*, 15(1–2): 121–35.

Sillitoe, K. and P.H. White. 1992. 'Ethnic Group and the British Census: The Search for a Question', *Journal of the Royal Statistical Society*, 155(1): 141–63.

Silverstein, Michael. 1998. 'Contemporary Transformations of Local Linguistic Communities', *Annual Review of Anthropology*, 27: 401–26.

Simoni, Alessandro. 2003. 'A Language for Rules, Another for Symbols: Linguistic Pluralism and Interpretation of Statutes in the Kingdom of Bhutan', *Journal of Bhutan Studies*, 8, 29–53.

Simpson, Andrew. 2007. 'Language and National Identity in Asia: A Thematic Introduction', in Andrew Simpson (ed.), *Language and National Identity in Asia*, pp. 1–30. Oxford: Oxford University Press.

Sutton, Peter. 1991. 'Educational Language Planning and Linguistic Identity', *International Review of Education*, 37(1): 133–47.

Theroux, Alexander. 1987. *An Adultery*. New York: Simon and Schuster.

Urciuoli, Bonnie. 1995. 'Language and Borders', *Annual Review of Anthropology*, 24: 525–46.

Van Parijs, Philippe. 2000. 'The Ground Floor of the World: On the Socio-Economic Consequences of Linguistic Globalization', *International Political Science Review*, 21(2): 217–33.

de Varennes, Fernand. 1996. *Language, Minorities and Human Rights*. The Hague: Martinus Nijhoff & Brill.

Wimmer, A. 2008. 'Elementary Strategies of Ethnic Boundary Making', *Ethnic and Racial Studies*, 31(6): 1025–55.

Yuval-Davis, Nira. 2004. 'Borders, Boundaries, and the Politics of Belonging', in Stephen May, Tariq Modood, and Judith Squires (eds), *Ethnicity, Nationalism and Minority Rights*, pp. 214–30. Cambridge: Cambridge University Press.

———. 2006. 'Belonging and the Politics of Belonging', *Patterns of Prejudice*, 40(3): 196–213.

Zolberg, Aristide. 2006. *A Nation by Design: Immigration Policy in the Fashioning of America*. Cambridge: Harvard University Press.

Zolberg, Aristide and Long Litt Woon. 1999. 'Why Islam is Like Spanish: Cultural Incorporation in Europe and the United States', *Politics and Society*, 27(1): 5–38.

Chapter 16

Who Belongs to Tibet?

Governmental Narratives of State in the Ganden Podrang

MARTIN A. MILLS

Figure 16.1
Geographical Domains of the *Chölkha Sum* Claimed by the CTA[1]

INTRODUCTION

On 21 September 1987, the Fourteenth Dalai Lama presented to the United States Congress his Five-Point Peace Plan for the resolution of the long-standing Tibet Question. The plan revolved around the transformation of the whole of Tibet into a de-militarized Zone of Peace. By 'the whole of Tibet', the Dalai Lama was referring to the 'three provinces' (*chölkha sum*) of what many refer to as 'ethnic Tibet': Ü-Tsang (including the domain of Ngari, or Western Tibet), Kham, and Amdo (see Figure 16.1). This distribution of regions is often presented as the 'traditional' parameters of ethnic or cultural Tibet by the Dalai Lama's Central Tibetan Administration (or 'Tibetan Government-in-Exile', henceforth CTA) in Dharamsala since coming into exile from Tibet in 1959, whose Assembly of Tibetan Peoples' Deputies, convened in 1960, contains elected representatives from these three regions.

However, as a basis for the Dalai Lama's diplomatic stance vis-à-vis China and the CTA's relationship with exiled Tibetans, the term remains extremely controversial. From 1913 to 1951, the government of the Dalai Lamas (called the Ganden Podrang, or 'Tushita Palace')—which came to an end in 1959—maintained effective political sovereignty over the area now called the Tibetan Autonomous Region (TAR), itself only around half of the so-called *chölkha sum*. The remaining territory of the *chölkha sum* includes not more than half the world's population of ethnic Tibetans, incorporated into the PRC provinces of Qinghai, Gansu, Sichuan, and Yunnan. The PRC government has consistently refused to recognize any 'Greater Tibet' (*bod chenpo*) beyond the domain of the TAR, ruling them out of talks with Dharamsala, and indeed has rejected the historical salience of the term:

> Why does the Dalai Lama insist on this groundless and impossible concept of "greater Tibet area"?[2]

Dharamsala's insistence on the *chölkha sum* regions as the basis for a wider ethnic unity of Tibetans, and therefore as a basis for claims of self-determination, has equally come in for criticism by academics and journalists who have argued that it involves a 'sleight-of-hand' that denies the true boundary of the Ganden Podrang's historical political sovereignty and elides the complex and long-lasting ethnic heterogeneity of the regions under debate (French, 2003: 13–14); that it denies the fact that these regions were rarely under anyone's systematic control (Samuel, 1993: 53–63, 139–45); that historically many of the inhabitants of Kham and Amdo were 'fiercely contemptuous' of Lhasa rule (Lopez, 1998: 197), rejecting even the nomenclature of 'Tibetan' (*bod pa*); and that such solidarities are the product of a post-1959 modernity, either within Tibet itself (Schwartz, 1994) or as the product of Dharamsala's own adoption of Western understandings of 'culture' (Lopez, 1998: 200).

At the same time, the *idea* of a Greater Tibet comprising three regions, far larger in extent than the TAR, is clearly of long historical standing, considerably pre-dating the rule of the Dalai Lamas, and found in texts such as the 13th century *Chronicle of Deu José* (LC, 3.1.1; see Dotson, 2006: 90) and the 14th century *Clear Mirror of Royal Genealogies* (*GSM*, see also Sørensen, 1994: 112). At the heart of this puzzle are two concerns: first, it is unclear what the relationship is between the idea of the *chölkha sum* and the broader distribution of Tibetan solidarities; and second, it is equally unclear how such ideas relate to actual events in Tibet's past. In this sense, the problem of the *chölkha sum* very much encapsulates the larger problem of what Shakya refers to as the 'crisis' of Tibetan identity (Shakya, 1993).

BELONGING AND IDENTITY

In what follows, some of the historical issues surrounding this clash of meanings shall be examined. It is not, however, the intention of this work to 'resolve' this aspect of the Sino-Tibetan issue. Ultimately, this issue is a matter of history, a history of who ruled whom (Sperling, 2004). Such debates are ones of ascription and assertion rather than objective fact. 'Sovereignty' after all cannot be measured in any empirical way: earth does not change colour or weight just because it is ruled by Beijing or by Lhasa, nor do the people on that earth change stature or constitution. The existence of flags, seals, and treaties only mean something to those that can read them and, upon reading them, be persuaded by them. In this sense, historical claims are merely acts of persuasion rather than evidence, depending upon mutual agreement of common terms and meanings, agreement which in this case is noticeably lacking.

It is not then the empirical 'reality' of historical claims or of putative (and ultimately inaccessible) 'identities' that is of concern here, but rather their genesis and meaning as active processes of thought and practice. Here, I will draw from Vikki Bell's distinction between *identity* as a quality intrinsic to a people and territory that acts as a means of securing political and economic claims, and *belonging* as a mode of performance that acts as the necessary precondition for identity claims (Bell, 1999: 3). For Bell, *all* intrinsic identity claims (the claim to *'be* Tibetan', *'be* Chinese', *'be* Indian', *'be* Muslim') have rhetorical rather than substantive existence, and logically depend upon more or less coordinated *performances of belonging,* which bring them into subjective being. Here, ontological identity claims act to obscure the conditions of their own genesis, by legitimizing them on the grounds that particular people, practices, and places intrinsically and always (or at least for a very long time) have 'had' a certain quality.

Bell's use of *performance* is of course highly suggestive. Let us imagine the performance of a play. In its genesis, a play begins with a multiplicity of inter-laced performances, gradually built up into a whole. In the beginning, each actor learns the lines associated with a particular part, the technicians work on the lighting and sound, whereas the props department busy themselves with elements of the scenery, costumes, and so forth. Only once these have been initially developed as individual strands are they progressively interwoven: the lines not simply said, but said as part of a concert of voices and intonations. Each of these elements 'belong' to the play, but are not identical with it, for there is presently no 'it' to be identical with. This interweaving, however, gradually builds up a sense not of individual components, but a progressively determining whole; in particular, of a *plot* or narrative that somehow constitutes the beating heart of the play itself, of which all the other components (individual lines and parts, costumes, props, makeup) are increasingly felt to be but *manifestations.* A fundamental shift in perception has therefore occurred: the identity, which was previously built up *as a consequence* of the various parts, transforms instead into their apparent *origin,* whose chimerical integrity is guaranteed by the existence of an organizing narrative logic, which, as the play is rehearsed more and more often, comes to dominate the parts, not vice versa. In equal measure, identity—emerging out of a series of performances of belonging—comes to be perceived and presented as the determinant of those performances.

This logic is hardly specific to Tibet: it applies equally to Beijing's claims that Tibet is 'inalienably and eternally' part of China, the VHP's claims to 'Hindu-ness' in India (Gold, 1991), or the Gush Emunim's assertions to a teleologically defined *eretz yisrael* (Aran, 1991).

In the Tibetan context, however, it allows us to build a history of belonging, which itself emerges out of how (in this case) the Tibetan government at Lhasa progressively built up a sense of its own history of state, around which notions of 'Greater Tibet' have been rendered concrete: from the early Ganden Podrang period of the Fifth Dalai Lama to the complex struggles of the mid-20th century, when Tibet came under the penumbra of Mao's People's Republic of China. What follows is therefore less an empirical history of rule (which is, I would argue, impossible) than a history of historicizing by the Ganden Podrang government, a portrait of a gradual indigenous interweaving of a series of strands of belonging retrospectively gleaned from the remnants of Tibet's shattered history, gradually interlaced over the course of 300 years to produce an underlying sense of identity and narrative. More than the mere 'invention of tradition' *ex nihil*, this is the progressive organization of existing histories of land, cosmology, kingship, conflict, and diplomacy into a progressive narrative of moral and ethical agency.

STATECRAFT AND THE EARLY GANDEN PODRANG (1642–1705)

The Ganden Podrang government came into existence in 1642 when the Mongolian prince Guśri Khan, who had spent five long years battling the enemies of his *guru* the Fifth Dalai Lama, conquered the neighbouring King of Tsang and offered the now unified lands of Tibet to the estate of his teacher. In alliance with Guśri Khan and his regent Sonam Rapten, the 'Great Fifth' then set about building a government at Lhasa, site of the great monastic universities of the Dalai Lama's own Geluk school of Tibetan Buddhism. Following in the footsteps of the Geluk's founder Tsongkhapa, the Fifth Dalai Lama: augmented the Lhasa Trülnang, Tibet's first 'governmental temple', at the heart of Lhasa; began the building of the magnificent Potala palace just outside the city; and, in 1653, embarked upon a lengthy state visit to the court of the Manchu emperor in Beijing, accompanied by a retinue of 3000 (Karmay, 2010).

In the performance of this statecraft, the Fifth Dalai Lama's government drew upon important precedents from Tibetan history as a way of signifying his links to Tibet's political and religious heritage: to the widespread indigenous mythology regarding the celestial *bodhisattva* Avalokiteśvara (in Tibetan: Chenresig), Tibet's patron deity; to the semi-mythical precedents of the imperial Yarlung dynasty of the ancient religion kings of Central Tibet; and to the long-standing relationship between Tibet's Buddhist schools and the Mongol royalty that now ruled China.

Avalokiteśvara and the Early Tibetan Kings

By the 17th century, Avalokiteśvara's place in Tibetan political and historical consciousness was deeply entrenched. One of the great *bodhisattvas* of Mahayana Buddhism, the Buddhist historical and revealed literature of Tibet had long regarded him as having been specifically assigned the 'barbarous Snow Land' by the Buddha Śakyamūni as his own field of salvation. While the cult of Avalokiteśvara seems to have truly taken hold in Tibet with the arrival of the Indian Buddhist luminary Atiśa (c. 982–1054) in the 11th century, texts emergent in this period—such as the 11th century *Pillar Testament (KKM)* and the hugely influential *Compendium of Mani*s *(MKB)*—describe the great *bodhisattva* overseeing the early birth of the Tibetan race, providing them with the rudiments of agriculture, and gradually coaxing them towards the life of religion. This mythology reaches its narrative zenith with the depiction of the rise of kingly power in Tibet. The great Yarlung kings of the 7th to 9th century—Songtsen Gampo (c. 618–49), Trisong Deutsen (c. 730–81), and Ralpacan (r. 822–39)—were presented both as manifestations of Avalokiteśvara and as founding Buddhism and the cult of the deity in Tibet, a cultural and political pinnacle that was brought down by the equally semi-mythical apostate king Langdarma.

These 11th and 12th century texts interpreted the rule of the early Yarlung *chögyel* ('religion kings'), and particularly the emperor Songtsen Gampo, as the work of Avalokiteśvara, and the king himself as the iconic earthly manifestation (*trülku*) of the deity.[3] The founding of the Lhasa Trülnang, Songtsen Gampo's key tutelary temple to Avalokiteśvara, was depicted as the product of a lengthy process of subduing the land of Tibet (depicted as a supine demoness—see Gyatso, 1989; Miller, 1998; Mills, 2007) to Buddhism, which involved building 'subduing temples' (*dulwa'i lhakhang*) both within the borders of the emperor's rule and in the surrounding territories, crossing much of the Tibetan Plateau,[4] a subjugation (*dulwa*) intimately associated with the power of Buddhist religious law, defended by Avalokiteśvara's wrathful forms. At the same time, the unity between the king and Avalokiteśvara was sealed with the construction of the royal palace at Lhasa on Marpori Hill (site of the present Potala), around the city's first, small temple to the deity. Kingly sovereignty was thus intimately associated with the powers of the deity, a theme essential to the self-understanding of the later Ganden Podrang (Ishihama, 1993). Intimately associated with this ritual and cosmological history were the military accomplishments of the Yarlung Dynasty, which saw the massive expansion of Tibetan political agency, from its early beginnings in the Yarlung Valley of Southern Tibet to the imposition of military strength across the Tibetan Plateau into Western China. The 14th century *Clear Mirror of Royal Genealogies (GLR)*, for example, records Yarlung victories over the A-zha territories north of Xining, with his successor Trisong Deutsen occupying Lanxiao, the capital of modern Gansu (Sørensen, 1994: 417–21). By the 14th century, these were broadly understood as the established boundaries of Yarlung hegemony. It is in the ancient Yarlung kingships, then, that the precedent as the *chölkha sum*—for a 'Greater Tibet'—is set.

Tibeto–Mongolian Relations

What of the origins of the actual terminology of the '*chölkha sum*', however? These lie in the 13th century, and are intimately associated with relations with the Mongol khans. The final fall of the Yarlung Dynasty in the late 9th century inaugurated a period of political fragmentation in Tibet, characterized by centuries of small, local kingships. Many political leaders at this time allied themselves with local and imported lineages of Buddhist practice, leading to the rise of the Sakya, Kagyü, and Kadam schools of Buddhism. This religious and political heterogeneity was, however, skewed by the arrival of the newly ascendant Mongol forces from the Northeast. In 1240, Mongol forces appeared, fresh from the almost complete annihilation of the Buddhist Tangut. Faced with potential destruction, and in response to Mongol demands, the scholar-monk Sakya Pandita travelled to the Mongol court with his nephews Pakpa and Chakna Dorjé. Impressed by the learning and powers of the Tibetan emissaries, Khubulai Khan eventually requested tantric initiation from Pakpa in 1265. In return for this, he offered the 'thirteen myriarchs' (*tri-khor*) of conquered Tibet to Pakpa as part of a patron–priest (*chöyön*) relationship. Combined, these myriarchs included Ü-Tsang and Ngari.[5] In 1276, on the eve of returning to Tibet, Pakpa received from the Khan the three administrative regions (M. *chölge*) of Tibet. The Tibetan word *chölkha* is a precise transliteration of the Mongolian *chölge*. Confusion exists as to what exactly the latter donation meant in geographical terms. According to Longdol Lama's late 18th century history of religious patrons for example, the *chölkha sum* were, respectively, Ü-Tsang, Amdo, and Kham (*MG*, fol. 5a); in contrast, in Ngorpa Konchok Lhundrup's much earlier history of Buddhism in India and Tibet, they are Ngari, Ü-Tsang, and Amdo-Khams (*GJG*, fol. 163—see also Tucci, 1989 [1941]: 86)). In more substantial contrast, Petech, using contemporary Chinese and Mongolian sources, identifies the three *chölkha* as Ngari, Ü, and Tsang—that is, *as not including Kham and Amdo* (Petech, 1980: 234; Petech, 1983: 190). Petech argues that this more limited geographical scope—which is effectively the same as the thirteen myriarchs—continues into the Ganden Podrang period (Petech, 1972 [1950]: 218).

This confusion is perhaps unsurprising. The 14th century saw the waning of Mongol power in Tibet, and eventually Sakya vice-regency on the Plateau was overthrown by the former Sakya administrator Changchub Gyaltsen (1302–64) who, in 1358, took the title of ruler and founded the Pakmodru Dynasty. While the true status of his *de jure* authority is unclear (see van der Kuijp, 2003), his administration was characterized by a movement away from Mongol rule: the myriarch system was restructured into a new system of *dzong* centred in the Yarlung Valley; the royal model of rule was reasserted, centred on a revivifying of old Yarlung imperial traditions; and Lhasa was re-valorised as the symbolic centre of Tibet. By the 15th century, the reality of these Mongolian administrative systems was textual, not lived.

GANDEN PODRANG UNDERSTANDINGS OF THE *CHÖLKHA SUM*

Under the new Ganden Podrang, this scattered indigenous history was brought together as a vision of the historical template for the performance of rule. For the Fifth Dalai Lama, these fragments were linked to a larger vision of 'the kingdom of Greater Tibet'[6] as a site of Avalokiteśvara's divine action that were largely coterminous with the boundaries of the Yarlung kingships, to which Pakpa's later actions were intimately associated. Pakpa became increasingly viewed through the lens of a larger biography of Avalokiteśvara's activities in Tibet. As Ishihama has shown in detail, the reign of the Fifth Dalai Lama between 1642 and 1682 was characterized by a systematic project of 'cosmological construction' that identified himself and his predecessors with the deity: through the regular performance of Avalokiteśvara empowerment ceremonies; through the detailed formulation of retrospective lists of pre-incarnations that led back not just to the 'First' Dalai Lama Gendundrup, but through multiple other figures such as the ancient religion kings of the Yarlung Dynasty, the great ritual protectors of Lhasa, and indeed Pakpa himself (see *D5NIV:* fol. 105b); and through the association of Avalokiteśvara's activities with the royal government of Tibet (Ishihama, 1993).

In this retrospective sense, *both* the Yarlung dynastic history and the later *chöyön* relations with the Mongols become part and parcel of a single heritage of 'Greater Tibet'. In his history of the royal governance of Tibet, the Fifth Dalai Lama recounts how Pakpa

> exercised mastery over the whole kingdom of the three *chölkha* of Greater Tibet, namely Ü-Tsang, the *chölkha* of religion; Upper mDo, the *chölkha* of men; Lower mDo, the *chölkha* of horses. (*GGD*, fol. 60a; see also Ahmad, 1995)

This idea of a Greater Tibet (that later came under Pakpa's authority) was also described within the Fifth Dalai Lama's biography as that territory within the aegis of Avalokiteśvara's protective action:

> The sublime protectors of the three families[7] looked out upon the kingdom of Greater Tibet with immaculate eyes: as for the upper part (called) Ngari, it was a land of elephants and deer; the middle part (called) Ü-Tsang, a land of deer and monkeys; and the lower part (called) Do-Khams, a land of monkeys and rock-dwelling demons. Moreover, the upper area was slate- and snow-mountains; the middle was rock faces and green meadows; and the lower part dense thickets of fruit trees and jungle. Because all moving creatures gave themselves up, without restraint, to such evil customs as taking life, they fell into the iron basket-like hell, which was the source of endless suffering, (situated) under these lands. Coming to know of this through the eye

of knowledge, the three Holy Ones discussed (the matter) and took the excellent decision to subdue it, for the first time, through the Lord of the World [an epithet of Avalokiteśvara]. Having changed to his thousand-armed, thousand-eyed form (Avalokiteśvara) came to the land of Lhasa. The hell which was there came to look like a place which put to shame the heart-ravishing pleasure-grove of the king of the gods. (*GGD*: 9–10)

It is, however, notable that the Fifth Dalai Lama's history distinguishes between Pakpa's *mastery*[8] over the three regions of Greater Tibet and the governmental obligation to the administration of law (understood as the "cessation of wrong-doing and the rewarding of virtue through law"[9]—*GGD*, fol. 60b) within the thirteen myriarchs of Ü and Tsang. Ultimately, this may well be a merely theoretical distinction, but it echoes a longer standing one, regularly evoked with reference to royal figures such as Songtsen Gampo as well as many systems of non-modern rule, between active political sovereignty and ritual suzerainty (Southall, 1988; Stein, 1980). Just as the myths of Songtsen Gampo portray him ritually subduing the land of Tibet with temples built far beyond his own borders (see above), in the same way the Ganden Podrang as a government accepted ritual responsibilities for the protection of the wider land of Tibet far beyond its effective political borders through, for example, the evocation of Buddhist protector deities in the performance of expelling rites (*torlok*) for the defence of the state and people against 'enemies of religion', and the performance of rites designed to perpetuate the geomantic subjugation of the land of Greater Tibet, such as through the regular distribution of *sa-ché* vases to ward off earthquakes, landslide, and hail (Mills, 2009). In a more passive way, the authority of Lhasa as a sacred centre existed implicitly in the general tendency of legal systems (of which there were many in Tibet) to ascribe their origins, however tenuously, to the ancient laws of Songtsen Gampo, despite a deeply felt rejection of the legal or political authority of the Ganden Podrang government (see, for example, Pirie [2008] for the Golok of Amdo).

A central component of this was the constitutional distinction between the religious authority of the Dalai Lamas and the political authority of their governments. As Ishihama notes in detail of the early Ganden Podrang, the Dalai Lama could not be regarded as 'head of state' in any modern sense, because of the important requirement that the secular concerns of government should not interfere with his religious duties. At the same time, the Dalai Lama was clearly superordinate to all government officers, who should follow his guidance (Ishihama, 1993: 42–44).[10] The Dalai Lamas' authority within the wider Tibetan Plateau was thus distinct both from the political sovereignty of his actual government and at the same time from that of the Geluk school of Buddhism of which he was a member. Certainly, the extent of his obligations stood in marked contrast to the Ganden Podrang's tax-raising powers and capacities for military defence, which were largely restricted to Central Tibet (CZ, 1989 [1830]; Surkhang, 1986); nor should it necessarily be equated with a general *popular* acknowledgement of sovereignty by the inhabitants of those areas.

To summarize therefore, while there may be some confusion in the historical sources as to the precise parameters of the original Mongolian designation of *chölkha sum*, the Ganden Podrang government of the Fifth Dalai Lama saw it as one of an overlapping set of individual components of sovereignty that, along with the actions of the early kings, constituted 'the kingdom of Greater Tibet', which was the field of Avalokiteśvara's cosmological obligation, and therefore the monarch's ritual obligation. These were not, however, the same as direct political control. These in turn were intimately associated with Tibet's diplomatic role within the patron–priest relationship with the Khans' Manchu inheritors.

None of these were new ideas in themselves, but they are threads that were drawn together in particular concert by the early Ganden Podrang. Combined, they served as a template for the manner in which Tibet was ruled from Lhasa; that is, for a set of parameters of what it understood as its *governmental obligation*.

1950–59: REUNITING GREATER TIBET?

Issues of space preclude a lengthy analysis of the deployment of the idea of Greater Tibet during the long twilight period that follow the death of the Fifth Dalai Lama: the multiple invasions of Tibet, the ransacking of Lhasa, the controversies over the Sixth Dalai Lama, the re-instigation of aristocratic rule between 1720 and 1750, the war with the Gorkhas, and the eventual relegation of Tibet to a Qing protectorate all served to undermine the authority of the Dalai

Lamas, who eventually became mere puppet rulers within an over-arching Geluk religious hierarchy (Petech, 1972 [1950]). Indeed, most Dalai Lamas during this period did not reach their majority. During this period, Manchu imperial reorganizations—particularly within Amdo—rendered the notion of a Greater Tibet largely moribund, or at least wholly theoretical. This situation largely continued through the rule of the Thirteenth Dalai Lama, whose expulsion of Chinese forces and representatives and declaration of independence from Manchu rule in 1913 had little power to include the regions of North-East Tibet. It is only with the turbulent early reign of the Fourteenth Dalai Lama that the notion of the *chölka sum* returned to ritual and political prominence.

Born to a farming family in Taktser village in distant Amdo in July 1935, the Fourteenth Dalai Lama was faced at a young age with the advance of Mao's People's Liberation Army, the fall of Chamdo, his own assumption of temporal powers, and the controversial signing of the 17-Point Agreement in 1951 (Goldstein, 1989). This was followed by eight years of protracted and tense negotiations with occupying PLA forces, the foundation of the Preparatory Committee for the Autonomous Region of Tibet (1954), a growing uprising in Eastern Tibet (1955–57), and finally the Lhasa Uprising itself, and his flight into exile (1959) (Goldstein, 2007; Shakya, 1999).

Early Chinese Communist Party policy following the invasion was not to destroy the Ganden Podrang government but to render it redundant by building up an alternative military administration in the region (Shakya, 1999). Given the wider anti-religious tendencies of Mao's political ideology, it is perhaps ironic that this served by default to reduce the Lhasa Government's functioning down to the one thing the communists could not replace—its religious and ceremonial authority. Indeed, this period saw the progressive reversal of the domestication of the Dalai Lama's own position within the Tibetan Government that had occurred during the long years of the Qing. While the protectorate period between 1720 and 1913 had seen the growth of assemblies, cabinets, and officers between the Dalai Lamas and direct rule (Goldstein, 1989), the 1950–59 period saw a dramatic reversal: the resignation of the Dalai Lama's two prime ministers in 1952, the sidelining of the established assemblies, and growing popular discontent with the aristocratic and monastic elites. All of this increasingly centred authority and loyalty on the young ruler.

Shifts in power within Lhasa were however eclipsed by growing resistance to Communist rule in Eastern Tibet. When this turned to full-scale rebellion, the Ganden Podrang's initial position was one of ambivalence, reflecting the narrowed political interests of its history as a protectorate. As Shakya notes:

> Despite cultural and religious affinity, the Lhasa regime clearly regarded the events in Eastern Tibet as outside their jurisdiction. (Shakya, 1999: 163)

Indeed, internal tensions amongst Tibetans were at times so bad that Phala, the Dalai Lama's chamberlain, would later comment that, had the March 1959 Uprising not occurred, civil war might ultimately have broken out between Lhasa and the Khampa rebels (Shakya, 1999: 193).

However, the growing flood of refugees from Eastern Tibet pouring into Lhasa, along with rampant inflation caused by the Chinese military presence and growing concern for the safety of the young Dalai Lama, critically changed this initially polarized dynamic between the inhabitants of Central and Eastern Tibet. This occurred through innovative performances of belonging focused on the Dalai Lama—actions that would both re-form the lapsed image of a wider Tibet and subtly shift its emphasis.

The Golden Throne and the People's Party

The first of these two actions occurred through the unification of the previously beleaguered and divided refugee fighters from Kham into a single fighting force, the so-called *Chushi Gangdruk*, or 'Four Rivers, Six Ranges',[11] which met in the Lhoka Region to the south of Lhasa in June 1958. A defining moment in the genesis of this group came in May 1957 when Gonpo Tashi Angdrugtsang, future leader of the Chushi Gangdruk, visited Lhasa to request a large-scale Kalacakra initiation from, and organize long-life offerings to, the young Dalai Lama. At the heart of these offerings was a 'golden throne',[12] for the funding of which representatives were sent to all parts of Tibet. The throne was eventually offered to the Dalai Lama at the Norbulingka Palace on 4 July.

This event has been interpreted as a sign of strictly *religious* devotion (e.g. Dunham, 2004: 195), but this obscures much of its constitutional significance (Dreyfus, 2005). Replicating the annual offering made by the Tibetan Government to the Dalai Lama as religious *guru*, it embodies the notion of *chösi zungdrel*: the hierarchical dependence of temporal power on religious blessing for authorization and legitimation. In particular, it also signifies and performs the Dalai Lama's *worldly sovereignty* over the domains of the celebrant. Gonpo Tashi Angdrugtsang described it as a means to:

> express the people's loyalty and confidence in the Dalai Lama's leadership and confirm his earthly sovereign powers. (Angdrugtsang, 1973: 51)

The fundamentally *constitutional* and government-centred nature of this offering can be seen in the manner in which Angdrugtsang, upon returning to Lhasa with offerings for the ceremony and key tribal chiefs from Lhoka, Kongpo, and Kham, held a secret meeting in which they all vowed to fight Chinese occupation—a vow made before an altar to Palden Lhamo, the principal protector deity of the Dalai Lama's government.

The golden throne thus constituted an important ceremonial link between the Dalai Lama and the wider field of Tibetans, many of them outside the now-established TAR, engaged in the growing struggle with the communists. To this day, the Chushi Gangdruk understand this event, and the guerrilla resistance that surrounded it, as *reconstituting* a greater mythic Tibet lost to political history since the fall of the imperial Yarlung dynasty under king Langdarma:[13]

> In appreciation of the Initiation and for the long life of His Holiness the Dalai Lama, a grand Tenshuk (Longevity) Offering Ceremony was performed by the Khampas. The offering of Tenshuk to His Holiness on the new golden throne was meant to symbolize the enthronement of His Holiness as ruler of the entire Tibetan territory and also for reaffirmation of faith in His Holiness as supreme being ... Upon the completion of religious ceremonies, the Khampa leaders and volunteer members gradually moved out of Lhasa in different routes towards the Lhokha area, south of Lhasa, and eventually assembled at Chaktsa Dri-Guthang (Chosen Rendezvous). The formal announcement of the formation of the Chushi Gangdruk (Land of Four Rivers and Six Ranges) Defend Tibet Volunteer Force was made on the 16th

of June 1958 and since then it is commemorated every year to mark the anniversary of Chushi Gangdruk. It was the first time that all the regions of Kham and the Khampas of all regions came together under one organization and fought under one banner since the splitting up of Tibet during the reign of the last and evil King, Lang [D]arma. (Chushi Gangdruk official website, http://www.chushigangdruk.org, accessed: 12 April 2010)

This link between the Khampa resistance and the Tibetan government was finally secured during the endgame of the Tibet Uprising in March 1959. The Dalai Lama's flight into exile took him initially through the Khampa-held Lhoka province, escorted by Khampa rebels. Reconvening his government at Lhuntse Dzong to the north of the Indian border, the Dalai Lama incorporated the Chushi Gangdruk into the Tibetan government structure, bestowing upon Angdrugtsang the government title of *magchi dzasag* (Shakya, 1999: 206), or minister of war.

The acceptance of the offering of the golden throne, combined with the incorporation of the Chushi Gangdruk into the Tibetan governmental structure, thus constituted a fundamental shift in the Ganden Podrang's fluid sense of its ceremonial and political sovereignty, incorporating Eastern Tibet as a part of its wider struggle to retain sovereignty.

An important second element of the growing conflict with the PLA forces was a shift from the established Ganden Podrang dependence on military forces, accumulated through the aristocratic structure and supported by protector deity-focused monastic ritual. The clear failure of these vectors to defend the Lhasa state combined with a growing popular sense that both the aristocracy and much of the monastic elite had failed to come out strongly enough in its defence, and particularly in defence of the young Dalai Lama. From 1952 onwards, Lhasa saw the growth of low-level 'people's associations' (*mimang tsongdu*) that were anti-Chinese, anti-communist, and highly critical of the established structures of the Ganden Podrang government (Goldstein, 2007: 317–40). By 1959, these associations, which comprised largely low-level traders, monks, and non-aristocratic Lhasa residents, became an important, if covert, lynchpin in the public strategies of the Dalai Lama's inner circle of advisors. It was these groups that organized the final, ill-fated defence of Dalai Lama's summer palace on March 1959 itself, a defence that was as much in opposition to what they saw as a treacherous aristocracy as it was to the PLA.

The role of these twin forces in the 10 March Uprising against the PLA forces—the *Mimang Tsongdu* in organizing the final defence of the Dalai Lama's summer palace and the *Chushi Gangdruk* in providing the principal route through Southern Tibet to the Indian border—emphasized the importance of the Tibetan *people*—many of them displaced from their original feudal lands—rather than established aristocratic and monastic structures in the defence of Tibetan sovereignty. In the final days leading up to the Lhasa Uprising, for example, the fraught question of loyalty to the Dalai Lama's government centred on a signature campaign, with all those supporting the uprising signing themselves as 'tsampa-eaters',[14] to distinguish themselves from the 'rice-eating' Chinese (Khétsun, 2008: 29).

TRANSFORMED BELONGING IN EXILE

This shift in emphasis would have important repercussions in exile, where the Dalai Lama increasingly emphasized the unity of Tibetans both within the domain of Greater Tibet as a whole and *as a people*. In clear contrast to the Ganden Podrang's views during the early days of the rebellion (see above), the Dalai Lama's earliest exiled statement—on 18 April 1959 from Tezpur, North India—included the argument that the PLA suppression of the 1955–56 Kanting Rebellion *in Kham* was a breach of the 17-Point Agreement (Norbu, 2001: 219):

> By the end of 1955 a struggle had started in the Kham Province and this assumed serious proportions in 1956. In the consequential struggle, the Chinese Armed Forces destroyed a large number of monasteries. Many lamas were killed and a large number of monks and officials were taken and employed on the construction of roads in China, and the interference in the exercise of religious freedom increased.

The Chinese authorities in Beijing rejected the statement, pointing out that these events occurred *outside* the Tibet envisaged in the 17-Point Agreement of 1951:

> The only fact it cited was the putting down of the rebellion by the Central People's Government in the former Sikang area in 1955. But

the whole world knows the Sikang area does not belong to Tibet at all. Previously it used to be Sikang Province and was later incorporated into Szechwan Province. (*New China News Agency*, 19 April 1959)

The Fourteenth Dalai Lama's emphasis on Tibetan unity deeply coloured his own speeches to the exiled community. In his address to refugee government ministers on 17 November 1959, for example, he chastised what he saw as an established tendency for regional and sectarian divisiveness:

> The single most important activity of the present time is solidarity and mutual harmony. For example, if the various traditional regions of Ü-Tsang, Kham and Amdo, the various monastic seats and local monasteries, the various military divisions and so forth are drawn into contention on account of [loyalty to] their names, this would be an exceedingly grave error! Tibetans may be perfectly amicable momentarily [because of] a shared suffering, but the main point is that we must become like an iron lump of concord and fellowship. (*SZND*, 2)

In the draft constitution formulated by the CTA in 1961 (ratified in 1963 as "Guidelines for a Future Tibetan Constitution"), one of the principal recommendations was the formation of an Assembly of Tibetan People's Representatives to act as a legislature, the first meeting of which was inaugurated on the 2 September 1960. It comprised 13 members, for which positions were allocated for three representatives from each of the 'three regions of Tibet'—Ü-Tsang, Kham, and Amdo.

There is much in this move that implies a shift from the Fifth Dalai Lama's vision of Greater Tibet as a *land* unified by Avalokiteśvara's moral obligation, towards the idea of a *people* unified by a common purpose. Indeed, many recent speeches by both the Dalai Lama and other prominent Tibetan religious luminaries imply a view that Tibetans as a *people* now carry that obligation in exile. Ultimately, however, the idea of Tibetans as a unified people constitutes an important foundation not merely of intra-cultural communications amongst Tibetans themselves but also inter-cultural representations on the international stage. In negotiations with Beijing, the question of the borders of Tibet, and the idea that the three regions should be treated as a whole from the perspective of the welfare of Tibetans as a people, has been a constant sticking point (Arpi, 2009: 154). Indeed, the Fourteenth Dalai Lama's public stance regarding negotiations has been increasingly focused on the theme of "the welfare and ultimate happiness of the Tibetan people" (Dalai Lama, 1980: 59n4).

More saliently, the question of Tibetans as a *people* defined by the *chölkha sum* has been a driving force of many exiled intellectuals. For example, Dawa Norbu, in his lengthy dissertation on the Sino-Tibetan question, legitimated the TGIE's claims to self-determination in terms of external, ethnological discussions about the unified nature of Tibetans as a people (Norbu, 2001: 341–42). The same holds true of TGIE officials: the TGIE's Minister for the Department of Home, Kalon Tashi Wangdi's 1997 essay on 'Self-Determination and the Tibetan Issue' clearly formulates Tibetan claims to self-determination in terms of internationally formulated ideas of ethnicity—of Tibetans as a 'people' in the United Nations and UNESCO sense (Wangdi, 1997).

CONCLUSION

In his work *Time and the Other*, Johannes Fabian argues that an unfortunate feature of anthropological practice is the tendency to bestow on others a cultural timelessness; an unmoving weight of tradition that serves to divest those Others of the kind of cultural agency that we would take for granted in any description of our own lives. In many respects, the over-determining anthropological notion of *identity* performs much the same function—although often used to valorise cultural voices, it also tends to ossify them. To extend the theatrical narrative introduced at the beginning, the *dramatis personae* of most plays contrasts the narrative evolution of certain central characters with the unchanging determinism of peripheral ones. Othello transforms, but Cassio and Iago remain ever the same. By the same token, we describe the West in terms of its *transformation*—according to narratives of modernity, freedom, civilization—but valorize and demonize Others (and there are few that have been so consistently Other than the Tibetans) in terms of their unchanging *identity*.

Above, we have traced some aspects of the multiple performances of belonging that the Ganden Podrang government at Lhasa and its exiled successor have deployed as part of their generation, less of a fixed cultural identity than of a *developing biographical narrative of state.* This narrative emerged out of the coordination of certain aspects of Tibetan history—the ascendancy of the ancient Tibetan kings, the ceremonial centrality of Lhasa, the *chölkha sum* as the constitutional basis of Pakpa's *chöyön* relation with the Mongols, and the rise of the Dalai Lamas—into the dominant narrative of the unfolding of Avalokiteśvara's obligation to Tibet. In the 20th century, this narrative has been both augmented and transformed with a growing concentration on the *chölkha sum* as the basis of Tibetans as a self-determining people.

Finally, it is instructive that many of these performances of belonging are built out of, and transformed by, histories of conflict: the Mongol supremacy of the 13th century; the Pakmodru coup d'état; Guśri Khan and the Fifth Dalai Lama's reunification of Tibet; and finally the Sino-Tibetan conflict of 1950–59. As Lan has described in detail regarding Zimbabwe's war of liberation, sovereign narratives of the relationship among religion, land, and the people are almost inevitably reinvented during times of war.

NOTES

1. *Source*: Website of the Central Tibetan Administration (http://tibet.net/map-of-tibet/), accessed April 2010.
2. *China Daily*, 2007.
3. See *KKM*, 302–5; *MKB*, 407–8.
4. On this myth, see (Mills, 2007; Miller, 1998).
5. For a listing of this gift of myriarchs, see (Tucci, 1989 [1941]: 85). Tibetan sources such as the *Vaidurya dKar po* and Shakabpa see it as occurring in 1253–54 and conferring 'supreme authority' over Tibet (Shakabpa, 1984: 65), Petech suggests 1265 arguing that it was 'largely theoretical' (Petech, 1983: 190). Tucci sees it as a form of 'nominal viceregency' (Tucci, 1949: 14).
6. T. *bod chen po'i rgyal khams.*
7. The bodhisattvas Vajrapani, Manjuśri, and Avalokiteśvara.
8. T. *mnga' sgyur.*
9. T. *nyes la chad pa dang bzang la bye ster ba sogs khrims kyi byed bo.*
10. This in many respects follows the long-standing Tibetan constitutional principle of *chösi-zungdrel*, 'the articulation of religious and temporal governance' (Cüppers, 2004).
11. The name *Chushi Gangdruk* was apocryphally chosen by Trijiang Rinpoche, the Dalai Lama's junior tutor, during the Monlam Chenmo Festival at Lhasa. I have, however, yet to confirm this.
12. The ceremony for this is called the *tenshuk zhabten* (T. *bstan bzhugs zhabs rten*).
13. See also Khétsun, 2008: 29.
14. *Tsampa* is ground-roasted barley, the principal foodstuff in Tibet.

REFERENCES

Tibetan References

CZ: *lCags-stag zhib-gzhung (The Iron Tiger Decree).* 1830 government tax settlement), eds. Ye-shes Tshul-krims, Ngag-dbang Chos-dar, sLob-bzang rGyal-mtshan, and sKal-bzang sGrol-dkar. Lhasa: Krung-go Bod-kyi shes-rig dpe-skrun-khang, 1989.

D5NIV: Sangs-rGyas rGya-mTsho. *Drin-can rtsa-ba'i bla-ma Ngag-dbang blo-bzang rgya-mtsho'i thun-mon-ma'i rnam-thar du-ku-la'i gos bzang las glehs bam gsum-pa'i las 'phro bzhi-pa* (Biography of the Fifth Dalai Lama, Vol. IV). TBRC No. W23956.

GJG: Ngor-pa DKon-mChok Lhun-Grub (1497–1557). *Dam-pa'i chos-kyi 'byung tshul legs-par bshad-pa bstan-pa'i rgya-mtshor 'jug-pa'i gru-chen.* Completed in 1692 by Bya-bral Sangs-rgyas Phun-tshogs (1649–1705). Ngawang Topgey, New Delhi, 1973.

GSM: bSod-nams rGyal-mtshan. *rgyal-rabs gsal-ba'i me-long (Clear mirror of royal genealogies).* Delhi: Tibetan Bonpo Monastic Centre, 1973. Tibetan Buddhist Resource Centre, Vol. 2645, work number 23770.

GGD: Ngag-dbang blo-bzang rgya-mtsho, *Bod-kyi deb-ther spyid-kyi rgyal-mo'i glu dbyangs* (Fifth Dalai Lama's History of Tibet, called *The Song of the Queen of Spring*), 1643.

KKM: *bka'-chems ka-khol-ma* (Pillar testament). Kansu'u mi-rigs dpe-skrun-khang, 1989.

LC: Lde'u Jo-sras. *Lde'u chos-'byung.* Lhasa, 1987.

MG: Klong-rdol bla-ma ngag-dbang blo-bzang (1719–94). *Bstan-pa'i sbyin-bdag byon-tshul-gyi ming-gi grangs.* In *The Collected Works of Longdol Lama.* Ed. (1973) Lokesh Chandra. New Delhi: International Academy of Indian Culture, pp. 1215–53.

MKB: *Maṇi bka'-'bum.* Vol. 1(E): *Bla brgyud gsol-'debs dang lo-rgyus skor sgrub-thabs-kyi chos-skor.* New Delhi, 1975.

SZND: Private Office of the XIVth Dalai Lama, *gZhung-zhabs mjal-thengs bzhi-pa'i thog stsal-ba'i bka'-slob, 17.11.1959.* In *Srid-zhi'i rnam 'dren gong-sa skyabs-mgon chen-po mchog nas slob-grwa khag sogs la shes-yon slob-sbyong byed sgo'i skor stsal-ba'i bka'-slob phyogs bsdebs bzhugs so//.* Vol. 1, 2000.

Other References

Ahmad, Zahiruddin. 1995. *A History of Tibet by the Fifth Dalai Lama.* Indiana University Oriental Series. Vol. VII. Indiana University Research Institute for Inner Asian Studies: Bloomington, Indiana.

Angdrugtsang, Gompo Tashi. 1973. *Four Rivers, Six Ranges: Reminiscences of the Resistance Movement in Tibet.* Dharamsala: Information and Publicity Office of H.H. the Dalai Lama.

Aran, Gideon. 1991. 'Jewish-Zionist Fundamentalism: The Case of the Gush Emunim (Bloc of the Faithful)', in R. Scott Appleby and E. Marty Martin (eds), *Fundamentalisms Observed*, pp. 265–345. Chicago: University of Chicago Press.

Arpi, Claude. Jahr. 2009. *Dharamsala and Beijing: The Negotiations That Never Were*. New Delhi: Lancer.

Bell, Vikki. 1999. *Performativity and Belonging*. Ort: SAGE Publications.

China Daily. 'An illusion called "greater Tibet area"', *China Daily*, 3 October 2007.

Cüppers, Christopher. 2004. *The Relationship between Religion and State (chos srid zung 'brel) in Traditional Tibet*. Lumbini: Lumbini International Research Institute.

Dalai Lama, XIV. 1980. *Collected Statements, Interviews and Articles*. Dharamsala: The Information Office of His Holiness the Dalai Lama.

Dotson, Brandon. 2006. *Administration and Law in the Tibetan Empire: The Section on Law and State and its Old Tibetan Antecedents*. Unpublished DPhil, Oriental Institute, University of Oxford.

Dreyfus, Georges. 2005. 'Are We Prisoners of Shangrila? Orientalism, Nationalism and the Study of Tibet', *Journal of the International Association of Tibetan Studies*, 1 (October): 1–21.

Dunham, Michael. 2004. *Buddha's Warriors*. New York: Jeremy P. Tarcher/Penguin.

French, Patrick. 2003. *Tibet, Tibet: A Personal History of a Lost Land*. Ort: Harper Perennial.

Gold, Daniel. 1991. 'Organised Hinduisms: From Vedic Truth to Hindu Nation', in Martin E. Marty and R. Scott Appleby (eds), *Fundamentalisms Observed*, pp. 531–94. Chicago: University of Chicago Press.

Goldstein, Melvyn. 1989. *A History of Modern Tibet, 1913–1951*. Berkeley: California University Press.

———. 2007. *A History of Modern Tibet, Vol. II: 1951–1954*. Berkeley: University of California Press.

Gyatso, J. 1989. 'Down with the Demoness: Reflections on a Feminine Ground in Tibet', in J. Gyatso (ed.), *Feminine Ground: Essays on Women in Tibet*. Ithaca: Snow Lion.

Ishihama, Yumiko. 1993. 'On the Dissemination of the Belief in the Dalai Lama as a Manifestation of the Bodhisattva Avalokiteśvara', *Acta Asiatica*, 64: 38–56.

Karmay, Samten. 2010. 'The Vth Dalai Lama's State Visit to the Manchu Imperial Court in Beijing in 1653'. A Garland of Many-Coloured Flowers Adorning the Snow Mountains: Conference to Celebrate Ten Years of Tibetan Studies at Oxford. Oxford, 24–25 June 2010.

Khétsun, Tubten. 2008. *Memories of Life in Lhasa under Chinese Rule*. New York: Columbia University Press.

Library of Tibetan Works and Archives. *Chölka-sum (the three provinces of Tibet) History*. 1999. Available online at http://ltwa.net/library/index.php?option=com_content&view=article&id=142&Itemid=107&lang=en (accessed: 20 May 2009).

Lopez, Donald. 1998. *Prisoners of Shangri-La: Tibetan Buddhism and the West*. Ort: Verlag.

Miller, Robert. 1998 'The Supine Demoness' (*Srin Mo*) and the Consolidation of Empire', *Tibet Journal*, XXIII(3): 3–22.

Mills, Martin A. 2007. 'Re-Assessing the Supine Demoness: Royal Buddhist Geomancy in the Srong btsan sGam po Mythology', *Journal of the International Association for Tibetan Studies*, 3: 1–47.

Mills, Martin A. 2009. 'This Circle of Kings: Tibetan Visions of World Peace', in Peter W. Kirby (ed.), *Boundless Worlds: Anthropological Approaches to Movement*, pp. 95–114. Ort: Berghahn Books.

Norbu, Dawa. 2001. *China's Tibet Policy*. London: Routledge.

Petech, Luciano. 1972 [1950]. *China and Tibet in the Early XVIIIth Century*. T'oung Pao Monographie I. Leiden: Brill.

———. 1980. 'The Mongol Census in Tibet', in Michael Aris and Aung Sang Suu Kyi (eds), *Tibetan Studies in Honour of Hugh Richardson*, pp. 233–38. New Delhi: Vikas.

———. 1983. 'Tibetan Relations with Sung China and the Mongols', in Morris Rossabi (ed.), *China Among Equals: The Middle Kingdom and its Neighbors, 10th–14th Centuries*, pp. 173–203. London: University of California Press.

Pirie, F. 2008. 'From Tribal Tibet: The Significance of the legal Form', in M. Freeman and D. Napier (eds), *Law and Anthropology*, pp. 143–63. Oxford: Oxford University Press.

Samuel, Geoffrey. 1993. *Civilized Shamans—Buddhism in Tibetan Societies*. Washington: Smithsonian Institute Press.

Schwartz, Ronald. 1994. *Circle of Protest: Political Ritual n the Tibetan Uprising*. London: Hurst & Co..

Shakabpa, Tsepon W.D. 1984. *Tibet—A Political History*. New York: Potala Publications.

Shakya, Tsering. 1993. 'Whither the tsampa-eaters?', *Himal*, 6(5): 8–11.

———. 1999. *Dragon in the Land of Snows: A History of Modern Tibet after 1947*. London: Pimlico Press.

Sørensen, Per. 1994. *Tibetan Buddhist Historiography: The Mirror Illuminating the Royal Genealogies*. Wiesbaden: Harrassowitz Verlag.

Southall, Aiden. 1988. 'The Segmentary State in Africa and Asia', *Comparative Studies in History and Society*, 30(1): 52–82.

Sperling, Elliott. 2004. 'The Tibet–China Conflict: History and Polemics', *Policy Studies* (East-West Center), 7. Available online at http://www.eastwestcenter.org/fileadmin/stored/pdfs/PS007.pdf).

Stein, Burton. 1980. *Peasant, State and Society in Medeival South India*. New Delhi: Oxford University Press.

Surkhang, W. 1986. 'Government, Monastic and Private Taxation in Tibet', *Tibet Journal*, 11(1): 31–39.

Tucci, Giuseppe. 1989 [1941]. *Indo-Tibetica IV.1: Gyantse and its Monasteries*, in Lokesh Chandra (ed.), *Titel*. Translated by Uma Marina Vesci. New Delhi: Aditya Prakashan.

———. 1949. *Tibetan Painted Scrolls*. Rome: La Libreria dello Stato.

Van der Kuijp, Leonard W. 2003. 'On the Life and Political Career of T'ai-si-tu Byang-Chub rGyal-mTshan (1302–1364)', in Alex McKay (ed.), *The History of Tibet*, pp. 425–66, vol. 2. London: RoutledgeCurzon.

Wangdi, Kalon Tashi. 1997. 'Self-Determination and the Tibetan Issue', *Tibetan Bulletin*, 1(4, July–August): 20–21.

Chapter 17

The Last Himalayan Monarchies

MICHAEL HUTT

...the realm I threaded together
was greater than that won by the sword.
—Shrawan Mukarung, 'Bise Nagarchi's Account'

INTRODUCTION

Much of the discussion of belonging in the Himalayas to date has dealt with themes of commonality, solidarity, and possession in relation to particular groups or communities, which are defined variously by the territory they inhabit, their ethnic or cultural identity, their religious affiliation and practices, and so on. In contrast to this, the following discussion does not focus upon belonging in relation to a group, but in relation to an institution (monarchy) and the individual (the monarch) who embodies that institution.

Although the world's more desperate states still throw up despots and dictators, the overall effect of political globalization has been a drastic reduction in the number of traditional monarchies in the world, and the reduction of monarchical power even in places where these institutions persist. This could be said to represent a global process of displacement or de-belonging of institutions that were once almost synonymous with particular nation states—or at the very least a process that has involved the renegotiation and redefinition of the terms on which monarchical belonging can be maintained.

Some of the special features of royal autocracies can be seen as strengths that make them more resilient in the face of socio-political change than non-monarchical autocracies. For instance, monarchies are less vulnerable to abolition by civilian or military coup d'état and they almost always preserve some degree of hereditary succession, which solves the problem of who is to be in control next. They also have their own unique exit options: a monarch can hold on to a permanent status as a constitutional head of state even if he loses all power. Furthermore, if a monarchy has existed for a long time it may have accumulated certain cultural rights and functions that cannot easily be reallocated to another institution or individual, and monarchies almost always have some measure of religious legitimation: medieval European monarchies ruled by divine right, protected by laws of lèse majesté; some Arab monarchies have the role of maintaining conditions in their realms that are conducive to the maintenance of Islam; the Nepali and Thai monarchies have had a similar role as Dharmarajas; and Bhutan's king is clearly Buddhist, though his religious role and status is less pronounced.

However, these features of monarchical autocracy can also serve to render monarchies more vulnerable. Although religious legitimation lends them strength, it is also important for the defender of a faith to maintain and preserve his own legitimacy, and not be outflanked or challenged by either fundamentalist or secularist forces. Similarly, succession can often amount to little more than a roll of the genetic dice and therefore brings with it certain dangers, which are heightened if intermarriage only takes place within a limited pool of elite families. Furthermore, a monarch's cultural rights and functions may relate to institutions and practices that come to be seen as archaic, exploitative, or symbolic of domination, and therefore become vulnerable to movements of social reform. And once a monarchy has been abolished, it is unlikely ever to be re-established.

THE LAST HIMALAYAN MONARCHIES

The kings of Ladakh, Sikkim, and several other once autonomous Himalayan realms are now mere figures of history. Until 28 May 2008 the Shahs of Nepal and the Wangchucks of Bhutan were the sole survivors; now only the Wangchucks remain. This discussion will seek to demonstrate that concepts of belonging can help us understand why it is that the monarch of one Himalayan nation state (Nepal) has been displaced and must now 'stand in the rain', whereas another (that of Bhutan) appears to have secured the future of his line for at least another generation. There are interesting parallels between the histories of these two monarchies, but there are also important differences.

The Shah dynasty claimed to be Rajputs who fled to the Himalayas from Chitaur in Rajasthan during the medieval period. They settled first in the Kaski area of what is now west-central Nepal, then spread eastward on two successive occasions. First one junior brother took control of Lamjung, then another, Drabya Shah, took control of Gorkha through the violent removal of its chieftain in 1559. Prithvi Narayan Shah of Gorkha embarked upon a military campaign during the 1740s, making the conquest of the rich and fertile Kathmandu valley his first objective. By 1814, when the first of a series of clashes with the British East India Company checked its expansion, Gorkha had succeeded in extending its territorial possessions to an area greatly in excess of present-day Nepal. Consequently, Prithvi Narayan Shah was subsequently invested with iconic status by Nepali nationalists as the father or 'unifier' of the nation state of Nepal, and the Shah monarchy provided a key element in the construction of a distinctive Nepalese identity. This did not prevent the Shah monarchy from being marginalized for over a hundred years, when the Rana family took charge, providing Nepal with hereditary prime ministers and reducing the kings to palace-bound figureheads until after the British, the Ranas' greatest supporters, had left the subcontinent.

Bhutan's Wangchuck dynasty is of much more recent origin. Ugyen Wangchuck of Tongsa founded his dynasty in 1907, 42 years after Bhutan's own border war with the British, and brought a long period of political instability and internal conflict to an end. Bhutanese sources frequently emphasize the 'contractual' nature of the Bhutanese monarchy, and the establishment of the monarchy is clearly one part of the adjustment Bhutan's elite had to make as it encountered and came to terms with the British colonial state (Aris, 1994; French, 1995). In Bhutan, it is the 17th-century Drukpa Kagyudpa monk Ngawang Namgyal who is revered as the creator or 'unifier' of the nation, thus occupying a place in the nationalist mythology that is comparable with Prithvi Narayan's in Nepal. Similar to the ancestors of Prithvi Narayan Shah, Ngawang Namgyal also came from outside the territory that became his realm: he fled southward from Tibet after a dispute over the succession to the position of head of the Drukpa Kagyudpa sect of Tibetan Buddhism. Ngawang Namgyal's bearded image may still be seen in almost every religious establishment in Bhutan, but the sixth mind incarnation of the Zhabdrung was quietly murdered by the state in 1931 after he had appealed to Gandhi for help to restore him to his former role and status (Wangchuck, 1999: 25–32). Many of his attributes and insignia (notably the Raven Crown) are now in the possession of the Wangchuck king. One could equate the Wangchucks with Nepal's Ranas if one took the view that both succeeded in marginalizing the founding lineage of their country, but here the similarity (even if it is accepted) ends. The Wangchucks' displacement of the Zhabdrung lineage appears to be permanent and since the reign of the third king their regime has been committed to a very particular mode of development and political modernization, whereas the Ranas' regime was not only temporary but also highly conservative. While the Wangchucks subsumed the cult of the nation's founding father because they knew that it would pose a threat to them if they did not—indeed, the fourth king, Jigme Singye Wangchuck, married the four nieces of the murdered Zhabdrung to repair relations between the two families—the Shahs' status as creators of the nation state of Nepal proved to be a liability when the very nature of that state came under challenge.

Despite the differences that exist between them, the Shahs and the Wangchucks both had to face the same dilemma during the last decades of the 20th century, as their realms opened up to the outside world and as the people dwelling within those realms turned from humble, illiterate, tribute-paying subjects into literate citizens who demanded more rights. In 1962, Mahendra Shah responded by attempting to create a system, the *panchayat vyavastha*, in which commoner politicians were admitted some right to participation, but which required them to subscribe to a royally ordained political order, and thereby controlled and circumscribed their activities. The failure of Mahendra's system of limited democracy can be attributed to its failure to assimilate the 'social forces produced by modernization' (Huntington, 1968), and to a consequent loss of legitimacy. The Wangchucks, meanwhile, have convinced the world that they are more progressive than the majority of their subjects.[1] Audible opposition to their government's policies has arisen only from one of the ethnic thirds of the population, the Lhotshampas or Bhutanese Nepalis, and this was dealt with through the simple measure of suppression and banishment during the early 1990s (see Hutt, 2003).[2] For the rest of the population, a latter-day Bhutanese version of Nepal's Panchayat system has been constructed in recent years to widespread international applause.

In the course of this discussion, we must consider both the belonging and the belongings of royal elites, and what happens when belonging is undermined or fails. Royal lineages the world over have faced the same challenges: to continue to *belong* to their nations as kings; to continue to retain their nations and states as their possessions, their *belongings*; to continue to maintain or impose upon their subjects a commonality and a collective allegiance that depends upon and includes them as monarchs. I will discuss the trajectory and fate of the Shah monarchy in some detail, touching upon contrasts with the Wangchuck case from time to time, and then summarize recent developments in Bhutan before drawing my conclusions.

COMMONALITY

Linguistic Commonality

The Shahs and the Wangchucks have both striven to construct models of their nations that are culturally homogenous, despite the objective reality of their ethnic, linguistic, and cultural diversity. In his much-cited 1984 article, Burghart identifies the designation of Nepali as the official language of Nepal, which he dates to c.1930, as the third episode in the process that led to the emergence of the concept of the nation state in Nepal (Burghart, 1996: 246). Nepali nationalist scholars have referred to Bhanubhakta Acharya's famous mid-19th century rendering of the *Ramayana* into Nepali as the 'emotional unification' of Nepal, building upon the political unification of the country under Prithvi Narayan Shah; during the Panchayat period in Nepal (1962–90), Nepali was strongly promoted as one of the three pillars of Nepali nationhood, alongside the monarchy and Hinduism. This monolingual model of what is so obviously a multilingual nation has come under sustained attack since the first Jan Andolan of 1990, and both the 1990 constitution of Nepal and the interim constitution promulgated in 2007 elevate the status of Nepal's other languages to that of *rastriya bhasa,* usually translated as 'languages of the nation', alongside the *rastra bhasa,* or 'official language of the nation', Nepali. In contrast, Bhutan's government has chosen to adopt Dzongkha as its national language, but tacitly recognizes that it is unlikely ever to perform all of the functions expected of it, not least because it remains the mother tongue of less than a third of the population and little more than a school subject for the rest. Its promotion of Dzongkha is therefore mainly of symbolic importance, as a marker of Bhutan's distinct and unique identity. In practice, much of the kingdom's business is conducted in English,[3] which is also the medium of all state education; this pragmatic approach greatly reduces the risk of opposition arising to national language policy from Bhutan's many linguistic minorities.

The linguistic commonality of Nepal's monarchs and subjects was thus predicated upon the assumption that they shared a common allegiance to Nepali, which was vigorously promoted by the government to the exclusion of all of the other languages spoken in Nepal. Once the primacy of Nepali came under attack, this commonality was also compromised. In Bhutan, a Dzongkha-speaking king presides over a polity that preserves and develops his language as a marker of its distinctive identity, but which simultaneously spreads knowledge of English across the population through its education and other policies.

Religious Commonality

Nepal was invested with a Hindu religious identity during the period of Gorkhali 'unification' and this was used to assert its distinctiveness vis-à-vis India, or 'Muglan'. The government's attempts to promote a more Sanskritized form of Hinduism during the last years of the Panchayat regime alienated minority ethnic hill groups, with the result that Nepal's status as a Hindu kingdom became a contentious issue in the aftermath of the 1990 Jan Andolan. However, it was still declared to be a Hindu kingdom in the 1990 constitution, just as it had been in the Panchayat constitution of 1962.

Sharma (2002: 22) argues that it was difficult to locate this Hinduness when the laws of the land were not derived from the *dharmashastra* and the state no longer supported or sanctioned a caste hierarchy: 'there has been a weakening of these elements and now it is only the kingship that remains the core Hindu institution' (ibid.). Nonetheless, Supreme Court decisions did continue to reflect a construction of Nepal as a Hindu state even after 1990, and Nepal's symbolic Hinduness was enshrined in symbols such as the ban on cow slaughter, the promotion of hill Hindu religious festivals such as Dasain, and a ban on proselytizing.

The Shah monarchy clearly knew that its chances of survival would be reduced if Nepal relinquished its Hindu identity. Gyanendra in particular went to some lengths to assert the Hindu character of his kingship. Lecomte-Tilouine notes that at his first Dasain as king in 2001, he visited every temple in Nepal that had a link to his lineage (2009: 234). It is also significant that Gyanendra sought to shore up the institution of monarchy after 2002 with visits to prominent shrines in India, where he was lauded by right wing Hindu organizations as the last Hindu monarch (see Ghimire, 2004; Lal, 2004).

Historically, royal elites have deployed and transmitted notions of 'cosmic order and transcendental hierarchy' (Cannadine, 1987: 3) as the means of ordering their terrestrial realms and sustaining their earthly dominance. The Hindu kings of Nepal participated in two separate hierarchies—the earthly and the cosmic—and their participation persuaded their subjects to bow to a polity that was manifestly unequal and unjust. According to Burghart, the world in which a Hindu monarchy makes sense is an interdependent one in which Brahmins, kings, and ascetics each assert their superiority in different contexts: the Brahmin in the organic universe, the ascetic in the temporal universe, and the king in the terrestrial universe:

> The terrestrial king saw himself as the divine protector of his subjects. In the form of the universal monarch Vishnu, he sat upon his throne in the centre of the kingdom; in the form of a self-existent person, he roamed at will throughout his realm. (1987: 238)

The Shah king was quite literally the 'body politic' and the auspicious body of the state was formed at the time of the coronation,[4] which took place over two days. On the first day, priests performed the *Vishnupuja*. They assembled 16 kinds of earth from different locations, attracted Vishnu to make himself present in a ritual vase (*kalasha*), then installed an image of Vishnu and conducted an *angapuja,* in which they venerated the 16 parts of Vishnu's body, beginning at the feet and working upwards. On the second day, the king was ritually besmeared with the 16 earths, beginning at the head and working downwards. Witzel provides an interesting explanation of the symbolism of the ritual besmearing. On the level of ritual topography, it established a relation between the king and earth of his realm; on the religious level, it imbued the king with the power of the location from which the earth was taken: soil from the top of a mountain was placed on his head, earth thrown up by bulls and elephants was placed on his arms, earth from an anthill was placed on his ears, and earth from a courtesan's doorway strengthened his procreative powers (Witzel, 1987: 446–47). The king was next sprinkled with waters of various qualities and from different places, and then anointed by four people, belonging to the four Hindu *varna*s,

> with clarified butter carried by a Brahmin in a gold pot, with milk brought by a Kshatriya in a silver container, with curdled milk brought in a copper vessel by a Vaishya, and by a Shudra, who brings honey in a wooden pot. (Lecomte-Tilouine, 2009: 205)

The king was therefore a recreation of the primordial being *purusa*, reconstituted by its different members, and a living embodiment of the Hindu *varna* hierarchy. 'The king constituted the kingdom as an encompassment hierarchy which possessed only one will. In this sense the king was everyone and therefore the only one', writes Burghart (1987: 248), and the functions of government were the limbs of the royal body politic, coordinated by the mind of the king. The king's embodiment of and terrestrial authority over the realm was reflected by the fact that only he was entitled to make gifts of land—to Brahmins, ascetics, and deities—and that his moral authority over the gifted land and its occupants continued, despite the fact that he had relinquished his proprietary authority over it.

Witzel (1987: 464–65) observes that the coronation ritual of the Shah king is supposed to be followed by the king making a procession around the city on an elephant and then a general audience at the palace, and that while Mahendra passed through the busiest parts of the city of Kathmandu after his coronation in 1956, Birendra 'merely skirted the town in the East' and concluded with a circumambulation of the Tundikhel parade ground—apparently the idea of a circumambulation of the whole city had been abandoned for security reasons. After Gyanendra had been crowned in June 2001, his entourage passed under armed guard through sullen crowds by the most direct route of return.

Writing in the mid-1980s, Burghart noted that although the ritual symbolism of the identity of king and realm persisted in native belief, it had lost its power to influence the believers: 'The pomp goes on, but there was a time when the pomp was also powerful' (1987: 269). He explains the 'change in the force of the idea' in terms of a transformation of the political economy. Land and labour were increasingly allocated by market forces, not by royal command, and the government of Nepal had become 'increasingly bound up with its citizens rather than its gods' (ibid.: 270). In 1990 the new 'democratic' constitution removed many of the king's powers, but he retained the status of commander in chief of the army, 'the most basic aspect of the role of a king, that of warrior'.[5] And this was the role in which the Shah monarchy took its last stand, as the Brahmin leaders of the Maoist insurgency fought to strip it of the last vestiges of its terrestrial authority (Lecomte-Tilouine, 2009: 226, 228).

One of the first acts of the reinstated House of Representatives in the aftermath of the 'second Jan Andolan' of March–April 2006 was to declare that Nepal would henceforth be a secular state, even before the interim constitution had begun to be drafted. It would appear to be a precondition for the success of a republican movement that a king's subjects should first lose their belief in the sense of shared commonality: the idea that *he is them and they are him.* The gap that has opened up between the ritually constituted Nepal of the four Hindu *varna*s that crowned its kings and the real Nepal of minority grievance, identity assertion, and equality discourse now yawns too wide to provide any basis for a Hindu monarchy. The Shah monarchy came to an end in 2008 because the Nepal that needed it, and gave it its raison d'être, had also ceased to exist.[6] The Maoist leader Baburam Bhattarai suggested in early April 2008 that the king would retain his 'cultural rights' (*sanskritik adhikar*), but this was swiftly contradicted by another leader, Ram Bahadur Thapa, and debate on the matter then seems to have been suppressed.[7] The definition of these 'cultural rights' was never clear, but most observers took this as a reference to the king's ceremonial duties at various national rituals, such as Indra Jatra, Bhote Jatra, and Dasain. Thus far, first the interim Prime Minister and then the President have stepped into the breach on these occasions. Perhaps one of the inevitable consequences of the abolition of the Shah monarchy will be that many of the traditions that affirm Nepal's national, Hindu identity and that also render Nepal exotic for visitors and observers from the outside world will slip into oblivion.

Bhutan's new constitution (at http://www.constitution.bt) stops short of defining Bhutan as a Buddhist state or identifying Buddhism as the state religion. Instead, it describes Buddhism as the 'spiritual heritage' of Bhutan (Article 3.1) and describes the Druk Gyalpo (the king) as 'the protector of all religions in Bhutan' (Article 3.2). The linkages between politics and religion are emphasized in its exposition of the *choe-sid-nyi* or 'Dual System'. For instance, Article 2.1 declares 'The Chhoe-sid-nyi of Bhutan shall be unified in the person of the Druk Gyalpo [King of Bhutan] who, as a Buddhist, shall be the upholder of the Chhoe-sid'. There has also been some blurring of Bhutan's national identity with the concept of the Buddhist trinity. The most important formulation expressing Bhutan's national commonality is that of the *Tsa Wa Sum*, the 'Three Roots' or 'Three Foundations', which mirrors the Buddhist trinity of the Buddha, the Dharma, and the Sangha in which a Buddhist takes refuge. The *Tsa Wa Sum* formulation dates back to the reign of Jigme Dorji Wangchuck, and was originally intended to signify 'Government, Country and People' (Phuntsho, 2004: 576); however, during the early 1990s it was increasingly rendered as 'King, Country and People', an entity to which the loyalty of Bhutan's Nepali population came increasingly into question.

However, despite the above and although it is clear that the king of Bhutan is a Buddhist, he is clearly not a 'Buddhist king' in the same way that the Shahs were Hindu kings. In Bhutan, the Central Monk Body, and not the king, is the sole arbiter on religious matters, and the Je Khenpo who sits at its head is the only individual accorded the same rank as the king.

Commonality of Origin

All of Nepal's several monarchies (Licchavi, Malla, Shah) have claimed to be of ancient or medieval Indian origin. After most of the Indian subcontinent to the south fell under first Afghan and Mughal and then British domination, this legitimized them in their status as Hindu rulers of the only unsullied Hindu realm—a commonality based on the fiction of shared Hinduness. Later, however, it made them vulnerable to nationalist republican assaults on their Nepali credentials, which undermined the monarchy's claim to commonality with the people of Nepal.

Marie Lecomte-Tilouine summarizes two versions of the arrival of the Shah family on what is now Nepali soil. According to the first, preserved in the 18th- and 19th-century Gorkha chronicles, the Shahs were Rajput survivors of the city of Chitaur in Rajasthan, which was destroyed in 1303 and again in 1567, who fled north to the mountains to 'protect their dharma' and save their lives, bringing their tutelary deity with them. She writes that '[r]ecent history has retained this version as it obviously serves a purpose—that of providing the Shah dynasty with a noble Rajput and Hindu origin' (2009: 101). An alternative version, preserved in the *Goraksaraja Vamsavali*, a text dated tentatively to the reign of Ram Shah (1614–36), has it that the Nepali line was established by a king whose dynasty were sovereigns of the Jambira fort. This king, Manmatha, abdicated and left to take refuge in the Himalayan forest, accompanied by his youngest son, Jaikhan. After the old king died, Jaikhan married in Lasargha (located in what is now the Gulmi district of western Nepal), where the people consecrated him as their chieftain; Lecomte suspects that his bride was a Magar princess. She argues that this version does not survive in later texts or oral traditions simply because it is too commonplace: 'it does not glorify Rajput heroism, does not present divine will in the choice of the new site for settlement, and cannot reinforce a national feeling' (ibid.: 102). Lecomte-Tilouine also identifies some striking parallels between the story of the Shahs' arrival in Nepal and the origin myths of the Maski Rana, a Magar lineage that provides the priests for the Alam Devi shrine at Lasargha. The shrine was traditionally visited once every five years by the reigning Shah monarch (by helicopter most recently). Thus, the royal family worshipped a Magar goddess as its lineage divinity, at a shrine where the priests shared the same origin story, located in a region that according to official history the Shahs had conquered only recently. The Shah lineage clearly has a relationship with the Magar ethnic group that has been played down in the official narratives, which prefer to play up its Rajput origins and Thakuri caste status.

This strategy of suppressing notions of local allegiance with an indigenous ethnic group made sense when the primary imperative was to emphasize the dynasty's pure Hindu character, legitimized by its descent from a line of prestigious Hindu kings. However, when the Hindu character of the Nepali state began to be challenged after 1990 and minority groups between to assert their separate non-Hindu identities, the Shahs' claim to belong in and to Nepal was weakened by the inescapable legacy of their much-vaunted Indian origins.

In contrast, the Wangchucks are universally believed to be descended from the 15th century Bhutanese culture hero Padmalingpa, the 'treasure revealer' (*terton*) who revealed the sacred Buddhist texts left by Padmasambhava. Padmalingpa is probably the most important Bhutanese religious figure after the Zhabdrung himself, and unlike Ngawang Namgyal he is untainted by any hint of foreign origin.

A further line of republican attack has been to cast doubt upon the king's efficacy as a preserver of sovereignty and to suggest that he is either in collusion with or selling the country out to foreign forces. In his famous *Kantipur* piece of 6 June 2001, the Maoist leader Baburam Bhattarai wrote that an important contribution of the Shah kings (from Prithvi Narayan Shah to King Birendra) had been 'to preserve Nepali independence and sovereign status from the hands of British imperialism and later from Indian expansionism' (Bhattarai, 2001). But now, the Nepali people would never accept 'the new Jigme Singye who has come to power by staging a Kot massacre', and whom Bhattarai described as 'the puppet of expansionist forces in the palace'. The fact that the editor and publisher of Kantipur were arrested on treason charges for publishing this article demonstrates the sensitivity of the issue (Hutt, 2006). Bhattarai's piece also reveals the extreme contempt with which the Nepali political left views the Bhutanese monarchy, which it accuses of selling out Bhutan's national interests to India. The suspicion that Nepal's leaders are always liable to compromise Nepal's sovereignty is also reflected in a more recent characterization of allegedly pro-Indian Nepali politicians as 'Lhendup Dorjes', a reference to India's absorption of Sikkim in 1974–75.[8]

Common Membership of a Moral Community

According to Lecomte-Tilouine, the Shah monarchy's Thakuri marriage practices were seen as incestuous and as further evidence of their foreign origins, but the Shah monarchy's loss of relevance and legitimacy is better explained in terms of the falling calibre of successive kings than by any public misgivings about its morality. While Mahendra was revered by many, Birendra was seen as avuncular but ineffectual. When the security forces were used against pro-democracy demonstrators in 1990, anti-king slogans such as

Birendra Chor Desh Chor ('thief Birendra leave the country') were briefly aired on the streets, but when Birendra stepped back and agreed to unban political parties and accept a constitutional status this period of serious unpopularity came swiftly to an end.

The moral character of the king really became a factor only after the enthronement of Gyanendra. At first this was because he came to power as a direct consequence of the palace massacre of 2001, the official explanation for which failed to convince many Nepalis, who preferred to sign up to one or another of a wide range of conspiracy theories.[9] Many refused to believe that a true Nepali son could ever kill his own mother and sister. The Nepali public's distrust of Gyanendra was matched only by its dislike of the crown prince, Paras, who was widely believed to be responsible for at least one fatal drunken-driving incident. Gyanendra was also disliked by many for his willingness to seek a military solution to the Maoist insurgency, unlike (they said) his brother Birendra, who was said to have been reluctant to set one Nepali against the other.

In 2005, the poet Shrawan Mukarung received a great deal of attention in the Nepali media for his public recitation of a poem entitled 'Bise Nagarchiko Bayan' ('Bise Nagarchi's Account').[10] Bise Nagarchi, a figure of Nepali historical folklore, is said to have been a tailor at the court of Prithvi Narayan Shah to whom the king turned for advice and counsel. Mukarung told me that he was inspired to write the poem after he visited the old palace at Gorkha, where it was explained to him that Bise Nagarchi's village had once stood on the site of the palace but was demolished to create space for its construction.[11] An extract from the poem follows (my translation):

Master!
Does your sword chop off heads now, or flowers?
I've been deluded.
Does your rifle shoot down thoughts, or people?
I've been deluded.
Did the subjects make this kingdom, or the king?
I've been deluded.
I've been in front of you now for 250 years,
Master!
How can I be a terrorist?

I've just gone mad, Master. Mad.

It's true, I may not have upheld Master's *Dibya Upadesh*,
I may have drunk raksi and declared
That I too won this country,
I may have called my sewing needle
The equal of Bhanubhakta's songs;
I may have shown my naked body
To those who wear the clean clothes I have tailored;
After I went mad I may even
Have insulted my own Lord.
Master!
Once a man has gone mad he makes excuses
Even to himself;
Where have they gone,
My offspring, the ones I laced into rags
For 250 years?
I may have wanted to search for them.
The pins that pricked my hands
And the blood that ran from them
Provoked me,
I may have decided that the realm I threaded together
Was greater than that won by the sword.
Master!
I am in your nation,
Along with the history of this soil,
How can I be a non-national?
I have gone truly mad Master!
Truly mad.

My head is spinning,
The ground is the sky,
The sky is the earth,
And as my eyes are dazzled
I see you with ten heads.
Oh, where are my feet?
Where is Bise Nagarchi?
Master! I've gone mad!

The poem was widely interpreted as a condemnation of Gyanendra for allowing the deaths of so many of his subjects in the conflict between the Royal Nepalese Army and the CPN (Maoist). Indeed, this may have been a more important factor in Gyanendra's growing unpopularity than the suspicion that he had some hand in his own brother's death. Only 24 per cent of those surveyed by Hachhethu et al.

(2008; see below) said they wanted an end to the monarchy because they suspected the king of involvement in the 2001 royal massacre, and only 9 per cent because they disliked Gyanendra and Paras.

POSSESSION AND ATTACHMENT

Monarchies have embodied nations, provided them with nationalist symbols, and preserved their sovereignty and borders. If nations are imagined communities, monarchies have usually been imagined embodiments of those communities. They and their supporters have claimed that they unify disparate nations and deliver progress and development.

In Panchayat-period Nepal the people expressed their love for the monarchy, and if foreign and Bhutanese media reports are to be believed they continue to do so in present-day Bhutan. However, *anciens régimes* collapse when their natural supporters are no longer bound by ideas of divine right, and no longer see monarchs as acting in their interests. In a recent opinion poll survey, Hachhethu et al. (2008: 49–53) found that 59 per cent of the 4,089 ordinary citizens in their sample were in favour of a republic, whereas 41 per cent wanted to retain the monarchy. The data reveal a radical shift in public opinion against the monarchy since 2004, when only 15 per cent of those interviewed favoured a republic. As the Nepali experience shows, republican arguments can gain force with great rapidity, especially when the monarch himself fulfils republican prophecies with the alacrity of Gyanendra Shah. Public sentiment (and, more importantly, the *public articulation of private sentiment*) can quickly change. As recently as in 2000, an Indian historian of the Shah monarchy felt able to state:

> In the Nepalese context, it seems that despite a transition from a monarchical form of government to a democratic one the institution of monarchy has deep socio-cultural and religious roots. The people of Nepal have great faith in the institution of monarchy. Even, during the 1990 movement for democracy, the institution of monarchy was not opposed by pro-democratic forces. The monarchy has not only been socially acceptable but has remained a cohesive force in the nation-building process of the country. It is true that the monarchy in Nepal has enjoyed an unbroken record of faith of the people, playing a cementing role, holding together divergent forces under one national

banner. Nepalese nationalism has grown and has been nurtured under the leadership of the Crown from the earliest times to the present day. (Shukla, 2000: 4)

Only 8 years later, the monarchy was gone.

Referring to the kingdom of Gorkha at the turn of the 19th century, Burghart defines two modes of royal ownership: of a territorial domain (*muluk*) described as the 'entire possessions of the king of Gorkha' and of a realm (*desa*) within which the king exercised his ritual authority. He identifies 1860 as the date at which the boundaries of the realm came to overlap with the boundary of the possessions, after which it became important to classify and incorporate Nepal's many ethno-linguistic communities, each of which inhabited its own 'country', and to create a definition of 'Nepaliness', which would be 'spread throughout the realm to its very borders with India and China' (1996: 258). Mahendra sought to introduce a distinction between king and state by introducing the concept of *desh-seva*, 'service to the country' in which both the king and the citizen would engage. He realized that it is dangerous for a king to consider himself the owner of the nation state over which he reigns—that is, to believe that it constitutes his *belongings*—because in another sense he is also the property of that nation, which can dispose of the monarchy altogether if it so chooses.

A republican movement must convince the nation that the king sees himself as its owner, that it does not belong to the king, and that it has no need for a king. Such a movement is greatly helped in the first of these by the fact that monarchies often preside over staggering concentrations of wealth (on the Nepal case, see Humagai, 2008). These concentrations of wealth cannot be preserved during a democratic transition, and republican rhetoric finds them a ready target. Here is one example of such rhetoric:

> Dear Nepali citizens and foreign lovers of Nepal, you might be wondering why Nepal is still poor when its countries of equal economic status have reached the sky with booming economic development. Let me try to answer—this is one of the reasons, I have recently found. Nepal is one of the poorest countries of the world but Nepal's king is the highest paid king of the world. The income of Nepali king Gyanendra Bir Bikram Shah Dev is 2,426 times higher than that of the Chinese president, 318 times higher than that of the Indian president, 301

times higher than that of the Pakistani president, 173 times higher than that of the Russian president, 57 times higher than that of the French president, 15 times higher than that of the British prime minister, 10 times higher than that of the American president ... the Nepali king earns Rs 61,91,00,000 (per capita income is Rs 16,560 = US$ 230). This means the Nepali king earns Rs. 19,878 times more than a citizen. Last year it was 37,385 times higher. Thus a citizen can earn as much as the king earns in a year only after working for 19,000 years or in 316 lives. Ho la! (Shyam Thapa, in Mulyankan Nov–December 2005; taken from Internet posting[12])

At its first full meeting on 19 May 2006 Nepal's reinstated House of Representatives stripped the king of his institutional possessions. It issued a proclamation that removed the words 'His Majesty's' (*Shri 5ko*) and 'Royal' (*shahi, rajakiya*) from every body of the state, and placed the army under civilian control. It also announced that the private property of the king would be taxed as per the law, that acts performed by the King could henceforth be questioned in the House of Representatives or in courts, and that the National Anthem would be changed.[13]

After Nepal was declared a republican state two years later, Gyanendra was required to leave Narayanhiti Palace. In the speech he gave on the day of his departure he stated that over the seven years of his reign he had no interest in anything but the sovereignty (*sarvabhaumsatta*), independence (*svatantrata*), self-respect (*svabhiman*), indivisibility (*akhandata*) of the country (*muluk*), and the institutional development of peace and democracy. He emphasized that all of his wealth was in Nepal, and that he did not own any movable or immovable property outside the country; he also denied that he had added to his wealth in any way during his reign.

Borgstrom identifies a 'correlation between traditional authority and formalised language':

Formalisation supports traditional authority by making argument impossible. It prevents action because it moves language to the realm of the non-historical, non-specific and ambiguous... Traditional authority must, in order to have any meaning at all, refer to a society in which leadership is endowed with sanctions that are not questioned; that is, a society in which power relations are treated as axiomatic. The successful use of formalised language confirms the stability of the power structure. That is why one cannot, as Bloch points out, argue with it, and why it has to be rejected altogether by an opponent. (Borgström, 1980: 36)

Gyanendra's loss of power and traditional authority was signalled by his use of language that was no longer 'non-historical, non-specific and ambiguous'. His leadership was no longer 'endowed with sanctions' and power relations were no longer axiomatic. As he departed, he gave a speech of self-justification that almost pleaded for understanding.

After the 2001 palace massacre, an increasing number of people began to believe that the end of the Shah monarchy was inevitable. Soon after the massacre the legend of Gorakhnath's curse became a matter for public discussion. Gorakhnath was an 11th century yogi who was believed to be the protector of the kingdom of Gorkha. According to the version of the legend that circulated in 2001 and thereafter, Prithvi Narayan Shah once came across Gorakhnath in a forest. The king offered some curd to the meditating yogi, who ate and then regurgitated it, asking the king to take it into his own mouth. Prithvi Narayan refused and as the regurgitated curd dribbled onto the king's ten toes, Gorakhnath uttered a curse, saying that because of Prithvi Narayan's pride his dynasty would be obliterated after ten generations. Birendra was the ninth descendant of Prithvi Narayan, and many concluded that the days of the Shah monarchy were therefore numbered. However, this interpretation seems to diverge quite radically from the original one, according to which Gorakhnath stated that Prithvi Narayan would become the ruler of the next ten places in which he set his feet.

Another popular tradition that was widely cited at this time was that of the sati's curse (satiko sarap), which people cited as a prediction of the end of the Shah lineage. The only reference to this in the standard literature comes in Hasrat (1970: 84), who states that the curse was laid by a queen of King Jagatjayamalla, who announced from her pyre the end of the Malla kings and the coming of the Shahs. What appears to have occurred here is that a number of myths dating back to the period of Malla monarchy in the Kathmandu valley as well to the early years of Gorkhali conquest and rule were conflated and re-deployed in the new context as inauspicious omens. Marie Lecomte-Tilouine also recalls being told by a Newar woman that the Shah dynasty would end soon, because there was no more room to hang the picture of the next king in the Pashupatinath temple.[14]

WANGCHUCK DEMOCRACY

Bhutan's monarchy appears to have secured at least a medium-term future for itself through a palace-sponsored process of democratization. In 1998 the king appointed a Council of Ministers, and a prime minister began to represent the country in overseas fora, instead of the king. In 2005 Bhutan's first written constitution was taken out to every district for a long and carefully guided process of comment, discussion, and consultation. The constitution provides for elections to a small upper house (the 25-seat National Council, with 20 members elected and 5 nominated by the king) and a 55-seat lower house, the National Assembly. Having stated earlier that he would abdicate when the elections were held in 2008, King Jigme Singye Wangchuck (the fourth Wangchuck king) actually abdicated in favour of his son Jigme Khesar Namgyel in December 2006.

A mock general election was conducted across the whole country in April 2007, with the electorate casting its vote for one of the four fictional parties (Druk Blue party, Druk Red party, Druk Yellow party, or Druk Green party), each of which had produced its own mock manifesto. Some 125,000 people voted in the mock election, representing around 28 per cent of eligible electors. The exercise was intended as a practice run that would familiarize voters and officials with a new electronic voting process.

A special feature of the new Bhutanese constitution is that while it allows for the establishment and registration of political parties for the very first time, and allows these parties to contest the first stage of its general elections, it allows only the two parties that garner the highest number of votes to move through to stage two. The party that wins the higher number of votes then forms the government, while the runner-up forms the opposition. Thus, Bhutan was setting out to establish a two-party democracy.

Druk Yellow won the primary round of the mock elections with 44 per cent of the total vote; in the second round it won all but one of the 47 constituencies. If media reports are to be believed, rural Bhutanese voters were not wholly convinced that democracy is what their country needs, partly because they knew that in neighbouring Nepal it was followed by widespread corruption, a violent insurrection, and the probable abolition of the Shah monarchy. The Yellow Party's landslide victory in the mock elections has been ascribed to the fact that it stood for 'culture and tradition', that yellow is the colour associated with Buddhism, and that it is also the colour of the ceremonial sash that may be worn only by the king and the Je Khenpo.

Only two parties contested the real National Assembly elections in March 2008: the People's Democratic Party (PDP), headed by the new king's uncle, and the Druk Phuensum Tshogpa (DPT), headed by the most recent chairperson of the Council of Ministers. Bhutan's Election Commission denied registration to a third party, the Bhutan People's United Party, allegedly on the grounds that its candidates did not possess the necessary competence, experience, or qualifications. This decision gave rise to some stridency even among bloggers on Bhutanese websites that are normally very strongly nationalistic and fiercely loyal to the establishment.

There was little to distinguish one party from the other in policy terms. The Druk Phuensum Tshogpa's website introduces its manifesto with these words:

> *In Pursuit of Gross National Happiness*
> *Growth with Equity and Justice*
> *We offer our unwavering allegiance to the sacred institution of monarchy, the life-force of our nation.*
> *We dedicate ourselves to realizing the vision of the Fourth Druk Gyalpo, His Majesty Jigme Singye Wangchuck, for a united, progressive and happy country.*
> *We shall be guided by His Majesty the King, Jigme Khesar Namgyel Wangchuck, in our pursuit of Gross National Happiness through a true and vibrant democracy.* (http://www.dpt.bt/manifestos_2008.php)

The People's Democratic Party's president introduces his party's manifesto thus:

> *Bhutan stands at a watershed. The Fourth Druk Gyalpo has placed the responsibility of governance in the hands of the people. In 2008, we will have for the first time in history a democratically elected government to take the nation forward.*
> *His Majesty the Fourth Druk Gyalpo stated in his last royal kasho: "As I hand over my responsibilities to my son, I repose my full faith and belief in the people of Bhutan to look after the future of our nation, for it is the Bhutanese people who are the true custodians of our tradition and culture and the ultimate guardians of the security, sovereignty and continued well being of our country".*

His Majesty the Fifth Druk Gyalpo also stated on the centennial National Day: "Today, in the womb of a strong and peaceful monarchy, we have begun to nurture the hopes of a vibrant democracy. It is this endeavour that we must henceforth uphold as our greatest priority—the success of democracy. For in the success of democracy lies the consolidation of our nation's achievements and the future happiness and well being of Bhutan".

The people from all corners of Bhutan told my colleagues and me, "We the Bhutanese must not fail to live up to Their Majesties' unconditional trust, and such noble expectations of us". (http://www.pdp.bt/)

There would thus appear to be no republican agenda in Bhutan, despite the posting of occasional attacks on the Internet. One such posting protests that there are no positions of any real political or economic importance in Bhutan that are not occupied either by Wangchucks or by their relatives; that none of Bhutan's business companies are owned by people from outside these circles; and that all of Bhutan's educational institutions are named after members of the Wangchuck family, while the contributions of the Zhabdrungs and the once-influential Dorji family are ignored.[15]

The popular media image of the benevolent and progressive monarch imposing progress and democracy on his unwilling subjects is surely a romantic simplification. These changes, which are radical in a Bhutanese context, were prompted by the ruling elite's recognition that the Bhutanese population is becoming increasingly educated and politically aware. One indication of this is that, against all predictions, the DPT won by a landslide in the general election, capturing 45 of the 47 constituencies. The PDP's president, Sangye Ngedup, who is the brother of Jigme Singye's four wives, was defeated in his own constituency. Several Bhutanese bloggers hinted that Sangye Ngedup was unpopular because his father had risen from relative obscurity to become one of Bhutan's richest businessmen solely because of his daughters' marriages to the former king (http://forums.bhutanobserver.bt/viewtopic.php?f=8&t=22). Another explanation was that PDP candidates had made too many references to the refugee issue during their campaigns. The two PDP MPs promptly resigned, protesting that voters had been unduly influenced by civil servants returning to their homes from the capital in order to cast their votes. These resignations opened up the prospect of Bhutan's new government ruling the country without any parliamentary opposition. However, they were swiftly withdrawn after an official inquiry announced that there had been no wrongdoing.

In 1992, King Jigme Singye Wangchuck told me during an audience at the Tashichö Dzong in Thimphu that in future the world would be surprised by the changes he was going to introduce. Independent research on the political culture of Bhutan is virtually impossible inside the country and much of the literature on Bhutan is guilty of exoticization. However, there are no real grounds for believing that the Bhutanese monarch is not popular among a majority of his subjects, and there is no indication of any serious challenge from within the country to him or to the system he heads. Now that his government has adjusted the country's demographic balance to ensure that the ethnic Nepali population does not gain political ascendancy, and has banished active ideological opposition from the land, he is able to embark upon genuine political reform at a pace that will probably secure the future of his line for another generation (and he is even relaxed enough to allow the representation of Nepali Bhutanese to increase once more). This does not mean that relations between the Bhutanese monarchy and the Bhutanese citizenry are not more nuanced and complex than they appear from a distance. However, there is clearly still a role for the monarchy to play in Bhutan, and the institution has been preserved through recourse to both pre-emptive ruthlessness and sensitive political foresight.

CONCLUSION

The Bhutanese monarchy has survived to this date in part because of the contractual relationship that exists between it and the Bhutanese nation state. The monarchy stands beside the nation and offers it its services, and can therefore present itself as an institution that serves a utilitarian purpose. At a popular level, Bhutanese nationalism is strong, and the insistence on a separate and distinctive Bhutanese cultural identity is sincere; the monarchy is certainly a part of this identity. However, on an economic and geopolitical level Bhutan's independence is severely circumscribed by India, and ultimately the future of the Wangchuck dynasty probably depends as much upon it delivering India's needs in terms of security and resources as it does upon the wishes of its people. Importantly, the Wangchuck monarchy does not embody or represent Bhutanese national identity to the same extent as the Shah monarchy embodied the national identity of Nepal. The monarchy belongs to the Bhutanese nation, but the public construction of its relationship with that entity is not one in which Bhutan is perceived as the possession of the king. As we have seen, there are some muted suggestions that this relationship exists mainly at the level of fiction and is in fact more exploitative than is commonly asserted. If this is true, it remains a convenient fiction nonetheless, in which a sufficient proportion of the small Bhutanese population have invested and from which they have gained enough for it to be maintained. In short, the Wangchuck monarchy belongs to the Bhutanese nation, which sees benefits in retaining it, whereas any suggestion that the king regards Bhutan as his possession is regarded as subversive.

Further west, the Nepali nation is being reshaped in a way that leaves no place or role for the Shah monarchy. The monarchy was too deeply embedded, both as an embodiment and as a possessor of the nation state, to survive these changes. A secular state does not need a Dharmaraja; a nation in which ethnic and regional elements and groupings are reasserting their distinctive identities has little time for a unifying monarch who symbolizes for so many a resented pattern of domination; and the cultural and ritual practices that call for the involvement of a king are now likely to wither away. The Shah king did not merely own or belong to his nation. He *was* that nation and all it contained—construed and constructed in a very particular way. The Nepali nation has decided to reconstruct itself, and it believes it can best do so without a king.

NOTES

1. See media reports, e.g. http://www.expressindia.com/latest-news/King-drags-Bhutan-into-democracy-first-elections/287130, http://www.legalserviceindia.com/article/l266-Monarchy-To-Democracy-In-Bhutan.html
2. Opposition to the government arose among the Sharchhop community of eastern during the mid-1990s, mainly on grounds of alleged economic inequalities between eastern and western Bhutan; however, this seems to have fallen away. See Amnesty International, 1998.
3. For instance, the anthropologist Richard Whitecross reports that Bhutanese government officials invariably prepare draft legislation in English and then translate it into Dzongkha. This is disseminated in both English and Dzongkha, but the Dzongkha version is treated as authoritative (Whitecross, 2006).
4. According to Burghart (ibid.: 269) 'Hail the realm, hail the king' (*jay desa, jay naresa*) was, in a way, saying the same thing twice over'.

5. It is significant that at cremation the royal corpse is carried to the pyre not by kinsmen but by Brahmins enlisted in the army.

6. It was curious that almost all Nepali media commentaries referred to it as the '239-year-old Shah dynasty', as if it was established in 1769.

7. In the earlier meeting with (RPP [Nepal] chairman Kamal) Thapa Prachanda had proposed that if the king voluntarily abdicated then he would be accorded a respectful place and could even be allowed to be active in politics. Dr Baburam Bhattarai had also said that if the king voluntarily gives up his throne then he would be given 'cultural rights'. The Maoist party later clarified that giving cultural rights to the King did not mean that he would remain as a cultural king. (http://nepalese-monarchy. blogspot.com/2008/05/thapa-meets-maoist-leadership-to-convey.html)

8. Dil Sahani, 'Lhendup Dorjeharu' in *Kalam* 17.1, Asar, 2066: 12–13.

9. Alternative explanations for the palace massacre continue to be published and circulated, 9 years after it occurred. See, for instance, Gyawali (2065 b.s.).

10. See, for instance, the article in the *Nepali Times* archived at www.nepalitimes. com.np/issue/2005/08/05/Review/670

11. Personal communication, Shrawan Mukarung, Kathmandu, 30 June 2009.

12. This English translation was posted on a large number of websites and blogs in early 2006. See, for instance, http://bignepal.com/forum/index. php?showtopic=969

13. A National Anthem Selection Taskforce (*rastragan chayan karyadal*) was appointed by the Minister of Culture, and this put out a nationwide call for citizens to send in compositions that would be considered for adoption as the new national anthem. 1272 submissions were received, and a composition by Pradeep Kumar Rai (aka Byakul Maila) was eventually selected. This makes no mention of the monarchy, nor of any of the other traditional symbols of the Nepali nation state, but instead stresses cultural diversity and inclusivity. The new anthem was given the taskforce's official approval on 20 April 2007 and declared the new national anthem by the House of Representatives on 3 August. The endorsement came after a long and acrimonious debate in the Nepali media about whether it was appropriate to adopt it when its author was found to have included a song by 'G. Shah' in an anthology he had edited some 4 years earlier.

14. I am indebted to Marie Lecomte-Tilouine for her advice on these myths and legends (personal communication via email, 2/6/2009).

15. http://lhapaa.wordpress.com/2007/05/15/the-wangchuk-economy

REFERENCES

Amnesty International. 1998. *Bhutan: Crack-Down on 'Anti-Nationals' in the East.* London: AI.

Aris, Michael. 1994. *The Raven Crown, the Origins of Buddhist Monarchy in Bhutan.* London: Serindia Publications.

Bhattarai, Baburam. 2001. 'Naya kotparva lai manyata dinu hundaina', in *Kantipur*, 6 June 2001.

Borgström, Bengt-Erik. 1980. 'The Best of Two Worlds: Rhetoric of Autocracy and Democracy in Nepal', *Contributions to Indian Sociology*, 14(1): 35–50.

Burghart, Richard. 1987. 'Gifts to the Gods: Power, Property and Ceremonial in Nepal', in David Cannadine and Simon Price (eds), *Rituals of Royalty: Power and Ceremonial in Traditional Societies.* Cambridge: Cambridge University Press.

———. 1996. *The Conditions of Listening. Essays on Religion, History and Politics in South Asia.* New Delhi: Oxford University Press.

Cannadine, David 1987. 'Introduction: Divine Rites of Kings', in David Cannadine and Simon Price (eds), *Rituals of Royalty: Power and Ceremonial in Traditional Societies.* Cambridge: Cambridge University Press.

French, Patrick. 1995. *Younghusband: The Last Great Imperial Adventurer.* London: HarperCollins.

Ghimire, Yuvaraj. 2004. 'Hindu ativadiko khelma raja', *Himal Khabarpatrika* (30 January–12 February): 32–38.

Gyawali, Arjun. 2065 b.s. *Darbar hatyakandko rahasya.* Kathmandu: Sachetan Manch.

Hachhethu, Krishna , Sanjay Kumar, and Jiwan Subedi. 2008. *Nepal in Transition: A Study on the State of Democracy.* Lalitpur: International IDEA.

Hasrat, Vikram Jit. 1970. *History of Nepal as Told by its Own and Contemporary Chroniclers.* Hoshiarpur: V.V. Research Institute Press.

Humagai, Mukul. 2008. 'Arabpati matra raja. Bhupu raja hune tarkharma raheka Gyanendra Shahko vyaparik bhavisya ke hola?' *Nepal.* 295, 27 May (Internet).

Huntington, Samuel P. 1968. *Political Order in Changing Societies.* New Haven: Yale University Press.

Hutt, Michael. 2003. *Unbecoming Citizens. Culture, Nationhood and the Flight of Refugees from Bhutan.* New Delhi: Oxford University Press.

———. 2006. 'Things That Should Not Be Said: Censorship and Self-Censorship in the Nepali Press Media, 2001–2002', *The Journal of Asian Studies,* 65: 361–92.

Lal, C.K. 2004. 'Ekkaisaum shatabdika raja Hindu samrat!' *Himal Khabarpatrika* (30 January–12 February): 39–41.

Lecomte-Tilouine, Marie. 2009. *Hindu Kingship, Ethnic Revival and Maoist Rebellion in Nepal.* New Delhi: Oxford University Press.

Phuntsho, Karma. 2004. 'Echoes of Ancient Ethos: Reflections on Some Popular Bhutanese Social Themes', in Karma Ura and Sonam Kinga (eds), *The Spider and the Piglet,* pp. 564–80. Thimphu: Centre of Bhutan Studies.

Sharma, Hari. 2006. 'Himal mat sarvekshan 2062 ko parinam "rajako shasan thik chaina"', *Himal Khabarpatrika* (29 March–13 April): 30–40.

Sharma, Sudhindra. 2002. 'The Hindu State and the State of Hinduism', in Kanak Mani Dixit and Shastri Ramachandran (eds), *State of Nepal.* Kathmandu: Himal Books.

Shukla, Deeptima. 2000. *Monarchy in Nepal.* Delhi: Kalinga Publications.

Wangchuck, Ashi Dorji Wangmo. 1999. *Of Rainbows and Clouds: The Life of Yab Ugyen Dorji as Told to his Daughter.* London: Serindia Publications.

Whitecross, Richard. 2006. 'Severing the Silken Knot? Buddhism, Constitutionalism and the Dual System in Bhutan'. Unpublished paper, presented at conference on 'Comparative Constitutional Traditions in South Asia', SOAS, London, 18–19 November.

Witzel, Michael. 1987. 'The Coronation Rituals of Nepal with Special Reference to the Coronation of King Birendra (1975)', in Niels Gutschow and Axel Michaels (eds), *Heritage of the Kathmandu Valley. Proceedings of an international conference in Lübeck, June 1985,* pp. 417–67. Sankt Augustin: VGH Wissenschaftsverlag.

Glossary

Adivasi	umbrella term for the 'indigenous', 'aboriginal' people of India/Nepal
anicca	Pali term for impermanence, one of the marks of existence along with suffering and not-self (Sanskrit: *anitya*)
baha	Newar Buddhist monastery
bari	non-irrigated field (Nepali)
Bahadur	a common Nepalese middle name, meaning 'brave'
Bahun	Nepali form of 'Brahman', the caste of priests
beijjat	dishonour, disgrace, despair (Nepali)
bhagne	to run away (Nepali)
Bharatiya Janata Party (BJP)	Indian People's Party
bampa	Thangmi hearth stone
bhoj	a Nepali term designating a ceremonial feast (Newari: *bhway*)
bhari bokne	to carry a load (Nepali)
bhikkhu	Buddhist monk
bidesh	foreign country (Nepali). In its common use, *bidesh* does not include India. *Bidesh janu* (Nepali) means to go and work abroad, India excluded
bisthapit	displaced people (Nepali)
bompo	a Tamang word used for shaman
Buddha Jayanti	holy day in Baisakh month (April–May) commemorating the birth, enlightenment, and death (complete enlightenment) of the Buddha

Bhutias	ethnic group in Sikkim made up of people of Tibetan ancestry
bodhisattva	Sanskrit Buddhist term for superior being intent on enlightenment
Changpa (Tibetan *byang pa*)	'Northerner', population of the Changthang highlands within Ladakh
Changthang (Tibetan *byang thang*)	'northern plains', a high-altitude plateau in western and northern Tibet extending into south-eastern Ladakh
chaure	colloquial Nepali word, mainly used in villages, to designate old wrinkled and skinny persons. The word means also useless or worthless persons as opposed to *jagire* and *lahure* that are considered to have value/worth (Nepali)
chaukidar	security guard
Chhetri	Nepali form of 'Kshatriya', the caste of warriors and rulers
Chogyal	former king of Sikkim
chölkha (Tibetan *chol kha*)	traditional 'province' of Tibet, derived from Mongolian term *chölge*
chölkha sum (Tibetan *chol kha gsum*)	three Tibetan provinces of Ü-Tsang (including Ngari), Kham and Amdo. Combined, they comprise *bod chenpo* ('greater Tibet').
chöyön (Tibetan *mchod yon*)	'patron–priest' relationship, established between Tibetan lamas and Mongol/Chinese rulers
chögyel (Tibetan *chos rgyal*)	'religion king', usually referring to one of the three great Buddhist kings of the Yarlung dynasty
chu	river in Lepcha language
crore	a unit in South Asian numbering systems equal to 10 million
dal-bhat-tarkari	classical Nepali meal of rice, lentil soup, and vegetable curry

Dalit	members of the lowest social status group in the Hindu caste system, traditionally regarded as untouchables, and recognized as Scheduled Castes in present-day India
darbar	palace
Darjeeling	hill district of the Indian state of West Bengal
Dasain	the biggest Hindu festival in Nepal corresponding to Durga Puja/Dussehra in India
dharma	Law of the Universe; duty, intrinsic nature of the things and their ought to be; the doctrine of the Buddha
Dharmashastra	Hindu scholastic texts related to the *dharma*, Sanskrit texts related to religious and legal duty
dharna	Hindi (and Nepali) word meaning sit-in protest
Dibya Upadesh	a Nepali text (1774). It contains King Prithivi Narayan's most important comments and instructions on rule and government
Druk	thunder dragon of Bhutanese mythology and a Bhutanese national symbol
dukha	hardship (Nepali)
dulwa (Tibetan 'dul ba)	ritual term for the subjugation of the land. *dulwa'i lhakhang* are temples devoted to this purpose
dzong (Tibetan dzong)	lit. fortress. Indigenous term for small-scale administrative district in Tibet
Ghale	an ethnic group found in Central Nepal, mainly around Gorkha
ghat	steps leading down to a holy river where ablutions and cremations are held
gharko awastha	household situation (Nepali)
ghumne	to wander (Nepali)

golsai	a variety of large cardamom
gundri	straw mat (Nepali)
Gurkha	soldiers from Nepal serving in the British and Indian armies, in the Sultanate of Brunei, and in the Singapore police. The word derives from the hill town of Gorkha
guru	a teacher; a respected, important person (in Sanskrit, lit. 'heavy')
Gurung	also known as Tamu, an ethnic group of Nepal
Guthi	among the Newars, a socio-religious type of organization. The word designated also the feasts organized by such groups.
halo jotne	ploughing a field (Nepali)
himal	high-altitude mountain
Hindutva	Hinduness, a movement advocating Hindu nationalism in India
Indra Jatra	Indra's festival, the main annual festival of Kathmandu old town
jagir	(Nepali) land tracts awarded to civil servants of the Nepali state in lieu of cash payment
jagire	salaried employment (Nepali)
janajati	'indigenous' nationality; the phrase currently used for Nepal's ethnic and historically marginalized communities, different from Hindu mainstream caste society
jan andolan	'people's movement' (Nepali)
Jyapuni	a female peasant from the Jyapu Newar caste
Kantipur	a Nepali daily newspaper (in Nepali). *Kantipur* is the old Nepali name of Kathmandu
kalasha	ritual vase
Khadi desh	Gulf countries, literally desert country
khaldo	hole in the ground (Nepali)

Kharnak (Tibetan *mkhar nag*)	'The Black Fort'; place name with a ruined fort; by extension, the high-altitude desert lying on the eastern edges of Zanskar
Kharnakpa	inhabitants of Kharnak; one of the three nomadic pastoralist groups living on the south-eastern edge of Ladakh
Kharnakling (Tibetan *mkhar nag gling*)	housing colony founded by pastoralist nomads, mainly from Kharnak, and located 10 kilometres from Leh town
kipat	(Nepali) traditional system of collective land tenure on the basis of ethnicity
Ladakhi (or Ladakhpa, *la-dvags-pa*)	inhabitants of Ladakh
lahure	those who went to enrol in foreign armies (it was sometimes used as a generic term to talk about those men who went to work outside Nepal and contributed to the households left behind) (Nepali)
lambu	a Western Tamang word designating a priest with responsibility for propitiating the divinities of the earth through sacrificial rituals
lek	a Nepali word for mountain
Lepcha	ethnic group of Sikkim
Lhochhar (Losar)	the Gurung (and Tibetan) New Year
Lhotshampa	Bhutanese Nepalis
Limbu	ethnic group found in the far East of Nepal and in Sikkim; part of the larger Kirat category
lupoon	Lepcha word for teacher
Madhesh	the Nepalese plain situated in the south of the country. Sometimes employed to in the Nepalese hills when speaking about India.
Magar	Nepal's second-largest ethnic group
Majhi	one ethnic group in Nepal, usually associated with fishing; fisherman

Mha puja	important familial ceremony of the Newars worshiping one's self and marking their New Year (November)
mimang tsongdu (Tibetan *mi mang tsong 'du*)	people's associations formed in the 1950s in Lhasa in opposition to Chinese occupation
momo	dumpling
muluk	country (Nepali)
Narmada Bachao Andolan	Save Narmada River Movement (India)
Nepal Bhasa	the term for the ancestral language of Nepal's Newar community, known also as Newari
nepalipan	Nepaliness
Newar	ethnic group to the Kathmandu Valley but now found spread throughout Nepal and beyond
OBC	Other Backward Classes, a category of the Indian state for those groups traditionally 'higher' than SC (Scheduled Tribes) but who are still disadvantaged, and used in providing affirmative action facilities.
OECD	Organization for Economic Cooperation and Development
Pahad	middle mountains
Pali	language of the Theravada Buddhist Canon
Panchayat system	in Nepal, the political autocratic party-less regime (1960/62–1990) regime. In Nepali: *panchayat vyavastha*
pandit	honorific title for a Hindu (Brahman) scholar and teacher learned in Sanskrit
PDS (Public Distribution System)	a network through which the Indian government sells subsidized products
paryatakiya kshetra	heritage village, tourist area (Nepal)
phedangma	a traditional Limbu priest
pirhi	veranda (Nepali)
puja	worship

pujari	priest, one who conducts worship
Pyangaon Bikas tatha Sanrakshan Samiti	local Development and Conservation/ Preservation Committee (Nepal)
rastra bhasa	official language of the nation
Rong	Lepcha word meaning ravine-folk or the dwellers of the valley
samabesikaran	'social inclusion' (Nepali)
sangha	monastery (in Sikkim)
satyagraha	Hindi word meaning truth-force and also used to refer to hunger-strikes as a mode of protest
satyagrahi	Hindi word referring to those who follow *satyagraha*
shastri	A learned person
sraddha	Hindu ritual performed for one's dead relatives and ancestors
svatantra	independence
sutta	the discourses attributed to the Buddha and contained in the second division of the Pali Canon
Tamang	one of the largest Nepali ethnic groups found mainly in Central Nepal, speaking a Tibeto-Burman language
Tihar	festival of light, a five-day-long Hindu and Buddhist festival celebrated in Nepal
Teej (Tij)	Hindu women's festival, celebrated yearly by women (Nepal)
tika	spot, most commonly of vermilion, placed on the forehead as a blessing
Thangmi	ethnic community of 40,000 with populations in Nepal's Sindhupalchok and Dolakha districts, as well as the Indian states of Sikkim and West Bengal (Darjeeling district)
Tharu	ethnic group of the Tarai region of Nepal and India

Theravada	the doctrine of elders, the only surviving school among the ancient schools of Buddhism and now the dominant form of Buddhism in Sri Lanka and Southeast Asia
thukpa	(Tibetan) noodle soup
trülku (Tibetan *sprul sku*)	incarnate lama and divine manifestation
Vajracharya	Newar Buddhist Tantric priest
Vajrayana	Tantric and esoteric Buddhist tradition, which appeared in India around the 7th century AD and later became the dominant form of Buddhism in Nepal and Tibet
vamshavali	A chronicle (for instance, tracing the origins of royal families)
varna	one of the four traditional Hindu socio-religious orders, comprising a number of castes
vihara	Sanskrit and Pali term for a Buddhist monastery of the Theravada religious tradition
vipassana	Buddhist meditation
Wangchuck	royal dynasty of Bhutan
yul (Tibetan *yul*)	in Tibetan, a village, a land, a region or a country. Any territory constituting a defined geographic reality and inhabited by a community

About the Editors and Contributors

THE EDITORS

Gérard Toffin is Director of Research at National Center for Scientific Research in France. In 1985, he created the CNRS team 'Centre for Himalayan Studies', where he was director until 1995. He has been carrying out research in Nepal since 1970 when he first came to Nepal to work as Cultural Attaché at the French Embassy. In addition to his own research on the Newars of the Kathmandu Valley, the Paharis, the Tamangs of western Nepal, the Parbatiya culture of the districts of Gulmi and Argha Khanchi in mid-western Nepal, and the Pranami sect in India and Nepal, he has directed, edited, and taken part in various anthropological research and publishing projects. He was the chief editor of the series 'Chemins de l'ethnologie' published by CNRS-Editions and Foundation Maison des Sciences de l'Homme, Paris, from 1993 till 2005. In May 2013, he received the Nai Derukh International Award in Kathmandu for his contribution to the study of Nepali culture and society.

Joanna Pfaff-Czarnecka is Professor of Social Anthropology at the Faculty of Sociology, Bielefeld University. The regional emphasis of her research is on the Himalayan region, South Asia, and on immigration societies of Central Europe. Her research interests range from political anthropology and anthropology of globalization to the nexus between inequality, social boundaries, and belonging. She has conducted extensive research in Nepal and India since 1979, which resulted in such publications as *Nationalism and Ethnicity in Nepal* (edited together with David Gellner and John Whelpton) and *Ethnic Futures: State and Identity in Four Asian Countries*, co-authored with Ashis Nandy, Darini Rajasingham-Senanayake, and Edmund Terence Gomez. She currently acts as Co-Director of the Interdisciplinary Research Centre (ZiF) at Bielefeld University and as member of the Senate of the German Research Foundation.

THE CONTRIBUTORS

Vibha Arora is Associate Professor, Indian Institute of Technology, Delhi.

Tristan Bruslé is Researcher, National Centre for Scientific Research (Centre for Himalayan Studies), France.

Ben Campbell is lecturer at the Department of Anthropology, University of Durham.

Pascale Dollfus is a social anthropologist and a CNRS Research fellow at the Centre for Himalayan Studies (UPR 299), France.

David N. Gellner is Professor of Social Anthropology at the Institute of Social and Cultural Anthropology and a Fellow of All Souls, University of Oxford.

Susan Hangen is Professor of Anthropology and International Studies at Ramapo College, NJ.

Sondra L. Hausner is University Lecturer in the Study of Religion, Fellow and Tutor of St. Peter's College, University of Oxford.

Michael Hutt is Professor of Nepali and Himalayan Studies, Centre of South Asian Studies, School of Oriental and African Studies (SOAS), University of London.

Chiara Letizia is Professor of South Asian religions at the University of Quebec in Montreal.

Martin A. Mills is Senior Lecturer and Head of Anthropology at the University of Aberdeen.

Mitra Pariyar is a doctoral student at Macquarrie University, Australia.

Blandine Ripert is a CNRS Researcher at the Center for South Asian Studies, EHESS-CNRS.

Jeevan R. Sharma is Lecturer in South Asia and International Development at the University of Edinburgh.

Sara Shneiderman is Assistant Professor of Anthropology and South Asian Studies, Yale University.

Bal Gopal Shrestha is a Research Associate of the Institute of Social and Cultural Anthropology, University of Oxford.

Bandita Sijapati is Research Director at the Centre for the Study of Labour and Mobility, Social Science Baha, and an Adjunct Professor at the Nepā School of Social Sciences and Humanities (Kathmandu).

Tanka B. Subba is the Vice-Chancellor of Sikkim University, Gangtok, Sikkim.

Mark Turin is Program Director of the Yale Himalaya Initiative and a Research Associate in South Asian Studies at Yale University.

Name Index